D0215593

TYPOLOGIES IN ENGLAND
1650-1820

Typologies
in England
1650-1820

PAUL J. KORSHIN

PRINCETON UNIVERSITY
PRESS

Publication of this book has been aided by a grant from
the Paul Mellon Fund of Princeton University Press

This book has been composed in Linotype Baskerville

Clothbound editions of Princeton University Press books
are printed on acid-free paper, and binding materials are
chosen for strength and durability

Printed in the United States of America by
Princeton University Press,
Princeton, New Jersey

Library of Congress Cataloging in Publication Data

Korshin, Paul J., 1939-
Typologies in England, 1650-1820.

Bibliography: p.   Includes index.
1.   English literature—18th century—History and criticism.
2.   Symbolism in literature.   3.   Typology (Theology)—
History of doctrines.   4.   Bible—Criticism, interpretation, etc.—England—History.   5.   Christianity and
literature.   6.   English literature—History and criticism.
I.   Title.   PR448.S94K6   820'.9'15   81-47139
ISBN 0-691-06485-7   AACR2

To Debra J. Thomas

I DEDICATE THIS BOOK.

"What neat repast shall feast us, light and choice
Of Attic taste, with Wine . . . ?"

Milton, Sonnet XXI

CONTENTS

LIST OF ILLUSTRATIONS

(following page 110)

ix

ACKNOWLEDGMENTS

BOOKS ON the literary applications of typology are a recent phenomenon; typology is not. Men have been trying to predict, prophesy, and prefigure the future for millennia, for perhaps as long as men have existed. While typology, in its formal sense, originally arose as a method of explaining sacred writings, first the Jewish, then the Christian Scriptures, structural anthropologists and mythologists have shown in recent decades that many ancient pagan religions also used prefigurative techniques. So the story that I have to tell, in its brief focus of one hundred and seventy years, has many ancient and respectable archetypes. Typology, as a venerable topic of study, has had cycles of interest; it is clear that we are in one now. I do not know how long the present cycle will last—earlier ones have endured for a century or more—but I think it is possible to show when it began. This latest bulge in the curve of interest in typology started in the 1930s with the theology of Karl Barth and Rudolph Bultmann and continued after World War II with that of Gerhard von Rad. Theological study of typology, since the late Cardinal Daniélou's *Sacramentum Futuri* appeared in 1950, has been considerable. Literary studies are equally recent: Erich Auerbach's "Figura" appeared in *Archivum Romanicum* in 1938, although Ralph Manheim's English version, which has had wide influence, appeared only in 1959; Perry Miller's discussion of typology in his introduction to Jonathan Edwards' *Images or Shadows of Divine Things* appeared in 1948. Since those modest but influential beginnings, hundreds of scholars have contributed to a growing bibliography of books and articles on many aspects of prefiguration in literature and in some of the other arts as well. Yet for all this scholarly and creative activity, most books and essays have focused on single authors, and my present book is the first that anyone has written about typology—or, as my title has it, *typologies* —in the literature of the English Enlightenment.

I have adopted my title from Mao Tse Tung (now Mao Zedong) who, in his *Little Red Book* of helpful aphorisms, said "Not one, not two, many Vietnams." Early in my studies of this subject, I realized that there were not one, not two, but many typologies. Since the subject of typology is as involved as it is ancient, the relevant terminology and the discussion of its applications can be complicated and at times—I regret—dry. However, I do not mean this book to be a dull one and, in fact, I was never bored while researching for and writing it. Since applications of typology can be and have been both elaborate and ingenious over the years, it would be fair to say that to perpetrate some of the prefigurative schemes that I have discovered must have involved an overactive imagination and a zealous belief in the types. To unravel and to try to understand some of the Enlightenment's use of prefigurative methods, then, has been challenging, exciting, and sometimes highly enjoyable. Certainly the research, all of which I did in the North Library of the British Museum (which Parliament transformed into The British Library early in my work), gave me the pleasure of spending many summers working at Seat 22, than which, for me, there is no greater scholarly enjoyment. Two Superintendents, Ian Willison and David Paisey, gave me every help and courtesy that a scholar could need, including sending me into the bookstack when my demands on the book-paging services became excessive. Nor can I forget the year—1977—when the books on the galleries of the Grenville salon and the King's Library became unavailable after the book fetchers' union decided that the catwalks were unsafe and how the Director General of the Reference Division, Dr. D. J. Richnell, saw to it that I got the books, somehow, brought from the dangerous heights by the devoted North Library staff.

I first began to think about typology in eighteenth-century literature in 1965, thanks to the references to the typology of the Deluge in Don Cameron Allen's *The Legend of Noah* (1949), but not until 1967, when Carey McIntosh casually remarked to me over a lunch at Leverett House that there was much typology in *A Tale of a Tub*, did I begin to consider the subject as more than material for a footnote. I did the bulk of the research for this book between 1972 and 1978 although, to a dedicated typologist, research into prefigurative methods and symbols seems never to end. Only in early 1973, when Earl Miner invited me to participate in a two-day seminar on the literary uses of typology that the Department of English at Princeton University was to sponsor in April 1974, did I realize that the typologies of English Enlightenment literature merited book-length attention. The nine other participants in the seminar, as well as the people who chaired the various sessions and commented from the audience, helped me to crystallize the form of this book at a crucial stage of my research. The subsequent publication of my contribution at the seminar in Earl Miner's meticulously edited *Literary Uses of Typology* (1977) gave me the benefit of further guidance from two specialist readers called in by Princeton University Press. Along the way, I have had unexpected *éclaircissements* from diverse sources. I am reminded now of Elliott R. Sober's helping me to work out the typology of character in 1972, of a remark that Stuart M. Tave made in a paper about Burke at a meeting in Minneapolis in May 1975 that led me to the typology of the French Revolution, and of Edward Hodnett directing me, later that year, to seventeenth-century editions of Aesop for their illustrations and enlightening scholia.

Portions of this book have appeared elsewhere in a form that I have now much changed. Part of Chapter 8 appeared in *Harvard English Studies*, Volume 1 (1970); part of Chapter 3 appeared in *Studies in Change and Revolution*, which I edited for Scolar Press, Ltd. in 1972; and portions of Chapters 5 and 9 appeared in *Literary Uses of Typology*. I am able to use these sections again in this volume with the permission of the Department of English and American Literature of Harvard University and the President and Fellows of Harvard College and by permission of the Princeton University Press.

The American Philosophical Society's Penrose Fund and the American Council of Learned Societies gave me grants-in-aid in 1970 and 1971 that allowed me, in those days of lower prices and modest inflation, to begin my work on this book; I wish to thank them now for their generosity. For permission to reproduce the illustrations that accompany this volume, I am indebted to the Trustees of the British Museum, The British Library, Lund Humphries Publishers, Ltd., The Pierpont Morgan Library, the Philadelphia Museum of Art, and Mr. and Mrs. David E. Zeitlin.

I HOPE THAT my notes and bibliography acknowledge all the scholarly assistance and—often—inspiration that I have obtained from learned people on three continents. But there is another kind of attention that I have been fortunate in having. A number of friends and colleagues, acting in various capacities and for various agents, read different versions of the entire manuscript of this book: Sheridan Baker, W. Bliss Carnochan, Stuart Curran, Earl Miner, Maximillian E. Novak, Gerard C. Reedy, S.J., Florence K. Sandler, Barbara H. Smith, and Joseph A. Wittreich, Jr. Let me thank them again and express the hope that they like what they read here, however much, or little, I may have regarded their numerous, patient criticisms and proposals for improvement. To the people who read portions of the manuscript—Geoffrey G. Harpham, Jocelyn Harris, and Mark Crispin Miller—an equal portion of thanks is due, along with a sense of wonderment that I allowed them to escape reading the whole typescript. And I have profited, finally, from the fruits of others' learning in many ways, especially from the guidance and support, at different times and venues, of W. J. Bate, David DeLaura, J. Paul Hunter, and Robert M. Lumiansky. Here, too, let me mention the help that I received from the late Edward L. Surtz, S.J. of Loyola University and—the one person who never wavered in his encouragement for eighteenth-century studies—the late James L. Clifford of Columbia University. My work with the Princeton University Press on the manuscript of this book—or portions of it—covers a period of more than six years, and during that time many members of the staff of the Press have dealt with me. Of these people, I would like to record my thanks to three in particular—Marjorie C. Sherwood, who, more than anyone else, made this book publishable; Judith May, who guided it skillfully through every stage of production; and Jan Lilly, who patiently heard my notions about design and then designed the final artifact —superb professionals all!

I have saved until last my largest debt—and I have done so only because I have already cited it on the third recto of this volume. It is to my wife and closest friend, Debra J. Thomas. She shared with me the joy of researching this book, the agonies of writing it, and the labor of typing it and, at last, she bore with me through several revisions that culminated in the Press's accepting it. Who would not judge of those delights, "and spare / To interpose them oft"?

The North Library
14 July 1980

ABBREVIATIONS AND
SHORT TITLES

FULL bibliographical information about every item cited appears in the first note that refers to the work. A reader wishing to locate the complete reference for a work should consult the main entry for it in the Index, where the relevant page number is given in parentheses. All works cited in the notes are indexed. A few books which are cited frequently are included in the abbreviations below.

Allen, *Mysteriously Meant*	Don Cameron Allen, *Mysteriously Meant: The Rediscovery of Pagan Symbolism and Allegorical Interpretation in the Renaissance*. Baltimore: Johns Hopkins Univ. Press, 1970.
BJRL	*Bulletin of the John Rylands Library*
ECS	*Eighteenth-Century Studies*
ELH	*ELH [Journal of English Literary History]*
ELN	*English Language Notes*
Frei, *The Eclipse of Biblical Narrative*	Hans W. Frei, *The Eclipse of Biblical Narrative: A Study in Eighteenth and Nineteenth Century Hermeneutics*. New Haven: Yale Univ. Press, 1974.
HLQ	*Huntington Library Quarterly*
JEGP	*Journal of English and Germanic Philology*
JHI	*Journal of the History of Ideas*
JWCI	*Journal of the Warburg and Courtauld Institutes*
Literary Uses of Typology	*Literary Uses of Typology from the Late Middle Ages to the Present*, ed. Earl Miner. Princeton: Princeton Univ. Press, 1977.
MP	*Modern Philology*
NCBEL	*The New Cambridge Bibliography of English Literature*
NED	*A New English Dictionary*
PMLA	*Publications of the Modern Language Association*
PQ	*Philological Quarterly*
RES	*The Review of English Studies*
TE	*The Twickenham Edition of the Poems of Alexander Pope*, ed. John Butt et al., 11 vols. in 12. London and New Haven: Methuen & Co. and Yale Univ. Press, 1939-69.

TYPOLOGIES IN ENGLAND
1650-1820

CHAPTER 1

Introduction: The Typological Propensity

A VISITOR FROM our century to early Enlightenment England—
England in the mid and later seventeenth century—if he
tarried long enough to taste the intellectual life of the period, would soon notice the large role that prediction of all kinds
played in the life of the nation. The human impulse to predict the
future, as anthropologists observe, is greatest in times of instability
and uncertainty. Primitive tribes and civilized peoples alike, no
matter how stable the body of received thought and tradition they
possess, strive more energetically to know what the future may hold
when the world around them appears unsettled and human affairs
in doubt. Our visitor to England, then, sometime between 1650 and
1680, would soon observe a propensity for prediction, whether
based on stories and events drawn from the past, on similarities
between present events and previous history, or on the possibility
that the present somehow suggested a fulfillment of an earlier prediction or prophecy. This modern visitor would soon recognize
some common ground between twentieth-century thought and the
intellectual attitudes of the last half of the seventeenth century.
For one thing, he would recognize that some of the predictive skills
of these early Enlightenment English were drawn from the Bible—
a book still popular in the twentieth century—but that the figuralism his hosts employed was based on the notion that the Bible was
historically true and that contemporary history was part of a seamless historical fabric continuous from biblical times. For another,
our guest would soon see that many of his more articulate hosts
readily believed there were predictive connections between biblical
times and their own and that they searched constantly for signs to
justify their beliefs. The modern visitor would also doubtless see

that, despite their great, and to him, unusual preoccupation with signs, shadows, figures of something past or yet to come, the seventeenth-century English lived, loved, swore, fought, and so on, rather like people in most other historical periods. They might take prediction and prefiguring seriously—as indeed they did—but, however much matters of this kind might obsess a few men and women, most people lived most of the time unconcerned as to what predictions might or might not come true.

My imaginary visitor is an ideal guest, innocent of preconceptions or expectations, as well informed about his own situation as he is about the past, and with a certain sense of humor concerning both. Perhaps it would be a mistake to think that my character represents the scholar, the historian of ideas, or the literary critic, for these inquirers into the texts and stories of the past sometimes lack the traits I have sketched for my traveler through time. As an inquirer into the figural history, especially the prefigurative side of that history, of the English Enlightenment, I know that my vision may be clouded by a felicitous hypothesis, my objectivity weakened by a yearning to find what I have come to seek. But for the seeker after details of the story of typology in the seventeenth and eighteenth centuries, there is a good deal to find. That few if any have sought to understand this chapter in the history of typological thought makes a scholar's search harder—there are no reliable guides—and more hazardous; it is easy to be misled by evidence that may turn out to be something less than the best evidence. Of one thing we may be certain: the history of typology over the last two thousand years is highly varied and fragmentary. The scholar confronts a plethora of material in many sources and, to be effective, must weave the evidence into a coherent historical and literary account.

From the time that the ancient Jews first started to use prefigurative language in prophetical statements about the future of their nation, these figures (which would not be named "types" until the Hellenization of Palestinian culture) have had a double purpose. Typology, the collective noun for the reading and learning of these signs, refers not only to the creating of prefigurative entities, but also to their interpretation. Typology is a method of decoding as well as a code, a science of exegesis as well as one of mysterious foreshadowing. A typologist is a person who interprets—or claims to interpret—an existing or presumed literary code as well as someone who speaks or writes in typological language or style. For most of its history, typology has been largely if not exclusively a method of encoding and interpreting religious texts and theological history. But in the middle of the seventeenth century in England, typology slowly began to change, to become secular in its applications, and to involve genres of literature other than the strictly religious. These genres are numerous, ranging from myth to political writings, from the prose character to the fable, from various kinds of poetry to prose narrative. The reasons for these changes, for this gradual secularizing of what had been almost exclusively a religious figuralism and exegesis, are numerous, and I shall not attempt to outline them now. They are the subject of the following chapters, in which I undertake to find the intellectual bases of typology in the literature of the English Enlightenment, broadly construed to cover the period from 1650 to 1820.

Typology in its strict, conventional sense had expanded by the middle of the seventeenth century to embrace imagery from pagan mythology and pagan literature. Hercules, Pan, Orpheus, Ceres, Achilles, Aeneas, and dozens of other characters became pre-Christian types of Christ. Theologians in search of the origins of Christianity found them in the lore, languages, and literatures of gentile theology and, as they found these origins, they decided that they must be shadowy types of the true religion that was still to come. Thus during the late Renaissance and early Enlightenment, typology becomes a deciphering of the encrypted codes of ancient civilizations. If, contemporary writers and scholars thought, the types were figures in a code, then someone must have encoded them. Here the seventeenth-century typologists had a fine example of encryptment that served them as their paradigm for all such potential codes—the hieroglyphics of Egypt. There was universal agreement that the glyphs represented a code that the Egyptian priests had made to preserve the secrets of their faith from unbelievers. If one set of ancient priests had acted thus, was it not likely that others had done the same? Were not the mysteries of Grecian religion equally obscure? Did not Jesus himself speak in parables that required explanation for vulgar ears? It was; they were; and he did. Since the hieroglyphs were a visual code, seventeenth-century typologists looked for visual signs or types in other kinds of graphic representation. The typology of emblem books, engraved title pages and book illustrations, paintings and typographic devices, iconography and iconology emerged gradually as early Enlightenment think-ers looked around them for predictive signs that might date from some earlier culture.

It is worth mentioning that many seventeenth-century English writers were fascinated with codes of all kinds. Writing in cipher was an old device, but the forerunner of modern stenographic shorthand, tachygraphy, dates from the mid-seventeenth century. It was common to treat any text, including Scripture, that required explanation as a code for which a *clavis* or key had to be produced before contemporary readers could understand it. Hence the late seventeenth and early eighteenth centuries are a period of "keys," "complete keys," guides to unlock the mysteries of dark or obscure authors, and efforts to decipher whatever some exegete deemed worthy of explanation. We may trace the unbroken skein of English fascination with dark authors from the mid-seventeenth to the early nineteenth century, from Sir Thomas Browne, Henry More, and Samuel Butler to Blake, Coleridge, and Shelley. Typology, as an exegetical tool, could perform a valuable function for those who hoped to extract meaning—often a prejudged, preferred meaning—from the works of mystics, cabalists, and hermeticists and from other curious writings. Hence, during the late seventeenth century, religious exegetes and then secular writers as well began to treat typology as a code left undeciphered by earlier cultures. We will find that these writers habitually and easily confuse typology with emblems, parables, signs, symbols, and hieroglyphics in their termi-nology. So great is this confusion that types become, in the language of semiology, figural enclaves with prefigurative or postfigurative purposes. Sometimes types look backward and forward simultane-ously. Even today, typology sometimes does not refer to prefigura-tive imagery or exegesis at all but rather describes the classification of phenomena in the manner of the sciences and the social sciences.[1]

In dealing with such a complex and potentially confusing topic

[1] It is usually obvious that "typology" means "classification" when one finds scientists using the term. However, one can easily be misled by its use in literary contexts. For instance, at one point in my researches I found a reference to and (with some difficulty) obtained a copy of Mihály Szegedy-Maszák's essay, "English Poetry in the Age of Sensibility: A Typological Approach," in *Studies in Eight-eenth-Century Literature*, ed. Miklós J. Szenczi and László Ferenczi (Budapest: Akadémiai Kiadó, 1974), pp. 117-87, only to discover that it was a detailed clas-sification of eighteenth-century verse according to ideas, aesthetic dimensions, genres, and style.

in intellectual history, there are, it seems to me, five possible approaches. The first is the strictly chronological treatment of typology, with a decade-by-decade survey of different authors, genres, and developments. The chief advantage that this approach offers is order; the reader finds materials about the 1660s in one place, about the 1720s in another, and so on. The second method of proceeding would involve individual authors and their works, in the order in which they appeared. Here, too, the advantage would be one of straightforward arrangement. A third possible method includes the examination of theories of typology over the period covered by this book. The fourth would be a study of typology according to the genres of literature in which it commonly appears. And the fifth approach that I considered is a strictly historical one, an attempt to write the history of typological thought in the English Enlightenment without regard for authors, genres, or decades. I rejected the first two methods as being limited and restrictive. Instead, I have chosen to follow a blend of the last three of these approaches—theories, genres, and the history of typology—with chapters devoted to each of these methods.

In the critical study of typological ideas and their applications to literature, this multivalent treatment of the subject is, so far as I know, still untried. Students of typology in the English Renaissance such as Barbara Lewalski (1966) and Mary Ann Radzinowicz (1978) have preferred to focus on a single author or a single work (in both cases the author is Milton and the works are *Paradise Regained* and *Samson Agonistes*). Steven Zwicker's book on the typology of kingship in Dryden (1972) is devoted, except for introductory material, to one author. The various studies of typology in colonial American literature and thought follow either the single author approach or the history of ideas method. My choice of method is dictated in part by the fact that the typological study of late seventeenth- and eighteenth-century literature is still a relative novelty. Except for specialized and partial views of a few authors and works, nobody has yet attempted a general survey of so broad a spectrum of typological texts and ideas as I shall take up in this book.

My second chapter, therefore, traces what may be, for readers conversant with Renaissance literature, familiar outlines of typological history from biblical times. I am interested in showing what the possibilities and limits of typological approaches to literature are, so I shall survey the different kinds of typology—conventional, applied, and abstracted—and suggest where, how, and under what

7

influences types are likely to appear in literary and other artistic contexts. This is a work about literature rather than its sister arts, but I feel obliged to point out the numerous visual manifestations of typology from 1650 to 1820, impressions that I hope the illustrations to this volume will strengthen. Part of the appeal of typology during this period is that it is closely associated with ideas of the Millennium and with natural human propensities to predictiveness. Hence I want to prepare readers for later chapters dealing with millenarian subjects and with what I shall call natural typology.

Anyone who deals with the subtleties of typological figuralism in Enlightenment, especially in eighteenth-century, literature must face the traditional view that such figural intricacies are alien to the thought of this period. The title of the final chapter of Don Cameron Allen's *Mysteriously Meant* (1971)—"The Rationalization of Myth and the End of Allegory"—suggests that its author firmly closes the gates on mystical imagery and interpretation at the end of the seventeenth century. Allen, of course, simply expressed an attitude that descended to him from intellectual historians of the pre-World War II era, although it remains a pity that such a gifted student of the arcana of literature should have rested his lance when he had a chance to tilt with the eighteenth century. This view is now something of a straw man that my readers will have to forgive me for erecting in these pages again; indeed, literary studies of eighteenth-century literature during the decade of the 1970s did much to show the strong continuity of the period with the literature of the middle and late Renaissance. My third chapter, then, is another kind of introduction to the study of typology in the seventeenth and eighteenth centuries, for it argues that literary and figural changes were widespread but that, nevertheless, the attractions of typological thought and imagery did not disappear. Their survival and the changes that typology underwent as part of that survival are the subject of the bulk of this book.

Typology, as I noted earlier, is an exegetical technique or, as I describe it at the beginning of my fourth chapter, "Typology as System," "a system of exegesis." This system has its own language, syntax, terminology, and semiology. The purpose of this and the following chapter, "The Development of Abstracted Typology," is to show how and in what kinds of texts we may expect to find typological thought at work. I shall argue that abstracted typology is the principal modification or corruption of conventional theological typology during the English Enlightenment and that its occurrence is common in many genres of literature. Yet there are also limits to the possibilities of typology. Looking for applications of typology is a legitimate historical and critical enterprise, but too zealous a search, too great a willingness to find prefigurative techniques in literature, may lead to, as Erasmus said of the union of his parents, the sacrilegious. I have defined my subject optimistically, as any scholar must do, but I have tried throughout to identify types and typological thought only when these resemblances appear in such a way in my subject matter that I think I can defend them to a skeptical audience. There will be some authors in whose writings typological thinking is fairly prominent while, during the same or subsequent years, there will be others equally exposed to typological methods and literature in whose writings we will find little or no typology. Defoe, for example, in the words of a recent critic, "shared with the majority of his readers the typological habit of mind involved not only in the assumption that Old Testament events prefigure those of the New Testament but, more generally, that the past offers archetypes of the present and future."[2] Not only does Defoe employ typology in his fictional narratives, but in *A Journal of the Plague Year*, which he represents as an accurate journal of a time in recent history, he includes events of 1665 as an historical type of a potential antitype in England of 1721. Yet a few decades after Defoe wrote, we will find that Samuel Johnson, who was also conversant with contemporary and past typological thought, seldom refers to typology *per se*. The principal influences on Johnson's theological thought include divines whose writings often include and discuss typology such as William Law, Samuel Clarke, Richard Baxter, Jeremy Taylor, and John Tillotson.[3] But typology, however central a topic it is to eighteenth-century Christianity, is not central to Johnson's *Sermons* or other writings; it would be pointless to promote resemblances for which there is scanty evidence.

In Chapters 6 through 9 I discuss four genres in which the presence of typology in one form or another is an especially interesting problem in intellectual and literary history. My subject in Chapter 6 is "Typology and Myth," and here I survey much, although by

---

[2] See Paul K. Alkon, *Defoe and Fictional Time* (Athens, Ga.: Univ. of Georgia Press, 1979), p. 40.

[3] James Gray, *Johnson's Sermons: A Study* (Oxford: Clarendon Press, 1972), pp. 47-130, mentions these figures and several other writers as Johnson's principal homiletic sources and models.

no means all, of the Enlightenment mythological speculation that involves a typological perspective. The mythologers became increasingly aware, during the eighteenth century, of the narrative forms that mythic documents took and of the narrative structure of the biblical texts that included the central Hebraic and Christian myths. The authors of lives or collections of biographies in the eighteenth century were able to impart a narrative structure to them, sometimes even recalling the typological properties of the hagiography or the martyrology. Thus it seems natural to turn from myth to the longer flight of narrative in Chapter 7, "Typology and the Novel." Some eighteenth-century novels employ typological characters, often derived from the popular *imitatio Christi* tradition; others use typological plots and stories. The Christ-like perfections or Satanic depravity of certain characters may derive from christomimetic traditions that were available to eighteenth-century writers, while there is also an active Protestant lore surrounding the acts of the English martyrology.[4] Prose fiction, I shall argue, is an ideal stage from which to present and debate prefigurative applications and topics, although I do not urge that as a result of my conclusions we should forthwith regard every eighteenth-century novel as a typological one. My eighth chapter, "Typology and Satire," takes up a divergent but important strain, the misuse or excessive use of typology. It is always fair to assume that the satiric object or methodology of a work is evidence that such an abuse actually existed and that a contemporary readership would have recognized it. So typological satire is evidence of the popularity and familiarity that the language of the types must have had in Enlightenment England. The fact that satirists from Butler to Byron occasionally used elements of prefigurative techniques to ridicule their opponents may say more about the pervasiveness of typologizing than the presence of types in prose fiction.

I devote only one chapter of this book, Chapter 9, "Typology and Prophecy," to the broad swath that millenarianism cuts across the European Enlightenment; an entire volume would just begin to do justice to this vast subject. Perhaps some areas of millenarian typol-

---

[4] Seymour Byman, "Ritualistic Acts and Compulsive Behavior: The Pattern of Tudor Martyrdom," *American Historical Review*, 83 (1978), 625-43, shows that the behavior of the Protestant martyrs, as Foxe chronicles it in his *Acts and Monuments*, often echoes christomimetic patterns in the accounts of early martyrs of the Church. Thus two of the streams of the *imitatio Christi* tradition —the Catholic and the Protestant—merge in English thought and tradition.

ogy are just a scholastic game involving the collecting of similarities between a prophetical text and an historical event. But we must somehow account for the remarkable persistence of this kind of typology and the great interest that important thinkers such as Newton, Hartley, Richard Price, and Coleridge took in it. Here the politics of typology is important, since some millenarians (Hartley among them) specified the conversion of the Jews to Christianity as a final antitype preliminary to the Millennium, while others stressed that wicked men in high places (presumably, public office) would be punished for their sins.[5] The prophetical style that we have all become acquainted with through the writings of Blake is hardly original with him—he was but a way-station on an almost endless millenarian railway—and I have attempted to study this tradition from 1650 to 1820. Here, however, the best that one chapter can do is to analyze elements of the tradition. Other writers can —and certainly will—devote volumes to the Millennium.[6] And millenarian visionaries who are persuaded that the signs of the times— the types or antitypes—tell them that the time is NOW will continue to be with us, too. The self-immolation of Jonestown, Guyana in 1978 revealed as much, and perhaps, as the second (some would say the sixth) millennium draws nearer to its end, we will see more evidence of the currency of typological millenarianism.[7]

Since typology, in its least conventional or most abstracted sense, deals with the human propensity to predict and to seek signs or

[5] See Mel Scult, *Millennial Expectations and Jewish Liberties: A Study of the Efforts to Convert the Jews in Britain, up to the Mid Nineteenth Century* (Leiden: E. J. Brill, 1978), pp. 35-89, for a discursive treatment of the subject of conversion. For an interesting study of early English eschatology during the period that gave rise to the most enduring millenarian movements of the last three centuries, see Bryan W. Ball, *A Great Expectation: Eschatological Thought in English Protestantism to 1660* (Leiden: E. J. Brill, 1975), *passim*.

[6] Frank P. Manuel and Fritzie P. Manuel, in their *Utopian Thought in the Western World* (Cambridge, Mass.: Belknap Press of Harvard Univ. Press, 1979), have an illuminating summary chapter on the forerunners of millennial speculation; see pp. 33-63.

[7] It is significant that the leader of an American fundamentalist Christian group called the Moral Majority—a body with ideological and exegetical attitudes strikingly similar to those of mid-seventeenth-century English millennial groups—believes that "this [i.e., the 1980s] is the terminal generation before Jesus comes" and that all the signs of the times point to the coming of the Millennium by the end of the twentieth century. See Frances Fitzgerald, "A Reporter at Large: A Disciplined, Charging Army," *The New Yorker*, 57, no. 13 (18 May 1981), pp. 60, 129-32.

prefigurations that desired events, once predicted, are about to happen, it can therefore concern itself with events and relationships that have little or nothing to do with the conventional origins of the device or methodology associated with it. In the eighteenth and early nineteenth centuries, I argue in Chapter 10, "The Typology of Everyday Life," there is a good deal of evidence that a number of writers in many different secular genres attributed prefigurative or typological qualities to many aspects of everyday life and letters. The universal typology of forms is grounded on the principles of conventional typology, but it seldom has anything to do with religion, religious ideas, or their applications. I trace the origins of this natural typology at least to Jakob Boehme, but the uses of this branch of figuralism embrace much popular literature as well as divinely inspired meditations. A common representation of natural typology involves the discovery of shadowing, prefiguring, or predictive elements in places where we might not expect to find them.

For example, Erasmus Darwin, through numerous analogies, advised his readers in the "Apology" to *The Botanic Garden* (1791), a poem on the economy of vegetation and the loves of the plants, that natural objects are allied to each other in many ways that may not be obvious. His explanation is a classic case of typology turned to everyday use:

> Many of the important operations of Nature were shadowed or allegorized in the heathen mythology, as the first Cupid springing from the Egg of Night, the marriage of Cupid and Psyche, the Rape of Proserpine, the Congress of Jupiter and Juno, Death and Resuscitation of Adonis, &c. . . . The Egyptians were possessed of many discoveries in philosophy and chemistry before the invention of letters; these were then expressed in hieroglyphic paintings of men and animals; which after the discovery of the alphabet were described and animated by the poets, and became first the deities of Egypt, and afterwards of Greece and Rome.[8]

Darwin is a respected naturalist, so we have to take him seriously, since he recites the received theory of the origins of the pagan gods with the added information that ancient myth prefigures Nature just as Egyptian religion prefigures the Greek and Roman. This text—and, to a greater extent, Darwin's long botanical poem—

[8] See Erasmus Darwin, *The Botanic Garden; A Poem, in Two Parts*, 2 vols. (London, 1791), I, vii-viii.

shows how one of the more curious ramifications of typology oper-
ated late in the eighteenth century, through a search for prefigurative elements or structures, figural enclaves in the great book of
nature.

This kind of prefigurative relationship is common in neoplatonic
texts, such as the following excerpt from Plotinus:

> Intellect indeed is beautiful, and the most beautiful of all
> things, being situated in a pure light and in a pure splendor,
> and comprehending in itself the nature of beings, of which in-
> deed this our material world is but the shadow and image; but
> intellect, that true intelligible world, is situated in universal
> splendor, living in itself a blessed life, and containing nothing
> unintelligible, nothing dark, nothing without measure. . . .[9]

The corrupted world of everyday life, then, is but a shadow, a type
of the perfectly clear, completely blessed, fully illuminated world
of intellect. Here, as always in such figural relationships, the types
are shadowy, dark, and imperfect, while the accomplishments or
antitypes are perfect. Thus writers of the Romantic period worked
typology into their perceptions of the world. Blake (whom this
passage from Plotinus influenced), Wordsworth, Coleridge, Shelley,
and no doubt others adapted typological styles and relationships to
their perceptions of nature. While I have written only a single
chapter on this aspect of my subject, I should note at this point
that, where the Enlightenment blends into the thought of the
Romantic era, there is a watershed in prefigurative thought that
provides abundant material for longer critical study. To aid other
students of typology, I have added, as Chapter 11, "Typology: A
Bibliographical Essay" to guide the interested reader to aspects of
the subject that I discuss rather briefly in this volume. Unlike Sacvan Bercovitch's "Annotated Bibliography" of typology (1972),
which will remain useful to all who study this topic, this chapter
analyzes rather than lists a wide variety of primary and secondary
sources. It may lead others, perhaps, to new typological fields that I
could not explore in this book.

Throughout its history, typology has been subject to excess,
whether from exegetes who have insisted on interpreting a single
prefigurative passage as if an entire work were typological or from

---

[9] *Five Books of Plotinus*, trans. Thomas Taylor (London, 1794), pp. 243-44.
Blake alludes to this passage in *Jerusalem*, Pl. 77. Cf. Kathleen Raine, *Blake
and Tradition*, 2 vols. (Princeton: Princeton Univ. Press, 1968), II, 189-210.

critics who have found types in works whose authors probably never intended them. It is possible genuinely to misread authorial intention, and I should note that I am as susceptible to such mistakes as any other mortal. One can minimize such critical self-delusion, however, by interpreting authorial intention with some strictness and by not reading a text typologically unless its author has "signed" it, that is, surrounded a presumed typological occurrence with hints that would have allowed all or at least some members of its contemporary audience to understand the prefigurative associations. It is difficult to go beyond this point into how much we can expect an audience in, say, the 1740s to know about biblical exegesis, classical mythology, iconography, and so on. It is also difficult to deal with the possibility that an author may, through his or her reading, have been so saturated with prefigurative lore that he or she might have used typology unconsciously. Several years ago, to take an interesting example, Maren-Sofie Røstvig argued that the central six books of *Tom Jones* embody a dramatized example of the Choice of Hercules, a well-known mythological story that Renaissance scholars often interpreted as a pagan type of the temptations of Jesus and of the difficult choices that the average Christian may face in life.[10] The problem with such an argument, however learned, is that we cannot be sure either that Fielding's readers were so deeply read in the iconographical lore of the Hercules legend that they would have made this identification or that Fielding himself intended to use this kind of typological structure without some palpable hints that he was doing so. Perhaps a Renaissance readership, smaller and better educated than an eighteenth-century audience, *would* have spotted such an intricate typological pattern. But the evidence that Fielding and his readers might have known about it is less persuasive.

Typological criticism of the visual arts is open to the same perils; however learned our guesses about the presence of prefigurative images, it is always preferable to have some announcement of artistic intention. The popularity of Victorian paintings featuring the rainbow—a type of the first Covenant with a long exegetical genealogy—may suggest, as a specialist in Victorian religious art has recently proposed, that painters of quasi-religious subjects were deliberately employing prefigurative imagery. No doubt some of them

10 See "*Tom Jones* and The Choice of Hercules," in *Fair Forms: Essays in English Literature from Spenser to Jane Austen*, ed. Maren-Sofie Røstvig (Cambridge: D. S. Brewer, 1975), pp. 147-77.

were, but we cannot be reasonably certain of such applications unless the painters tell us so in some way, as indeed they often do.[11] The art critic can feel more certain of the twentieth-century artist Graham Sutherland's frequent use of the thorn motif as a pre- or postfigurative image, since Sutherland himself remarked that the thorn was not only a feature of structural design in his works but "a sort of paraphrase of the Crucifixion" with associations of cruelty and martyrdom (see Figure 27).[12]

Beyond such certainties, the study of typology must inevitably be speculative. Types abound in art and literature, and it would be a relatively easy matter to collect them, as some of the pre-Nicene Church fathers and the seventeenth-century classifiers of types did. But merely collecting types, while it is an action involving discernment, is not necessarily to be seen as sophisticated critical activity. Thus it is always well to seek an indication from an author that he or she is actually employing typological figuralism. Typology, as I have said already—and will say many times more in the following pages—is a code, a series of signs, a silent language perceived most readily by those on the inside. It is possible, I think, to interpret this language to those on the outside and that, at last, is the purpose of this book.

[11] On this subject, see George P. Landow, "The Rainbow: A Problematic Image," in *Nature and the Victorian Imagination*, ed. U. C. Knoepflmacher and G. B. Tennyson (Berkeley and Los Angeles: Univ. of California Press, 1977), pp. 341-69.

[12] See "Obituary: Mr. Graham Sutherland," *The Times* (London), 18 February 1980, p. 14.

CHAPTER 2

The Possibilities and Limits
of Typology

THE TITLE of this book requires a certain amount of explanation, with regard both to meaning and to scope. Typology is not a new concept; it comes down to us over almost two millennia of literary study and criticism. Even before the term itself was introduced, the concept behind it had literary applications stretching back several centuries before Christ, where formal typology begins. Scholars have long recognized that typology, once solely a branch of nonliteral scriptural exegesis, has broad literary applications. Today, an author who turns his or her attention to literary typology treads a path which begins with early criticism of Dante and one which has seen especially many pilgrims in the last twenty-five years. My title, however, mentions not "typology" but "typologies," for I plan to show that there are several kinds and many uses of typological figuralism in English literature. The chronological focus of the present work is deliberately broad so that it will embrace three, possibly even four, distinct periods of our literature. My contention is that this mode of figuralism, which was so popular in the Middle Ages and the European Renaissance that it is appropriately regarded as characteristic of those eras, increased in subtlety and methods of application during the Enlightenment, which I have interpreted broadly to include a span of years both before and after the limits of the eighteenth century. The pivotal period of my attention is this century, which encompasses but does not entirely constitute the Enlightenment in England and Europe. This study would be incomplete without some scrutiny of the typologies of Marvell, Milton, and Dryden in the seventeenth century and of Blake, Coleridge, and Shelley in the nineteenth. Typology is a subject that benefits from comparative study, but its place in the Continental Enlightenment is beyond the limits of my inquiry here, although I shall refer to many European authors in the course of my investigation. In one sense, this book might be subtitled "the survival of typology," but to do so would be question-begging. I seriously doubt that there has ever been any question that Christian typology, employed in biblical exegesis and for homiletic purposes, has ever ceased to be with us. The most uninvolved study of the Old and New Testaments, at any time in modern history, must emphasize the prefigurative relationship between the Old and the New; indeed, even to name the two parts of the Bible "Old" and "New" involves an exercise in typological imagination.[1] Typology, then, as an aspect of Christian education and belief, never faded from the human imagination although, as we shall see, there would be numerous quarrels about its proper intention, meaning, and use. What did survive, throughout the eighteenth century and on into the nineteenth, was something more complicated than the typology that is so central and necessary to Christianity. As one kind of typology, the theological, gradually expanded into other kinds, and changed through new uses in imaginative literature, what survived from the European Renaissance throughout the late seventeenth and eighteenth centuries was a complex mode of literary figuralism which, until very recently, we have hardly noticed as part of the eighteenth-century intellectual experience.

I shall not rehearse the old view that eighteenth-century English literature is lacking in the intricacies and subtleties of the literature that both preceded and followed it. Sometimes it is helpful to have fallacy to ridicule, but this particular argument has been thoroughly demolished a number of times over the last twenty years by scholars who have successfully demonstrated that the imagistic texture and imaginative depths of eighteenth-century texts recall the Renaissance and anticipate the nineteenth century in numerous ways. That the literary texts of a given culture form a demonstrable continuity is a concept which I shall take as a truism (no matter what a small minority of recidivists may think). However, until barely a decade ago, students of the eighteenth century seemed unaware that typology pervades not only the theology but the imaginative literature of the period as well. So important a work as

---

[1] See Earl Miner's "Afterword" to *Literary Uses of Typology*, p. 370.

Ernest Lee Tuveson's *Millennium and Utopia* (1949), whose focus is one of the most typologically involved subjects of the seventeenth and eighteenth centuries, makes no mention whatever of prefigurative techniques.[2] So influential a study as Earl Wasserman's *The Subtler Language*, which first appeared a decade later, is silent about the typological qualities of the major poems which it so intelligently reads. And as lately as 1969, Maynard Mack's *The Garden and the City*, our major recent reading of Pope's later poetry, passes by the typological qualities of Pope's late verse. Obviously, I could cite many other examples as well. I do not wish to detract in any way from the achievements of these and other recent scholars by citing what they have failed to do or what they have not mentioned. I am interested in suggesting, rather, that typology has not been part of the usual scholarly perspective on eighteenth-century literature until very recently. Many students of the period have accepted the widely promulgated view that, with the advent of the age of reason, all aspects of English literature swiftly became clear, logical, precise, and rational ("rational," in this context, is understood to mean devoid of mysticism and arcana). The few scholars who have taken an interest in eighteenth-century mysticism have done so with an eye to showing how such currents in the thought of the period lead to Romanticism; often they describe their findings as evidence of pre-Romanticism. Desirée Hirst, for example, studies eighteenth-century strains of the Kabalah, other aspects of Jewish mysticism, Quietism, and Swedenborgianism, and gives the impression that mysticism and arcana are part of an underworld of contemporary thought.[3] Until quite recently, indeed, there was no reason for eighteenth-century specialists to mention an aspect of figuralism like typology. Typology, many scholars have assumed, is an element of mysticism that appears only in a limited number of theological contexts.

In this respect, students of theology and history have established the field for literary scholars to enter after them. Historians like D. P. Walker and Clarke Garrett have shown how the infatuation

[2] *Millennium and Utopia: A Study in the Background of the Idea of Progress* (Berkeley and Los Angeles: Univ. of California Press, 1949). Tuveson talks around the subject on many occasions without ever specifically mentioning prefigurative techniques.

[3] See her *Hidden Riches: Traditional Symbolism from the Renaissance to Blake* (London: Eyre & Spottiswoode, 1964), pp. 162-267. Hirst does not deal with typology except in a few peripheral comments.

of the age with mysticism and millenarianism stresses typological views of large bodies of texts. Students of religion and myth have made us aware of the intense struggle within established religion over typology and Scripture prophecies, over the origins of myth and its relation to other literature, at different points in the century. And most recently, specialists in language have shed important light on types as forms of early symbolism. In the field of American studies, historians and literary critics have long been aware of the importance of typology and other kinds of figuralism in the colonial and postcolonial periods. Now, led by others, it is possible to study prefigurative forms and structures in eighteenth-century English literature itself. I shall view the problem from a new and different angle and shall attempt to show that typology exists and, indeed, is popular in forms of imaginative literature where it is seldom if ever mentioned.

As part of the explanation of the title of this book, I should add that, while I shall talk a great deal about theological writings from 1650 to 1820 and refer to and quote from a number of them, my primary focus is other than theological. In the sermons, exegeses, apologetics, and miscellaneous religious writings of the eighteenth century, the existence of typology is not—and never has been—open to the slightest argument. Its presence and history have been outlined, to some extent, by Fairbairn and Farrar, but no one has undertaken a systematic study of eighteenth-century religious typology in this century.[4] Perhaps the fact that theological typology is so clear, except for the controversies over prophecy, has made detailed study unnecessary; or perhaps the relatively minor contributions to biblical exegesis by eighteenth-century English religious writers have rendered the subject unfit for inquiry. My focus, instead, will be on the many genres of literature in which typology, typological

---

[4] Frederic W. Farrar, *History of Interpretation* (New York, 1886), deals mainly with Continental theology. Patrick Fairbairn, *Typology of Scripture, or the Doctrine of Types investigated in its principles* . . . , 2 vols. (Edinburgh, 1845-47), devotes part of his first volume to the eighteenth century, but he, too, turns the bulk of his attention to the Continent. Thomas R. Preston, in two forthcoming essays, deals afresh with typology as part of biblical hermeneutics in eighteenth-century England and underscores its links with literature: see his "Biblical Criticism, Literature, and the Eighteenth-Century Reader," in *Books and Their Readers in Eighteenth-Century England*, ed. Isabel Rivers (Leicester: Leicester Univ. Press, 1982). I am grateful to him for allowing me to consult in manuscript his still unpublished essay, "From Typology to Narrative: The Rewriting of Sacred History in Eighteenth-Century England."

imagery, and prefigurative structures, characters, and plots play a part. My method, of necessity, will often be circumstantial, but this need will give me many opportunities to show how greatly the literature and thought of the period were indebted to a figural tradition whose survival, persistence, and recurrence are considerable.

At this point, it may be useful for me to say that the discovery of typological subtleties, patterns, structures, and methodologies in a large body of literature does not by itself transform minor writings to works of genius. An obscure novel or poem which, after my analysis, scholars may agree to be written in a typological mode, will not therefore become an important work by a major genius. As an intellectual historian, my purpose is to trace the history of an important, hitherto neglected figural mode in many genres of eighteenth-century literature; I do not wish to create new reputations for works long forgotten or to argue that certain works, now that we can see how intricate they are, are therefore intrinsically more worthy of attention. However, it is my hope that the kind of study which this book embodies will bridge the gap between studies of seventeenth- and nineteenth-century literature, both of which have for some time been regarded as fit subjects for similar analysis. Perhaps my efforts here will promote cognate inquiries, over the next decade, into the figural backgrounds of eighteenth-century texts. Typology is a system of exegesis; when its methods are applied to literature, typology often becomes a predictive structure. A growing awareness of such structures and of literary codes like typology has stimulated literary studies in the last few years and, in various ways, this book is meant both to refine the study of such structures and codes and to enlarge our perception of them in eighteenth-century English literature.

This discussion can benefit from a prolepsis, and I take this opportunity to add one, for my study cannot—and is not intended to —cover all aspects of typology, whether theological or abstracted, within the period of its focus. For example, I shall say very little about the presence of typology and typological structures and codes in the visual arts of the eighteenth century. The subject is a large one, long known to art historians, but only in the last decade or so have scholars started to identify the presence of types in the various arts. A major exception to this trend is the study of stained glass in churches; the *Corpus Vitrearum Medii Aevi*, a vast compilation on which work was started before the Second World War, inaugurated a major trend in the study of church architecture. Indeed, one need only examine the stained glass panels in English churches, cathedrals, and chapels from Canterbury and King's College Chapel to the Wren churches of the late seventeenth and early eighteenth centuries to appreciate how thoroughly their architects understood the visual qualities of typology.[5] Typology made its impact felt in other arts as well, from the grandest history paintings to more modest prints and emblems. The popular genre of paintings dealing with the Christ-like death of a leading statesman or general, for example, often employed typological materials. Benjamin West's astoundingly popular *Death of Wolfe* (1763) frames itself on the biblical accounts of the mourning of Christ and follows the style of well-known sixteenth- and seventeenth-century deposition scenes.[6] John Singleton Copley contributed to the genre with his *The Death of the Earl of Chatham* (1779-81) and so did John Trumbull with his *The Death of General Warren* and *The Death of General Montgomery* (both 1768).[7] These, and other similar paintings, had an enormous extended audience through the sale of prints. The typological structure of a painting with a deposition scene may seem fairly obvious; but the painters of the century also demonstrated that less familiar typological groupings and structures made appropriate subjects for large canvases. Copley's *Watson and the Shark* (1778), for example, has recently received a persuasive typological reading, and there can be little doubt that students of eighteenth-century painting and portraiture will continue to detect prefigurative structures and groupings of figures drawn from earlier Christian iconography in the art of the period.[8] Large history paintings

5 John M. Schnorrenberg, "Anglican Architecture, 1558-1662: Its Theological Implications and Its Relation to the Continental Background," unpub. doct. diss., Princeton Univ., 1964, discusses some of the typological aspects of Church architecture in the century before Wren. The usual medieval arrangement of stained glass, followed into the nineteenth century, was to depict scenes from the Old Testament (types) on the left side of the nave and parallel scenes from the New Testament (antitypes) on the right side, but there are many variations in existence. The idiosyncratic design of many of Wren's masterpieces, of course, does not permit such an arrangement.

6 See Joseph Burke, *English Art, 1714-1800* (Oxford: Clarendon Press, 1976), pp. 245-47 and Pl. 70A.

7 See *American Art: 1750-1800. Towards Independence*, ed. Charles F. Montgomery and Patricia E. Kane (Boston: New York Graphic Society, 1976), pp. 87-88, 98-100.

8 In Irma B. Jaffe's essay, "Ethics and Aesthetics in Eighteenth-Century American Art," forthcoming in *The American Revolution and Eighteenth-Century Culture: Bicentennial Essays*, ed. Paul J. Korshin (New York: AMS Press,

on biblical themes also employ typological materials, continuing a trend that painters had favored since large-scale artistic patronage started in renaissance Italy. West's painting, *Elisha Raising the Shunammite's Son* (1766) and Benjamin Robert Haydon's *Christ's Triumphant Entry into Jerusalem* (1820), like many other contemporary paintings on biblical subjects, are rich in typological materials.[9]

The great popularity of collections of iconography in the eighteenth century (thanks to the efforts of Ronald Paulson and others, we are just coming to realize the importance of Ripa's *Iconologia* and contemporary collections of emblem books) is another fruitful area for typological study (see Figure 20).[10] Paulson points out that, long before native English editions of Ripa started to appear, English artists were thoroughly indoctrinated in the literary and visual traditions surrounding Ripan iconography. Since the Bible, other sacred texts, and Christian contexts inevitably loom large in these traditions, it is inevitable that typological structures would have entered the language of eighteenth-century art in this way. Artists of the age read widely as well and, as a group, must have been thoroughly aware of the use of prefigurative structures in the literature of their time. Art as royalist propaganda, from the time of Rubens's Banqueting House ceiling and Inigo Jones's designs for Charles I's court masques, had flattered monarchical hopes and aspirations by introducing suggestive analogies from christological traditions; we are now beginning to realize that many of these parallels form yet another chapter in the history of the typology of kingship. The eighteenth-century graphic artist, finally, in the role of book illustrator, had the opportunity to illuminate some of the

---

Inc., 1982). See also Roger B. Stein, "Copley's *Watson and the Shark* and Aesthetics in the 1770s," in *Discoveries and Considerations: Essays in Early American Literature and Aesthetics presented to Harold Jantz* (Albany: State Univ. of New York Press, 1976), pp. 85-130, and Charles Mitchell, "Benjamin West's *Death of General Wolfe* and the Popular History Piece," *JWCI*, 6 (1966), 20-33.

[9] See Robert Rosenblum, *Transformations in Late Eighteenth-Century Art* (Princeton: Princeton Univ. Press, 1967), pp. 53-54, on West's painting. On Haydon's painting, see Walter Jackson Bate, *John Keats* (Cambridge, Mass.: Harvard Univ. Press, 1963), pp. 111-13, 643, and Haydon's own *Description of Christ's Triumphant Entry into Jerusalem* (London, 1820).

[10] See Ronald Paulson, *Emblem and Expression: Meaning in English Art of the Eighteenth Century* (Cambridge, Mass.: Harvard Univ. Press, 1975), pp. 8-10, 14-15.

prefigurative scenes from the popular poems and novels of the century (see, for example, Figure 14). As we study further the illustrators of *Paradise Lost* and *The Seasons* and especially the art of Blake, I think that we are certain to perceive many previously unnoticed typological scenes. Nor should we neglect another popular mode of graphic art, the eighteenth-century medal. Its study, from Addison to Snelling and beyond, was far more than an avocation for the dilettante, and the medal's two-faced structure bore a striking resemblance to the two-testament structure of the Bible. Eighteenth-century medals have not been systematically studied in recent years, but even a cursory acquaintance with existing collections will reveal numerous uses of prefiguration, even to the point of introducing scriptural quotations and allusions (see Figures 30-33). Although I shall make occasional, highly scattered, references to visual typology in the following chapters, the tradition is so important, so rich and varied, that it merits separate examination by specialists in the visual arts.

At this stage, I should mention again that the term *typology* does not always have a figural connotation. It has acquired, in the last few decades, a wide currency in the quantitative branches of the social sciences, where it usually refers to categorizing phenomena according to types of behavior or other distinguishing characteristics. In this sense, *typology* means "classification." In such contexts, so far as I can ascertain, there is no suggestion whatsoever of the extensive figural applications of the term and, indeed, its use in this way appears even to be the result of social scientists' desires to use complex-sounding terminology (a failing of which literary critics, myself included, are by no means innocent); surely "classes" would do as well and would cause no confusion between the different purposes of humanists and social scientists. However, it is pointless for me to complain, since *typology* has also entered the lexicon of literary scholarship in the social scientist's sense of the world.[11] Clearly typology, in any number of senses, is with us to stay.

The use of figural typology differs from country to country and period to period, so a useful distinction for us to bear in mind is the degree of its secularization within a given culture. Typology is drawn into secular contexts relatively late in the eighteenth cen-

[11] For example, David Lodge, *The Modes of Modern Writing: Metaphor, Metonymy, and the Typology of Modern Literature* (London: Edward Arnold, 1977), is a study of, among other things, classification rather than prefiguration.

tury in France and Germany, in the first because the threat of blasphemy until the time of the French Revolution was a real one, in the second because a popular secular literature developed quite slowly in the last half of the eighteenth century.[12] In America, too, we will find that a secularized typology scarcely appears at all before the early Federal Period, with a much greater flowering to follow in the nineteenth century.[13] But in England, which had settled its principal religious problems and the main questions of political succession by the end of the seventeenth century, a favorable climate existed for experiment with new literary forms and methodologies. Older figural modes like typology which, as I shall show, survived the seventeenth century virtually unchanged in structure, would become suitable for experimental use in secular genres of literature. It is possible that some eighteenth-century typologies are practically unconscious but, whether by accident or deliberately, types certainly enter early into secular use. A few brief examples will illustrate the kind of secularizing I have in mind. Consider, for instance, Mary Astell's description of a women's monastic retreat in *A Serious Proposal to the Ladies* (1694). In a context that is both religious and secular, she calls the retirement "a Type and Antepast of Heav'n."[14] This is a standard secularized application, with a religious context still evident. Let me give an example of another kind. Swift, writing to Bolingbroke and Pope from Dublin in 1729, recalls his political prominence in London twenty years before, and makes another kind of allusion:

> My greatest misery is recollecting the scene of twenty years past, and then all on a sudden dropping into the present. I remember when I was a little boy, I felt a great fish at the end of my line which I drew up almost on the ground, but it dropt

12 See Frei, *The Eclipse of Biblical Narrative*, pp. 149, 155-56.

13 On nineteenth-century American secularization of typology, see Karl Keller, "Alephs, Zahirs, and the Triumph of Ambiguity: Typology in Nineteenth-Century American Literature," in *Literary Uses of Typology*, pp. 274-314, and Mason I. Lowance, Jr., *The Language of Canaan: Metaphor and Symbol in New England from the Puritans to the Transcendentalists* (Cambridge, Mass.: Harvard Univ. Press, 1980), pp. 294-95, where the author mentions secularizations of typological modes in the writing in Whitman, Faulkner, Frost, Mailer, and Robert Lowell.

14 Mary Astell, *A Serious Proposal to the Ladies, for the Advancement of their True and Greatest Interest*, 2 parts in one vol. (London, 1694), I, 42. "Antepast" here means "foretaste" (see *NED*); it is, curiously, the same word as "antipasto," which is a foretaste to a meal or a type of an entrée.

in, and the disappointment vexeth me to this very day, and I
believe it was the type of all my future disappointments.[15]

The religious context is nonexistent here; Swift is smooth, conversational, and entirely correct in his use of what I will later call
abstracted typology. The occurrence is too trivial for it to have any
special meaning for our knowledge of Swift's figuralism, although
we know from *A Tale of a Tub* that he had a superb working
knowledge of all aspects of typology. Indeed, there is probably a
self-deprecating mood of irony at work in this personal recollection.

Typology, in its two-thousand-year history, has risen, declined, risen
again, and then repeated the entire process in another cycle. Its
popularity has varied considerably over the centuries. We know
now, thanks to the twentieth-century theological studies of Daniélou
and others, that typology was central to the thought and exegesis of the pre-Nicene Church.[16] In Augustine and post-Augustin-
ian theology, typology merged with allegorical and other tropological forms of interpretation, a phenomenon that continued, with
minor variations, until the Reformation. During the seventeenth
century, typology acquired new force, for the Protestant reformers
found it an effective method for using the facts of salvific history to
emphasize the rectitude of their cause and their independence from
Rome. This second rise of typology ultimately led to much far-
fetched and inventive analogizing; as a consequence, typological
exegesis began to fall into disrepute in eighteenth-century Europe.
During the seventeenth and eighteenth centuries, in the hands of
the exegetes, typology gradually began to alter its nature completely. In the religious sphere, theologians who would no longer

[15] *The Correspondence of Jonathan Swift*, ed. Harold Williams, 5 vols. (Oxford: Clarendon Press, 1963-65), III, 329 (5 April 1729).

[16] See Jean Cardinal Daniélou, S.J., *Sacramentum Futuri* (Paris: Beauchesne,
1950), trans. Engl. as *From Shadows to Reality: Studies in the Biblical Typology
of the Fathers*, trans. Wulstan Hibberd (London: Burns & Oates, 1960); *Origen*,
trans. Walter Mitchell (New York: Sheed & Ward, 1955); and *The Development
of Christian Doctrine before the Council of Nicaea*, Vol. I, *The Theology of
Jewish Christianity*, trans. John A. Baker (London: Darton, Longman, & Todd,
1964), and Vol. II, *Gospel Message and Hellenistic Culture*, trans. John A. Baker
(London: Darton, Longman, & Todd, 1973).

use typology as a method for reading Scripture started to turn it toward the study of the general basis of symbolic language and the comparative study of religions. At the same time, a great secularizing of typological applications began; we start to find secular writers using typological themes and *schemata* in nonreligious contexts in literature. The process that I describe here briefly is a slow one that takes place over more than a century. Theological typology fell under renewed suspicion in the nineteenth century, along with a gradual growth of intolerance toward the convoluted methods of exegesis with which it had traditionally been associated. Yet we are now witnessing the third rise of typology. The growth of twentieth-century historical and archeological inquiry into Christian origins and the history of religions coupled with the heightened ecumenical fervor of the last thirty years has brought typological thinking into new focus again. From this new trend my study takes its direction.

My focus, the Enlightenment, means that I shall study the second rise of typology, the period of its first great secularization, and the phenomena in intellectual history that bring about these changes. The ecumenical attitudes of our own age are important to my inquiry, for they have led to an awareness in modern literary scholarship that typology is broader in application than its theological origins would suggest. Modern theologians are now interested in typology, in the words of an authority on Old Testament prophecy, as "one of the essential presuppositions of the origin of prophetic prediction. In addition, it is a characteristic of the road by which early Christianity came to terms with its Old Testament heritage."[17] In a similar way, literary scholars, especially those concerned with deciphering the texts and cultures of the past, have come to regard typology as the key to a number of literary and historical codes. Thanks to Perry Miller and Sacvan Bercovitch, we are aware that typology was part of the cipher in which American Puritans encoded their aspirations for the new nation.[18] And thanks to Theodore Ziolkowski, Northrop Frye, and Frank Kermode (among many others), we have become more aware of the uses of typology in modern literatures.[19] As typology becomes a more popular subject

[17] See Gerhard von Rad, *Old Testament Theology*, trans. Engl. D.M.G. Stalker, 2 vols. (New York: Harper & Row, 1962-65), II, 367.

[18] See especially Sacvan Bercovitch, *The American Jeremiad* (Madison: Univ. of Wisconsin Press, 1978), pp. 93-131.

[19] See Ziolkowski, *Fictional Transfigurations of Jesus* (Princeton: Princeton Univ. Press, 1972), pp. 3-29; Frye, *Anatomy of Criticism* (Princeton: Princeton

of literary study, attempts to define it multiply. Almost every twentieth-century study of typology includes a chapter or several pages
of definition; the efforts that result range from sound philological
scholarship to the use of the term in religious exegesis and to discussion of its nontheological applications.[20] I owe much to these
definitions, but I also find that virtually every one of them is limited in perspective to a single field or subject.

The cornerstone of contemporary typological study is the precept
that typology begins with the New Testament. As K. J. Woollcombe
observes in an influential essay, "The origins of typology are to be
found in the way the New Testament writers handled the Old
Testament prophecies."[21] Nearly every modern student of the subject goes on to point out that typology is an ancient mode of Christian symbolism, that St. Paul and the Evangelists introduced and
gradually elaborated it, and that in the early Church a number of
fathers, from Origen to Augustine, perfected its manifold applications. We are right, I think, to agree that typology early developed
into a mode of figuration and signification in which both type and
antitype, the foreshadowing and that which is shadowed forth, possess historical reality and vitality. The Greek word τύπος itself is
rather ambiguous, for it can refer to either the original or the copy,
but in typological exegesis scholars almost universally agree that the
type is the Old Testament prefiguration of a New Testament fulfillment, whether a person, a place, an event, or a texture of events.
Definitions of typology, however, almost always fail to point out
that this figural mode is not exclusively Christian but pre-Christian.
It is true that exegetical typology, as we understand it today, derives
from the efforts of St. Paul and his followers to demonstrate to the
Jews and Gentiles of first-century Palestine (and later, of other
parts of the ancient world) that Jesus Christ was the Messiah promised in the Old Testament prophecies. But it is essential to note
that typology is a form of nonliteral predictive exegesis or explana-

---

Univ. Press, 1957), pp. 186-206; Kermode, *The Genesis of Secrecy: On the Interpretation of Narrative* (Cambridge, Mass.: Harvard Univ. Press, 1979), pp. 23-47
(on the Book of Mark; Kermode speaks of typological exegesis without actually
calling it such).

[20] For the philological side of the definition, see Ursula Brumm, *American
Thought and Religious Typology* (New Brunswick: Rutgers Univ. Press, 1970),
pp. 20-23. There are many similar definitions.

[21] See "The Biblical Origins and Patristic Development of Typology," in *Essays
on Typology*, ed. G.W.H. Lampe and K. J. Woollcombe (Napierville, Ill.: Alec
R. Allenson, Inc., 1957), p. 49.

tion and that, as such, it was not original with the Apostles. St. Paul, as he himself stresses in his address to the multitude in Jerusalem (Acts 22.3), was schooled in the Jewish law by Gamaliel. He was, as one commentator notes, "a rabbi converted to a Christian evangelist."[22] Hence Paul was acquainted with rabbinic or midrashic exegesis, a nonliteral (i.e., figural) form of interpretation that includes prophetic and predictive reading of Old Testament texts. Midrashic predictive exegesis is either historical or eschatological. As Wolfson describes it, Jewish "historical predictive interpretation is an attempt to find in scriptural texts predictions of future events already known to the interpreter to have taken place either in Biblical or post-Biblical times"; Jewish eschatological predictive interpretation is "the attempt to find in Scripture non-literal meanings referring to events which are to take place in the end of days, such as the advent of the Messiah, the Messianic age, the world to come, and the resurrection of the dead."[23] The methods of Jewish nonliteral predictive interpretation, then, are closely analogous to Pauline typology, and they were familiar in the ancient world not only in rabbinic writings but also in the Hellenistic Jewish writings of the ancient Near East that borrowed from rabbinic traditions. The exegeses of Philo, for example, are indebted to Greek philosophic interpretation, and employ nonliteral interpretation to discover hidden meanings in Scripture in much the same way that Greek exegetes found the hidden senses in Homer. Although there is no etymological link between rabbinic midrash and Greek allegorism, it is certain that the allegorical exegeses of the early Fathers readily adopt both Jewish historical and eschatological nonliteral interpretation. Christian typology subsumes aspects of both of these methods of reading.

The Jewish past of typology reaches the Renaissance and post-Reformation along three roads in the history of ideas. The first route is through Pauline exegesis, the refinements of the Fathers, and the further refinements of the medieval church.[24] The second is through the introduction, in Christian Europe, of the study of

22 See Joseph Bonsirven, S. J., *Exégèse Rabbinique et Exégèse Paulinienne* (Paris: Beauchesne, 1939), p. 348; cf. pp. 68-76, 328-30.

23 Harry Austryn Wolfson, *The Philosophy of the Church Fathers. Vol. I: Faith, Trinity, Incarnation*, 3rd ed., rev. (Cambridge, Mass.: Harvard Univ. Press, 1970), pp. 26-27; see Wolfson's entire chapter on "The Allegorical Method," pp. 24-72.

24 See the helpful essay of Henri de Lubac, S.J., " 'Typologie' et 'Allegorie'," *Recherches de Science Religieuse*, 34 (1947), 180-226.

the rabbis in the sixteenth and seventeenth centuries. Some of this interest focused on Jewish mysticism, especially on cabalism, but there is a gradually increasing knowledge of midrashic typology as well, particularly among English writers like Milton who were well read in Continental theology or in the rabbis themselves.[25] The third source for European knowledge of pre-Christian typology is the hermetic writings, the ancient theology whose study attained cultic proportions in the seventeenth century. In England, during the period covered by this book, Ralph Cudworth, Edward Stilling-fleet, Andrew Ramsay, William Warburton, and a large following of eighteenth-century mythologers were aware of at least one, sometimes several, of these sources for pre-Christian typology. Enlightenment messianism and millenarianism often confuse elements from all three sources so that it is difficult to separate the various strands in order to trace them back to their originals. The Enlightenment search for Christian origins, which I shall examine more closely in Chapter 6, inevitably deals with pre-Christian types and typological exegesis. Consequently, when eighteenth-century theologians like David Hartley and Jacob Bryant began to find in ancient typology a basis for a universal symbolism, common to all cultures and languages, they were dealing with typology in terms that should remind us of twentieth-century semiology. Typology becomes a code, a sign language, which all people had once understood but which the linguistic confusion of Babel had transformed into a welter of conflicting sounds and images. Today we readily understand the quest for a universal sign language.[26] The typologists of seventeenth- and eighteenth-century Europe understood what they were looking for less clearly, so we will find that they dabbled in many topics, some of them germane, others irrelevant. Christian iconography, hermetic symbolism, hieroglyphics, the imagery of freemasonry, Greek and Roman decoration, emblems, pagan pictographs —all are jumbled together in a long procession of learned works from the seventeenth through the early nineteenth centuries. It is not my purpose in this book to analyze all of this literature but rather to trace, using a great deal of it, from serious theological works to didactic and less didactic secular genres, the many ways in

25 Harris Francis Fletcher's two studies, *Milton's Semitic Studies and Some Manifestations of Them in His Poetry* (Chicago: Univ. of Chicago Press, 1926) and *Milton's Rabbinical Readings* (Urbana: Univ. of Illinois Press, 1930), are important guides to Milton's absorption of midrashic exegesis.

26 Among many works on the subject, see Pierre Guiraud, *Semiology*, trans. George Grass (London: Routledge & Kegan Paul, 1975), pp. 1-4.

which the elusive codes of typology appear, disappear, and reappear in new forms.

 3

Let me now discuss the uses and implications of typology that will be important to this work. The first might be called *conventional typology*. This aspect of the term is well illustrated in the Gospels and in the Epistles of St. Paul and the elaborations of those uses that the pre-Nicene Fathers and Augustine made. Typology, according to Hebrews 10.1, is embodied in the law of the Old Testament, "having a shadow of good things to come, and not the very image of those things"; Adam, according to Romans 5.14, "is the figure of him that was to come"; Israel and its tribulations are to be interpreted as a foreshadowing of the fulfillment that would come later in Christ (1 Cor. 10.1-4). These and a number of similar typological texts establish the basis for interpreting certain passages of the Old Testament as prefigurations of Christ.[27] Some of the figural readings that the Evangelists and St. Paul employ derive from midrashic exegesis. The early Fathers, most notably Origen, were not content to leave typology as they found it. They expanded its scope considerably, so that many Old Testament events became, for them, prefigurations of the life of Christ; they interpreted many of the smallest details of the Pentateuch as types of the Church, the spiritual life, the sacraments, and—significantly—of post-New Testament Christian history.[28] The early Fathers, in broadening the contexts of typology far beyond what the New Testament had presented, were attracted by the probative possibilities of prefiguration: to look back over the documents of the past and to find in them prophecies that had been fulfilled since the writing of those very documents made them seek ever more zealously for types of Christianity whose mere hints were now established fact. Typology, in other words, very early acquired an historical purpose, just as the predictive figurations of the rabbis served historical needs for the Jewish people. The typological elaborations of medieval fourfold

---

[27] For a full listing of all the typological texts in the New Testament, see Barbara K. Lewalski, *Protestant Poetics and the Seventeenth-Century Religious Lyric* (Princeton: Princeton Univ. Press, 1979), pp. 111-12.

[28] See Daniélou, *Origen*, pp. 161-62, and *Gospel Message and Hellenistic Culture*, pp. 200-11, 221-28, 237-55, 257-71, etc.

exegesis do little to change the bases of conventional typology, but the codification of centuries of glosses in medieval commentaries and texts, of which Nicholas of Lyra's *Biblia Sacra cum glossa ordinaria et postilla* is the most detailed, made volumes of typological lore available to later generations of exegetes. Indeed, it is possible to read through the annotated Bibles of the sixteenth and seventeenth centuries, which derive from medieval compilations, and to find a typological gloss for virtually every text in the Old Testament.

The Protestant reformers of the sixteenth century did not reject the Church's typological stratifications of Scripture, but they did modify the direction of conventional typology significantly to embrace contemporary and future history. They continued the practice of typological exegesis with respect to Old and New Testament texts, but they also intensified the process, which started as early as Clement of Alexandria and Eusebius, of drawing analogies between Old Testament types and contemporary history. This analogizing, which some students of the seventeenth century call *correlative typology*, most commonly involves implied parallels between such Old Testament figures as Moses, Joshua, and David, and contemporary monarchs, statesmen, and other worthies.[29] These Old Testament types had their traditional antitypes in the life and works of Jesus, and thus to relate them to postbiblical events is to introduce an after-the-fact typology, or postfiguration. Marvell's use of Davidic typology in writing about Oliver Cromwell, for example, makes Cromwell a postfiguration of a type. Dryden uses postfigurative typology with the David story in *Absalom and Achitophel*. Protestant typologists also elaborated conventional typology in a second way by regarding their own history as an antitype of Old Testament history or typological events. Israel's deliverance from captivity in Egypt or in Babylon, from the Red Sea's threat of deluge, or from wanderings in the wilderness became, for many Protestants and especially for English Puritans, living prefigurations of their own struggles. This sort of typology comes to involve the search for the New Jerusalem and, as such, it is central to the Puritan experience in the New World.[30]

Typology permeated all aspects of the Puritan experience in England and America, but it was far from being ubiquitous. Writers

29 See Lewalski, *Protestant Poetics*, pp. 129-38.
30 See the essays in *Typology and Early American Literature*, ed. Sacvan Bercovitch (Amherst: Univ. of Massachusetts Press, 1972).

who introduce typology into their writings, whether religious or secular, have always done so selectively. All Christians are conscious of typology and some of its implications, but those who choose to make typological references or parallels in published writings have a reason for using this kind of figuralism. A popular English kind of postfigurative typology is that which appears in sermons commemorating the martyrdom of Charles I. January 30th, or Martyr's Day, sermons were a staple of the English scene from the 1660s until the early nineteenth century; perhaps as many as a thousand examples of the genre survive. In view of the typological possibilities of the Regicide, it is surprising that so few of these sermons actually elaborate christological parallels. One might suggest that the Christian experience was such that every auditor or reader would automatically have understood the typological qualities of Charles's execution; but if all Christians had this understanding, then it would have been needless for preachers and exegetes to mention it at all. Typology implies a perceived relationship on the part of the reader or exegete; it is an intensified mode of *figura*, a mode that writers have traditionally used for historical and literary purposes to strengthen an existing proof. The evidence for Christianity, so far as seventeenth- and eighteenth-century writers were concerned, was sufficient for all reasonable people to accept, but the perception and communication of typological relationships helps to intensify the evidences of the Christian religion. Typology, as I shall show later, simply underscores, in the world of *figura*, the predictive relationships that form the basis of much human experience. If we trace the frequency of typological references in chronological terms, we will find that religious writers tend to have recourse to typological arguments more often during periods of national and spiritual crisis. In English history, such high points of typological discourse occur during the Civil Wars, in the 1670s and '80s, during the lengthy controversy over Scripture prophecy in the 1720s and '30s, and around the time of the American and French Revolutions. This kind of Protestant typology, which often has a religious context but just as commonly has political or literary associations as well, displays sufficient modifications of conventional typology to merit a different name. In this book, I shall describe such figuration as *applied typology*.

A third form of Protestant typology is messianic or millenarian prefiguration. Jewish eschatological typology, as early as the seventh century B.C., had concerned itself with predictions or signs of the

Messiah.[31] Jewish apocalypticism frequently has to do with the Messiah's coming, with the end of recorded time, and with the establishment of a perfect kingdom. An early Christian occurrence appears in Mark, when the four leading disciples—Peter, James, John, and Andrew—ask Jesus "privately" of the coming of the Messiah and his works: "Tell us, when shall these things be? and what shall be the sign when all these things shall be fulfilled?" (Mark 13.4). Jesus' answer is explicit; he speaks of the time of great tribulation and of the second coming of the Son of Man (Mark 13.24-27). In speaking thus, Jesus recalls familiar themes from Jewish messianism. Christian exegetes, as they worked the typology of apocalypse into the fabric of their beliefs, clearly borrowed from the Jewish eschatology; readings of the Book of Revelation nearly always point to the historical typology of Jesus' second coming.[32] Protestant millenarian typology differs from that of the Catholic Church in that it tends to regard the apocalyptic predictions of the Old and New Testaments as types whose antitypes are to come not at some unspecified future date but whose fulfillments are to be found in recorded history.[33] One of the features of this kind of applied typology is a careful study of biblical and postbiblical chronology in order to determine the precise time of the Millennium, a serious endeavor that enlisted the efforts of theologians and scientists alike from Joseph Mede to Sir Isaac Newton to Joseph Priestley. Millenarianism may be the form of typology that has the most popular appeal and that touches popular literature—pamphlets, chapbooks, inspirational narratives—most thoroughly.

[31] On Jewish messianism, see Gershom Scholem, "Toward an Understanding of the Messianic Idea in Judaism," in his *The Messianic Idea in Judaism and Other Essays on Jewish Spirituality* (New York: Shocken Books, 1971), pp. 1-36, as well as the following essays in the same collection; and Maurice Vernes, *Histoire des Idées Messianiques depuis Alexandre jusqu'à l'Empereur Hadrian* (Paris: Sandoz et Fishbacher, 1874), Chaps. I-III.

[32] See Daniélou, *The Theology of Jewish Christianity*, pp. 377-404, an excellent chapter on early Jewish-Christian millenarianism, and H. Bietenhard, "The Millennial Hope in the Early Church," *Scottish Journal of Theology*, 5 (1953), 12-30.

[33] See Lewalski, *Protestant Poetics*, p. 129; Clarke Garrett, *Respectable Folly: Millenarianism and the French Revolution in France and England* (Baltimore: Johns Hopkins Univ. Press, 1975), pp. 121-43, and more generally, *Puritans, the Millennium, and the Future of Israel: Puritan Eschatology, 1600-1660*, ed. Peter Toon (Cambridge: James Clarke, 1970), and Bernard Capp, *The Fifth Monarchy Men: A Study in Seventeenth-Century English Millenarianism* (Totowa, N.J.: Rowman & Littlefield, 1972).

Historical applications of typology draw the figural mode away from its original exegetical purpose and, in seventeenth- and eighteenth-century England, there is a distinct secularizing of prefigurative styles of imagery. This form of typology—*abstracted typology*, as I call it later in the book—may sometimes retain overtones of its original Christian purpose. It appears in secular literature in various ways: in characters and moralized fables, in stories that recall typological relationships from biblical and other literatures, in analogies to pagan types, in mythological discussions that blossom from the search for Christian origins, in narratives with prefigurative or typological patterns, and even in satirical works that ridicule the presumed excesses of inspired figuralist reading. Since abstracted typology is the principal subject of this book, I shall say little about it at this stage of my discussion. The evidence for abstracted typology is sometimes very strong, as for example in seventeenth-century character books, whose figures of virtue and vice often derive directly from typological sermons, or in the moralized bodies of commentary that accompany contemporary collections of fables. But the evidence for abstracted typology is not always so satisfying, and sometimes, as for instance in prose narrative, we may find typological patterns or isolated strains rather than completely structured prefigurative stories. In this respect, my search for typological materials in prose fiction is part of the twentieth-century critical quest for cultural and intellectual patterns in texts from the past for which the chief evidence is often no more than the presence of accepted archetypes, understood patterns, and recognized codes. "Typological thinking," as a recent theologian writes,

> is in itself very far from being an esoteric form of proof which belongs only to theology. It rises out of man's universal effort to understand the phenomena about him on the basis of concrete analogies, an effort to which both philosophers and poets of every age have devoted themselves.[34]

Hence typological patterns in poetry, especially shorter poems, and in short pieces of narrative prose are relatively common and easy to identify. Typological patterns in longer narratives at first seem more difficult to justify, but modern scholars have readily discerned precisely such structures in longer works like Du Bartas's *Divine Weekes*, Milton's *Paradise Lost* and *Paradise Regained*, Bunyan's

---

[34] Von Rad, *Old Testament Theology*, II, 364.

longer religious allegories, Blake's major prophecies, and Shelley's *Prometheus Unbound*. The authors of these works found Christian —and allied—typological traditions helpful, for various reasons, but one of the most important reasons why they used it was that typology is an intensifying figural mode which clarifies and persuades an audience about the point to which it relates. I hope to show later in this volume that the presence of typological patterns in eighteenth-century prose narrative is real, has a definite purpose, and does not require special mystic spectacles to read.

Typology is linked indissolubly to prophecy, and here, too, the typological applications that I shall study in this book have their own peculiar use. There is much evidence that writers during the late Renaissance and the seventeenth century came to regard prophecy as a unique genre.[35] Indeed, a fascination with the prophetic vision, the Pisgah-sight, and the visionary seer as poet link Renaissance and Romantic literature. Not every prophecy is typological, but there is often a prefigurative side to the prophetic vision, especially when the prophecy has to do with the Millennium. The Enlightenment debate about the Millennium, as I shall show later, was intense and long-winded; it embraces a diverse group of writers from enthusiastic millenarians like Richard Brothers (who claimed an audience with God) and Joanna Southcott (who believed herself —erroneously, as it turned out—impregnated by the Holy Spirit with the Shiloh, the man-child of Revelation 12.5) to exact scientists like Newton and Whiston, who were attracted by the chronological detail of Scripture prophecy. Millenarian prophecy, particularly that which derives from folk traditions, usually involves the prefiguration of a Savior-style person with awesome powers and total suzerainty over the earth; shadows abound in such visions, and both type and antitype play a large popular role.[36]

Thus a working definition of typology must take cognizance of the pseudo-theological applications of the prefigurative mode that occur throughout the eighteenth century. We may see aspects of prophetic typology in many kinds of literature: visionary dreams (*The Pilgrim's Progress, Robinson Crusoe*), mock-prophetic visions (*The Dunciad*), the *vates*-figures of Gray, Smart, and Blake, and

[35] See Joseph Anthony Wittreich, Jr., *Visionary Poetics: Milton's Tradition and His Legacy* (San Marino, Calif.: The Huntington Library, 1979), pp. 3-5.
[36] For an excellent account of the popular tradition of prophesying, see J.F.C. Harrison, *The Second Coming: Popular Millenarianism, 1780-1850* (New Brunswick: Rutgers Univ. Press, 1979), pp. 11-38.

popular pamphlets and dissenting tracts promising the perfect world of the Millennium. The prophet always claims to hold the key to secret writings, hidden signs, or a silent language. These are artifacts which the non-*illuminati* perceive without comprehension, but the prophet glimpses the types and shadows within them and speaks, often announces, the truth and fulfillment that are to come. In the sense that prophecy holds forth the coming of some greater man, the accomplishment of some greater event, or the arrival of a better world than the present time can afford, its structure is strongly typological. In this context, then, it forms a major part of prefigurative tradition in the years from 1650 to 1820.

The complexity of typology in seventeenth- and eighteenth-century England was made possible, in part, by its careful classification and codification. With a zeal that might have pleased the scientific taxonomists of the next century, seventeenth-century Protestant theologians collected types and separated them into categories: personal types, perpetual types, occasional types.[37] The writings of these codifiers form a genre in itself, the typological handbook. These handbooks are by Protestant, usually Anglican, clergymen; as the seventeenth century waned, they are the work entirely of Dissenters. Their authors—among them are William Guild, Thomas Taylor, John Everard, Thomas Worden, Benjamin Keach, and Samuel Mather—drew in part on the Protestant reformers of the sixteenth century, chiefly Luther and Calvin, but more on the systematic classifiers of the seventeenth century like Johannes Cocceius and Salomon Glassius.[38] These encyclopediae could not have been meant for easy reading; they are rather reference works for the authors of sermons and popular treatises. Nevertheless, few of them had only a single edition, and some appeared as many as ten times, even as late as the nineteenth century. While this learned tradition

[37] This classification is that of Samuel Mather in *The Figures or Types of the Old Testament* (1683); other codifiers adopted similar taxonomies.

[38] William Guild, *Moses Unveiled* (1650), Thomas Taylor, *Christ Revealed: or the Old Testament Explained* (1635), later revised as *Moses and Aaron, or The Types and Shadows of our Saviour in the Old Testament Opened and Explained* (1653), John Everard, *The Gospel Treasures Opened* (1653), Thomas Worden, *The Types Unvailed, or, The Gospel pick't out of the Legal Ceremonies* (1664), Benjamin Keach, *Tropologia: A Key to Open Scripture Metaphors* (1681), and Mather's work cited in note 37 are the principal English handbooks. Cocceius' *Summa Doctrinae de Foedere et Testamento Dei* (Leyden, 1648) and Glassius' *Philologia Sacra*, 5 vols. (Jena, 1623-26), were widely read and influential in England.

doubtless permitted ready access to the typology of Scripture, it also encouraged writers to locate prefigurative relationships outside of the world of the Bible in the great book of nature. *Natural typology*, as I refer to it, has other roots as well, whether in the doctrine of pagan resemblances among things or the mystical associationism of Jakob Boehme, but its significance for my study lies in its serving as a basis for the finding of predictive relationships in the world and in texts outside a strictly religious context. Boehme's inspiration permits him to see types of the divinity in the dawn, the innocence of animals, the simplicity of youth, the beauty of plants and flowers, and the like. In the eighteenth century, David Hartley, Christopher Smart, William Cowper, and later Coleridge would carry the analogies of natural typology much further. Ultimately, with Coleridge, an artistic creation is the antitype of a shadow or an idea of creation in the mind and, in such formulations, typology blends with and becomes almost indistinguishable from semiology, more a pattern of symbolic thought than religious prefiguration.

 4

To the theologian seriously concerned with the exegetical values of biblical figuralism, nonscriptural applications of typology can be very dangerous.[39] To the intellectual historian seeking to chart the presence of various forms of typology in the thoughts and texts of a portion of our past, the manifold adaptations of the prefigurative mode in imaginative literature are one of the many challenges that studies of Enlightenment thought present. In the following chapters, I shall mix the familiar with the new, and shall urge readers to take a somewhat different perspective on the past, "to rearrange familiar objects in a new pattern from a new angle of vision."[40] I shall devote most of my attention to typology in its literary contexts from 1650 to 1820, for the movement of the types in eighteenth-century England is always from the rigid theological prescriptions of the mode to considering it as an integral part of the figural experience of everyday life. Hence what is most interesting

[39] For this view, see G.W.H. Lampe, "The Reasonableness of Typology," in *Essays on Typology*, pp. 35-38.

[40] See Edmund S. Morgan's review of Bercovitch's *The American Jeremiad* (1978), "The Chosen People," in *The New York Review of Books*, 26, no. 12 (19 July 1979), 33.

to the intellectual historian of typology in the English Enlightenment is not its survival, more or less unchanged, in religious contexts (although this survival is important), but its gradual application, by many literary hands, in a number of genres. The skill of
those hands, as we shall see, varies considerably, and so, too, will
uses of typology. As it grows and changes, typology accommodates
itself to both literary and historical situations and so gives rise to
structures that endure for many decades and that, in some ways,
are with us still.

CHAPTER 3

Figural Change and the Survival
of Typological Tradition

STUDENTS OF the seventeenth century have long been in agreement about the profound changes that occurred in the theory and practice of literature in the last half of the century. It is impossible to discuss English literature of this period without some reference to the transformations between metaphysical and Augustan, or from the Renaissance to the neoclassical age. These, and other similar synthetic inventions of critical nomenclature, have come to dominate our thinking about the causes of the change from the styles and methods of the earlier to those of the later seventeenth century. If we accept that there were such intellectual matrixes as the Renaissance or the neoclassical frame of mind, it is not difficult to suggest reasons for the difference between them. Various causes, usually conveniently general, have been proposed. The rise of scientific thought, the Civil War and the political instability it created, the Commercial Revolution, the growth of rationalism, the religious turmoil of the century—these concepts are pressed into service in the great task of explanation. There is no doubt that such generalities do produce literary change. But because broad concepts almost always contain inconsistencies, partial truths, and built-in fallacies, they are imperfect tools for historical examination. In this chapter, I intend to avoid them as much as possible, and to study only one important aspect of this literary transformation, the question of *figural change*. The changes in figuralism, its deployment, and the theories concerning it are substantial. They are not universal, however, so it will be necessary to temper the analysis of the imagistic transformation by the introduction of a control. This is its corollary, *the survival of tradition*, particularly *typological* tradition.

Some years ago, Lawrence Stone proposed a tripartite method for the study of seventeenth-century historical change.[1] It involves the search for a hierarchy of causes which he calls long-term preconditions, middle-term precipitants, and short-run triggers. He applies them primarily to the complex of events around the beginning of the English Revolution in the early 1640s. This methodology requires us to conceive of historical change as dependent upon substrata of other significant events, some quite recent, others relatively distant. Literary historians think in the same way, but without such a carefully wrought method as Stone's; much more is left to chance. In the study of literature it has often seemed more important to study the "sources" for a theme or an idea than to attempt to rank such causes in terms of their relative immediacy. It is possible, however, to single out a group of significant intellectual influences that had a powerful effect upon seventeenth-century writers in causing them to make aesthetic decisions in favor of one figural method and against another. The principal qualities of earlier seventeenth-century figuralism are well known. The complexity, predilection for obscurity, love of paradox, use of complex rhetorical and grammatical devices, interest in symbolism, and allusions drawn from various learned traditions of the past which characterize this period have become commonplaces of recent scholarship.[2] They require no further identification here.

There can be no "typical" early seventeenth-century image, but many, if not most, examples of metaphysical or baroque English poetry will be found to have some or all of the qualities I have just mentioned. The learning of Donne may often be patristic, that of Vaughan hermetic, and that of Henry More neoplatonic, but the

[1] See Lawrence Stone, "The English Revolution," *Preconditions of Revolution in Early Modern Europe*, ed. Robert Forster and Jack P. Greene (Baltimore: Johns Hopkins Univ. Press, 1970), pp. 55-108, esp. p. 65.

[2] Among the most prominent studies in the learned tradition of seventeenth-century imagery is Don Cameron Allen, *Image and Meaning: Metaphoric Traditions in Renaissance Poetry* (Baltimore: Johns Hopkins Univ. Press, 1960; rev. ed. 1968). For a good recent sampling of essays, see *Seventeenth-Century Imagery: Essays on Uses of Figurative Language from Donne to Farquhar*, ed. Earl Miner (Berkeley and Los Angeles: Univ. of California Press, 1971), and *Illustrious Evidence: Approaches to English Literature of the Early Seventeenth Century*, ed. Earl Miner (Berkeley and Los Angeles: Univ. of California Press, 1975), pp. 41-69, 71-89. Also influential for its exposition of the multitude of learned sources for imagery is Ruth Wallerstein, *Studies in Seventeenth-Century Poetic* (Madison: Univ. of Wisconsin Press, 1950), esp. pp. 181-277.

presence of profound, frequently obscure, erudition in all of these poets cannot be disputed. The same would be true of the vast majority of their contemporaries. In the later seventeenth century, particularly after the Restoration, as the standard schema of literary history describes it, a simplifying reaction began to reject the prevalent trend of imagistic erudition and obscurity. Few of the poets of the Restoration and eighteenth century, despite strong contrary evidence, have much reputation for learning or scholarship. From the information we have about the reading and libraries of Oldham, Dryden, Swift, Pope, and Johnson, their learning was considerable, but the belief persists that they excluded ostentatious erudition from their verse.[3]

Although there *was* extensive figural change in the second half of the century, it is wrong to assume that poetic learning in any way decreased or that what happened to figurative language or methodology can properly be described as simplification. Other terms in common use for the imagery of the later period such as clarity, perspicuity, plainness, and so on, do not describe the change we are talking about. They merely label what several generations of literary historians have decided took place. Concepts such as simplicity and clarity refer to the reader's ease or difficulty of comprehension, not to the intellectual bases of imagery. Since we cannot resurrect a seventeenth-century audience, still less ascertain precisely what a hypothetical group of this kind would have understood, simplification of imagery is a concept whose full significance we cannot entirely recapture. In order to set the stage for understanding what happened to typology in late seventeenth-century literature and life, it may be useful to examine some of the reasons why figural techniques, of which typology is one, changed at all, what qualities resisted change or adapted to new literary conditions, and why. Let me look at some literary preconditions to which seventeenth-century authors responded.

 2

The most important of the long-term preconditions for later seventeenth-century figural change is the tradition of Renaissance Christian humanism. Renaissance antiquarianism, the study of pagan

---

[3] Recent writings on several of these authors have started to emphasize their learning; a good example is Phillip Harth, *Contexts of Dryden's Thought* (Chicago: Univ. of Chicago Press, 1968).

myth, the primitive anthropology of early mythographers like Giraldi, Conti, and Cartari, and the Christianizing tendencies of sixteenth- and seventeenth-century editors of the classics laid the groundwork and provided much of the source material for poetic learning.[4] Mysteries, foreshadows and types of Christianity, and pagan distortions of the Hebraic ancestors of the primitive Church were considered to be everywhere. We find very little distrust of mystery before 1650, but much thereafter. The learning of the Renaissance mythographers, with its tendency to find evidences of the Christian religion in many ancient pagan texts, must be seen as a long-term precondition for the changes of the last half of the century. This tradition culminates in subtle, polymathic works like Athanasius Kircher's voluminous studies of eastern (most notably Egyptian) mythology, Samuel Bochart's *Geographia Sacra*, and Gerhard Vossius' *De Theologia Gentili et Physiologia Christiana*.[5] As we will see, there would be two kinds of reaction to this tradition. One, the parodic, represented by satiric works like *Hudibras*, *A Tale of a Tub*, and the Scriblerian writings, rejects and burlesques etymological, mythological, and other pedantries. The other, the skeptical, modifies mysterious interpretations, but continues to accept those aspects of them that appeared to be supported by sound evidence. Milton, for example, avoids the ornamental use of pagan myth but continues to employ the typologies that were closely associated with the Christianity of the pagan *mythos*.[6] Marvell's use of classical myth is insignificant, except when it can be infused with a Christian theme. Dryden seldom introduces classical mythology without the added artifice of hinting at its Christian, often typological, overtones. Similar evidence exists in the practices of many other writers.

A second long-term precondition for figural change is to be found in post-Reformation scriptural exegesis. Mystical interpretation, strongly favoring figural readings, is so common in the century be-

---

[4] See Allen, *Mysteriously Meant*, p. 233 and, in gen., pp. 201-47.

[5] Many of Kircher's works deal with Oriental mythology. See particularly *Oedipus Ægyptiacus*, 3 vols. in 4 (Rome, 1652-54), *Obelisci Ægyptiaci . . . interpretatio* (Rome, 1661), and *Sphynx Mystagogus* (Amsterdam, 1676). Bochart's *Geographia Sacra, seu Phaleg et Canaan* (Caen, 1646) is one of the first early applications of the etymological method to mythology; Vossius' *De Theologia Gentili* (1641), most easily available in his *Opera*, ed. Isaac Vossius, 6 vols. (Amsterdam, 1695-1701), Vol. V, is the earliest important study of the origins of idolatry.

[6] See, Allen, *Mysteriously Meant*, pp. 293-94.

fore 1650 that it scarcely requires illustration. Anglican hermeneutics had already, by Hooker's time, sought to moderate the four-
level spiritual reading of the medieval Church, but the "mistakes"
of mystical exegetes would not be exposed until the Restoration,
and even then, exposure did not necessarily mean rejection. The
ready availability of mystical authors throughout the late seventeenth and eighteenth centuries made a revival of mystical interpretation possible at any time. Just as Boehme would be reprinted
in the 1760s and '70s, in an edition which influenced Blake and
Coleridge, so the mystical readings of the early Fathers would be
made current again in the nineteenth-century Ante-Nicene Library.
English Puritanism would reform this moderation still further,
seeking the "one sense of Scripture which could both explain and
instruct." Searching for literalism of meaning, Puritan hermeneutics "repudiated imagination in the primary procedures of exegesis"
as well as "in the secondary procedures of homiletical and devotional exploration."[7] Puritan exegesis, as detractors like Swift argued, was often guilty of a misplaced literalism by attributing historical verity to inspirational *aperçus*. To the Anglican rationalists
of the Restoration, this practice was sublime demagoguery; their
hermeneutics concentrated on obtaining a proper balance between
the mysteries and literalism.[8] Figural reading of Scripture continued in Anglicanism, but it was to move, especially after the Restoration, toward a moderate style which took fewer risks. Figuralism,
in other words, was permissible if there was some historical justification for it. The diligent theological antiquarianism of scholars
and historians from Edward Stillingfleet and Theophilus Gale to
William Warburton, Jacob Bryant, and George Stanley Faber
sought to uncover acceptable verifiable evidence for this kind of
modified mystical interpretation. This entire process evolves gradually in the century and a half after 1650. Its development is clearly
slow enough to qualify it as a long-term influence upon imagistic
practice.

[7] U. Milo Kaufmann, *"The Pilgrim's Progress" and Traditions in Puritan
Meditation* (New Haven: Yale Univ. Press, 1966), p. 41. For an excellent appraisal of Puritan hermeneutics, see pp. 25-60.

[8] The best study of Anglican rationalism is that of Irène Simon, *Three Restoration Divines: Barrow, South, Tillotson*, Bibliothèque de la Faculté de Philosophie et Lettres de l'Université de Liège, fasc. 181 (Paris: Société d'Editions
"Les Belles Lettres": 1967), pp. 75-148. See also Phillip Harth, *Swift and Anglican Rationalism: The Religious Background of "A Tale of a Tub"* (Chicago:
Univ. of Chicago Press, 1961), *passim*.

These long-term precipitants, which I have outlined in general terms, consist of a great number of particularities verifiable from numerous works on mythology or biblical exegesis. The science of etymological interpretation, for instance, by which a skillful linguist could "discover" similarities among texts in half a dozen languages, did not begin with Bochart, although he carried it further than any others. The ancient historians, among them Strabo and Tacitus, the pre-Nicene Fathers, and the early writers in the patristic tradition had made etymology a familiar tool for mystical reading long before the Renaissance. Few seventeenth-century writers could have been unfamiliar with the method; it is still undergoing ridicule as late as *Gulliver's Travels, The Memoirs of Martinus Scriblerus,* and *Tristram Shandy.* The entire mystical tradition, then, formed over a century of scholarship and commentary, is unlikely to have had immediate causative effects upon the change in English figural—and typological—methodologies. The leisurely pace of its transmission from the Continent to England in a steady trickle of books and manuscripts disqualifies mysticism as a rapid catalyst of change. We must look to intellectual trends which developed more quickly, over a period of twenty to thirty years, and whose influence upon change, while less cumulative, is perhaps equally great.

The middle-term precipitants are not isolated from the long-term and the short-run factors; they do not occur exclusively in a separate band of time. Although most of those that will interest us fall between 1640 and 1670, some overlap and interrelate with other factors in a complex way. These factors are not all intimately involved with typology and the typological style, but they will affect the way writers both secular and clerical introduce types into their works. Three of the most important influences that I want to take up here are: the Civil War and its immediate aftermath, the Commonwealth; the growing distrust of mystical (including metaphorical and stylistic) excess; and the intensification of empirical methods of scholarly inquiry.

The effect on imagery of England's political instability between 1642 and 1660, while it is difficult to gauge precisely, is nonetheless considerable. The bitterness and violence of the Royalist-Parliament controversy is, more than anything else, responsible for the extreme satirical bitterness of Cleveland and the political poetry of Cowley, Davenant, and Marvell. Cleveland is a fine example of the violent figural reaction to political heresy, for his favorite method of attack is to outdo the excesses of his sectarian opponents with a mocking and snarling obscurity. Perhaps it is fitting that, after he ceased to write satire, Cleveland was the drinking companion of another great ridiculer of the mystics, Samuel Butler, with whom, as Aubrey tells us, "he had a clubb every night." He wrote virtually all of his popular satires of the 1640s, like "Smectymnuus," "The Mixt Assembly," "The Rebell *Scot*," and "On the Archbishop of *Canterbury*," with a deliberate obscurity far more difficult than anything the Parliamentary polemics could hope to attain. The prologue to "The Rebell *Scot*" is particularly harsh, but in its learned catachreses we can see a disgust with the involved argumentation of contemporary politico-religious debate.[9]

The Civil War years saw the beginning of the first crude newssheets and a crescendo of party polemic (witness the 22,000 items in the catalogue of the Thomason Tracts), so for sheer accumulation of materials the period is unique in literary history before the eighteenth century.[10] Most studies of seventeenth-century imagery tend to concentrate on poetry and literary prose. Nevertheless, even a random survey of the materials associated with the English Revolution indicates how greatly controversy inclines men to figural excess. The frequency with which the high pitch of enthusiasm and zeal is criticized during the Civil War years and the Interregnum is significant. It is not confined to controversial works like Edwards's *Gangræna* (1646), Hobbes's critique of abuses of language in *Leviathan*, Meric Casaubon's condemnation of feigned enthusiasm in *A Treatise concerning Enthusiasme* (1655), Cowley's strictures on false wit in the preface to his *Poems* (1656), and numerous similar utterances after the Restoration.[11] I do not wish to underestimate the importance of general social unrest as a middle-term

[9] See *The Poems of John Cleveland*, ed. Brian Morris and Eleanor Withington (Oxford: Clarendon Press, 1967), p. 29, esp. lines 1-26. The entire poem is learnedly obscure in a parodic way.

[10] The phenomenon of "the groaning press" has often been noticed. See the *Catalogue of the Thomason Tracts in the British Museum, 1640-1661* (London: The British Museum, 1908), p. xxi.

[11] There has been no sustained study of abuses of language in the Restoration, but Richard Foster Jones devoted great attention to the reform of pulpit oratory. For example, see his "The Attack on Pulpit Eloquence in the Restora-

influence on figural change. It is clear, however, that when men of letters greeted the Restoration of Charles II as a "general calme" and a return to sanity, they must have been thinking of what they hoped to see in language and style as well as in politics and religion.[12]

The growth of a distrust of mysticism, while it is localized enough in time to qualify as a powerful middle-term precipitant of figural change, does not begin until after the middle years of the century. We find little criticism of mysticism and its typological curiosities before 1660: Henry Reynolds could still mount the search for undermeanings in *Mythomystes* (1633); Alexander Ross and the various editions of his typological masterwork, *Mystagogus Poeticus*, belong to the 1640s and '50s; Henry More encourages the quest in *Conjectura Cabbalistica* (1653); Thomas Vaughan's mystical and magical writings of the 1650s strongly promote obscurity; and the translations of Boehme's mystical writings belong mainly to the 1640s and '50s.[13] The attack upon excessive obscurity and riddling mysticism, however, is practically contemporaneous with these developments. When a poet of the late metaphysical school like Bishop Henry King belabors stylistic and imagistic enthusiasm as "precipitate Barbarism" and uses his considerable eloquence to ridicule the florid style he had once favored himself, it is an event worthy of our notice.

In a visitation sermon that he delivered at Lewes in 1662, King finds mystery close to heresy:

> Hard and Intricate Riddles in Divinity have no use but to rack the Brain, Not to Inform, but to Pose the Understanding.

---

tion: An Episode in the Development of the Neo-classical Standard for Prose," *JEGP*, 30 (1931), 188-217.

12 Images of calm, peace, the halcyon, etc. appear in nearly all the verse tributes that poets offered to King Charles upon his return, from *Astræa Redux* to Waller's *To the King, upon His Majesty's Happy Return*. Samuel Parker, for example, in his *History of His Own Time* (London, 1727), pp. 1-2, writes, "When *Charles* the second was return'd to the kingdoms of his ancestors, to the great joy of almost all his subjects, we hop'd for a golden and better than *Saturnian* age . . . and [that] the perfect tranquility of the Nation would continue at least for several generations."

13 The popularity of Jakob Boehme is paradigmatic of the vogue of mysticism in England. His works were translated into English by various authors and published in London between 1645 and 1662. See the *NCBEL*, II, cols. 1658-62.

To deliver my full meaning, the *Plain, Positive, Catechistical Doctrine of the Church,* as it is most Easie and Familiar, so most *Sound* and Orthodox.

How many by over-bold searches after the Abstruse Mysteries of Faith, and Hid Decrees of God, have quite blinded themselves, and perplexed others?[14]

Later, in a somewhat more sweeping condemnation, he declares, "All sin is an obliquity, and the habit of Vice, *Prophaneness, Adultry, Murther, Lying, etc. are contrary to sound Doctrine."* "Obliquity," or divergence from moral rectitude, doubtless also refers to the viciousness of a flawed style.[15] King is but one of a number of pulpit orators who employ the homiletic discourse for the purpose of criticizing the overwrought figuralism of ecclesiastical prose. Tillotson, Barrow, and South do very nearly the same thing. W. Fraser Mitchell and Irène Simon have ably commented on the seventeenth-century transformations in pulpit oratory.[16] But it is also necessary to link this development to a broader attitude within much of the intellectual community regarding the proper use of imagery, both in prose and poetry.

For a stronger attack upon the seductive dangers of mysticism, we may turn to the writings of Samuel Parker. His strictures upon Neoplatonism are among the most explicit of the Restoration. In his *Free and Impartial Censure of the Platonick Philosophie* (1666), Parker quite characteristically treats the mystics as enthusiasts, zealots, fanatics, and madmen, while representing orthodox Anglicans who are untainted by schism as sober, sound, judicious, "pragmatick," and reasonable.[17] Platonism, because of its *"Enthusiastick Fanaticisme,"* is dangerous doctrine indeed: "What Pestilential Influences the Genius of *Enthusiasme* or opinionative Zeal has upon the Publick Peace, is so evident from Experience, that it needs not be prov'd from Reason." But, worst of all, the Platonists compound

---

[14] *A Sermon preached at Lewis in the Diocess of Chichester. . . .* (London, 1663), p. 36. See also pp. 19-21, 27-28, 34-35, and 42-43.

[15] See *NED,* s.v. "Obliquity," 4; cf. figurative senses for "Oblique" and "Obliquely."

[16] See W. Fraser Mitchell, *English Pulpit Oratory from Andrewes to Tillotson* (London: S.P.C.K., 1932), *passim,* and Simon, *Three Restoration Divines,* pp. 1-73.

[17] This distinction is typical of all of Parker's controversial writings and also of his *History of His Own Time.*

the confusion between truth and mystery by their flagrant abuses
of language:

> Instead of pure and genuine Reason, they abound so much
> with gaudy and extravagant Phancies. I that am too simple or
> too serious to be cajol'd with the frenzies of a bold and un-
> govern'd Imagination cannot be perswaded to think the
> Quaintest plays and sportings of wit to be any true and real
> knowledge. I can easily allow their Discourses the Title of
> *Philosophical Romances* (a sort of more ingenious imperti-
> nencies) and 'tis with this estimate I would have them read:
> But where they pretend to be Natures Secretaries, & to under-
> stand all her Intrigues, or to be Heavens Privadoes, talking of
> the Transactions there, like men lately drop'd thence, encircl'd
> with *Glories,* and cloathed with the Garments of *Moses & Elias,*
> and yet put us off with nothing but rampant Metaphors, and
> Pompous Allegories and other splendid but empty Schemes of
> speech, I must crave leave to account them (to say no worse)
> Poets & Romancers.[18]

Parker's critique of figurative language, especially of the abuse of
Christian, platonic, hermetic, and Egyptian mysticism, is quite
comprehensive. His attack also includes a condemnation of ecclesiastical writers who assumed the role of popular prophets—"cloathed
with the Garments of *Moses & Elias*"—for the Puritan millenarianism of the 1640s, while it never reached its former heights after the
Restoration, continued its threat of prophetic excess. That this figural excess is often typological is significant for my inquiry, since
it shows that Anglican writers included typology in their criticism
of *stylistic* excess at the same time that they continued to employ
typology as an *exegetical* tool in reading Scripture. Parker's work
articulates other themes to which he and his colleagues would return often in the next decade.

In 1670, to take another example, Parker would find the Non-
conformists guilty of similar linguistic and imagistic subterfuges,
this time broadening his scope to include *all* abuses of wit, particularly in secular literature. Religious zealotry, he suspects, has

---

[18] *A Free and Impartial Censure of the Platonick Philosophie, Being a Letter
written to his much Honoured Friend, Mr. N. B.* (London, 1666), pp. 73-74.
See pp. 73-115 *in toto* for one of the strongest censures of the philosophical and
linguistic bases of platonism and neoplatonism. Parker is especially contemptuous of Egyptian and other hieroglyphic learning.

spread to "the young Nurslings, and small Infantry of the Wits, the wild and hair-brain'd Youths of the Town."[19] Parker's opponents are not specifically devotees of mysticism, but their manner shows all the familiar signs of devotion to its usual methods. They have perverted "all Religion into unaccountable Fansies and Enthusiasmes, drest it up with pompous and empty Schemes of speech, and so embrace a few gawdy Metaphors and Allegories, instead of the substance of true and real Righteousness."[20] Parker, who was secretary to Gilbert Sheldon, Archbishop of Canterbury, was one of the first ecclesiastical writers before Swift to enlarge the attack upon figural abuses to include the intellectual errors of secular literature. His writings are suggestive of the negative reaction to mystical interpretation in the decade following the Restoration, but they display an increasing disquiet with a figural style that had been popular for more than a century. Dissatisfaction with literary methodologies is a slow-growing phenomenon. Hence it is interesting to see how widespread are the attitudes which Parker voices.

The height of the popularity of mysticism, especially of mystical exegesis of Scripture, has been variously estimated to embrace the 1580s or to include the period from 1640 to 1660.[21] There are scattered early objections to the figural excesses inherent in such methodologies. Bishop Wilkins, in *Ecclesiastes*, favors less obscure methods of interpretation. John Hall disagrees with the absurdities of obscure figural interpretations in *The Grounds and Reasons of Monarchy Consider'd* (1650-51): "And I am to note . . . the Poorness, or, to say better the Blasphemy of the Argument which flourishes out Kings as the Types of Divinity, and verily lavishes some

[19] See *A Discourse of Ecclesiastical Politie* (London, 1670), pp. xxii-xxxiii (pp. xxiv through xxxi are skipped in the numeration). The "Preface to the Reader" is devoted mainly to a study of abuses of wit, language, and figures of speech.

[20] *Ibid.* p. 74. Cf. pp. 76-77: "For were men obliged to speak Sense as well as Truth, all the swelling Mysteries of Fanaticism would immediately sink into flat and empty Nonsense, and they would be ashamed of such jejune and ridiculous Stuff as their admired and most profound Notions would appear to be, when they want the Varnish of fine Metaphors and glittering Allusions."

[21] See William G. Madsen, *From Shadowy Types to Truth: Studies in Milton's Symbolism* (New Haven: Yale Univ. Press, 1968), pp. 38-48. Madsen himself does not draw this conclusion, but he suggests it. What he does not conclude Earl Miner has stated more cogently in "Plundering the Egyptians, or, What We Learn from Recent Books on Milton," *ECS*, 3 (1969-70), 302-303. Barbara K. Lewalski, finally, in "Typological Symbolism and the 'Progress of the Soul' in Seventeenth-Century Literature," *Literary Uses of Typology*, pp. 79-80, reaffirms the focus of recent scholarship on mid-century figuralism.

Metaphysics to prove that all things have a natural tendency to Oneness."[22] The arguments of the neo-Harringtonians, or of Marvell in *An Account of the Growth of Popery and Arbitrary Government* (1677), were based in part on the fear that obscurity of political reasoning might cloak a return to the tyranny with which they identified the pre-Civil War years. The strongest attacks upon mystical exaggerations, however, appear after the Restoration. It is difficult to determine how influential some of these works are, but the fact that they articulate a general trend in figural matters suggests that they answered the demands of an audience. One of the most significant of these attacks is John Spencer's *A Discourse concerning Prodigies* (1663).

Spencer's little book (it is just over a hundred pages long) is characteristic of the attempts by Restoration political and religious writers to strip natural phenomena, events, and persons of any special aura of mystical symbolism. Meric Casaubon had made a similar effort during the Interregnum regarding enthusiasm; his *Treatise concerning Enthusiasme* (1655) decisively rejects the divine qualities attributed to enthusiastic outbreaks by various mystical fanatics. Spencer was faced with a similar problem, the tradition that many natural phenomena were to be interpreted as special numinous symbols, arcane prophecies, or types. "God was pleas'd heretofore," he writes, "(suitably to the non-age of the Church) to address himself very much to the lower faculties of the Soul (Phancy and imagination); accordingly we finde Prophecies deliver'd in vehement and unusual schemes of speech, such as are apt greatly to strike upon and affect the imagination."[23] Hence the "most splendid types and symbols" of the Old Testament. Spencer no longer considers such a structure of symbolism necessary in the modern world; those who continue to insist on its existence are at best anachronistic, at worst fanatic.

[22] *The Grounds and Reasons of Monarchy Consider'd: And Exemplify'd in the Scotish Line*, in *The Oceana of James Harrington, and His Other Works* (London, 1700), pp. 5-6 (each item is separately paged). John Toland, who edited the 1700 edition of Harrington's works, included Hall's *The Grounds and Reasons of Monarchy Consider'd*, with a note to the reader that it was not by Harrington but by John Hall of Durham and Gray's Inn. See *The Political Works of James Harrington*, ed. J.G.A. Pocock (Cambridge: Cambridge Univ. Press, 1977), p. xii.

[23] *A Discourse concerning Prodigies: wherein the Vanity of Presages by them is reprehended, and their true and proper Ends asserted and vindicated* (Cambridge, 1663), p. 11.

But they which talk of and look for any such vehement expressions of Divinity now, mistake the temper & condition of the Oeconomy which the appearance of our Saviour hath now put us under; wherein all things are to be managed in a more sedate, cool, and silent manner, in a way suited to and expressive of the temper our Saviour discover'd in the world. . . . The mysteries of the Gospel (today) come forth cloth'd in sedate and intelligible forms of speech; the minds of men are not now drawn into ecstasie by any such vehement and great examples of Divine Power as attended the lower and more servile state of the world.[24]

Although Spencer does not rule out prophecy and typology, he is quite specific about limiting the tendency of the human mind to draw parallels and analogies between the historical past and the present. An Old Testament allegory like *Absalom and Achitophel*, which is illustrative without insisting upon figural analogies between Judea and England, would be acceptable. But the Puritan typologizing which argued that the difficulties of the ancient Jews foreshadowed the hardships of seventeenth-century sectarianism strains credibility.

Religious writers like Spencer, Parker, and Eachard seldom confine their observations solely to the theological sphere. They have a proleptical skill in anticipating secular objections by extending their arguments into other precincts of the world of learning. Spencer broadens his scope to embrace an aggressive consideration of contemporary figural practice:

The Opinion I now contest is so receptive of Argument against it, that there is less need of any to press it further, especially considering the great Advocates thereof are so much under the command of a mighty imagination, which delights in *conjugates* and *parallels* and *symbolizing instances*, so much that it usually makes them or finds them in Nature. Now we shall ever finde, that all persons which take up opinions from their own Poetical Genius and busie phansie, are impregnable to the assaults of reason: the Rosy-crucians acted so hugely by imagination in *Philosophy*, some kinde of *Chymists* in *Medicks*, the *Cabalists* in Scripture-expositions, *Enthusiasts* in Religion, *Figure-casters* in Astrology, are so invincibly resolved upon their hypotheses, that (like him in the story) when their hands,

[24] *Ibid.*, pp. 11-12.

those little reasonings wherewith they hold them, are cut off, they will *mordicus defendere,* hold them with their teeth, biting and reviling language, thrown upon their opposers and neglecters. They are entertained with pleasant and easie dreams and therefore are angry with those which attempt to awaken and discompose them.[25]

The *"conjugates* and *parallels,* and *symbolizing instances"* represent both the materials and the techniques of figural excess, while the series of offenders reads like a preview of the deranged abusers of religion and learning in *A Tale of a Tub.* This topic is a persistent theme of Spencer's *Discourse.*

Whether in religion, civil affairs, or the arts, the tone of mystical excess, of attaching strange meanings to events and literary texts, is a constant sign of political and mental instability. Of course, the writers of the early Restoration did not completely deny the existence of symbolic meanings. Far from it: the practice of seeking symbolic qualities in the world was an obsession, and the method of drawing parallels was among the most popular games of the last half of the century. As John Wallace has observed, this game was regularly revived and was "always played most earnestly when times were bad and another great crisis had occurred."[26] The difference between the techniques of the mystics and those of more judicious writers like the Anglican rationalists is largely a matter of restraint. Spencer admits the existence of symbolism in nature (the growth of plants in springtime from their dead roots, for example, prefigures the Resurrection to man), but he condemns mystical hyperbole. In the same way, Thomas Fuller, who sees the destruction of Jerusalem as a type of the Last Day, refuses to press matters further and declines to see Jerusalem as a type of the militant church.[27] Attitudes like these are important in bringing about the development of new imagistic methodologies.

The condemnation of religious zeal is seldom restricted to religion alone. Catachresis in theology is similar enough to mystical excess in literary prose and poetry to allow us to interpret many religious texts in terms of secular affairs. Pulpit oratory that used false flowers of rhetoric to entice an audience is as dangerous as

---

25 *Ibid.,* p. 18.

26 "Dryden and History: A Problem in Allegorical Reading," *ELH,* 36 (1969), 279.

27 See Thomas Fuller, *A Pisgah-Sight of Palestine and the Confines Thereof* (London, 1662), p. 320. For the visual side of Fuller's typology, see Figure 10.

florid and figurative verse calculated to arouse the passions. As Dryden would later put it, "A man is to be cheated into Passion, but to be reason'd into Truth."[28] Dryden's observation in *Religio Laici* comes at the end of a century of doubt concerning the role of figuralism in poetry. The subject had set off a Renaissance debate on the propriety of poetic fictions and on the utility of poetry itself.[29] Herbert's famous justification of poetic plainness, in "Jordan (I)," suggests a movement away from baroque magnificence toward clarity and simplicity which continues among the Cavalier poets in the middle third of the century. Davenant, for example, comments frequently in the Preface to *Gondibert* (1651) on the hermeneutic difficulties caused by excessive wit, conceits, and fancy.[30] But he also associates these forms of excess with religious mystery, inspiration, and the dissembling of spiritual enthusiasm. While Davenant was not a foe of the use of Christian themes in poetry, he constantly opposes the affected zeal and stylistic obscurities of English sectarianism. His most important statement on the matter, printed after the Restoration, is only one of numerous attacks upon the abuse of mysticism made by poets later in the century. In his poem "To my Friend Mr. Ogilby, upon the Fables of Aesop Paraphras'd in Verse" (1668), Davenant argues, drawing on an old and familiar Christian tradition, that God's presence may be read in the world, "his easier Book," wherein his miracles are conveyed "in Natures Text." This is part of the argument, dating back at least to Philo and Origen, which provided one of the earliest theoretical justifications for mystical interpretations of Scripture.

The ancient world, however, was less given to imaginative interpretation than its reputation would suggest. Like the theological critics of mysticism, Davenant feels that the early Fathers and other critics were temperate: "Then usefully the Studious World was wise, / Not learn'd, as now in useless subtilities." The distinction is important: primitive wisdom, drawn from the empirical evidence

[28] *Religio Laici*, "Preface." See *The Works of John Dryden*, ed. H. T. Swedenberg *et al.* (Berkeley and Los Angeles: Univ. of California Press, 1956-   ), II, 109.

[29] See, for example, Russell Fraser, *The War Against Poetry* (Princeton: Princeton Univ. Press, 1970), for discussion of the attack, chiefly Puritan-centered, upon poetry in the late Renaissance and seventeenth century to the beginning of the Civil War.

[30] *Sir William Davenant's Gondibert*, ed. David F. Gladish (Oxford: Clarendon Press, 1971), pp. 4, 5-7, 18, 19, etc.

of Nature, was less likely to delude the unwary than the second-
hand or circumstantial evidence presented in mystical writings and
scholastic conundrums. The change for the worse at the present is
the result of ignorance, pride, and contentious obscurantism:

> But now the gravest Schools through Pride contend;
> And Truth awhile, at least themselves defend.
> So vext is now the World with Misteries,
> Since prouder Mindes drest Truth in Arts disguise;
> And so Serene and Calme was Empire then,
> Whilst Statesmen study'd Beasts to govern Men.
> Accurst be *Ægypts* Priests, who first through Pride
> And Avarice this common Light did hide:
> To Temples did this Morall Text confine,
> And made it hard, to make it seeme Divine:
> In Creatures formes a fancy'd Deity
> They drew, and rais'd the mysterie so high,
> As all to reach it did require their aid;
> For which they were as hir'd Expounders, pay'd.
> This Clouded Text, which but to few was known,
> In time grew darker, and was read by none;
> So weak of Wing is Soaring Mystery;
> And Learning's light goes out, when held too high.[31]

This passage, like most of Davenant's poetry, has been neglected,
but its implications for our understanding of figural change in Restoration poetry are considerable. The rejection of Egyptian mythology is only part of the story, for the study of Oriental and Egyptian idolatry and hieroglyphics, although it was widespread among
learned people in the seventeenth century, does not have vast influence on the *thematic* materials of English poetry at this time.[32]

[31] "To my Friend Mr. Ogilby," *The Works of Sir William Davenant, Kt.*
(London, 1673), p. 308.

[32] The poets were familiar with Egyptian mythology, as Milton's allusions
in *Paradise Lost* and Dryden's in *The Hind and the Panther* will readily indicate. The extensive researches of Kircher (see note 5, above) were well known
in England. See also Liselotte Dieckmann, *Hieroglyphics: The History of a
Literary Symbol* (St. Louis: Washington Univ. Press, 1971), pp. 100-28, and
Allen, *Mysteriously Meant*, pp. 107-33 ("The Symbolic Wisdom of the Ancient
Egyptians"). Among the poets, Butler satirizes mysticism in *Hudibras*, I.i.529-32;
cf. his character, "An Hermetick Philosopher," in *Samuel Butler, 1612-1680:
Characters*, ed. Charles W. Daves (Cleveland: The Press of Case Western Univ.,
1970), pp. 139-59, for a tirade against the mystics.

Obscurantism ("This Clouded Text") and the pretended mysticism of pagan mythology were, for Davenant, more broadly representative of seventeenth-century abuses of the information vital to an enlightened understanding of the institutions of religion and government. The false mysteries, steganography, and hieroglyphics of "*Ægypts* Priests" are devices that the ancient clergy deliberately introduced to make difficult matters which should be open. The very obvious fact that many of the workings of government in seventeenth-century England were secret from public view could be defended, as it always has been in all societies. But Davenant is unable to accept mystery-mongering in religion and the world of the arts. Mythological allusion will not disappear from poetry as a result of objections like these. However, there will be a change in the articulation of the mythological *figura* during the last years of the century. This development is partly due to the attack upon mysticism that I have traced here. An equally important part of the transformation is the consequence of the clarification and Christianizing of ancient myth, a subject that I shall later relate to the survival of figural tradition. Pagan philosophy and myth, while they could be criticized for their obscurity and idolatry, were also recognized as the principal bases of Old Testament and Christian history. A writer like Theophilus Gale could attack the errors of pagan philosophy in *The Court of the Gentiles*, but he also affirmed that much Christian learning was derived from the ancient Hebrews and from Oriental religion, and gave careful attention to extracting what he regarded as useful from pagan philosophy and science.[33]

Gale is part of the late seventeenth-century tradition of scholarly antiquarianism which, impelled by a methodology that was at least partially empirical, carried on researches into the origins of religion and government. Many of these scholars were gifted in the Oriental languages. They made considerable use of their linguistic abilities as they sought to trace the Christian threads back through ancient learning. While they are not mystics, Stillingfleet, Bochart, Spencer, and Vossius often show a degree of imagination in their historical

---

[33] See *The Court of the Gentiles: or A Discourse touching the Origin of Human Literature, both Philologie and Philosophie*, 2nd ed., 4 vols. (Oxford, 1672-77), I, 424-34, 434-39, 440-48. See also Allen, *Mysteriously Meant*, pp. 70, 74-75. Gale's first two volumes derive Western learning from the ancient Hebrews, beginning with Moses; Vol. III exposes the errors of pagan philosophy, and Vol. IV collects what Gale deemed worthwhile from pagan thought.

studies which may be said to stretch the concept of empirical evidence past the point of credibility. More important, however, is that these men and many other antiquarian scholars like them do make a conscious attempt to sift whatever historical evidence is available to them. They are often responsible for proliferating errors, but their central effort was to explain the mysteries of the past by subjecting them to rational examination. The scholarly tradition of "opening" mysteries, which Swift parodies so successfully in *A Tale of a Tub*, is one of the significant middle-term precipitants for seventeenth-century figural change. However many mistaken associations this search produced, it is responsible for the increase in Restoration consciousness that what seemed mysterious was often capable of sensible explanation. Some of these researches were quasi-scientific, like Browne's *Pseudodoxia Epidemica* (1646); often they were what then passed for experimental science. Others, especially after 1650, are serious scientific treatises, including the writings of chemists like Elias Ashmole and Robert Boyle, botanists like Nehemiah Grew and John Ray, mathematicians like Newton and John Wallis, experimental naturalists like Robert Hooke and John Woodward, and a host of medical writers on topics that ranged from anatomy to mental disease. The most impressive result of this change in scholarly investigation is the gradual fostering of the belief that the mysterious could be explained.

Such scholarship had broad appeal, and was often imitated in the nonscholarly world. John Dunton's *Athenian Mercury*, in the 1690s, for instance, purported to answer all questions dealing with the mysteries of natural science and philosophy. The popularity of books elucidating the secrets of state and government was enormous. To understand this trend one has only to read through compilations like *Cabala, Sive Scrinia Sacra: Mysteries of State and Government. . . . Wherein such Secrets of Empire, and Publick Affairs, . . . are clearly represented* (1654).[34] The methodology of these popular works is sometimes little more than a parody of what philological, historical, and scientific scholars were doing, but it indicates the effect which the emerging tradition of scholarly investigation must have had upon the public imagination. In thematic terms, the influence of this tradition upon imaginative literature is obvious, for

[34] The later editions of *Cabala* (1663, 1691) are considerably enlarged with new "secrets." For a visual representation of cabalistic techniques, see Figure 7.

starting with the late seventeenth century the effect of scientific ideas is great and constantly increases.[35]

It is more difficult to determine the precise impact of the new empirical scholarship upon imagistic usage. Certainly there was an increase in the number and complexity of scientific images in English poetry. With regard to imagistic quality and relative difficulty, we can say that the development of these new methods of scholarly inquiry helped to evolve a poetics of inquiry. Poems which deal with the examination of a given topic, in the way that *Religio Laici* and *The Hind and the Panther* deal with the nature of religious belief, various verse arts of poetry discuss the genres, and verse comments on politics analyze the issues, owe their manner and existence at least in part to this tradition of empirical, historical examination. The literary critics and stylistic reformers of the last half of the century are consistent in their emphasis on imagery that was relatively easy to interpret. Obscure texts hinder rational inquiry and limit an audience's comprehension of both argument and exposition. Complaints about the abuse of imagery, as we have seen, are very common during this period. It should be clear, I think, that one reason for these objections was that the spirit of empirical inquiry, even in so exalted a genre as the pindaric ode, was profoundly inhospitable to imagery and language that were unclear. In the short term, this change in scholarly methodology is barely perceptible. But in the middle term, over a period from about 1650 to 1680, the accumulation of evidence is substantial. Hence we may say that one of the important influences on figural change in the mid-seventeenth century revolt from the baroque and the obscure styles of imagery which characterize metaphysical poetry was undoubtedly the new methodology of learned inquiry. At the same time, however, I should observe that metaphysical poetry continued to be published throughout this period. Herbert's *The Temple* appeared first in the 1640s, but there were many editions of this work and of *The Priest to the Temple* between 1650 and 1680. Editions of Cleveland's extreme metaphysical poems were numerous. Henry Vaughan's major works were all published after 1650. The first collected edition of Marvell's poetry, in which virtually all of his metaphysical poems first appeared, is dated 1681.

---

[35] See, for example, W. Powell Jones, *The Rhetoric of Science: A Study of Scientific Ideas and Imagery in Eighteenth-Century English Poetry* (Berkeley and Los Angeles: Univ. of California Press, 1966), *passim*.

Scientific and rational learned inquiry, then, had a gradual effect on literature and did not quickly dispel earlier poetic traditions.

The fabric of literary history does not separate readily into such factors as long-term preconditions and middle-term precipitants. These influences upon imagistic change clearly coexist and often may be congruent. To identify the short-term causes of the kind of change I have been analyzing is difficult, for innovations in the arts, unlike historical events, are seldom so rapid that they may be said to have immediate catalysts. Lawrence Stone has identified what he calls the short-run triggers for the English Revolution in the critical events of the years 1639-42.[36] But can we find analogous influences on a complex literary, stylistic, and intellectual transformation which was accomplished gradually, over a period of about half a century? When the change under examination develops so slowly, there will be no single critical period distinguishable for containing short-run triggers. Methods of studying political and social revolutions will not apply. However, in a protracted period during which a gradual alteration in figural techniques was underway, there are often briefer points of intensification, particular occurrences or clusters of events that have a strong and immediate effect upon literature and the other arts.

During the seventeenth century after 1640, then, while the various general influences that I have discussed were working to change writers' theories of imagery, there are a number of events of transcendent literary importance that have an intense and rapid effect upon literature and its imagery. They are events which readily lent themselves to literary treatment or which, like the expiration of the Licensing Act in 1695, otherwise affected the intellectual climate. In a curious way, perhaps because the outpouring of emotions they caused was so intense, they tended to evoke conservative literary reactions. Poets writing on these subjects turned often to older, established styles of figuralism. The first such event is the judicial murder of the Earl of Strafford, in May 1641. Not only did this execution inspire much contemporary literary attention,

---

[36] See Lawrence Stone, "The English Revolution," *Preconditions of Revolution in Early Modern Europe*, pp. 103-107.

but it would still be alluded to over a century later as a major catalyst of the Civil War. Strafford's execution inspired the splendid
analogizing of *Coopers Hill* (1642) and, both in poetic themes and
their imagistic presentation, provoked much contemporary allusion
and drawing of parallels.[37] The Regicide had a similar but much
more dramatic effect upon imagery, for in order to justify or con-
demn it, its apologists and detractors had to ransack the storehouses
of analogy. These two events of the 1640s have the most pronounced influence upon the literary method of drawing parallels of
any political happenings of the century. The Regicide led to an
outpouring of typology. Many writers saw Charles I as a postfiguration of the martyred Savior, a relationship which the 1662 revision
of the Prayer Book would strengthen. Royalists treated Cromwell as
a type of Satan or as the Great Beast of Revelation, but he had his
defenders, among them Milton and Marvell, who compared the
Lord Protector to such Old Testament types of the Messiah as
Joshua and David. The Restoration and the Coronation of Charles
II (1660-61), like the Regicide, touch every branch of literature,
from sermons and pamphlets to the ecstatic panegyrics written on
both occasions. Poets writing about these events quite spontane-
ously reintroduce the Golden Age analogizing and classical parallels which had been so common in Elizabethan literature. Other
events or clusters of events which had a strong short-term effect
upon imagery include the critical years of the Popish Plot and the
Exclusion Crisis, the train of historical circumstances leading up to
the Glorious Revolution, and the expiration of the Licensing Act
in 1695, which permitted satirists a new freedom in their commentary upon political affairs.

These "intensifying" events have one thing in common. Their
immediate effect upon literary imagery is thematic, content-ori-
ented, and, ultimately, superficial. That is, the subject-matter or allusive spectrum of literary metaphors and similitudes underwent
change, but the structural basis and linguistic heart of the Renaissance figural tradition remained intact. The method of drawing
correspondences that is so characteristic of later seventeenth-century
imagery is not radically different from the complexities of Renais-

---

37 C. V. Wedgwood, *Thomas Wentworth: First Earl of Strafford, 1593-1641*
(London: Jonathan Cape, 1961), pp. 337-99, and Brendan O Hehir, *Harmony
from Discords: A Life of Sir John Denham* (Berkeley and Los Angeles: Univ.
of California Press, 1968), pp. 28-53, provide full details of the trial and execution of Strafford, the surrounding controversy, and the literary backlash.

sance symbolism. It is only likely to be less mysterious. The linguistic equations of simile and metaphor, at least in the short run, remain practically unchanged. To illustrate: the Restoration as an event provoked, in the short period of about one year, a number of literary responses containing imagistic adornments. There is an impressive richness of themes, with subject matter drawn from Homer, Virgil, the classical myths, and the Old and New Testaments. But the analogic method which makes possible most of these comparisons differs very little from the allegorizing, symbolizing, and paralleling of Renaissance imagistic traditions. Poets from Denham and the Cavaliers on to Dryden and the satirists of William III's troubled decade seldom alter the traditional structural bases for linguistic and thematic association.

This common experience and tradition helps explain why a poem like "Upon Appleton House" seems to exist in two worlds, the first the Renaissance syncretism of Marvell's reading, the other the practical theater of political and historical correspondences. Consider the following stanza:

> Out of these scatter'd Sibyls Leaves
> Strange *Prophecies* my Phancy weaves:
> And in one History consumes
> Like *Mexique Paintings*, all the *Plumes*.
> What Rome, Greece, Palestine, ere said
> I in this light *Mosaick* read.
> Thrice happy he who, not mistook,
> Hath read in *Natures mystick Book*.
>
> (LXXIII)

If we expound this passage with an emphasis on the last line, it is easy to interpret it as an example of the symbolic treatment of curious learning familiar to Renaissance antiquarian scholarship. The net of allusion here is indeed wide, and the knowledge required for adequate interpretation obscure. But the stanza is also a fine example of the seventeenth-century methodology of correspondence. The prophetic qualities of the sojourn in the wood (a traditional *topos* for obscurity) are historical parallels to the three principal sources for seventeenth-century political analogizing, the history of biblical times, of ancient Greece, and of the Roman Empire. Nature as a book lying open to the exegete is our imagistic concept with medieval origins and a respectable Renaissance genealogy, but it was common in the Restoration and eighteenth century as well.[38] The doctrine of typological correspondences that forms the basis of Marvell's series of images here and elsewhere in "Appleton House" is similar to the types that Dryden employs in "To the Duchess of Ormonde" or "To My Honour'd Kinsman" and that Prior employs in *Carmen Sæculare*, poems written about fifty years later. In the history of imagistic change in the last half of the century, these are not isolated examples.

In the long-term and middle-term perspectives, I have noted a great deal of thematic alteration and considerable shifting in the depth of academic and scholarly background to imagery. When we get down to the closer quarters of imagistic reaction to immediate historical or literary catalysts, we find that certain elements of seventeenth-century imagery are startlingly resistant to change. This resistance is what I have called the survival of tradition, or, in the context of this chapter, the survival of typological tradition. We have seen how imagistic change was promoted by new theories of scriptural exegesis, and how political events and fashions in the world of scholarship contributed to the transformation of the thematic side of imagery. But the structural basis of figurative language remained fundamentally the same throughout the century and, in a similar way, the basis of Christian worship, which in its day-to-day celebration provides much of the foundation for typology, also remained constant. For Anglicans, the 1662 revisions of the Book of Common Prayer changed nothing central to Christian belief and did nothing to affect the essentially typological basis of the relationship between the two Testaments, the prophecies, resurrection, and so on.[39] And among Catholics and the various Protestant sects, we must remember that typology was even more popular than in the Anglican Church. Let me now examine several qualities of early seventeenth-century typological imagery that retained their importance and vitality during and after the last half of the century.

38 William Kinsley makes this point in "The *Dunciad* as Mock-Book," *HLQ*, 35 (1971), 29-47.

39 On the durability of all forms of Christian worship in the seventeenth century, see Horton Davies, *Worship and Theology in England: From Andrewes to Baxter and Fox, 1603-1690* (Princeton: Princeton Univ. Press, 1975), pp. 363-404, who shows that, while the 1662 revisions of the Prayer Book had the potential for much alteration in external forms of worship, in fact few major changes were made. Donald Greene, "Latitudinarianism and Sensibility: The Genealogy of 'The Man of Feeling' Reconsidered," *MP*, 75 (1977-78), 181-83, also comments on the durability of most forms of Anglican worship in the late seventeenth and eighteenth centuries.

5

In the analysis of literary change, it is customary to single out what I have called the "significant intellectual influences" likely to affect writers at a given time that could have caused them to make aesthetic decisions different from their previous practice. I have suggested what some of the most powerful extrinsic influences during the later seventeenth century were. But no study of change can be complete without some attention to non-change or continuity. Just as on the stage of history the vast transformations of the century are accompanied and perhaps accentuated by the survival of tradition, so in the literary milieu we may observe similar phenomena. With respect to the nation's history, this tendency is evident in a number of ways. For example, throughout the eighteenth century there was a slow but steady movement of the population away from the country toward the cities and large towns, yet the tradition of a family's having roots in the country, a closeness to the land, lingers on. Starting from the late seventeenth century, especially the reign of William III, a gradual administrative revolution takes place that transforms government operations, but the old traditions of the patronage system remain and, if anything, are strengthened during the eighteenth century.

Scholars have long noticed that something similar happens in literature, but the phenomena of change and the survival of tradition have never been thoroughly examined. Literary historians have shown that the metaphysical conceit does not perish with the passing of the school of Donne. Although it may be less obscure, its structural basis survives in the poetry of Dryden, Pope, and their contemporaries. The private mode of metaphysical verse is gradually displaced by a more politicized public style. But the poetic tradition that permits poets to discuss their own private lives, personalities, and aspirations in their work continues long after "affecting the metaphysics" had been discredited.[40] However, it would be tautological to regard the continuance of a class of image such as the conceit as evidence for the survival of an older figural tradition. In order to understand why certain kinds of imagery resisted change, we must look instead for qualities of seventeenth-century

[40] For an excellent discussion of the public and private modes in seventeenth-century poetry, see Earl Miner, *The Metaphysical Mode from Donne to Dryden* (Princeton: Princeton Univ. Press, 1969), pp. 3-47.

thought that helped to create the characteristic speech of the poetry of the late seventeenth and early eighteenth centuries.

While many aspects of Renaissance style and imagery weakened and were transformed or replaced during the century, one part of the old figural tradition that successfully withstood radical change was typology. Medieval and Renaissance applications of typology were so many and various that it is hard to name another imagistic technique so widespread in early seventeenth-century England. As the result of a number of able critical studies, we have recently come to recognize that typology is pervasive in early and mid-seventeenth century poetry, from Shakespeare and Donne through Herbert, Vaughan, Marvell, and Milton.[41] It was a tremendously popular method of exegesis with Catholic, Anglican, and Puritan theologians alike. In secular literature, the scriptural types played a part in the writing of history, the interpretation of ancient mythology, and the study of antiquities. The completely orthodox, Augustinian view of history as a gradual unfolding of the New Testament theme of redemption, as presented originally in types and shadows to the select *illuminati* of the Old Testament, when applied to contemporary history permitted considerable free interpretation and mystical distortion of everyday events.[42] Typology lent itself easily to the abuses I mentioned earlier as characteristic of excessive mysticism. Some Anglican divines—Andrew Willett, Henry Hammond, John Wilkins, and others—counseled moderation, but for many writers both secular and religious typology was the fatal Cleopatra for which they lost the world of rational exegesis, and were content to lose it. Whereas mystical abuses of language and imagery were subjected to abundant criticism and as a result gradually declined, the typological tradition did not weaken in the least during the period of our interest. If anything, it would

[41] In addition to works cited elsewhere in the notes, see Barbara K. Lewalski, *Milton's Brief Epic* (Providence, R.I. and London: Brown Univ. Press, 1966) and *Donne's Anniversaries and the Poetry of Praise* (Princeton: Princeton Univ. Press, 1973), Richard D. Jordan, *The Temple of Eternity: Thomas Traherne's Philosophy of Time* (Port Washington, N.Y.: Kennikat Press, 1972), Rosemond Tuve, *A Reading of George Herbert* (Chicago: Univ. of Chicago Press, 1952), and Ira Clark, " 'Lord, in thee the *Beauty* Lies in the *Discovery*': 'Love Unknown' and Reading Herbert," *ELH*, 39 (1972), 560-84.

[42] There have been many valuable contributions to the literature of typology, especially in the last few years, such as Madsen's fine study (see note 21, above). See, for example, Maren-Sofie Røstvig, "Images of Perfection," in *Seventeenth-Century Imagery*, ed. Miner, pp. 1-24, esp. pp. 4-6, 9-10.

acquire greater subtlety of application during the last years of the century.

It is interesting to see how broad the applications of typological imagery were. Earlier in the century, John Gaule wrote: "When, and in what, was not Christ typed, or prophecied? Each type was a silent Prophecie of him; each Prophecie a speaking Type. All things in Holy Writ were said by, of, or for him; The Word of God implying, or unfolding nothing more, then God the Word."[43] Exegetical typology is not always this sweeping, but it appears everywhere, in interpretations of every book of both Testaments, and even in postbiblical documents like the Creed.[44] Sermon-literature is frequently typological: the annual martyrology sermons on the anniversary of the Regicide were tailor-made for the subject. During and after the Commonwealth years the method continued unabated. The death of Cromwell, the Coronation of Charles II, the Fire of London, and other signal events were seen as types.[45] As the typological treatment of Cromwell shows, the method did not have to be confined to anointed kings. Indeed, a nice touch to the Cromwell legend was furnished by the contemporary historian who reported that the Jews of Asia Minor, hearing of Cromwell's martial greatness, sent three rabbis as emissaries to England to ascertain whether Oliver was descended from the Jews in any way, thinking that he might be the Messiah (Cromwell was often compared with messianic Jewish figures).[46] Other historians simply read all past history as vast typological cycles representing a prospect of good things to come, a process that began with scriptural history and widened, in concentric circles, to include ecclesiastical and finally

[43] *Practique Theories: or Votive Speculations upon Jesus Christs Prediction. . . .* (London, 1629), p. 21.

[44] John Pearson, *An Exposition of the Creed* (London, 1659), pp. 523, 542-44, 554-57, exemplifies many of the commonplace qualities of typological exegesis.

[45] See *The Unparalleled Monarch. Or, the Portraiture of a Matchless Prince* (London, 1659), pp. 9-10, 54, 61-62, and Sig. I6ᵛ; *A Collection of Several Passages concerning his late Highnesse Oliver Cromwell. . . .* (London, 1659), p. 20; and Thomas Sprat, "To the Happy Memory of the Most Renowned Prince, Oliver, Lord Protector," in *Three Poems upon the Death of his late Highness Oliver* (London, 1659), p. 29 (Stanza 16; each poem is separately paged). On the typology of the Fire of London, see Seth Ward, *A Sermon Preached before the Peers in the Abbey Church at Westminster, October 10, 1666* (London, 1666), pp. 1, 2, 4.

[46] This account is found in François Raguenet, *Histoire d'Olivier Cromwell* (Paris, 1691), pp. 322-24.

secular history as well.[47] Of all the biblical prophecies the books of Daniel and Revelation affected views of secular history most profoundly. As I will show in detail later (see below, Chapter 9), the millennial prophecies would be intimately associated with contemporary eschatologies. With the assistance of impassioned pulpit oratory, the English public would be able to read Revelation in particular side by side with contemporary history. Events that boded ill could be seen as apocalyptic, as antitypes of the prefigurations in Scripture and, finally, as types themselves of yet a greater Millennium.[48]

The imagistic exuberance of typology spread to poetry. During the period of the century when the predominant figural tradition was undergoing the well-known changes which I have discussed above, the complexities of secularized typological imagery continue to be popular. Dryden's first Restoration panegyrics are often typological, as is much secular poetry of the 1660s, but his poetry of the 1690s, instead of containing less of this kind of imagery, is even more intricately involved with secularized types. The odes, his lines on Purcell, the literary epistles to Congreve, Kneller, Ormonde, and Driden, and even his translations reveal the typological imagination keenly applied.[49] It would be easy to multiply examples of the dramatic survival of this aspect of early seventeenth-century figural traditions. But it is more important to inquire into the reasons for its continuance in the face of striking figural change all around it. The first reason, I suggest, is that typology was a logical imagistic system, for it involved no unexpected yoking of contraries or sudden linguistic catachreses. It is sound, reliable, predictive, and easily capable of comprehension. The traditional rising motion of the type, from darkness to light, the part to the whole, doubt to truth, promise to fulfilment, and death to resurrection,

[47] Particularly relevant to this process is John Edwards, *A Compleat History or Survey of all the Dispensations and Methods of Religion*, 2 vols. (London, 1699), I, 3.

[48] Popular millenarianism has attracted much scholarly attention in recent years. See, for example, Christopher Hill, *The World Turned Upside Down: Radical Ideas during the English Revolution* (London: Temple Smith, 1972), pp. 70-85, and *Milton and the English Revolution* (New York, Viking Press, 1978), pp. 279-84, and the excellent bibliographical note to J.F.C. Harrison's *The Second Coming*, pp. 263-66.

[49] For earlier discussion of Dryden's typology in the 1690s, see my *From Concord to Dissent: Major Themes in English Poetic Theory, 1640-1700* (London: Scolar Press, 1973), pp. 197-98, 202-207, 209-12.

was well accommodated to poetic themes in the century. It was easily parodied, too, as we can see from *Hudibras, A Tale of a Tub,* and *The Dunciad.* But it is clear that it survived partly because it was needed. Second, typology helped justify pagan symbolism, much of which, by the end of the century, was identified with Old Testament or Christian types and symbols.[50] Finally, the typological tradition survived because it accorded so perfectly with the popular imagistic games of drawing parallels and making analogies. Types were reliable emblems, drawn from the most satisfactory of books, corroborated by the irrefutable evidence of the New Testament. Since typology was familiar even to an unsophisticated audience, it provided the late seventeenth-century writer with a shorthand of allusion with which the common reader was acquainted and which therefore required a minimum of explanation or self-exegesis. Mystical obscurity withered because it was difficult; typology, potentially equally mysterious, resisted figural change because it required very little knowledge of hermeneutics to use it or to decipher its meaning.

6

A recent commentator on seventeenth-century typology notes "the seamless continuity in the history of familiar political types" throughout the century, but more specifically in the years just after the Restoration.[51] In fact, for the reasons which I have mentioned above, typological codes persisted throughout the crucial thirty-year period 1650-80 during which so much other figural change took place. The critical event of the Regicide, as I noted earlier, furnished contemporary writers with a ready-made martyrology, one which Milton notices in *Eikonoklastes* (1649) but which even his formidable polemical talents could do nothing to prevent:

---

50 The association of the pagan myths with Hebraic and Christian theology has many Renaissance antecedents. For example, see John Spencer, *De Legibus Hebraeorum Ritualibus et earum rationibus, libri quatuor,* 2 vols. (Cambridge: 1727), I, 201-13. The fashion continues during the eighteenth century and, through the writings of the mythographer Jacob Bryant, informed the thought of the English Romantics. See Bryant's *A New System, or, An Analysis of Ancient Mythology,* 3 vols. (London, 1774-76), II, 200-201, 272, 285, 296-97, 528-30.

51 See Steven N. Zwicker, "Politics and Panegyric: The Figural Mode from Marvell to Pope," in *Literary Uses of Typology,* p. 128.

And heer may be well observ'd the loose and negligent curiosity of those who took upon them to adorn the setting out of
this Book [i.e., *Eikon Basilike* (1649)]: for though the Picture
sett in Front would Martyr him and Saint him to befool the
people, yet the Latin Motto in the end, which they understand
not, leaves him, as it were a politic contriver to bring about
that interest by faire and plausible words, which the force of
Armes deny'd him. But quaint Emblems and devices begg'd
from the old Pageantry of some Twelf-nights entertainment at
Whitehall, will doe but ill to make a Saint or Martyr.[52]

There would be other voices raised against the Charles I-martyr
typology from time to time, including such distinguished writers as
the Harringtonian John Hall and Defoe, but it continues to be a
popular figural mode until well after 1700. Indeed, after the Restoration, the restored Anglican clergy resumed the same, familiar
Old Testament typology for Charles II that Puritan divines had
used to celebrate the establishment of the Commonwealth a decade
earlier.

Millenarian typology, which the controversialists of the 1640s
had used to complement their enthusiasm for social change, also
continues unabated after 1650.[53] On the Puritan side, such figuralism forecasts the time, always soon to come, when the community of the Saints will achieve its long sought perfection; on the
Royalist side, millennial typology reflects the longing of many for
the monarchy and, after its return, the widely felt view that there
was a perfection to be found in monarchical rule. For example,
Abiezer Coppe's *A Fiery Flying Roll* (1650), a piece of popular
prophecy by a well-known Ranter and extremist Leveller, is but
one of a number of Revelation-inspired calls to repentance before
the arrival of the Millennium. The pamphlet contains some interesting millenarian typology that is, in a sense, timeless; one finds
similar examples in the 1640s and in the 1790s. Coppe records his
encounter, while out riding, with "a most strange deformed man,
clad with patcht clouts," to whom he felt mystically drawn to give
all his money as if his silver and gold had risen up in judgment

[52] *Complete Prose Works of John Milton*, III (New Haven: Yale Univ. Press,
1962), 342-43.

[53] On the Puritans' attitudes toward social change, see Michael Walzer, *The
Revolution of the Saints: A Study in the Origins of Radical Politics* (Cambridge,
Mass.: Harvard Univ. Press, 1965), pp. 1-21.

against him. "This is a true story," he adds, "most true in the history. Its true also in the mystery. And there are deep ones coucht under it, for its a shadow of various, glorious, (though strange) good things to come."[54] The mystery, we learn, foreshadows the great leveling that is to come at the Day of Judgment, for the leveling theme accords well with the idea of apocalypse. Marvell, much less an enthusiast than Coppe, similarly introduces millennial typology into his poems about Cromwell, first in "An Horatian Ode upon Cromwel's Return from Ireland" (1650) and again, more impressively, in *The First Anniversary of the Government under O. C.* (1655). In this long poem, Marvell's typology of Cromwell habitually compares the Lord Protector to Old Testament types of Christ, but frequently in contexts that suggest not simply Christ the Savior but rather Christ the deliverer of the world from Antichrist. Hence Cromwell, in cleansing England of those who "sing Hosanna to the Whore" (113), ridding the world of "Kings that chase the Beast" (124), pursuing "the Monster [of Popery] thorough every Throne" (128), is a prefiguration of Christ's actions at the time of Apocalypse, when the Millennium shall ensue.[55] Parliamentary rule was widely supposed to be the scourge that would bring about the Millennium, with Cromwell as its chief agent.

The contemporary literature on the death of Cromwell and that on the Restoration of Charles II provide a neat counterpoint on the continuity of typology. Marvell, in *A Poem upon Death of O. C.* (1658), presents an apotheosis of Cromwell in terms of Old Testament typology:

> There [in "the bright abysse"] thy great soule at once
>   a world does see,
> Spacious enough, and pure enough for thee.
> How soon thou Moses hast, and Joshua found,
> And David, for the sword and harpe renown'd;
> How streight canst to each happy mansion goe . . .[56]

Marvell proceeds from type to type, from one kind of revelation

---

[54] See Abiezer Coppe, *A Fiery Flying Roll: A Word from the Lord to all the Great Ones of the Earth . . . Being the last Warning Piece at the dreadfull day of Judgement* (London, 1650), 2 parts, ii, pp. 4-6.

[55] See *The Poems and Letters of Andrew Marvell*, ed. H. M. Margoliouth, 3rd ed., 2 vols. (Oxford: Clarendon Press, 1971), I, 322-23, for the gloss pointing out that a substantial portion of the poem (lines 99-158) "takes its colour from the apocalyptic prophecies of Dan. 7-8 and Rev. 12-20."

[56] Lines 291-95.

(Moses, the figure of wisdom) to a second, Joshua, who figures forth martial prowess, to David, the ultimate king-harmonist-Christ type. Cromwell's death is not the occasion for a millennial prophecy, but rather for a further covenant and for the opportunity for "calme peace [to succeed] a war." Dryden's poetry of the 1660s— chiefly *Astræa Redux* (1660), *To His Sacred Majesty* (1661), and *Annus Mirabilis* (1667)—invokes scriptural typology similar to that of Marvell's. In *Astræa Redux* Dryden observes of Charles II, "Thus banish'd David spent abroad his time, / When to be Gods Anointed was his Crime" (79-80), and a few lines later we see the King as a second Adam, or type of Christ, while in *To His Sacred Majesty* Charles is the figure of Moses. Dryden writes here, "As Heav'n of old dispenc'd Cælestial dew, / You give us Manna, and still give us new" (23-24). Jewish history is as important to the Royalists as it had been to the Puritans, for the cyclical patterns of exile, captivity, and return that characterize the story of Israel in the Old Testament had ready typological applications to contemporary England. Cromwell and his circle discussed the readmission of the Jews into England in 1655-56, since their exposure to the Gospel might lead to their conversion to Christianity, and their conversion—whenever it might take place—was understood to be a sign of the Second Coming.[57] Dryden returns to the narrative of Jewish history at great length in *Absalom and Achitophel* (1681), the poem whose typologies are the most profound of all his works. David and his story prefigure the history of Charles II and the Exclusion Crisis, but Dryden deals more subtly with Jewish history than most scholars have supposed. The doctrines of the Jews—the London mob in the poem—are the way of error, just as erroneous Jewish doctrine prefigures heresy in Christian times, and Dryden clearly associates the moody, headstrong, murmuring race of the Jews with Achitophel, his Satan-type.[58] Yet I should also note the millennial tone with which *Absalom and Achitophel* ends, with

[57] See Christopher Hill, *Antichrist in Seventeenth-Century England* (London: Oxford Univ. Press, 1971), pp. 114-15, for comment on the conversion of the Jews.

[58] Robert D. Moynihan has kindly allowed me to use an unpublished essay entitled "Anti-Jewish Stereotypes: Dryden's Matrix of Caricature for the Restoration and Eighteenth Century," where he suggests that Dryden does not simply use an allegorical framework of Jewish history, but also responds to contemporary attitudes, both Jewish and Christian, toward messianism, the conversion of the Jews, and the errors of Jewish belief.

"Henceforth a Series of new time began" (1028) and an allusion to Virgil's Messianic Eclogue. Earlier in the poem Dryden shows us Absalom as a false messiah ("Thee, *Saviour*, Thee, the Nations Vows confess" [240]: "The Croud . . . / With lifted hands their young *Messiah* bless" [727-28]), a mistaken antitype, and a false prophet. Appropriately, he concludes his poem with a hint of the true prophecy associated with his David-Charles II figure, a true monarch and a genuine type.

The most important literary figure in the continuity of typological tradition in the second half of the seventeenth century is undoubtedly Milton. His typological scope is wider, far wider, than that of almost any other English writer of his age, and the influence of his practice on eighteenth-century attitudes toward figuralism is enormous. Scholars have noticed the importance of Miltonic typology for the English Romantic poets but, curiously, no one has yet studied how much Milton's methods meant for Enlightenment thought.[59] Milton uses conventional typology with easy familiarity in his theological treatise, *Christian Doctrine*, and he makes different applications of prefiguration in his poetry from the early "On the Morning of Christ's Nativity" (1629) to *Samson Agonistes* (1671).[60] I have little to add to the extensive studies of Milton's typology in *Paradise Regained* by Northrop Frye and Barbara Lewalski, in *Paradise Lost* by William Madsen and many others, in *Lycidas* by Joseph Wittreich, and in *Samson Agonistes*, in a most interesting study, by Mary Ann Radzinowicz.[61] Radzinowicz neatly summarizes the main school of twentieth-century study of Miltonic typology. These scholars, she writes, "argue that Milton saw history as a redemptive process; the one just man was contained within history to be the vehicle of typological teaching, but he also stood outside history by achieving higher vision than the historical, so

[59] The influence of Milton on Blake has attracted considerable attention. See Joseph Anthony Wittreich, Jr., *Angel of Apocalypse: Blake's Idea of Milton* (Madison: Univ. of Wisconsin Press, 1975), pp. 13-34, 103-29.

[60] See *Christian Doctrine*, I.xxviii, in *Complete Prose Works of John Milton*, VI (New Haven: Yale Univ. Press, 1973), 542-62, for some of Milton's use of conventional typology.

[61] See Frye, "The Typology of *Paradise Regained*," *MP*, 53 (1956), 227-38; Lewalski, *Milton's Brief Epic, passim*; Jonathan Goldberg, "*Virga Iesse*: Analogy, Typology, and Anagogy in a Miltonic Simile," *Milton Studies*, 5 (1973), 177-90; Madsen, *From Shadowy Types to Truth, passim*; Wittreich, *Visionary Poetics*, pp. 163-64; and Radzinowicz, *Toward Samson Agonistes: The Growth of Milton's Mind* (Princeton: Princeton Univ. Press, 1978), pp. 273-311.

as to be himself the vehicle of exemplary teaching."[62] Other scholars have claimed that Milton evolves his own doctrine of progressive typological revelation which we can trace through his writing,
especially the major poems. Much of Miltonic scholarship is devoted to showing how he developed the ideas of his three major
poems from his earlier work and his extensive reading. Accordingly, views of his prefigurative methods show that the typology of
his "Nativity" hymn is plain and unadorned, that of *Lycidas* obscure and prophetic, that of *Paradise Lost* profoundly visionary,
that of *Paradise Regained* intimately involved with the accomplishments of Christ the Antitype, and that of *Samson* an ultimate representation of the typological figure in history. Certainly Milton's
typology becomes more elaborate and difficult to interpret over the
course of his entire career. But more central to the scope of this
chapter is the way in which Milton's typology contributed to the
continuity of this figural mode in the seventeenth and eighteenth
centuries.

Milton's typological applications, of course, illustrate the survival
of prefigurative techniques during the years from 1650 to 1680. But
they do more, for his typology very quickly started to influence
contemporary writers. Dryden's use of *Paradise Lost* in *Absalom
and Achitophel*, for instance, is well known, but it is particularly
interesting to note that Dryden must have derived the poem's typology, at least in part, from Milton's representation of Satan, who is
the figure for Achitophel, and of Adam, the just man in history
who is type of Christ and figure for Charles II (David).[63] The typology of *Paradise Lost* clearly inspired some of Pope's typological
invention in *The Dunciad*, but it is less widely recognized that
Pope's *Messiah* also owes some of its conception to Milton's poetical
treatments of the Messiah. A number of eighteenth-century epics,
both English and German, on Old Testament and christological
themes, which I shall discuss in a later chapter, derive their typology from that of Milton's two epics. Long before Blake and other
English Romantic poets regarded the poet Milton as a poetical
visionary or a prophet with a typological story to tell, eighteenth-
century English writers saw that Milton's career as poet could be

---

[62] *Ibid.*, p. 309.

[63] Anne D. Ferry, in *Milton and the Miltonic Dryden* (Cambridge, Mass.:
Harvard Univ. Press, 1968), studies the relationship at length, but ineptly and
without historical depth, making no reference to the messianic parallels or to
other contemporary literature. See esp. pp. 119-21.

reckoned in typological terms. In the late 1730s the political writer William Guthrie, an early associate of Samuel Johnson, produced "The Apotheosis of Milton, A Vision," one of the first works to attribute divinely inspired prophetical powers to Milton.[64] Blake would carry the apotheosizing of Milton to its greatest lengths at the end of the eighteenth century and the beginning of the nineteenth. Eighteenth-century editions of Milton's collected works, as well as of the individual epics, frequently include commentary and, by the end of the century, these books begin to acquire an encyclopedic quality, with many of them containing the *notae variorum editorum* as seventeenth-century syntagmata had done.[65] Another kind of interpretation accompanied many eighteenth-century editions of Milton, that of the book illustrator, and here, too, decades before Blake's extensive graphic typologizing of Miltonic themes, there is persuasive evidence for the survival and nurturing of an earlier figural tradition.[66] This brief glance at only three of the many writers who actively used typology during the latter seventeenth century will suggest, I think, that not only is typological continuity evident from many points of view but that the writers of the period employed prefigurative techniques with a good deal of innovation.

The continued popularity of typology in later seventeenth-century poetry does not represent the only survival of earlier tradi-

[64] Guthrie's work appeared in the *Gentleman's Magazine*, 8 (1738), 223-35, 469, 521-22; 9 (1739), 20-21, 73-75. Sir John Hawkins, in his 1787 edition of Samuel Johnson's *Works*, erroneously attributes this piece to Johnson (see Volume XI).

[65] Richard Bentley's commentary to his edition of *Paradise Lost* (London, 1732) is almost entirely concerned with textual emendation, but the notes of Thomas Newton's edition, 2 vols. (London, 1749), J. Merchant's, 2 vols. (London, 1751), and Raymond de Saint Maur's, 2 vols. (London, 1775), are extensive and pay specific attention to Milton's typology. Most of these notes, plus commentary from other sources, may be found in H. J. Todd's edition, *Poetical Works of John Milton; with the principal notes of the various commentators*, 6 vols. (London, 1801).

[66] Wittreich, in *Angel of Apocalypse*, p. 286, mentions many of the eighteenth-century illustrators of Milton. For a full study, see C. H. Collins Baker, "Some Illustrators of Milton's *Paradise Lost* (1688-1750)," *The Library*, 5th ser., 3 (1948), 1-21, 101-19. Collins Baker, I should note, deals with only one Miltonic work; illustrating all of the poems was a flourishing craft.

tions. An examination of figural change must also recognize that the smaller components of literature, such as theories of grammar, language, and the cognitive bases of words themselves, are also important. Although I shall not deal with these topics here, I will observe that the maturing of the English language during the seventeenth century and the contributions of lexicographers and other historians of English words, grammar, and usage play a vital part, still largely unassessed, in imagistic change.[67] However, whether poetic discourse is private or public, inward or outward, complex or plain, learned or simple, the mental operations involved in its creation are basically the same. The long-term preconditions and middle-term precipitants of figural change are, as I have suggested, broad movements of ideas that leave the basic materials of literature, the fundamentals of language and grammar, virtually unchanged. The transformations they produce are analogous to contemporary changes in architectural styles: the surface results and sometimes even the method of construction changed, but the building materials remained essentially the same. Hence I have introduced the concept of the survival of tradition, as demonstrated by the continuance of typologizing, to serve as a control. It is meant to illustrate that the figural change of the later seventeenth century, which scholars have always regarded as a major transformation in English literary history, exceeded in profundity only by the evolution of Romanticism in the next century, is quite conservative in nature.

Typology, then, outlasted the seventeenth century but, at the end of the century, it was not a dying mode or a recidivist style that hinted at archaism. By its very continuance, even as other aspects of early seventeenth-century literary style changed or disappeared, typology itself underwent many changes. These changes are suggestive of the subtlety and sometimes hard-to-understand codes that obtained in late seventeenth- and eighteenth-century literature. The importance of typology to the literature of the period is evidence of how closely this literary mode figures in the language of undermeanings of the age; it is desirable for us to seek to understand its transformations. At the beginning of the seventeenth century, typology

---

[67] For example, such important historical studies as Richard Foster Jones, *The Triumph of the English Language* (Stanford: Stanford Univ. Press, 1951) and DeWitt T. Starnes, *Renaissance Dictionaries* (Austin: Univ. of Texas Press, 1954) are not concerned with showing how changing ideas of language or the expanded role of the dictionary affected imagery.

had been largely a phenomenon of theological interpretation and writing; it appeared in creative literature mainly in theological contexts. At mid-century, typology had already gained approval in much religious and in some secular poetry, as well as in political contexts and controversy (aided, most notably, by the Regicide). By the end of the century, typological references and structures had become common poetic materials, and were starting to appear in literary prose. Still further adaptations would come in the eighteenth century. Each step of the way is illuminating, for at every juncture we will garner new evidence of the uncommonly rich complexity of eighteenth-century literature, its continuity with the Renaissance, and its gradual accumulation of the intellectual heritage it would pass on to English Romanticism. Typology, originally a single technique in the armory of biblical scholarship, expands into a system of reference and a literary-historical code ripe for deciphering.

CHAPTER 4

Typology as System

1

TYPOLOGY IS a system of exegesis. It is probably the most enduring of the hermeneutic techniques employed by the primitive Christians to elucidate the relationships among the mysteries of the Old Testament, the revelation of the emerging text of the New Testament, and the perplexities of recent history. From the very beginning of its existence, typology was associated indissolubly with signs, images, symbols, and an entire figural tradition; the word itself (τύπος) stood for the interpretation of signs, for the clarifying of the obscure.[1] Typology is also closely associated with the fulfillment of prophecy, for it serves both as *prefiguration* of the goals or expectations of prophecy and as *postfiguration* or a representation of a prophecy that has been achieved. As such, typology is also part of rabbinic exegesis and was regularly employed in pre-Christian times by Jewish exegetes. The early Fathers had to deal with typology, for typological exegesis had been employed not simply by such an authority as the Pauline Epistles, but in the Gospels themselves: it was clear to them that it was a designated, even a sanctified interpretative guide that no Christian could ignore. The development of typological methodologies in biblical hermeneutics, while very complex, is well known to church histo-

[1] There is no history of typology *per se*. Among the many works which deal extensively with it, the most helpful include F. W. Farrar, *History of Interpretation* (New York, 1885), *passim*; *Essays on Typology*, ed. G.W.H. Lampe and K. J. Woollcombe, which contains Woollcombe's "The Biblical Origins and Patristic Development of Typology" and Lampe's excellent "The Reasonableness of Typology"; and Daniélou's *Sacramentum Futuri*. Sacvan Bercovitch's "Annotated Bibliography" of writings concerning typology, in *Typology and Early American Literature*, ed. Sacvan Bercovitch, pp. 245-337, is the most complete bibliography ever attempted.

rians, theologians, and (increasingly) to nontheological scholars, including historians and literary critics.[2]

At the start, I should mention that typology, in its exegetical sense, was early amalgamated or conflated with figuralism and figural traditions and, along with such terms as shadow, allegory, and parable, became one of the principal means of nonliteral biblical interpretation. In biblical typology, an event, a person, a sign, or occasionally a text or literary device is understood, by exegetes and informed readers alike, to assume a predictive or prefigurative quality with regard to later events. Such readers regard a type not just as a figure or symbol of something that is to come or as a part of something that will be completed later but as a sort of metaphorical promissory note, a partial literary figure whose fullness will be revealed afterwards. A type answers to the fundamental human need to hope that the future will give more than the past or present has yielded, and it impinges closely upon the predilection of historical writers, including literary historians, to analogize between events in different ages and cultures. Moreover, when it is construed broadly, with small regard for the requirements of biblical interpretation, typology can acquire fantastic ramifications which challenge both historian and literary critic. Indeed, precisely because typology is so close to the basic human predictive need, it has long been used very loosely, at times almost with abandon. In this respect, typology is like other systems of exegesis, in which the validity of an interpretation depends upon the meaning of key terms like "metaphor," "symbol," "structure," "allegory," and so on. Since my interest in this study is the application of typology to literary contexts primarily *outside* the sphere of biblical exegesis, it may therefore be helpful for us to examine this system in several parts. I would distinguish at this point among *conventional* typology, *applied* typology, and *abstracted* typology.

Conventional typology deals principally with biblical situations. In scriptural exegesis, it has traditionally been concerned with demonstrating the existence of typological relationships between the Old

---

2 The history of typological terminology is complicated; for further discussion, see Chapter 5. "Typology" is often used synonymously and confused with many other terms; the most common analogues are "figural" and "figuralism."

and New Testaments. Since it is such a popular hermeneutic device, this might appear to be the simplest of the three categories. While it is true that typology tends to be above religious struggles and persecutions, it is not immune to controversy. For example, the influential mystical exegesis of Origen, the fourfold method of the medieval Church, and the extensive typologizing of late medieval scriptural commentary were not entirely acceptable to Reformation and post-Reformation theologians. Medieval commentaries continued to be readily available, in large compilations of biblical criticism, to Renaissance and seventeenth-century exegetes and, as we will see later, schools of interpretation developed which would use conventional or biblical typology in highly exaggerated ways. Mystics like Jakob Boehme and Thomas Vaughan, scientists or pseudo-scientists like Paracelsus and Lord Herbert of Cherbury, and members of unorthodox Christian sects employed typology to wrest strange meanings and curious relationships from the body of existing learning.

In the seventeenth century, we start to encounter the theological debate about the acceptability of typology as a hermeneutic method: in certain cases it had become so common and was employed so inventively that it was decried as a brand of excessive, mystical exegesis. The view of John Gaule, mentioned earlier, once practically orthodox, would later seem extreme.[3] Gaule's notion that Christ was prefigured in virtually everything of importance in the Old Testament would be too much to accept. Hence Anglicans throughout the late seventeenth and eighteenth centuries would hesitate to adopt so sweeping a definition or would have important reservations to make about it. In terms of the Bible itself, Gaule's pronouncement would continue to be acceptable to many, but the intermingling of religion and politics in seventeenth-century England gradually transformed typology into a polemical device with broad nontheological implications.[4] Typology would continue to be an acceptable form of exegesis in contemporary theology (indeed, twentieth-century theologians use it), most often for homiletic or historical purposes, but the point at which theologians and other literate people begin to dispute the propriety of its application is

[3] See C. A. Patrides, *Milton and the Christian Tradition* (Oxford: Clarendon Press, 1966), pp. 128-30.

[4] Steven N. Zwicker, *Dryden's Political Poetry: The Typology of King and Nation* (Providence, R.I.: Brown Univ. Press, 1972), pp. 16-23, discusses political typology in seventeenth-century contexts.

crucial. As so often happens in the history of literary interpretation, a dispute about a method of exegesis is an indication that an important evolution has started to take place. In the case of pure or biblical typology, the evolution can be described as follows: a simple and relatively straightforward hermeneutic device begins to develop into a set of loosely correlated principles or a *system* which still bears a resemblance to its original form and purpose but which will now be put to other, applied uses.

The corruption of biblical typology and the development of applied typology did not happen suddenly in the Reformation and its immediate aftermath. Applied typology had arisen in ancient times: the Church Fathers had not hesitated to apply typological methods to the interpretation of pagan literature and mysteries. The early Christian view of the *Odyssey* shows applied typology at work. Odysseus' escape from the Sirens (*Odyssey*, XII) by being bound to the mast was seen as a pagan mystery that prefigured Christian salvation. Odysseus' mast was a pagan type of the Cross, Odysseus a type of the Christian who, cleaving to the wood of the Cross (itself a powerful symbol of death and resurrection), would sail through the waters of destruction to salvation.[5] Applied typology was not confined to the classics of pagan literature, although they come in for their share of such treatment. The *Iliad*, the *Aeneid*, and the *Metamorphoses* were the most popular classical fields for playing the game of analogy. The position of the analogists, so ably presented by Don Cameron Allen, was that ancient pagan literature was written by informed pre-Christians in a code whose mystical signs could be deciphered and read by someone with a thorough knowledge of ancient symbolism and nonliteral interpretation, especially typology. The formal bases of this kind of exegesis, however much they might be ridiculed by later, especially Enlightenment, skeptics, would nevertheless endure until the nineteenth century and, in certain aspects of the techniques of Lévi-Strauss and modern structural anthropology, they are with us still. There are scattered hints that the pre-Christian pagans may have known about typology, although they did not have a name for the mode as they used it. For example, Plutarch identifies a Homeric allusion to Agamemnon's boldness (*Iliad*, III.179) as a

---

[5] See Hugo Rahner, *Greek Myths and Christian Mystery* (London: Burnet & Oats, 1963), pp. xvii, xxi; cf. Chapter 6, note 6, below.

prefiguration of Alexander's martial genius.[6] Unfortunately, such hints are quite rare. The human tendency to predict the future or, with the aid of hindsight, to read the texts of the past as if their authors were blessed with prophetic knowledge, is probably at work here; genuine typology would come later.

Typology, in the conventional sense, involves historical interpretation of both Testaments: the events of the New were not just foreshadowed but justified by the events of the Old Testament (for the visual linking of the Testaments, see Figures 5, 12, and 13). Thus the victory of Christ and his Church vindicated the prefigurative qualities of the Old Testament types. Historical events, in other words, may readily be interpreted as the successful afterlife of mysterious prognostications, perhaps originally unnoticed or misunderstood by all but the illuminated. A historian who has the inclination to see the end of his account as the fulfillment of its suggestive beginnings can therefore impart a typological framework or structure to history. This is typology in its best applied sense. It is present, in this way, in Eusebius' *Church History*, a work whose central apologetic idea is that the triumph of Christianity is the culmination of a historical process that began with the mysterious prophecies and signs of the Old Testament. Moreover, the historians of antiquity generally conceived of history as a progression from shadowy beginnings to a glorious fulfillment, for historians, then as now, were often apologists for an established government or certain accepted ideas, and conceived it useful to describe the present as an antitype held forth by the past.

In its applied sense, then, biblical typology could be used for various literary purposes, not all of them necessarily religious. Applied typology is particularly common, for example, in political literature. The analogizing of kings or other rulers to Christ, familiar in the Middle Ages and Renaissance, reached a culmination in seventeenth-century England, when applied typology was often employed in literature of all kinds to describe figures like Charles I (the Martyr King) and Cromwell (the Davidic King).[7] The reli-

[6] A. J. Maas's article, "Types in Scripture," *Catholic Encyclopedia*, XI, 107, identifies this allusion, but of course there is no reason to believe that Plutarch knew anything about prefigurative methods of exegesis.

[7] See Zwicker, *Dryden's Political Poetry*, pp. 48-55, and Joseph A. Mazzeo, "Cromwell as Davidic King," in his *Reason and the Imagination* (New York: Columbia Univ. Press, 1962), pp. 29-55.

gious significance of the typological relationship is never completely forgotten in these situations: writers were conscious that
their audience knew full well that Adam, Moses, Joshua, David,
and so on were traditionally regarded as prefigurative of Christ.[8]
Seldom indeed do we encounter an authorial statement in imaginative literature that a type or a typological relationship is being
used, except in profoundly religious or (the opposite extreme)
clearly parodic contexts. So Milton refers to types in *Paradise Lost*,
where the import is one of high seriousness, and Dryden does the
same in *Mac Flecknoe*, where the situation is jocular.[9] But these are
exceptions; applied typology in other works by these authors and in
Donne, Herbert, Vaughan, Marvell, and scores of other writers
from Spenser to Pope is seldom labeled as such. In the seventeenth
century, we will often find applied typology in public poetry, where
the element of historical vindication would be likely to have the
maximum political impact. There is a good deal of distortion in
this category of typology, for the prefigurative purposes of the biblical variety are often absent. Whereas readers of Scripture could
readily comprehend how Moses foreshadowed Christ or how the
Israelites' crossing of the Red Sea prefigured redemption from sin
through Christ, Dryden's David (Charles II) in a poem like *Absalom and Achitophel* was less obviously a typing of Christ. What we
have instead in Dryden's case is a kind of postfiguration, in which
the poet introduces a type to refer us *back* to an accepted typological relationship at the same time that the figure of David reminds
us that, in biblical times, he also prefigures the greater accomplishment of his Christian antitype. Such figural juggling may seem
baffling, if not obscure, to a generation like ours, trained in rational
analysis of imagery, but it was entirely acceptable to and conform-

---

[8] The large seventeenth-century compilations of Scripture metaphors and
other source books for typological imagery leave no doubt that these identifications were widely, if not universally, made. See, for example, Griffith Williams,
Seven Goulden Candlesticks (London, 1624), p. 258. Samuel Mather, *The Figures
or Types of the Old Testament* (Dublin, 1683), in a long section called "The
Gospel of the Personal Types" (see 2nd ed. [London, 1705], pp. 51-136) sums up
all the personal figural associations for the century.

[9] Milton's chief allusion to typology in *Paradise Lost* is at XII. 300-306, on
which see the commentary of Madsen, *From Shadowy Types to Truth*, pp. 48-53.
The reference in *Mac Flecknoe* is to lines 29-34, but the scholia by H. T. Swedenberg, Jr. in *The Works of John Dryden*, II, 315, are disappointing.

able with post-Renaissance figural and iconographical traditions.[10] The excesses of applied typology naturally provoked objections during the seventeenth century; not every contemporary reader would accept figural distortion. Milton and John Hall objected to the typology of martyrdom that appears in accounts of the death of Charles I and so, half a century later, did Defoe. At least one of the answers to *Absalom and Achitophel* takes serious issue with Dryden's David-Charles II typology. So among literary men, as among orthodox Christians, there is discernible evidence that some writers—relatively few—found the survival of Renaissance typological figuralism offensive, blasphemous, or both.

A similar zest for analogy made possible the most interesting variety of applied typology, the mythological, whose many permutations I shall discuss in detail in Chapter 6. This kind of typology is probably most common, certainly best known, in the visual arts. The materials of pagan mythology, as art historians including Jean Seznec, André Grabar, and Rudolf Wittkower have shown, were easily adaptable to Christian iconography, whether in sculpture, painting, stained glass, the decorative arts, manuscript illumination, or book illustration. The explanation of pagan mythology in Christian terms dates from patristic times, so it is natural that the central figures of myth were very early regarded as types of Christ amidst the wilderness of paganism (see Figure 4).[11] Orpheus became the healing Christ, the Good Shepherd, the divinely inspired musician-magus, the type of the Resurrection. Hercules became the suffering, martyred Christ, the subduer of symbolic evil, the performer of seven miraculous tasks.[12] The ingenuity of eager exegetes left few

[10] A helpful view of the figural associations of seventeenth-century iconography is D. J. Gordon, "Ripa's Fate," in his *The Renaissance Imagination: Essays and Lectures*, ed. Stephen Orgel (Berkeley and Los Angeles: Univ. of California Press, 1975), pp. 51-74.

[11] Jean Seznec, *The Survival of the Pagan Gods: The Mythological Tradition and Its Place in Renaissance Humanism and Art*, trans. Barbara F. Sessions (Princeton: Princeton Univ. Press, 1953), is relevant throughout. See also André Grabar, *Christian Iconography: A Study of Its Origins* (London, 1969), pp. 137-46, who discusses Old Testament typology but is confused about accurate terminology.

[12] On Hercules, see Seznec, *The Survival of the Pagan Gods*, pp. 11, 154-55; the identifications are commonplaces by the mid-seventeenth century, as Alexander Ross's article in *Mystagogus Poeticus; or The Muses Interpreter*, 6th ed. (London, 1675), pp. 167-72, clearly demonstrates. See also Rahner, *Greek Myths and Christian Mystery*, pp. 3-45. Late seventeenth-century examples of this ty-

myths free from a Christian tincture. Pre-Renaissance explanation
of pagan myth in typological terms is usually inspirational: there
was much emphasis on similarities between the pagan "type" and
scriptural history, usually with little or no effort at proof. Scriptural
exegetes, after all, were generally scrupulous in defending a typological reading or identification. Even so copious an annotator as
Nicholas of Lyra, who codified typological exegesis from patristic
sources for generations of later scholiasts, had explained *why* he
thought most of his types were worthy of the distinction. In contrast, the leading Renaissance students of classical mythology, Giraldi, Natales Comes, and Vincenzo Cartari, were usually content to
point out types in their discussions of myth without explanation or
corroboration. The inspirational method was picked up in the English Renaissance; a good example is Alexander Ross's *Mystagogus
Poeticus; or The Muses Interpreter* (1647). Ross stresses the most
tenuous analogies between classical myth and Christ; he is, indeed,
more of a symbolist than a typologist. His popular work, however,
helped to establish a Christian basis for many seventeenth- and
eighteenth-century mythic allusions. Not every mythic allusion is
ipso facto typological: the matter must be decided by thematic and
contextual factors. Dryden's Orpheus figure in his "Ode on the
Death of . . . Purcell" (1696) is a type, as the situation reveals. His
passages about Charles II in *Annus Mirabilis* are identified as typological by subject matter, style, and action. Mythic allusions after
1700 are seldom so clear: contexts are sometimes typological, sometimes distorted for parodic purposes, as they will be in *A Tale of a
Tub, The Rape of the Lock,* and *Jonathan Wild.* The element of
contextual distortion is a matter that must be reserved for later
discussion.

Renaissance mythography was not limited to inspirational link-
ings of the pagan and Christian. In an important way, it helped to
set the basis for the typological system that we find so frequently in
later literature. The essence of all typology is a logical progression
from cause to effect, from type to antitype; like all thematic modes
of reference or exegesis, its structure is concrete and highly reified.
In a given situation, of course, the typologist may suggest a relationship founded on mystical rather than genuine correspondence. This

pology occur in Dryden's poetry: he uses the Orpheus type in "An Ode, on the
Death of Mr. Henry Purcell" (1696) ("We beg not Hell, our *Orpheus* to restore"
[16]) and the Hercules type in Threnodia Augustalis (1685) ("Our *Atlas* fell indeed; But *Hercules* was near" [35]).

is where the contributions of Renaissance and seventeenth-century writers on myth are significant. Their search for mysterious meanings and adumbrations of Christianity in pagan myth relates to that of earlier Christians, but it is not always inspirational. Often, in fact, it is quite scientific, orderly, and logical. In analyses of Christian origins, typology is a natural method to employ, for it is in many ways a logical and rational system. In the efforts of scholars like Bochart, Vossius, Kircher, and many others to interpret pagan mythology as an obscured version of Old Testament history we find a great impetus for the typological system of post-Renaissance literature. The Dutch scholar Vossius, for example, who wrote the first detailed study of the origins of pagan idolatry, provided a solid scholarly foundation for literary men who wanted to allude to the pagan myths while stressing their Old Testament (and hence typological) analogues. The labors of the French linguist Bochart, whose specialty was etymological relationships (some of them real, most of them imaginary) among the Oriental tongues, established most of the pagan pantheon as mere linguistic distortions of the Old Testament patriarchs, many of whom were widely accepted as types of Christ. Hence an allusion to Saturn, Neptune, or Jupiter could be regarded as another name for Adam, Noah, or Moses, all of whom had definite prefigurative roles in Christian thought (see Figure 8). Kircher, a German Jesuit who lived in Rome, devoted many years to deciphering (incorrectly, as it turned out) Egyptian hieroglyphics and sought out secret writings (steganography) in music and magnetism as well. He made the quest for Christian symbolism in *all* mysterious documents fashionable for more than a century after his death. Even after more enlightened study had shown Kircher's Egyptological efforts to be wrong, scholars of the later eighteenth century continued to refer to his works respectfully. And these polymaths are only three from among many learned men who undertook systematically to explicate the mysteries of earlier, pre-Christian civilizations in terms that often required the use of applied typology to make the past comprehensible to the Christian mind.

The more fanciful, inspirational applied typology, with its overtones of mysticism and enthusiasm, declined somewhat in popularity in late seventeenth-century England. For one thing, it was too closely associated with Continental mysticism and English nonconformism to be free from controversial implications. For another, systematic study of pagan myth led Protestant apologists to asso-

ciate it with the alleged idolatries of Roman Catholicism. We find
the Anglican apologist Edward Stillingfleet devoting a long chapter
of his early work, *Origines Sacrae* (1662), to showing that pagan
mythology was a distortion of Hebraic history (and hence typological). But later in his career Stillingfleet spent much of his time
defending Anglican doctrines, as did other apologists, and idolatrous devotion to pagan mythology was one of his most prominent
targets. In the years from about 1700 to about 1740, students of
mythology became increasingly rational, not only in England but
on the Continent as well. Allen calls this process "the rationalization of myth," and there can be no doubt that it was quite a general movement.[13] Writers on antiquity, from Huet and Graevius
to Gronovius and Blackwell, tend to treat ancient mythology as a
body of superstitious phenomena rather than as the mystic matrix
of Christianity. Allusions to mythical figures in English poetry
after the first quarter of the eighteenth century seldom, I think,
have the contextual qualities of applied typology. The association of typology and myth, as I will show in Chapter 6, continues
in the eighteenth century in other ways. We continue to find applied typology, of course, as, for instance, with Pope's Man of Ross
(*Epistle to Bathurst*) or Wharton, a negative type (*Epistle to Cob-
ham*). We may notice a recollection of the typological qualities of
animals (an old exegetical practice which Dryden had employed
to advantage in *The Hind and the Panther*) in Gay's *Fables*,
but there the contexts are not theological. However, as the impetus
for applied typology diminishes, a new one gradually replaces it.
This is the movement toward abstracted typology, a latecomer to
the figural scene, which is derived from its predecessors.

 3

Perhaps the central characteristic of abstracted typology is its total
dedication to the symbolic properties of all things. Most important
is the conception of the world as a book lying open for interpretation, which originates at least as early as the Old Testament.[14]

[13] See *Mysteriously Meant*, pp. 279-311. As I will show later (see below,
Chapter 6), the study of myth is rationalized only on the surface; the allegorical
spirit would live on long after 1700.

[14] The notion is a commonplace; it is discussed at length by Leo Spitzer,
"Classical and Christian Ideas of World Harmony," *Traditio*, 2 (1944), 409-64.

Origen is not the first, but he is among the most prominent, of the early Christians to treat natural circumstances or occurrences as symbolic of theological qualities.[15] The discovery of correspondences between worldly and divine things is often simply the result of a pious search for resemblances between past and present to justify an existing body of doctrine. But the quest can also become a more intricate attempt to unravel strands of mystery from the fabric of the world. In this way, an exegete could easily deploy a typological hermeneutic to explain a text, a story, or a natural circumstance. The first typologists, for example, found mystical shadows of Christ and his Church not simply in Old Testament persons, but also in candlesticks, priestly vestments, animals, and astronomical phenomena, to mention only a few of the more obvious. Numerous figural texts in both Testaments were interpreted typologically, that is, they were taken as evidence that it was permissible to read types in the broadest possible sense. One of the chief Pauline typological references, that "the law having a shadow of good things to come, and not the very image of the things" (Hebrews 10.1), allowed the exegetes to take the entire Mosaic Law, or any part of it, in a prefigurative sense. A typological system began to evolve as early as the second century, at least in the theological sphere, when the primitive Church adopted the symbolic manner of teaching religious doctrines common among the Egyptians, the Gnostics, and the Greek and Roman mystery religions.[16] The ostensible political reason for this move was to make Christianity more palatable to heathen groups which the Church sought to convert. The figural result was more interesting, in that it ensured a wider popularity for the doctrine of correspondences outside the strictly theological sphere.

Egyptian religion, with its copious lore based on actions, signs, images, and other sensible representations, contributed more to later figural traditions than other early sources of mystery. By the

[15] See Daniélou, *Origen*, pp. 182-84. Other important pre-Nicene exegetes who, following Paul and Philo, used types in their readings of Scripture, are Justin Martyr, Irenaeus, Clement of Alexandria, mainly in the *Stromata*, and Tertullian. Wolfson, *The Philosophy of the Church Fathers*, p. 63, observes succinctly, "With Clement and Origen the nonliteral method of interpretation in Christianity reached its fullest development." There have been many studies of Philo's figuralism; for a convenient summary, see Samuel Sandmel, *Philo of Alexandria: An Introduction* (New York: Oxford Univ. Press, 1979), pp. 17-18, 160, 168-70.

[16] See J. L. Mosheim, *An Ecclesiastical History, Ancient and Modern*, 2 vols. (London, 1765), I, 101-102.

late European Renaissance we often find *hieroglyphics*, in the correct Egyptian sense, used practically interchangeably with accepted literary terms like *type, figure, image, emblem*, and *symbol*. In this way, Egyptian mythology differs from the Hellenic (and hence Roman) tradition, which laid its principal stress on mythic persons. The mythographers and figuralists did not ignore the Egyptian gods: they are a frequent topic of discussion in the Renaissance and afterwards among euhemerists and Oriental scholars. But nothing could equal the power that the hieroglyphic tradition exerted upon Western minds. Hieroglyphics were not simply a secret writing or a code; they were pregnant with mystical significance as well. In England, the word is in use by the late sixteenth century (1586, according to the NED), and it begins to acquire transferred senses rapidly. By 1635, Francis Quarles, in the preface to his *Emblemes*, could write:

> An Embleme is but a silent Parable. Let not the tender Eye checke, to see the allusion to our blessed SAVIOUR figured, in these Types. In holy Scripture, He is sometimes called a Sower; sometimes a Fisher; sometimes a Physitian: And why not presented so, as well to the eye, as to the eare? Before the knowledge of letters, God was knowne by *Hieroglyphicks*; And, indeed, what are the Heavens, the Earth, nay every Creature, but *Hieroglyphicks* and Emblemes of His Glory?

The hieroglyphic, here used analogously with other kinds of figures, including emblems, parables, and types, becomes a key to mysterious knowledge. Quarles follows a considerable earlier tradition in reading hieroglyphics typologically.[17] His significant addition to this background is the proposal that the entire creation may be viewed as a sign, or an infinite series of signs, of divine glory (see Figures 1-3).

He is not alone in holding to this belief: it permeates most documents in the English and Continental emblem tradition.[18] We find the idea elsewhere, expressed in approximately the same way. A later seventeenth-century writer on myth and antiquity, for example, in a discussion of the Egyptian mysteries, makes the by now familiar figuralist analogy:

[17] (London, 1635), Sig. A3ʳ. On the earlier tradition, see Dieckmann, *Hieroglyphics*, pp. 48-61.

[18] See, in general, Arthur Henkel and Albrecht Schöne, *Emblemata* (Stuttgart: J. B. Metzler, 1967).

Every name is an abbreviation of a Thing, but it is not able to give such a perfect *Idæa* of the Properties and hidden Qualities of the Things intimated, as the picture of them in a witty *Hieroglyphick*. The Great Creator of all things hath been pleased to discover unto us in this manner the Divine pleasure and all the excellencies of his Being. In the Old Testament the Mysteries of the Gospel were delivered to the Children of *Israel* in Types and Figures. And in the great Book of Nature God teacheth us by Mysterious Impressions of himself by Natural *Hieroglyphicks*, by certain significant Images of his Glorious Being.[19]

Contextually, this is a theological observation. But its implications are immense, for the author, the French Jesuit Pierre Gaultruche, establishes correspondences (1) between traditional (i.e., Egyptian) hieroglyphics and "Natural *Hieroglyphicks*" and (2) between the typological figuralism of the Old Testament and the phenomena of "the great Book of Nature." The association of theological typology and natural hieroglyphics grows from descriptions like this one. There is even more to the relationship, for this passage portends the growth of a figural system based on a typological analogy between things and events, past, present, and future, which can function completely independently of the theological sphere. Abstracted typology, as it will develop in English literature, will at first appear in theological or quasi-theological contexts: this is why the seventeenth- and eighteenth-century upsurge of interest in comparative religion is relevant to its spread. But, as we will see, the typological system functions equally well in contexts where natural religion or the religion of nature is central (as in Blake, Wordsworth, Shelley, Browning, and Ruskin), and ultimately, in situations where there is no particular religious context at all.[20]

Typology, I said at the beginning of this chapter, is a system of exegesis, a complex and often multifaceted method of interpreting certain texts or stories that have descended to a given period from

[19] Pierre Galtruchius, *The Poetical Histories: being a compleat Collection of all the Stories necessary for an understanding of the Greek and Latine Poets* . . . , trans. Marius D'Assigny, 2 vols. (London, 1671), II, 156. For some of the visual bases of natural hieroglyphics, see Figure 9.

[20] See George P. Landow, "Moses Striking the Rock: Typological Symbolism in Victorian Poetry," in *Literary Uses of Typology*, pp. 315-44, for discussion of Victorian uses of literary typology; on Blake, Shelley, and Wordsworth, see below, Chapter 9.

the past. The Old Testament in the hands of the exegetes of the early Church was an ideal subject for adumbrative reading; not only were there many specific mandates for such a system in the New Testament, but the facts of early Christian history could often be taken as antitypes or confirmations of certain earlier shadows. There is also evidence that the ancient (i.e., pre-Christian) Jewish interpretation of the Hebrew Bible employed types.[21] Midrashic and patristic exegesis, however, while they relied extensively on non-literal methods (indeed, Wolfson believes that nonliteral exegesis had risen to such heights by the time of Clement and Origen that afterwards nothing new happened among the Fathers with regard to scriptural interpretation), find their predictive materials, both fore-shadowings and antitypes, in theological texts. Abstracted typology is generally unsuitable to the interpretation of theological texts (conventional typology existed for that purpose). It cannot be readily used to suggest a theological meaning in a nontheological text— this is the purpose of applied typology. Most seventeenth-century political typology is what I would call applied. For example, Dryden's presentation of Charles II as David augments the King's role with some of the christological significance that David's name would naturally imply. Most applied typology appears to have been created for this express christological purpose. The writer who introduces abstracted typology into a literary work, unlike the conventional and (to a lesser extent) the applied typologists, has ceased to be an interpreter of past mysteries (any method of exegesis has as a major purpose the solution of dark or problematical parts of a text). He is not concerned with decoding or deciphering a difficult text such as the Bible or one of the ancient philosophers (Plato and Plotinus had been fruitful ground for Renaissance typologists). Theological matters are not his central interest, yet such an author may simultaneously have an ethical or moral purpose for using types. The eighteenth-century novelists who introduce abstracted typology into their books, such as Richardson, Fielding, Goldsmith, Mackenzie, Smollett, and Godwin, were clearly aware that their methods had a didactic tendency and would enforce existing religious and ethical values, but their contexts are not primarily theological. Such a writer, then, has become both creator and exegete at once: he is the fashioner of his own mysteries and, by introducing a typological schema, simultaneously provides the key to their inter-

---

21 See Wolfson, *The Philosophy of the Church Fathers*, pp. 27-28 on midrashic nonliteral interpretation (and cf. pp. 24-43, *passim*).

pretation. To interpret such texts accurately, we must recognize the presence of the typological system and try to understand how it works.

We begin to glimpse a typological system in the attempts of the Renaissance euhemerists to christianize pagan myth. This exegesis is a species of applied typology, since the figures of pre-Christian fable were unmasked as types of Christ. The christianizing of myth had pretty well run its course by the last half of the seventeenth century. Stillingfleet's *Origines Sacrae*, the last major English work to follow the Renaissance polyhistors, is highly derivative, and it did not produce imitators. A new kind of mythological writing develops toward the end of the century: the scholarly study of pagan societies, an early species of what we now call comparative religion. There are a number of English and Continental treatises on the subject, all from the period after 1680.[22] These are mainly pious, Christian works, usually written by priests or divines, whose burden was to show how pagan religions prefigured the only true faith. There is no need to categorize them here, for their typology, which appears frequently, is clearly applied, or used for theological purposes. The study of pagan myth *qua* myth, as a body of belief and story unique and separate from Christianity, is an outgrowth of deism and seventeenth-century empiricism.[23] At first glance, it might seem that works like Cudworth's *True Intellectual System of the Universe* (1678) or the writings of Fontenelle and Bayle, by studying ancient religion as something distinct from Christianity, would discourage the zeal of typologists. They did not—in fact, they did almost the reverse. Cudworth, for instance, in his examination of the Orphic mysteries, discovered that they tended to exalt a single deity and even showed evidence of a sort of trinitarian thought.[24] These phenomena were not specifically types of persons or circumstances within Christianity, but they *were* types nevertheless; although the antitype was not always named, it usually was obvious. Rational inquiries into myth, which increased in the first half of the eighteenth century, were barren of Renaissance mystery-mongering.

Yet a new form of nonliteral interpretation employing typology

[22] I discuss works in this interesting tradition in Chapter 6.
[23] On the attitudes of deists and freethinkers toward myth, see Frank Manuel, *The Eighteenth Century Confronts the Gods* (Cambridge, Mass.: Harvard Univ. Press, 1959), pp. 57-81, 129-48.
[24] See *The True Intellectual System of the Universe* (London, 1678), pp. 299-306.

comes into existence all the same. Scholars no longer regarded symbolic passages in ancient texts and religions as mysterious adumbrations of Christianity; instead, they examined them as if they were part of a code which, since someone had rationally encoded them, could be rationally decoded with the aid of the proper key. The "key" had great appeal to eighteenth-century European audiences; it actually forms a subgenre of some prominence. "Keys" and "complete keys" abound in the late seventeenth and eighteenth centuries. These works have not yet been systematically examined; while they vary greatly, they share a common concern with identifying correct names and places. The "keys" to the ancient world's code were to be found, contemporary scholars believed, in a thorough knowledge of ancient languages, customs, and religions. For example, Thomas Blackwell, the author of the most rational, skeptical eighteenth-century account of Homer (a deeply mysterious writer to the Renaissance), found that myth was a figural tradition independent of any relationship to Christianity. "It is certain," writes Blackwell,

> that Mythology, as it now stands, is not to be understood without a wide and accurate Knowledge of the *religious Rites* of the several Nations from whom the *Greeks* received their Gods, because upon some significant Ceremony concerning the Nature, or traditional Tale concerning the Exploits of the Divinity depends the Key to the Legend, and sometimes the very *Name* of the God himself. As the early *Egyptian* Rites were established by Law, were all recorded, were all typical and symbolical, the Type or Symbol came by an easy Transition, not only to signify obscurely, but directly to express the Thing typified: a grand Source of Error and Incertainty in the Foundation of the Allegory![25]

We do not know that the ancient Egyptians had any notion of typology and neither did Blackwell. But this uncertainty does not prevent him from finding an extensive typology in every aspect of their religion. Typology becomes a universal, abstract system for Blackwell, having no relationship to a future antitype; it is simply a branch of figuralism. "If *Heaven* and *Earth*, *Ocean* and *Slime*, *Ether* and *Air*, *Fire* and *Water* be human persons deified, of what Type, or Symbol, or any one Thing in the Universe may we not say

[25] Thomas Blackwell, *Letters concerning Mythology* (1748), 2nd ed. (London, 1757), pp. 190-91.

the same?"[26] This is neither pure nor applied typology, for there is no concrete area of reference; Nature provides an inexhaustible stock of symbolical material, some of which, Blackwell believes, is typological. We might put it differently: a typological scheme or system appears in certain elements of the past and in certain texts. It is predictive and prefigurative, but not in a Christian context. This nonreferential typology, subsumed as it is within a larger figural system, should not be mistaken for ordinary symbolism (although it is a variety of symbolism). It is more properly typology abstracted from its traditional contexts but retaining some of the foreshadowing quality that is so attractive to the human desire to predict the future based on the evidence available from the past or present.

Even more appropriate to the subject of abstracted typology are the writings of the eighteenth-century mythographer Jacob Bryant, whose works would be extremely popular with the English Romanticists. Bryant emphatically rejected euhemerism and the christianizing of pagan myth, and he refused to accept that ancient legends might stem from linguistic distortions of the Hebrew Scriptures. Nevertheless, he continually suggests that mythological figures and, more importantly, persons or incidents from the historical past, are nonreferential or abstracted types (see, for example, Figure 19). His *A New System; or, An Analysis of Ancient Mythology* (1774-76) is an important source book for later typologists. Better still is his *Observations and Inquiries relating to various parts of Ancient History* (1767), a straightforward study, in a series of brief essays, of selected ancient problems. It contains a chapter on the "Mystical Offering," through human sacrifice, of the ancient Phoenicians, which Bryant examines dispassionately, with historical detachment, and until his conclusion, no figuralism. Then he shifts his focus strikingly:

> I have been obliged to take these pains, in order to determine, who the deity was whom the *Phenicians* are supposed to have copied in this particular of human sacrifice: and at the same time to show, that nothing could have preceded for them to imitate; but that what they did was *a type and representation of something to come.* It is the only instance of any sacrifice in the gentile world, which is said to be mystical; and it is attended with circumstances, which are very extraordinary. . . . These sacrifices therefore *had no reference to anything past,* . . .

[26] *Ibid.,* p. 212.

but alluded to a great event, to be accomplished afterwards. . . .
The mystical sacrifice of the *Phenicians* had these requisites,
that *a prince was to offer it; and his only son was to be the
victim*: and as I have shewn, that this could not relate to anything *prior*, let us consider, what is said upon the subject, as
future, and attend to the consequence. For if the sacrifice of
the *Phenicians* was a *type* of another to come; the nature of this
last will be known from the representation by which it was
prefigured.[27]

Bryant is careful not to name any antitype for the mystical sacrifice
(modern anthropologists would hesitate to assign a relationship at
all), but he is deliberately suggestive. The Christian context appears to be present, but the precise referent is absent, so that
Bryant's typology remains an abstracted interpretation imposed
upon a situation from ancient history. Bryant is but one of a number of eighteenth-century mythographers who, while skeptical of
the mystical qualities of the ancient past and inclined to seek natural causes for occurrences formerly thought to be miraculous, argued that events in the historical past were prefigurations of later
happenings. The students of religious cults, including Richard
Payne Knight, Antoine Pernety, Sir William Jones, Charles Dupuis,
and George Stanley Faber, often sought analogues for Christianity
in the customs of pre-Christian religions. When they found them,
as they could hardly fail to do, they frequently described them in
the language of typology. Secular historians were likewise fascinated
with the predictive possibilities of the past and sometimes they, too,
introduce prefigurative structures, as do Joseph Priestley, C. F. de
Volney, and Burke (if only to refute them). I will discuss the effect
of typology on mythology and prophetic history in more detail later
(see Chapters 6 and 9). For the moment I wish simply to emphasize
the presence of a system of abstracted typology in nontheological
contexts. It is a significant aspect of eighteenth-century figuralism,
whose offspring and cousins we will find in all branches of English
literature.

If a work of literature is to qualify as art, it must move beyond the
sphere of the literal. All art is symbolic in some sense: the ancient

---

[27] *Observations and Inquiries relating to various parts of Ancient History*
(Cambridge, 1767), pp. 291-92.

distinctions between poetry and history are clearly relevant. If interpreters of the past can treat history symbolically (there are few who do not do so), then writers of imaginative literature are even more likely to create similar patterns. The typological system which I have suggested for interpretative works and commentary is a special sort of rhetorical view of the past, and it is usually presented as an attempt to discern certain well-defined relationships in history. The system functions similarly in the creative arts, particularly literature.[28] Conventional and applied typology have appeared in imaginative literature since the Middle Ages. Most early literary typologies fall into one of these categories. The age of typological abstraction begins about the middle of the seventeenth century in England and on the Continent, for at about this time scholars, historians, and the authors of creative literature begin to perceive nontheological typological patterns or structures in events and the world generally.

It is important that we should not treat abstracted typology as if it had universal applicability. Not every instance of prophecy, foreshadowing, or prediction can be allowed to qualify; the concept's interpretative value would evaporate under such circumstances. Abstracted typology is valuable only when it illuminates authorial intention and deepens our perception of the meaning of a work. When can we be reasonably sure that abstracted typology is present in a literary work? I think that there are at least five possible categories. (1) When the general circumstances of an event (position, local color, details of story, etc.) parallel Old Testament or New Testament typical events, but without specific theological treatment. Pope's Man of Ross (*Epistle to Bathurst*) who strikes the rock that water may run forth, is an abstracted type; he may also be what R.P.C. Hanson calls a situational type.[29] Henry Mackenzie's Harley, the Man of Feeling, who takes on a poor soldier's burden with the greatest pleasure in the world, is an abstracted type and so, as I will suggest in Chapter 7, are Goldsmith's Vicar, Godwin's Caleb Williams, and a number of other characters in fiction.[30]

[28] Typology also plays a prominent role in the visual arts, as I have suggested in various places, especially Chapter 2, above; its role in manuscript illumination and stained glass is widely appreciated. It has been argued that typological correspondences exist in music: see Manfred Bukofzer, "Speculative Thinking in Medieval Music," *Speculum*, 17 (1942), 165-80.

[29] See R.P.C. Hanson, *Allegory and Event: A Study of the Sources and Significance of Origen's Interpretation of Scripture* (London: SCM Press, 1959), p. 15.

[30] For a relevant article, see my essay, "Probability and Character in the Eighteenth-Century Novel," in *Probability, Time, and Space in Eighteenth-Cen-*

(2) When a generalized mythological story, whether allegorized or not, analogizes a myth or scriptural story that is generally accepted as typological. The allegorical myths that Johnson presents on a number of occasions in *The Rambler* are often analogous to typical stories; the myth of Shelley's *Prometheus Unbound* and those of Byron's *Sardanapalus* and *Cain* clearly parallel typological stories. (3) When, in a nontheological situation, an author uses an icon, emblem, or other pictorial image closely associated with one of the type-myths. This category can be overextended, so contextual factors are important. Not *every* harp is the harp of David, obviously, but if the song and the harmony struck off parallel the Davidic situation, as in Gray's "The Bard" or Coleridge's "The Aeolian Harp," we may be dealing with a category of abstracted typology. (4) When the actions or life-style of a fictional character parallel— either wholly or partially—those of a type-figure or a type-myth. Steele's leading character in *The Christian Hero*, the Apostle Paul, is a good example. Also appropriate are Robinson Crusoe, Clarissa Harlowe, Sir Charles Grandison, and Smollett's Ferdinand Count Fathom. This category also can work in reverse: a character who parallels a negative type (equivalent to the Antichrist, or Satan), like Fielding's Jonathan Wild or Byron's Manfred, would be an abstracted type. (5) When a natural circumstance, such as a landscape, or other natural object is presented as prefigurative, though in non-Christian terms, of some greater event or consummation. Ordinary foreshadowing or prophecy will not do: the motion from the circumstance to what it holds forth must embody the traditional *rising* motion of conventional biblical typology. This category receives a great impetus from the seventeenth-century emblem tradition, which exploited the concept of the world as symbolic book, and from the popular mystical writings of Jakob Boehme, who stressed the typological correspondences between natural phenomena and religious belief. Equally important are studies of natural religion like William Turner's *Compleat History of the Most Remarkable Providences* (1697). Turner is a theologian, and his work cannot be called abstracted typology, but his belief that everyday natural phenomena are but partial earthly signs of far greater heavenly and divine wonders nourishes the attribution of prefigurative qualities to natural images. Abstracted typology, then, flowing from theologi-

---

tury Literature, ed. Paula R. Backscheider (New York: AMS Press, Inc., 1979), pp. 63-77.

cal sources, becomes a significant addition to European figural traditions by the later seventeenth century.

My principal interest in this chapter is to show how an awareness
of the typological system can advance the interpretation of literature, so I shall give a few instances for illustrative purposes, with
fuller discussion to follow in later chapters. Often a poem or a
novel that has been undervalued or whose meaning has been misunderstood can be substantially clarified as a result of such awareness. Dryden's first poem, for example, "Upon the death of the
Lord Hastings" (1649), seldom read sympathetically, is usually regarded as enthusiastic baroque praise with an encomiastic conclusion. Dryden addresses the dead Hastings' fiancée, whom he calls a
"*Virgin-Widow*," as follows:

> With greater than Platonick love, O wed
> His Soul, though not his Body, to thy Bed:
> Let that make thee a Mother; bring thou forth
> Th' *Idea's* of his Vertue, Knowledge, Worth;
> Transcribe th' Original in new Copies; give
> Hastings o'th' better part: so shall he live
> In's Nobler Half; and the greate Grandsire be
> Of an Heroick Divine Progenie. . . .
>
> (97-104)

It is interesting to observe the analogy, in "*Virgin-Widow*," to an
accepted typological figure, Mary. The mystical spiritual marriage
reminds us of the medieval exegetical tradition (which Dryden
would have known from his acquaintance with Nicholas of Lyra)
of Marian typology.[31] The Virgin is seen as prefigurative of the
Church, as a type of triumph over sin (lust), and as a sacramental
image. Hastings' widow, in conceiving the "*Idea's*" of his qualities,
is explicitly typological, since a type would normally shadow forth
later images (cf. *NED*, s.v. "Idea" *sb.*, 7a, where the word means
"figure, form, likeness, image"). The rising motion of Dryden's passage, with the wedding between the virgin and the dead man's spirit
leading to "an Heroick Divine Progenie," is obviously typological,
yet the situation is not specifically religious. Rather, Dryden has
quite deliberately presented a secular story in terms of a typological
situation.

31 On the typology of Mary, which was obviously most popular in the Middle
Ages, see Robert B. Burlin, *The Old English Advent: A Typological Commentary* (New Haven: Yale Univ. Press, 1968), pp. 20-21.

Dryden is such a consummate typologist that I shall ignore his applied (mainly political) typology for the present; it is an important part of his figural contribution, but more readily identifiable than the abstracted typology at the end of *Annus Mirabilis* (stanzas 293-304). Consider the ostensibly prophetic view of London's future:

> Me-thinks already, from this Chymick flame,
>   I see a City of more precious mold:
> Rich as the Town which gives the *Indies* name,
>   With Silver pav'd, and all divine with Gold.
>
> (St. 293)

This is no ordinary prophecy, however, for the context is one of visionary prefiguration in which both the Fire ("this Chymick flame") and the golden city of the future are analogous to the destruction of the Temple and the prefiguration of the Heavenly Jerusalem. The situation is secular. But the accompanying freight of imagery makes the vision typological, in the abstracted sense.

There is a great deal more abstracted typology in Dryden's odes of the 1680's and '90s: the freedom of the ode form lends itself easily to prefigurative patterns. His most complex and obscure presentation of abstracted types comes, I think, not in an ode but in his epistle "To Sir Godfrey Kneller" (1694). There is much prefigurative imagery in this poem's progressive view of painting. Dryden introduces one passage specifically on shadows (14-21) in painting that is consistent with a typological system of exegesis, while his progress-piece on the history of painting fits the pattern as well. It begins with an allusion to the myth that Prometheus breathed life into the first man: *"Prometheus*, were he here, wou'd cast away / His *Adam*, and refuse a Soul to Clay" (22-23). Just as Adam is a type of the second Adam, Christ, so Prometheus, the fire-stealer and propagator of the arts, and himself a potent pagan type of Christ, is only a shadowy type of Kneller's greatness. This is exactly the way the poem turns out: "By slow degrees, the Godlike Art advanc'd; / As Man grew polish'd, Picture was inhanc'd" (35-36). By bringing in Kneller's gift to the author, the picture of Shakespeare, Dryden enlarges his typological framework to embrace literature as well. Finally, we learn that Kneller's consummation is a little way off yet (145-53), and that the true test of the quality of his painting will be Time:

More cannot be by Mortal Art exprest;
But venerable Age shall add the rest.
For Time shall with his ready Pencil stand;
Retouch your Figures, with his ripening hand.
Mellow your Colours, and imbrown the Teint;
Add every Grace, which Time alone can grant:
To future Ages shall your Fame convey;
And give more Beauties, than he takes away.

(174-81)

Dryden wrote few more patently secular poems than the Kneller epistle. There is no contextual evidence of his familiar applied typology (as in the epistles to the Duchess of Ormonde or his cousin John Driden). But the presence of a typological system in the poem is unmistakable: it is the mortar that unifies the whole. If we fail to recognize the existence of the system, the poem (which deserves extended analysis) falls into a series of disjunctive episodes. With the typological schema as the thread that runs through the entire text, "To Kneller" becomes a coherent, prefigurative statement about the history of painting, past, present, and future.

Pope employs abstracted typology in several different ways. His *Messiah* and *Windsor Forest* both contain pertinent examples. Perhaps his best known example is that of the Man of Ross, in the *Epistle to Bathurst* (249-90). Others have noted the analogy between the Man of Ross's actions and those of typical figures ("From the dry rock who bade the waters flow"—254—is an obvious postfiguration of Moses), so Pope's typological intention would appear evident. But *To Bathurst* also contains a negative abstracted type, Sir Balaam, whose moral depravity and universal evil parallel the kind of behavior we would associate with Satan. Abstracted typology fills *The Dunciad* as well, although it is distorted, inverted, and parodic. The conclusion to Book IV, for instance, is a parodic figural analogy to the Last Judgment; it is one of Pope's distorted types, introduced within the framework of abstracted typology. And the satires of the later 1730s yield other examples, particularly *Epilogue to the Satires*, Dialogues I and II, where England is analogized to an Egypt, a Babylon, a venal pagan land. In any theological discourse the significance of these typological places would be obvious; in satiric poetry the point is clear enough, too, but our knowledge of the typological schema makes the author's intention

97

more vivid. Pope does not write extended typological narrative, as Dryden does; he prefers the isolated abstracted type. However, as with other satirists who use abstracted typology (Cleveland, Butler, Swift), the element of parody is important to his method.

The notion of a typological system, while few writers define it as such, continues to be part of English figural traditions in the later eighteenth and nineteenth centuries. In its conventional and applied senses, poets with close theological or numinous concerns like Smart and Blake bring it up often in their works. The various categories of abstracted typology occur, as I have mentioned, in Romantic poetry as well, usually as part of a deliberate effort to introduce prefigurative images or themes. The subject and mythic associations of *Prometheus Unbound*, to take one clear case, are conducive to typological methods and interpretation, and Byron's dramas sometimes can be read in this way.[32] The concept of typological places, a form of situational typology, develops in the Romantic era; it is related to the seventeenth-century treatment of Egypt, Babylon, wandering, and captivity as types of contemporary misfortunes. This aspect of abstracted typology had been popular with eighteenth-century American Puritans, who had identified their mission and its physical location in biblical terms. Jonathan Edwards described America as "the *millennium* state" shadowed forth in the Book of Revelation; Emerson would later see the new nation as a "moral wilderness" that prefigured the New Jerusalem; and Thoreau used Walden Pond for both pre- and post-figurative purposes.[33] Wordsworth's account of the Simplon Pass in *The Prelude* (VI. 621-40) is an outstanding typological landscape (see Chapter 9, below). Ruskin would later make similar sympathetic readings of history and interpret the destinies of Venice and Tyre as types for nineteenth-century England.[34] The section from *The Prelude* on the Simplon Pass is important because it advances the frontiers of traditional nature imagery from standard symbolism, in which natural objects or locations *represent* abstractions, to typology, in

[32] Byron's drama *Sardanapalus* clearly invites typological reading; see Jerome J. McGann, *Fiery Dust: Byron's Poetic Development* (Chicago: Univ. of Chicago Press, 1968), pp. 228-43. McGann, in what is basically a close reading of the play, unfortunately makes nothing of the typological qualities of Byron's hero.

[33] See Sacvan Bercovitch, *The Puritan Origins of the American Self* (New Haven: Yale Univ. Press, 1975), pp. 154-57 (on Edwards), 159-61 (on Emerson), and 161-62 (on Thoreau).

[34] See George P. Landow, *The Aesthetic and Critical Theories of John Ruskin* (Princeton: Princeton Univ. Press, 1971), p. 349.

which they *prefigure* greater events, concepts, or abstractions. For Wordsworth, a long catalogue of sublime alpine effects is

> all like workings of one mind, the features
> Of the same face, blossoms upon one tree;
> Characters of the great Apocalypse,
> The types and symbols of Eternity. . . .

He sacramentalizes nature, and scans the great book of the Creation like a literary critic reading a text, finding "Characters," "types," and "symbols"—literary terms—in his exegesis. Wordsworth was not alone among nineteenth-century poets in employing the language of types in nature poetry. He would be followed by Clare, Tennyson, Browning, and the authors of secular hymns. Most of these writers fall outside the scope of this study but, without citing other *topoi*, it is possible to suggest that, by the early nineteenth century, typology is not simply a system, but a *creative* system at that.

Typology was originally an interpretative device, formidable in broadness of application, capable of much fanciful distortion. Some distortion, as we have seen, was intentional (although not necessarily malicious): to hold that the bondage of the Jews in Egypt prefigured the persecution of seventeenth-century Puritans is to sharpen a typological axe on the whetstone of controversy. Much typology answers to the fundamental human need to establish predictive patterns between past and present and between present and future. A predictive or prophetic rhetoric, when it is expressed in terms of discrete condensations of events, or signs, becomes a form of figuralism. Long before the authors of the New Testament assigned prefigurative value to Old Testament events and persons, typology had played a significant role in Jewish interpretation. Its existence, ultimately, may have to be explained as a psychological and perhaps an anthropological phenomenon.

When we leave the realm of pure or conventional typology, where it functions as a system of exegesis, we must deal with a creative and changing system. Typology is no longer merely exegesis, but to a reader without a knowledge of its exegetical tradition it would be close to meaningless. It is transformed into a literary system, the conscious application of a figural method of interpretation to the imitation of reality. In what respect, then, is typology any different from other kinds of figuralism, such as symbolism, pictorialism, metaphor, or any of the rhetorical figures used typologically? Why should it be singled out for special treatment? The answer is that typology is not merely a kind of figuralism or imagery. Simultaneously, it is also a widely accepted hermeneutic device, one that interpreters employ deliberately in both religious and secular contexts. Hence most writers who introduce a typological schema into a passage, a poem, a chapter, or a novel, are conscious that they are using a figural technique that combines the mystery of metaphor and the secret of interpretation. In one plausible sense, the occurrence of typology as system in literature is at once both image and interpretation. Ordinarily, a figural device requires another method of explanation to interpret it. We cannot explain a metaphor with another metaphor; to do so *could* qualify as an explanation, but it would probably complicate rather than clarify. But we *can* employ hermeneutic typology to explain the types that occur in literature. In fact, the only way that we can grasp the meaning of what I have called abstracted typology is by reading it in its own terms, prefiguratively and predictively. A greater awareness of the complex ways in which writers deliberately and unconsciously deploy what Ruskin called "the language of types" in imaginative literature will open an important new dimension in literary criticism and literary history.

Of the three kinds of predictive figuralism which I have discussed in this chapter, it is clear that two categories, *applied* and *abstracted*, are of more immediate significance to eighteenth-century English literature than *conventional* typology. Applied typology, where types are used in nontheological writings but in religious contexts, and abstracted typology, in which types are used in secular contexts and in which prefigurative structures and patterns become important, are not perfect entities. The definitions I have framed for them are not airtight; they may overlap at times, much as the definitions for other typological terms sometimes are slightly congruent. Of the two, abstracted typology is the more complex and gives rise to the more creative applications, especially in the kinds of writing I discuss in Chapters 6-8, myth, fiction, and satire. As a result of this complexity, it will be necessary to devote an entire chapter to the rise and embroidery of this unique figural mode.

CHAPTER 5

The Development of
Abstracted Typology

EXEGETES HAVE traditionally employed interpretative typology for prefigurative or postfigurative reasons, either to justify a certain reading of a text or event by alluding to a desired future circumstance, or to support a favorite interpretation by arguing that it fulfills something prophesied or predicted in the past. If we wish to interpret Graham Greene's whiskey priest in *The Power and the Glory* as a postfiguration of Jesus,[1] then this typological interpretation does not *predict* so much as it *completes* an unseen hermeneutic sequence started at some time in our distant cultural past. With another Christ figure, Richardson's Sir Charles Grandison, we would be justified in viewing this paragon as a prefiguration, a typical figure foreshadowing the greater perfections of some urbane, socialized, quintessentially gentleman Jesus. The behavior and situation of Greene's trapped priest dimly replay a few scenes from the New Testament: his humility and the humaneness of his predicament impress many readers with the similarity of everyday life to the Christian situation everywhere. The cold typology of *Sir Charles Grandison*, on the other hand, is difficult for twentieth-century readers to relate to life, but for Richardson's audience, Sir Charles was the perfect Christian, a character plucked from the pages of a typological homily. The failure of *Grandison*

---

[1] See Theodore Ziolkowski, *Fictional Transfigurations of Jesus*, pp. 221-23. Cf. John J. White, *Mythology in the Modern Novel: A Study of Prefigurative Techniques* (Princeton: Princeton Univ. Press, 1971), pp. 11-14. Both Ziolkowski and White use the concept of prefiguration loosely, yet both emphasize the likelihood that a type or a prefigurative myth would evoke a familiar pattern for the reader.

with its original public is curious: sermons were popular in the eighteenth century.[2] Perhaps Sir Charles's perfections were unrealistic, making him appear too similar to that other frequently typologized Charles, the one whom the eighteenth-century public was accustomed to see prefigured and postfigured in annual martyrology.[3] Their popularity apart, the two novels cited give examples of a typological mode of reference considerably removed from *traditional* theological concerns. Neither Greene nor Richardson is writing homilies or works of Christian apologetics. Their typologies are therefore *abstracted*, drawn away from the theological field of action, although there may be religious significance in the way each is introduced. Literary historians of the last twenty years have shown how pervasive and acceptable typological imagery was in seventeenth-century English literature. What is responsible for the change that led to the development of abstracted typology? This is the question to which I hope to offer some answers in this chapter.

 2

Four factors play a large role in the gradual rise of abstracted typology. The first is a seventeenth-century confusion of terminology that, in its narrowest range, caused typology to expand its area of reference. Pierre Legouis has protested against the "abuse" of typology in criticism of seventeenth-century literature: it should always, he argues, involve the study of types and antitypes.[4] So it should. But seventeenth-century writers themselves were often indistinct in their application of types: sometimes the word "type," in a theological context, describes an emblem, a hieroglyphic, a heraldic device, a historical painting, a portion of a picture or portrait, an engraved title page, or a purely representative device like a symbol (see Figures 1-3).[5] Our seventeenth-century forebears were torn between belief in the realities of messianic persons and the potentially pre-

2 On the reception of *Grandison*, see Alan Dugald McKillop, *Samuel Richardson, Printer and Novelist* (Chapel Hill: Univ. of North Carolina Press, 1936), pp. 215-25.

3 The annual Martyr's Day sermons still require more study, despite the helpful essay by Helen W. Randall, "The Rise and Fall of a Martyrology: Sermons on Charles I," *HLQ*, 10 (1947), 135-67.

4 "Some Remarks on Seventeenth-Century Imagery: Definitions and Caveats," in *Seventeenth-Century Imagery*, ed. Miner, pp. 192-93.

5 Francis Quarles, in the Preface to his *Emblemes*, provides a good example of the confusion by using "Types" synonymously with "Emblemes," "Parables," and "Hieroglyphicks." See Sig. A3ʳ.

figurative qualities of a welter of signs. It is well to remember that the period of this terminological confusion, the century from 1625 to about 1725, was not so exclusively an age of print as our own. The reading experience of the average literate person was augmented by a rich visual iconography, one far different from what the modern reader knows. The lists of objects in *A Tale of a Tub* and other works had visual, often prefigurative, life for Swift's audience. Books explaining visual devices, pictorial details, even the decorative qualities of architecture, were common. Some are sophisticated, like emblem books. Others, like Ripa's *Iconologia* (literally the *stories* of visual images), books of coins and medals, and antiquarian compilations like those of Gronovius and Graevius, vary in appeal.[6] Even such a keen observer as Johnson was affected by the confusion: one of his *Dictionary* definitions of "typical" is "figurative of something else" (the absence of a designation for *pre*figuring or foreshadowing is significant).[7]

Confusion over terminology can lead to difficulties. This, too, has happened with abstracted typology, as with that problem of historians called "the fallacy of prediction by analogy."[8] Seventeenth- and eighteenth-century historians, seeking analogies from the past to vindicate events and governmental policies in their own time, sometimes propose that ancient history may foreshadow the present. The Puritans in particular delighted in seeing the persecutions that they suffered because of their position as an unpopular minority as the antitype of the persecutions of the Israelites in Egypt, or as an antitype of the persecutions carried on against the primitive Christians by Rome.[9] Scholars in other branches of learning have found

---

[6] The first English edition of Cesare Ripa's *Iconologia: or Moral Emblems* did not appear until 1709; there was another edition in 1778. However, there were as many as a dozen Continental editions during the eighteenth century. Dieckmann, *Hieroglyphics*, pp. 48-99, surveys a generous portion of the literary tradition surrounding these devices.

[7] Martin Kallich, "Swift and the Archetypes of Hate: *A Tale of a Tub*," *Studies in Eighteenth-Century Culture*, 4 (1975), 43-67, provides an egregious modern example of this confusion. Kallich rashly interprets "type" to mean "any symbol," which allows him uncommon latitude in interpreting Swift, since he assumes the corollary to be true ("any symbol" = "a type"); he seems unaware of Legouis's caveats (see above, note 4).

[8] The coinage, so far as I know, is David Hackett Fischer's; see his *Historians' Fallacies: Toward a Logic of Historical Thought* (New York: Harper & Row, 1970), pp. 257-58.

[9] Here is a twentieth-century example of this variety of abstracted typology: "Cortez's plight in Mexico foreshadowed Richard Nixon's plight in Washington"

predictive analogy helpful; often it is evident that they are using a methodology derived from abstracted typology. Linguists, for example, at one time believed that the grammar and syntax of Indo-European languages could be taken as a type of the morphology of other, more primitive tongues.[10] This belief, highly speculative, caused linguists to "generate" grammatical structures for nonliterary languages by constructing antitypes that were *predicted*, as it were, by Western languages.

There is nothing that the modern student of figuralism can do to prevent such enthusiasm; indeed, to a considerable extent, its very existence in the past makes our inquiries necessary. In seeking the *raisons d'être* for abstracted typology, however, we must bear in mind that the original meaning of "type" and "typology" includes a connotation that is more than verbal or literary. Types are always *signs* whose meanings would be known to those fortunate enough to "read" the code they embody and of which they are a part. The meaning of abstracted typology is conveyed through words with an imagistic, pictorial, visual, or symbolic effect or by an author's introducing names, characters, places, or events that would induce an audience to regard them as prefigurations of something else. The English audience, advised by Dryden that their restored monarch, Charles II, had been "forc'd to suffer for Himself and us," or that the King was like "banish'd *David*," or that he had been made "at his own cost like *Adam* wise," is being instructed that a typological code (a rather simple one, it happens) is in operation.[11]

In the 1730s, Pope acquaints his audience with his typological purposes, as in the *Epistle to Bathurst*, in a different manner. We become aware that the Man of Ross is a typological character because of his Moses-like actions in the text and because of the long footnote that Pope added in 1735. The reader was encouraged to see Sir Balaam as a type of sin (or as a negative type) because of the signals Pope scatters about his text to suggest that this is no ordinary sinner but one who postfigures and also prefigures a known pattern. The associations with the Judas-character are telling: he accepts a bribe from France to betray his country (or master), his friends at Court forsake him and he "hangs," and finally,

---

(Russell Baker, "Moods of Washington," *New York Times Magazine*, 24 March 1974, p. 72). This may be self-parody.

[10] See, for example, J. van Ginneken, *La réconstruction typologique des langues archaïques de l'humanité* (Amsterdam, 1939).

[11] Dryden, *Astræa Redux*, lines 50, 79, 113.

"sad Sir Balaam curses God and dies" (396-402). Pope's situational details leave no doubt of the extra-verbal, typological qualities his figure possesses. Fielding, still differently, emphasizes the typological qualities of certain characters, like Joseph Andrews or Squire Allworthy, by events: Joseph is chaste under trying circumstances, Allworthy is forgiving. The figure surrounded with symbolic detail, then, is the special handiwork of an author using abstracted typology. A character or a situation which would otherwise lack prefigurative force is thus transformed into a typological sign.

This distinguishing stamp separates genuine abstracted types from narrative or logical devices like predictive analogy. For signs are not just words. In a literary medium, they are *expressed* through words, but they have special cognitive status, like numbers. Susanne K. Langer comments, "Numbers seem to have a special status; their symbolic expression by numerals, which every reader verbalizes according to his own language, shows that number concepts are not ordinary elements of vocabulary, but may long have been conceived and conveyed by non-linguistic symbols, and perhaps had a history of their own in our cerebral evolution."[12] Signs, as they appear in literature, may also be regarded as "non-linguistic symbols"; they have a life of their own outside and beyond a text in which they may appear.

A reader, for instance, who comes upon the figure of Joshua in a poem about Cromwell could well expect that Joshua's military qualities would suggest something about Cromwell's martial skills. If the same reader, any time between 1650 and 1750, finds a pagan worthy like Hercules in a text about an English sovereign, he might well remember that Hercules was a pagan type of Christ. This identification would very likely cause him to predict certain qualities of the sovereign in question. A reader in 1749 who picked up a poem called *The Vanity of Human Wishes* might recall that the character of Cardinal Wolsey had lately been used to symbolize the faults of overweening political power; for such a reader, then, "Wolsey's end" could prefigure or, as it happens, postfigure the fall of some more recent power-grabbing statesman.[13] These figures would qual-

[12] Susanne K. Langer, *Mind: An Essay on Human Feeling*, 2 vols. (Baltimore: Johns Hopkins Univ. Press, 1967-72), II, 349.

[13] See *The Vanity of Human Wishes*, lines 99-128; Wolsey was a character for Sir Robert Walpole. Since the historical details of Wolsey's fall were well known to the contemporary reader, it seems likely that the Wolsey-character functioned in a prefigurative manner for an eighteenth-century audience, shad-

ify semiotically as non-linguistic symbols, which can be shifted about from one text to another, always keeping the same approximate significance. True abstracted types always retain something of the sign. Like numbers, they are in a class by themselves, expressed through the medium of language, but usually visual or semiological, working on a plane separate from language. They may be seen as a sort of nonvisual iconography.

Not every word-picture, however, can be so classified. Typological events, persons, and places are distinct from other imagistic materials, for they are, as A. C. Charity puts it, events with an afterlife.[14] The circumstances of abstracted typology have an accepted and acknowledged history of their own; a writer who used an abstracted type could expect—or hope—that some of his audience would spot the connection. Those who believe that late seventeenth- and eighteenth-century writers drank deep from the cup of clarity may take issue with me here. How, it may be objected, could writers who strove to *narrow* the hermeneutic gap between author and reader possibly be guilty of hidden meanings?[15] My answer is that the cup must have contained some dregs, or that it somehow intoxicated— the constant interplay of allusions, complex wordplay, and deliberate political obscurities in the literature of this period suggest nothing else. Like the typological inscriptions in medieval and Renaissance paintings, some of these types must have escaped the attention of many seventeenth- and eighteenth-century readers.[16]

Semioticists call the elements of a code "semantic enclaves." The abstracted types I am discussing here are such units, typological clusters which probably were not completely clear for every member of the audience. The mysterious youth of unknown genealogy who appears often as a character type in the gothic novel, later in the eighteenth century, may have seemed nothing more than a roman-

---

owing forth the fall of Walpole. See Maynard Mack, *The Garden and the City: Retirement and Politics in the Later Poetry of Pope, 1731-1743* (Toronto: Univ. of Toronto Press, 1969), pp. 133, 159, 205.

[14] See Charity, *Events and Their Afterlife: The Dialectics of Christian Typology in The Bible and Dante* (Cambridge: Cambridge Univ. Press, 1966), pp. 1-4.

[15] For discussion of the "hermeneutic gap," see my *From Concord to Dissent,* pp. 7, 72, 79, 196.

[16] For a particularly interesting treatment of this largely unnoticed aspect of typology, see Mieczsław Wallis, "Inscriptions in Paintings," *Semiotica,* 9 (1973), 1-28, especially 11-14, 16-17, 27. Also helpful is T.S.R. Boase, "A Seventeenth-Century Typological Cycle of Paintings in the Armenian Cathedral at Julfa," *JWCI,* 13 (1950), 323-27.

tic hero to many middle-class readers. To the informed reader, however, the character of Theodore in *The Castle of Otranto* (1765), with his sacrificial and redemptive qualities and his other christomimetic overtones, could have seemed a type of the suffering deity. The fact that the "semantic enclave" of such a character might pass unremarked by some readers does not negate its existence even if only the twentieth-century exegete reports on it. A code can lose its significance rapidly, as we can see from the heavy annotation Pope's editors gave his works only a few years after his death. Pope, as I have suggested, was good at using semantic enclaves. Less than twenty years after some of his best abstracted typology, which he had presented in the 1730s without any explanation, Warburton felt compelled to add much explanation to its occurrence in his 1751 edition of Pope's *Works*. The confusion in terminology I mentioned earlier, then, caused writers of the later seventeenth and eighteenth centuries to lose sight of the theological distinctions which governed typology as a system of biblical exegesis. Types, emblems, hieroglyphics—all came to be used synonymously. Thus, farther from the fount, the stream at random strayed.

The second important cause of abstracted typology, closely related to the terminological factor, was the politicizing of theological contexts, particularly in the last half of the seventeenth century. As early as the 1650s John Hall objected sharply to typologizing kingship at every possible opportunity, but his complaints were little heeded.[17] Perhaps the decline of divine-right theories aided this secularizing process more than anything else. The Coronation of Charles II led to an outpouring of Old Testament and messianic typology from poets and poetasters alike,[18] but as the divine-right susceptibilities of the Stuart house declined and as the king-making powers of Parliament rose, the picture changed. Later coronations called forth fewer biblical types (Adam, Noah, Moses, Joshua, David) and more abstracted typological figures from classical mythology (Hercules, Amphion, Timotheus, Orpheus) and secular classical history (Alexander, Caesar, Cato). There would be yet another transformation in the eighteenth century to the types drawn from

[17] See Hall, *The Grounds and Reasons of Monarchy Consider'd* in *The Oceana of James Harrington, and His Other Works* (London, 1700), pp. 5-6.

[18] Gerard Reedy, S.J., "Mystical Politics: The Imagery of Charles II's Coronation," in *Studies in Change and Revolution*, ed. Paul J. Korshin (London: Scolar Press, Ltd., 1972), pp. 19-42, discusses many of the typological variations in the coronation verse tributes.

English history: Alfred, Edward the Confessor, Edward III, and Henry V.[19]

It is interesting to note how the subjects or reference points of typology change as it becomes less theological and more abstract. The typology of the Old Testament figures had been established by centuries of exegesis: it was based on a strong Christian belief in the unity of the two Testaments. That drawn from classical mythology was no novelty: the search for mysterious Christian meanings in pagan texts during the late Middle Ages and Renaissance had succeeded in giving Christian citizenship to the heroes of ancient myth, even though they lacked the birth certificates of natives.[20] An unfettered Christian holism led Samuel Bochart to declare that the pagan gods were Old Testament patriarchs by birthright. Less adventurous but dutiful antiquarians like Gerardus Vossius, Athanasius Kircher, John Spencer, and Edward Stillingfleet at least gave pagan myth an acceptable rationale and genealogy. From the assumed unity of Christian and pagan myths, it was a short step to the belief that secular history is predictive, and that the histories of ancient Greece and Rome, and of the great kings of the Middle Ages and Renaissance, might hold forth some special lesson to seventeenth- and eighteenth-century England. The maturing of English history in the first third of the eighteenth century—the work of many writers from Temple to Rymer and Rapin—established the characters of England's historical past as patterns for present emulation. Narrative history was *expected* to inform politics. When Sir William Temple, in his *Introduction to the History of England* (1695), stressed the similarities between William the Conqueror and William III, his contemporaries noted the postfiguration of the Prince of Orange with approval.[21]

[19] The panegyric verse available from the coronations of Charles II, James II, William III, Anne, and George I reveals much fluctuation and uncertainty in the use of Old Testament types and classical figures. William III and the first two Georges are sometimes seen as postfigurations of Roman or English rulers (not exclusively in favorable terms). In non-coronation verses, we can note the introduction of historical typology at least as early as the 1630s. The memorial volume for Edward King, *Justa Edovardo King naufrago, ab Amicis moerentibus* (Cambridge, 1638), contains an untitled and unsigned poem which compares King, by punning on his last name and his first name, with "Edward the Confessour, or the Saint" (see pp. 8-9).

[20] Allen, *Mysteriously Meant*, Chapters 8 and 9 (pp. 201-78), offers an account of the symbolic interpretations of Renaissance mythographers that is unlikely to be surpassed.

[21] See Abel Boyer, *Memoirs of the Life and Negotiations of Sir William Temple* (London, 1714), p. 413. It should be noted that there is no "fallacy of

The use of an abstracted typology came about as a result of
secular historians' efforts to parallel their subject with sacred history. Church historians from the time of Eusebius had done the
same. There can be little doubt that historians and early political
scientists adapted typological practice to their methods. Even titles
are expressive: consider Henry Nevile's *Plato Redivivus, or a Dialogue concerning Government* (1681), whose subtitle runs as follows—"Wherein, by observations drawn from other Kingdoms and
States, both ancient and modern, an endeavour is used to discover
the present politic distemper of our own; with the causes and
remedies." Three speakers, a physician, a noble Venetian, and an
Englishman, hold a discussion on statecraft; their talk turns (inevitably) to what is wrong with the state of affairs in seventeenth-
century England:

> And you would have good store of practice in your former
> capacity, if the wise custom of the ancient Greeks were not
> totally out of use. For they, when they found any craziness or
> indisposition in their several governments, before it broke out
> with a disease, did repair to the physicians of state . . . and
> obtain'd from the same good Recipes, to prevent those seeds
> of distemper from taking root, and destroying the publick
> peace. But in our days, these signs or forerunners of diseases
> in state are not foreseen, till the whole mass is corrupted; and
> that the patient is incurable, but by violent remedies.[22]

To understand Nevile's lament about the shortsightedness of the
present, we have to bear in mind that seventeenth-century exegetes
of the Pentateuch habitually insist that the ancient Hebrews were
well enough informed to be able to interpret correctly the foreshadowings of the Messiah in their surroundings and situation. The
patriarchs, in other words, understood the language of the types.

In these latter times, the argument runs, men have to be guided
to a proper interpretation of prefigurative signs; the old vision has
failed. Hence Nevile shows the ancient Greeks as informed readers
of "signs," of "forerunners" of diseases or civil instability. Not only
does his dialogue stress the uses of abstracted typology in running

---

predictive analogy" at work here or in similar situations; the eighteenth-century
historian was not trying to show a cause-and-effect relationship between past
history and the present. Rather, he would be trying to justify the actions of a
modern ruler, such as James II or William III, as acceptable *postfigurations* of
past times.

[22] Henry Nevile, *Plato Redivivus*, 4th ed. (London, 1763), p. 12.

the state, but he also presents early historical events or circumstances as prefigurative desiderata. One of the purposes of Nevile's republican tract was to show that the vision of classical government had vanished from Stuart England. What he does for republican Greece others would do for ancient Rome, for the obsession with the success or failure of previous governments was a national concern. For example, Walter Moyle's "Essay on the Constitution of the Roman Government" (c. 1710) shows at some length "the Reasons of the Corruption and Ruin of the *Roman* Commonwealth." Moyle's "Reasons" have a bearing on Stuart England, for every one of them is predictive of flaws in the English monarchy.[23] Secular historians, then, contribute substantially to the spread of abstracted typology, principally by their willingness to treat history as something parallel to Scripture, as something possessed of a unified purpose and a narrative consistency. The past is a series of chronicles scattered with *significant events and characters* which, if properly understood, would enable Englishmen to predict correct solutions for the present.

 3

A third factor in the movement toward abstracted typology is what I shall call the post-Restoration expansion of the number of genres using typology. During the first half of the seventeenth century, the most common locations of typological imagery are biblical exegesis, Christian apologetics, homilies, divine poetry, the pastoral, the epic, and ecclesiastical history. The last of these was already a form of abstracted typology, for the belief that the history of the Church in antiquity foreshadowed religious history in the Reformation and afterwards, held by more than a few church historians in the seventeenth century, is an innovative, noncanonical use of the device.[24]

23 *The Works of Walter Moyle, Esq.*, 2 vols. (London, 1726), II, 99-148, especially p. 132.

24 Church historians also sometimes regarded themselves as fulfilling a role that had been hinted at in former ages. See, for example, Paolo Sarpi, *The Historie of the Councel of Trent*, trans. Nathanael Brent, 2nd ed. (London, 1629), "Dedication," Sig. ¶6r-v. See also Laurence Echard, *A General Ecclesiastical History* (London, 1702), pp. 3, 32; Basnage's *History of the Jews, from Jesus to the Present Time*, trans. Thomas Taylor (London, 1708), p. vii; and cf. Benjamin Keach, *Antichrist Stormed: or, Mystery Babylon the Great Whore, and Great City, proved to be the present Church of Rome* (London, 1689), pp. 103-16, for a polemical use of historical typology.

1. Emblem of a snake, from George Wither,
A Collection of Emblemes, Ancient and Moderne. . . . (London, 1635).
By permission of The British Library. The figure of a snake with its tail
in its mouth (Book 3, Illus. 23), symbolizes eternity and,
according to Wither, typifies the year and its rebirth.

2. A horned figure of Moses on a mount of vision—Mount Pisgah or Mount Zion—being lifted heavenwards by a pair of hands, presumably a suggestion of the intervention of divine vision. From George Wither, *A Collection of Emblemes, Ancient and Moderne.* . . . (London, 1635), Book 3, Illus. 36. By permission of The British Library.

3. Emblem of a palm tree, from George Wither,
A Collection of Emblemes, Ancient and Moderne. . . . (London, 1635),
Book 3, Illus. 38. By permission of The British Library.
According to Wither, "For, many wayes, [the palm] fitley typifies,
/ The *Righteous-man*, with his properties."

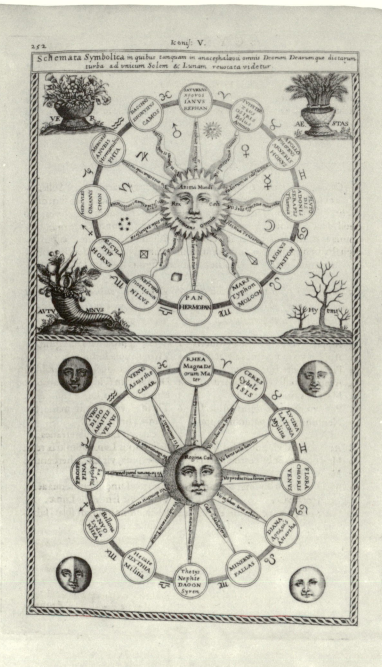

4. A schematic drawing (Iconis: V) showing how the pagan deities derive from a small set of pre-Christian types, from Athanasius Kircher, *Obeliscus Pamphilus* (Rome, 1650). By permission of The British Library. The sun and the moon, in Kircher's analysis of ancient mythology, were common pre-Christian attributes of many religions; he interpreted such figures in the Egyptian hieroglyphics as mystical prefigurations of Christianity.

5. Untitled engraving (c. 1650) comprising illustrations of various
typological passages from the Old and New Testaments. The Peel Collection,
Volume I. By permission of The Pierpont Morgan Library. The passages
that the engraver cites—John 1.51, Gen. 35.14, Gen. 28.16, and
Heb. 13.14-16—either prefigure the sacrifices of Christ or foreshadow
an afterlife through Christ.

6. "Statui Isidis Multimammae," from Athanasius Kircher,
Oedipus Ægyptiacus, 3 vols. in 4 (Rome, 1652-54),
Volume I. By permission of The British Library. Kircher's
engraver envisaged the Egyptian goddess Isis as having
many breasts, rather like the more extravagant
representations of Ceres, whom exegetes such as Ross saw as
typical of Christ and the Church.

7. "Iconismus Inferendus," from Kircher's *Oedipus Ægyptiacus*, Volume II.
By permission of The British Library. This magnificent chart from Kircher's *magnum opus*
represents the extreme of his typological thinking. The "Arbor mystica" from Paradise
shows how the seventy-two names for God in seventy-two countries lead, cabalistically,
to Hebrew characters which themselves lead to the name of Jesus the Messiah.

Iouis siue Panos Hierogly‑
phica repræsentatio.

A Facies rubicunda, caloris vis in Mundo.
B Radiorum cœlestium in sublunaria vir‑
C Elementa masculina.   (tus.
D Potestas in annũ omnesq; reuolutiones.
E Virtute eius omnia fulciuntur.
F Dominium in firmamentum, seu fixa‑
   rum stellarum sphœram.
G Terra (elementum fœmin.) hispida
   plantis, satis, arboribusque.
H Aquæ & liquoris fons (elem. fœm.) ri‑
   gatione fœcundans terram.
I Agei, segetes, aliaque vegetabilia.
K Harmonia 7. Planetarum.
L Aspera & inæqualia montes indicant.
M Vis fœcundatiua.
N Stabile fundamentum.
O Vis ventorum, & celeritas in agendo.

Ta‑

8. "Jouis sive Panos Hieroglyphica repræsentatio," from Kircher,
Oedipus Ægyptiacus, Volume II. By permission of The British Library. The qualities of
Pan—for Kircher, a pagan type of Christ—are anatomized to represent
the governing forces of the Creation.

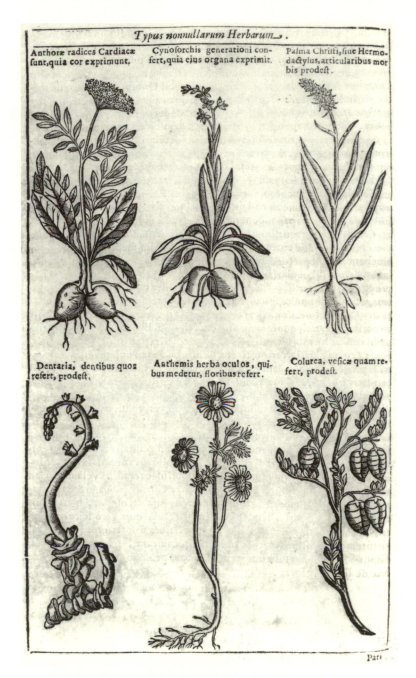

Anthoræ radices Cardiacæ funt, quia cor exprimunt,

Cynoforchis generationi confert, quia ejus organa exprimit.

Palma Chrifti, fiue Hermodactylus, articularibus morbis prodeft.

Dentaria, dentibus quos refert, prodeft.

Aathemis herba oculos, quibus medetur, floribus refert.

Colutea, veficæ quam refert, prodeft.

Pari

9. "Typus Nonnullarum Herbarum," from Kircher,
Oedipus Ægyptiacus, Volume III. By permission of The British Library.
Kircher, here influenced by Boehme and other mystical writers,
shows how certain plants are signs—types—of parts of the human body,
part of the analogical game that makes natural typology possible.

10. The engraved title page to Thomas Fuller, *A Pisgah-sight of Palestine and the Confines thereof. . . .* (London, 1662). By permission of The British Library. The engraving with a medley of biblical themes, like this one, is common in the seventeenth century. One of Fuller's texts—Num. 13.24—may be seen as typological of Palestine, and another—Zech. 4.3, the vision of the golden candlestick and the seven lamps—as typological of the Messiah.

THE MYSTERIOUS CALENDER

Taken from the Original, above 30 years since found in the Pyramids of EGYPT symbolically representing the Glorious and Immortal acts & mighty Atchievm.ts of the somuch fam'd & never to be
forgotten Hero's Valarous HUZ the elder & of no lefs renown'd Pollitick BUZ his own Brother.

Infcrib'd to the Reverend Dr. A ____ Regius Profeffor of Hieroglyphicks in the famous Univerfity of
Bagdet whofe profound knowledge (as his Mythological works plainly demonftrate) in the Myftical Learning of the Egyptians & great forefight of future events hath Blazon'd his fame from Pole to Pole & juftly plac'd him
amongft the Magi.

G	F	E	D	C	B	A
Sund	Mond	Tuefd	Wed	Thur	Frid	Sat
Apr	Sep	June	Feb	Aug	May	Jan
			Mar			
July	Dec	June	Nov	Aug	May	Oct
1	2	3	4	5	6	7
8	9	10	11	12	13	14
15	16	17	18	19	20	21
22	23	24	25	26	27	28
29	30	31		Env.		

EXAMPLE *When* G *is the Dominical Letter, You have All the* SUNDAYS *of that* YEAR, viz: *The* 1.st 8.th 15.th 22.d & 29.th *of April & July
are* SUNDAYS, *so are the* 2.d 9.th 16.th 23.d & 30.th *of* Sep.t & Decemb.r &c. *When* F *You have all the* MONDAYS, *when* E *all the* TUESDAYS, *When*
D *the* Wednefd.y C *the* Thurfd.y B *the* Frid.y And A *the* Saturd.y *In* LEAP YEARS *there are always* 2 Dominical Letters, B & A *are the* 2
Dominical Letters *for the* YEAR 1704. B *Holds to* S.t MATTHIAS *Eve (Feb 24.) And Shews the* Fridays, A *Serves all the* Reft *of the* Year
And Shews the Saturdays, The Months with a Point Underneath have 31 Days.

By Hader Camber Bazer High Preft & Primier Minifter to the most Illustrious Prince Pretzgianni.

11. "The Mysterious Calendar" (1704), from The Peel Collection, Volume I.
By permission of The Pierpont Morgan Library. A satirical representation of a jumble of
hieroglyphics that mocks the prefigurative qualities that the seventeenth-century polymaths
assigned to them. "The Reverend Dr. A_____" is probably Athanasius Kircher himself.

In the Great Legislator veil'd, Survey
The Twylight to the Savior's glorious Day;
When Shadows to the Substance must resign,
And Truth with unrebated Splendor shine.

12. Frontispiece to Samuel Wesley, *The History of the Old and New Testament attempted in Verse*, 3 vols. (London, 1705-21), Volume I. By permission of The British Library. The frontispiece to the Old Testament implies the prophetical powers of Moses and presents types of Christ and the Crucifixion in the sacrificial lamb and the sacrificial altar.

Behold unveil'd the Heav'nly Wisedom here!
See where She shows ye Cross, ye Thorns, ye Spear!
The Everlasting Gospel in Her Hand
Unseald: Let him that Readeth Understand!

13. Frontispiece to Wesley's *The History of the Old and
New Testament*, Volume III. By permission of The British Library.
In the frontispiece to the volume containing the New Testament,
the engraver, J. Sturt, shows the accomplishment of the
Old Testament type of Christianity in the unsealed
"Everlasting Gospel" and points out a type of the Crucifixion—
the crown of thorns—and types of redemption—the Cross and
the spear that wounded Christ's side.

14. "Christian leaves the City of Destruction," from the first
illustrated edition of Bunyan's *The Pilgrim's Progress*, . . . , 22nd ed.
(London, 1728). By permission of The British Library. In Sturt's engraving,
Evangelist, himself a living type of redemption, directs Christian
upwards toward the wicket gate and the shining light.

15. "A View of the New Jerusalem" (1740), from The Peel Collection,
Volume II. By permission of The Pierpont Morgan Library. A Wesleyan print—the two
preachers who warn of the wrath to come are Wesley and Whitefield—in which sound
Christian doctrine prefigures both the New Jerusalem and the Tree of Life
of the Book of Revelation.

16. The frontispiece to Thomas Broughton, *An Historical Dictionary
of all Religions from the Creation of the World to this Present Time*,
2 vols. (London, 1756), Volume I. By permission of The British Library.
A medley of religions, from pagan idolatries to Islam, Judaism, and
Christianity, with Moses and the tablets of the law and Christianity taking the center.
The sun of God, partly obscured by clouds, is a traditional
visual type of the notion that pagan mythologies and other errors
simply overlay but do not change the one true religion.

17. "The Tree of the Soul" from *The Works of Jacob Behmen*, 4 vols.
(London, 1764-81), Volume I. By permission of The British Library.
The figures illustrating Boehme's principles are the contribution of William Law.
The soul of man as represented by this tree, according to Boehme, is a type of the
pure heavenly soul of Jesus. One branch of the tree, which also
represents the generation of Adam and the faith that grows from the grain
of mustardseed, leads to the fire world, and another leads to
paradise, but the tree itself reaches to divine glory and majesty.

18. "Hieroglyphicks of the Natural Man" (1771), from The Peel Collection, Volume IV. By permission of The Pierpont Morgan Library. A parodic representation of the barren fig tree (Matt. 21.18-20, Luke 13.6-9), here nourished by Satan and Death. The barrenness of the fig tree is a sign of faith in God; the rich crop of vices on this parodic tree is a visual type of lack of faith.

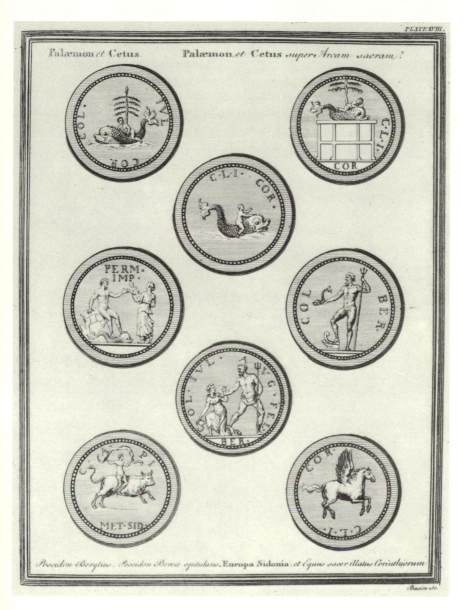

PLATE XVIII.

Palæmon et Cetus.   Palæmon et Cetus super Arcam sacram?

Poseidon Berytius. Poseidon Beroæ opitulans. Europa Sidonia et Equus sacer illatus Corinthiorum.

Basire sc.

19. "Palæmon of Corinth borne up at sea by a Cetus," from
Jacob Bryant, *A New System, or, An Analysis of Ancient Mythology*, 3 vols.
(London, 1774-76), Volume II. By permission of The British Library.
Bryant noted that Palamon's being saved from drowning by a whale,
upper left and center top, might be seen as a pagan type of
Jonah and the whale.

20. Four iconographical figures, from George Richardson, *Iconology;
or, A Collection of Emblematical Figures, Moral or Instructive*, 2 vols. (London,
1779), Volume I, Plate LI. By permission of The British Library. The figures are,
clockwise from the upper left, Prophecy, Theology, Mythology, and Iconology.
Prophecy "has a veil over her face, to indicate that the ancient prophecies of
holy Scripture were frequently delivered under enigma's and typical
representations." Iconology's roll of symbolic writings characterizes
"this ancient method of conveying truth," which gave rise to
hieroglyphics, emblems, symbols, and types.

Frontispiece.

*Look what a fine morning it is. — Insects,
Birds, & Animals, are all enjoying existence.*

Published by J. Johnson. Sept.ʳ 1.ˢᵗ 1791.

21. William Blake's frontispiece to Mary Wollstonecraft's
Original Stories from Real Life, 2nd ed. (London, 1791). By permission of
The British Library. Blake evidently intended the cruciform shape
of Mrs. Mason, with her two pupils, to foreshadow the
Christian teachings of the book.

22. "Presages of the Millenium" (c. 1791), from The Peel Collection, Volume XII. By permission of The Pierpont Morgan Library. A satirical representation of Brothers' prophecies and Nathaniel Brassey Halhed's support of them. The Crown and Parliament here are joined as millenarian scourges; in the horse's tail appears the figure of Edmund Burke as a winged serpent.

24. "Hercules and the Carter," from *The Fables of Aesop*, trans. Samuel Croxall, 2 vols. (London, 1793), Volume II. By permission of The British Library. This fable, a non-Aesopic addition to the collection, was thought to shadow forth Christian moralism to the pagans. The carter, who importunes Hercules in vain to draw his cart from the mire, is a sign to Christians, "whose reason should be enlightened by revelation," to avoid making the same error.

23. "The Fowler and the Ring Dove," from *The Fables of Aesop*, trans. Samuel Croxall, 2 vols. (London, 1793), Volume I. By permission of The British Library. Aesop's original has the fowler wounded by the snake as he prepares to kill the dove, but Croxall adds the death of the fowler because of his wickedness. The application suggests that this fable is a type of evil deeds and stresses that Providence may retaliate upon men for their iniquity.

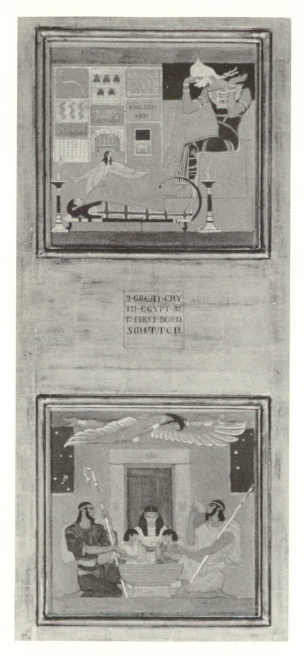

Π·GREAT·CRY
ΙΠ·EGYPT·AΠ
Τ·FIRST·BORΠ.
SΦΙΡΤΕΠ.

25. Violet Oakley, *The Life of Moses* (1929), an altar screen at the
Samuel S. Fleisher Art Memorial, Philadelphia. By permission of the Philadelphia Museum
of Art. The central panel shows the infant Moses in the arms of Pharaoh's daughter;
the side panels are illustrations of scenes, almost all of them typological, from the
life of Moses. The bottom panels include (far left) Moses carving the ten commandments
and (far right) Moses striking the rock. The Oakley altarpiece is a rich example of
twentieth-century visual typology.

26. (Above) Violet Oakley, *The Life of Moses* (1929), detail, showing two of the
typological scenes—the plague of the smiting of the firstborn son (above) and the first
Passover—from the life of Moses. By permission of the
Philadelphia Museum of Art.

27. Graham Sutherland, *Thorn Tree* (1945), oil on canvas, from the
collection of Sir Kenneth Clark; by permission of Lund Humphries & Co., Ltd.
Sutherland, in studying to execute his commission for the Northampton *Crucifixion* (1946),
made a number of studies of thorns that served him as prefigurations of the
sufferings of Christ on the Cross, a striking example of the way twentieth-century artists
have continued to employ visual typology. See Douglas Cooper, *The Work of Graham
Sutherland* (London: Lund Humphries & Co., Ltd., 1961), pp. 32-33.

28. "Abraham Offering Isaac" (c. 1780), a biblical type-
scene on a Staffordshire dinner plate. Designed by the
Staffordshire potter John Turner (d. 1787), a contemporary
and friend of Josiah Wedgwood, the plate, along with its
companion piece (Fig. 29), was painted in Holland. By permission
of Mr. and Mrs. David E. Zeitlin of Merion, Pa.

29. "The Dipping" (c. 1780), John Turner's application of a
typological event to an unidentified infant's christening.
The presence of the dove of the Holy Spirit is a typological
motif that the artist borrowed from Renaissance sources.
By permission of Mr. and Mrs. David E. Zeitlin.

30. A medal by George Bower struck on the occasion of the
discovery of the Rye House Plot, 1683. By permission of the
Trustees of the British Museum. On the obverse Charles II is
represented as Hercules reposing on the lion's skin; to complete
the pagan typology, the hydra has seven heads—those of the
committee of six who saw to the redress of grievances, plus
Satan, as spiritual head of the conspiracy.

31. A medal commemorating the coronation of George I, 1714,
by the Hanoverian engraver Nicholas Seeländer. By permission of
the Trustees of the British Museum. Each letter of the legend on the
obverse side is an emblem with a brief Latin compliment to the
King surmounting it; several of these emblems are typological,
including the R in Georgius formed of a pelican feeding
her young with her own blood and the R in Rex
formed of St. George and the Dragon.

32. A medal commemorating the death of Matthew Tindall,
the Deist, 1733. By permission of the Trustees of the British
Museum. Tindall's early works attempted to vanquish the Roman
Catholic Church, alluded to in the pagan typology of the obverse,
where Tindall, book in hand, overcomes the Hydra;
on the reverse, a pelican that wounds its own breast
surmounts an obelisk.

33. A medal commemorating George II's defeat
of the Rebels in December 1745. By permission of the
Trustees of the British Museum. On the reverse,
Truth, armed with an open Bible, vanquishes the
Hydra, whose heads include those of the Pretender,
the King of France, the Devil, the Pope, a cardinal,
and a bishop. The allusion to the pagan typology of
Hercules is common in English medallism.

34. A medal commemorating Napoleon's convening of
the Sanhedrin in 1806, reproduced from Ismar Elbogen,
History of the Jews after the Fall of the Jewish State
(Cincinnati, 1926). The reverse shows Napoleon
receiving the tablets of the law from a rabbi;
the typological parallel is to Moses receiving
the law on Mount Zion.

By the last half of the century, however, typology becomes attractive to the practitioners of other literary genres, especially to satirists, character writers, the authors of prose and verse fables, and, perhaps most important, the writers of prose narrative. None of these genres is new to the late seventeenth century, but all change enormously after about 1650. The increased sophistication of satire, for instance, particularly in cultivating new rhetorical strategies, naturally leads satirists to seek fresh methods of ridicule. Typology is susceptible to parody for, as we know from seventeenth-century Anglican, Puritan, and Roman Catholic exegesis, it is capable of being abused by the exegete. Since much Restoration and early eighteenth-century satire has a theological basis, it is not surprising that satirists found the distortions of typology attractive as methods of ridicule.[25] Cleveland, Butler, and Swift all find distorted typology useful for attacking the excesses of Puritanism. The minor scribblers who swarm through the pages of *Poems on Affairs of State* afford other examples. In *The Dunciad*, Pope creates the most consistent distorted typologies of all, and his *First Epistle of the Second Book of Horace Imitated* ("To Augustus") is scarcely less successful.

We would be unlikely to turn to the Theophrastan characters of the early seventeenth century for abstracted typology, but this genre, too, becomes less moral and more satiric as the century progresses. The sobriety of Joseph Hall gives way to the wit and nastiness of Butler, and with Butler comes the distortion of accepted prefigurative forms for satiric purposes. The late seventeenth-century efflorescence of fables contributes to the growth of abstracted typology in interesting ways, as I shall show later. The prose or verse fable, whether Aesopic or modern, not only provides a stage for typological characters and beasts, but it revives the *glossa* and the *moralia*.[26] Typological readings often lurk in the *glossa ordi-*

[25] On typological satire, see my essay, "Swift and Typological Narrative in *A Tale of a Tub*," *Harvard English Studies*, 1 (1970), 67-91, and see Chapter 8 below.

[26] Animal symbolism was amazingly popular in the seventeenth century, as is demonstrated by the numerous editions of Wolfgang Frantz's *Historia Animalium Sacra* (1612). The first part of Frantz, "De Quadrupedis," was translated by "N.W." as *The History of Brutes* (London, 1670), and the work itself was gradually enlarged "cum Commentariis & Supplementis, Observationum ex recentiori Historia naturali, Similitudinem, Emblematum, Hieroglyphicorum . . ." into an enormous syntagma. There were at least ten editions by 1712. A helpful study of beast symbolism (and relevant typology) is Beryl Rowland,

naria to the vulgate Bible (a work which continued to be available in seventeenth-century England); so, too, do they crop up in the lengthy prose explanations which accompany many collections of fables. The commentaries may be even more important than the fables themselves and are frequently much longer than the texts they illustrate.

The genre that expands more than any other after 1660 is prose narrative or, more properly, prose fiction. With an early writer of fictional narrative like Bunyan, typological situations (as in *The Pilgrim's Progress* and *The Holy War*) may remind us more of the sermon than of the novel. The contemporary sermon writer would use Old Testament types to demonstrate or underscore a certain Christian doctrine (such as the truth of the prophecies). But Bunyan is a leader in encouraging abstracted typology in fiction, and for one very persuasive reason: his complex typologies are highly appropriate to the requirements of the novel; they are invented scenes and little predictive dramas, Christian and biblical in their subject but original in their presentation.[27] His fictional types are structural units (cf. "semantic enclaves") which prefigure later plot developments. Nor are they accidental foreshadowings: Christian's sojourn at the House of the Interpreter and the death and instantaneous resurrection of Faithful play deliberate prefigurative roles. Bunyan is echoing Puritan homiletics, meditations, and confessional autobiography, but those who follow him are themselves influenced by Bunyan's narrative style and literary figuralism.

The eighteenth-century novel provides a field for a unique literary operation, the blending of two alien literary forms and methodologies, the character and the type. The *character*, if we think of it in Theophrastan terms, is Grecian, pagan; it portrays a single, representative specimen of a generalized class of individuals that are—and always will be—everywhere the same. The *type* is Christian,

---

Animals with Human Faces: A Guide to Animal Symbolism (Knoxville, Tenn.: Univ. of Tennessee Press, 1973).

[27] There are many typological promises vouchsafed to Christian which help the reader to predict the conclusion of the book. The events and prophecies which take place at the House of the Interpreter are among the most vivid such scenes. See *Grace Abounding to the Chief of Sinners and The Pilgrim's Progress*, ed. Roger Sharrock (London: Oxford Univ. Press, 1966), pp. 161-69. This section ends with a typological Pisgah-sight. *The Holy War* is often typological in the scenes involving Emmanuel's mission and the promises regarding the paradisiacal future of Mansoul. See the ed. of James F. Forrest (New York: New York Univ. Press, 1967), pp. 75, 131, 132 (for typological riddles), 161-62, 169, 253, 280.

prefigurative, a structural unit relating closely to the great drama of the promise of Christian salvation. Both of these literary forms and methods, as I have suggested, are popular about 1700. In the expansion of prose fiction during the eighteenth century, there occurs a blending of these two elements, of pagan and Christian, character and type into a new literary device, the *character type*. We use the term all the time, yet without adequate recognition of its origins or purpose. It is related, I think, to the stock characters of Renaissance drama; these personages are often prefigurative. Predictive characters existed in Roman drama, especially in comedy, and they are common, too, in Renaissance and seventeenth-century comedy. We can identify a good number of characters whose qualities are predictable and who thus form prefigurative units. The fool, the faithful servant, the overreacher, the miser, the young man impatiently awaiting a legacy, the clown, the sharper (Autolycus is surely the type of dramatic confidence men), the drunken squire (from Sir Tunbelly Clumsy to Squire Western, they are all alike), and a number of others—all are stock characters whose behavior a contemporary audience could confidently predict. The term, "character type," in fact, is a nineteenth-century invention: the first distinctions of the word "type" to refer to "a general class of individuals" date from the 1840s.[28]

However, although the formal literary term is relatively recent, the prefigurative phenomenon it expresses appears to be mainly a seventeenth- and eighteenth-century development. The early English novelists had the many character books, sketches, and political polemics of the previous century ready at hand; stock "characters" abound in the fiction of Defoe, Richardson, Fielding, Smollett, and a score of lesser novelists.[29] What we have hitherto ignored is that many, if not most, of these characters were immediately recognizable to an audience well-acquainted with character books, literary emblems, iconology, and other signs, predictive or nonpredictive. As soon as a reader identified and classified a fictional person as a representation of a known "character," he or she would be able to

[28] See *NED*, s.v. "Type," *sb.*¹, 5a, 6, 7ab, quots.

[29] Benjamin Boyce, *The Theophrastan Character in England to 1642* (Cambridge, Mass.: Harvard Univ. Press, 1947), is the standard work on the early character; see also Boyce, *The Character Sketches in Pope's Poems* (Durham, N.C.: Duke Univ. Press, 1962), pp. 44-59. La Bruyère's *Caractères*, translated as *The Characters, or Manners of the Age*, 2nd enlarged ed. (London, 1700), was widely used as a source for character sketches, augmenting Theophrastus and the English character books.

predict the person's behavior. This action was possible because the characters in the early English novel frequently are also abstracted types. Not every fictional person can be so identified, and the process of prediction is made difficult by variations in behavior. But Lady Booby and Lady Bellaston, Blifil and Ferdinand Count Fathom, Lovelace and Sir Hargrave Pollexfen, Roxana's fool husband, the misanthropic Sir Matthew Bramble, and dozens of others perform more or less as we would be likely to predict if we were acquainted with the contemporary *characters* each of them represents. They are not so much *prefigurative personages* as they are *predictive structures*, a knowledge of which serves to foreshadow information about the novel to its audience. The *character type*, then, becomes a standard eighteenth-century fictive entity whose behavior could be predictive, whose place in a work of fiction an audience would probably understand without special authorial commentary. Such developments in the novel are a principal reason why abstracted typology flourished after 1700.

The last of the four factors that influence abstracted typology involves the theological controversy of the early eighteenth century over the meaning of the Old Testament prophecies. This topic may seem distant from English literary history; it is still a matter primarily for discussion among theologians.[30] Yet it is a part of the intellectual tapestry that includes questions of prefiguration and character typing in imaginative literature. The controversy begins with Deist attacks upon the mysteries of religion in the 1690s. I cannot go into the intricacies of the debate in detail here, and to summarize the burden of a book like John Toland's *Christianity Not Mysterious* (1696) is beyond my powers of condensation. It may be said, however, that in questioning the mysteriousness of Christianity, Toland casts doubt on the importance of "figurative Words, Types and Ceremonies" to modern believers.[31] They may have been

---

[30] For a thorough (but poorly organized) study of the controversy, see James O'Higgins, S.J., *Anthony Collins: The Man and His Works* (The Hague: Martinus Nijhoff, 1970), pp. 155-99.

[31] See John Toland, *Christianity Not Mysterious: or, A Treatise shewing That there is Nothing in the Gospel Contrary to Reason, nor above it: and that no Christian Doctrine can be properly call'd A Mystery*, 2nd ed. (London, 1696), p. 66; cf. pp. 72-73.

mysterious in antiquity, but they were perfectly intelligible in the eighteenth century.[32] He strikes out broadly against figuralism:

> Every one knows how the Primitive *Christians*, in a ridiculous imitation of the Jews, turn'd all Scripture into Allegory; accommodating the Properties of those Animals mention'd in the *Old Testament* to Events that happen'd under the *New*. They took the same Liberty principally with Men, where they could discover the least Resemblance between their Names, Actions, or State of Life; and carry'd this Fancy at length to Numbers, Letters, Places, and what not. That which in the *Old Testament* therefore did, according to them, represent any thing in the *New*, they call'd the *Type* or *Mystery* of it. Thus TYPE, SYMBOL, PARABLE, SHADOW, FIGURE, SIGN, and MYSTERY, signify all the same thing in *Justin Martyr*.[33]

Seldom has the terminological confusion I mentioned above been more clearly stated.

The controversy was to go on for more than thirty years, aided by the annual Boyle lecturers, and by numerous theological publications. Discrepancies in biblical quotations and in scholarly methods would be exposed; the sound evidentiary methods of Richard Simon would help cast considerable doubt on the accuracy of the Old Testament prophecies. Anthony Collins, the Deist whose *A Discourse of the Grounds and Reasons of the Christian Religion* (1724) is probably the most significant work in the controversy, holds that a prophecy has one immediate literal fulfillment, and that the notion of a long-term fulfillment is nonsense. He argues that the child promised in Isaiah 7.14 was Isaiah's son, not the Messiah, and elsewhere he is scornful of vague attempts to impose an artificial unity upon the two Testaments by inventive typologizing.[34] Yet Collins, paradoxically, is not out to destroy typology; he is eager to establish its justifiable limits. The inventions of patristic writers like St. Clement of Alexandria, who thought that the myth of the phoenix could be taken as a type of the Resurrection, are unconvincing.[35] But Collins's defense of typology, one of the most curious in the eighteenth century, has been unjustly neglected:

[32] *Christianity Not Mysterious*, pp. 102-103.

[33] *Ibid.*, p. 115.

[34] See Anthony Collins, *A Discourse of the Grounds and Reasons of the Christian Religion* (London, 1724), pp. 45-46, 51; cf. O'Higgins, *Anthony Collins*, p. 166.

[35] *A Discourse of the Grounds and Reasons of the Christian Religion*, p. 231.

> It seems therefore most destructive of christianity to suppose; that *typical* or *allegorical arguing* is in any respect *weak and enthusiastical*; and that the Apostles always argu'd in the matter of *prophesies* according to the literal sense of the *prophesies* and the way of reasoning used in the schools: since it is most apparent; that the whole Gospel is in every respect founded on *type* and *allegory*; that the Apostles in most, if not all cases reason'd *typically* and *allegorically*; and that, if the Apostles be suppos'd to reason always after the *rules* used in the schools, and if their writings be brought to the test of those *rules*, the books of the Old and New Testament will be in an *irreconcileable state*, and the *difficulties* against christianity will be incapable of being solv'd.[36]

The "rules" to which Collins refers are the imaginative methods of interpretation used by the ancient Jews and early patristic writers. Two things are clear from this passage: Collins opposes the figural extravagance of the more extreme typological exegetes, and he is aware that, without the typological reasoning that Christian apologists have traditionally used to reconcile the Old and New Testaments, "the *difficulties* against christianity will be incapable of being solv'd." Without typological reasoning, then, there would be no Christianity. Collins is clearly ironical in this passage, just as other Deists adopted ironical rhetoric in dealing with what they thought were weak points in standard Christian apologetics. But he is not out to destroy Christianity, and this is why, I think, he notes that *"typical* or *allegorical arguing* is . . . *weak and enthusiastical."* Collins had spotted the weakness in much typological argument—its proneness to imaginative connections without any evidentiary foundation for them—and his sound criticism of this quality may have led to the more careful scrutiny of the historical bases for typology that followed in the 1730s.

The effect of his position, and of the Deist-inspired controversy, leads to a new movement to find rational bases for typology. Warburton's *Divine Legation of Moses Demonstrated* (1738-41) and

---

[36] *Ibid.*, pp. 269-70; cf. Collins's entire Chapter 10, entitled "Typical or Allegorical Reasoning defended against Mr. WHISTON; wherein is a digression that compares together the allegorical Scheme and Mr. WHISTON's literal Scheme, and that proves his literal Scheme false and absurd." William Whiston's *Essay towards restoring the true Text of the Old Testament* (London, 1722) is strongly deistical. O'Higgins, curiously, ignores this chapter completely in his study of Collins.

John Jortin's *Remarks on Ecclesiastical History* (1751-53), respected works by members of the Church establishment, show how the controversy established abstracted typology more firmly than ever before. Warburton confuted and rejected the idolatrous animal worship of the ancient Egyptians, but argued that there was a rational basis for making the images of external nature prefigurative and predictive.[37] Jortin was dubious of excessive typologizing, but conceded that if the prophets had accurately "foretold the things relating to Babylon, Tyre, etc."—and, so far as Jortin was concerned, they had—then it was reasonable to accept their types and signs of the Messiah as well. "A Type," he said convincingly, "is a rough draft, a less accurate pattern or model, from which a more perfect image or work is made."[38] The basis for abstracted typology is as clear here as it had been in Anthony Collins's rhetorical question in 1724: "For what is a *Poetick Description* fulfill'd, but a Typical Prophesy *fulfill'd?*"[39] Neither statement has an entirely theological context; the figural transformation from typology as exegetical system to typology as imagistic technique is nearly complete. Let me turn now to an examination of several stages on which the scenes from abstracted typology are played.

 5

Among the most natural subjects for typology is kingship. In seventeenth-century England, when the destinies of Church and state were closely linked and when civil instability constantly threatened, the urge to typologize the monarchy seems to have been greater than at any other time in English history since the Reformation. Poets were prepared, beginning with the Restoration, to write flattering verse panegyrics of the Stuart house, but, as I said earlier, Old Testament typology waned gradually as the fortunes of the Stuarts—and the century—petered out. Davidic typology remained popular long after Edenic and Noahic imagery had fallen into desuetude, perhaps because of the flawed nature of David himself.

[37] For a convenient summary of Warburton's position, see Burton Feldman and Robert D. Richardson, *The Rise of Modern Mythology, 1680-1860* (Bloomington, Ind.: Indiana Univ. Press, 1972), pp. 112-13.

[38] See John Jortin, *Remarks on Ecclesiastical History*, 5 vols. (London, 1751-53), I, 183 and, in general, I, 179-97.

[39] *A Discourse of the Grounds and Reasons of the Christian Religion*, pp. 238-39.

William and Mary, like Charles II before them, were seen as post-figurations of Moses when they arrived in England, and one of the elegists of Mary at her death in 1695 would recall the Mary-Moses comparison.[40] But the later Stuarts seldom inspired such lyricism. Classical, rather than Christian, mythology was deemed more suitable. John Willis, of New-Inn Hall at Oxford, greeting the birth of the Prince of Wales (the future Old Pretender) in 1688, saw the new arrival as a "Messenger of Peace," but his christomimesis is otherwise modest. Somehow, pagan typology seemed more appropriate:

> If a new Hydra dares our World molest
> This Prince shall crush the many headed Beast.
> Our Jove no more shall lead his Hosts to fight,
> The Son shall Conquer in the Fathers right.[41]

The analogy of the male infant to the infant Hercules, popular in visual iconography, was a standard typological allusion in poems about royal princes.[42]

An alternative for the panegyrist eager to typologize without bringing up the touchy question of divine right was the abstracted type from classical history. One of the Cambridge versifiers on the landing of William and Mary remembered that Julius Caesar had landed in England, too (and forgot that Caesar's fortunes there had been indifferent):

> The Mighty *Julius* whose illustrious Name
> Till now stood first in the Records of Fame;
> Who by his Courage kept the World in awe,
> Was but a Type of the Divine *Nassau*.[43]

The funerary exercises at William III's death could not match this extravagance, but among the small number of poems written on the

---

[40] See Robert Smithies, "On the Late Happy Revolution: A Pindarique Ode," st. 9, in *Musae Cantabrigienses Serenissimus Principibus Wilhelmo et Mariae* (Cambridge, 1689), Sig. a3ᵛ; see *Lachrymae Cantabrigienses in Obitum Serenissimae Reginae Mariae* (Cambridge, 1695), Sig. Zzᵛ (untitled ode by Bart. Stote).

[41] See *Strenae Natalitiae Academiae Oxoniensis in Celsissimum Principem* (Oxford, 1688), Sig. T2ʳ⁻ᵛ.

[42] There are other examples, like the poem addressed to Anne, later Queen, on her marriage to George Prince of Denmark. See *Hymenaeus Cantabrigiensis* (Cambridge, 1693), Sig. R3ᵛ-4ʳ (untitled verses by William Ayloffe). For medallic images of a king crushing the hydra, see Figures 30 and 33.

[43] *Musae Cantabrigienses*, Sig. C1ᵛ (untitled verses by Richard Stone). I owe this reference to Earl Miner.

death of Anne (published, almost as an afterthought, in 1716) was a "Pindarique Ode" containing the following stanza:

> *Vespasian*, whose Imperial Name
> Triumphant rides upon the Wings of Fame
>   That measur'd Time's swift Hand,
>   Not by the Ebb and Flow of Sand,
> But the more reg'lar Motions of his Mind,
> Which ev'ry Beat, struck Blessings to Mankind,
> No more Illustrious Shade shall mention'd be,
>   But as the Type of Thee.[44]

The straining for a typological association here suggests not so much the weakness of abstracted types as it does the enervation of the Stuart myth. The panegyric verse addressed in the next half-century to the Hanoverian kings was bland, lacking in the tumid enthusiasm of the seventeenth-century paean.

The typology of kingship did not die out quite yet, for there remained a much more fertile field—the Martyr's Day sermon. Perhaps as many as a thousand of them survive, including a great many for the first sixty years of the eighteenth century. Charles the Martyr had obvious christological properties; for many of the homilists, he was both postfiguration and foreshadow, both antitype and type.[45] Sometimes, as in Joseph Trapp's 1729 sermon, the typology is hesitant and even flawed:

> Tho' I am very far from making an exact Parallel between [Christ's] Sufferings, and those of our Royal Martyr, which would be Blasphemy indeed; (and, whatever had been insinuated, Nobody, that I know of, ever *did* make such a Parallel) yet I cannot understand where the Blasphemy, or even Indecency, or Impropriety, lies in making some Sort of Comparison between them.[46]

Trapp, curiously unaware of the vast number of exact parallels that

[44] *The Loyal Mourner for the Best of Princes: Being a Collection of Poems Sacred to the Immortal Memory of her Late Majesty Queen Anne* [ed. John Oldisworth?] (London, 1716), p. 41. The verses are by W. Paul.

[45] See, for example, Thomas Fothergill, *The Reasonableness and Uses of Commemorating King Charles's Martyrdom* (London, 1753), pp. 4-5. It is noteworthy that this kind of typology continued to be employed over a century after Charles's death.

[46] *A sermon Preached . . . at the Cathedral Church of St. Paul on Friday, January 30, 1729* (London, 1729), p. 1.

had been made in the previous eighty years, but aware of the controversy in the 1720s over the use of typology, avoids using the term itself, and contents himself with simply suggesting that Charles the Martyr was a postfiguration of the crucified Christ. At times of great national crisis, when it was natural to draw parallels, Charles's martyrdom would be seen as a prefiguration of all the nation's present troubles, as in Edward Banyer's 1747 sermon:

> National Sins deserve national Judgments, and unrepented of in the Course of Providence, sooner or later, their own Punishment. The Truth of which, to a serious Observer of Occurrences for near a Century past, will easily appear, since there are hardly any national Misfortunes within that Compass of Time, which are not natural Consequences of the Wickedness of this Day. To this, as to their proper Source, are owing all our Disputes and Animosities, every Cause of our Fears real or imaginary; and it depends much upon our future Behaviour, whether God shall spare, or go on to inflict his Judgments.[47]

Banyer evidently has in mind the troubles of the '45. His method, not uncommon in Martyr's Day sermons, is to treat the Regicide as a prefiguration of future troubles; typology, in these contexts, becomes a helpful guide for those who would like to cast blame for events in recent history. Throughout the 1740s and 1750s we continue to find sermons which see the king in terms of minor Old Testament types like Daniel and Jonah.[48]

One remarkable quality in eighteenth-century Regicide sermons, relatively uncommon in the genre during the last half of the seventeenth century, is the tendency for homilists to draw a "character" of Charles I, usually as the perfect Christian ("Christianus Perfectus"), less frequently as the picture of the good magistrate. Edward Young, for example, in his 1729 sermon, draws a "Character of a Good Prince," and, before his abstracted typology begins, compares Charles I to David, Aemilius Lepidus, Cato, Alcibiades, and Pericles. Clarendon's famous character of the King, in his *History of the Rebellion* (1702-04), had been favorable, but it was not exactly a whitewash. Young's vision of the Good Prince is different:

[47] *A Sermon Preached Before the Right Honourable the Lord Mayor . . . Jan. 30, 1746-7* (London, 1747), p. 18. Banyer sees the 1745 troubles in Scotland as antitypes of the martyrdom.

[48] A good instance is Samuel Johnson, *A Sermon Preached in the Parish-Church of Great Torrington, On Sunday, the Thirtieth Day of January, 1742* (London, 1745), pp. 2-3, 6-7, 8-10. Johnson was the Vicar of Great Torrington.

He labours for the Good, wakes for the Care, feels for the Wants, lives for the Glory, or sets Death at defiance for the Preservation of the Whole. The Good Prince is the *Eye* of Government that never closes; the *Hand* of Government that is never weary; the *Heart* of Government that never ceases pouring out the Vital Streams of Prudence and Good-will; to feed, and support the *Publick Safety*, and *Publick Peace*.[49]

The good prince is obviously a type, but in Young's context he might almost be a character in a novel. Images of Christian perfection, inspired in part by Steele's *Christian Hero* (1701) and by the popular *imitatio Christi* tradition that flourished in the eighteenth century, are important in English fiction; in Young's vivid homily we may glimpse the vital link between the abstracted type in a quasi-theological situation and the same figure in literature.

Young is not alone in seeing the martyred Charles as a type whose chief significance has been abstracted to the concerns of everyday life. One of the more reflective homilists, John Whalley, in his 1740 Martyr's Day sermon, meditates on the prefigurative qualities of his subject:

Indeed this is the most noble End, as well as the properest Use to be made of all History, to teach us that best sort of Wisdom, a practical Wisdom, by transmitting down to us the Actions of our Forefathers, that so by an attentive Consideration of their bad and good Conduct, together with the Causes and Consequences of both, we may come to know by what most likely Means we are to avoid the one, and imitate the other. . . . The Life and Actions of the Divine Author of our Holy Religion are set out to us in the Gospel History, as a Pattern for our Imitation.[50]

Charles I, the homilist concludes, speaking to all of us through his sufferings, is both Christ's typical postfiguration and an abstracted type, presented to us as the perfect Christian. Characters of perfection appear in many other sermons, but their typological associations are seldom so obvious as when they relate to kingship. The

[49] *An Apology for Princes, or the Reverence due to Government* (London, 1739), pp. 48-50. Young's iconographical allusion to "the *Eye* of Government" recalls Matt. 6.22, Luke 11.34, Eccles. 2.14, and Job 11.4.

[50] *A Sermon Preached before the House of Commons . . . Jan. 30, 1739/40* (London, 1740), pp. 1-3.

typological "character" in the sermon now brings me to a consideration of the character books themselves.

Joseph Hall, the first English character-writer, recognizes the universal qualities of his art. In his "Premonition of the Title and Use
of Characters," he describes the evolution of his form: "The Divines
of the olde Heathen were their Morall Philosophers: These received the Acts of an inbred law, in the *Sinai* of Nature, and delivered them with manie expositions to the multitude: These were the
Overseers of maners, Correctors of vices, Directors of lives, Doctors
of vertue, which yet taught their people the body of their naturall
Divinities, not after one maner."[51] The character was an acquired,
highly specialized piece of knowledge, but, as Hall understands the
genre, it is more than mere information. He says that the learned
men who specialized in this branch of knowledge "bestowed their
time in drawing out the true lineaments of every vertue and vice,
so lively, that those who saw the medals, might know the face:
which Art they significantly termed Charactery. . . ." The allusion
to medals is doubtless inspired by the Greek origin of the word,
meaning "to engrave." That Hall should mention medallic art is
significant, since Renaissance numismatists were agreed that medals
embodied a special sign language of their own.[52] It is not necessary
for us to inquire into the mysterious qualities of old coins. It is
enough that Hall sees the prose character as a kind of sign, which
would allow its viewers to "know the face," for this suggests that as
early as 1600 characters were thought to be predictive. Hall's *Characters of Vertues and Vice* are, in fact, strongly prefigurative
throughout. The characters of Vices are drawn in such a way that
the reader, once acquainted with a certain kind of viciousness,
would be able to anticipate its ramifications, predict its behavior.

[51] Joseph Hall, *Characters of Vertues and Vices in two Bookes* (London,
1608), Sig. A4ʳ. See the entire Preface, Sig. A4ʳ-6ᵛ. Hall sees Theophrastus, the
founder of his genre, as a kind of Moses figure, and the character writer as a
dispenser of typological wisdom. Isaac Casaubon, whose *editio princeps* (Leyden,
1612) of Theophrastus inaugurated modern study of characters, makes no such
claim; see his "Prolegomena," pp. 83-92.

[52] On medallic symbolism, see Allen, *Mysteriously Meant*, pp. 256-62, and
Ernst H. Kantorowicz, *The King's Two Bodies* (Princeton: Princeton Univ.
Press, 1957), including the illustrations. See also Figures 30-33.

The characters of Virtue are more obviously typological and christomimetic.

Perhaps one brief example from Hall's collection will tell us how the predictive, typological character functions in the seventeenth century. Here is "The Characterism of the *Faithfull man*":

> Examples are his proofes; and Instances his demonstrations. What hath God given, which hee can not give? What have others suffered, which hee may not bee enabled to endure? is hee threatned banishment? There he sees the Deare Evangelist in Pathmos cutting in pieces; hee sees Esay under the saw. Drowning? hee sees Ionas diving into the living gulfe. Burning? he sees the three children in the hote walke of the furnace. Devouring? hee sees Daniel in the sealed den amids his terrible companions. Stoning? hee sees the first Martyr under his heape of many gravestones. Heading? loe there is the Baptists necke bleeding in Herodias platter. He emulates their paine, their strength, their glorie. . . . He is not so sure he shall die, as that he shall be restored; and outfaceth his death with his resurrection. . . . In common opinion miserable, but in true jugement more than a man.[53]

Not only does Hall specifically compare the faithful man with a number of traditional Old and New Testament types and figures, he emphasizes that this character itself is typological, for the person he figures forth is only a shadow of what he *shall* be. Hall's homiletic style, with its biblical overtones, may seem stiff and unattractive to the reader of imaginative literature. His characters of Vices are less rigid; there is a compelling variety about evil. Here, too, his declared purpose of providing the *signs* that will acquaint the reader with the entire character is central.[54] Just as Hall's virtuous characters tend to foreshadow Christ-like perfections, his vicious types prefigure full-blown, satanic evils.

Typological characters are common homiletic devices. One popular sermon writer, for instance, giving a character of the cunning hunter, asserts that "The wicked oppressors of the world are here Typed and Taxed." A character of the plain-dealing man, which

[53] *Characters*, pp. 23-25. The characters of the humble man (pp. 27-31) and "Of the good Magistrate" (pp. 57-62) are also typological, even to the point of echoing biblical texts commonly linked with Christ.

[54] See Hall's characters of "The Hypocrite" (pp. 71-77), "The *Profane*" (pp. 93-97), "The Flatterer" (pp. 113-18), and "The Envious" (pp. 167-73).

takes Jacob as its exemplar, suggests that his behavior foreshadows that of *all* plain-dealing men ever since.[55] Sermon-characters, chiefly associated with aspects of Christian behavior, are a standard rhetorical device well into the eighteenth century.[56]

Character books become progressively larger and more elaborate during the course of the seventeenth century and, although the popular appeal of this kind of literature tended to preclude much theorizing about character types, we may occasionally find a telling description. The Overburian characters, often satirical and abusive, conclude with a brief apothegmatic account, "What a Character is." This little theoretical coda emphasizes that the genre is meant to make a deep impression (the etymological sense of the word) on the reader and to function as a sign that will leave "a strong seale in our memories." One recalls the semiological terminology—"semantic enclaves." But the character is more: "Character is also taken for an Ægyptian Hieroglyphicke, for an imprese, or a short Embleme; in little comprehending much. To square out a Character by our English levell, it is a picture (reall or personall) quaintly drawne, in various colours, all of them heightened by one shadowing."[57] This is a terminology we have come to recognize as prefigurative, as deliberately conceived for typological purposes. Sir Thomas Overbury, it might be noted, was not writing for ecclesiastical preferment or apologetic glories: his collection was intended to do nothing more than what most of these modest duodecimos and sextodecimos aimed at—to entertain a literate but not necessarily pious audience.

Earle's *Micro-Cosmographie* (1650), often regarded as the best of the seventeenth-century collections (Butler's characters, which are without peer, did not appear until 1759), begins to show resemblances to actual individuals from the world of fiction. The sign-like, semiological qualities I have noted occur continually, but now the names of characters become more explicit. Earle's character of

[55] See *The Works of Thomas Adams. Being the Summe of His Sermons, Meditations, and Other Divine and Morall Discourses* (London, 1629), pp. 116, 131. Adams, who was a Puritan, delivered a series of "character" sermons in the second decade of the seventeenth century which seems to have been much imitated.

[56] A case in point is Samuel Clarke who, like Thomas Adams, devoted many sermons to subjects like "The Character of a Good Man" or "The Excellency of Moral Qualifications." See *The Works of Samuel Clarke*, 4 vols. (London, 1738), I, 147, 154-59, 237-42, 248-53, 266-70.

[57] Sir Thomas Overbury, *His Wife. With Additions of New Characters, and Many other Wittie Conceits*, 11th ed. (London, 1622), Sig. Q4^r.

"The Worlds Wise Man" evokes Bunyan's Mr. Worldly Wiseman and Fielding's Jonathan Wild ("His conclusion is commonly one of these two; either a Great Man, or Hang'd").[58] His contemplative man, his skeptic in religion, his "good old Man," and his "Prophane Man" are all exemplars of character types which were the common coin of the world of English fiction by the early eighteenth century. The religious aura in which Hall and homiletic authors like him were wont to enwrap their character sketches gradually diminishes, but its typological properties linger on.

In the development of abstracted typology whose course I have been attempting to chart, the elements of religious prefiguration, whether positive or negative ("positive" means christic typology; "negative" refers to images which foreshadow Satan or satanic evils), are less important than the methodology of prefiguration itself. "A *Type* is a mould or a pattern of a thing," wrote Anthony Collins in support of "Typological Prophecys."[59] He then proceeds to give a theological context and application to this helpful definition, but we need not accompany him. For, in the imaginative literature of which character writing is an undoubted part, the definition of "character" is practically the same as Collins's description of a "type." And what the character writers present in their limited theorizings, they practice. My suggestion, then, is that the predictive qualities of the seventeenth-century character type sustain and inform later fictional creations. In eighteenth-century prose fiction, from the brief stories in the periodical essay (those of Addison and Johnson come to mind), to the longer, unstructured narratives of Defoe, to the carefully plotted craftsmanship of the century's major novelists, abstracted typology is a constant presence.

 7

The distinguishing quality of abstracted types is that, unlike mere words, they embody *signs* recognizable to a literate audience; they have a life beyond the text in which they are incarcerated. It is easy to see how this rule applies with character types, for the character is a unit that, under certain circumstances, may establish semiologi-

58 John Earle, *Micro-Cosmographie. Or, A Piece of the World Characteriz'd; In Essays and Characters* (London, 1650) pp. 69-71. See also Samuel Butler, *Characters*, ed. Daves, pp. 5-12, for brief remarks on all the major character books.
59 *The Scheme of Literal Prophecy Considered* (London, 1726), p. 345.

cal communication between the author and the reader. Yet another area of abstracted typology involves the *fable*. Here, at first glance, it might seem that typology of any kind would be impossible. Yet such was not the case in the eighteenth century. The fable genre may have been more popular from 1690 to 1750 than at any other time in our literary history. Its many practitioners firmly believed that it possessed special semiological qualities that distinguished it from more recently developed genres. Virtually all commentators agreed that, in Addison's words, "Fables were the first Pieces of Wit that made their Appearance in the World, and have been still highly valued, not only in times of the greatest Simplicity, but among the most polite Ages of Mankind."[60]

The definition in Johnson's *Dictionary* emphasized the fictive nature of the fable, but also noted that it was a story or the "contexture of events" which constitutes the plot of a work of literature. It was further agreed that the fable gave a partial, figurative, frequently allegorical vision of the truth; it was similar to the parable, unprepossessingly simple, yet filled with latent meaning. Seeking to mitigate this apparent simplicity, one translator of Aesop, Edmund Arwaker, assured his readers that fables were not merely for children, but were a special vehicle for conveying truth, whether moral or satirical. For "few can contemplate Truth, in its full Splendour, but must have it convey'd to them by *Mediums*, and its Beam let gently in upon them, as it were through Chinks and Crannies."[61] Other versions of Aesop took a similar view, insisting that fables were eminently suited for the instruction of children but that they were inherently figural, profoundly laden with emblematic meaning (see, for example, Figures 23 and 24). It was inevitable that in an age when figural interpretations were the rule rather than the exception writers would realize that fables were both condensed behavioral guides for all readers and typological, predictive, stories or plot-signs.

The most popular English version of Aesop was that of Sir Roger L'Estrange, which appeared in nearly a score of editions from the later seventeenth to the eighteenth centuries. The work snowballed as it passed from one edition to the next, accumulating materials

---

[60] See *The Spectator*, ed. Donald Bond, 5 vols. (Oxford: Clarendon Press, 1965), II, 219-20 (No. 183).

[61] *Truth in Fiction: or, Morality in Masquerade, A Collection of Two Hundred twenty-five Select Fables of Aesop, and other Authors* (London, 1708), pp. ii, iv-v, vi. The entire Preface (pp. i-xvi) is relevant.

from other fabulists, scholia, and a large body of moral reflections. L'Estrange saw his work as thoroughly symbolic:

> For there's Nothing makes a Deeper Impression upon the Minds of Men, or comes more Lively to their Understanding, than Those Instructive Notices that are Convey'd to them by Glances, Insinuations, and Surprize; and under the Cover of some *Allegory* or *Riddle*. But, What can be said more to the Honour of This *Symbolical* Way of Moralizing upon *Tales* and *Fables*, than that the Wisdom of the Ancients has been still Wrapt up in *Veils* and *Figures*; and their Precepts, Councels, and salutary Monitions for the Ordering of our Lives and Manners, Handed down to us from all Antiquity under *Innuendo's* and *Allusions*? For what are the *Ægyptian Hierogliphicks*, and the whole History of the *Pagan Gods*; The Hints, and Fiction of the Wise Men of Old, but in Effect, a kind of *Philosophical Mythology*: Which is, in truth, no other, than a more Agreeable Vehicle found out for Conveying to us the Truth and Reason of Things, through the *Medium* of *Images* and *Shadows*.[62]

Particularly important to L'Estrange, Dryden, and other English fabulists was the association of the fable with the biblical parable; if Jesus taught symbolically, might not the fable of antiquity do the same? L'Estrange's placid acceptance of the symbolical interpretations of the ancient gods sounds like a rich serving of Stillingfleet with a healthy dose of Alexander Ross. Yet his credulity need not be emphasized; the work of the scholarly antiquarians, such as Richard Bentley, who would demonstrate the inauthenticity of Aesop during the 1690s, had little effect upon those who wished to find figural readings in old books.[63] Nor would what Don Cameron Allen calls "the rationalization of myth" have such a widespread effect in the eighteenth century as one might expect. L'Estrange's *Aesop*, complete with this highly figural preface, would continue to be reprinted *in toto* for fifty years.

It is clear from the remarks just quoted that L'Estrange took advantage of the terminological confusion over typology current in the seventeenth century. He goes on to clarify matters substantially:

[62] *Fables of Aesop and other Eminent Mythologists: with Morals and Reflexions*, 2 vols. (London, 1694), I, Sig. A2ᵛ.

[63] On Bentley's role in the Phalaris controversy, see J. E. Sandys, *A History of Classical Scholarship*, 3 vols. (Cambridge: Cambridge Univ. Press, 1903-05), II, 403-405.

How much are we Oblig'd then, to those Wise, Good Men, that have furnish'd the World with so sure, and so Pleasant an Expedient, for the Removing of All These Difficulties [of teaching moral precepts]! And to Æsop in the First Place, as the *Founder*, and *Original Author*, or *Inventer* of This Art of Schooling Mankind into Better Manners; by Minding Men of their Errors without Twiting them for what's Amiss, and by That Means Flashing the Light of their Own Consciences in their Own Faces. We are brought Naturally enough, by the Judgment we pass upon the Vices and Follies of our Neighbours, to the Sight and Sense of our Own; and Especially, when we are led to the Knowledge of the Truth of Matters by *Significant Types*, and *Proper Resemblances*.[64]

The fables, then, instruct prefiguratively, by presenting the reader with a situational type which, by thorough acquaintance, will enable him to interpret proper behavior under similar circumstances. L'Estrange's hundreds of fables (the two-volume collection contains nearly 500) are carefully planned to be interpretative in this way. Like all other versions of Aesop, they are obscure, but the moral reflections, which their author called "Emblems," remove all ambiguities. Sometimes the commentary runs on for ten pages, as in the fable called "A Horse and an Ass," where the proud and contemptuous behavior of the Horse, who scorns the humble Ass, becomes a type of the miserable behavior of all proud men.[65] We can go on to multiply examples by the score: fables of "A Cock and a Diamond" (an emblem of industry and moderation), of "A Dog and a Shadow" (a type of excessive desire), of "A Fowler and a Partridge" (the bird is a type of the guilty sinner), of "A Crow and a Dog" (on false religion), and many others.[66] I much doubt that eighteenth-century readers purchased their copies of L'Estrange's *Aesop* solely because of the work's moral scholia. Yet the edition was frequently reprinted and expanded over a period of nearly half a century while other contemporary English versions of Aesop enjoyed considerably less popularity. Perhaps—and at this point I can only speculate—the scholia to L'Estrange's edition made it attrac-

---

[64] *Fables of Aesop*, Sig. A3ʳ.

[65] *Fables of Aesop*, 7th ed. (London, 1724), I, 45-53 (Fable 38).

[66] *Ibid.*, I, 1-2 (Fable 1); I, 6-8 (Fable 6); I, 148-49 (Fable 132); I, 192-93 (Fable 179). The moral is frequently a christianizing of a pagan situation, almost always in explicitly typological terms.

tive as a moral guide for the education of children (Locke, in *Some Thoughts concerning Education*, had recommended Aesop for young children) in a period of our literary history before the rise of children's literature.

The *corpus* of Aesop's original fables was insufficient to satisfy eighteenth-century tastes for moral dicta. So the book was swelled with contemporary, Aesop-like tales, which differ mainly in that they are political in application. Perhaps the best of these is L'Estrange's "Kingdom of the Apes," where the reflection informs us that "It is the proper Business of *Mythology* to point out and Represent the Images of Good and Evil, and under those Shadows to Teach us what we ought to do, and what not."[67] Fables, in other words, contain both positive and negative types, either foreshadowing desirable, Christ-like behavior, or evil, satanic traits. They are a kind of "social" typology. The fable can even become a vehicle for historical interpretations (Gay's verse fables are notable for their success in this sphere). Samuel Croxall's translation of Aesop, in the "Application" to the well-known Aesopic fable, "The Wind and the Sun," waxes ecclesiastical:

> Persecution has always fix'd and riveted those Opinions which it was intended to dispel; and some discerning Men have attributed the quick Growth of Christianity, in a great Measure, to the rough and barbarous Reception which its first Teachers met with in the World. I believe the same may have been observ'd of our Reformation: The Blood of the Martyrs was the Manure which produc'd that great Protestant Crop on which the Church of *England* has subsisted ever since.[68]

Croxall's genius was smaller than that of L'Estrange, who was never so bald in attributing typological relationships. Perhaps the lack of deftness in Croxall's touch suggests how common abstracted typology had become by the 1720s, and how traditional it was for the fable to be a vehicle for historical prediction and fictive prefiguration. The end of my story is not an ending—typologies do not end, they only *foreshadow* endings—but is another proposal. I propose that the abstracted typology practiced by the fabulists helps establish a prefigurative style that would be used freely and with immense facility for the rest of the eighteenth century.

[67] *Ibid.*, I, 444, and see pp. 444-47.
[68] Samuel Croxall, *Fables of Aesop and Others, Newly done into English, with an Application to each Fable* (London, 1722), pp. 76-77.

As I have suggested in the foregoing pages, the shape of the pre-figurative style in the eighteenth century is closely linked with the language of signs, with the semantic enclaves of character and fable, with the visual, and with that most human desire to predict the future. It has been plausibly argued that typological patterns of thought exist in all societies and in all centuries. If we limit our quest to mere predictiveness, this may indeed be so. But the language of types in this period works through a recognizable code—a type always has an antitype, an antitype always presupposes a type somewhere in its past. The prefigurative style, when we find it, will have an extra-verbal quality about it, for types are, after all, signs. Here, for example, is the kind of typological text contemporary readers could have enjoyed:

> Nature *labours* with its utmost Diligence upon this corrupted dead Earth, that it might generate Heavenly Forms and Species or Kinds; but it *generates only* dead, dark, and hard Fruits, which are no more than a mere Shadow or Type of the Heavenly.

Or, if they continued in the same work:

> Further, if you will consider the heavenly Divine Pomp, State, and *Glory*, and conceive how it is, and what Manner of Sprouting, Branching, Delight, and Joy there is in it, view this World diligently, and *consider* what Manner of Fruit, Sprouts, and Branches, grow out of the *Salitter* of the Earth, from Trees, Plants, Herbs, Roots, Flowers, Oils, Wine, Corn, and whatever else there is that your *Heart* can find out; *all* is a *Type* of the heavenly Pomp.[69]

True, this is a seventeenth-century translation of Jakob Boehme's *Aurora* (trans. English 1620), but I am quoting from the eighteenth-century edition ascribed to William Law, from the very copy which belonged to Coleridge.[70] Boehme's comment is one example

[69] "Aurora: The Day-Spring, or, Dawning of the Day in the East," in *The Works of Jacob Behmen; the Teutonic Theosopher*, ed. G. Ward and T. Langcake, 4 vols. (London, 1764-81), I, pt. 1, 42-43. See Figure 17 for one of William Law's illustrations to Boehme.

[70] Coleridge's annotated copy, now in the British Library, has the shelfmark C.126.k.1.

of the many typological interpretations of the seventeenth century which retained popularity and influence in the next century and a half. To an acquaintance with Boehme we may ascribe, in part, the typology of natural existence that we find in Smart, Cowper, Wordsworth, and Shelley.

The prefigurative style will involve a blending of Christian and pagan, as in the typological character or in the christianizing of fabulistic plot structures in the novel. The allegorical essays in *The Rambler*, to take a prominent case, which we have long taken as evidence for Johnson's adherence to Renaissance traditions, may be something quite different. In one of them, Johnson falls asleep, and dreams that he walks through a landscape which, to our eyes, appears unbelievably emblematic and prefigurative, complete with images of a Dantesque wood and an Edenic vale. The figure of Religion appears and saves the dreamer from a melancholy doom by assuring him that good behavior, as it were an *imitatio Christi*, will bring him to eternal happiness:

> To such a one the lowliest self-abasement is but a deep-laid foundation for the most elevated hopes; since they who faithfully examine and acknowledge what they are, shall be enabled under my conduct to become what they desire. *The christian and the heroe are inseparable*; and to the aspirings of unassuming trust, and filial confidence, are set no bounds.[71]

The Christian and the hero—Christ and Hercules or, indeed, Everyman—the prefigurative qualities of two entire classes of images are here blended into one. The foreshadowing and emulation of Christian heroism, after all, are what typology is all about.

The prefigurative style, finally, will involve specifically contemporary achievements, as we may see in Richard Glover's "Poem on Sir Isaac Newton" (1728). Newton's scientific accomplishments, Glover proclaims, surpass anything the ancients could do. But he does not put his message in terms of *praise*; he expresses Newton's glory as the consummation of a type in the person of an antitype. The poet addresses Nature:

Thee the wise
Of ancient fame, immortal PLATO's self,
The Stagyrite, and Syracusian sage,

[71] *The Works of Samuel Johnson* (New Haven: Yale Univ. Press, 1954-   ), III, 241 (*Rambler*, No. 44; italics added).

From bleak obscurity's abyss to raise,
(Drooping and mourning o'er thy wondrous works)
With vain inquiry sought. Like meteors these
In their dark age bright sons of wisdom shone:
But at thy NEWTON all their laurels fade,
They shrink from all the honours of their names.
So glimm'ring stars contract their feeble rays,
When the swift lustre of AURORA's face
Flows o'er the skies, and wraps the heav'ns in light.[72]

The abstracted typology here has all the usual chaperones: a *type* (Plato, Aristotle, the other ancients), an *antitype* (Newton), and the traditional and necessary *extra-verbal signs* (the meteors, which are prophetic signs; the dawn = the Sun = Newton, with a sideways glance at Christ). Pope, perhaps, put it more neatly: "Nature, and Nature's Laws lay hid in Night. / God said, *Let Newton be!* and All was *Light*."[73] From type to antitype in two lines: it would be hard to better that.

---

[72] Glover's poem is prefixed to Henry Pemberton's *A View of Sir Isaac Newton's Philosophy* (London, 1728). See Sigs. [a]3ʳ⁻ᵛ. See Marjorie Hope Nicolson, *Newton Demands the Muse: Newton's "Opticks" and the Eighteenth Century Poets* (Princeton: Princeton Univ. Press, 1946), pp. 13-14.

[73] "Epitaph. Intended for Sir Isaac Newton, in Westminster Abbey" (c. 1730).

CHAPTER 6

Typology and Myth

MYTH WAS a subject of absorbing interest to the seventeenth and eighteenth centuries. Its meanings are diverse and complicated, and the subject underwent considerable change from the middle of the seventeenth century to the early nineteenth century. Hence the relation of typology to myth, which begins in the first centuries of the Christian era and which has never been simple, is both interesting and varied during this period. Until about 1700, *myth* meant mainly the inherited body of pagan mythology, principally Greek and Roman, which had been handed down to modern times from a number of conflicting classical and postclassical sources.[1] At the same time that myth carried this meaning, however, other myths, not specifically identified as such, existed, such as the myth of kingship and the myth of the state. According to the structures of these myths, sovereign and *civis* were analogized, by way of a number of devices both subtle and obvious, to heroic figures and virtuous commonwealths of the past. Students of English history and literature are familiar with comparisons of English sovereigns to personages like David, Alexander, Julius Caesar, Augustus Caesar, the Apostle Paul, and Christ. The figures in the analogies are usually historical, but the analogies themselves, rich in figuralism and often unctuous with flattery, assume the status of myths. The myth of the state received its essential characteristics from political writers at all points of the political spectrum, so that texts comparing England with Eden or Athens, Augustan Rome or Renaissance Florence, Egypt or Babylon, were common, especially in the seventeenth century. While the traditional view of myth as pagan story coexisted with contemporary mythologies,

[1] See Feldman and Richardson, *The Rise of Modern Mythology*, p. xxi.

a process familiar to the European Enlightenment, whereby myths are transformed, die, and are reborn, went on incessantly. Demythologizing, to use the barbaric jargon of a twentieth-century school of theology, and *re*mythologizing helped to ensure that notions latent with meaning for seventeenth-century poets and scholars would evoke nothing but scorn a century later.[2] In the century and a half after 1700, the spirit of historical inquiry and the rise of historical antiquarianism in studies both theological and secular help to account for sweeping changes in myth. We will find that myths of king and state are often turned to ridicule, and that the stories and theologies of all pagan countries will be intensively searched for new analogies to England, its religion, and its form of government. In all of these undertakings, typology plays a part.

The association of typology with myth begins in the first century, as the founders of Christianity sought to discover hidden philosophic meanings in Scripture. Philo and Paul found in the midrashic method of the rabbis, according to which certain Old Testament texts acquired nonliteral, predictive meanings, a useful exegetical system for linking the two Testaments, and interpretative typology was born.[3] While the early Fathers believed in the literal truth of the texts with which they dealt, the application of typology and the search for hidden types in them suddenly transformed them to the status of myths. An allegorist like Origen, for example, was able to create an entirely separate narrative account of and meaning for numerous biblical texts by the use of typology; the literal Bible was seen to harbor a hidden and secret story with its own arcane meaning. The ancient world did not have analytical definitions for *myth* in the sense that we have them today, but the typological exegeses of the Fathers "uncovered" what we may now identify as myths in the historical accounts and especially in the narrative portions of the Old Testament.[4]

[2] See Frei, *The Eclipse of Biblical Narrative,* p. 133; cf. Sanford Budick, *Poetry of Civilization: Mythopoeic Displacement in the Verse of Milton, Dryden, Pope, and Johnson* (New Haven: Yale Univ. Press, 1974), pp. 5-6. The modern theological jargon derives from the writings of Rudolf Bultmann and his followers.

[3] See Wolfson, *The Philosophy of the Church Fathers,* pp. 24-72, *passim,* on allegorism, figuralism, and typological exegesis from Justin Martyr to Jerome, and esp. pp. 24-32.

[4] On Origen, see Wolfson, *The Philosophy of the Church Fathers,* pp. 58-64 ("With Clement and Origen the non-literal method of interpretation in Christianity reached its fullest development."—p. 62), and Daniélou, *Origen,* trans. Mitchell, pp. 160-62.

Early Christian apologists sensed the similarities between some of the major figures of the pagan pantheon and central persons in the Old and New Testaments and, from the second century and the time of Eusebius and Tertullian, writers on Christianity began to regard these analogies in a light favorable to their cause. Pagan gods and demigods such as Adonis, Aesculapius, Apollo, Bacchus, Hercules, Mercury, Minerva, Neptune, and Prometheus became figural predecessors of the genuinely typological figures in the Old Testament. The medieval justification for the study of pagan literature was derived from arguments that dated at least from Clement of Alexandria's *Stromata* and numerous texts of St. Augustine. The great writings of paganism were prized because they inculcated morality and philosophy worthy of Christian contemplation, but they were valued as well because they included numerous types of Judaism and hence of Christianity.[5] Of all the Greek mythological narratives, the *Odyssey* provided the strongest analogies with the Christian experience, no doubt because Odysseus' pilgrimage-like voyages bore a strong resemblance to the progress of Christian life. Typology appears in unusual places in this context: Odysseus' adventures with the Cyclops and his dalliance with Circe proved as fruitful of analogy to Christianity as did the more obvious story of the Sirens.[6] Odysseus' having himself tied to the mast of the ship in order that he might resist the blandishments of the Sirens (*Odyssey*, XII) was seen as a pagan type of Christ's allowing himself to be crucified; just as Odysseus offers himself as a "sacrifice" to save his companions, so Jesus offered himself as a sacrifice for the redemption of mankind.[7] Achilles, immortal in all but his heel, Adonis gored by the boar, Aeneas in his visit to the underworld, Hercules in his labors and his fiery death, and many other familiar mythic characters found ready parallels to Christ. But Christian exegetes were not satisfied only to point out the parallels; in order to demonstrate that Christianity as a religion was historically inevitable, they stressed that these figures were types of Christ and his mission. Even the pagans, had they known enough to decipher the code inherent

[5] See Allen, *Mysteriously Meant*, pp. 4-5 and, in general, pp. 1-20; cf. pp. 90-93.

[6] Rahner, *Greek Myths and Christian Mystery*, pp. 286-300, gives a detailed account of the typologizing of the Homeric writings. Eustathius, the twelfth-century Byzantine commentator on the *Iliad* and *Odyssey*, gave the search for Christian analogues in Homer its major medieval impetus. See J. E. Sandys, *The History of Classical Scholarship*, I, 420-22.

[7] The typology appears most clearly in Maximus, *Homiliae, Patrologia Latina*, LVII, 339.

within their own stories, would have recognized the foreshadowing of Christianity.

The wisdom of the pagan mythologers and, later, of the authors of the Old Testament would provoke much discussion in the European Enlightenment. This discussion, indeed, would be far from amiable, and I will not be able to cover it here in detail. It will be sufficient to say that the search for typological parallels to Christianity in pagan mythology continued virtually unabated until late in the seventeenth century. To doubt the existence or veracity of the pagan types was, in effect, to deny the foreknown quality of Christianity and to risk being accused of atheism. Until the later seventeenth century, when men such as Milton, John Hall, Richard Simon, and Pierre Bayle spoke out openly against drawing typological parallels or challenged the foundations on which typologizing was established, the search for typological undermeanings in pagan mythology increased steadily in sophistication.[8] That the typologizing of pagan myth strained credulity is obvious, but to describe the excesses of this method, as does a recent commentator, as "downright ridiculous" may miss the point completely.[9] The typologists, particularly those of the seventeenth century, were no more excessive in their figuralism than the sonneteers of the *cinquecento* had been, and the mere fact that there is frequently no evidentiary foundation for their typology does not vitiate them as subjects for our attention. Sometimes, especially in recent years, it has seemed that abnormal psychology leads to more interesting results than do studies based on irrefutable evidence. And we must be grateful to the enthusiastic typologists of pagan myth for several things. First, they stressed typological *analogies* between static figures from pagan myth and static situations in Christian history. Adonis, gored, dies, and his dead body is transformed into a flower; thus Adonis becomes a type of resurrection. Orpheus' music causes his flock to follow him tamely; thus Orpheus is a type of the Good Shepherd (John 10.1-16). As a result of this aspect of the mythologizers' read-

[8] Allen's account in *Mysteriously Meant*, although it is often unaware of the typologizing of the mythologers and exegetes, remains the best recent study of this trend.

[9] In his introduction to *Poems on the Reign of William III* (Los Angeles: William Andrews Clark Memorial Library, 1974), Augustan Reprint Society Publ. No. 166, Earl Miner finds some late seventeenth-century figuralism painful (pp. iv-v). But, to be fair to the enthusiasts of the 1690s, we should at least concede that Pauline typology, to take only one earlier instance, was an even more cunning concoction.

ing, we are now able to identify numerous brief typological passages in English literature and to understand them more fully
within their contemporary contexts.

Second, the mythographers stress a certain number of typological
stories, longer accounts in fable and legend which, they deemed,
bore a prefigurative resemblance to some of the biblical narratives.
The paralleling of the *Odyssey* to the story of Jesus, of Virgil's
fourth *Eclogue* to the Old Testament prophecies, and of the Prometheus legends to christological sacrifice are just three examples.
What is important about these stories is that they allow for the
introduction of typology into *narrative* situations. For the student
of literature, typological narrative is the most important manifestation of typology, since narrative is extended, reasonably coherent,
and deeply meditated. The close similarity of many pagan myths
and legends to early romance and, as romance evolved, to certain
forms of the novel is important in the study of typological forms
in the English novel. Finally, the Renaissance mythographers
stressed the encrypted nature of typology: typological structures in
pagan myths were often seen as deliberately encoded messages for
modern genius to decipher. Deciphering, as I shall show later, plays
a fascinating role in the story of typology and myth in the period
covered by this study.

The study of pagan mythology in England around the middle of
the seventeenth century was still viewed with the utmost seriousness. Untouched as yet by the withering scorn of Deists such as
Pierre Bayle, Bernard Fontenelle, John Toland, and John Tren-
chard, the pagan stories could still be interpreted for their mysterious undertones and hidden Christian meanings. The seventeenth-
century mythologer wrote with the consciousness of more than two
centuries of learned commentary; often he found it easier to abstract his examples from a well-known and readily available source.
But among those most accomplished in the field are three writers
whose originality affected the study of myth for more than a century, the German Jesuit Kircher (who spent most of his time in
Rome), the French scholar Bochart (whose colossal learning later
procured him a summons to the court of Sweden), and the Dutch
polymath G. J. Vossius (whose son Isaac found life more comfort-

able in England).[10] Of the three, Kircher has recently emerged as the most important thinker, for his studies of hieroglyphics and of other symbolic languages have rendered him a subject of curiosity to twentieth-century students of linguistic history and early semiotic systems.[11] Bochart's *Geographia Sacra, seu Phaleg* (1646) is yet to have its day (it may yet), but for his contemporaries Bochart's etymological expositions of pagan myth were powerfully convincing. Vossius, easily the most genuinely learned of the three, contributed *De Theologia Gentili* (1641), a work whose intention is better served by its subtitle, *de origine ac progressu idololatriae*. Rather than dwell upon linguistic similarities in the names of the pagan deities, Vossius drew upon his extensive knowledge of primitive religions (based on reading that would later be the envy of Jacob Bryant and George Stanley Faber) to show how the physical or structural similarities of the ancient gods and of ancient theodicies were post-Old Testament corruptions crafted without malicious intent by the Egyptians, Syrians, Greeks, Romans, and so on.[12]

Since these Renaissance polymaths took care to document their works with copious annotations and quotations from the best writers and (whenever they were available) original documents, their brand of scholarship met with wide approbation, in England as elsewhere. We may get a clear notion of how this kind of scholarship was received from Edward Stillingfleet's *Origines Sacrae: or A Rational Account of the Grounds of the Christian Faith* (1662), which includes, amidst a lengthy justification of the divine authority of the Old Testament, a helpful chapter "Of the Origin of the Heathen Mythology." "Rational," for Stillingfleet, means "the reverse of atheistical," hence Christian, so his title is somewhat tauto-

[10] Bochart and Vossius, despite the enormous relevance of their work to many aspects of seventeenth-century humanism, have received little twentieth-century attention, but Kircher has been the subject of an interesting recent biography, P. Conor Reilly, *Athanasius Kircher, S. J.: Master of a Hundred Arts, 1612-1680* (Rome: Edizioni del Mondo, 1974).

[11] See, for example, Jacques Derrida, *Of Grammatology*, trans. Gayatri Chakravorty Spivak (Baltimore: Johns Hopkins Univ. Press, 1976), pp. 74-81; James Knowlson, *Universal Language Schemes in England and France, 1600-1800* (Toronto: Univ. of Toronto Press, 1975), pp. 6, 8, 13-15, etc. Two recent interpretations of Kircher are Erik Iversen, *The Myth of Egypt and Its Hieroglyphics in European Tradition* (Copenhagen: Gad, 1961), pp. 89-98, and R.J.W. Evans, *The Making of the Habsburg Monarchy, 1550-1700: An Interpretation* (Oxford: Clarendon Press, 1979), pp. 433-43, an excellent study of the *Oedipus Ægyptiacus*.

[12] See Allen, *Mysteriously Meant*, pp. 68-71.

logical; its secondary meaning is "based on truthful evidence." Stillingfleet's sound evidence, in his account of the pagan deities, is largely a redaction of Kircher, Bochart, and Vossius, with occasional but minor allusions to lesser writers. Speaking of the Noahic narratives, he shows his broad scope at once:

> The memory of the Deluge it self we have already found to be preserved in the *Heathen Mythology*; we come therefore to *Noah* and his posterity. Many parcels of *Noah's* memory were preserved in the scattered fragments of many Fables, under, *Saturn, Janus, Prometheus,* and *Bacchus. Bochartus* insists on no fewer than 14 *Parallels* between *Noah* and the *Heathen Saturn,* which he saith are so plain, that there is no doubt but under *Saturn, Noah* was understood in the *Heathen Mythology. Saturn* was said to be the common Parent of *Mankind,* so was Noah; *Saturn* was just a King, *Noah* was not only righteous himself, but a Preacher of righteousness; The Golden *Age* of *Saturn* was between *Noah* and the dispersion of *Nations.* . . .[13]

Never for a moment questioning his sources, Stillingfleet moves swiftly to show the confusions of Noah with the other pagan gods and, later, he performs similar operations for other figures from the pagan pantheon. It is significant, for our purposes, only to note that Stillingfleet turns his analytical gaze almost exclusively upon the typological figures of the Old Testament, so that their heathen identities are actually pagan types.

Stillingfleet wrote to reaffirm the truth of the Bible and hence of Christianity, to confute atheism, and to demonstrate the mistakes of Roman Catholicism. Many of his contemporaries who dealt with typology and myth had similar intentions, but not all. One who did not was Alexander Ross, whose *Mystagogus Poeticus* (1647), while much influenced by the Continental scholarship on myth, goes far beyond the scholiasts into the realm of poetical mythology. Ross's mythological handbook, somewhat in the tradition of earlier Renaissance works of this kind, is an alphabetical guide to all major pagan deities and figures from Greek and Roman literature. For each figure he analyzes, Ross presents a commentary that begins with the literal and proceeds to the figural interpretation, ending (when necessary and appropriate) with the typological. Typology was, for Ross, the highest form of figuralism, since it relates directly

[13] *Origines Sacrae,* 5th ed. (London, 1680), pp. 552-53.

to Christ. His typologies are important for establishing the basis of typological narrative, since he is much attracted by the typological qualities of characters in classical literature. Achilles, for example, Ross saw as a pagan type of baptism, but "Christ is the true *Achilles*."[14] The adversary Hector was another type, while Aeneas was "the *Idea* of a perfect Prince and Governor" (the good magistrate is often seen in seventeenth-century character books and sermons as a type of Christ).[15]

Not all pagan types prefigured Jesus alone. In fact, Ross reserves his most illuminating analysis for a different kind of figuralism, as we may see from his discussion of the goddess Ceres:

> *Ceres* is a type of Gods Church, which is a grave Matron in rustick apparel, as being of little esteem in the world, having only the Spade of Discipline in her right hand, and from her arms hangs a basket full of the seeds of Gods word. By this hand stand two Husbandmen, the one turning up the ground with a spade, the other sowing the seed. On her left hand (which holdeth the Hook and Flail of Correction and Excommunication) stand two other husbandmen, the one reaping and the other threshing. These are her Ministers whose office is to rout out, and pull down, to build and plant; she sits upon the Ox of Patience and labour, with a Crown of Wheat-Ears upon her head, as having power to distribute the Bread of Life. Her Breasts are open, and stretched forth with the sincere Milk of Gods Word; over her right side, *Juno* is dropping down rain, and over her left, *Apollo* shineth, to shew, that by the heat of the Sun of Righteousness, and influence of Graces from Gods Spirit, she doth flourish and fructifie. Christ is truly *Ceres*; which having lost mankind, being carried away by the Devil, he came, and with the Torch of his Word, found him out; and being drawn with the flying Serpents of Zeal and Prudence, dispersed his Seed through the World, went down to Hell, and rescued us from thence.[16]

It must be said for Ross that, however good his intentions, his logic often defies interpretation. His presentation of Ceres (of which this excerpt is but a small part) has a pictorial quality that his other descriptions seldom have in such detail, if at all. It is not icono-

[14] *Mystagogus Poeticus; or The Muses Interpreter* . . . , 6th ed. (London, 1675), p. 3.
[15] *Ibid.*, p. 15; cf. pp. 13-15.   [16] *Ibid.*, pp. 68-69.

logical in the sense that Ripa's *Iconologia* presents its images, for Ripa does not deal with the pagan deities and his *moraliter* eschews description of his engravings (Ross's work is unillustrated). It is clear that Ross is working from a complex image, or perhaps a composite of several images, but that he does not expect his audience to have the picture before them. The popularity of moralized illustrations, thanks to the emblem tradition, was considerable at the time that Ross wrote.[17] Emblem writers, as I noted earlier, often confuse a number of pictorial and figural terms; Ross's account of Ceres is especially helpful precisely because it does *not* confuse terms.[18] His Ceres is symbolic, but the symbolism is neatly wrapped in a typological cocoon, the Church on one side, Christ on the other. But the richness of his examples—he will often give as many as twenty different interpretations of a pagan figure—is sometimes confusing, for Ross could interpret pagan mythology both *in bono* and *in malo*. Thus, one of his readings of Hercules presents him as a prefiguration of Satan, although Ross afterward stresses that "Christ is truly *Hercules*." The value of Ross's contribution is not his fantastical sense, but his careful association of typology with visual signs, with a traditional symbolism, to demonstrate that the coincidence of predictive meaning is not accidental but deliberate.[19]

Ross and the arcane scholars whose work he helped to popularize believed that pagan theology, because of a number of linguistic, historical, and cultural confusions, did no more than to distort the "original" Hebrew narratives which, as all readily agreed, prefigured the life and works of Christ and his church. So the gods of the pagans, many of which already bore considerable similarities to key Hebrew and Christian figures, became types in the best sense of the term. Poets and men of letters, political apologists and historians knowingly introduced figures from Graeco-Roman mythology into their writings with prefigurative intentions. It is difficult, in

[17] Besides the well-known source books on emblems, such as Henkel and Schöne's *Emblemata*, it is appropriate to mention here the equally important tradition of illustrated editions of Aesop's *Fables*, with their moralizing passages on the accompanying woodcuts which are often much more elaborate than the cuts in emblem books, and also the tradition of Ripa's *Iconologia*. For a possible visual analogue to Ross's Ceres, see Figure 6.

[18] On the confusion of terms by emblem writers, see Quarles's preface, quoted above, Chapter 4, section 3.

[19] For another discussion of Ross's typology, see Earl Miner, *The Restoration Mode from Milton to Dryden* (Princeton: Princeton Univ. Press, 1974), pp. 332-34.

the rarefied atmosphere of twentieth-century scholarship, for any of us to recapture the pressures and methods of literary composition three centuries ago. I know of no successful attempt to do so; the semifictional accounts that make the effort convince very few people of their accuracy. We can see the relative nonchalance with which Dryden introduces the typology of the Phoenix into his first poem, "Upon the death of the Lord Hastings" (1649)—"Thus, without Young, this *Phoenix* dies, new born" (80)—as no more than a casual allusion. If Dryden did not study Ross's handbook, it matters very little, for he could have obtained the knowledge of this pagan type of the resurrection from any one of many classical source books used in the last form at Westminster (where, in 1649, he was still a student). At about the same time, Marvell could employ pagan typology in "An Horatian Ode upon Cromwel's Return from Ireland" (c. 1650), with his references to the heroes of pagan Rome; while we cannot imagine what artistic struggles Marvell underwent before deciding on this particular style of poetic flattery, we do know what an easy choice of referents it must have been, for such images were common. Marvell's well-known "Amphion" passage from *The First Anniversary of the Government under O. C.* (1655) contributes to the aura of elegant praise, but the image itself had a long genealogy:

> Such was that wondrous Order and Consent,
> When *Cromwell* tun'd the ruling instrument;
> While tedious Statesmen many years did hack,
> Framing a Liberty that still went back;
> Whose num'rous Gorge could swallow in an hour
> That Island, which the Sea cannot devour:
> Then our *Amphion* issues out and sings,
> And once he struck, and twice, the pow'rful Strings.[20]

A moment later, Marvell will recall the harmony of David and, still later, will evoke the familiar millennial typology of the books of Daniel and Revelation (lines 99-110).[21] The popularity of this sort

---

[20] *The First Anniversary*, lines 67-74.

[21] *The Poems and Letters of Andrew Marvell*, ed. H. M. Margoliouth, 3rd ed., 2 vols. (Oxford: Clarendon Press, 1971), I, 322-23. The scholia dealing with millennial Puritanism, the reign of the Saints, and its figural qualities are by now considerable. Christopher Hill, *Antichrist in Seventeenth-Century England* (London: Oxford Univ. Press, 1971), pp. 98-115, is attentive to the years of Marvell's major poetry.

of figuralism, as Christopher Hill has shown, was enormous, and pagan typology obviously accorded well with contemporary schemes of praise. Thus, while we have little basis for speaking authoritatively as to the artistic milieu in which a seventeenth-century writer would decide to introduce typologies, whether pagan or Christian, plain or abstracted, it should be clear that any literary process for which there are hundreds of surviving examples must have been one with which people were comfortable.

I stress the ease with which Marvell and Dryden (as well as Waller, Denham, Cowley, Milton, Butler, Oldham, and many other poets) used pagan typology because I want to suggest that what attracted them was an "old" style of figuralism which derived from the Renaissance syntagmata and encyclopediae of classical mythology. This kind of allusion, against which Dr. Johnson would declaim in his *Lives of the English Poets* toward the end of the next century, while it would continue to ornament polite verse for a half century more, lost its acceptability and strength later in the seventeenth century. In part, this decline had to do with attacks from the pulpit and elsewhere upon excessive ornamentation in literature of all kinds. But, more to our purpose, the change in the use of pagan typology is also associated with the rise of English deistical thought. The Renaissance mythologists, in their search for Christian origins, found a polytheism whose gods were nothing more than Hebrew and Christian types under other names. Once a scholar learned the code, as Kircher, Bochart, and Vossius all claimed to have done, deciphering could follow. The Deists asked harder questions of the past than the old mythologists had done. Frank Manuel concisely summarizes the problems confronting Deism: "the startling conformities among heathens ancient and modern and the even more disturbing fact that pagan rituals and beliefs showed marked resemblances to the Judaic and Christian rituals and ceremonial practices" raised the question of why God had allowed such monstrous perversions of His being to exist, much less to flourish for centuries, in the world.[22] In trying to answer, Deists, from the 1670s to the 1730s, would cast themselves in the role of caustic critics, even ridiculers, of the orthodox Christian views on prefiguration. The Deists especially attacked the absurdities of pagan theodicies, and demonstrated how preposterous it was that the Universal Author could have allowed such a nasty bunch of charlatans to prefigure a

[22] *The Eighteenth Century Confronts the Gods*, pp. 58-59; pp. 57-64 make an excellent contribution to the subject.

religion so perfect as Christianity. Pagan typology was one aspect of the "old" explanation of paganism which suffered, although typological figuralism, as I have already shown, survived in a new guise.

Hence the Deists undertook to strip the mysteries from the foundations of the Christian religion: "Christianity not mysterious" was a byword in more ways than one for their inquiries. The supreme example from the 1670s was the influential Ralph Cudworth, whose massive confutation of pagan atheism, *The True Intellectual System of the Universe* (1678), set the tone of much inquiry for the next seventy-five years. Cudworth would have nothing whatsoever to do with the "old" school of mythology; he never cites its major practitioners except to point out their mistakes, and instead bases his study of pagan theology on a complete return to the original documents. His central theorem is that all the pagans were, in reality, covert Christians; nor does he carry out "an ex post facto conversion [of the ancient pagans] to Deist Christianity."[23] He does contend, however, that pre-Christian paganism was *"Polyonymous"* and *"That the Supreme God amongst the Pagans, was . . . worshipped under several Personal Names*, according to several *Notions* and *Considerations* of him . . . ."[24] The pagan gods, it then follows, could not be types of Christ and Christianity, for they were derived from the natural attributes of things rather than from distortions of Old Testament names. It might seem that a writer like Cudworth would defeat figuralism entirely, but such is not the case; indeed, without intending to do so, he provided one of the fields of study which eighteenth-century mythographers would find most fruitful of typology.

Cudworth was not content to show that all pre-Christian pagans were, in the basic qualities of their theodicies, monotheistic; he went further and argued that the religious systems of the ancient Egyptians, Persians, and Greeks were trinitarian as well. True, the trinity of divine attributes or essences acknowledged by the ancient Platonists was hypostatic rather than personal, but the persons of the Christian Trinity also represented essences. Cudworth never has to tell us that Christianity is an antitype of earlier mystery religions, but he suggests as much when he shows that it is a fulfillment of imperfect notions of God glimpsed centuries earlier.[25] Influenced

<hr>

[23] *Ibid.*, p. 60.
[24] *The True Intellectual System of the Universe*, p. 477.
[25] *Ibid.*, pp. 546-51, 612, 631-32.

by Cudworth's methodology, many eighteenth-century mythographers undertook full-scale investigations of the theodicies of different pagan sects in quest of religious structures which might in some way be seen as embryonic forms of Christianity. Unlike Cudworth, they would often refer to them in specifically typological terms. But the closest Cudworth comes to such a position is in his "Preface," where he promises to prove

> That the *Pagan Theologers* all along, acknowledged *One Sovereign* and *Omnipotent Deity*, from which all their other *Gods* were *Generated* or *Created*; we have thereby not onely Removed the forementioned *Objection* out of the way [i.e., that the pagans were polytheists]; but also Evinced, That the Generality of mankind, have constantly had a certain *Prolepsis* or *Anticipation* in their Minds, concerning the *Actual Existence* of a *God*, according to the *True Idea* of him.[26]

The *"True Idea"* of God is, of course, the trinitarian monotheism of Christianity. For Cudworth to suggest that "the Generality of mankind" have always had an anticipation of this idea creates, in effect, pagan shadows and prefigurations of the later-to-be-fulfilled truth of Christianity. Although Cudworth does not bother to say so, the structural basis of this argument is practically identical with that which Renaissance commentators had employed to show how the shadowy religious beliefs and ceremonies of the Old Testament prefigured the accomplishment of all the hints and anticipations in the New.[27] Hence Cudworth, and with him some of the Deists that followed him, while almost never mentioning typology, which represented the "old" style of syncretic mythology they rejected, did not entirely abandon its central structural concepts.

The English Deists were not the only group of writers who were critical of typology. Throughout the seventeenth century, and with

---

[26] *Ibid.*, "The Preface to the Reader," Sig. **1ᵛ-**2ʳ. There are a few full-length studies of Cudworth, but Frances Yates, *Giordano Bruno and the Hermetic Tradition* (London: Routledge & Kegan Paul, 1964), pp. 427-31, discusses some of Cudworth's influence on studies of Egyptian mysticism.

[27] There are numerous examples. Andrew Willett, *Hexapla in Genesim* (1605), 3rd ed. (London, 1632), pp. 143, 197-98, 199-212; *Hexapla in Exodum* (London, 1633), pp. 132, 172, 484, 493, 563, 707-708; and Thomas Taylor, *Moses and Aaron, or the Types and Shadows of the Saviour in the Old Testament opened and explained* (London, 1653), p. 22, show how the Old Testament figures and ceremonies are merely partial ideas and representations of the New Testament fulfillments.

increasing harshness as the crescendo of Puritan protest mounted, Anglican theologians had objected to the inventiveness of much applied typology in its pure, exegetical sense. Moderate typological interpretations, those which did not stretch the sense of Scripture beyond probability, continued to be acceptable, and poets, of whom Dryden is perhaps the most fruitful example in the last half of the century, made much use of typology in certain kinds of contexts. Dryden found typology well accommodated to his celebrations of human merit, particularly to panegyrics of men of state. His early Restoration poems of praise, *Astræa Redux* (1660), *To His Sacred Maiesty* (1661), and *To My Lord Chancellor* (1662), all employ scriptural typology in the applied sense, and one of them, *To His Sacred Maiesty*, not only opens with a typological passage, but has a typological structure as well.[28] And we will find Dryden using typology in many other contexts, from the political (*Absalom and Achitophel*) to the religious (*The Hind and the Panther*) to fables in translation ("The Character of a Good Parson").[29] Given the facility with which Dryden employed typological imagery, then, in which he is very much the equal of such splendid practitioners of the methodology as Donne, Henry Vaughan, and Milton, it is surprising to note how rarely he introduces pagan typology, that which was derived from seventeenth-century ideas of myth, into his writings.

The Stuarts were often favored with analogies drawn from mythology; Dryden, in his long and unpindaric odic farewell to his patron Charles II, *Threnodia Augustalis* (1685), chooses to make his typology pagan as well as Christian. The sudden death of Charles, he tells us, was like a West Indian hurricane, an unexpected burst from a calm sea,

> As if great *Atlas* from his Height
> Shou'd sink beneath his heavenly Weight,
> And, with a mighty Flaw, the flaming Wall
>   (As once it shall)

[28] I have discussed these poems in *From Concord to Dissent*, pp. 113-15.

[29] There has been much discussion of Dryden's typology in these contexts, especially in Zwicker, *Dryden's Political Poetry, passim* and Miner, *The Restoration Mode*, pp. 325-29, 331-35. Zwicker's recent essay, "Politics and Panyegyric: The Figural Mode from Marvell to Pope," in *Literary Uses of Typology*, pp. 115-46, focuses mainly on Dryden's earlier poetry, and has unfortunately little to say about the interesting figuralism of his last decade, the 1690s, when Dryden's Jacobitism is an important influence.

Shou'd gape immense and rushing down, o'erwhelm
    this neather Ball;
So swift and so surprizing was our Fear:
Out *Atlas* fell indeed; But *Hercules* was near.[30]

The passage is subtle, combining three types, two classical and one
Christian. Atlas, the pagan Titan whose fall prefigures an apocalyptic dissolution, reminds Dryden's audience that the sovereign's
death may be a type of the Millennium. Hercules, the standard
pagan type of Christ, here represents the military leader the Duke
of York, now James II. Charles's death foreshadows not an episode
in the life of Christ but the unknown future as typed out by the
Book of Revelation. Indeed, Atlas is one of the few pagan types
that Dryden could have presented to achieve such a figural goal.
The Hercules figure for the new king suggests the similarity of the
pagan worthy to Jesus in taking on mighty tasks and great sufferings for the benefit of his people. Dryden liked to treat of James
II in terms of the sovereign's presumed humility: at one point in
The Hind and the Panther (1687), he types out James as "A Plain
good Man, whose Name is understood" (III.906)—James as the
perfect husbandman, yet with a hint of the pagan warrior. *Threnodia Augustalis*, as its title suggests, is rich in Roman imagery, and
its typology is more inventive than most examples of its kind. Late
in the poem, Dryden plainly calls the late Charles "That all forgiving King, / The type of him above" (257-58) and, recalling
Charles's exile, adds, "his ungrateful Country sent / Their best
Camillus into banishment" (266-67). Typological references to historical figures from the classical past are not uncommon, especially
to Alexander, Caesar, and Augustus, but I know of no parallel reference to the military leader Camillus.[31] Before the end of the
poem, Dryden manages to compare Charles once to Moses (425-28)
and again to Hercules (as *"Alcides,"* 447; cf. 446-64); again, the
pagan type is far more elaborate and inventive than the traditional
theological type, which is perfunctory.

Despite his consummate ability to manipulate pagan types, I
would observe that Dryden is nevertheless careful not to overdo it.
He mixes mythological allusions with Christian and Hebrew types

[30] *Threnodia Augustalis*, lines 39-45. For an amplification of this typological
reading, see *The Works of John Dryden*, III, 305.

[31] On Camillus, see the *Oxford Classical Dictionary*, s.v. "Camillus (1)," pp.
198-99. Livy, *Ab Urbe Condita*, 5.49.7, describes the military leader Camillus as
"parens patriae conditorque alter urbis."

and with unexpected parallels, several of them figural, from Roman history. Seldom indeed does Dryden use pagan typology after 1685. One of the very few instances occurs in *An Ode, on the Death of Mr. Henry Purcell* (1696), where he compares Purcell, "The God-like Man," with the christic and salvific Orpheus:

> We beg not Hell, our *Orpheus* to restore,
>   Had he been there,
>   Their Sovereigns fear
>   Had sent Him back before.
> The pow'r of Harmony too well they know,
> He long o'er this had Tun'd their jarring Sphere,
>   And left no Hell below.[32]

Not twenty years earlier, Cudworth helped to deflate the typological qualities of the orphic mysteries by assuring his readers that "there never was any such man as *Orpheus*, but only in *Fairy-land*, and that the whole *History* of *Orpheus*, was nothing but a mere *Romantick Allegory*, utterly devoid of all Truth and Reality."[33] The Orphic theology, he concludes, was not a pagan faith after all; its worshipers believed in a hypostatic trinity similar to that of Christianity. So Dryden's using the story of Orpheus' harmonizing of Hades as a pagan type for Christ's harrowing of Hell is an elegant tribute, but it scarcely betokens strong commitment to pagan mythology for typological purposes.

In 1696, Dryden had just four years to live but, in sheer volume, more than half of his poetic output was still to come, in his translation of the works of Virgil (1697) and the *Fables* (1700). He uses the typology of classical myth sparingly, if at all, in these last years, although he had many opportunities to do so. The figure of Alexander in *Alexander's Feast* can be interpreted typologically, but such a reading is not central to the purpose of the poem. Dryden's version of Virgil's *Fourth Eclogue* which, later, in the hands of Pope, becomes a distinctly typological poem, takes no advantage of the occasion to draw parallels; they had, after all, been made for hundreds of years, often to excess, and Dryden's *Virgil* does not much attempt to sharpen contemporary theological and political axes.[34] Aeneas' tour of the underworld, with his father's shade as cicerone,

---

32 *Ode*, lines 16-32. See also my *From Concord to Dissent*, pp. 197-98, and p. 198, note 40.

33 *The True Intellectual System of the Universe*, p. 294; cf. pp. 294-306.

34 On mystical readings of Virgil, see Allen, *Mysteriously Meant*, pp. 135-62.

presents another grand opportunity for classical myth to merge with typology, for the episode had been seen by some Renaissance exegetes as a sort of Pisgah-vision.[35] Here, according to some interpretations, Aeneas is the type and the Roman worthies, down to Marcellus and the doomed son of Augustus, are his antitypes, but Dryden makes nothing of these exciting possibilities. Ready at hand was a recent seventeenth-century Pisgah-sight, the one occupying much of *Paradise Lost*, Books XI and XII, which Milton transforms into an important piece of typological narrative, but it would be wrong to imagine any parallels between Milton and Dryden in this respect.

In his translations for the *Fables*, it is noteworthy that Dryden ignored the books of the *Metamorphoses* dealing with such matters as the creation of the world and the genealogy of the gods, where pagan types might readily have been introduced. The typological passages we find in the *Fables*, in "To the Dutchess of Ormond," "To John Driden, of Chesterton," and in "The Character of a Good Parson," are very good indeed, but they are examples of biblical typology in applied literary contexts. It would be fair to say that pagan types had been closely associated with praise of the Stuart kings and that for Dryden to have used them more than he does in the 1690s would have laid him open to the charge of Jacobitism.[36] After the turn of the century, the figures of pagan myth are seldom used as types in the "old" style, in the manner of the Renaissance mythologers, except for purposes of parody and satire. The anonymous *The Golden Age* (1702), to take a deservedly obscure example, is an imitation of Dryden's translation of Virgil's *Fourth Eclogue*, with the original (Dryden's translation) and the "imitation" printed on facing pages. The poem, mercifully brief, begins with the pagan type of Saturn and suggests that the Golden Age has returned again with the succession of Anne, but the bulk of the poem is a satire upon those corrupt features of the preceding iron age that may yet remain.[37] It is difficult to fit Anne into the pre-

[35] See *Virgil's Æneis*, in *The Poems of John Dryden*, ed. James Kinsley, 4 vols. (Oxford: Clarendon Press, 1958), III, 1227-32 (VI.1021-1226).

[36] George Watson, "Dryden and the Jacobites," *TLS*, 16 March 1973, pp. 301-302, is the most recent person to examine this aspect of Dryden, but in insufficient detail; more study is clearly needed. Steven Zwicker's still unpublished study of the 100 plates to Dryden's translation of Virgil, which I have not yet seen, will enrich our knowledge of his Jacobite phase and, I hope, of his typological methods.

[37] *Poems on Affairs of State: Augustan Satirical Verse, 1660-1714*, ed. George DeF. Lord et al., 7 vols. (New Haven: Yale Univ. Press, 1963-75), VI, 449-65.

dictive structure of Virgil's eclogue; if we are to see Anne as a type of a messianic king, presumably, in the Virgilian framework, then the antitype would be none other than the Pretender. Pagan typology had seen better days.

 3

The last years of the seventeenth century and the first decade or so of the eighteenth are often regarded by historians of ideas as a turning point in regard to attitudes toward pagan mythology. Allen sees the period as one characterized by "The Rationalization of Myth and End of Allegory"; Feldman and Richardson see the forty years starting with 1680 as the beginning of modern mythology.[38] As early as 1633, in his "Elegy upon the Death of Doctor Donne," Thomas Carew praises Donne for banishing the "train / Of gods and goddesses" from his own and the poetry of his age, but foresees that his followers will exalt the "old idols" once more. Carew gently exaggerates, of course, since the period of Donne's greatest poetic activity, 1590-1610, marks a high point of classical allusion in English poetry, and Carew's "Elegy" is itself rich in references to pagan literature and deities. There is little doubt that the prevailing tendency in the available evidence is toward employing myth for ornamental rather than allegorical or moral purposes. Addison, for example, in *Spectator* No. 523, ridicules modern poetry that attempts to praise greatness in terms borrowed from classical mythology:

> At . . . times when I have searched for the Actions of a Great Man, who gave a Subject to the Writer, I have been entertained with the Exploits of a River-God, or have been forced to attend a Fury in her mischievous Progress, from one end of the Poem to the other. When we are at School it is necessary for us to be acquainted with the System of Pagan Mythology, and may be allowed to enliven a Theme, or point an Epigram with an Heathen God; but when we would write a manly Panegyrick, that should carry in it all the Colours of Truth, nothing can be more ridiculous than to have Recourse to our *Jupiters* and *Junos*.[39]

[38] See Allen, *Mysteriously Meant*, pp. 279-311; Feldman and Richardson, *The Rise of Modern Mythology*, pp. xix-xxvii.
[39] *The Spectator*, IV, 361-64 (30 October 1712).

Pope, in "An Essay on the Life, Writings, and Learning of Homer," prefaced to his translation of the *Iliad* (1715), regarded Homer's pagan theology as a serious matter for the ancient world, and as embodying "true Sentiments for Profit [and] Allegories for Pleasure"; he does not Christianize Homeric mythology, and justifies the use of myth as consistent with "the *Marvellous.*"[40]

However, we ought not to conclude that, as the allegorical qualities of classical mythology lost ground in the minds of English and Continental poets and men and women of letters, the typological possibilities of myth were abandoned lock, stock, and barrel. For, as I have shown in Chapter 4, typology survived into the Enlightenment along with the other major figural traditions of the seventeenth century, although its form and purpose were much changed. Dryden, as I noted above, does not seem to exploit the potential for typology in his translation of Virgil which earlier commentators on the *Aeneid* had found so attractive. But Dryden had read the exegetes, and he was entirely aware of the search for hidden Christian meanings in the classical literature of Greece and Rome. As he observes in "The Dedication of the Æneis," "*Augustus* is still shadow'd in the Person of Æneas, of which I shall say more, when I come to the Manners which the Poet gives his Hero," clearly a statement sensitive to the predictive aspects of the poem. A moment later, Dryden explains that Virgil's problem was to create a perfect prince and to insinuate that Augustus, masquerading as Aeneas, was such. He could not accomplish this goal too openly, for the flattery would be obvious; instead, Virgil makes Aeneas exemplary for his piety: "Knowing that Piety alone comprehends the whole Duty of Man towards the Gods, towards his Country, and towards his Relations, he judg'd, that this ought to be his first Character, whom we would set for a Pattern of Perfection."[41] To present a living monarch as a pattern of perfection was a Renaissance and seventeenth-century commonplace which, from the time of Elizabeth, had both prefigurative and postfigurative implications; poets and other writers gave the technique new wings after the "martyrdom" of Charles I. Thus, while Dryden cannot endorse figures from pagan myth or history as types in the Christian sense, he is aware of the predictive structure in Virgil's literary relating of Aeneas and

[40] *The Iliad*, trans. Pope, in *The Poems of Alexander Pope*, 11 vols. (London: Methuen & Co., 1939-69), VII, 70. Pope, like Erich Auerbach, sees Homer and the Old Testament as similar in "pure and noble simplicity" (VII, 18).

[41] *Poems*, III, 1016, 1018, 1020.

Augustus. The ancient myths might lose their value as moral and allegorical precursors of Christianity, but they begin to obtain new value as evidence of typological structures in other systems of thought than the Judeo-Christian. As we have seen, even as the first seventeenth-century skepticism about pagan mythology began, writers as distinguished as Bacon, in *De Sapientia Veterum*, Cudworth, and Sir Isaac Newton stressed the instructive value of myth.[42] The stories it had to tell might be improbable, if not actually offensive, but the structures of myth often gave examples that were applicable, in various ways, to the concerns of the Enlightenment.

The rise of the comparative study of religion is closely associated with, if not synonymous to, the early Enlightenment analysis of myth. This study was pursued with much vigor on the Continent by scholars such as Pierre-Daniel Huet, Louis Thomassin, and Joachim Bouvet.[43] The polymathic Kircher was their guide, for his volumes on Egyptian and Chinese hieroglyphics (the Chinese character-writing was thought to be hieroglyphical, and the Chinese to have derived their learning from Egypt) appeared to be filled with evidence of correspondences between pagan religions and Christianity. I shall not pursue the study of comparative religion here since, in this respect, it has been superbly documented by Frank Manuel and D. P. Walker, but I shall refer to hieroglyphics later in this chapter.[44] The early students of comparative religion broadened the familiar mythological spectrum to include the myths of ancient Egypt, Persia, India, and China, establishing patterns of inquiry that would remain unchanged until the first third of the nineteenth century and that may still be glimpsed today in post-Frazerian mythological studies and in the relatively new discipline of comparative folklore.[45] Although these writers saw themselves

[42] The Cambridge Platonists, including Henry More and Cudworth, were avid searchers after the instructive purposes of myth. On Bacon, see Paoli Rossi, *Francesco Bacone* (Bari, 1957), pp. 206-10; and on Newton see P. M. Rattansi, "Newton and the 'Pipes of Pan,'" *Notes and Records of the Royal Society of London*, 21 (1966), 126-27.

[43] D. P. Walker, *The Ancient Theology: Studies in Christian Platonism from the Fifteenth to the Eighteenth Century* (Ithaca, N.Y.: Cornell Univ. Press, 1972), pp. 214-28, discusses the fascinating complexities of seventeenth-century French comparative theology.

[44] Manuel, *The Eighteenth Century Confronts the Gods*, pp. 24-53, 57-70, and Walker, *The Ancient Theology*, pp. 194-230, are particularly relevant here.

[45] For helpful discussion of mythological studies after Frazer, Theodor H. Gaster, *Myth, Legend, and Custom in the Old Testament* (New York: Harper

as following in the polymathic tradition of Vossius and Kircher, we may quite properly regard them as employing structural methodologies. Their method is to seek cognate structures, or constellations of belief and ritual, in apparently dissimilar bodies of non-Christian theology.

Against this background, the search for similar structures, particularly those which, in the opinion of these new exegetes and their followers, appeared to prefigure (and therefore to confirm the validity of) the gospel miracles, narratives, and New Testament Christianity, could be carried out on a broad front. Let me consider for a moment the example of Richard Steele's *The Christian Hero* (1701), ostensibly a defense of Christianity over pagan morality. Steele's examples of pagan morality are the characters of Julius Caesar and Cato the Censor, both of whom he dismisses as defective because of their lack of genuine religious faith. By contrast, the examples of Jesus and the Apostle Paul stress that suffering, meekness, and devotion are the emblems of true greatness. Steele traces St. Paul's career through the Book of Acts with close attention, and focuses on the healing of the lame man at Lystra (Acts 14.8-18): "This Miracle alarm'd the whole City, who believ'd their Gods had descended in Human Shapes: *Barnabas* was immediately *Jove*, and *Paul* his *Mercury*: The Priest of *Jupiter* now is coming to sacrifice to 'em with Oxen and Garlands; but they ran into the Multitude; we are Men like you, are subject to the same Weakness, Infirmities, and Passions with your selves."[46] The significance of this brief episode, and of the entire history of St. Paul as given by Steele, is that it illustrates the rejection of paganism and pagan typology at the very historical point when the first mass conversions of the Gentiles were beginning.

Steele will go on to propose that the true heroism is the imitation of the life and works of Jesus, the Apostles, and the Martyrs: the

---

& Row, 1969), pp. xxv-xxx, xxxix, is illuminating. The *locus classicus* for this subject is Sir James G. Frazer, *Folklore in the Old Testament*, 3 vols. (London: Macmillan, 1918).

[46] *The Christian Hero*, ed. Rae Blanchard (London: Oxford Univ. Press, 1932), p. 54. Steele may be recalling Satan's second temptation of Christ in *Paradise Regained*, IV.195-284, where Milton has Satan tempt Christ with the learning of the Hellenistic world, especially that of Athens. But Satan's allusion to Socrates (IV.274) allows Milton to undermine the temptation without Satan's realizing his mistake, for Socrates was a type of Christian learning and—because of his death—of Christ's meekness in accepting suffering. See Lewalski, *Milton's Brief Epic*, pp. 241-49.

eighteenth-century Christian can, with a long glance at the *Imitatio Christi* and at the manuals of religious instruction and behavior of the 1680s and '90s, become a postfiguration of the Savior and, simultaneously, a prefiguration of his own later perfections in the afterlife.[47] Interestingly, Steele finds a strong, if imperfect, parallel in the writings of a pagan author, Seneca, whom he quotes from L'Estrange's translation of the *Morals*: "A good Man is not only the Friend of God, but the very Image, the Disciple, the Imitator of him, and the true Child of his Heav'nly Father" (p. 62). Seneca is right in every respect except in his unwillingness to sacrifice his comfort, even his life, to his beliefs (the Christian, or at least St. Paul, would have done so). We see Steele reject pagan mythology as spurious in his summary of Acts 14 but, in finding a partial parallel, imperfect yet suggestive, to the true Christian position in the writings of a pagan philosopher, we also may see how the search for typological structures could unearth useful metals in strange mines. If Steele's efforts have any validity, then we should be able to find similar efforts to uncover typological structures for modern (i.e., eighteenth-century) behavior in other pagan texts. I have dwelled on Steele because of the importance of *The Christian Hero* to later eighteenth-century narratives. Since the central constituents of narratives are plot and character, the influence of writers like Steele and others in the *imitatio Christi* tradition on the typology of narratives will have great significance, as I will show later (see Chapter 7).

The Christian Hero gives us highly condensed exemplars of both typological narratives (the stories of St. Paul and Jesus are ideally predictive of the Christian life) and typological characters. If characters from pagan mythology could be converted into pre-Christian examples of heroes and good men worthy of emulation, then the same could be done with greater ease to characters from Christian story. We will constantly find examples of this process in the writings of the most popular religious authors of the century. Isaac Watts, whose *Psalms of David* and *Hymns* easily make him one of the most popular single religious writers of eighteenth-century England, wrote a lengthy treatise entitled *Humility represented in the Character of St. Paul*, which stresses at some length that, as Christ was Paul's pattern, so christomimesis is the proper rule of life for

---

[47] On the reforming tradition of religious manuals, see *The Christian Hero*, ed. Blanchard, pp. ix-xi.

all Christians.[48] John Wesley thought that religion was "an *uniform following* of Christ, an entire inward and outward conformity to our master"; it is a view he expresses in many ways in more than a dozen works.[49] The typology of character gradually became a staple of Protestant writing, whether religious or secular; the method which Steele helped to popularize in England became even more popular, at about the same time, in America.[50] Thus when Johnson said, half a century later, "The christian and the heroe are inseparable," he was articulating a belief that was so widely accepted by those who read and wrote Christian narratives that the relationship between the two entities had ceased to be cryptic. When such relationships lose their mystery, they become harder to decipher for they are harder to perceive.

The beginning of this inseparability is difficult to spot exactly. The first confusing (or should I say, blending) of pagan and Christian heroism has been traced variously to Ficino, to Boccaccio's *Genealogie deorum gentilium*, or to the first commentators on Homer and Virgil, Eustathius and Servius. I do not have the space to run these sources down; nor if I did, would the resulting compendium tell us anything new. Let me start, for purposes of this chapter only, with the author to whom I have alluded often in earlier chapters, Samuel Bochart, the leading Protestant etymologer of the seventeenth century. Bochart's mythmaking seems incredible to us today—indeed, it seemed incredible to students of the subject two hundred years ago, too—but respectful references to his work dot the *glossa marginalia* of seventeenth- and early eighteenth-century volumes of sermons, exegesis, and mythography. In his *Geographia Sacra, seu Phaleg et Canaan* (1646), Bochart discovered the

---

[48] See Isaac Watts, *Works*, 6 vols. (London, 1753), II, 317-51, esp. pp. 349-51. Watts, it should be noted, elsewhere argued that the figural style of the Old Testament was no longer necessary: "I am fully satisfied, that more honour is done to our blessed Saviour, by speaking his name, his graces, and actions, in his own language, according to the brighter discoveries he hath now made, than by going back again to the *jewish* forms of ritual, and the language of types and figures." See "Preface" to *The Psalms of David Imitated in the Language of the New Testament* in *Works*, IV, xvi. Watts's assessment of the figural language of the New Testament is curiously neglectful of the highly figural gospel parables and the Book of Revelation.

[49] My reference here is to Wesley's *A Plain Account of Christian Perfection, as believed and taught by the Rev. Mr. John Wesley from the year 1725, to 1765*, 3rd ed. (Bristol, 1770), p. 4.

[50] See Bercovitch, *The Puritan Origins of the American Self*, pp. 34-35.

great similarity between the roots of the Hebrew names for the patriarchs and the names for the pagan gods in half a dozen ancient languages, in all of which he was proficient. Not everything that he suggested was new: in the sixteenth century, the similarity—we would almost say *structural* similarity—between Noah and Saturn had been noted. Bochart's great virtue was that his writings could render possible an even closer link between pagan deities and the Judeo-Christian histories and types than could be forged earlier, for he sought and found a bond in the very building blocks of narrative and history, words. The seventeenth-century fascination with Babel and its aftermath, and with the possibility of establishing a universal "character" or language, made Bochart's discovery especially welcome.[51] The ancient languages themselves had now been verified as a reliable guide to comparative religion: the heroes of pagan myth were tied neatly into the standard package of biblical exegesis. A few years later Huet, in his *Demonstratio Evangelica,* could show how all the pagan gods derived from Moses, and were, in fact, identical with Moses.[52] Thus just as Enlightenment skepticism about pagan myth was starting to develop, a process which would lead to the discrediting of pagan heroism by authors like Steele, hard-working exegetes were creating the basis for treating myth with new respect as a series of predictive structures for universal narrative.

Bochart's etymological game of parallels temporarily reduced typology to nothing more than an elaborate word game. The effect of this kind of analogizing may be seen in the writings of Protestant exegetes for the rest of the seventeenth century. No less a figure than Samuel Mather, in *The Figures or Types of the Old Testament* (1683), one of the most formidable typological handbooks ever compiled, probes deeply for verbal and linguistic parallels be-

[51] John Wilkins appropriately entitled his study of the subject *Essay towards a Real Character and a Philosophical Language* (1668), employing a word, "character," which simultaneously described the predictive qualities of writing, iconographical symbols, and actual persons. See Knowlson, *Universal Language Schemes,* pp. 15-27, 224-28, and Russell Fraser, *The Language of Adam: On the Limits and Systems of Discourse* (New York: Columbia Univ. Press, 1977), pp. 1-40, *passim* (this is an entire chapter, somewhat unstructured, called "The Legacy of Nimrod").

[52] See *Demonstratio Evangelica* (Paris, 1678), pp. 68-115. There were many later editions (but no English translation) of Huet's popular work. The etymological tradition was also popular in England, Germany, and Holland; see Manuel, *The Eighteenth Century Confronts the Gods,* pp. 110-17.

tween Old and New Testament to strengthen his doctrine of typology.[53] Thomas Taylor, Benjamin Keach, and much later, Patrick Fairbairn, in works of differing intentions, all show or comment on the marked influence of the etymologizing school of typology; in this way, they give credence to the association of the pagan gods and heroes with biblical figures on a linguistic basis alone.[54] If mythological figures, simply because they were presumed to be linguistically similar to Old Testament types, could become types themselves, then it would be only a question of time before someone would create a typological story or narrative involving such figures.

I am not trying to force the existing evidence to reflect inevitabilities that do not exist. We should remember that, while this process of terminological and name confusion is going on, the authors of character books and fables, as I have already suggested, are busy finding predictive qualities in their stories. At the same time, again in the later seventeenth century, the writers of long fictional romances, in both French and English, often stress salvific scenes and symbolic character names with clear prefigurative purposes. Those who, like Steele, defend the narrative and intellectual consistence of Scripture over pagan myth implicitly recognize that mythological stories are not without their virtues, so long as we agree that these virtues are, cumulatively, less than those of Christian history. An apologist like Anthony Blackwall, while praising the typological relationship between Old and New Testament, specifically sets forth to prove "the several advantages which the sacred Writers of the new Testament have over the foreign Classics [i.e., pagan myth and classical epic]." Yet Blackwall's defense of biblical typology, by the very fact that he thought it necessary to write it, suggests how seriously people regarded their classical myths as late as 1725.[55] That Blackwall could praise typology as he does in 1725, at the height of the debate over the validity of Scripture prophecy, may not add much excitement to the political aura of that contentious decade, but it does open a further path of inquiry into the subject

[53] *The Figures or Types of the Old Testament*, 2nd ed. (London, 1705), pp. 53, 66, 68, 71, 76, 86, 104, 109-10, etc.

[54] See Thomas Taylor, *Moses and Aaron*, pp. 1-21; Benjamin Keach, *Tropologia: A Key to Open Scripture Metaphors, in Four Books* (London, 1682), *passim*; and Fairbairn, *The Typology of Scripture*, I, 17-20.

[55] *The Sacred Classics Defended and Illustrated: or, An Essay humbly offer'd towards proving the Purity, Propriety, and true Eloquence of the Writers of the New Testament* (London, 1725), pp. 349-50; cf. Part II, chap. viii.

of typology and myth. This topic is the study of pagan myth and its predictive elements in the age of Enlightenment skepticism.

Pagan myth "old style," as we have seen, was mysteriously prefigurative of Christianity, with no questions asked and few reasons given. This happy relationship was entirely appropriate to the syntagmatic learning of the Renaissance and seventeenth century. The syntagma was a vast compilation, a *gazophylacium* (as it was sometimes called) or treasure-house of items of learning, like entries in a vast unarranged catalogue. Its compilers, whom Swift ridiculed in *A Tale of a Tub* as the creators not of literary works but rather as the cooks of ragouts and olios, loved similarities and parallels of all kinds. Among the many relationships which they encouraged, that between pagan myth and Christian typology is the one most interesting to me in this study, but it is only one of many. As the old method of drawing parallels slowly withered, the methods of typology lingered in some places, as in certain branches of Protestant biblical exegesis, and were gradually transformed elsewhere, as in character writing, fables, and romance. The new, scientific scholarship of philologers, antiquarians, lexicographers, and Christian apologists led, as we have seen, to the search for predictive and linguistic structures. The new quest for Christian origins was every bit as sincere as the old, but it employed new techniques and was less naive (some might even say less crass). Nobody would be so far-fetched as poor Alexander Ross (now much maligned), but for those bold enough to make the search, rich analogies would come to light.

Samuel Mather, writing of his doctrine of the personal types, codified the typological individuals in the Old Testament more thoroughly than any of his predecessors, but it would be more than a century before anyone would specifically describe these typical figures as predictive characters. Late in the eighteenth century, Sir William Jones uses terminology which we would now identify as semiological in discussing how the personal types of the Old Testament are *signs* specially endowed with meaning concealed from all but enlightened interpreters. Jones takes "the two Characters of *Jonah* and Solomon" (Luke 11.29-32) as character-signs predictive of Jesus' resurrection.[56] Jones's preeminent knowledge of Persian and Indian languages and mythology gives his comments on secret languages and predictive signs great significance, for decoding the secrets of Oriental myths became one of the leading intellectual games of the later eighteenth century. The first students of romance saw in its methods, particularly the weaving of plot and the use of symbolic characters, a close parallel to the creation of ancient myth. Myths, we should bear in mind, did not merely *happen*; they were deliberately *framed* in order to conceal from the general public subjects of vast importance. Thus Bishop Hurd tells us that Spenser did as much with *The Fairie Queene*:

> He gave an air of mystery to his subject, and pretended that his stories of knights and giants were but the cover to abundance of profound wisdom.
>
> In short, to keep off the eyes of the prophane from prying too nearly into his subject, he threw about it the mist of allegory: he moralized his song: and the virtues and vices lay hid under his warriours and enchanters. . . .
>
> And this, it must be owned, was a sober attempt in comparison of some projects that were made about the same time to serve the cause of the old, and now expiring Romances. For it is to be observed, that the idolizers of these romances did by them, what the votaries of Homer had done by him. As the times improved and would less bear his strange tales, they *moralized* what they could, and turn'd the rest into mysteries of *natural Science*. And as this last contrivance was principally designed to cover the monstrous stories of the *pagan Gods*, so it served the lovers of Romance to palliate the no less monstrous stories of *magic and enchantments*.[57]

The mysterious traditions that had grown up around Homer were well known to Hurd's audience, so it is hardly surprising that he finds Spenser employing allegory for a similar purpose. Clara Reeve,

[56] See *A Course of Lectures on the Figurative Language of the Holy Scriptures, and the Interpretations of it from the Scripture Itself* (London, 1787), pp. 37-39.

[57] *Letters on Chivalry and Romance* (London, 1762), pp. 114-15. It is noteworthy that the language Hurd uses to describe Spenser's mythmaking ("to keep off the eyes of the prophane from prying too nearly into his subject") is virtually identical with that which seventeenth-century mythographers used to describe the *raison d'être* for the Egyptian hieroglyphics.

a few decades later, while subscribing to euhemeristic doctrines, agreed that "the heathen Mythology," which had started as "the History of mortal men, and their actions," had been deliberately obscured as "the Veil of Allegory concealed and altered facts, till they could no longer be traced, and at last were lost in fable and obscurity."[58]

Hurd and Reeve are important because they suggest how widely dispersed were the notions that the ancient myths (originally, Greek and Roman; later all myths are included) involved some kind of encoding for purposes of concealment and that the central facts of these myths, could they only be uncovered, would be predictive of Christian history. We can find this attitude as early as Pierre Gaultruche's (Galtruchius) *The Poetical Histories* (1671) in Maurice D'Assigny's English translation. Galtruchius thought that ancient myths and fables were superstitious confusions, but his translator was not satisfied with this approach, and added to his version an entire treatise on Egyptian hieroglyphics, setting forth clearly the theory of deliberately encoded myths which, when deciphered, bear a powerfully prefigurative relationship to Christianity. Galtruchius' work is a handbook in the Renaissance tradition; it makes no attempt to create new myths as the authors of romance were supposed to be doing. Such creative works do exist, however, and one of the best of them falls into the period when the "new style" of interpreting mythology was at the height of its popularity.

The work I have in mind is Andrew Michael Ramsay's *The Travels of Cyrus*, originally written in French (1727), and popular at the time it appeared (seven editions in a dozen years).[59] Ramsay is more a philosopher than a novelist, but his novel is valuable to students of typology and myth because he was among the first people, if not the first person, to assimilate the ideas of the seventeenth-century English mythological tradition exemplified by Cudworth and by the French school of the same period, of which Huet and Thomassin are the best known practitioners.[60] Like D'Assigny in his translation of Galtruchius, Ramsay also adds a treatise on ancient "theology and mythology" (the two are now bracketed, a distinct advance over the later seventeenth century) where, among other topics, he lavishes much attention on hieroglyphics. The main por-

[58] *The Progress of Romance*, 2 vols. (London, 1785), I, 15.
[59] See *A Checklist of English Prose Fiction, 1700-1739*, comp. William H. Mc-Burney (Cambridge, Mass.: Harvard Univ. Press, 1960), pp. 77-78.
[60] See Walker, *The Ancient Theology*, pp. 231-40.

tion of *The Travels of Cyrus* is an impressive typological narrative. Ramsay presents his hero as a world traveler at the time of Nebuchadnezzar. Cyrus visits with important historical and biblical figures, accompanied by the Hebrew philosopher Eleazar who helps interpret the different religions of the ancient world. In the course of two chatty volumes of travel and talk, we get expositions of Zoroastrianism, Hermeticism and the religion of ancient Egypt, the Persian religion, Greek, Cretan, and Babylonian theology, and finally the Hebrew religion. Cyrus gradually realizes that all the religions of the ancient world are conformable to each other, and that they are equally prefigurative of the Jewish (and, as Ramsay knew his readers would realize, the Christian) religion. The prophet Daniel enters the story, and reminds Cyrus that Isaiah had prophesied of him *by name* at least one hundred and fifty years earlier.[61] Indeed, Isaiah's prophecy of Cyrus (Is. 44.28-45.1), "That saith of Cyrus, He is my shepherd, and shall perform all my pleasure," gives Cyrus a messianic title ("anointed"). It is unique in the Old Testament because Cyrus is the only gentile type of Christ.

The "Preface" to the fourth English edition, which may be by Ramsay or by his translator Hooke, stresses the prefigurative qualities of ancient religions, through their representations in myths, and argues that "The Author of Cyrus has only wrought into a *connected system* the most beautiful hints of antiquity, in order to unfold the great principles of religion, and shew that all nations had from the beginning some idea of those principles more or less confus'd."[62] The narrative of Cyrus' travels and education in ancient religion has one central theme, Ramsay's conception of "a middle God, who was to expiate and destroy moral evil by his own great sufferings" (I, viii). Later, at the end of the novel, Daniel assures Cyrus that "the ancient tradition of Noah concerning this grand sacrifice [i.e., of a Messiah, the great Immanuel] was what suggested to all nations the first thought of offering victims to THE MOST HIGH as types of that perfect holocaust."[63] The sentiment is a fa-

[61] See *The Travels of Cyrus*, 4th ed., 2 vols. (London, 1730), II, 214. This "much enlarged" edition is, in fact, much changed from Nathaniel Hooke's original translation (1727), but I have been unable to determine whether Ramsay collaborated with his translator in making his extensive revisions.

[62] *Ibid.*, I, viii-ix (italics added). Systematic schemes of learning are characteristic of early eighteenth-century scholarship; see Michel Foucault, *The Order of Things: An Archaeology of the Human Sciences* (New York: Pantheon Books, 1970), pp. 56-58.

[63] *The Travels of Cyrus*, II, 235.

miliar one; practitioners of "old style" mythology habitually adopt it, basing their position on the Bochartian view that pagan theologies, in the post-Babel confusion of tongues, have cognate or etymologically similar names for their gods, all of which derive from the Old Testament patriarchs. But Ramsay's position is not language-related; it is derived from the "new style" mythological notion that the "tradition" of Noah had become a legend common to all ancient folklores. In the school of comparative religion, Ramsay's Cyrus functions both as exemplar and as teacher. Similar redemptive structures occur in all the religions in which Cyrus receives instruction; they are typological in other cultures, just as they are in the Judeo-Christian tradition.

The accompanying "Discourse upon the Theology and Mythology of the Ancients," which fills the last half of the second volume, is an extended gloss upon *The Travels of Cyrus*. The novel includes a number of scenes in which Eleazer and Daniel prophesy to Cyrus on historical events which the eighteenth-century Christian reader would know had been completed; they are historical types with recognizable antitypes. The "Discourse" is scholarly, with scholia referring to the favorite pagan authors on myth, like Plato, Iamblichus, and Plutarch, and to the leading seventeenth-century polymaths, like Kircher, Vossius, and Cudworth. But the message is fundamentally the same: "that there are Traces of the principal Doctrines of *revealed religion* with regard to the *three States of Nature* to be found in the Mythology of all Nations."[64] Ramsay uses the Chinese, whose logographical script had fascinated the polyhistors of the previous century, as a summary example of his system:

> The *Chinese* books speak likewise of the Sufferings and Conflicts of *Kiuntsé*, just as the *Syrians* do the Death of *Adonis*, who was to rise again to make Men happy, and as the *Greeks* do of the Labours and painful Exploits of the Son of *Jupiter* who was to come down on Earth. It looks as if the Source of all these Allegories was only an antient Tradition common to all Nations, that the middle God, to whom they all give the Name of *Soter* or *Saviour*, was to put an End to Crimes by his great Sufferings. But I do not lay a Stress upon the Notion, my Design being only to speak of the Traces that appear in all Reli-

[64] *The Travels of Cyrus. . . . To which is annex'd A Discourse upon the Theology and Mythology of the Ancients*, 2 vols. (London, 1727), II, part ii, 2.

gions of a Nature *exalted, fallen,* and *to be repaired* again by a Divine Hero.

These Truths run equally through out the Mythologies of the *Greeks,* the *Egyptians,* the *Persians,* and *Indians,* and the *Chinese.*[65]

Cudworth, as I noted above, thought that the evidence of paganism would prove that "the Generality of mankind, have constantly had a certain *Prolepsis* or *Anticipation* in their Minds" concerning trinitarian monotheism and the central notions of Christianity, but, like the other scholars of his age, he studied pagan *mythology* as if it were a combination of errors. Ramsay, on the other hand, studies pagan *religion.* Cudworth suspects that there may be similar beliefs among all religions; Ramsay, like the other early students of comparative religion, is concerned only to find similar structures. For Ramsay, the universal tradition of belief in a savior or redemptive figure, which all nations but those in the Judeo-Christian orbit have obscured and altered by their fables, firmly establishes all of pagan myth as typological once again. The typology is of a different kind from what it had been in the Renaissance, but the meaning of "types" as the eighteenth-century students of myth use it has barely changed at all.

The fascination of the eighteenth century with fables of all kinds derives, in part, from the belief that these stories often carried down to the present important shadows of Christianity from the distant past. The heavily annotated, much glossed editions of Aesop I discussed in Chapter 5, the numerous collections of other, post-Aesopic fables, and the zeal with which scholars and other writers of the last two-thirds of the eighteenth century sought out and collected materials relating to the folklore of northern Europe, the Orient, and the Americas are all related more closely than we have hitherto realized to the typological interpretation of myths.[66] As Thomas Blackwell would realize before 1750, "*Mythology* in gen-

---

[65] *Ibid.,* II, part ii, 132-33.

[66] Study of the fable has not kept pace with that of other genres. The only recent work, Thomas Noel, *Theories of the Fable in the Eighteenth Century* (New York: Columbia Univ. Press, 1975), pp. 1-13, acknowledges the popularity of the genre, but is unfortunately confined to Aesopic fables only. I emphasize that eighteenth-century writers and audiences were not interested in fables only because they were of typological importance. As Noel and others point out, fables were also popular as allegorical comments on contemporary life, as children's stories, and, no doubt, as entertainment.

eral, is *Instruction conveyed in a Tale*. . . . But it is not strictly confined to *Narration*: Signs and Symbols are sometimes brought in play, and Instruction is conveyed by significant Ceremonies, and even by material Representations."[67] The terms "signs," "ceremonies," and "rites" are often used synonymously in writings on comparative religion at this time; they are almost always typological. Blackwell proceeds to state confidently that the study of mythology is now impossible without a full and accurate knowledge "of the *religious Rites* of the several Nations from whom the *Greeks* received their Gods; because upon some significant Ceremony concerning the Nature, or traditional Tale concerning the Exploits of the Divinity depends the Key to the Legend, and sometimes the very *Name* of the God himself."[68] Myth, then, has become an encoded fable with a typological key; ceremonies and rites convey vital information about religious belief through a symbolical language. The beginning of these mythological riddles is Egypt:

> As the early *Egyptian* Rites were established by law, were all recorded, were all typical, the Type or Symbol came by an easy Transition, not only to signify obscurely, but directly to express the Thing typified: a grand Source of Error and Incertainty in the Foundation of the Allegory! But besides the original Type, any remarkable part of the divine Service, any mystical Mixture as in the Rites of *Ceres*, any striking Posture as in the Feasts of *Pan*, any uncouth Garb of the *Hierophant* or Priest, or any uncouth Quality ascribed to the *Numen*, was enough to fix an Epithet, and the Epithet to wear gradually into a Name.[69]

Typology, or a kind of prefigurative structure, plays a major role in the development of all myths, whether Egyptian or later. We have come some way from the "old style" mythographers' notion that the pagan gods were the worthies of the Old Testament masquerading under other names. Now we learn that the plain and simple types of primitive religions have been distorted and mystified; through a grand confusion of signs as epochal as the great vowel shift, the types became obscure and deciphering them was made necessary. Blackwell may seem an extreme example of an eighteenth-century unwillingness to abandon the language and methods of the previous century, but we may reasonably regard him

---

[67] *Letters concerning Mythology* (1748), 2nd ed. (London, 1757), p. 70.
[68] *Ibid.*, pp. 189-90.   [69] *Ibid.*, p. 190.

as a precursor of Sir James G. Frazer. Indeed, Blackwell goes a good deal further in *Letters concerning Mythology*, and makes some fairly revolutionary postulations on natural typology, or the prefigurative qualities of physical phenomena, but this is matter for a later section of this study. Nor is Blackwell alone in his search for the key to ancient legends, for a knowledge of the code with which ancient signs (and types) had been disguised. Indeed, the quest for this particular grail had already been underway for more than a century by students of hieroglyphics. Since the mysteries of the glyphs had long been associated with both ancient mythology and with typology, it will now be appropriate to examine the relationship between the two.

The link between typology and myth in the seventeenth century, as we have seen, emphasized how myths, through confusions in language and story, actually embodied pre-Christian types. By the middle of the eighteenth century, the scholars, poets, and novelists who dealt with myth had put that notion, which they regarded as mistaken, far behind them. Now myths were confusions of a once common tradition, but still prefigurative in the same way that types look forward to the future. The difference between the two schools is a matter of hermeneutics or of a theory of interpretation, and the unifying factor between the two attitudes toward myth is the new belief in prefigurative *signs*. Blackwell thought that myths were *"Instruction conveyed in a Tale,"* but he carefully added that the tale was sometimes presented in a language of signs. Here we have a reversion to classical typology of the early Christian era, when exegetes were fully conscious of the Greek meaning of types (literally *signs*). But we have ideas more significant at work here, too, for in the mid-seventeenth century the terminological confusion which helped feed the growth of abstracted typology had created a close association between the *structural* signs that embody typology as we know it and the *physical* signs that make up certain kinds of writing and languages.[70] Primitive methods of writing, especially hieroglyphics, attracted the attention of the learned as early as the sixteenth century. I shall not give the history of Europe's long flirta-

---

[70] On the terminological confusion, see above, Chapter 5, sections 2 and 7.

tion with early alphabets, secret scripts (steganography), ciphers (shorthand and tachygraphy), and idealized languages here; it would be very interesting, but much of the work has already been done elsewhere.[71] The popularity of all of these topics in the seventeenth and eighteenth centuries was considerable, and the association of these sign systems with typology is an ever-present fact.

Types, as I mentioned earlier, are semantic enclaves of a kind. The seventeenth-century students of language and writing systems, schooled as they were in theology and its system of codes, frequently associated typological codes with language codes. While the Egyptian hieroglyphic was not the only language code known and studied in the seventeenth century, it was the one most often associated with a religious sign language or, to use other terms, with a deliberate effort on the part of a priesthood to encrypt the secrets of religious belief in a special code.[72] Hieroglyphics embodied the religious secrets of the ancient Egyptians, encoded to preserve them from corruption at the hands of an impure laity. They must have been concealed, reasoned such adept decoders as Henry More and Cudworth, because these religious beliefs, prefigurative as they must have been of monotheistic Christianity, would have been unwelcome in an increasingly idolatrous country. Hence to decode them would be to discover the typological qualities inherent in ancient Egyptian mythology which everyone knew were there all along anyway. So the decipherers reasoned. Had not Moses, who had more to do with the encoding of Old Testament types than anyone else, been educated by the Egyptian sages in their wisdom? Were not many of the most common hieroglyphic pictographs

71 I would emphasize that this study has not been exhaustively undertaken by a single scholar. On early alphabets, see Derrida, *On Grammatology*, pp. 74-81; on steganography, see Athanasius Kircher, *Polygraphia Nova et Universalis et Combinatoria Arte Detecta* (Rome, 1663); on tachygraphy, see Thomas Shelton, *Tachygraphy* (London, 1641), and *The Diary of Samuel Pepys*, ed. R. C. Latham and W. Matthews, 9 vols. (Berkeley and Los Angeles: Univ. of California Press, 1970-76), I, xlvii-liv; and on idealized languages see Bishop Wilkins, *An Essay Towards a Real Character and a Philosophical Language* (London, 1668). See also Barbara Shapiro, *John Wilkins, 1614-1672: An Intellectual Biography* (Berkeley and Los Angeles: Univ. of California Press, 1969), pp. 207-23, and Knowlson, *Universal Language Schemes*, pp. 9-26.

72 Madeleine V. David, *Le débat sur les écritures et l'hiéroglyphe au XVIIᵉ et XVIIIᵉ siècles, et l'application de la notion de déchiffrement aux écritures mortes* (Paris: S.E.V.P.E.N., 1965), Chaps. 1 and 2 (esp. pp. 34-40), shows that the prevalent attitude toward hieroglyphics in the seventeenth century was that they were cryptographic. A satiric view of hieroglyphics is also possible; see Figure 11.

representations of natural phenomena? Was it not already clear, thanks to the speculations of Jakob Boehme, that the very signatures of things were abundantly prefigurative of numerous aspects of Christianity? Did not this more-than-accidental similarity demonstrate that the Egyptian magi knew all about Christianity, and used this simple code to prefigure its glorious achievements to the *adepti*? He had; they were; it was; and it did.

The blending of the two systems—structural signs and physical signs—becomes more intricate still. Symbolical writing, whether hieroglyphic or logographic in the Chinese way, was usually described as a "character"; the word sometimes appears in the titles of the learned works that discuss these codes. *Character*, in its original sense, meant an impression or an engraving, and so would be appropriate to describe writing. But it also had the wide meaning in the seventeenth and eighteenth centuries of a certain specialized genre of writing (which I discussed earlier), itself often strongly prefigurative, at least to contemporary minds. The association of the two meanings of *character* (the first a method of writing in script or picture, the second an iconic image of a brand of human behavior) is anything but fortuitous. A pictographic character was a compressed image or the signature of a person or thing; a prose character was also a compressed image of a certain kind of person, a behavioral signature. Both Thomas Vaughan, in his *Magia Adamica* (1650), and Jakob Boehme, in more than a dozen mystical works, argued that the world was filled with mystically prefigurative signs.[73] Henry More, in *Conjectura Cabbalistica*, found numerous correspondences between man and the world, man and the heavens, and argued "Thus did Divine Providence by natural *Hieroglyphicks* read short Physick-Lectures to the rude Wit of Man."[74] Boehme's intentions would be much augmented in the lavishly illustrated edition of his collected works published in the eighteenth century, a work whose elaborate fold-out (and, in some copies) hand-colored plates brought out many prefigurative associations between nature and man that the master himself never intended; I have already mentioned the influence of this edition on William Blake.[75]

[73] See Dieckmann, *Hieroglyphics*, pp. 77-84.

[74] *Conjectura Cabbalistica, or a Conjectural Essay of Interpreting the Mind of Moses* (1653) (London, 1713), p. 57.

[75] The full reference is *The Works of Jacob Behmen, The Teutonic Theosopher*, 4 vols. (London, 1764-81). The term "signature of things," used by hieroglyphologists in the mid-seventeenth century, derives from Boehme's work

We have already seen how Alexander Ross responded to the hieroglyphic tradition in his graphic depictions of the pagan gods. About the same time, many other writers made similar associations that were even more specific in their Christian sensibility. Jeremy Taylor, for example, in urging the imitation of Christ on his readers, noted that "the life of JESUS is not described to be like a picture in a Chamber of Pleasure, onely for beauty and entertainment of the eye, but like the Egyptian Hyeroglyphicks, whose every feature is a precept, and the Images converse with men by sense, and signification of excellent discourses."[76] Such christomimetic qualities of hieroglyphics are commonly stressed. D'Assigny, who augmented his English translation of Galtruchius' *The Poetical Histories* with "A Short Collection of the Famous Mysteries of the Egyptians, named Hieroglyphicks," tried to show that the Christian prefigurative qualities of hieroglyphics paralleled those of the pagan myths. "But the *Egyptian Priests*," he wrote, taking a popular line,

> unto whom it did belong to teach, did not suffer their Doctrines without a shaddow, or some dark Emblem. Their manner was to discover unto their Auditors the Mysteries of God, and of Nature in *Hieroglyphicks*, which were certain visible shapes and forms of Creatures, whose inclinations and dispositions did lead to knowledge of the Truths, intended for Instruction. All their Divinity, their Philosophy, and their greatest secrets, were comprehended in these ingenious characters, for fear that they should be prophaned by the inquisition and acquaintance of the Common People. . . . The Great Creator of all things hath been pleased to discover unto us in this manner [i.e., by concealed signs] his Divine pleasure, and all the excellencies of his Being. In the Old Testament the Mysteries of the Gospel were delivered to the Children of *Israel* in Types and Figures. And in the great Book of Nature God teacheth us by Mysterious Impressions of himself by Natural Hieroglyphicks, by certain significant Images of his Glorious Being.[77]

De Signatura Rerum, translated into English as *Signatura Rerum* (London, 1657).

[76] *The Great Exemplar of Sanctity and Holy Life . . . described in The History of the Life and Death of . . . Jesus Christ* (London, 1649), Part i, 10.

[77] Galtruchius, *The Poetical Histories . . . unto which are added Two Treatises, One of the Curiosities of Old Rome . . . the other containing the most remarkable Hieroglyphicks of ÆGYPT*, By Marius D'Assigny, 2 vols. (London, 1671), II, 154, 165 (quoted above, in part, in Chapter 4; cf. Chapter 4, note 19).

D'Assigny's conflation of hieroglyphics and types is not new; it echoes other terminological amalgamations of the earlier seventeenth century. This tendency to use different terms to express similar prefigurative conceptions, as I pointed out in Chapter 5, multiplies the opportunities for abstracted typology. Moreover, in the context of mythology, natural typology assigns predictive importance to phenomena analogous to the prefigurative qualities which generations of exegetes had assigned to figures in non-Christian mythology. The seventeenth-century mythographers were united in believing that some, if not all, myths, were meant to embody recognizable qualities of natural phenomena. A popular reason for the evolution of hieroglyphics was, and for a long time would continue to be, that the pictographic characters originally had represented elements in external nature which, over the centuries, became the objects of idolatrous worship. Thus D'Assigny's statement has the force of confirming the presence of prefigurative myths (or types) within the vehicle of the hieroglyphic. The natural hieroglyphic will develop gradually, over more than a century, into one of the major bases of Romantic typology; the *imitatio Christi* tradition and devotional theology will both play a large part in its evolution. I shall examine the first of these influences in more detail in Chapter 7. As for books of devotion, especially those which instructed the contemporary Christian in the duties of a Christian life and in the crises that one encounters in the Christian pilgrimage, we can find evidence of the prefigurative qualities of natural phenomena from the time of Bunyan forward. A popular manual on how to deal with the fears of death, to take a good instance of natural typology, helps confirm the existence of an afterlife by enumerating nine separate natural signs that foreshadow resurrection. These include the rising of the sun, the waxing of the moon, the arrival of spring, trees breaking into leaf, seeds sprouting, the rebirth of birds like the phoenix from their ashes, the rebirth of insects from the ground, and the awakening of beasts from hibernation.[78]

The bridge between hieroglyphics, whether natural or Egyptian, and the predictive uses of myth had been hinted at throughout the later seventeenth century. It remained for Ramsay and Warburton to complete its construction. Ramsay's Cyrus does not merely hear

---

[78] Charles Drelincourt, *The Christian's Defence against the Fears of Death*, trans. M. D'Assigny, 4th ed. (London, 1701), pp. 432-34; see, in general, pp. 422-65 for numerous other natural types.

of ancient religions in his *Travels*; he receives ocular proof of many pagan ceremonies as well. During Cyrus' stay in Egypt the high priest explains to him the ceremonies of Egyptian worship, including the inevitable hieroglyphics which represent the Egyptian trinity (Osiris, Isis, and Horus), itself a type of the Christian Trinity.[79] Ramsay lifts his notions of hieroglyphics and myth directly from Cudworth, although somewhat more concisely than in the fifty folio pages Cudworth devotes to the subject.[80] Cudworth simply acknowledges that the Egyptian hieroglyphics, in one way or another, represent virtually every one of their many deities. Since he goes to great lengths to show how the Egyptian gods are identical with those of Greece and Rome, all of them inevitably become mythological types. *The Travels of Cyrus*, then, reaffirms the association between hieroglyphics and myth which the Neoplatonists (Cudworth and More) and the polymaths (Vossius and Kircher) had first discovered between 1640 and 1680.

The major eighteenth-century English writer on hieroglyphics, Warburton, differs from the seventeenth-century school in that he cannot accept a mystic origin for sign languages. In *The Divine Legation of Moses Demonstrated* (1738-41), as I noted in Chapter 5, he had argued that typology, one of his important sign languages, must have evolved naturally, as a result of the very nature of language, cultivation of speech, and symbolic action. Hieroglyphics, which for Warburton form a chapter in the evolution of writing, or grammatology, must have come about in a similar way. In this respect, Warburton would have agreed with Vico, who was aware that hieroglyphics or similar totemic symbols existed in many cultures around the world.[81] Both Warburton and Vico also are in agreement that hieroglyphics were not an invention of the Egyptian priests and philosophers to conceal their esoteric wisdom from vulgar minds. Warburton's description of the rise of hieroglyphics par-

[79] *The Travels of Cyrus*, 4th ed. (London, 1730), I, 138-42. Cf. Walker, *The Ancient Theology*, pp. 246-47.

[80] *The True Intellectual System of the Universe*, pp. 308-55. Ramsay doubtless drew as well on Kircher's *Obeliscus Pamphilus* (Rome, 1650) and *Oedipus Ægyptiacus*, 3 vols. (Rome, 1652-54), two great treasure troves of what then passed for hieroglyphical exegesis and deciphering.

[81] See *The New Science of Giambattista Vico*, 3rd ed. (1744), ed. Thomas G. Bergin and Max H. Fisch (Ithaca, N.Y.: Cornell Univ. Press, 1968), pp. 140-43 (¶¶432-36). Vico incidentally thought that family codes or totemic symbols led to the development of coats of arms; in this context, I should note that heraldry is a form of iconology that often uses visual representations of types.

allels his study of the rise of typology. In primitive times, the first speakers were forced to supply the deficiencies of speech (i.e., entities for which there was as yet no vocabulary) "by apt and significant *Signs*."[82] Early metaphors, Warburton found, were often forms of hieroglyphics used prefiguratively; the symbolic language of Old Testament prophecy would yield many examples of old hieroglyphics which the prophets introduced for typological reasons. In this context, he writes: "To instance only in the famous Prediction of *Balaam: There shall come a* STAR *out of* Jacob, *and a Sceptre shall rise out of* Israel [Numb. 24.17]. This Prophecy may possibly in Sense relate to *David*, but, without doubt, it belongs principally to *Christ.*" Here, Warburton noted, the Hebrew culture recalled Egyptian hieroglyphics, in which a star denoted God.[83]

Since hieroglyphics corresponded to types in their development, in the same way the rise of fables and myths relates to the spread of symbolic signs. The fable, Warburton thought, was a highly specialized kind of symbolic speech. The fables of the Egyptians had been expressed in a naturally evolved code of glyphs or pictographs. Analogously, the myths of antiquity (with their numerous typological properties) were also an elaborate code, beyond hieroglyphics, but still distantly recalling this visually symbolic speech. The myth or fable was nothing more than "a kind of Speech which corresponds in all Respects, to writing by *Hieroglyphics*, each being the symbol of something else understood."[84] Warburton's reasoning is clever but tortuous. Ultimately, his purpose is to demonstrate that the wisdom of the ancient Egyptians, as transferred from Egypt to Hebrew (and hence, prefiguratively, to Christian) culture and religion through the agency of Moses, is one of the bases of the Christian religion. Warburton is a serious Christian apologist, so his discussion of hieroglyphics and myth is subordinate to his more workmanlike goals. He never suggests, as Ramsay does, that symbolic languages, hieroglyphics, and types might have any narrative pos-

---

[82] *The Divine Legation of Moses Demonstrated*, II, 82-83. The long section of Book IV (II, 66-206), entitled "The high antiquity of *Egypt* proved from their *Hieroglyphics*," was translated into French as *Essai sur les hiéroglyphiques des Egyptiens* (Paris, 1744); its influence in France was far more profound than in England. See Derrida, *Of Grammatology*, p. 332. Condillac, in his *Essai sur l'origine des connoissances humaines*, 2 vols. (Amsterdam, 1746), II, 178-82, quotes Warburton approvingly and, in general, subscribes to the bishop's theory of hieroglyphic origins.

[83] *The Divine Legation of Moses*, II, 148-49.

[84] *Ibid.*, II, 91-92; cf. II, 87-94.

sibilities. But his most important contribution, for purposes of this study, is his insistence that the predictive fables of antiquity arose naturally from a language of signs, at first hieroglyphic, later more broadly symbolic. The study of typology and myth has many peculiar configurations, of which the hieroglyphical is among the most curious. Yet the language of signs has a role to play in typological narrative, and we will hear more of it later.

During the eighteenth-century debates on myth, a trend toward simplicity and naturalness gradually emerges. Myths, the new euhemerists assured their audience, were not the corruptions the mythographers of the previous century thought them; they had evolved naturally, in the process of linguistic development and through the growth of civilized peoples. The external representations of myths, whether iconic (hieroglyphics, other pictographic writings, ancient art) or legendary (the actual stories of the generation of the gods and their exploits), paralleled languages and societies. The cultivation of speech and the elaboration of civil order created complications in figuralism and the texts which contained it, but now, it would have seemed, all was plain. Surely if authors so diverse in temperament as Vico and Warburton could agree on such a complex subject we might expect that the matter could be settled. Vico's contribution cannot be conveniently summarized here; instead I shall allude to other studies which do him more justice than I can and focus instead on what his perceptions do for the relationship between typology and myth.[85] Vico's comments on myth are not concentrated in one portion of his *Scienza nuova*; they are scattered widely through the work which, indeed, refers to aspects of ancient mythology on almost every page. The single fact in the physical history of the world on which Vico's theory of myth depends is "that the universal deluge covered the whole earth."[86] This event, dimly recalled in the history of every nation, led to the

[85] See Feldman and Richardson, *The Rise of Modern Mythology*, pp. 50-55; Manuel, *The Eighteenth Century Confronts the Gods*, pp. 149-67 (a flowery, vivid discussion); and David Bidney, "Vico's New Science of Myth," in *Giambattista Vico: An International Symposium*, ed. Giorgio Tagliacozzo (Baltimore: Johns Hopkins Univ. Press, 1969), pp. 259-78.

[86] *The New Science of Giambattista Vico*, p. 72 (¶194).

first fables of the distant past; these fables embodied the first heroes and heroines, who were necessarily titans. Vico had a zest for comparative religion: he noted carefully that every gentile nation had its Jove and its Hercules, fabulous histories about them, and pantheons of other immortals and demi-immortals surrounding them. Hence the first theologies, starting in ancient Egypt, were historical accounts interspersed with fables, "to which later generations, growing ashamed of them, gradually attached mystical interpretations."[87] The myths which we know today, together with all symbolical representations relating to them, developed slowly, and their origins are always capable of being discerned by systematic study. More than anything else, the *Scienza nuova* is a study of the development of societies and here, too, Vico shows that mythologies made an important contribution to the process of socialization. With great ingenuity, he derives ancient institutions such as law, marriage, education, and household discipline from vestiges of the mythic past.

His entire Book II, "Poetic Wisdom," consists of Baconian apothegms that illustrate conclusively how civil societies, their customs, and their arts coalesced gradually from the age of fable and the myths which sprang from the fabulous past. Indeed, the four-hundred-odd paragraphs in this book contain literally hundreds of examples, many more than I can adequately discuss in this short account. All is tremendously systematic and logical; there are few echoes of the inchoate methodology of the seventeenth-century mythographers in Vico's sober, well-reasoned analyses. Vico never mentions typology *per se*; the pagan myths for him lead not to their antitypes in Christianity, but rather to a more sophisticated modern world. His favorite mythological figure is surely Hercules, who appears in a number of contexts. However, while the mythographers of the previous century regarded Hercules as one of the leading pagan types of Christ, Vico treats him as the original of later myths, not as a prefiguration of the Redemption. Indeed, Jesus plays very little role in Vico's system; the leading events of Christian drama interest him not at all. Bayle would have been delighted with the secularism of the third edition of *Scienza nuova* (1744). Only in his love for etymology does Vico weaken, and admit a brief glimmer from Bochart's dark lantern into his clearly illuminated universe. He concludes Book II with modest eloquence:

[87] *Ibid.*, pp. 72-76 (¶¶ 193-223).

We have shown that poetic wisdom justly deserves two great and sovereign tributes. The one, clearly and constantly accorded to it, is that of having founded gentile mankind. . . . The other, concerning which a vulgar tradition has come down to us, is that the wisdom of the ancients made its wise men, by a single inspiration, equally great as philosophers, lawmakers, captains, historians, orators, and poets, on which account it has been so greatly sought after. But in fact it made or rather sketched them such as we have found them in the fables. For in these, as in embryos or matrices, we have discovered the outlines of all esoteric wisdom. And it may be said that in the fables the nations have in a rough way and in the language of the human senses described the beginnings of this world of sciences, which the specialized studies of scholars have since clarified for us by reasoning and generalization.[88]

The central themes of the typology-myth relationship after the middle of the eighteenth century are new analogies and retained obscurities. Vico represents the first of these themes but not the second. He has banished obscurity and mysticism completely from the systematic study of myth (it is perhaps a shame that this banishment was not more permanent). But he has not done away with the tried and true method of drawing parallels. Vico's new analogies are wonderfully simple. The fables of antiquity, which are embodied in myths, provide the sketches, embryos, or matrices for all wisdom, which in Vico's work is the "world of the sciences." His language is not ostensibly predictive, yet to eighteenth-century readers it was in fact prefigurative. A three-hundred-year-old tradition of prefiguration had made familiar the notion that types, or sketchy, shadowy representations, held forth or prefigured their full-fledged, complete antitypes. The movement was always from shadowy types to truth, from the sketch to the completed painting, from the vague sign of an idea to the completed system of ideas. So the paradox of Vico's logical and unmystical account of the perfecting of human science is that his method of describing this evolution employed the terminology of traditional figuralism.

Vico was not alone in contributing new analogies to the study of myth. An impressive series of savants, including Joseph Butler, Warburton, David Hartley, Jacob Bryant, George Stanley Faber, and others too numerous to mention, inspired by the logical preci-

[88] *Ibid.*, p. 297 (¶779).

sion with which scientific study could dismantle the mysteries of the universe, would find that the materials of fable or myth, whatever their origins, had prefigurative qualities. In the seventeenth century, no student of myth could fail to notice how closely a pagan god such as Saturn typed out Christ and the Christian situation. The deistic analogists of the next century were figuralists, too, but their typology was less theological in its suggestions; their analogies would usually lead to a more abstracted typology. Bishop Butler, for example, deals very little with typology in the strict theological sense, but he does note that a number of historical facts supply evidence for the genuineness of Christianity. Prophecies, he finds, can often be demonstrated from civil history. "Now there are two Kinds of writing," he tells us, "which bear a great Resemblance to Prophecy, with respect to the matter before us; the Mythological, and the Satyrical where the Satyr is, to a certain Degree, concealed."[89] Butler, I should add before I go any further, is a subtle writer, by far the cleverest of the eighteenth-century analogists (the title of his work suggests as much, and he is the only writer to mention analogy so prominently). If a satire, Butler decides, refers to a fable or parable without any prefigurative connection to anything else, *the mere fact that its author cites this allusion is sufficient proof that he intended a prefigurative connection to be made.* Unfortunately, Butler supplies no examples of this unique method of analogizing. And why should he? No doubt he thought that to mention the most far-reaching use of analogy yet devised was *ipso facto* proof of its existence. His interpretation of prophetical writings is equally inventive:

If a long Series of Prophecy, is applicable, to the present State of the Church, and to the political Situations of the Kingdoms of the World, some thousand Years after these Prophecies were delivered, and a long Series of Prophecy delivered before the Coming of Christ, to him; these things are in themselves a Proof, that the prophetick History was intended of Him, and of those Events. . . . yet it is to be remembered further, that the ancient Jews applied the Prophecies to a Messiah before his Coming, in much the same Manner as Christians do now: And that the primitive Christians interpreted the Prophecies respecting the State of the Church and of the World in the last

[89] *The Analogy of Religion, Natural and Revealed, to the Constitution and Course of Nature* (London, 1736), p. 251.

Ages, in the Sense, which the Event seems to confirm and verify.[90]

The reasoning is plain enough: prophetical writings have been in use for thousands of years; we have abundant evidence that early prophecies about the present state of Christianity were accurate types, since we may see about us living evidence of their antitypes; therefore writings that are substantially like prophecy, such as myths, also have sound prefigurative qualities. Butler, like the other apologists of his generation, was reluctant to dismiss the materials of pagan mythology as utterly worthless. These writings, after all, were just too "good" to be valueless; why not turn them to the great designs of Christian apologetics? True, Butler does not actually say that pagan myths are typological. No eighteenth-century analogist, especially if he also happened to be a bishop of the established church, would venture to say as much. Instead, he implies that mythological writings, as a genre, operate in the same way as, or, in twentieth-century terms, are structurally similar to, the accepted typological prophecies of the Old Testament.

From Butler forward, we will notice a new element in the treatment of typology and myth. It is the new, logical application of analogy, based, as Butler's title tells us, on the "constitution and course of nature" or, in somewhat different terms, on the design of all created things, whether they be natural phenomena or products of the human sciences. Butler's follower David Hartley, who strongly affirmed the veracity of typology through the "argument from design," continually asks, "How could these types *not* be true?"[91] Just try, says Hartley, to apply the typological passages from Scripture and the typological events and persons from myth and history to some person other than Christ. "If design be excluded, these ought to be equally, or nearly so, applicable to other persons and events; which yet, I think, no serious considerate person can affirm. Now, if chance be once excluded, and the necessity

[90] *Ibid.*, p. 252.

[91] A systematic study of the "argument from design" has yet to be made. For ancillary comment, see Martin C. Battestin, *The Providence of Wit: Aspects of Form in Augustan Literature and the Arts* (Oxford: Clarendon Press, 1974), pp. 143-47. The "argument from design" is in part derived, as Battestin observes, from physico-theology, but the theological tradition of Butler and Hartley reveals an important application of it. In this context, see Robert H. Hurlbutt 3d, *Hume, Newton, and the Design Argument* (Lincoln, Neb.: Univ. of Nebraska Press, 1965), pp. 43-64.

of having recourse to design admitted, we shall be instantly compelled to acknowledge a contrivance greater than human, from the long distances of time intervening between the prophecy and the event."[92] Hartley argues persuasively for the existence of natural typology, which for him becomes a method for proving the truth of Christianity because of the prefigurative qualities of natural phenomena (see above, Chapter 5). Like Butler and, for that matter, like many seventeenth- and eighteenth-century readers of the Book of Revelation, Hartley includes secular history in his typological schema. Just as pre-Christian, Jewish history prefigured New Testament events, so certain prophetical books, particularly Daniel and Revelation, have had recognizable antitypes in postbiblical secular history. Indeed, Hartley concedes, with a touch of millenarianism, some of the antitypes are still to come. He believes that ancient myths are a distortion of actual secular history (a familiar view, held by Warburton, Blackwell, and Bryant) and that, as such, they may also be involved with the predictive structures of ancient prophecy. But myth is not Hartley's major focus. Instead, he sees the ancient fables, somewhat in the manner of Vico, as a corruption of the secular histories of different peoples. He does pause to study Jewish history in considerable detail and, after a lengthy examination, concludes, "The whole history and institutions of the *Jewish* people, when interpreted by Christianity, are types and prophecies of a future state."[93] If the secular history of the Jews can be viewed typologically, just because it happens to be the subject of the Old Testament, then what bar was there to viewing the secular history of the pre-Christian gentiles in the same way? Cudworth and Ramsay's *Travels of Cyrus* had started just such a trend and, in the hands of Jacob Bryant, master mythographer and typologist extraordinary, there would be no limits to the scope of the inquiry.

Bryant's reputation in his own time was considerable. He wrote about difficult passages in Scripture, on the testimonies of the ancient historians, and on antiquarian topics in general. He was anything but a popular writer, yet his *A New System, or, an Analysis of Ancient Mythology* (3 vols., 1774-76) appeared three times in his own lifetime and had wide appeal in condensed, handbook form. Much of Bryant's effectiveness derives from his very secularity. He does not argue for the truth of Scripture by pointing to revelation

---

[92] *Observations on Man, His Frame, His Duty, and His Expectations*, 3 vols. (London, 1791), II, 158-59.
[93] *Ibid.*, II, 394.

or by arguing for commonsense interpretations of biblical prophecy. Quite the reverse: he presents his audience with evidence (or what passed for evidence) drawn from throughout the ancient world, from many ancient religions, and in a number of languages to support plausible inferences about the Old and New Testaments. He was, if I may distort terminology for a moment, a scientific euhemerist, and his studies have a just claim to be ranked among the first efforts at comparative religion. Bryant's "evidence" does not stand up to twentieth-century scrutiny, but it convinced a wide spectrum of readers in the later eighteenth century. He did not rely only on interpretations of ancient texts or his considerable facility in the Oriental languages; *A New System* is laden with pictorial evidence, too, in the form of tables, inscriptions, and elaborate engravings, all the standard *apparatus criticus* of eighteenth-century antiquarian studies. *A New System* falls into the class of works that were so expensive to produce that they could be published only by subscription or with the support of a wealthy patron. Bryant enjoyed the second of these props in the form of the lifelong patronage of the Duke and Duchess of Marlborough. And, in James Basire's engraving shop, where the plates for *A New System* were prepared, there was a young apprentice named William Blake, who assisted in the work and who is now believed to have engraved at least one of the plates himself. Blake, as we know from his own works and other sources, read Bryant's *magnum opus* (although he never mentions the smaller studies), and always refers to him with approbation. We know that Coleridge read and annotated *A New System* and that Shelley used it, along with many other books on myth, when he studied the background for *Prometheus Unbound*. Bryant was influential, then, and at his best, he can be very cogent.

His often fantastic philology and excitement over hieroglyphics show that he had derived some of his enthusiasm from Bochart and Kircher, but he had also read Warburton, Vico, and Hartley, from whom he derived a certain degree of skepticism. Bryant sees all pagan mythology as a series of permutations of ancient "hieroglyphics," but, following Warburton, he subscribes to the grammatological theory of their evolution—they are an early form of writing later invested with a mysterious aura.[94] Like Vico, he thought that the recollection of a universal deluge dwelled deep in the collective memory of every gentile nation and, with this notion as the cornerstone of his inquiries, he searched the surviving materials of pagan

---

[94] See *A New System*, II, 528-30.

myth and secular history for evidence that might prefigure Christianity. Such evidence, of course, would have to be in the form of signs which only a polymath learned in many ancient cultures could decipher, but Bryant was equal to the task. His *Observations and Inquiries relating to various parts of Ancient History* (1767), a study of selected problems in various ancient cultures chosen because of their special similarity to Christian practices, finds many similarities between mystical offerings in pagan rites and Judeo-Christian ceremonies. Bryant sees such curiosities not as historical accidents (he would never admit that he had preselected only a few examples from thousands of years of recorded history) but as abstracted types. "What they did," he says of the Phoenicians' ritual sacrifice of their king's only son, "was *a type, and representation of something to come.*"[95] Inspired by this success, Bryant combs pagan history for other accounts of human sacrifice and, happily, finds that most of them are prefigurative of the Messiah. After all, he reasons, recalling the argument from design, such an aggregate of circumstances could hardly be the result of chance.

This argument is a strain that runs through all of Bryant's works. The similarities between pagan myth and ritual and Judeo-Christian typology are too numerous and widely scattered to be mere accidents. Therefore they must of necessity be signs of the future, prefigurations of later events. Bryant's range is wide, from the pre-Christian mysteries to the history of early antiquity, and always he looks for recognizable types and antitypes. Josephus, for example, whose account of Jesus some had suspected to be a later forgery, was in fact an accurate historian, an historical witness, as Bryant thought, to the accomplishment of the types that had foreshadowed Jesus' mission and the founding of his Church.[96] Bryant always treats the Old Testament types as absolute historical facts, although he acknowledges (with a nod at Bishop Lowth's great study of Hebrew poetry) that the strongly figural mode of Jewish prophecy and poetry renders some of the types obscure. Yet the search for hidden truths can have no limits: had not Aristotle written that "the rudest block of marble contains a latent sculpture"?[97] When an antiquarian is motivated by such generous principles, we should not

[95] *Observations and Inquiries relating to various parts of Ancient History*, p. 291 (italics in original). See also pp. 267-85.

[96] *Vindiciae Flavianae: or, A Vindication of the Testimony given by Josephus concerning our Saviour Jesus Christ* (London, 1777), p. 12.

[97] See *A Treatise upon the Authenticity of the Scriptures and the Truth of the Christian Religion* ([Cambridge,] 1791), p. 90; cf. pp. 43-61, 146-49.

wonder that he makes intriguing discoveries or that he uncovers splendid new analogies. Yet, like Butler, Hartley, and other Christian apologists, he finds the excesses of deism unacceptable. In *A Treatise upon the Authenticity of the Scriptures* (1791), Bryant quotes Pope's "Universal Prayer," the hymn of deism, disapprovingly:

> Father of All! in every Age,
> In every Clime ador'd,
> By Saint, by Savage, and by Sage
> Jehovah, Jove, and Lord!

He correctly sees the poem as a deistical version of the Lord's Prayer, and criticizes Pope's view, "that *all* rites, however base, and *all* idolatry, however gross and shocking, related ultimately to the worship of the one true God."[98] The key words here are "all" and its repetition. Bryant's analogizing, at last, has its limits: *some* pagan rites relate to Christianity, shadow it forth, but not by any means *all*. Thus restrained, the master typologist would continue, in a variety of works, to seek figural analogies in pagan myths and secular history which prefigure his favorite subjects. Since my principal interest in this chapter is the relationship between typology and myth, I do not list his analogies, however interesting they may be, unless they shed light on his typological methods. Late in his fruitful career, Bryant makes a helpful remark about one of his inquiries which illuminates his typological method in a way which even *A New System* fails to do. Toward the end of a discussion of the typology of Jonah, he observes that Jonah's ordeal "in the body of the Cetus" for three days

> was made a type, and in a manner a test, of Christ's being three days and three nights in the bosom of the earth; [we should] reflect upon the dignity of the personage, who made the declaration [as Jesus himself does, Matt. 12.40]. Our Saviour would never have founded truth upon a fable, nor applied for evidence to a Galilean novel; for, if the history is not true, but a devised tale, it must be esteemed little better.[99]

If a type receives the approval of the New Testament or some other

---

[98] *Ibid.*, p. 11 (italics added).

[99] *Observations upon Some Passages in Scripture, which the Enemies to Religion have thought most obnoxious, and attended with difficulties not to be surmounted* (London, 1803), p. 249.

unquestioned authority, then the literary source in which it is contained must be true. Bryant's analogizing worked two ways, from type to antitype, and also from antitype to type. Hence some of his typologizing of myth is accomplished in reverse; Bryant works from a Christian source to find a pagan prefiguration. The freedom with which the late eighteenth-century academic mythographers treated their subject would provide many fruitful analogies for the mythmakers of English Romanticism.

The last of the English mythographers to uncover new typological parallels in the religion of the gentiles is Faber. Others would follow in the footsteps of Bryant and Sir William Jones, content to accept their learned commentaries without expanding them, but Faber, a voluminous author, obscure clergyman, and ardent Christian apologist, whose numerous studies of the ancient gods were popular in the nineteenth century, deserves special attention. His masterwork, *The Origin of Pagan Idolatry*, seems at first to be arranged like a vast seventeenth-century syntagma, an interminable collection of separate treatises but, to the curious twentieth-century reader, it is something more. Faber does have a coherent arrangement and a cohesive argument, which he states concisely at the end of his third volume: "Thus an insidious attempt of antichristian unbelief is shown to be completely nugatory: and thus, *in every particular*, the old theology of the gentiles is found to bear witness to the truth of Divine Revelation."[100] The essence of Faber is simple enough: the ancient pagans, in their ignorance of the world around them, delighted to veil the simplest truths in the language of mysterious allegory to make the religions based on them more venerable. Adam and Noah, after the confusion of tongues which is Nimrod's legacy, became the prototypes of the pagan gods. Since Adam, Noah, and virtually all prediluvian biblical figures are types of Christ, all pagan mythology is typological. Faber directs special obloquy at Babel, for he sees it as responsible for the linguistic confusion which is the type of all pagan mythologies. It is the task of mythographers to interpret the hidden codes which lie at the heart of all myths; thus, for Faber, typology becomes very much a secret language, with its own signs, images, and visual symbols. From Faber's innocent beliefs come the association of typology with iconography, hieroglyphics, freemasonry (Faber's *Origin* was popu-

---

[100] *The Origin of Pagan Idolatry ascertained from historical testimony and circumstantial evidence*, 3 vols. (London, 1816), III, 661 (italics added).

lar with nineteenth-century Masons) and, in our own century, the study of all bodies of arcane symbolism. The writings of the prolific Arthur Edward Waite, which deal with Boehme, Paracelsus, hermeticism, neoplatonism, magic, freemasonry, and other aspects of unaffiliated mysticism, owe most of their perceptions of the pagan-Christian nexus to Faber, and Waite is just one of a number of twentieth-century mystics who keep the old analogies warm.

Bryant had been willing to concede that *some* pagan sacrifices were types of the Crucifixion and Resurrection. But for Faber *all* pagan sacrifices "ought to be deemed . . . *typical* of the sacrifice of Christ."[101] In the same way, all pagan rites and mysteries have a common source and prefigure their Christian parallels. Cognizant of the literary interests of his age, he allows his attention to wander to romance and, in an unusual chapter entitled "On the Origination of Romance from old mythologic Idolatry," Faber tries to collect together scattered notions on secular, ecclesiastical, and magical romance.[102] He does not have a key to all romances similar to his key to all mythologies, but he acknowledges that selected kinds of legends are clearly typological. For example, stories dealing with a hero who is exposed in an ark or some other sacred or mystical vessel derive from the Moses story and may be decoded as typological. Romances dealing with a sacred lake, presided over by a fairy or female divinity, must derive from gentile recollections of the deluge, and they, too, may be read in prefigurative terms. Faber's concern with narrative genres is important, since it antedates by a century and a half the critical concerns of a number of recent scholars. His work, enthusiastic and overzealous though it may be in its apologetics, is important for my study for another reason: Faber's holistic view of ancient mythology, which subsumes all pagan idolatries to one purpose, acquires such coherence that portions of *The Origin of Pagan Idolatry* become a typological narrative.[103] Just as Faber found the very nature of language to generate figuralism and, thus, to lead to the introduction of typology, he seems to have found the essence of typological myths to generate predictive and prefigurative forms of literature.

[101] *Ibid.*, I, 488; cf. I, 488-96.
[102] *Ibid.*, III, 314-55.
[103] See especially the final chapter (III, 630-61), "Respecting the Mode in which Pagan Idolatry originated. . . ."

7

It is appropriate to end this chapter with a discussion of Faber, for there has been no student of typology and myth who has come quite so close as he did to the concerns of literary scholarship today, which are literary texts themselves. All earlier mythographers had been concerned with the events which constitute any number of fabulous stories, but not with the actual texts containing those stories. Students of myth prior to the nineteenth century are theologians and Christian apologists; literary criticism is ancillary to their concerns. Occasionally one of the scholars whom I have been discussing will mention a literary genre (Butler, Warburton, Bryant, and Faber all do so) but, with the possible exception of Faber, they have illustrative ends in mind and they are not primarily literary critics. Scholars had not yet learned to see fables, myths, and legends in terms of genre, motif, and literary structure. However, as I noted in Chapter 2, there is abundant evidence that, by the seventeenth century, English writers had come to regard prophecy—especially apocalyptic prophecy—as a self-contained genre. Typology was an important element in the strategy of prophetic writings and, consequently, the eighteenth-century mythologers often did deal with the structural qualities of myth without actually announcing that they were doing so. During the century and a half covered by this chapter, as I have suggested, English and Continental students of myth and literature engaged in a long-term debate on the nature of pagan myth and its relationship to both Christian and secular history. Attitudes toward myth change radically. During the same period, theologians debated the relevance of prophecy and typology to bodies of Christian belief and, again, there are radical changes. One constant which emerges from both debates is the endurance of typology—an insistence upon predictive structures, whether they are found in fabulous stories or in natural phenomena, is widespread.

The vast majority of the writers on whom I have focused in this chapter see myth in typological terms because they are interested in strengthening the intertexture between paganism and Christianity. If we take a backward glance over the century, we can see that the fervor of Christian apologetics rises rather than falls. It is hardly surprising that scholars should seize upon myth to help prove the truth of Christian religion. The evidentiary techniques of empirical science, the skepticism of deism, and the open ridicule of freethinking combined, over a long period, to lower the esteem in which established religion was held. The eighteenth-century physico-theologians, analogists, and supporters of universal design set out to restore the dignity of established religion from its detractors, and the inquiries of the mythographers are consistent with this defense. From the Boyle Lecturers at the end of the seventeenth century to the apologists of the early nineteenth century, there is a new concern with origins.[104] The very term becomes a kind of structural entity, as poets and mythographers alike concern themselves with myths of creation and preexistence. As we shall see, biblical epics will compete unequally with the mythological genius of Blake and Shelley, and stories with mythic structures will become popular with contemporary audiences. The mythographers are always concerned with the relationship of pagan story to the Bible itself, for the historical accuracy of biblical narrative was still widely accepted and many students of myth obviously believe that such realistic qualities as they can adduce in it will help further to corroborate the truth of scriptural narratives.[105] Much of the analogizing that goes on as part of this noble inquiry is sheer imposture but, if I may formulate some of the positive qualities of the mythological study of this period, the quest for typological parallels leads to some good ends for the student of literature.

First, the study of myth, however bizarre its conclusions and relationships, nourishes an interest in literary realism. Students of biblical narrative often point out that the New Testament does not scruple to tell even the most unflattering stories about Jesus and his disciples, including most notably the disciples' doubting and betrayal of their master. If the narrative were anything but true, would not its authors have suppressed such episodes? Inspired by the verisimilitude of the Bible, the mythographers looked for elements in pagan mythology which could be supported by external evidence. From Cudworth to Faber, there is a gradual growth in the theory of natural typology. Predictive structures exist as part of the nature of created things; primitive fables embody these structures; the signs or symbols of such entities inhere naturally in the narra-

104 On the Boyle Lectures, see Margaret C. Jacob, *The Newtonians and the English Revolution, 1689-1720* (Ithaca, N.Y.: Cornell Univ. Press, 1976), pp. 162-200, 273-74.

105 See Frei, *The Eclipse of Biblical Narrative*, pp. 152-54 and, in general, pp. 142-54. See also my review of Frei in *ECS*, 11 (1977-78), 274-80.

tives formed from them. Despite a century of skepticism, men of letters and religion once more accept the heritage of paganism and proceed to transmit it.

Second, and last, the typological qualities of myth as perceived by the scholars who discovered and the divines who helped propagate them relate closely to that most popular of eighteenth-century literary genres, prose fiction. If mythic structures were analogous to certain biblical circumstances, then both myths and the Bible could bear witness to numerous qualities within the eighteenth-century novel. We have seen that typological characters abound in the literature of our period, but the typology of narrative and, in particular, of the novel itself is a larger subject. I have just sketched the history of the relationship of typology to myth in the period from 1650 to 1820; inadequate though any such survey can be to the complexity of the topic, it is but a foundation for the study of typology and the novel.

CHAPTER 7

Typology and the Novel

F ROM EARLIEST times, typology has been important to writers
and interpreters of narrative. The first exegetes introduced
typology, both for interpretative purposes and to stress the
consistency between two bodies of narrative, the Old and New Testaments. As the exegetes of the pre-Nicene era came to appreciate
the prefigurative and structural possibilities of the device which
they had developed, they began to introduce typological structures
and relationships into narratives of their own. Exegetical typology,
as Daniélou observes, reveals analogies which unify both Testaments, "bestowing as it were the signature of God on his work, and
guaranteeing the authenticity of Scripture."[1] Hence the introduction of typological patterns into nonbiblical narratives, fashioned
by the Fathers for various theological purposes, would tend to corroborate their accuracy and cogency. St. Irenaeus, in his *Adversus
Haereses*, a work which would be popular with seventeenth-century
anti-Puritan polemicists, not only stresses the typology of Scripture
in his defense of primitive Christianity; he sees himself and his
book as postfigurations of the apostolic mission and as prefigurative
of the ultimate triumph of the Church. Eusebius, in his *Preparitio
Evangelica* and *Demonstratio Evangelica*, fuses the typology of
Scripture with the essence of his own works, representing them as
antitypes of what had been foreseen in biblical prophecy, that is,
the foundation and prosperity of the Church of the Gentiles.[2] A
sense of historical typology pervades another kind of narrative,

[1] *From Shadows to Reality*, p. 30; on Irenaeus as a typologist, see esp. pp.
30-47.

[2] See *The Proof of the Gospel, being the Demonstratio Evangelica of Eusebius
of Cæsarea*, trans. W. J. Farrar, 2 vols. (London: SPCK, 1920), II, 235-36.

Eusebius' *Historia Ecclesiastica*, where the author considers the present accomplishments of the Church as having been foreshadowed by the types of the New Testament. Just as the priesthood of the Old Testament prefigured that of Jesus, so Christ's life and the establishment of his Church prefigure the Christianity of Eusebius' time, A.D. 324.[3] Eusebius also has the habit of concluding each book of his history with a recapitulation showing just how much of each given type of the Church had been accomplished by the current stage of his narrative.

The imposition of a predictive structure, whether borrowed from the Bible or from exegetical traditions, upon any narrative, or the incorporation of prefigurative details into a narrative work, becomes a common quality of postpatristic literature and continues through the Middle Ages and Renaissance. As I have already noted, the exegetes of pre-Christian pagan literature were quick to discover (or to imagine they had discovered) typology in classical antiquity, starting with Homer. But Christian authors from Augustine to Dante suffused their longer works with predictive imagery. Often such imagery was specifically typological, as in Augustine's *Confessions* or the *Divine Comedy*. On other occasions it was merely implied, but the collecting of the typological commentary of almost a millennium into great syntagmata like the *Biblia Sacra cum Glossa Ordinaria* made even tacit types readily accessible to authors. By the time of Nicholas of Lyra, the figural or typological sense was a standard method of reading Scripture. The Bible itself, as the best known example of prose narrative for centuries of readers, is often explicitly typological, and certain books of the Bible, especially Genesis and Exodus, the prophets (with an emphasis on Daniel and Jonah), the four Gospels, and Revelation, were widely accepted as prefigurative narratives.[4] By the mid-seventeenth century, these biblical narratives had already started to lend themselves to certain kinds of stories. Bunyan, for example, whose narratives usually include much prefiguration and other Christian iconography, creates characters who embody biblical qualities and who wander through typological landscapes, performing acts

3 See *The Ecclesiastical Histories of Eusebius, Socrates, Sozomen, and Theodorit*, trans. and abr. Samuel Parker, 3rd ed. (London, 1729), pp. 47-48.

4 See Frei, *The Eclipse of Biblical Narrative*, pp. 24-37. Frei's Chapter 7, "Apologetics, Criticism and the Loss of Narrative Interpretation," pp. 124-54, is central to an understanding of eighteenth-century conceptions of biblical narrative.

which emblematize well-known typological episodes from both Testaments. Not only does Christian carry on a physical pilgrimage which is a recognizable imitation of that of the Jews in Exodus, but he also accomplishes a pilgrimage of faith analogizing those states of mind suggested in the New Testament. *The Pilgrim's Progress* and some of Bunyan's other narratives were published in a form which specifically recalls the theological sources of early typological narratives. Bunyan's works often include a typological gloss, a marginal guide to bring freshly to the reader's mind relevant biblical texts and cross references. The gloss survives in some eighteenth-century novels only in the brief "arguments" that sometimes appear at the heads of chapters; Bunyan's use of marginal comments, so far as I know, is unique among writers of fiction.

Allusions to biblical narrative are frequently almost universal in their application. For example, there is a specific reference to the typology of Jonah in *Robinson Crusoe*, but the Jonah emblem and type were so widely understood and identified that we may safely expect to find them behind almost every allusion to a shipwreck and the safe recovery from it. Biblical materials furnish a tremendous number of iconographical sources for the author of narrative; some of these allusions, inevitably, are typological, and authors who draw on these materials thus bring typology into their works. It would be reasonable to say that biblical narrative traditions underlie many typological allusions in post-Renaissance narrative. I would stress, however, that the use of typology in narrative is not always simple or simple-minded. I will discuss its many difficulties and subtleties in the hands of eighteenth-century narrative artists later in this chapter. But at this point it may be useful to mention that biblical typology, when it is abstracted to narrative situations, particularly in the novel, is usually accompanied by a visible sign language or iconography to alert the reader to its presence. Typology is a kind of prefigurative code that many, indeed most, readers from 1650 to 1820 were capable of deciphering.[5] But most readers will not interpret a given text typologically unless they know that the code is present in the text they are reading. To trace this code and the signals that authors used when they intended their readers to look for it is the purpose of this chapter.

---

[5] These dates are not inclusive: the English audience before 1650 was aware of typology, too. After 1820, it would be fair to say that typological awareness declines slightly among the by now much larger reading public.

Equally important to narrative typology is the broad and popular subject of myth. As I have already shown, all of the eighteenth-century mythographers, from the skeptics like Bayle and Vico to the most credulous searchers for Christian origins, were aware of the typological possibilities of pagan myth. Several of them, more perceptive than the rest, actually focus on the typological basis of myths. Ramsay, whose *Travels of Cyrus* is more philosophical novel than mythography, went so far as to cast his narrative as a typological quest for the foundations of Christianity. His Cyrus receives a series of prefigurative homilies from various pagan and Jewish guides; the book is an extended typological gloss on ancient myth. Richard Hurd and Clara Reeve, in their studies of romance, show an awareness of the prefigurative qualities of romantic narrative. In this respect, they were following *A Treatise of Romances and their Origin* (1672), the work of the supreme French typologist Huet, whose biblical exegesis and *Demonstratio Evangelica* employ typology with easy familiarity.[6] Still later, Faber, early in the nineteenth century, attempted to classify romance into a series of themes or motifs, for some of which he was able to find typological associations. Indeed, all mythological motifs are related to the general technique of prefiguration, especially with regard to such structural entities as character and plot. Even in twentieth-century narrative, it is argued, authors introduce myths with prefigurative and post-figurative intentions on the assumption that the ideal reader "can still be expected to be familiar with most prefigurations beforehand, just as the novelist himself was when he wrote the work."[7] Thus Fielding's analogies to pagan heroes in *Tom Jones* or Richardson's allusions to ancient worthies in *Sir Charles Grandison* could reasonably be expected to strike an eighteenth-century reader with prefigurative force. Neither author left anything to chance, however, for Fielding seldom leaves his mythological allusions without an explanation, while Richardson always adjusts the context to show his pejorative views of pagan heroism.

6 See *A Treatise of Romances and their Original* (London, 1672). Huet derives romances originally from Egyptian hieroglyphics (pp. 12-13); after giving a potted history of romance as it was known in the 1660s, he stresses (pp. 96-98) that some romances deliberately "couch a hidden meaning," in the manner of Jesus' parables. For Huet, some examples of the genre merit exegesis, and his analogy with the parables suggests that he must have thought that the texts of certain romances might be prefigurative in the same manner.

7 See John J. White, *Mythology in the Modern Novel*, pp. 11-12.

Mythological allusions, then, can be prefigurative in two ways in eighteenth-century novels. An allusion to a well-known pagan type of Christ like Hercules or Prometheus draws an obvious kind of prefiguration into the orbit of a story. In a more complicated way, an allusion to a mythological character who is not necessarily typological can cause readers who are familiar with the story of this character to predict a certain conclusion. An allusion to a character from myth can therefore *function* prefiguratively without actually *being* an accepted pagan type. Swift's reference to Sinon at the end of *Gulliver's Travels*, Part IV, is such an allusion: for the reader familiar with Sinon's treachery, the quotation from Virgil functions to help predict Gulliver's own mendacity. Sterne's mythological allusions, like Butler's before him, often have a similar purpose. Pagan mythology, however, seldom has more than an allusive presence in eighteenth-century narrative, except perhaps in specialized works like *The Travels of Cyrus*. The great popular interest in myth during the century, as illustrated by the numerous dictionaries, handbooks, and iconographical guides to the subject which appeared, often in multiple editions, is enough to suggest that it embodies a narrative tradition with many prefigurative overtones available to authors and readers alike. A reading public that was generally acquainted with the typological qualities of myth would have little difficulty in deciphering prefigurative codes and structures in other kinds of narrative.

In an earlier chapter (see Chapter 5, section 6), I briefly discussed the prefigurative and behavioral structures that are often inherent in the concept of character during the seventeenth and eighteenth centuries. The authors and compilers of the early character books do not go out of their way to include typological characters in their collections, but a few clearly prefigurative descriptions appear in every work. Most seventeenth-century character books epitomize vices and other human imperfections; occasionally we will find characters of evil so pronounced as to be Satanic, or *negative* types of a kind. In this sense, a negative character type would be one whose evils are such that they prefigure or postfigure those of Satan, the Antichrist. The eighteenth-century novel, as we shall see, will produce a number of characters whom we can classify in this way: Jonathan Wild, Lovelace, Sir Hargrave Pollexfen, Squire Thornhill, and Falkland all come to mind as evil men whose villainy has no clear origin and whose chief delights consist in producing suffering in others. The good character, while rare in the character books

themselves, has a distinct and frequent existence in sermon literature, political didacticism, and early biography. Edward Young's
"Character of a Good Prince" (1729) is a fine example of christomimetic characterization with obvious typological intentions.[8] The
Good Prince is more than a postfiguration of the Good Shepherd;
he is also a fit subject for imitation. Young writes, "He is as *Perfect*,
and truly Great as possible; not only for his Subjects *general* Good,
but for their *personal* Glory. . . . A *Subject* to *such* a Prince may be
a Character of Dignity. . . ."[9] A subject who copies such a character
is an imitation of the Savior, a prefiguration of the perfections of
the resurrected man.

Students of character, throughout the seventeenth and eighteenth
centuries, would stress the christological basis of good behavior.
Some writers argue that imitation of the divine perfections is an
absolute necessity for salvation; others are more specific and speak
only of the imitation of Christ's perfections. Tillotson, in a well-
known passage, similar to the one which Richardson would include
as a typological tailpiece to *Sir Charles Grandison*, is concerned
with the divine perfections:

> Would we but often set God before our eyes and represent
> to ourselves those excellent and amiable *perfections* of the di-
> vine nature, which are so comfortable and beneficial to us, and
> to which we stand so infinitely obliged . . . that by the pattern
> of *perfection* itself, and the example of him who is so much
> above us . . . we might be provoked to be so affected towards
> one another . . . as we have always found God to be towards
> us, and as we desire he should still continue; and miserable
> creatures are we, whenever he ceaseth to be so, if this example
> of his goodness and patience towards us do not transform us
> into the image of the divine *perfections*, and prevail upon us to
> imitate those excellencies which we have so much reason to
> approve and admire, and be in love withal.[10]

Tillotson speaks of patterns of perfection in general, but his typological message is that imitating the divine perfections will make
the most desirable human character. Elsewhere he is more explicit

[8] See above, Chapter 5, section 5, on Martyr's Day sermons in the eighteenth
century.

[9] *An Apology for Princes, or the Reverence due to Government*, p. 45.

[10] *The Works of the Most Reverend Dr. John Tillotson*, ed. Thomas Birch,
3 vols. (London, 1752), II, 508.

on the importance of the good man's character and the imitation of Jesus' perfections.[11] Character need not always be christomimetic in order to be typological. Perhaps characters so drawn are too perfect for credibility; this was one of the criticisms leveled against Richardson's Sir Charles Grandison. The christomimetic character, thus, may be too *obvious* to have any fictional value, but perfect imitations of Christ are as rare in novels as they are in life. The Boyle Lecturers, for example, who were required to demonstrate the truth of Christianity against all other religions, often found in the typological narratives of the Old Testament strong corroboration of the historical foundation of the Scriptures. One of the annual lecturers, George Stanhope, alludes to the typical persons of these narratives with a characteristic sense of certainty:

> All the Persons who were types of Christ were not so in all, but in some particular regards only; (*David*, for the purpose, in his Afflictions, and *Solomon* in his Glory:) So nothing hinders why the Prophecies which had an Eye to Both [i.e., to two senses of interpreting prophecy—the first sense being the christological, the second the literal], might not in some Passages respect Both; (the One in a strict, the Other in a qualified Sense,) in some the Antitype only, in some again the Type only, and not the Antitype at all: By reason the Person Typical, though he did in some, yet did not in the Circumstances there mentioned, sustain the Character of a Type.[12]

Stanhope's crabbed prose does not enhance his difficult subject. It is, in fact, a statement dealing with what other divines called "partial types," according to which an Old Testament person with some strongly nontypological traits, like David's lasciviousness, could still be a type of Christ in part. Stanhope describes such figures not as historical personages but in characterlike terms. It is through theoretical statements about typology like this one that we may sense the development of the view that nonhistorical individuals—such

11 See, for example, *Works*, I, 128, 155-56; II, 147-53; III, 213-34.

12 George Stanhope, "The Christian Interpretation of Prophecies Vindicated" (Sermon VIII of the Boyle Lectures, 1701-02), in *A Defence of Natural and Revealed Religion: Being a Collection of the Sermons preached at the Lecture founded by the Honourable Robert Boyle, Esq.*, ed. S. Letsome and J. Nicholl, 3 vols. (London, 1739), I, 729. This passage is the earliest I have found in which "character" and "type" are used in such close conjunction, suggesting the later term, "character type."

as the characters in a prose narrative—could have prefigurative properties just as the persons in the Old Testament do. These examples merely foreshadow the enormous contemporary tradition of typological characters in forms of narrative with which the eighteenth-century audience for prose fiction would have been familiar.

Young's "Character of a Good Prince" is part of a Martyr's Day sermon, an exceptionally popular genre from 1650 to 1800. We do not know the exact number of such sermons preached; the number printed must have been close to 1,000. Probably only the best examples of the genre ever found their way into print and, of course, the best of these would have been preached a number of times, reprinted, and collected in complete works or other compilations.[13] Sermons commemorating Charles I's martyrdom are not the kind of narratives I am studying in this chapter. The service in the Book of Common Prayer, however, called "Form of Prayer for the Thirtieth of January," is accompanied, in all folio and most quarto editions of the Prayer Book during the late seventeenth and eighteenth centuries, by a lengthy prose narrative of the life, government, persecution, trial, and death of King Charles I. From 1662, when the newly revised Prayer Book first included the form of prayer for 30 January, to the end of the eighteenth century, there were three to six editions of the Prayer Book every year, with at least one folio or quarto edition every year. Editions in smaller formats generally contain a condensed version of the narrative. This historical account, which would have been common knowledge, in its many editions, among a vast number of Anglican communicants, does to the story of Charles I what Foxe's *Acts and Monuments* and other ecclesiastical histories of the Church had done for the primitive martyrs and victims of persecutions from the early Church until the Reformation. The anonymous author or authors of this narrative present Charles I as "the very soul of a wise and good Prince, and a Pattern of true Christian Patience and Courage."[14] The account of Charles's trial stresses some of the christological overtones which

---

[13] The British Museum Catalogue of Printed Books lists about 500 in the Appendix to Charles I; there are hundreds more under other headings. Provincial printing is barely represented in the British Library's General Catalogue (hereafter referred to as GK3); the new *Eighteenth-Century Short-Title Catalogue* will doubtless discover other specimens.

[14] See William Nicholls, *A Comment on the Book of Common Prayer* (London, 1710), Sig. Yy1ʳ. Nicholls simply reprints the standard Prayer Book text with additional notes.

Martyr's Day sermons were accustomed to display, especially his persecution at the hands of Cromwell's troops. The order of prayer itself includes a number of typological texts from the New Testament and, if anything, even more strongly enforces the typology of Charles I. That Richardson was aware of Charles I's history is evident from a brief episode in *Sir Charles Grandison*, where the Della Porrettas assure Sir Charles that the marriage agreement by which he would marry Clementina is apparently modeled on that drawn for the marriage of Charles I and Henrietta Maria of France.[15] What is significant for my purposes now is that the typology of England's Martyr King, which was widely accepted during our period, was presented to a large audience not only in annual homilies but also in an historical narrative in which the character of the King assumes a prefigurative role similar to the kinds of narrative typology which I shall shortly be examining in prose fiction.

 2

The character of the good Christian or, more simply, the character of the good man, is adumbrated by the seventeenth-century character books and augmented by Martyr's Day sermons and the Prayer Book narrative associated with them. We will see this individual, in both male and female forms, in several varieties of prose narrative from about 1670 to the early nineteenth century. Scrutiny of novels written after 1820 will likewise yield many interesting examples. We can get an idea of what contemporary writers intended by such characters from a sermon by Samuel Clarke, originally preached about 1710. In this text Clarke, who had yet to fall into disrepute for his unorthodox views on the trinity, takes a common homiletic subject, the character of one of the Apostles (in this case, Barnabas) and from it proceeds to a statement on character:

> The word, *Good*, in this character of a *good* man, is used sometimes in a way expressive of *Virtue in general*, as opposed to *all Wickedness* or *Vice*; and sometimes as denoting a *particular Kind* or *Degree* of *Virtue*, as distinguished by degree of Excellency above *other* Virtues. In the *former* sense of the word, a *good man* stands opposed to a *vicious* or a *bad man*: In the

15 See *Sir Charles Grandison*, ed. Jocelyn Harris, 3 vols. (London: Oxford Univ. Press, 1972), II, 219, 674.

latter sense, a *good man* stands distinguished, by way of Eminence or Superiority, above other even *just* and *righteous* persons.[16]

Clarke's good man is similar to other types found in contemporary sermons, but this excerpt is significant because it equates goodness with virtue and because it suggests that this character, while standing above other righteous persons, need not necessarily embody total Christian perfection. There exists a substantial body of sermons on Christian perfection, but the perfect man or woman is not often an attractive subject for serious prose fiction (children's literature is quite another matter). So Clarke establishes sound and realistic guidelines for those who might wish to create literary characters in the mold of his good man. He also enunciates for the eighteenth century the theme of the virtuous man as essentially equivalent to the perfect Christian for purposes of emulation. The virtuous character, we will find, is far more attractive as a fictional possibility than the absolute paragon of perfection. Even Sir Charles Grandison, who comes as close to the *Christianus perfectus* as any character in an eighteenth-century novel, thinks that he has faults. And Grandison, by virtue of his marriage to Harriet Byron, is revealed to us as something less than perfection, even though Richardson goes to some pains to delineate Sir Charles's mental anguish over whether it would be right for him to marry. Typologists had agreed since the seventeenth century, however, that a figure of Christ need not be like him in every particular; no type, after all, could be so complete as its antitype.

Seventeenth-century attitudes toward the good man or the character of the good man had been much influenced by Jeremy Taylor's *Rule and Exercises of Holy Living and Dying* (1650-51), which emphasizes the supreme desideratum of Christian perfection. Taylor's imitators were more or less rigid in the degree of perfection they considered acceptable. William Law, for instance, in *A Practical Treatise upon Christian Perfection* (1726), after declaring that "All Christians are required to imitate the Life and Example of Jesus Christ," concedes that we are "not called to the same manner of Life, or the same sort of Actions," but rather "to the same Spirit

16 *The Works of Samuel Clarke, D. D.*, 4 vols. (London, 1738), I, 267. Clarke preached a number of sermons on this subject: see I, 154-59, 237-42, 334-49, 420-25, 438-42 (on "The Character of the Messiah").

and Temper."[17] Taylor himself, in a companion-piece to *Holy Living*, had urged, "So we should *put on Christ*, and imitate the whole body of his Sanctity, conforming to every integral part, and expresse him in our lives, that God seeing our impresses, may know whose image and superscription we bear, and we may be acknowledged for sons when we have the tire and features, and resemblances of our elder Brother."[18]

Theological and secular themes converge here for, throughout the seventeenth century, "impress" was synonymous with *characteristic quality* or *character*. The theme is pervasive in theological writings of all kinds during the eighteenth century, with the emphasis varying according to the purpose and denomination of whoever happened to be pronouncing it. Fundamentalist and evangelical writers tend to insist on "an *uniform* following of Christ, an *entire* inward and outward conformity to our master" (to use Wesley's phrase).[19] Wesley, again, expected his followers to aspire to his own austere brand of Christian perfection. "He thinks, speaks, and lives," he wrote in *The Character of a Methodist*, *"according to* the Method laid down *in the Revelation of* JESUS CHRIST."[20] Isaac Watts, whose Calvinism was relatively mild in comparison to Wesley's Arminianism, proposed, as other Anglicans did, the imitation of one of the Apostles. Steele had done the same in *The Christian Hero*, a work which grows out of this theological tradition. Watts, in his treatise, "Humility represented in the Character of St. Paul" (one of Steele's choices in his essay), simply stresses the qualities of Paul (and later of Jesus) that are attainable by the ordinary Christian, by Everyman. "Let us follow and observe him in the progress of Life," he writes of Jesus and, in a thumbnail sketch of Christ's life, he points out not the saintly perfections but rather the humble temper which would have been easily within the reach of the bulk of his middle-class London congregation.[21] Moreover, one of the

---

17 (London, 1726), pp. 462-63; cf. Chap. XIII, pp. 461-98.

18 Jeremy Taylor, *The Great Exemplar of Sanctity and Holy Life according to the Christian Institution* (London, 1649), Part i, p. 5. For contemporary meanings of "Impress," see *NED*, s.v. "Impress," sb.¹ 2a.

19 See John Wesley, *A Plain Account of Christian Perfection*, p. 4. Cf. pp. 8, 33, 90.

20 *The Character of a Methodist* (Bristol, 1742), p. 16. On Wesley's insistence on "sinless perfection," see Ronald A. Knox, *Enthusiasm: A Chapter in the History of Religion, with special reference to the Seventeenth and Eighteenth Centuries* (New York: Oxford Univ. Press, 1950), pp. 540-43, and see his portrait of Wesley, pp. 422-58.

21 *The Works of Isaac Watts*, 6 vols. (London, 1753), II, 249; see II, 317-51.

most popular of all eighteenth-century presentations of Christ's life is *Paradise Regained*, published during the course of the century in more than twenty separate editions and many times more with Milton's poetical works. The Son's extreme privations in *Paradise Regained* might have been rather difficult for a comfortably well-off London audience to imitate, but Milton does not propose the Son as an emulative figure in the same way that à Kempis does the life of Christ.

Without doubt the largest body of contemporary material dealing with the theme of Christian perfection is the *De Imitatione Christi* of Thomas à Kempis. Between 1650 and 1800 there were at least a dozen separate fresh English translations, all of which were reprinted from two to twenty times. The work's bibliographical history is far from complete; so far, however, it is clear that there were well over one hundred English editions of à Kempis's work during this period in one translation or another. The *Imitatio*, incidentally, which had been quite popular in the Renaissance, would be even more widely printed in nineteenth-century England. It was such a common book, in fact, that, while it is often mentioned, it is almost never quoted during our period, always a sign that authors assume a widespread acquaintance with a work. The most popular translation was that of George Stanhope (1698); other translators include Dryden's antagonist Luke Milbourne (1697), Richard Challoner (1737), and John Wesley himself (1735). The central motion of the *Imitatio* is tropological, since à Kempis argues that all aspects of the Christian life should be a postfiguration of Christ. The first post-1650 translator, known only as "F. B.," sets out the task in broad terms:

> Now there is nothing more precious, more dear to God then his own Image, his own Life from which Wicked men are said to be estranged. . . . And as there is nothing higher, nothing more excellent then the *Participation of the Divine Nature*, then the resemblance of God who is the first and Supreme Excellency, then *the Imitation of Christ* who is the highest, the most perfect and lovely Pattern and Idea of all purity and holinesse. Besides there is nothing more essentiall to the constituting of a true Christian, then the denying of himself, the taking up of his Crosse, and following of Christ.[22]

22 *The Christians Pattern; or a Divine Treatise of the Imitation of Christ*, trans. F. B., rev. John Worthington (London, 1657), "To the Reader," Sig. ¶ 3$^{\text{r-v}}$.

Almost all subsequent translations and editions of the *Imitatio* contain similar prefatory exhortations. Only Wesley goes to greater lengths to explain the significance of à Kempis's work for the eighteenth-century reader. His lengthy, clear preface points out that the mysteries of the "inward kingdom of GOD" cannot be known by those who derive their knowledge merely from commentaries but rather must be known from experience, by actually *living* the life of Christ. "This," Wesley writes, "is that inward, practical, experimental, feeling knowledge, so frequently commanded by [à Kempis]."[23]

The *Imitatio* is frequently typological as well, emphasizing that the Christian may be responsible for a self-created postfiguration of Christ which functions as a foreshadowing of the still greater perfections to which he or she will attain in the afterlife. A Kempis lists individual characteristics that imitate Jesus (Book I), proceeds to give a certain number of christomimetic character types, such as that "Of a good peaceable Man" (II.3), and then devotes his longest book (Book III) to specialized Christian qualities. His fourth and last book is devoted to good Christian behavior and the Christian virtues; its first chapter (IV.1), on preparations for the Eucharist, contains the most protracted typological passages in the entire work. An excerpt from Luke Milbourne's verse translation will show the extent of the typology:

> Yet all the Sacrifices there [i.e., in the Sanctuary of the
>   Church]
> Were but the Types of that revolving Year,
>   In which *Incarnate God* should fall,
> The great Atonement, and should *perfect All.*
>   That great Atonement, Bread and Wine
> To us exhibit in a Mode Divine;
>   What Flames should then enlarge my Heart,
> When in my Saviour I expect a Part?
> How should I dress to meet my bleeding Lord
> While every Type great Kings and Saints of old ador'd?[24]

Milbourne's version of à Kempis's typology is expansive, for he enlarges the figural significance of the communion ceremony to in-

23 *The Christian's Pattern; or, A Treatise of the Imitation of Christ*, trans. John Wesley (London, 1735), pp. xx-xxi.

24 *The Christian Pattern Paraphrased: or, The Book of the Imitation of Christ . . .* , trans. Luke Milbourne (London, 1697), pp. 264-65; cf. pp. 261-69.

clude the entire Christian year and, in a curious way not present in any other translation, he implies that types of Christ are universal and that "the Kings and Saints of old" paid due reverence to a galaxy of prefigurations. These earlier types are the so-called "legal types" of Mosaic Law. Another translator, Stanhope, brings still another element to the drama of the *Imitatio*: "How poor and despicable were those Legal Sacrifices, whose greatest Excellence and Commendation was, that they typified and foretold That One only perfect and sufficient Sacrifice upon the Cross, which in this Sacrament we at once commemorate and apply the Virtue to our selves?"[25] In other words, Old Testament typology was but a shadowy prefiguration of the Crucifixion, whereas the Eucharist itself is a clear, recognizable postfiguration, an unshadowed type. If the patriarchs were types of Christ, then what is today's Christian? In an oblique manner, the Christian who follows à Kempis's rules, as one who knowingly acts out a typological ritual of old, is a greater type still. As so often happens in the history of Christianity, *imitatio Christi* is equivalent to *typus Christi*. This equation, I should note, is unusual for, in the strict sense of the *imitatio* theme, the *imitatio Christi* is not typological *per se*. Typology, in the old fourfold interpretation of Scripture, involves belief or faith, whereas the notion of *imitatio Christi* involves moral allegory, the *quid agas* sense of Scripture, what Christians should do and the kind of life they should try to lead. During the late seventeenth and early eighteenth centuries, however, there is a proliferation of English texts emphasizing proper patterns of behavior at the same time that there are many confusions and conflations of figural language. As a result of this double trend, the formerly clear distinctions between typological reading and moral allegory start to blur. Hence these two senses of Scripture are often joined and, in many eighteenth-century contexts, the *imitatio Christi* theme becomes identical with a postfiguration of Christ.

What à Kempis's devotional work might have left unclear about the typology of Holy Communion "The Order for the Administration of the Lord's Supper" in *The Book of Common Prayer* must have made abundantly obvious to a still larger eighteenth-century audience. Liturgical typology was a matter of much antiquity by the eighteenth century. Virtually all the exegetes of the Pentateuch

---

[25] *The Christian's Pattern: or, A Treatise of the Imitation of Jesus Christ*, trans. George Stanhope (London, 1698), p. 283.

allude to the typological apparatus of Mosaic Law, Jewish ritual and worship, and especially of the Passover. In so doing, they were simply following an exegetical *modus operandi* that began in pre-Nicene times, as early as Origen's *Homiliae in Genesin*. The Prayer Book, in its "order" for Holy Communion, thus skims the cream from a lengthy series of interpretations while alluding simultaneously to not one but several cognate narratives. Communion was seen as a symbolic reenactment of the Last Supper, but it was also understood to represent an antitype of the sacrifice of Isaac, the Mosaic legal sacrifices, and the Passover, to mention only a few of its better known types. The Prayer Book would give every communicant a chance to join in symbolic celebration of Christ's presence: "for then we dwell in Christ, and Christ in us; we are one with Christ, and Christ with us."[26] For those who did not partake of communion (and according to statistical studies of the period, the number of noncommunicants swelled considerably during the eighteenth century), the Prayer Book or one of its numerous abridgments was so widely owned that almost every literate person could have been acquainted with this physical rendition of the *imitatio Christi* theme.[27]

The *imitatio Christi* theme, then, was both widely known and strongly typological. Reminders of its prefigurative qualities were everywhere in seventeenth- and eighteenth-century England, whether in coins and medals which stressed a kinship between sovereign and Lord, in annual sermons on England's presumed christomimetic Martyr King, in the liturgy of the established church and, ultimately, in narratives having no ostensible relationship to any of these bearers of iconographical likeness. The character tradition, as nourished by popular compilations, is especially influential on later forms of narrative: there is more than an accidental resemblance between the Theophrastan-style characters of good and evil and the stock situations of middle-class perturbation chronicled so successfully in Richardson's *Familiar Letters on Important Occasions* (1741). There is another aspect to the eighteenth-century literary character sometimes overlooked—the transition from the brief, usually satiric, mainly pre-1700 Theophrastan character to those,

26 *The Book of Common Prayer* (London, 1713), Sig. M3^r.

27 On the number of people to take communion, see J. Wickham Legg, *English Church Life from the Restoration to the Tractarian Movement* (London: Longmans, Green, & Co., 1914), pp. 37-41. Legg's statistics on the number of communicants are very fragmentary.

almost all post-1700, derived from La Bruyère. Let us look at an early eighteenth-century La Bruyèrian character of "An Honest Man":

> *God* is his *Father*; *Religion* his *Mother*; *Truth* is his *Friend*; *Chastity* his *Companion*; *Justice* his *Practice*; *Honour* his *Reward*; *Sincerity* his *Wife*, which he Loves above all Others: His *Children* are *Complacency, Good Humour, Love* and *Confidence*: His *Brethren* and *Kinsfolk, Angels* and *Good Men*: *Hypocrites* are his *Antipodes*; the whole *Creation* is his *Servant*; *Sin* and *Devils* his *Slaves*. . . .
>
> He is as *Firm*, as a *Rock*; as *Bold*, as a *Lion*; as *Mild*, as a *Lamb*; as *Wise*, as a *Serpent*; as *Harmless*, as a *Dove*; as *Constant*, as a *Turtle*; as *Rare*, as a *Phoenix*. . . .[28]

This passage is perhaps the ultimate expression of the *imitatio Christi* theme. The cascade of nouns embraces a dozen christomimetic qualities and the adjectival qualities recall Scripture closely. Not only is the "Honest Man" an ideal Christian, but he is also both pre- and postfiguration, type and antitype in one. The opening words, *"God* is his *Father,"* show us that this character is a type. All that follows emphasizes the predictive structure of the character: the honest man is himself a prefiguration of the goal to which devout Christians should aspire, but at the same time the author establishes for the character its own internal prefigurative qualities. The first identification (*"God* is his *Father"*) leads us to expect, to be able to predict, all the subsequent qualities, for they are naturally associated with such a complete type of Christ.

The anonymous author of *The English Theophrastus* could not have expected that his audience would regard typological characters like this one as genuinely representative of contemporary mores. Not court nor town nor city could ever have produced a real person so perfect as this "Honest Man." However, the value of such creations for writers and students of literature is considerable. In homilies and other theological writings, as we have seen, clergymen were accustomed to sketch patterns of perfection similar to this patently exaggerated figure. These character sketches were doubtless useful for didactic purposes and as acceptable pictures of the *imitatio*

---

[28] *The English Theophrastus: or the Manners of the Age. Being the Modern Characters of the Court, the Town, and the City*, 3rd ed. (London, 1708), pp. 383-84.

Christi theme, a topic which had real value in the processes of Christian instruction, catechism, and conversion. Characters were useful, too, in certain historical and political narratives. The full-length descriptions of Charles I, for example, or of Oliver Cromwell in books dealing with the crises of the seventeenth century or in contemporary biographies helped to associate Charles, in the minds of contemporary readers, with Christ and Cromwell with Satan. This is a figural tradition contemporary with both men which survives into the eighteenth century. But characters stressing the perfection of virtue or the deformity of vice will be most important in imitative works, in fictional narratives of various kinds.

Typological characters, then, are a relatively common literary phenomenon in the late seventeenth and eighteenth centuries. Of such creations, those with christological or christomimetic properties are most popular; doubtless the pervasiveness of the *imitatio Christi* tradition accounts for their frequency. A corollary, the negative typological character (that is, one prefigurative of satanic evil), also exists: we see this figure quite often in the character books which, after all, concentrate on vices, and as the villainous person in a variety of literary works; Richardson's Lovelace is undoubtedly part of this tradition. The characters in the Theophrastan and La Bruyèrian compilations have no lives of their own. Even in the character books, typological characters are little more than epitomes; they are predictive, but only in the sense that they may serve as structural guides to a certain kind of behavior. Within a prose narrative, however, a typological person may assume a larger significance, often (but not always) functioning both as a predictive structure for a preferred kind of behavior and as an agent whose presence helps to prefigure events later in the plot of the work itself. At the start of this chapter, I looked at some of the traditions —biblical, mythological, characterological—that cast a typological shadow over prose narrative. Now it is appropriate to ask some questions about these narratives themselves. What sorts of narratives are likely to include typological characters or to be otherwise prefigurative? Do novels, in particular, contain sustained typological patterns? Does the typological parable or story play any role in the prose fiction of the period?

I showed earlier (see Chapter 5, section 2) that typological patterns frequently occur in secular historical and political works.
Sometimes such instances are nothing more than allusions to widely
accepted types. On other occasions, as in collections of lives like
Foxe's *Acts and Monuments*, individual typological accounts were
clearly meant to remind audiences of the *imitatio Christi-typus
Christi* theme and to hold up a pattern of good Christian behavior.
Church history, as we saw with Eusebius, could also be typological,
and so could other religious chronicles. Jacques Basnage, for example, whose *Histoire des Juifs* (1707) was translated into English
in the year it appeared in France, sees a typological pattern to Jewish history from the time of Jesus to the present.[29] Basnage was not
alone in assigning the Jews figural significance, and the Jews of
Europe and Asia in the seventeenth and eighteenth centuries never
ceased to believe in the possibility of a Messiah, an antitype to the
promises of the prophets. Indeed, historians of all kinds were fond
of regarding the Jews as a people whose history was typological, a
practice which would attain its most refined performance with
David Hartley in the middle of the century and which would continue until long after the turn of the nineteenth century. The Book
of Revelation had considerable influence on the typology of history,
for it was regarded as a typological prophecy of secular history since
the time of Jesus. Some commentators also regarded it as the history
of the world from the Creation to the Apocalypse, expressed in a
symbolic code whose understanding would help to prepare mankind for the arrival of Judgment Day. Revelation hurls the types
out of their customary religious contexts into the arena of historical interpretation, and secular historians of various persuasions
took many liberties in regarding historical events as the antitypes
or fulfillments of apocalyptic prophecy.[30]

The most fertile field for narrative typology is undoubtedly the
novel. There are several reasons why this is so. The fictive milieu
gives an author who may be disposed to manipulate prefigurative
events the opportunity to create predictive characters and plots, to
imitate existing figural accounts and, often under the disguise of
verisimilitude, to produce more effective and moving prefigurative
structures than could an historian who must be bound by rules of

29 See Jacques Basnage, *The History of the Jews, from Jesus Christ to the
Present Time*, trans. Thomas Taylor (London, 1708), p. vii.

30 For a more thorough discussion of the effect of the Book of Revelation on
typological narratives, see Chapter 9.

evidence, however vague. The storyteller, in other words, has more narrative options than the historian does. The novelists of our period, with a wide choice of typological subjects, characters, fables, and exegeses of all kinds available to them, did not need to be confined to telling bald, unembroidered tales. Defoe, as he reflects through the person of Crusoe on his subject's earlier voyages and on the kind of account he has rendered of them, has cause to scorn narratives which are false but whose authors or tellers make them *appear* to be true. After all, Crusoe assures us, there can be no doubt of the veracity of *his* story: has he not told it himself precisely as it happened? "Supplying a Story by Invention," he insists, "is certainly a most scandalous Crime" (and one of which Defoe is also guilty).[31] How, then, is Defoe not a false tale-teller like those whom he has his hero censure? He is ready with an answer: *Robinson Crusoe* is a special kind of story, a true history with didactic intentions:

> The telling or writing a parable, or an allusive allogorick [*sic*] History is quite a different Case, and is always Distinguisht from this other Jesting with Truth; that it is design'd and effectually turn'd for instructive and upright Ends, and has its Moral justly apply'd: Such are the historical Parables in the holy Scripture, such the Pilgrims Progress, and such in a Word the Adventures of your fugitive Friend, *Robinson Crusoe.*[32]

Perhaps it is just as well that the third volume of *Robinson Crusoe* proved so unpopular; had this excerpt been more widely read, Defoe's audience might have seen the entire novel as a theological tract. For a moment, I think, in this passage, Defoe and his narrator merge into a single person—Defoe absorbs Crusoe's identity just long enough to let us see that his prose narrative is acceptable as a true story because it follows the methods of the biblical narratives and of Bunyan's symbolic spiritual biography of a Christian's pilgrimage through life. Defoe's mention of "the historical Parables" shows that he is thinking about the historical truths of the New Testament. His joining the parables with Bunyan is strong evidence that he saw his own narrative achievement as similar to those two great exemplars of typology—the life of Christ and the life of a Christian.

31 *Serious Reflections during the Life and Surprising Adventures of Robinson Crusoe: with his Vision of the Angelic World* (London, 1720), p. 113.
32 *Ibid.*, pp. 115-16.

The patterns for typological narratives, then, if we are to accept the testimony of a practitioner of the style like Defoe, are the great inventories of typology: the Bible and stories about the Christian life and the imitation of Christ. These are not the only sources available, and certainly they are not the only patterns which contemporary novelists used, but they are among the most important. Allegorical narratives dealing exclusively with theological subjects are therefore among the earliest precursors of fictional typology. *The Pilgrim's Progress* and *The Holy War*, to take just two of Bunyan's many relevant works, contain much typology, usually for illustrative purposes. *The Pilgrim's Progress* comes close to being a consistent typological narrative: the work is arranged as a series of prefigurative scenes, with a constant movement from darkness to light. Christian, at the start, lives in the City of Destruction, benighted and surrounded by sin; Bunyan marks his progress (a *progress* is itself a kind of prefigurative movement) in several ways. First, we see Christian's gradual ascent to light (Interpreter: "Do you see yonder shining light?" Christian: "I *think* I do."); then we follow the gradual enlargement of his perceptions of his human predicament from the partial sight of the type to the full revelation of the antitype, and we are drawn into a book-long drama of resurrection, from Christian's being doomed to certain death in the City of Destruction to his attaining eternal life in the Heavenly City.[33] The act of enlarging one's perceptions, thus allowing a transition "from shadowie types to truth" (to use Milton's phrase), would later be adopted by Blake in his concept of the cleansing of the perceptions. Christian's sight is at first extremely clouded and limited, but he gains vision, adventure by adventure, and the book concludes with several Pisgah-sights, one of the oldest of typological structures. *The Holy War* is a more rigid book than Bunyan's classic and, consequently, its typologies are more obvious than those of *The Pilgrim's Progress*. The allegory, which embodies the temptation of Mansoul by Diabolus and the city's ultimate redemption by Emmanuel, could be interpreted by even the least literate members

---

[33] See above, Chapter 5, note 27, and cf. Bunyan's comment in his "Apology":

> Was not Gods Laws,
> His Gospel-laws in olden time held forth
> By Types, Shadows, and Metaphors?

See *Grace Abounding to the Chief of Sinners and The Pilgrim's Progress*, p. 142. The entire "Apology," pp. 139-45, is a strong defense of biblical tropology.

of Bunyan's audience.[34] The typological narrative is contained in the fact that this allegory is plainly prefigurative of the Christian's redemption from sin by the Messiah. The Immanuel of the Book of Isaiah is a type of the Savior which would be comprehensible from the text of *The Holy War* even without Bunyan's many marginal glosses. On the whole, Bunyan is a sophisticated typologist only in *The Pilgrim's Progress*, but the prefigurative elements in his works are numerous, and his considerable influence on later narratives is doubtless responsible for some of the more subtle typological structures in the eighteenth-century novel.

There are many other religious narratives with typological qualities, but most of them are far less proficient than Bunyan's. Some of these texts, which vary from straight didacticism to the confessional-autobiographical style, deserve our attention, for they illustrate one of the most obvious directions which typological narrative can take, one which will appear in the works of novelists from Defoe and Richardson to Goldsmith and Godwin. The controversialist and well-known typologist Benjamin Keach, for example, uses prefigurative techniques throughout his *Antichrist Stormed* (1689), a polemical pseudo-historical narrative attacking the Roman Catholic Church. Keach carries the typological promises of the New Testament, especially the Book of Revelation, into contemporary life and history and finds, among other wonders, that "literal *Babylon* in *Chaldea*, was a Type or Figure of *Rome* Papal or the *present Church* of *Rome*, and *that in many particulars*."[35] He is confident that those New Testament prophecies still uncompleted will be "made good in the Antitype as it was in Type" sooner or later, but preferably sooner. Thus, while the purpose of Keach's narrative is patently polemical, his principal method is typological.

Keach wrote other semifictional narratives which are relevant to our theme. His *War with the Devil* (1674), in which a young man takes part in several long dialogues, written in crude couplets, with Conscience, different vices and virtues, the Devil, and Jesus himself, is a good example. The religious message is one that we will find in many later narratives of conversion: there are many signs or promises of salvation vouchsafed to the doubting Christian to confirm his

---

[34] On the typology of *The Holy War*, see Chapter 5, note 27. See also Emmanuel's concluding speech to Mansoul for Bunyan's version of the typology of salvation—*The Holy War* (London, 1682), pp. 388-97.

[35] *Antichrist Stormed: or, Mystery Babylon the great Whore, and great City, proved to be the present Church of Rome* (London, 1689), pp. 103-16.

faith and speed his conversion. In Keach's rather transparent dialogues, it is Jesus who tidily assures the wavering youth that all the types will be fulfilled in him.[36] The most popular of Keach's religious narratives are a pair of little books, *The Travels of True Godliness* (1683) and *The Progress of Sin*, written after he had completed his massive compilation of all known types, *Tropologia* (1682). *The Progress of Sin* is somewhat the better work, since it concludes with the triumph of Ungodliness, or Sin, followed by a sudden reversal, the trial and sentence of Sin by a court of the righteous. As Apollyon, or Satan, gives Sin his commission early in the book, Keach artfully mingles types and antitypes. The narrative theme is an account of how Sin, at various times in recorded history, has succeeded in getting Jews and Christians to ignore the signs (or types) sent to forewarn them of the Messiah and his mission.[37] Keach is almost always the heavy-handed moralist, concerned mainly with the theological message rather than with the art of narrative, yet this strain of typology, which involves the use of obviously religious emblems and many biblical citations, will recur in more polished works as diverse as *Robinson Crusoe* and *Sir Charles Grandison*.

Another typological precursor of the novel is the autobiographical account of the spiritual life, usually including a thorough treatment of the author's regeneration from sin and complete conversion. In this class of works we will find diaries, spiritual autobiographies, and such books as Bunyan's *Grace Abounding to the Chief of Sinners*, Baxter's *Reliquiae Baxterianae*, and the anonymous *An Account of Some Remarkable Passages in the Life of a Private Gentleman* (once attributed to Defoe).[38] Bunyan's autobiography contains all the usual ingredients of this genre: we learn

---

[36] *War with the Devil: or the Young Mans Conflict with the Powers of Darkness*, 4th ed. (London, 1676), pp. 86-92.

[37] *The Progress of Sin: or, The Travels of Ungodliness*, 6th ed. (London, 1763), pp. 48-51.

[38] G. A. Starr, *Defoe and Spiritual Autobiography* (Princeton: Princeton Univ. Press, 1965), pp. 3-50, devotes a long and informative chapter to a group of these works. Starr does not suggest that spiritual autobiographies have prefigurative qualities, as I do here. I should emphasize that all autobiography has certain predictive qualities, but secular autobiographies, unlike the religious or spiritual side of the genre, usually (but not always) lack figural or confessional passages and any other potentially typological features. See Paul Delany, *British Autobiography in the Seventeenth Century* (New York: Columbia Univ. Press, 1969), pp. 107-15, 172.

of his abandoned sinfulness, ungodliness, and scoffing at religion, of the signs of conversion that he ignored so that he could sin on, of the signs that finally moved him to begin his regeneration, and at last of his constant faithfulness. During the process of Bunyan's conversion, typological texts and discoveries abound; the movement of the book is clearly one from darkness to light, from damnation to a promise of eternal life, and so on.[39] Baxter has less to say about his personal sinfulness than Bunyan, but he often discusses his pain and suffering in fulfilling his ministry in christomimetic terms. At one point, he tells us that his health is so poor that he must undergo a daily resurrection: "I die daily, and yet remain alive."[40] The *imitatio Christi* theme is omnipresent, even though Baxter's work is more an *historia sui temporis* than a spiritual autobiography. The Private Gentleman's *Account* also proceeds in the traditional way, carrying us through the author's life from a sinful youth to a repentant middle age to a preachy level of mature experience. This systematized structure of religious education will appear in mature novels like *Robinson Crusoe* and, in a secular sphere, in *Tom Jones* and the adventure stories of Smollett. Like other practitioners of this genre, the Private Gentleman profits from good reading and, it is interesting to note, among his books is L'Estrange's translation of Aesop's *Fables* with commentary, which he dutifully reads on Sundays "with wondrous delight." But his reading fails to banish his doubts until he comes across Thomas à Kempis, after which he begins the slow process of regeneration, painfully advancing from spiritual darkness to *éclaircissement*. The climax of his conversion comes when he realizes that Satan's attacks against him are really leveled against the devil's true enemy, Jesus. Thus the narrator becomes a Jesus figure, a postfiguration, and his account assumes the qualities of a pilgrimage of faith as a type-story of the universal Christian condition. "To conclude with something Practical," the author rounds off the main part of his work by summarizing the

[39] For example, Bunyan considers the typological implications of Esau's repentance, the restoration of Job, and the typology of Hebrews 12; see *Grace Abounding . . . and The Pilgrim's Progress*, pp. 73, 80, 84. There are many other relevant examples in Bunyan's writings.

[40] See *Reliquiae Baxterianae: or, Mr. Richard Baxter's Narrative of the Most Remarkable Passages of his Life and Times* (London, 1696), Part iii, pp. 192, 198. Baxter integrated the typology of his own life with expectations of the Millennium. See William M. Lamont, *Richard Baxter and the Millennium: Protestant Imperialism and the English Revolution* (London: Croom Helm, 1979), pp. 30-32.

mechanics of conversion, which, with its emphasis on the *imitatio Christi* theme, shows that he took his à Kempis seriously.[41] These first-person narratives are long, rambling, and structurally flawed, but they sometimes adumbrate the more finished first-person accounts of a fair number of eighteenth-century novels. The typology of these early works is often protracted and far from artless. The later novel will be more subtle.

There is another strain of narrative typology which would be popular in fictional accounts (some of them very dubious contributions to the genre of the novel) in the first half of the eighteenth century. Whereas Bunyan, Keach, and their novelistic successors embody types, predictive characters, and prefigurative structures within an entire work, there is a group of popular narratives in which typology occurs at sporadic intervals but which are predominantly nonfigurative in style. Such works are adventure stories or *chroniques scandaleuses* which include an occasional Christian reflection as a slight genuflection in the direction of respectability. Penelope Aubin's *The Life of Madam de Beaumont* (1721), an outstanding example of this class of works, is a tale of endangered female chastity in which miraculous preservations, incredible coincidences, and preposterous speeches combine to save the heroine, an unspoiled beauty who has spent most of her life in a suspiciously well-furnished cave in Wales, from ravishment by a series of coarse fellows. We hear that God and Providence have been watching her all the time, which helps to explain her comfortable cavern, but this tepid moralizing is unconvincing, and the author knows it. Therefore she adds a typological paragraph at the very end of the novel on the role of Providence as deliverer and the wonderful ways, some of them strongly reminiscent of Old Testament types, in which God rewards virtue and punishes vice.[42] A book which is essentially a romance of adventure attains religious status only by virtue of a typological scene tacked on at the end. Jane Barker's *Exilius: or, The Banish'd Roman* (1715) is prevented by its pagan setting from dealing openly with Christian themes, but its various stories are nevertheless structured on topics of moral interest to the contemporary audience. Barker's heroines thus become types of per-

---

[41] See *An Account of Some Remarkable Passages in the Life of a Private Gentleman* (London, 1708), pp. 34, 78, 92-94, 166-77.

[42] See *The Life of Madam de Beaumont* (London, 1721), p. 142. God's power to "give Food upon the barren Mountain" echoes the typological preservation of the Israelites from starvation in Exodus.

secuted innocence whom it is possible to see as deliberate prefigurations.[43] Characters subjected to persecution at the hands of ill-intentioned people but who somehow manage to bear up under the strain form an interesting prefigurative subclass in the world of the eighteenth-century novel. Often they are women (usually young and sexually attractive women), for the models of the early female martyrs and saints had proven that christomimesis need not be confined solely to men. Barker's heroines, Clelia and Clarinthia, share the persecuted-woman role with such later wonders of Christian resistance to persecution as Pamela, Sarah Fielding's Mrs. Heartfree, and Charlotte Summers, heroine of the anonymous *The History of Charlotte Summers* (1749). The persecuted man can often respond to threats with physical violence, a counterplot, or an escape; the persecuted woman can escape, as Clarissa flees her parents' home and later escapes her seducer by her death, but most frequently her patience, discretion, and humility must be her shield. In the case of Barker's *Exilius*, a narrative with little ostensibly religious matter acquires typological force because of the carefully plotted use of prefigurative characters.

The narrative of adventure, of which the picaresque novel is perhaps the most visible example, is notable for its attraction to theological concerns. The theme of religious conversion, from which there is occasionally backsliding, is a common one in European picaresque fiction. The central character in Von Grimmelshausen's *Simplicissimus* has an intense conversion, followed by a monastic retreat; Lesage's Gil Blas renounces his sinful past; Guzmán, in Alemán's novel, turns from his vicious life and embraces religion; and both *Moll Flanders* and *Colonel Jack* include the theme of religious conversion.[44] In the later eighteenth century, as I will discuss further on, we will find an occasional dedicated rogue, like

[43] John J. Richetti, *Popular Fiction before Richardson: Narrative Patterns, 1700-1739* (Oxford: Clarendon Press, 1969), p. 235, notes that the persecuted maiden in *Exilius* is "a divine messenger whose beauty and saintly presence both prove and prefigure the truth and joys of religion in this life and the next." See also pp. 230-36.

[44] The scholia dealing with picaresque fiction are very extensive. On religious themes in picaresque novels, see Richard Bjornson, *The Picaresque Hero in European Fiction* (Madison, Wis.: Univ. of Wisconsin Press, 1977), pp. 24-27, 46-51, 120-24, 166-68, 189-91. On the conversion theme, see A. A. Parker, *Literature and the Delinquent: The Picaresque Novel in Spain and Europe, 1599-1753* (Edinburgh: University Press, 1967), pp. 42-44, 89-93, 104-106, 107-108, 122-23, 129-30.

Smollett's Ferdinand Count Fathom, who undergoes a religious conversion, but the more usual pattern for such novels calls for a sprinkling of religious morality applied here and there and a moral conclusion to keep the work from being entirely profane.

An occasional adventure narrative, less self-conscious than the picaresque, adopts the same methods. *The History of the Long Captivity and Adventures of Thomas Pellow* (1739?), whose authorship remains a mystery,[45] may serve as an instance of the irreligious narrative sweetened with the fortuitous addition of typological materials. Pellow goes to sea as an eleven-year-old boy; his adventures include his captivity and mistreatment by and escape from the Moors. He is forced to "convert" to Mohammedanism to avoid tortures even worse than those to which the Moors subject him. At intervals, the narrator reminds his audience that he is still a Christian, and alludes to the governance of God or Providence, but essentially *The History of Thomas Pellow* is a guileless account of the vicious mores of another religion interspersed with occasional religious reflections. These reflections are not quite sufficient to elevate young Pellow to the level of a persecution-figure; a narrative undertaken with no typological purpose seldom acquires one. However, after nearly four hundred pages of adventures largely devoid of an ethical sense other than the desire for self-preservation, the author concludes his text as follows:

> To look back upon, and seriously to consider the Years of my Captivity, is so frightful and amazing, that all must allow that nothing but the *Almighty Protection* of a *great, good, all-seeing, most sufficient*, and *gracious* GOD, could have carried me through it, or delivered me out of it; therefore, to HIM be the *Glory, Honour*, and *Praise*, and may HE so order my Heart, as always to continue a *lively Remembrance* thereof, and so order my Ways, to live up to HIS *Divine Precepts*, during the Remainder of this *Mortal Life*; that after all these my Sufferings ended here, I may be crowned with a *glorious Immortality*, in the Kingdom of HEAVEN.[46]

45 The British Library's GK3 catalogues the work under Thomas Pellow (shelf mark G. 14628). See Richetti, *Popular Fiction before Richardson*, pp. 107-10, and *A Checklist of English Prose Fiction, 1700-1739*, comp. William H. McBurney (Cambridge, Mass.: Harvard Univ. Press, 1960), p. 107.

46 *The History of the Long Captivity and Adventures of Thomas Pellow* . . . (London, [1739?]), p. 388. There are other scattered allusions to religious piety; cf. pp. 15, 161-63, 192.

The hint of the *imitatio Christi* theme in this passage (imitating the perfections of God, when no member of the Trinity is specified, is invariably taken to refer to the emulation of Christ) is modest, and there is little preparation earlier in the narrative to lead us to expect it, but it is enough to show that the narrator would like us to consider his character as imitating the divine perfections. Does such a reference, appearing almost as an afterthought to a work without any hint of figuralism, make a narrative typological? Obviously not, but it probably does demonstrate that the prefigurative style has become so common, so widespread, by the second third of the eighteenth century that the author of a narrative of personal adventures saw such a conclusion as completely acceptable.

Less than a decade after this Christian ending to a novel that is otherwise mainly secular, Richardson would write, in the "Postscript" to *Clarissa. Or, the History of a Young Lady*, that his work was "designed to inculcate upon the human mind, under the guise of an Amusement, the great Lessons of Christianity, in an Age *like the Present*," when it appears that audiences expect poetic justice at the conclusion of a work of fiction rather than that "which God, by Revelation, teaches us." "The History," he continues, "or rather, The Dramatic Narrative of CLARISSA, is formed on this Religious Plan; and is therefore well justified in deferring to extricate suffering Virtue till it meets with the Completion of its Reward."[47] The novel, as Richardson took great pains to point out, was capable of teaching religious truth and morality by its whole text; he would have disapproved of narratives which were religious because of a few pious passages or a devout conclusion. The novel with a typological story, of which *Clarissa* is the longest, if not best, example from the eighteenth century, has its origins in seventeenth-century religious romance, in pious biographies, and even in the hagiographical tradition of the Renaissance.

By the late seventeenth century, we begin to encounter typological narratives which are patently religious. For example, Robert Boyle's romance, *The Martyrdom of Theodora, and of Didymus* (1687), tells of the suffering of a pair of Christian lovers at the hands of the Romans because they refuse to repudiate Christianity. Martyrdom always associates itself with typology; Boyle's novel is no exception to this rule. The book contains many references to the example and imitation of Jesus' perfections, and the Christian hero-

---

[47] *Clarissa. Or, The History of a Young Lady*, 7 vols. (London, 1748), VII, 425-26.

ism of both leading characters strongly underscores the use of typological persons in early prose fiction. Theodora and Didymus, imprisoned and threatened with death, have a chance to escape their persecutors, but they ignore it, with Theodora somewhat more steadfast in her resolve to die than her lover. Both of them, but especially Theodora, enunciate the *imitatio Christi* theme, and agree to "imitate, as well as own him, whatever it cost them."[48] Didymus, answering a Roman soldier who urges him to abandon his faith, merely stresses "the Power and Honour of Suffering for Him, and of imitating him [i.e., Jesus]"; their Savior becomes a silent exemplar of perfection, nearly a character in the novel. Indeed, the author manages to introduce almost every popular typological theme from contemporary sermons and exegesis: his characters are prefigurations of heavenly glories, they postfigure Jesus' death, they even prophesy typologically that Rome will become Christian.[49] Martyrdom, to be sure, is a somewhat specialized aspect of the typological character, one which we will seldom find in the contemporary novel; Clarissa Harlowe is the principal example of heroic Christian tragedy in prose fiction. As we saw with Barker's *Exilius*, and as the eighteenth-century mythographers eagerly suggested, pagan persecutions or sufferings were often seen as typological of the treatment of contemporary sects like the Puritans. Behn's Oroonoko, whom the other slaves in Surinam worship as a god and whom even his captors rename "Caesar," is another pagan hero with an aura of the Christian martyr. True, Oroonoko does not really sacrifice himself for anyone, although we can view his leadership of the slaves' revolt as a species of pagan heroism. His heroic resistance and brutal execution are not typological, at least not in the contexts which Behn gives for these events, but his death is strongly reminiscent of some of the martyrdoms we read of in Foxe.[50]

Narratives that focus on the castaway or other solitary survivors of disaster (the shipwreck is the most frequent event in this category) have a venerable genealogy, as episodes from the *Odyssey*, the *Aethiopica* of Heliodorus, and the *Decameron* show. We will find the typological possibilities of such stories fulfilled most im-

[48] *The Martyrdom of Theodora, and of Didymus* (London, 1687), p. 19.

[49] *Ibid.*, pp. 169, 170, 176-77, 225, 227-28, 230.

[50] See Aphra Behn, *Oroonoko: or, The Royal Slave*, in *The Histories and Novels of the Late Ingenious Mrs. Behn* (London, 1696), pp. 53-54 (each contribution to the volume is separately paginated).

pressively in *Robinson Crusoe*. An important variation to this subgenre is the story of the already committed castaway who does not
need to undergo a Crusoe-like conversion. Peter Longueville's *The
English Hermit* (1727), a work which shows the influence of Defoe,
is the story of a self-sufficient hermit named Philip Quarll who
spends fifty years on an uninhabited island off the coast of Mexico.
The novel has some features in common with *Crusoe*, including
prophetic dreams with millennial (and hence typological) intima-
tions, providential intervention, and a general sense of preservation
amidst many dangers.[51] Quarll's adventures, except for his symbolic
dreams, are not explicitly figural, but scattered allusions to typological stories from the Bible strengthen the book's prefigurative
style. On one occasion, the hermit compares a ship that tries un-
successfully to rescue him to the Ark (Noahic typology); another
time, after reflecting upon his prosperity, the narrator comments,
"In this most blessed State he thinks of himself as Adam before his
fall, having no Room for Wishes, only that every Thing may continue in its present Condition."[52] To achieve a state of prelapsarian
purity and sinlessness is no minor achievement; it is among the supreme typological events. The author, in the tradition of Bunyan
and Keach, prefaces his text with a set of verses "On the Hermit's
Solitude":

> 'Tis with content Quarll lives, he's truly blest,
> Has nought to dread, nor is with nought distrest;
> Prays for his Country, and its present Prince,
> That he may reign in Heaven, when call'd from Hence.
> Here, in these lonely Shades, he just uprose,
> A Type of Resurrection to disclose;
> A Resurrection from a Wat'ry Hell,
> Where Shoals of Terrors strove which should excell.

[51] Richetti, *Popular Fiction before Richardson*, pp. 96-104, gives an interesting
interpretation of this novel as parallel to *Robinson Crusoe*.

[52] [Peter Longueville,] *The English Hermit, or the Unparallel'd and Surprizing Adventures of one Philip Quarll* (London, 1727), pp. 215-16, 220, 243. The
authorship of the work is uncertain; see Arundell Esdaile, "Author and Publisher in 1727: *The English Hermit*," *The Library*, 4th ser., 2 (1922), 185-92,
who argues that Longueville is the author, but that one Edward Dorrington
published a pirated first edition. Esdaile is probably wrong; except for the
preliminaries, the text of both "editions" is identical. The work was one of the
more popular *Robinsonaden*, with more than 19 editions during the eighteenth
century in Great Britain and North America as well as Dutch, French, and
German translations.

A Resurrection, Emblem of the Last,
Which will recall our ev'ry Guilt that's past. . . .[53]

The English Hermit, as this excerpt suggests, is a crude narrative, carelessly written and ungrammatical in a way that would have embarrassed a craftsman like Defoe. Typological passages, however, buttressed with the signs (emblems, biblical allusions) that would assure a contemporary audience that prefiguration was present, are numerous. Longueville is not capable, I think, of producing a well-structured narrative embodying typological patterns, but that such a coarse, popular, work should exist at all is evidence that, by the 1720s, the typological style was a common, perhaps even a *necessary* ingredient of certain kinds of prose fiction.

The factors that I have mentioned in this section—typological allusions in secular history, in personal memoirs, in pious reflections and works of devotion, in popular romances, and in accounts of individual suffering—take effect gradually, over a period of half a century. They do not affect every piece of prose fiction published in England, but their growing influence marks an important period in the history of literary figuralism. The prefigurative trend in prose narrative is not an isolated phenomenon; it parallels figural trends in other kinds of literature. From 1695 to 1745, for example, the period when the *imitatio Christi* theme lends itself to the frequent appearance of typological characters in fiction, more than fifty English editions of à Kempis's *De Imitatione Christi* were published, more than one a year. The moralized character, which is often typological, starts to appear in the first two decades of the eighteenth century, the very period when collections of characters with commentary and the moralized English translations of Aesop were especially numerous—at least one such work appeared, on the average, every year. Typological prophecies, sometimes with a chiliastic slant, start to appear in novels between 1715 and 1725, the years when the controversy over scriptural prophecy flourished. The rage for figural predictions (some of them instances of prefiguration) in the novel which starts about the time of *Robinson Crusoe* must also be linked with the rise of figural predictions in diaries, almanacs, calendars, and other ephemeral publications of the early eighteenth century and with the steady popularity of millenarianism.[54]

[53] *The English Hermit*, p. 4.

[54] An examination of the tens of thousands of surviving pieces of ephemera for this period is beyond the scope of this book. The largest collection, so far

4

From the typological precursors of eighteenth-century fiction, we come to the principal exemplars of this figural mode: from the foothills to the mountains. In the next three sections, I shall discuss no more than twenty works, a dozen in some detail, the others briefly. Every major novelist of the century except Sterne will appear in the following pages and, if I were to widen the focus of this chapter, dozens of lesser authors could appear as well. Typology in the eighteenth-century novel has three kinds of existence. First, there are novels with typological patterns or structures inherent in their form. Second, there is a class of novels which include one or more typological characters; it is a large class indeed, for characters embodying a prefigurative structure or prefigurative qualities are common in the literature of this period. Finally, I will discuss several works which actually embody typological stories. I should emphasize at the start that many of the texts that I shall deal with are works for which numerous other interpretations and kinds of readings have been proposed. The purpose of this chapter is not to offer new and different exegeses of these novels but to enlarge our understanding of them by showing the existence of their typological dimension which has, until now, gone almost entirely unnoticed.

Perhaps *Robinson Crusoe*, of all eighteenth-century prose narratives, is the ideal example of a typologically patterned novel. Defoe, as we have long been aware, was influenced by aspects of typological tradition. The spiritual biography, the emblematical life story or narrative, and a homiletic and exegetical religious background rich in prefigurative elements all blend into his best works.[55] As Paul K.

---

as I know, is at the British Library; its exact size is not yet known. Diaries (e.g., *The Gentleman's Diary* [1742-1840]), almanacs (e.g., *The Court and City Register* [1742-1809], *Dade* [1604-1701]), and calendars regularly include instances of prognostications, predictions, and iconographical figures—such materials clearly were common coin in the eighteenth century.

[55] See Starr, *Defoe and Spiritual Autobiography*, pp. 33-38; and J. Paul Hunter, *The Reluctant Pilgrim: Defoe's Emblematic Method and Quest for Form in Robinson Crusoe* (Baltimore: Johns Hopkins Univ. Press, 1966), pp. 93-124. This chapter, entitled "Metaphor, Type, Emblem, and the Puritan 'Allegory,'" discusses typology only very briefly (pp. 99-101), but is nevertheless an important statement on figuralism in the novel to which I am much indebted in this present chapter. See also Robert W. Ayers, "*Robinson Crusoe*: 'Allusive Allegorick History,'" *PMLA*, 82 (1967), 399-407, a strongly religious reading of Defoe's figuralism. Pat Rogers, *Robinson Crusoe* (London: G. Allen

Alkon has recently observed, "Defoe shared with the majority of his readers the typological habit of mind involved not only in the assumption that Old Testament events prefigure those of the New Testament but, more generally, that the past offers archetypes of the present and future."[56] Alkon finds typology a helpful method for solving some of the many puzzles of Defoe's chronological "placing" of events in his narratives; both Defoe and his audience were familiar enough with typology to be able readily to accept—and to understand—prefigurative events, scenes, and characters in prose narratives without quibbling about imprecision in historical or chronological timing. In fact, by the time Defoe turned his hand to his major prose narratives, he was nearly sixty years old, and must, like his contemporaries, have been hearing about types and antitypes from exegetes and millenarians for most of his life. The millenarian prophecies of the Bible, to the eighteenth-century reader, were types with any number of possible antitypes throughout post-biblical time, up to and including the present. What we twentieth-century readers might call an "archetype" Defoe and his audience would call a "type." Today, readers might not think of an archetype shadowing forth later events, but for Defoe's audience types always imply that which they prefigure later in time or—in literary situations—later in a text. What is true of a typologically patterned novel like *Robinson Crusoe*, then, would be true in a lesser way of some of Defoe's other prose narratives.

The story of the shipwrecked victim saved from destruction, as Crusoe is saved, is a plain postfiguration of the Jonah-type, one of the most common types of Christ's Resurrection to be used in the eighteenth-century sermon. That Crusoe is the sole survivor of *three* shipwrecks instead of the more usual one intensifies the Jonah identification.[57] Crusoe is a typological character in other ways, too. He violates the laws of filial obedience, scorns religion, and pharisaically discredits the near-miracle by which he grows his first shoots

---

& Unwin, 1979), pp. 51-72, discusses religious and allegorical readings of the work, noting (pp. 63-66) a few of its typological possibilities, but urging restraint on those who would "make the correspondences too strict and . . . drown the text in scriptural allusions of doubtful relevance" (p. 63).

[56] See *Defoe and Fictional Time*, p. 40.

[57] See *The Life and Strange Surprizing Adventures of Robinson Crusoe* (London, 1719), p. 15, where another sailor urges Crusoe not to go to sea again: "*As you made this Voyage for a Tryal, you see what a Taste Heaven has given you of what to expect if you persist; perhaps this is all befallen us on your Account, like* Jonah *in the Ship of* Tarshish."

of corn—we can readily see him as an unbeliever or an apostate. But he undergoes a protracted religious conversion, thus becoming a postfiguration, if not of the Apostle Paul, then of the universal redeemed sinner. The process of conversion, in seventeenth-century devotional and sermon literature, is always the step whereby the errant Christian becomes a partial type of Christ by attaining some of his divine perfections. In his postconversion serenity, it is true, Crusoe undertakes a vendetta against different groups of cannibals, but Defoe did not regard this attitude as inconsistent with his hero's new-found faith. Crusoe is as "fearful of seeing [the cannibals], as of seeing the Devil himself," for the heathen people's "Hellish Degeneracy" is so extreme that they perform pagan sacrifices of a sort.[58] The cannibals, Satan-like, are thus, collectively, a negative type. It is therefore appropriate for Crusoe to try to thwart them and to save their intended victim and, since the rescue of Friday from sacrifice recalls God's intervention to prevent the sacrifice of Isaac, typological as well. The novel also includes prophetic dreams and a second conversion (that of Friday, from paganism to Christianity). When Crusoe, after his early misfortunes, recalls his "father's *Prophetick discourse*," he adds that his woes thus far "were but a Taste of the Misery I was to go through."[59] So typological incidents and emblems, of which these are but a sampling, interspersed throughout the narrative, are an essential part of Defoe's great work.

The presence of a number of types or typological scenes—indeed, the novel is a succession of prefigurative episodes—is not enough by itself to make *Robinson Crusoe* a novel with a typological pattern. Defoe gives the book such an arrangement the way Bunyan does in *The Pilgrim's Progress*—by framing his story to fit a typological subject. For Bunyan, the pilgrimage of human life is a figuration of the individual's struggle to achieve salvation; Christian's story, as I said earlier, is both pre- and postfiguration of the life and mission of Christ and of the Savior's perfections. In Defoe's case, the central figuration of *Robinson Crusoe* is *deliverance* which, for Crusoe himself, operates on several levels. He must undergo deliverance from disaster (shipwrecks), from captivity by the Moors, from his own sinfulness, and from his island. Numerous references to the subject in the text of the novel corroborate Defoe's overarching structure. He would later note that he regarded *Crusoe* as "an allusive alle-

[58] *Ibid.*, pp. 195-96, 199, 201.
[59] *Ibid.*, p. 20; cf. p. 5 for the "truly Prophetick" discourse of Crusoe's father.

gorick History" in the style of New Testament parables or *The Pilgrim's Progress*. In what way does he make the work so? The key, I suspect, lies in his treatment of the theme of deliverance. Crusoe, in his religious meditations, turns often to the subject of his miseries and, despite his suffering, his preservation from death. He sees that his opposition to his father's "excellent Advice . . . was, *as I may call it*, my ORIGINAL SIN."[60] Like Adam, Crusoe's disobedience has exiled him from a life of comfort to one of adversity. All that the Old Testament patriarchs were given to comfort them with the possibility of redemption were the signs or types which are everywhere in the text of the Pentateuch but, according to the standard exegetical view, few of them before Moses understood what the types meant. Crusoe, thinking of how Providence has delivered him from "so many unseen Dangers," muses on deliverance:

> This renew'd a Contemplation, which often had come to my Thoughts in former Time, when first I began to see the merciful Dispositions of Heaven, in the Dangers we run through in this Life. How wonderfully we are deliver'd, when we know nothing of it. How when we are in (a *Quandary*, as we call it) a Doubt or Hesitation, whether to go this Way, or that Way, a secret Hint shall direct us this Way, when we intended to go that Way; nay, when Sense, our own Inclination, and perhaps Business has call'd to go the other Way, yet a strange Impression upon the Mind, from we know not what Springs, and by we know not what Power, shall over-rule us to go this Way; and it shall afterwards appear, that had we gone that Way which we should have gone, and even to our Imagination ought to have gone, we should have been ruin'd and lost.[61]

The "secret Hint[s]" save Crusoe from many disasters. They are evidently behind his accidentally landing from the shipwreck on the side of the island which the cannibals practically never visit, and are responsible for his being saved during the earthquake and again from the strong currents that seize his canoe during one of his misguided efforts to escape. Crusoe himself never learns what these mysterious signs are; like the postlapsarian Adam, deprived of revelation, he knows that they are there, but no more.

Defoe saw no reason to deprive his audience of such insights, so he scatters prefigurative hints here and there throughout his narra-

[60] *Ibid.*, p. 230.
[61] *Ibid.*, p. 207.

tive. I have already mentioned his use of the Jonah and Edenic types, but the most obvious type of deliverance is that of the Jews from Egypt. Crusoe, unlike the Jews and like Milton's Adam, is always certain that he will be saved; he longs for companionship so that he can "learn some Knowledge . . . of the Place where I was, and of the probable Means of my Deliverance."[62] Later, when he has several companions to help him escape, one of them, the Spaniard, urges moderation: "You know, says he, the Children of *Israel,* though they rejoyc'd at first for their being deliver'd out of Egypt, yet rebell'd even against God himself that deliver'd them, when they came to want Bread in the Wilderness."[63] Defoe gives no intimation that his hero understands this "secret Hint" any more than he understands the other typological promises of his deliverance, but of course there is no reason for a character in a prefigurative drama to be his own exegete (only Jesus, of all such characters, is fully aware of the types that surround him). Since Defoe himself is the child of a Puritan exegetical tradition in which typology played a large role, it is reasonable for him to reflect that tradition in his fictional narratives. Just as seventeenth-century Puritans were accustomed to regard their position in England as a captivity of sorts, as a postfiguration of the Jews in their various captivities and adversities, so Defoe makes *Robinson Crusoe* into a novel in the same typological pattern. When Crusoe finally sees "my Deliverance indeed visibly put into my Hands," he tells the captain of the vessel that "I look'd upon him as a Man sent from Heaven to deliver me." It is a neat ending to the parable of Robinson Crusoe's sufferings, which Defoe first mentions on page two and with which he is almost continually concerned thereafter. It is worth noting that Defoe gives his audience a foreshadowing of this deliverance much earlier, in the key passage where Crusoe opens his Bible "casually." "The first words that occur'd to me were these, *Call on me in the Day of Trouble, and I will deliver, and thou shall glorify me.*"[64] As Crusoe makes his final computation of the length

62 *Ibid.,* p. 234.

63 *Ibid.,* p. 292.

64 *Ibid.,* pp. 323-24, 110. The biblical quotation, Psalms 50.15 (slightly misquoted: ". . . and I will deliver *thee* . . .") and, indeed, the entire 50th Psalm, have typological significance. Henry Hammond, *A Paraphrase and Annotations upon the Books of the Psalms* (1659), 2nd ed. (London, 1683), Sig. a1^r, discusses the typological aspects of the Psalms in detail. Hammond sees Psalm 50 as a prefiguration of the Messiah (pp. 148-49).

of time he has spent on the island, he observes that he has been "deliver'd from this second Captivity" much as the exegetes referred to the delivery of Israel from its two captivities, the Egyptian and the Babylonian.[65] The typological pattern of the novel is complete: what Defoe has foreshadowed on dozens of occasions he has accomplished in full.

Defoe continues to use typological patterning as a device in *A Journal of the Plague Year*. In *Crusoe*, his sufferer is a man who is far from perfect, one who has sinned in a way recognizable to all and whose individual deliverance is the result of a personal religious experience. But in *The Plague Year* the sinner is an entire urban population, perhaps an entire people, for in Old Testament imagery cities are frequently a synecdoche for a whole nation. When the work concerns an individual like Robinson Crusoe, the typological pattern in which he is involved deals with sin, expiation, conversion, repentance, and deliverance. For a heterogeneous group, Defoe is more comfortable with a different kind of typological pattern, that of deliverance from the threat of apocalypse. Signs of apocalypse appear in the Bible long before the Book of Revelation; from patristic times, exegetes interpreted the plagues of Egypt and the prophecies of Jeremiah and Daniel as types of Judgment Day. Defoe is conscious of these types, for he refers to them all on various occasions, and his narrator, the saddler "H.F.," is more aware than Crusoe of the types which embrace his story. When he opens the Old Testament to Psalms 91.1, he interprets the text typologically, as a sign from God that he will be delivered from the plague.[66] Yet the types of messianic deliverance are not seen by all. H.F. goes on to foreshadow doom:

---

[65] *Robinson Crusoe*, p. 320. The typological patterning of *Robinson Crusoe* may be something of a puzzle, for Defoe, after all, has Crusoe declare that he was not a very religious man, at least not before his isolation on the island. But Defoe does not completely accept typology on all occasions. We know, for example, from his *A New Test of the Church of England's Loyalty: Or, Whiggish Loyalty and Church Loyalty Compar'd* ([London,] 1702), p. 12, that he considered typological parallels between Charles I and Christ to be "Blasphemous," although he does call Charles I "that blessed Martyr." Contemporary hostility to the excesses of political typology is fairly common, so it is significant that Defoe's objection is not to typology *per se* but to its excessive political application.

[66] *A Journal of the Plague Year* (London, 1722), pp. 15-16. Interpreters of the period usually treat Psalm 91 as one promising messianic deliverance and resurrection. See Hammond, *A Paraphrase and Annotations*, pp. 263-64.

> But I must go back to the Beginning of this Surprizing Time, while the Fears of the People were young, they were encreas'd strangely by several odd Accidents which put together, it was realy a wonder the whole Body of the People did not rise as one Man, and abandon their Dwellings, leaving the Place as a Space of Ground designed by Heaven for an Akeldama, doom'd to be destroy'd from the Face of the Earth; and all that would be found in it, would perish with it. I shall Name but a few of these Things. . . .[67]

The description of apocalyptic destruction is a typological dramatization of the prophecies of Revelation: the saddler makes it appear as if the great antitype of Revelation were about to come to pass. Of course, the people of London *are* wicked, and they do *not* arise and abandon their city, for the black trumpet of doom will be understood by few. Defoe then follows with a series of predictions, both true and false, some of which the saddler accepts, others of which he lets pass without comment. The follies and brutal behavior of the people as destruction stares them in the face are analogous to the behavior of the citizens of Nineveh, one of the Old Testament pagan cities whose destruction was seen as a type of sin, hell, and death. The analogy to Nineveh is doubly typological because, in the Book of Jonah (3.2-10), Jonah prophesies to the residents of Nineveh that their city "shall be overthrown." The Ninevites repent, and God does not destroy their city after all. The type of Nineveh would tell Defoe's eighteenth-century audience what they already knew, that the London of 1665 was also spared. Other apparently typological episodes round out the structure of *The Plague Year*. We have, for instance, the story of the poor man, "a serious, religious good Man," who does not abandon his contagion-stricken family, but rather serves them from afar during their illness. He is probably a type of the Christ figure, as the shepherd who does not abandon his flock (most of the London clergy, Defoe carefully notes, *had* abandoned theirs). We hear, at great length, the story of three poor men who flee the plague; with them, Defoe enunciates a collective pattern theme: "Their Story has a Moral in every Part of it, and their Conduct, and that of some who they

[67] *Ibid.*, p. 23. On Akeldama, the field of blood where Judas killed himself, see Acts 1.19.

join'd with, is a Patern for all poor Men to follow, or Women either, if ever such a Time comes again."[68]

A Journal of the Plague Year, then, is a narrative whose typological pattern, like that of *Crusoe*, is one of deliverance from the threat of destruction. Thus Defoe undertakes to show that the plague was an apocalyptic warning, a type of the ultimate judgment to come:

> I would be far from lessening the Awe of the Judgments of God, and the Reverence to his Providence, which ought always to be on our Minds on such Occasions as these; doubtless the Visitation it self is a Stroke from Heaven upon a City, or Country, or Nation where it falls; a Messenger of his Vengeance, and a loud Call to that Nation, or Country, or City, to Humiliation and Repentance according to that of the Prophet *Jeremiah*, xviii. 7, 8. . . . Now to prompt due Impressions of the Awe of God on the Minds of Men on such Occasions, and not to lessen them it is that I have left those Minutes upon Record. . . .[69]

The signs of apocalypse are also calls to repentance, but the humble, artless saddler is no sermonizer, no officious canter of religious visions; he simply gives his observations of things. Defoe has his narrator allege that London's deliverance from the plague was accomplished by "the immediate Finger of God," but he insists that his book is not a sermon but a history.[70] *The Plague Year* is not a typological exegesis, one which explains the types in *another* text. Rather, it is a self-contained typological narrative which creates its own shadows of apocalypse and redemption from it and which contains and meticulously interprets its own predictive structures.

The City of Destruction, as Bunyan would have said, like Defoe's London, is a type of apocalypse from which only a timely conversion and repentance can redeem us. Defoe is the first urban novelist but, while his city is far more realistic than those of Bunyan, Keach, and the Puritan autobiographers, he does not abandon the parable-like structure of which, in *Robinson Crusoe*, he was so proud. With both of his typologically patterned narratives, the structure so central to the Puritan—and Christian—experience is the key to an understanding of the work. Both *Crusoe* and *The Plague Year* deal

---

[68] *Ibid.*, p. 140; cf. pp. 140-72. For the episode of the poor man who does not forsake his family, see pp. 123-27.

[69] *Ibid.*, p. 222.

[70] *Ibid.*, p. 285; cf. pp. 282-84 and see Exodus 8.19.

in different ways with apostasy, threats of destruction and death, repentance, and the promise of salvation. Defoe's purposes in writing each work obviously differed, but the parables behind the two are strikingly similar. At the end of the first volume of *Robinson Crusoe*, the hero's conversion and individual prefigurative story are complete, but he leaves his island peopled with unconverted rascals. And, once London has been delivered from the plague, and the saddler has presented his secular homily on the types of destruction and redemption, the Court returns from exile at Oxford and its licentious existence resumes (parallel to that of George I's court in 1722). Some prophecies, Defoe no doubt thought, are best left unfulfilled. Blake, who would prophesy the New Jerusalem from the perspective of an equally fallen London some eighty years later, would have agreed.

When Moll Flanders, the heroine of Defoe's next (after *Crusoe*) major fictional narrative, finally completes the circle that returns her to Newgate, her birthplace, Defoe makes very little of the antitype of the many foreshadowings of Moll's doom with which he has provided us. True, Moll surveys the scene and notes that "all the dreadful croud of Afflicting things that I saw there; joyn'd together to make the Place seem an Emblem of Hell itself, and a kind of Entrance into it."[71] And, true again, *Moll Flanders* (1721) antedates the typologically structured *Journal of the Plague Year* by a year. Yet in many ways Defoe was already experimenting with new styles of architecture for the novel form he was evolving. Accordingly, while we do see many foreshadowings of Moll's future, they are seldom attended by the existing methodology of prefiguration. Even Moll's repentance is perfunctory compared to Crusoe's drawn-out spiritual regeneration; there is no *sortes Virgilianae* with the Bible and, indeed, Moll never reads or quotes from Scripture at all. Defoe assures us, in his "Preface," that the whole relation is "applied . . . with the utmost care to vertuous and religious Uses," but now he evidently wished his readers to deduce the religious applications with less homiletic prompting than *Crusoe* had used.[72] The

71 *The Fortunes and Misfortunes of the Famous Moll Flanders, &c.* (London, 1721), p. 337.

72 *Ibid.*, p. viii. Henry Knight Miller, in a forthcoming essay, "Some Reflections on Defoe's *Moll Flanders* and the Romance Tradition," in *Greene Centennial Studies*, ed. Robert R. Allen and Paul J. Korshin (Charlottesville: Univ. Press of Virginia, 1982), argues for a much stronger Christian interpretation of *Moll* than I have given here, and notes Defoe's typological patterning of the plot.

entire work, he adds a moment later, is one from every part of which "some just and religious *Inference* is drawn, by which the Reader will have something of Instruction, if he pleases to make use of it."

Defoe thus heralds the end of the typologically patterned narrative he had presented in *Crusoe* and which he would reintroduce, in a somewhat altered manner, in *The Plague Year*. The narrative patterned on the central events of the Christian life, which Defoe derived from seventeenth-century sources, was stiff and ill-suited to the demands of dialogue and characterization, and did not readily accommodate subplots. We will not find this kind of abstracted typology in the novel very often beyond the 1720s. Ramsay's *The Travels of Cyrus* (1727), as I have noted, is a narrative with a typological structure, but it belongs to an entirely different tradition from that in which Defoe is working. Moreover, Ramsay's *Cyrus* does not inspire imitators except in the peripheral sense that it may be related to later mythographical studies of Christian origins. Nor do other, more allegorical narratives lead to much in the way of typological patterning. *Rasselas*, for example, is an allegory of the choice of life whose characters discover that the choice of eternity makes more sense. Johnson's novel deals with its hero's flight from an earthly paradise, the pilgrimage of the four main characters to Cairo, where all the vanities of Ecclesiastes are centered, and their gradually learning that the pilgrimage does not necessarily lead to happiness. Salvation, Johnson seems to be suggesting, is found through self-knowledge and by achieving personal sanity, not by various trials of the will against external foes. The conclusion leads back to the beginning, as Rasselas and his entourage plan to return to Abyssinia. Johnson employs a familiar pattern—one of quest and return—in *Rasselas*, but it is doubtful that he had a formal prefigurative purpose in mind when he wrote it.

Johnson's earlier, much shorter, narrative, "The Vision of Theodore, the Hermit of Teneriffe" (1748), contains some of the ingredients which other writers had employed with figurative skill—a vision and a hermit—and Johnson's hermit, to help matters, does have a kind of Pisgah-sight. He dreams, and behold, an angelic being offers him instruction if he will "look round . . . without fear": "I looked and beheld a mountain higher than Teneriffe, to the summit of which the human eye could never reach."[73] The

---

[73] *The Works of Samuel Johnson, LL. D.*, 9 vols. (Oxford, 1825), IX, 164.

mountain of Existence, as Johnson calls it, is populated with allegorical beings representing the vicissitudes of human life. There is a Bunyanesque straight and narrow way to the mountaintop, unattainable without following Religion, and there are a number of paths to the caverns of Despair, where most of the voyagers on the mountainside appear to tend. For Johnson's allegorical humans, the climb through existence is "the toil of their pilgrimage," a standard typological *topos* in narrative forms.[74] While the bulk of the events in "The Vision of Theodore" are not prefigurative, the piece nevertheless shows how a typological structure could be adapted to an entire (though brief) narrative. "The Vision," in its entirety, is an interesting exercise in typological iconography, including some of the standard devices that Ripa had used and which George Richardson, Ripa's chief English follower, would elaborate.[75] But as a typologically patterned work, "The Vision of Theodore" suffers by comparison with other similar narratives because it is so short, consisting mainly of brief descriptions for allegorical and iconographical purposes. Perhaps its chief value for students of typology is that it shows what the narratives of Bunyan and Defoe might be like if they were completely stripped of their episodes. Novels with prefigurative structures will continue to appear from time to time in the second half of the eighteenth century, but they will not be the main source of typology in the novel. For the wider road, we must turn to novels with typological characters.

I suggested earlier that, in the eighteenth century, certain literary characters function as *predictive structures* (see Chapter 5, section 6). When such characters appear in novels of our period, a reader's

---

[74] *Ibid.*, IX, 169. On the theme of pilgrimage in Johnson, see *Rasselas*, Chap. xi, and cf. Thomas M. Curley, *Samuel Johnson and the Age of Travel* (Athens, Ga.: Univ. of Georgia Press, 1976), pp. 169-82.

[75] See George Richardson, *Iconology; or, A Collection of Emblematical Figures*, 2 vols. (London, 1779), I, i-vii. Compare Johnson's figure of Innocence (*Works*, IX, 165, with Richardson's *Iconology*, I, 84-85; Plate XL, Fig. 155); Education (*Works*, IX, 168, with *Iconology*, I, 100; Pl. XLVII, Fig. 181); Religion (*Works*, IX, 170, with *Iconology*, II, 136-37; Pl. C, Fig. 387); Melancholy (*Works*, IX, 174, with *Iconology*, II, 109-10; Pl. XCI, Fig. 352); and Despair (*Works*, IX, 173, 175, with *Iconology*, II, 27-28; Pl. LXII, Fig. 238). See also Figure 20 in this volume.

knowledge of the larger class or type of which they are specimens enables him or her to predict how they are likely to behave. Not all fictional characters fall into this category, but for those that do, the *character type*, as we now call this kind of fictional creation, would be prefigurative for those who recognized it. One reason why we respond so rapidly to stock situations and personages in many kinds of literature (as well as in farce, vaudeville, burlesque, television, and so on) is that we are affected by both the ability and the normal human tendency to predict human behavior and character traits based on what we already know. I call this tendency *the typology of everyday life*, and I will discuss it at greater length in Chapter 10. We still need to learn a great deal about how the eighteenth-century audience responded to prefigurative characters in the novel. Whether all readers knew enough about typology to recognize it when it appeared in fiction is a question that will always puzzle students of the period. However, I think that the level of recognition was high, even among less educated readers, for typology occurs with frequency in many popular devotional works and in much ephemeral literature. The evidence I have collected thus far will be sufficient to persuade some, perhaps many, twentieth-century readers of how widespread the *imitatio Christi* tropology was in eighteenth-century literature and life, and how readily even a reader who did not have a formal education could spot these types when they did occur. It is noteworthy, in this context, that the typological facility of the self-educated Richardson is in some ways greater than that of the classically educated Fielding.

It is crucial to my argument at this point to show why the typologically patterned narrative, in the style of *The Pilgrim's Progress* or *Robinson Crusoe*, lost popularity and was replaced by novels with other typological methodologies. The explanation is that the more sophisticated audiences of the second third of the century (while they continued to read Bunyan, Defoe, and a host of similar writers) evidently were attracted by novels with more secular themes than Bunyan and Defoe had provided. Defoe himself turned to a more worldly kind of fiction after 1722. The character of the Christian Hero, as Steele had proposed it, could be popular for a while, but it required elaboration. By 1735, George Lillo's play of this title is flat and uninteresting; typological characters, to be attractive to a contemporary audience, had to be furnished out so that they seemed like characters in real life, probable characters, rather than illustrations to a sermon. The typological character also had to be sufficiently credible to withstand ridicule. Typological satire begins in the mid-seventeenth century with the efforts of that pair of ridiculers of mystery-mongering, Cleveland and Butler. There would be a rash of such satire in the late 1720s and 1730s, starting with *The Dunciad Variorum*. The greatness of kings and ministers, butter for the seventeenth-century typologist's bread, would be a favorite subject on which Fielding and Pope would attack the establishment. Richardson discovered, to his embarrassment, that Pamela's chastity, which made her, in the eyes of some readers, a postfiguration of that Christian saintliness which could convert the ungodly, simply made her a huge joke to many others. So the typological character, to be persuasive and probable, had to be less forced and less obvious than it had been earlier in the century.

One possible solution was Fielding's in *Joseph Andrews* (1742). There can be little question that Fielding deliberately created the typological dimensions of Parson Abraham Adams and Joseph himself. The biblical Joseph was understood to be a type of Christ, and Fielding's attractive youth clearly has christomimetic qualities. In his leisure time in the Booby household, he "had read the Bible, the *Whole Duty of Man*, and *Thomas à Kempis*," but he reads silly chronicles, too.[76] Joseph's chastity is completely resolute, but he is far from perfect. He likes his ale, trades punches and cudgelings with miscellaneous thugs, and empties a jordan on the head of an intruder (if Sir Charles Grandison so much as uses a jordan, we do not hear of it). If he is a fictional transfiguration of Jesus, he fills this role in its comic as well as its serious aspects. Joseph even delivers an oration on charity, complete with allusions to Pope's famous Christ type, the Man of Ross, and to Fielding's favorite *Christianus perfectus*, Ralph Allen. "I defy the wisest Man in the World," he declaims, "to turn a true good Action into Ridicule. I defy him to do it." But Parson Adams has nodded off and snores loudly through this homily (so much for Shaftesburian preaching).[77] Joseph is an "intended Martyr," but only to Mrs. Slipslop's wrath—typology becomes slightly jocular.[78] Parson Adams is another postfiguration

---

[76] See *Joseph Andrews*, ed. Martin C. Battestin (Oxford: Clarendon Press, 1967), p. 24. Thomas Stackhouse, *A New History of the Bible from the Beginning of the World to the Establishment of Christianity*, 2 vols. (London, 1737), I, 324, emphasizes the typology of the biblical Joseph; other commentators actually stressed the kinship between the narratives of Joseph and Jesus Christ.

[77] *Ibid.*, p. 234; cf. pp. 233-35. The notion that true goodness could not be turned to ridicule derives from Shaftesbury's *Characticksticks*.

[78] *Ibid.*, p. 34.

—of Christ as servant to the poor, healer of the sick, shepherd to his flock (he takes the injunction "Feed my sheep" [John 21.17] literally), and teacher of the true faith. On twenty-three pounds a year, he practices and inculcates the values of primitive Christianity. But Adams is a Christian hero on the human scale: he is ill-dressed and unpolished in manner and boring as an ecclesiastical speaker. Unlike the patriarch Abraham, who does not lament God's order to sacrifice Isaac, Adams, while delivering a discourse on this very subject, hears that his youngest son has just drowned; naturally, and predictably, he bitterly laments his loss, just long enough to become believable. At this point his son, like the Isaac-type, is restored to him.[79] Few novelists of the eighteenth century would employ typology on such a human scale.

However, when Fielding gets down to sober dealings with *figura*, as he does at the conclusion to *Joseph Andrews*, he does not try to undercut the typology of the work. The double recognition scene involving Fanny and Joseph would be a page from romance were it not for the prefigurative qualities of the event. Mr. Wilson, Joseph's real father, suddenly excited,

> embracing [Joseph] with a complexion all pale and trembling, desired to see the Mark on his Breast; the Parson followed him capering, rubbing his Hands, and crying out, *Hic est quem quaeris, inventus est, &c. Joseph* complied with the Request of Mr. *Wilson*, who no sooner saw the Mark, than abandoning himself to the most extravagant Rapture of Passion, he embraced Joseph, with inexpressible Extasy, and cried out in Tears of Joy, *I have discovered my Son, I have him again in my Arms.*[80]

Joseph becomes a complex prefiguration here. Adam's quotation from Scripture (actually an approximate recollection of two texts) associates Joseph with the risen Savior. Mr. Wilson's excitement recalls the narrative parable of the return of the prodigal son (Luke 15.11-32), a passage that stresses the typological qualities of repentance. Finally, the scene looks back to Joseph's self-revelation to his eleven brothers and later to Jacob, all of whom had thought him long dead (Gen. 45, 46). As early as the Middle Ages, exegetes of Genesis had regarded the recognition scene in Genesis 45 as a type

[79] *Ibid.*, pp. 308-10.
[80] *Ibid.*, p. 339. Adams's Latin text is a conflation of Matt. 28.5-6 and Luke 24.5-6, both passages that announce the resurrection of Jesus.

of Jesus' appearing to his eleven remaining Apostles after his death and resurrection.[81] Since Fielding has already established Joseph Andrews as a postfiguration of Joseph in Egypt, he must have expected his audience to identify Joseph's other prefigurative qualities in this important scene. Indeed, this passage has iconographical qualities as well, for Mr. Wilson knows his son from "the Mark on his Breast," which closely approximates Jesus' fifth wound, one of the marks by which the resurrected Jesus makes himself known to the Eleven on several occasions (this scene is the subject of several heroic seventeenth-century paintings). Recognition scenes, I would note, are part of the stock materials of romance, whether Christian or pagan, and the discovery of a missing child long thought dead was as popular in the fourteenth century (as a number of examples in *The Decameron* show) as in the eighteenth. Fielding's structural pattern of exile, initiation, and return is an ancient one. But the recognition scene in *Joseph Andrews* contains some unusual biblical echoes as a result of the characters of Joseph and Parson Adams. Earlier in the novel, Fielding had juxtaposed comic and serious elements when alluding to the typological qualities of his characters, but here, in the penultimate chapter of the book, he is very much in earnest. One can scarcely ask for a better example of the typology of character, but I would stress at this point that Fielding's novelistic structure itself is not prefigurative in the same way as is that of *Robinson Crusoe*. *Joseph Andrews* represents a new departure in the application of typology to the English novel.

Following Fielding's work, and in part because of it, we will find a number of novels with typological characters, not the least of which is *Tom Jones*. Fielding must have intended his readers to notice the typological qualities of Mr. Allworthy, a fictionalized

---

[81] The resurrected Jesus appears to the eleven on several occasions; see Matt. 28.16-20, Luke 24.36-49, John 20.24-29, and Acts 1.3-9. See Henry Ainsworth, *Annotations upon the Five Bookes of Moses, the Booke of the Psalmes, and the Song of Songs* . . . (London, 1639), p. 154. Richard Kidder, in *A Demonstration of the Messias*, in *A Collection of the Sermons preached at the Lecture founded by* . . . *Boyle*, I, 140, comments, "It cannot be denied, that the most *Holy* and *separate* Persons in the Old Testament, were *Types* of the *Messias*: Such was the *High Priest*; such was *David*, by whose name the *Messias* is sometimes called; and such was *Joseph*, who was *separate from his Brethren*." Nicholas of Lyra's gloss to Gen. 45 states that Joseph's revealing himself to his father is a sign of the incarnation of Christ and to his brothers is a sign of Christ's gathering his Apostles. See *Biblia Sacra cum glossis, interlinearia et ordinaria, Nicolai Lyrani postilla*, 7 vols. (Venice, 1588), I, 111ᵛ-112ᵛ.

Ralph Allen of Bath, and of Tom himself, exiled from Allworthy's Paradise Hall. *Adamus exilius* prefigures a later return to paradise after the resurrection (or a *figura* of resurrection, like repentance), and of course Tom does return in the end, when he is revealed to be Allworthy's nephew and heir (to make Jones the *son* of Allworthy would have carried resemblances too far, and Fielding was wary of overstressing typology). Fielding's sister Sarah, in *The Adventures of David Simple* (1744), creates a series of character types with Bunyanesque qualities and names like Orgeuil, Spatter, and Varnish. In his preface to the second edition of this book, Fielding specifically links his sister's character-drawing techniques to Theophrastus and La Bruyère.[82] He could have said a good deal more than he does about Sarah's use of typological characters, with reference especially to her hero, who bears his deprivations and sufferings without complaint and with Job-like patience. The conclusion to Book V, where the author notes that David Simple's sorrows are insufficient to subdue the Christian mind, is relevant:

> For, like *Job, David Simple* patiently submitted to the temporary Sufferings alloted him: and, from a Dependence on his Maker, acquired that Chearfulness and Calmness of Mind, which is not in the Power of the highest worldly Prosperity, without such a Dependence, to bestow.[83]

The Job-tropology here is effective, although the novel ends with David's death rather than with the restoration of his family and property. For this reason, the typology of character in *David Simple* is less biblical than that of *Joseph Andrews*. David is a postfiguration, in part, of Job's patience, but his real significance is as a type of the perfect Christian whose true hope is in the world beyond the grave. Thus his final thoughts on his life and career are the utmost statement of Christian humility and a close, though unskillful, representation of the *imitatio Christi* theme. The character with Job-like qualities would come to a richer fruition in *The Vicar of Wakefield*, and the *Christianus perfectus* would reach its apogee with *Sir Charles Grandison* (Richardson knew Sarah Fielding and had read her novels). Thus Sarah Fielding's typology serves as a useful bridge between the more biblical prefigurations of the early part of the century and the secularized portraits that predominate after 1750.

[82] See *The Adventures of David Simple*, ed. Malcolm Kelsall (London: Oxford Univ. Press, 1969), p. 7.
[83] *Ibid.*, p. 334.

The secularized typological character appears, to give one well-known example, in Henry Mackenzie's *The Man of Feeling* (1771), a self-confessed "fragment" of great sentimental reputation. Mackenzie's Man of Feeling, Harley, is not entirely devoted to sensibility for the sufferings of others (although these consume a good portion of the book). Harley, overtaken by "romantic enthusiasm," offers to assist a crippled old man (Mr. Edwards): "There is that in your appearance which excites my curiosity to know something more of you: in the mean time, suffer me to carry that knapsack." Mr. Edwards has been a soldier, not a mariner, but in Harley's burst of romantic ardor to learn more about the man's past we get a brief foreshadowing of the aged wanderer with a story of great privation to tell which Coleridge would exploit in *The Ancient Mariner*. The old man objects; his shoulders are used to the weight. " 'Far from it,' answered Harley, 'I should tread the lighter; it would be the most honourable badge I ever wore.' "[84] The Man of Feeling's active benevolence consists, both here and elsewhere in the novel, in assuming the burdens of others less fortunate than himself; it recalls at least one quality of the good Christian: "Bear one another's burdens, and so fulfil the law of Christ" (Galatians 6.2). Harley goes on to be the sole rescuer and support of the pitiable old soldier and, because we hear of the unfortunate man's sufferings at some length, with much weeping from all concerned, the story is often regarded as a tear-jerker. Who would want to deny such an obvious conclusion? Yet Mackenzie also gives us a much sentimentalized version of the *imitatio Christi* theme in the figure of Harley. Consider this passage from the conclusion:

> He [i.e., Harley] was buried in the place he had desired. It was shaded by an old tree, the only one in the church-yard, in which was a cavity worn by time. I have sat with him in it, and counted the tombs. The last time we passed there, methought he looked wistfully on the tree: there was a branch of it, that bent towards us, waving in the wind; he waved his hand, as if he mimicked its motion. There was something predictive in his look! Perhaps it is foolish to remark it; but there are times and places when I am a child in those things.[85]

That the Man of Feeling, so much a type of Jesus, should have something "predictive" about him is consistent with the christologi-

84 *The Works of Henry Mackenzie, Esq.*, 8 vols. (Edinburgh, 1808), I, 158-60.
85 *Works*, I, 243-44.

cal nature of his wanderings, preachings, and diverse acts of charity, which are secular miracles of a sort. If Harley is a prefiguration, however, he is without emblematical qualities—his typology is so far abstracted that he lacks the usual signs that we are accustomed to relate to in such characters.

Another kind of typological character occurs in novels where an occasional allusion or an undefined sense of prophecy provides a hint of predictiveness. The example of Congreve's *Incognita* (1692) may be useful here. At the very start of the book, Congreve describes his hero in typological terms:

> Aurelian was the only Son to a Principal Gentleman of Florence. The Indulgence of his Father prompted, and his Wealth enabled him, to bestow a generous Education upon him, whom he now began to look upon as the Type of himself; an impression he had made in the Gayety and Vigour of his Youth, before the Rust of Age had debilitated and obscur'd the Splendour of the Original.[86]

The father sees his son as a postfiguration of himself as a young man, an observation common enough in fiction. But the specific mention of typology, the only one in the novel, is unlikely to be accidental and, in fact, Congreve's text is liberally strewn with predictive imagery and structures.[87] To return to the mainstream of eighteenth-century fiction, we can find a similar aura of predictiveness in certain gothic novels. *The Castle of Otranto* (1765), to take the first example of the genre, is a romance of mystery, but the fulfillment of an ancient prophecy is central to solving its intricate puzzles. The prophecy is plain enough: *"That the castle and lordship of Otranto should pass from the present family, whenever the real owner should be grown too large to inhabit it."*[88] The ghost of the murdered Alonso (the true owner) lurks about the castle; when his heir appears unrecognized in the person of Theodore, Manfred, the usurper, is struck by the youth's resemblance to the murdered man. Thus we have a clear hint that Walpole is using a typological

---

[86] *Incognita: or, Love and Duty Reconcil'd. A Novel* (London, 1692), p. 1.

[87] See *Incognita*, pp. 2 (Don Fabio is "reviv'd in the Person of his Son"), 40-41 (Incognita as a postfiguration of Venus), 65 (Leonora as Eve), 81-82 (Aurelian as "the Sacrifice to Expiate [his father's] Offences past"), 93 (Aurelian as deliverer of Incognita), and 117 ("the most probable Idea of the Prototype").

[88] Horace Walpole, *The Castle of Otranto*, ed. W. S. Lewis (London: Oxford Univ. Press, 1964), pp. 16-17.

code: Theodore is a postfiguration of his father, and his presence will be vital to solving the riddle of the ancient prophecy. Theodore, who has lived in obscurity until a series of miraculous events brings him into prominence, fits the familiar christomimetic pattern of a type. He has suffered greatly, he is nearly a victim of Manfred's villainy, and at one point he even offers himself as a sacrifice to Manfred's wrath. There is a hint of millennialism as Theodore prepares to enter into his righteous dominions. As the Castle of Otranto splits asunder, the observers within "thought the last day was at hand."[89] The Apocalypse, in traditional exegesis, is indeed a typological event of the first order, the second coming of Christ. At this juncture in the narrative, Walpole restores Theodore to his patrimony.

Gothic romance, with its propensity for antique settings and shadowy mysteries, proves an attractive subject for this kind of vague, often faintly ludicrous, typology of character. Clara Reeve's most popular venture into gothic exaggeration, *The Old English Baron* (1777), also contains abundant prefigurative material. Reeve tells the story of one Sir Philip Harclay, a fifteenth-century baron whose Christian qualities are outstanding, and who sets out to restore the true heir of the murdered Lord Lovel to his rightful patrimony. The novel is full of prophetic hints, often put rather crudely; the expectation of great events, hidden workings toward some great end, and prophetic dreams help to create the aura of prefiguration. The true heir, a youth called Edmund, is modestly styled "child of Providence!—the beloved of Heaven!" and Sir Philip sees in him "the forerunners of some great events."[90] Young Edmund, like Walpole's Theodore, acts his figural role to perfection. He is the perfect Christian at a time in history when most such people resided in cloisters; he is distinguished for his meekness, humility, and other virtues and, because of his goodness, he suffers the scorn and hatred of his detractors and enemies, as any good postfiguration of Jesus would. Like Christ, he is later discovered, raised to his proper rank, and triumphantly restored to his estates.

A later development of the gothic novel is the novel of horror, of which Mary Shelley's *Frankenstein; or, The Modern Prometheus* (1818) is perhaps the best known example. Shelley uses typological

[89] *Ibid.*, p. 108.
[90] See *The Old English Baron: A Gothick Story*, 4th ed. (London, 1789), pp. 144, 175. Earlier editions of the novel are entitled *The Champion of Virtue: A Gothick Story*.

patterning and characterization quite clearly, as her subtitle suggests, for Prometheus is a well-known pagan type of Christ. Frankenstein, her modern figure of Prometheus, has discovered the mysteries of creation and, like his classical namesake, is able to create life from chaos. His first and only effort is the famous monster, whom Shelley calls a "dæmon," and whom she devises as a clear postfiguration of Milton's Satan. The Miltonic allusions are numerous, but the dæmon's postfiguration of Satan is undoubtedly clearest in the confrontation scene between Frankenstein and monster near the summit of Mont Blanc. The monster assures Frankenstein that he did not ask to be born and that, while he is very wicked just now, he was benevolent to start with, his soul glowing with love and humanity:

> Remember, that I am thy creature: I ought to be thy Adam, but I am rather the fallen angel, whom thou drivest from joy for no misdeed. Every where I see bliss, from which I alone am irrevocably excluded. I was benevolent and good; misery made me a fiend. Make me happy, and I shall again be virtuous.[91]

The typology of *Frankenstein* is suggestive and far from theologically perfect but, after all, Shelley's purpose was not a religious one. Her intention was to write a story, perhaps nothing more than a tale, perhaps a ghost story, about the mysteries of creation, a subject much discussed in the early nineteenth century. She chose to make her mad scientist a postfiguration of the pagan creator and Christ-type, Prometheus, and her Frankenstein suffers mental pangs not dissimilar to the physical pain of the Titan. The fact that contemporary iconography often pictured Prometheus bound alive to a crucifix makes the typology of *Frankenstein* convincing, however incomplete a recollection of the traditional typological relationship the book gives. The gothic novel, with its peculiar brand of Christian Hero, is a much larger genre than these few examples can suggest and, of course, the christological character is not universal in these works. Perhaps the most important contribution of the gothic novel to the field of typology is the element of historical perspective. Most typological characters, until the gothic revival, appear in novels of the contemporary scene; the gothic romance gave authors a chance to adapt prefigurative techniques to a different historical milieu.

[91] *Frankenstein; or, The Modern Prometheus*, ed. James Rieger (New York: Bobbs-Merrill, 1974), p. 95.

If ever the Christian Hero may be said to appear in the novel, then Richardson's *Sir Charles Grandison* (1753-54) must contain his greatest prototype. As I have already mentioned, it may be difficult for the twentieth-century reader to relate Richardson's quintessentially gentleman Jesus to real life, and *Grandison* was less popular with its original audience than Richardson's earlier novels had been. The character of Sir Charles Grandison, however, is a logical step in the evolution of narrative typology. Indeed, Richardson is obsessed with the nature of *character*; the correspondents in his novels—but most of all in *Grandison*—speak of it constantly. As early as his *Familiar Letters on Important Occasions* (1741) Richardson had experimented with clusters of letters on certain aspects of Christian behavior; these structural units tend to become situational or behavioral types, akin to those in collections of fables and character books. The *Familiar Letters* contain no openly typological clusters, but some groups of letters tend to inculcate or suggest behavioral codes or structures, for use in appropriate circumstances, with a strongly Christian tincture.[92] Both parts of *Pamela* and (as we will see later in this chapter) *Clarissa* deal with the typology of character in different ways. But in *Sir Charles Grandison*, Richardson's proudest achievement was the entirely believable character of the good Christian: "What," asks Harriet Byron late in the work, by now Lady Grandison, "is the boasted character of most of those who are called HEROES, to the un-ostentatious merit of a TRULY GOOD MAN? In what a variety of amiable lights does such a one appear? In how many ways is he a blessing and a joy to his fellow-creatures?"[93] Richardson seldom allows the reader to forget Sir Charles Grandison's Christian perfections for more than a few pages; even when his hero is absent from England on missions of healing and benevolence in Italy and elsewhere we hear of him constantly in exchanges of letters between other characters. The superlatives applied to Grandison almost endanger his character. Richardson even flatters his hero through his typography—as a skilled printer, he could, and did, pull out the typographical stops for Sir Charles. Italics, several sizes of capitals, and italic capitals

---

[92] See *Familiar Letters on Important Occasions*, ed. Brian W. Downs (London, 1928), pp. 15-20 (on courtship), 56-57 (a father forgiving an ungracious son), 105-108 (a steward relieving a poor tenant), and many other exchanges on matrimony, filial obedience, debts and debtors, parents and children, masters and servants, and so on.

[93] *The History of Sir Charles Grandison*, III, 462.

crowd the descriptions of him. If Sir Charles is so perfect as Richardson makes the world think him on literally scores of occasions, then there is a risk that the character might become fatuous and intolerable, but Sir Charles never becomes a bore. Indeed, the postfigurative typology associated with Grandison may well be the most intense ever created in an English novel. A few instances must suffice.

Grandison, first, refuses to duel with various malefactors, whom he invariably disarms by the force of his persuasion. One character compares him to *"The godlike man"*; he is "accustomed to do great and generous things"; he speaks with a Christ-like openness and simplicity; he bestows his benevolence, in a number of parable-like episodes, on those less fortunate than he, yet Richardson never reveals how a man no more than thirty years of age can be instinctively trusted on financial and related matters by so many people. Grandison is "a general *Philanthropist* [whose] whole delight is in doing good"; he is *"The Friend of Mankind,"* "a Prince of the Almighty's creation" and, finally, "THE MAN . . . The Man of Men."[94] The subtle use of biblical tags brings Grandison into our consciousness as a reincarnation of Jesus. Someone says of him, "Let me show you, that the *Prophet* HAS *honour with his countrywoman"* (see Matt. 13.57), as if Grandison's very being were prophetical of something greater to come. Harriet Byron, in an inspired piece of rodomontade, compares him to Adam, but thinks that if Grandison *had* been Adam, he would have "left it to the Almighty, if such had been his pleasure, to have annihilated his first Eve, and given him a second."[95] The second Adam, Christ, as St. Paul had reasoned, would not succumb to the temptations of the flesh, and the teachings of the New Testament confirmed that Jesus could resist every kind of temptation. Harriet Byron twice sees herself as an Eve figure, though perhaps somewhat improved; while *she* is capable of resisting temptation, she still thinks of herself as imperfect and unworthy of Grandison.[96] Yet Richardson somehow had to make Grandison a probable character; he manages to achieve this desideratum by the romantic entanglement of his hero with Clementina della Porretta. The della Porrettas are an Italian version of the Harlowes—insolent, proud of their ancestry, and unyielding and uncompromising in everything. Clementina's

[94] *Ibid.*, I, 290; I, 209; II, 61, 70, 236, 436.
[95] *Ibid.*, II, 169, 609.   [96] *Ibid.*, II, 2-6, 609.

infatuation with Grandison makes their marriage all but a necessity, except for the fact that his Protestantism is unacceptable to her rigidly Catholic family. Clementina's mental instability leads to a period of enthusiastic madness, and Grandison seems about to relent and to embrace Catholicism, but the lady has a change of heart, the marriage is forgotten, and Grandison finally leaves Italy tempted but unfallen. Grandison is not *quite* perfect, then, for he has been saved from compromising his religion by several lucky accidents. What rescues the character from fatuousness are his minor flaws (Grandison can become quite passionate with genuine villains, and he more than once mentions his pride) and the fact that he is never on the scene long enough to make his goodness seem smarmy. The female correspondents, especially the rather overdrawn Harriet Byron, often become cloying—too much rant proceeds from Harriet's pen for her to remain completely credible. But it is no more possible to dislike Grandison than it is possible to dislike the character of Jesus. Grandison, then, is a personification of the completely good man, the character of the virtuous Christian drawn at full length.[97]

In *Clarissa*, Richardson often deals with Christianity as if it were a series of iconographical episodes. The Christianity in *Grandison* is less subjective and, therefore, more preachy and didactic. Grandison himself usually teaches parabolically, by example rather than by precept, and Richardson leaves much of the moralizing and homilies to Harriet. Nevertheless, he could not resist writing a sermon of his own on the theme of typological prefiguration but, since there was no place where he could insert it in the novel without making the text ridiculous, he thoughtfully adds his *moralium* in "A Concluding NOTE by the EDITOR." The virtuous man, he thought, the Christian Hero of Steele's tract, actually was possible

---

[97] Margaret Anne Doody, in *A Natural Passion: A Study of the Novels of Samuel Richardson* (Oxford: Clarendon Press, 1974), undertakes the most thorough study of Grandison to date (see pp. 240-76, *passim*). While she emphasizes, in much detail, that Grandison is an eighteenth-century model of virtue, she does not respond to the powerful typological message of the novel; see esp. pp. 271-72. See also Jocelyn Harris, "Learning and Genius in *Sir Charles Grandison*," in *Studies in the Eighteenth Century, IV: Papers presented at the Fourth David Nichol Smith Memorial Seminar, Canberra 1976*, ed. R. F. Brissenden and J. C. Eade (Canberra: Australian National Univ. Press, 1979), pp. 167-91, and, " 'As if they had been living friends': *Sir Charles Grandison* into *Mansfield Park*," *Bulletin of Research in the Humanities*, 83 (1980), 360-405, especially pp. 390-98 on the paradisal park in *Grandison* and the typology of the novel.

in real life and, as I have suggested earlier, the popularity of à Kempis, of discussions of exemplary character, and of sermons on the imitations of the Creator's perfections shows conclusively that many of Richardson's contemporaries thought so, too. Moreover, such Christian excellence was possible now (as it had been in apostolic times) "amidst all the infection of fashionable vice and folly":

Sir CHARLES GRANDISON is therefore in the general tenor of his principles and conduct (tho' exerted in peculiarities of circumstances that cannot always be accommodated to particular imitation) proposed for an Example; and, in offering him as such, were his character still more perfect than it is presumed to be, the Editor is supported by an eminent Divine of our own country.

'There is no manner of inconvenience in having a pattern propounded to us of so great perfection, as is above our reach to attain to; and there may be great advantages in it. The way to excell in any kind, is, *optima quaeque exempla ad imitandum proponere*; to propose the brightest and most perfect Examples to our Imitation. No man can write after too perfect and too good a copy; and tho' he can never reach the perfection of it, yet he is like to learn more, than by one less perfect. He that aims at the heavens, which yet he is sure to come short of, is like to shoot higher than he that aims at a mark within his reach.

'Besides, that the excellency of the pattern, as it leaves room for continual improvement, so it kindles ambition, and makes men strain and contend to the utmost to do better. And, tho' he can never hope to equal the Examples before him, yet he will endeavour to come as near it as he can. So that a perfect pattern is no hindrance, but an advantage rather, to our improvement in any kind.'[98]

The text, which is from Tillotson, is only one of dozens available to Richardson in the Archbishop's many sermons on the divine perfections and on the *imitatio Christi* theme, so we must suppose that he selected his example with great care to set off Grandison's perfections and to emphasize his high degree of probability. Since no type could ever, by definition, be the equivalent of its antitype, it

[98] *Sir Charles Grandison*, III, 466. The quotation is from Tillotson's sermon, "Concerning our Imitation of the Divine Perfections," which I cited above in note 10. See Tillotson, *Works*, I, 506-507.

was therefore appropriate for Richardson to draw the character of his Christian Hero a little lower than the angels. The typology of Sir Charles appears most clearly in one of his letters to Harriet Byron after their engagement to be married. Sir Charles, explaining his gratitude to Clementina della Porretta, his almost-wife, reasons as follows:

> Shall not the man who hopes to be qualified for the Supreme Love, of which the purest Earthly is but a type, and who aims at an universal benevolence, be able to admire, in the mind of Clementina, the same great qualities which shine out with such lustre in that of Miss Byron?[99]

If we follow this passage to its logical conclusion, Richardson is saying that all of the virtuous actions of Grandison—and, for that matter, of the other good men and women in the novel—are to be interpreted as prefigurations of the antitypes which are to come in the next world.

I should emphasize that *Sir Charles Grandison*, for all the typology of Sir Charles, never quite becomes a typologically patterned narrative. The work is too long and miscellaneous for such coherence, and Richardson was trying to do too many things with it for the book to attain such an orderly structure. As if to emphasize that character rather than pattern is his chief concern, Richardson also draws typological characters in Harriet Byron and Sir Hargrave Pollexfen, the villain of the piece, of whom we see a great deal in the first two volumes, but very little thereafter. Pollexfen, unlike Lovelace, has no endearing qualities; he is a negative type, a pre- and postfiguration of Satan pure and simple. From the beginning, when he tries to abduct Harriet from a masquerade, and when Grandison rescues her from his talons without even drawing his sword, we see Pollexfen as "the very worst Lucifer of all"; "in wickedness, in cruelty, . . . every man's superior"; as a "tyger-hearted man" (the tiger was often associated with wrath, cruelty, and evil).[100] Pollexfen goes so far as to call himself "a man of *natural violence*"; his evil rubs off on his colleagues Bagenhall and Merceda, both of whom later die miserably. The ultimate anguish is reserved for Pollexfen, who reappears in Volumes 6 and 7 as the type of the impenitent sinner (the Judas figure), violent in his denunciations of Grandison (the Jesus figure), eager for the prayers of

99 *Sir Charles Grandison*, III, 155.
100 *Ibid.*, I, 150, 157, 162.

the pious, a false professor of Christianity, and finally dead without certainty of redemption.[101] If Pollexfen is less wicked than Lovelace, it is only because his crimes are less severe and because we see less of him in the novel than we do of the villain of *Clarissa*. Neither villain nor hero in *Sir Charles Grandison* is so completely evil or so completely good as he might have been. The typological qualities of their characters thus have an important function, since a type, whether of good or evil, always points to some greater accomplishment in the future.

Richardson was disappointed that his last novel was not more of a commercial and critical success but, for my purposes in this study, the book has an interesting influence on the typology of character. Sir Charles's perfections inspired other novelists to try to create the flawless man. Even before the final volumes of *Grandison* appeared, early in 1754, there was one anonymous imitator, with a two-volume work entitled *Memoirs of Sir Charles Goodville and his Family: in a series of letters to a friend* (1753). The hero is only a faint shadow of Grandison, but the work does contain an occasional short tale set into the narrative as an illustration of the natural goodness of man.[102] The Christian gentleman, modeled in one way or another on Richardson's character of Sir Charles, rapidly becomes a fixture in the later eighteenth-century novel. Heroes capable of good humor and benevolence, from Goldsmith to Godwin, owe something to Grandison.

But the typology of character reaches a high point with *Sir Charles Grandison*; later imitations of him seldom show such an ethical and religious perfection. Fanny Burney's *Evelina* (1778) may afford us the best example of this tendency. Burney's contemporaries were quick to compare her novel with *Grandison* and, to be sure, there are grounds for valid comparison. If Evelina Anville (later Belmont) is a less innocent Harriet Byron, then Lord Orville, the novel's perfect gentleman, is a much watered-down Sir Charles. Christian reflections and biblical tags, very much a part of *Grandison*, evaporate completely in *Evelina*, and we see religion only in the distant person of Evelina's guardian, the Rev. Mr.

---

[101] *Ibid.*, III, 142-44, 461-62.

[102] One of these exempla deals with a clergyman who turns over his income to his former benefactor, who has unluckily gone bankrupt. The generous vicar is a postfiguration of Christ, but the episode seems largely meant to prove that selfishness is not innate to humanity. See *The Memoirs of Sir Charles Goodville*, 2 vols. (London, 1753), I, 266-74.

Villars. Things keep happening to Evelina: strange men accost her in public places, prostitutes jostle her in "Marybone-gardens," yobs and miscellaneous rubberneckers bray after her in the street, embarrassingly déclassé relations mortify her before Lord Orville himself (Evelina will later turn out to have a noble father, but the Branghtons are related on her mother's side), and an impertinent Hargrave Pollexfen figure named Sir Clement Willoughby pursues her with unwanted rakish attentions. It is hard to imagine how Harriet Byron, an orphan who has led a sheltered life, would have survived such incivilities, but Evelina, another orphan who has led a sheltered life, gets along all right. Indeed, the achievement of Burney's novel is that its female author recreates, in a way Richardson could never have done, what it was like to be an innocent young woman at the mercy of an army of impostors. Lord Orville does not marry Evelina until her true father, who thinks another woman is his daughter, recognizes her and showers her with paternal caresses and bank drafts. "It seldom happens that a man, though extolled as a saint, is really without blemishes; or that another, though reviled as a devil, is really without humanity," writes one of Burney's characters.[103] The typological qualities of Lord Orville, for he is a postfiguration of Jesus, are therefore not on the exalted level of Grandison's. Orville is the best man in the book—engaging, polite, charming, attentive, benevolent—gentleman Jesus as courtier. We may glimpse the contrast in other ways, too. Richardson follows Harriet Byron's marriage to Sir Charles with an entire volume of active Christian magnanimity and benevolence. Burney takes care of her comedy with dispatch. After arranging Evelina's marriage to Orville, she ends *Evelina* with a scene of genuine burlesque, in which a jesting sea captain who has been present at the festivities ridicules the foppish Mr. Lovel by presenting him with a monkey "fully dressed and extravagantly *à-la-mode*."[104] If a fop is a figure for a dressed-up monkey, then perhaps the reader may be justified in seeing, in Burney's episode on "this charming replica of man," a clever figural joke.

I do not mean to imply that the typological character in its fullest

---

[103] See *Evelina, or the History of a Young Lady's Entrance into the World*, ed. Edward A. Bloom (London: Oxford Univ. Press, 1968), p. 158. On its similarities to *Sir Charles Grandison*, see *Critical Review*, 46 (1778), 202-204. The anonymous reviewer wishes that more novels dealt with characters outside of the nobility and gentry.

[104] *Ibid.*, p. 400; cf. pp. 399-400.

sense ceased with Richardson; to do so would be to ignore the obvious prefigurative qualities of a number of pieces of nineteenth-century fiction. However, after *Sir Charles Grandison*, this aspect of narrative typology would never be quite the same again. A final example may demonstrate the transformations of figuralism later in the eighteenth century—Godwin's *Caleb Williams* (1794). Godwin was no stranger to typology. The members of his radical circle in the 1790s used it frequently in their writings; prefiguration is an important ingredient of the prophetical texts that proliferated during and after the French Revolution; and Godwin's novel *Fleetwood, or the New Man of Feeling* (1805) owes its leading character to Richardson and Mackenzie.[105] In *Caleb Williams*, Godwin skillfully manipulates the typology of character in a manner for which there are few precedents in the eighteenth-century novel. The first volume consists almost entirely of the history of Mr. Falkland as told to young Caleb by an older fellow-servant, Collins. Falkland, we learn, in the years before his present state of detached and suffering melancholy, was a minor Sir Charles Grandison. The younger Falkland had been capable of settling duels without drawing his sword (one of Sir Charles's most imitated qualities); during an Italian journey an adversary describes him as "this god-like Englishman"; and he believes in benevolent and charitable actions rather than empty words.[106] As a foil to Falkland, Godwin gives us Squire Tyrrel, and if ever there was a negative type, it is he. Tyrrel's "rooted depravity" and unyielding desire for vengeance against those less fortunate than himself make him a type of evil. The quarrel between these two characters comes about when Falkland objects to his neighbor's inhuman treatment of one of his tenants. The two exchange the following words:

> Mr. Falkland [says Tyrrel], it would be quite as well if you would mind your own business, and leave me to mind mine. I want no monitor and I will have none.
>
> You mistake, Mr. Tyrrel; I am minding my own business. If I see you fall into a pit, it is my business to draw you out and

---

[105] The epigraph to each of the four volumes of *St. Leon: A Tale of the Sixteenth Century* is as follows: "Ferdinand Mendez Pinto was but a type of thee, thou liar of the first magnitude," which comes from *Love for Love*, II.v. See Congreve, *Works*, 3 vols. (London, 1710), I, 358.

[106] *Things as They Are; or, The Adventures of Caleb Williams*, 3 vols. (London, 1794), I, 34-35, 33, 151-56 (in which Falkland rescues the denizens of a burning house).

save your life. If I see you pursuing a wrong line of conduct, it is my business to set you right and save your honour.[107]

One can scarcely imagine a better example of active benevolence; Falkland seems more and more the Grandison figure. After an argument in which Tyrrel brutally beats the unresisting Falkland, Tyrrel is mysteriously murdered. In a development which seems to complete Falkland's typological character, Godwin makes him a persecution figure as well. Falkland comes under suspicion and is tried for the murder but, after he delivers a powerful speech, filled with Christian humility, to the court, the jury acquits him. Falkland's address to the court represents the height of Christian meekness and self-sacrifice; we may well be reminded of Peter's address, inspired by the holy spirit, to the Pharisees (Acts 4.5-12). Afterwards, his cheering neighbors welcome him back to his village in a scene of "enthusiastic adoration" that parallels Christ's entry into Jerusalem and that establishes the persecuted but now exonerated man as a postfiguration of Jesus.[108] Later, the tenant on whose behalf Falkland had intervened, thus causing the fatal quarrel with Tyrrel, is found guilty of the murder and is hanged.

As a political novelist, however, Godwin was dedicated to displaying the injustice of "things as they are" and, as we learn in the second volume, Falkland is in fact guilty of the murder of Squire Tyrrel for which he had been acquitted. Caleb Williams, the sole possessor of the truth, now finds himself the object of Falkland's intense persecution, and the typology which Godwin had appeared to construct in the first volume is abruptly reversed. Caleb's "adventures" involve his efforts to escape the unstinting vengeance of his former patron. During a *mélange* of episodes that would be picaresque if Falkland's pursuit of Caleb were not so deadly serious, Caleb gradually emerges as a figure of the persecuted sinner. Now Godwin parallels Falkland to Satan, and the feckless Caleb, surrounded by prophetic signs of his destruction, becomes the suffering Christian groping through life's pilgrimage for salvation. Seized at last for a crime he has not committed, Caleb tries to reveal the secret of Falkland's murder which he has long regarded as the way in which he can prove his own innocence:

Till now I had conceived that the unfavourable situation in which I was placed was prolonged by my own forbearance [in

---

107 *Ibid.*, I, 126.   108 *Ibid.*, I, 282-86, 287-88.

keeping Falkland's guilt of murder a secret]; and I was determined to endure all that human nature could support, rather
than have recourse to this extreme recrimination. That idea
secretly consoled me under all my calamities: a voluntary sacrifice is chearfully made. I regarded myself as allied to the army
of martyrs and confessors; I applauded my own fortitude and
self denial; and I pleased myself with the idea, that I had the
power, though I never hoped to employ it, by an unrelenting
display of all my resources to put an end at once to my sufferings and persecutions.[109]

Caleb is a flawed postfiguration; he endures persecution and a great
deal of suffering but, unlike the martyrs of the Church, he plans to
play his final card when it is necessary to save himself. Martyrs have
traditionally shown greater consistency than this. Caleb, according
to Godwin's theories of political justice, must suffer because he is a
servant, while his persecutor, a rich man, can escape retribution
from the law. Until *Caleb Williams*, the novelists of the age had
preferred to make their Jesus figures men of wealth and title or
basically strong people from the middle walks of life who managed
to struggle upward to Christian perfection. Godwin's neat reversal
of this comfortable equation is devastating to the traditional use of
typological characters. The French Revolution helped to remind
novelists that Jesus had been a man of humble birth and profession,
and while Caleb Williams cannot comfort himself with more than
a shadowy sense of moral rectitude, at least Godwin's novel turns
our attention to the typological possibilities of people of low estate.
Neither Caleb nor Mr. Falkland are perfect typological figures:
"things as they are," at best, permit only a flawed typology.

 6

The final category of typology in the novel, novels with typological
stories, embraces its predecessor, the novel with typological characters, for most prefigurative accounts are made possible by the presence of persons who fit the typological schemas that I have been
discussing in this chapter. Richardson's masterwork, *Clarissa*, the
eighteenth-century's ultimate example of a religious novel, is built
around the two central characters of Clarissa and her seducer, Love-

[109] *Ibid.*, III, 192-93.

lace, both of whom have strong typological qualities. Richardson even assigns them type names, reminiscent of Bunyan and the Puritan moralities: *Clarissa* is the superlative of perfection (yet she is not perfect), while *Lovelace* (or "Luvless," as one of his semiliterate servants writes his name) is bereft of the love of God, a lack which leads him to his doom. But the novel is more, far more, than a presentation of typological characters. Clarissa, it is true, is a fallen angel who flees from her father's house, her Eden, receives her father's implacable curse, is deceived by her seducer, and later undergoes a thorough and complete Christian repentance, strictly according to the accepted handbooks and homilies. Later, as a soul already in grace, she can forgive her persecutors—her cruel, avaricious family and her maniacal seducer—and so is free to meditate on Scripture and to expound sacred mysteries. And Lovelace, just as clearly, is drawn to represent Satan, whether the attractive and idealized figure of *Paradise Lost* or the unvarnished tempter of homily and tract. As Clarissa represents a typological character in the *imitatio Christi* and the *Christianus perfectus* traditions, so Lovelace is a negative type, prefigurative of every kind of moral vice, a foreshadowing of Satan. The overall plan of *Clarissa*, however, is so broad that it encompasses much more than the two leading characters. The stories of the Harlowes, of Lovelace and his profligate friends, of the brothel-keeper Mrs. Sinclair (perhaps another Bunyanesque touch—her sin is the most *clear* of any character in all of Richardson) and her whores, of Lovelace's aristocratic connections, and innumerable other details of contemporary life surround them, so that *Clarissa* lacks a coherent typological structure, in the manner of *Robinson Crusoe*, even as it possesses a larger typological presence than a novel where the typology is confined mainly to characters, like *Joseph Andrews* or *Sir Charles Grandison*.[110]

The novel does, however, contain two typological stories which are very much a part of Christian tradition: the account of the sinning Clarissa, her sufferings as a result of her sin, her long self-realization, repentance, and martyr-like death, and the story of the evil man, Lovelace, who can never repent and so must die a Judas-

[110] John A. Dussinger, "Conscience and the Pattern of Christian Perfection in *Clarissa*," *PMLA*, 81 (1966), 236-45, esp. 236, soundly elucidates the importance of the novel's religious theme and the central importance of repentance (without mentioning the book's typological possibilities), but suggests that *Clarissa*'s design is so broad that the theological argument is subsumed by episode.

like death. The martyrology of Clarissa is never in doubt from the time that she finally frees herself from "the enemy of [her] soul" until her death and, afterwards, the exciting climax of the reading of her will; she is very much, in Dryden's phrase, "a great emblem of the Suffering Deity."[111] Lovelace, for his part, whom Richardson compares with sin, demons, hell, Satan, and other types of sin in scores of passages, is, finally, unable to repent. "LET THIS EX-PIATE!" he ejaculates on his deathbed, but he has "refused ghostly attendance, and the Sacraments in the Catholic way" (he dies in Austria, a Catholic country), so we must assume that his idea of expiation is insufficient, in religious terms, to save him.[112] Indeed, Richardson, in the collection of "instructive sentiments" from *Clarissa* which he published three years after the first edition, under the heading "Repentance. Contrition" adds, in black letter for spe-cial emphasis, "Lovelace lived not to repent!"[113] Richardson's hint in this volume of addenda suggests that he was unsympathetic to the view that Lovelace, who temporarily loses his sanity after Cla-rissa's death, had at least started a partial repentance.[114] Lovelace does promise to undergo spiritual regeneration on a number of occasions, but basically he remains a scoffer against religion, a scorn-ful figure of the atheist or apostate whom all the forces of eigh-teenth-century divinity, from the Boyle Lecturers on, marshaled themselves to confute. Lovelace fits the caricature perfectly: he goes to church for the show of it or to seduce young women, he cites scraps of Scripture out of context for purposes of ridicule, he be-littles sober divinity. When, after the rape, Clarissa recalls for Anna Howe Lovelace's various stratagems, she remembers how he had imposed two strumpets upon her as his aristocratic cousins. When they visit her in her temporary refuge at Hampstead, an elaborate charade takes place. "The grand deluder" leaves Clarissa with "the pretended ladies" and, at the other end of the room, peruses a book "which, had there not been a preconcert, would not have taken his

111 See *Annus Mirabilis,* "To the Metropolis of Great Britain," a clearly typo-logical passage.

112 *Clarissa,* VII, 414-15.

113 *Letters and Passages restored from the original manuscripts of the History of Clarissa. To which is subjoined, A Collection of . . . moral and instructive sentiments . . .* (London, 1751), p. 290.

114 Dussinger, *PMLA,* 81 (1966), 237, ignoring Richardson's statement, thinks that Lovelace "undergoes a significant change when his conscience is awakened enough to feel despair, if not repentance, for the horrendous act against Clarissa."

attention for one moment. It was *Taylor's Holy Living and Dying.*
. . . He approached me, with it in his hand—A smart book, This,
my dear!—This old divine affects, I see, a mighty flowery style upon
a very solemn subject. . . ."[115] Clarissa correctly perceives that Lovelace knows nothing about this popular book of devotion, one of the
most widely read such works of the era, but simply scoffs at it.

Other moral writers who dealt with atheism often posit a scene
in which the atheist is suddenly brought to his or her senses by a
supernatural occurrence, a great cataclysm, or even the innocence
of a child; in Defoe's writings, for example, we see all of these circumstances work as forces of conversion. But nothing can convert
Lovelace: even Clarissa's religious experience and figural language
are foreign to him. A telling passage comes late in the last volume,
when the stricken Clarissa, visited by Lovelace's friend Belford, tries
to make it clear to him that she never wants to see her persecutor
again. Lovelace and Belford have seen one of her letters, in which
she innocently states that she hopes to return to her parents' house
and to be reconciled to her family. Clarissa asks Belford for the letter (which exists at this point in Lovelace's transcript):

> Nay, sir, said she, be pleased to read my letter to yourself—I
> desire not to see *his*—and see if you can be longer a stranger to
> a meaning so obvious [Belford is writing to Lovelace].
> I read it to myself.—Indeed, Madam, I can find nothing but
> that you are going down to Harlowe-Place to be reconciled to
> your father and other friends: And Mr. Lovelace presumed that
> a letter from your sister, which he saw brought when he was at
> Mr. Smith's [Clarissa's last refuge, where Lovelace had tried to
> visit her], gave you the welcome news of it.
> She then explained all to me, and that, as I may say, in six
> words.—A *religious* meaning is couched under it, and that's the
> reason that neither you nor I could find it out.
> Read but for my *father's house, Heaven*, said she, and for the
> interposition of my dear blessed friend, suppose the *Mediation*
> of my *Saviour*; which I humbly rely upon; and all the rest of
> the letter will be accounted for.[116]

Lovelace and Belford cannot accept this kind of interpretation;
they are incredulous, even scornful of such analogizing. The passage
is important because it is the sole instance in the entire novel of

[115] *Clarissa*, VI, 58.   [116] *Ibid.*, VII, 81-82.

Richardson's glossing one of his own texts, displaying a method of exegesis which is closely allied with typological reading of Scripture. Richardson had said, in the "Postscript" to the first edition of *Clarissa*, that the novel was formed on a "Religious Plan"; in this excerpt, he demonstrates to his audience how to interpret his religious meaning. The gloss served several functions. First, it provided Richardson's eighteenth-century audience with a signal that he was thinking of Clarissa's plight in terms of a typological code and, second, it furnishes a key to permit us to decipher that code. Clarissa speaks of returning to her father's house as her voyage to Heaven; thus we may also see that her temptation away from Harlowe Place by one of Lovelace's many satanic stratagems is indeed equivalent to her fall from a sinless innocence.

Clarissa's friends and family reject her until the moment of her death—their letters of forgiveness come too late. Like Job, who is similarly bereft of friends, family, and property, she never abandons her sublime faith in God and, like Job, she is a type of Christ. The Job story, indeed, was seen in eighteenth-century England as one of the most dramatic typological accounts in the Old Testament; more than the other types of the Old Testament, Job is a narrative character with particular relevance to the Christian life.[117] The exegetes saw Job as the type of true Christian fortitude and faith in adversity and it is clear that Richardson wants us to regard Clarissa in a similar light. That Clarissa's sex was different from Job's created no difficulty for Richardson; that her adversities are peculiarly feminine did not disqualify her for the role of Christian hero. Clarissa's heroism is perhaps at its greatest when, throughout the final two volumes, her radiant piety and virtue, as communicated by Belford to Lovelace, are so overpowering that the enemy of her soul does not dare to come to see her, despite his ardent protestations that he *must* see her. Throughout these last six weeks of her life, Clarissa fortifies herself by paralleling herself to Job (even Belford and Lovelace see that much); her meditations, of which Rich-

[117] See Simon Patrick, *The Books of Job, Psalms, Proverbs, Ecclesiastes, and the Song of Solomon, paraphrased* (London, 1727), p. 59, where Patrick describes Job as a prophet among the gentiles; "Preface," Sig. a2ᵛ, quoting St. Jerome (Sigs. a1ʳ-b2ᵛ); Matthew Henry, *An Exposition of the Old and New Testament*, 6 vols. (Philadelphia, 1829), III, 10, 38, 133, 192. Patrick's study of Job first appeared in 1697, Henry's exposition in 1725. The typology of Job, noted as early as pre-Nicene times, is emphasized perhaps most of all in the *glossa* and *moralia* of Nicholas of Lyra, readily available in the eighteenth century in Poole's *Synopsis Criticorum*.

ardson actually prints only four in the novel (the others he adds in his *Meditations* of 1750), are pieced together from her biblical reading, but most of all they derive from Job. Her third meditation, for instance, the one which demonstrates to all that her repentance is complete, begins with Job's fifth answer to Bildad: "How long will ye vex my soul, and break me in pieces with words?"[118] In a dozen other texts, Richardson analogizes Clarissa's situation to that of Job, either by direct quotation of biblical originals or by describing her heroic extenuation of will under the most arduous circumstances. The typology of Clarissa's story, however, does not rest only upon a similarity to the narrative of Job. As the key to Richardson's typological riddle suggests, she relies upon the mediation of Jesus, whom she calls upon with her last breath; her death has clear resemblances to the marriage of the soul to its heavenly Bridegroom.[119] The central story of *Clarissa*, then, is unmistakably typological. Clarissa's death accomplishes the upward movement from her earliest phase, when she merely studies the imitation of Christ (one of the books in her library at Harlowe Place is Thomas à Kempis), to a true expression of the *imitatio Christi* theme and a complete union with Jesus—from type to antitype in seven volumes![120] Relentlessly parallel to the apotheosis of Clarissa is the negative typology of Lovelace, who moves gradually but steadily downward in the progress of his villainy. The iconography of Lovelace always stresses his physical attractiveness, like one of the sons of light, but Richardson never fails to ally him to perdition, which is where, if we accept his last defiant letter to Belford, he may be assumed to end his career.

The typology of *Clarissa* is based upon two stories. The first is that of Clarissa. By the end of the first volume she is a sacrifice to Harlowe family greed, a "fallen angel" in the very bosom of her family; yet, even after her temptation and further humiliation at Lovelace's hands, she manages to achieve repentance and salvation. The other is that of the unrepentant rake in whose character Richardson sought to display the fatal dangers of rooted depravity. One

[118] Job 19.2; see *Clarissa*, VI, 380-81. Richardson composed thirty-six meditations for Clarissa, later published separately as *Meditations Collected from the Sacred Books* (London, 1750); cf. Dussinger, *PMLA*, 81 (1966), 240-41.

[119] Doody, *A Natural Passion*, p. 174, makes this observation, including what may be one of the few references thus far in Richardson scholarship to typology; she sees Lovelace, in a curious misuse of terminology, as "a kind of Satanic anti-type" to Clarissa. The sense, if not the understanding, of typology is here.

[120] See *Clarissa*, II, 166, an exchange between Arabella Harlowe and Clarissa: "'Have you not a Thomas à Kempis, sister?' . . . 'I have, Madam.'"

of Richardson's greatest achievements in *Clarissa* is undoubtedly his success in subsuming his religious purpose within a predominantly secular presentation. Secular, too, is the next major novel to embody a typological story, Smollett's *Ferdinand Count Fathom* (1753). Smollett's villainous rake, whose adventures are sometimes regarded as a kind of picaresque fiction, has much in common with Lovelace, although his crimes are more numerous and a good deal worse.

The typological story of *Ferdinand Count Fathom* is built around the Judas-like wickedness of the impostor Fathom who, among many other crimes, betrays and tries to destroy his benefactor, Count Renaldo de Melvil, the novel's Christ-figure. Smollett surely meant his audience to regard Fathom as the very type of the hardened sinner, a villain as remorseless as Lovelace, whose worst depravity is his sexual promiscuity and his willingness to seduce and destroy innocent women. Smollett's novel, however, has a curious and unexpected turn to it—its religious plan, every bit as decisive as Richardson's, is to show a repentant rake, to make Count Fathom into a kind of regenerate Lovelace. Thus when Fathom is plotting his worst crimes, Smollett makes us aware that even the most depraved criminal is not without some tincture of humanity. On one occasion, for example, after Fathom hatches some especially despicable plot and seals it with a vow, Smollett notes that an oath "is commonly the cement of every conspiracy, how dark, how treacherous, how impious soever it may be. A certain sign that there are some remains of religion left in the human mind, even after every moral sentiment hath abandoned it; and that the most execrable ruffian finds means to quiet the suggestions of his conscience, by some reversionary hope of Heaven's forgiveness."[121] Smollett scatters other signs, or foreshadowings, of his hero's forthcoming repentance about the book, in order to lay some foundation for the event and to mitigate its suddenness when it actually takes place. The novelists of the mid-eighteenth century seem to think that a contemporary audience would not accept so unsophisticated a repentance as that of Moll Flanders; a good deal of doctrinal sincerity, both before and after the fact, would be necessary to make penitence more convincing. Moll can assure her readers that she and her husband are finally sincere penitents for the wicked lives

---

121 *The Novels of Tobias Smollett*, Shakespeare Head Edition, 11 vols. (Oxford, 1925-26), VII, 44-45.

they have lived, but Smollett gives the common reader of the 1750s more demonstration than that.

Here it is important to stress the typology of repentance in the Christian scheme of things. Hooker, who seldom favors flowery language, is especially eloquent on the subject:

> Repentance . . . may be without hyperbolical terms most truly magnified, as a recovery of the soul of man from deadly sickness, a restitution of glorious light to his darkened mind, a comfortable reconciliation with God, a spiritual nativity, a rising from the dead, a dayspring out of the depth of obscurity, a redemption from more than the Egyptian thraldom, a grinding of the old Adam even unto dust and powder, a deliverance out of the prisons of hell, a full restoration of the seat of grace and throne of glory, a triumph over sin, and a saving victory.[122]

Nearly every term of Hooker's equation is typological itself or refers to a typological passage in Scripture; later Anglican writers would reinforce this typological pattern throughout the seventeenth century. The most searching study of repentance is undoubtedly the work by one of Clarissa's favorite authors, Jeremy Taylor, *Unum Necessarium, or the Doctrine and Practice of Repentance* (1655), a handbook-style approach to the subject complete with meticulous exposition of the particular kinds of sins and their proper expiation. Taylor, like Hooker, sees repentance as a prefiguration to the Christian in this life of the greater promise of total redemption and eternal salvation in the afterlife. There was ample foundation, then, for a late and sudden repentance like that of Smollett's Count Fathom, provided that it be accompanied by appropriate signs of reformation.[123]

When Fathom's repentance comes, then, it is not a surprise but a circumstance for which Smollett has prepared his audience, for the type of the satanic villain could hardly be transformed into the type of the converted sinner without suitable foundations. Fathom must be imprisoned for his crimes and, as his punishment looms, signs of his reformation start to appear: "I begin to feel myself overtaken by the eternal justice of heaven!" he cries, and we hear

[122] *The Laws of Ecclesiastical Polity*, VI.v.5, in *The Works of Richard Hooker*, ed. John Keble, 7th ed., rev. W. M. Church and F. Paget, 3 vols. (Oxford, 1888), III, 62.

[123] See *Unum Necessarium*, in *The Whole Works of Jeremy Taylor*, ed. Reginald Heber, rev. Charles Page Ellen, 10 vols. (London, 1847-54), VII, 115-16, 126-27, 159, 178, 199-200, 232, 370-71.

that, "for the first time, his cheeks were bedewed with the drops of penitence and sorrow." But this incipient regeneration is too easy and painless to cure a sinner of Fathom's magnitude beyond a doubt of recidivism. Before he can replace his stony heart with a heart of flesh (Ezekiel 11.19), his hardships and privation must be sufficient to convince the man whom he has most injured, Renaldo, to become his redeemer.[124] Renaldo rescues Fathom from prison, brings about his cure from the illness which seemed certain to kill him, dispenses pardon instead of exacting vengeance, welcomes the now-converted sinner to the ranks of the elect even as he warns him sternly against a lapse of morals, and in every way appears as a type of Christ. Fathom's lamentable state in this key chapter exemplifies all the conditions which writers on repentance cite as prerequisites for spiritual regeneration. His failing health (he is clearly on his deathbed, although his is not a deathbed repentance), his nakedness, physical misery, and squalor, his severe remorse and self-mortification, his fears of eternal vengeance—all these things point to a dramatization of the penitent's last hours. Once Fathom hears of his deliverance, he recovers just enough to deliver a little typological homily:

> Blessed be God! (he cried) for having defeated the villainy of him who sought to part such lovers [i.e., Renaldo and the aptly named Monimia]. Dear sir [Fathom addresses the true physician, symbolic priest], will you add one circumstance to your charity, and bear to that happy couple . . . the respects and remorse of a sincere penitent, whom their compassion hath raised to life. I have been such a traitor to them, that my words deserve no regard. I will not therefore use professions. I dare not hope to be admitted into their presence. I am indeed ashamed to see the light of the sun: how then could I bear the looks of that injured family! ah, no! let me hide myself in some obscure retreat, where I may work out my salvation with fear and trembling, and pray incessantly to heaven for their prosperity.[125]

---

[124] See *Fathom* in *Novels*, VIII, 160-64. Smollett seems to stress the sincerity and genuineness of Fathom's conversion, but Thomas R. Preston, in "Disenchanting the Man of Feeling: Smollett's *Ferdinand Count Fathom*," in *Quick Springs of Sense: Studies in the Eighteenth Century*, ed. Larry S. Champion (Athens, Ga.: Univ. of Georgia Press, 1974), pp. 223-39, argues that the conversion may be fraudulent, for "in the society Smollett depicts it is almost certain that a villain remains a villain" (p. 238). If this dictum is correct, then religious conversion in eighteenth-century England requires close reinterpretation.

[125] *Novels*, VIII, 280.

Fathom's actions and demeanor recall Taylor's character of the regenerate person in *Unum Necessarium* who has conquered his fleshly lusts and devotes his whole being to his salvation;[126] Renaldo has literally "raised [him] to life," the strongest proof of the *imitatio Christi* theme. Fathom's very language recalls the traditional phraseology of the penitent: he fears the light of the sun, and he can think only of seeking his salvation in great obscurity.[127]

Smollett was a master of the picaresque, as his first two novels show. In *Ferdinand Count Fathom*, his third, he makes convincing picaresque noises; recent students of the genre have been impressed, and at least one critic has seen the book as the last eighteenth-century work in the picaresque tradition.[128] Perhaps so, but then we would have to concede that the character of the picaro has changed under the pressure of time and manners. Fathom's story is clearly that of a rogue, but he is not the social delinquent of earlier picaresque fiction, capable of committing harmless pranks and monstrous crimes with equal moral vacuity. One might as well call Lovelace a picaro. Fathom never sins without an editorial comment from Smollett to show that his story is coded for some higher significance, for *Ferdinand Count Fathom*, like other novels with typological patterns, characters, or stories, is rich in religious sign language. Like other fiction of the 1750s, such as *Amelia, Sir Charles Grandison*, and *Rasselas, Fathom* has a symbolic purpose but, more than these others, it embodies the systematic method of typology within its central fable.[129] Other novelists of the age were content to draw typological characters; Smollett, less a student of theology than Fielding, Richardson, or Johnson, chose otherwise. The repentance of Fathom is most improbable, if we think of it in terms of real-life criminals and calculate statistics of recidivism but, in the

---

126 See Taylor, *Works*, VII, 370-72 (*Unum Necessarium*, VIII.vi.42-44).

127 Cf. John 3.20, "For every one that doeth evil hateth the light, lest his deeds should be reproved," and Philippians 2.12, "Wherefore, my beloved, . . . work out your own salvation with fear and trembling." Smollett uses biblical allusions with great frequency in *Fathom* and even more in his later novels; there are more than 400 biblical allusions in *Humphry Clinker*. I owe this information to Thomas R. Preston.

128 Parker, *Literature and the Delinquent*, p. 127, sees *Fathom* as "the last European novel of any consequence that is directly within the tradition started by *Guzmán de Alfarache*."

129 Eric Rothstein, *Systems of Order and Inquiry in Later Eighteenth-Century Fiction* (Berkeley and Los Angeles: Univ. of California Press, 1975), argues persuasively (pp. 1-21) that many novels of the period have in common systematic methods of inquiry and revelation, such as "analogy" and "modification."

contexts of biblical narrative, where typology originates, we are not given the opportunity to doubt the reform of the sinful. Jesus says to the woman taken in adultery, "Go and sin no more" (John 8.11); our understanding must be that she reforms, just as surely as we must believe that those whom Jesus heals are indeed made whole. The persuasiveness of Smollett's typological story in this novel is clearest, I think, in the final chapters, especially Chapter 57, where biblical tags drawn from the prophetical books and the New Testament crowd in thickly upon us. In this chapter, the typology of the savior-figure, Renaldo, and of the restored sinner, Fathom, becomes most evident. Smollett thought again of the credibility of the penitent rake, for he brings Fathom back in his last novel. Late in *Humphry Clinker* we come across Fathom, living in the north of England under the new name of Grieve, as an honest apothecary (in his earlier life, he had actually impersonated a physician). We learn that he is "a sincere convert to virtue," "unaffectedly pious," who performs "all the duties of a primitive Christian."[130] In the context of Smollett's last novel, this brief description may not awaken any figural impulses in the reader but, viewed as a conclusive period to the story of Fathom, it serves as impressive evidence that Smollett did indeed regard the central story of *Ferdinand Count Fathom* as a typological fable.

The most simple as well as the most affecting typological story in an eighteenth-century novel is undoubtedly that of one of the century's most transparent books, *The Vicar of Wakefield*. The simplicity of Goldsmith's novel, coupled with its enormous popularity until the end of the nineteenth century and beyond, has caused scholars to study it closely in an effort to ascertain the secret of its art. The Vicar's primitive Christianity has hardly gone unnoticed, while some readers have discovered comic, ironical, and satirical sides to his story. Since it is possible to find many such elements in *The Vicar of Wakefield*, such readings are not without force, but only recently has Martin Battestin persuasively demonstrated the analogies between Goldsmith's work and the Book of Job, with its strong typological strain.[131] Goldsmith's novel-writing predecessors of the 1740s and '50s had seen the importance of verisimilitude, and strove to create real situations and probable characters. Goldsmith,

---

130 See *Humphry Clinker* in *Novels*, X, 239-41.

131 See *The Providence of Wit*, pp. 193-214. Battestin's entire chapter, "Goldsmith: The Comedy of Job," shows how the story of Job, as interpreted by contemporary exegetes, is analogous to the trials of the Vicar and his family.

on the contrary, writes as if he were entirely unconcerned by such fictional motives. Neither the Vicar nor any of the other characters in the book could have persuaded an eighteenth-century audience that this was an attempt to imitate reality accurately. The Vicar's sufferings, credulity, foolishness, pride, and Christian steadfastness are most improbable, united in one person. The Elihu-figure in Goldsmith's retelling of the Job story is the mysterious Mr. Burchell, who for the bulk of the novel is the person who tests the faith of the Primrose family and, more particularly, of the Vicar. Burchell turns out to be Sir William Thornhill, the novel's Christ. Burchell's disguise makes him one of the most unusual types of Christ in eighteenth-century literature. Yet we must also concede that the book's simplicity is its greatest virtue: Goldsmith never said that he sought to create a realistic novel with complex, highly probable characters.

The key to the typological story of *The Vicar of Wakefield* may well be one of the most obvious in all the novels that I have discussed in this chapter. It occurs in Goldsmith's humble "Advertisement":

> There are an hundred faults in this Thing, and an hundred things might be said to prove them beauties. A book may be amusing with numerous errors, or it may be very dull without a single absurdity. The hero of this piece unites in himself the three greatest characters upon earth; he is a priest, an husbandman, and the father of a family. He is drawn as ready to teach, and ready to obey, as simple in affluence, and majestic in adversity. In this age of opulence and refinement whom can such a character please? Such as are fond of high life will turn with disdain from the simplicity of his country fireside. Such as mistake ribaldry for humour will find no wit in his harmless conversation; and such as have been taught to deride religion will laugh at one whose chief stores of comfort are drawn from futurity.[132]

The notion that the leading character draws his chief stores of comfort "from futurity" suggests that, for Goldsmith, all the action of the novel is but a prefiguration of a larger, more accomplished scene of life in some future state. And, indeed, for the Christian, the narrative of life was nothing but a prefiguration of futurity, a preparation for an eternal life in the hereafter. That Goldsmith's hero

[132] *The Vicar of Wakefield*, 2 vols. (Salisbury, 1766), I, Sig. [π]2ᵛ.

is not a simple character but, in fact, a blend of "the three greatest characters upon earth" is another clue to the typological story of *The Vicar of Wakefield*. His latter-day Job, the Vicar, unites in himself three qualities of the Christ whom he is meant to typify: Jesus as minister, Jesus as shepherd, and Jesus as the leader of the Church. The key to Goldsmith's typological code sounds almost too portentous for the novel's simplicity, but the Vicar does represent each of these three characters at different times in the story.

The Vicar's comedy is also his tragedy. In his simplicity, he cannot see the traps set out to delude him, and so misunderstands the people he meets. As Battestin observes, "Paradoxically, though Job is the very type of the Christian hero, he is not without faults."[133] Thus Dr. Primrose misreads many of the signs that he encounters in the course of the narrative, especially those relating to Mr. Burchell. When the Primroses are prosperous, the Vicar sees Burchell as "a man of broken fortune," "a poor forlorn creature," and even "a middle aged man of broken fortune."[134] Burchell later emphasizes his "secret reasons" for persuading the Primrose daughters to avoid the company of Squire Thornhill and his harlots, but the Vicar obstinately ignores his suggestion and fails to ask what the secrets may be. Only after the Vicar recovers his older daughter, seduced and abandoned, does Olivia open his eyes: "I am convinced," she tells him, "that he was ever our warmest sincerest friend."[135] Dr. Primrose's occasional blindness to the world around him is more than balanced by his essential benevolence, both in good times and bad. When Burchell first visits the Primroses, the Vicar eloquently delivers a brief homily on the Christian duty of hospitality, and assures his family, "The greatest stranger in this world was he that came to save it." Burchell, thus compared to Jesus, is clearly a shadowy type, early in the novel, of the antitype as which he will stand revealed in the final three chapters. Goldsmith's dramatic irony here is that the Vicar himself proposes a typological sign without understanding it. Dr. Primrose compounds his folly early in the second volume when once again he comments significantly, yet unaware of his meaning, on his story. The Primroses have just learned that Squire Thornhill plans to marry Miss Wilmot; the Vicar, with Job-like resignation, prefers the circle of his family, however they may suffer, to the glittering life of the

---

[133] *The Providence of Wit*, p. 201.
[134] *The Vicar of Wakefield*, I, 52, 53, 80.
[135] *Ibid.*, II, 47.

wealthy. The scriptural analogy is to Job 21, Job's sixth answer to his three friends, but Goldsmith goes further and gives his hero a typological speech on good and evil and on the nature of narrative: "Almost all men have been taught to call life a passage, and themselves the travellers. The similitude still may be improved when we observe that the good are joyful and serene, like travellers that are going towards home; the wicked but by intervals happy, like travellers that are going into exile."[136] As we have noted, seventeenth- and eighteenth-century exegetes and preachers commonly speak of the Christian life as a pilgrimage, and Goldsmith alludes to this notion in his "similitude" here. The improvement of the figure tells us that the pilgrimage of life leads to a goal, either toward home or toward exile. In the context of *The Vicar of Wakefield*, this passage is yet another sign to Goldsmith's audience that the narrative itself is prefigurative, and that the Vicar's typological story leads to the usual end for all good people, "towards home."

The metamorphoses and disguises of *The Vicar of Wakefield* come to an end in Chapter 11 of the second volume. We have seen Burchell change from a young man of about thirty to a middle-aged man without fortune; now he is transfigured into the youthful (and eminently marriageable) Sir William Thornhill. In the novel's secular world, Sir William redeems the Vicar from his debts, saves him from prison, and even heals his burnt arm with one of his miraculous prescriptions. In Goldsmith's typological story, Sir William is a kind of epitomized Sir Charles Grandison, the antitype toward which the entire story of disguise and adversity has been tending. When the Vicar's son George recognizes Burchell as Sir William Thornhill, Goldsmith comments as follows:

> Never before had I seen anything so truly majestic as the air [Sir William] assumed upon this occasion. The greatest object in the universe, says a certain philosopher, is a good man struggling with adversity; yet there is still a greater, which is the good man who comes to relieve it.[137]

The typological structure of *The Vicar of Wakefield*, then, has two principal characters working along similar lines rather than at cross-purposes (as do Clarissa and Lovelace or, in a slightly different way, Count Fathom and Renaldo de Melvil). The Vicar, like Job, is a type of Christ, but he is never entirely aware of his situation; like the Israelites, he ignores many signs during his wanderings which

[136] *Ibid.*, II, 73-74. [137] *Ibid.*, II, 173.

are there on purpose to comfort him. Thornhill, his redeemer, whom we see disguised as Burchell, is that more perfect minister to the good man who ultimately relieves his adversity.

Goldsmith's typological story is different from those in the two novels I have already discussed in this section, for it is the first one to contain two types of Christ, different yet interwoven. The Vicar dominates the novel, for we see with his eyes and hear everything in his voice. If Battestin is correct—and I am persuaded that he is—Goldsmith's eighteenth-century audience recognized the Job-figure in the Vicar and understood his prefigurative qualities. Mr. Burchell, too, is part of an established contemporary tradition, the secular man fulfilling the requirements of the *imitatio Christi* theme. Isaac Watts, speaking of the young Jesus, comes close to describing Goldsmith's Burchell:

> And when he began his ministry, he travelled through the country on foot to preach his divine gospel, when he might have been borne on the wings of angels. He was content with mean lodging in the tents of fishermen, and sometimes the Lord of Glory had not [*sic*] where to lay his head. He never accepted but of one gaudy day in the period of his life, and then his highest triumph was to ride upon the colt of an ass into *Jerusalem*: . . . An obscure life on earth vailed the majesty of the king of heaven.[138]

Burchell's humility is his principal characteristic; he is disguised in the world of the novel to intensify the typological theme, so that his revelation may dramatize the messianic qualities at which Goldsmith has hinted from time to time.[139] Here, too, Goldsmith was comfortably within a long homiletic tradition of sermons on the truth of the Old Testament prophecies and the character of the Messiah. A standard argument of such sermons would be to prove that all who are faithful to God are, figuratively, sons of God, so that the character of Jesus can have continual postfigurations in the persons of those who successfully imitate him.[140]

One of the key words to describe *The Vicar of Wakefield*, which Goldsmith himself uses in his "Advertisement," is "simplicity." In

[138] "Humility represented in the Character of St. Paul," *Works*, II, 349.

[139] On the element of disguise in the novel, see Curtis Dahl, "Patterns of Disguise in *The Vicar of Wakefield*," *ELH*, 25 (1958), 90-104, a thorough study which unfortunately sheds little light on the problem.

[140] See, for example, Samuel Clarke's sermon, "On the character of the Messiah," *Works*, I, 438-42.

novels that have typological stories, as I have already observed, the typological fable is a small, although by no means insignificant, part of the whole work. Typology, we must always remember, is not simply a system of exegesis; it is also a method of figuration or figuralism. In the oldest figural works, like the books of the Old Testament, the figural coexists with the literal style. As Erich Auerbach points out, the literal or realist style of narrative, which later in the Christian era becomes known as *sermo humilis*, is the basic style of the entire Bible, including the biblical narratives; the figural style, which in many cases throughout the Bible is typological, is encapsulated within the larger framework of the narrative.[141] The functioning of typological stories in eighteenth-century novels which, thanks to the studies of Battestin and Rothstein, we are now coming to see as systematic narratives, is similar to the way in which figuralism operates in the Bible. In a novel like *The Vicar of Wakefield*, the typological story of the Vicar and his afflictions and of Mr. Burchell-Sir William Thornhill is just as simple as the hint in the "Advertisement" suggests it will be. Surrounding this narrative pattern and, for some readers, obscuring it, are the many episodes which make up the action of the book. Some of these episodes are complex—the "Whistonean controversy" scene has recently provoked discussion[142]—but they are not necessarily part of the typology. Typological characters, as I said in Chapter 5, are predictive structures of a special kind. In the same way, the typological stories in certain novels of the eighteenth century are also predictive or prefigurative patterns. No novelist that I am familiar with takes the trouble to spell out the purpose of such prefigurative patterns, so we may have to content ourselves with a surmise. In Goldsmith's own words, typological stories may well have been intended to remind the contemporary audience that their "chief stores of comfort are drawn from futurity."

Typological characters, patterns, and stories are not limited to the novel in eighteenth-century England, but occur in other genres with

141 See Erich Auerbach, *Literary Language and Its Public in Late Latin Antiquity and the Middle Ages*, trans. Ralph Manheim (Princeton: Princeton Univ. Press, 1965), pp. 50-56.

142 See Howard D. Weinbrot and Eric Rothstein, "The Vicar of Wakefield, Mr. Wilmot, and the 'Whistonean Controversy,'" *PQ*, 55 (1976), 225-40.

considerable frequency. I will discuss some of these occurrences—
such as those in the lyric, satire, biblical epic, and prophetic verse
—in later chapters. Another genre, more closely related to the
novel, where typological motifs have some importance is children's
literature. Since literature meant specifically for children flourished
in the later part of the century, more or less coincidentally with the
appearance of much secularized typology in novels, it deserves our
attention here. Scaled-down versions of the Bible, children's catechisms and prayerbooks, and works meant to inculcate infant devotion, such as Bunyan's *A Book for Boys and Girls: or Country
Rhimes for Children* (1686), were not uncommon before mid-century; these books, and others like them, often deal with typology.[143]
But the creation of typological stories for children begins in earnest
with the later eighteenth century and the writings of Maria Edgeworth, Anna Laetitia Barbauld, Mary Wollstonecraft, and Thomas
Day.[144] Certainly the children's book was an ideal place for the
simplicity of many typological characters and stories.

Moreover, as Isaac Kramnick has noticed, many of the authors of
the early collections of children's stories were dissenting clergymen,
usually Methodists, or were closely associated with dissenting circles
and groups possessing radical political opinions. This circumstance
may in part account for the fact that many stories in these volumes
deal with feats of unusual endurance and piety on the part of the
poor child, who is often an orphan (we should note that the child of
unknown parentage can always be analogized to familiar types like
Melchizedik), or with a pair of youthful exemplars, one rich and inclined to malice, the other poor and inclined to virtue. Systematic
study of the many hundreds of volumes which make up the body
of children's literature in the late eighteenth and early nineteenth
centuries has scarcely begun, but it is already evident that many of
the stories that were standard fare for children are imitations or

---

[143] Bunyan's work, reprinted many times in the eighteenth century as *Divine
Emblems: or Temporal Things Spiritualized*, complete with crude illustrations,
contains some typological iconography, as does his *Emblems for the Entertainment and Improvement of Youth* (London, 1750).

[144] On the development of the children's book, see the standard history, F. J.
Harvey Darton, *Children's Books in England: Five Centuries of Social Life*, 2nd
ed. (Cambridge: University Press, 1958). For the original impetus for this section,
I am indebted to Isaac Kramnick's Clark Library Seminar paper, "Children's
Literature and Bourgeois Ideology: Observations on Culture and Industrial
Capitalism in the Later Eighteenth Century," in *Culture and Politics from
Puritanism to the Enlightenment*, ed. Perez Zagorin (Berkeley and Los Angeles:
Univ. of California Press, 1980), pp. 203-40.

condensations of fables in moralized versions of Aesop like that by Richardson, reworked characters of Theophrastus and other character writers, and sometimes even condensed versions of well-known books.[145] In the last third of the century, enterprising writers also published abridged versions of certain novels for the use and education of children. Among these efforts are, of course, *Robinson Crusoe* and *Pamela*; a more surprising abridgment for the young is that of *Sir Charles Grandison* by Francis Newbury (1769) and later by Mary Wollstonecraft as *Young Grandison* (1790), which is a translation of an earlier German version of the novel back into English.

The nucleus of this vast literature may be glimpsed by examining a few characteristic works, of which Thomas Day's *The History of Sandford and Merton* (1783-89) is one of the best. Day's work, which swelled, through installments, to three volumes, proved that the annals of the poor are neither short nor simple. A poor boy, Harry Sandford, and a rich boy, Tommy Merton, come together, despite their utterly different circumstances and personalities, and receive instruction from the local clergyman, a Man of Ross figure named Mr. Barlow. The story is a glorification of the simple virtues of the poor and the modest, which emerge triumphant over the jaded tastes and luxurious life-style of the gentry. True Christianity, Day wants his audience to know, resides among working people, and just as the common folk embody all the Christian virtues, especially hard work, so the gentry shamelessly pursue all vices, even after they have been demonstrated to be injurious and depraving to soul and body alike. The true aristocracy are the virtuous Cincinnatus-figures among the working class. That the novel should have stretched to three volumes shows how Day worked to prove his points, which he does through a series of episodes in which Harry's virtue completely overcomes Tommy's vices. I should add that Day gives his poor lad every practical advantage, including common sense, mechanical skills, and an even temper; the rich youth degrades his colleague in one way only, by exercising the skills of "polite" society and the raillery of the drawing room.

Such a work could have succeeded perfectly well without the addition of typology, but Day obviously found typological patterns

[145] Thomas Day's *The Children's Miscellany* . . . (London, 1788), contains a condensation of Longueville's *The English Hermit*, entitled "The History of Philip Quarll," pp. 194-339, previously unknown to cataloguers; Day deletes much of the book's circumstantial detail, but retains all the religious sections, including much typology.

and structures useful for didactic purposes. Thus we should not be surprised to find that the poor boy, Harry, even before the instruction of the book begins, already has a thorough understanding of Christ and his Apostles (the theme of primitive Christianity is common in children's books) and knows that they are examples to be emulated (the *imitatio Christi* theme is pervasive in such literature). On one occasion, Harry is indirectly responsible for a huntsman on horseback's losing a hare which he has been pursuing; the man, angered, brutally lashes the boy with his riding crop, leaving him badly hurt. This is the sort of scene in which Day specializes: at once the patrician Tommy comes to his friend's aid, crying out for vengeance. Harry's mild response is characteristic: "Indeed, if I had been a man, he would not have used me so; but it is all over now, and we ought to forgive our enemies, as Mr. Barlow says Christ did; and then perhaps they may come to love us, and be sorry for what they have done."[146] The hare that Harry has rescued is a type of Christ, familiar to all contemporary readers, but Day stresses his typological character in Harry's remarks.

Episodes like this one, in which Harry is always the Christ-figure and Tommy is always governed by self-interest, are but one way in which Day instructs. Another is by internal stories, usually fables which the clergyman-teacher, Mr. Barlow, reads to the boys and on which they are then invited to comment. A pair of these, entitled "The Good-Natured Little Boy" and "The Ill-Natured Boy," exemplify the *imitatio Christi* theme almost too well; the distinctions between the typological fable of the pious lad and the vicious pranks and hard usage of the ill-natured brat are those between black and white.[147] A third method is by presenting the clergyman (the Good Shepherd figure) as the *Christianus perfectus.* So Mr. Barlow is "a worthy servant and follower of Jesus Christ himself," a modest friend of the poor, living proof of the divinity of disinterested benevolence, Sir Charles Grandison on the village level. We have seen such characters before: the Vicar of Wakefield is such a man, and Clarissa, before she flees her family, devoted a set number of hours every week to visits to the poor and to relieving their distress. *Sandford and Merton* is far from believable—typological fables often propose idealized exemplars for our imitation—and is sometimes actually incredible. After three volumes of morality, the

[146] *The History of Sandford and Merton, A Work intended for the Use of Children,* 3 vols. (London, 1783-89), I, 83-85; cf. I, 11-12.

[147] *Ibid.,* I, 136-42, 143-53.

rich lad, Tommy, finally gets the point and resolves, as he puts it, "to apply myself to the study of nothing but reason and philosophy."[148] In Day's fantasy world, even ten-year olds can aspire to wisdom.

Day was the philosopher of children's literature, although it would be fair to say that all of his philosophy is expressed in less than twenty pages of the first volume of *Sandford and Merton*. Most authors in the tradition confined themselves either to brief tales or to condensed fictional narratives of youthful education. Mary Wollstonecraft's *Original Stories from Real Life* (1788) is in fact one story, the account of sisters named Mary and Caroline, aged fourteen and twelve (it is rare in children's books to learn the age of a child character), whose mother has died and whose father places them for proper education with a Mrs. Mason, "a woman of tenderness and discernment."[149] Wollstonecraft's mission is much clearer than Day's, as she tells us in her preface: "Systems of theology may be complicated, but when the character of the Supreme Being is displayed, and He is recognized as the Universal Father, the Author and Centre of Good, a child may be led to comprehend that dignity and happiness must arise from imitating Him; and this conviction should be twisted into—and be the foundation of every inculcated duty."[150] The key to complicated systems of theology, then, is the imitation of the divine perfections, a tenet which the book reinforces at every possible juncture. In other words, the creation of tropological characters among children is a necessary part of education; the *imitatio Christi* theme becomes part (is "twisted into" the very fabric) of not only the education of children but also of books about children's education. Wollstonecraft could just as well be glossing the children's books of Edgeworth, Day, Barbauld, and John Aikin, although these other writers lack her clear dedication to a religious theme.

The second edition of *Original Stories* (1791), printed by the radical publisher Joseph Johnson, contains six engravings by Blake, including a typological frontispiece (see Figure 21). This first plate of the book shows the elongated form of Mrs. Mason, her arms spread so that her shape is a cruciform, above the lowered

148 *Ibid.*, III, 256.
149 *Original Stories from Real Life; with conversations calculated to regulate the affections, and form the mind to truth and goodness*, 2nd ed. (London, 1791), p. vii.
150 *Ibid.*, p. vi.

heads of the two girls. As an accompaniment of the facing title page, this frontispiece, with the sign of the cross and the message of salvation through Christ, prefigures the contents of the work which, in story after story, show that the imitation of Jesus and the simple virtues of primitive Christianity are the way to salvation.[151] Mrs. Mason is a kind of female Sir Charles Grandison. She is comfortably well-off, and can afford to relieve the distresses of the poor; moreover, she is a model of the iconographical themes that the frontispiece figures forth. She teaches the girls to follow the central Christian themes of meekness, humility, charity to the unfortunate, and uncomplaining suffering. Since every action in the book, in Wollstonecraft's words, is "twisted into" an understanding of the Supreme Being, we must expect to find that Mrs. Mason can extract a typological meaning from virtually every episode. No scene can be too trivial for such a figural drama, and I could cite many examples. One that is somewhat unusual, because of what it tells us about children's literature, is an interesting homily on pain. Caroline, the younger sister, is stung by a wasp and, like any twelve-year old, she cries at the pain. Mrs. Mason moralizes thus: "I am sorry to see a girl of your age weep on account of bodily pain; it is proof of a weak mind—a proof that you cannot employ yourself about things of consequence. How often must I tell you that the Most High is educating us for Eternity?"[152] She goes on to show that pain is simply a foreshadow of eternity, and that children must learn to accept suffering as a preparation for later life, death, and futurity. No doubt Wollstonecraft is alluding here to women's sufferings and ability to bear pain (she herself died in childbirth in 1797), but she is also among the first (if not the first) to hint that childhood is a preparation for and prefiguration of adulthood and eternity. Later writers, especially Wordsworth in the "Immortality" ode, will have more to say about the typology of childhood. In the contexts of narrative, however, it is sufficient to note that the authors of children's books found it appropriate to their purposes to employ several different kinds of typology, of which typological characters and typological patterns are the most usual, as an integral part of their educative and fictional methods.

[151] For comment on Blake's illustrations to the second edition of *Original Stories*, see Martin Butlin, *William Blake* (exhibition catalogue, Tate Gallery, 9 March-21 May 1978) (London: Tate Gallery, 1978), p. 47.

[152] *Original Stories*, p. 156; cf. pp. 156-60.

The multifarious uses of typology in eighteenth-century fiction emphasize an old truth, that religious instruction has never been confined to catechisms, sermons, and other theological texts. The pleasant instruction of every form of narrative continues, nay intensifies, in the eighteenth century, for the exegeses of professional theologians could never reach so large an audience as the novel. Those interested in Christian apologetics early recognized this fact, and even before Johnson's famous dictum on the didacticism of the novelist in *Rambler* 4, Defoe, Richardson, and Fielding had devised their own methods for conveying religious instruction in prose narrative. That these methods often involved typology is a matter of much interest for commentators like myself, but this circumstance is part of a long-term trend in English figuralism. This trend provides for a secularization and popularization of sacred metaphor and for a heightened public awareness of the naturalness, even of the historical inevitability, of such figural techniques as typology. The mythologers and theologians of the mid-eighteenth century, as we have seen, were aware of this trend, and shaped their canvas to its force. Novelists, cognizant of contemporary tastes and closely attuned to the popularity of prefigurative styles, seem to have followed closely. Typology gradually comes to be seen as a quality that is universal in all societies, part of the human condition. Samuel Clarke, in an early eighteenth-century sermon on "The Nature, End, and Design of the Holy Communion," observes that the sacrament of the Lord's Supper recalls the Passover, another typological ceremony, and realizes that such commemorative ceremonies are found in all societies:

> And accordingly we find in the Histories of All Nations, that something like This was their usual manner of keeping up in their Minds a Sense of great and remarkable blessings; of preserving the Memory of their most eminent Benefactors; and of making effectual the Laws and particular Precepts, such Benefactors have thought fit should be perpetually observed.
>
> AND now, This is the Method which God has been pleased to make use of with *Us Christians* likewise. The Sacrifice of the Death of Christ . . . was a Blessing, of which the deliverance of the People out of *Egypt*, and their passage through the *Red Sea*, was but a Type and Figure.[153]

[153] Clarke, *Works*, I, 348; cf. 344-49.

We would now understand Clarke's observations in the light of structural anthropology, and we would interpret his statement as an assertion that prefigurative ceremonies, or rites, can be found in all human cultures. But Clarke was by no means alone in hinting at the universality of typological situations in the eighteenth century. Other divines join him, and the texts of Boehme, Hartley, and later Coleridge testify abundantly to a growing awareness that the structure of human learning and experience is predictive and, therefore, typological in a secular way.

Biographers and autobiographers, as I noted earlier in the case of Baxter, often noted the analogies of human life to the typological framework of the Bible or to the more generalized typology of life as a pilgrimage. No doubt one of the reasons why Boswell exaggerated Dr. Johnson's religious devotions (at times of his life when Johnson actually ignored religious duties) and intensified his account of Johnson's final sufferings was to bring his version of Johnson's life into conformity with the tradition of Christian heroism (a well-known branch of typology). In another sphere, Methodist followers of Wesley were encouraged, sometimes even enjoined, to keep a daily journal and to memorialize in narrative form the relationships between daily life and one's spiritual accomplishments.[154] The novelist, whose genre derives from and parallels those of the biographer and autobiographer, the diarist, and the memoirist, inevitably employs similar figural devices in creating his or her narrative. The eighteenth-century novelist, as we have seen, inherited the figural system of typology, found it popular, and used it. Martin Battestin has written of

> the idea that fiction, like all art, is an imitation of ideal nature, a rendering by means of analogy, type, and figure of the universal human comedy, whose author is Providence, whose actors, however faulty their performance, confess the efficacy of the rational virtues, and whose formal character is the product of the highest artifice—harmony, symmetry, the full consent of things.[155]

Eighteenth-century assumptions about narrative unquestionably include this idea, although the narratives themselves also include a

---

[154] See Isabel Rivers's fascinating study, " 'Strangers and Pilgrims': Sources and Patterns of Methodist Narrative," *Augustan Worlds: New Essays in Eighteenth-Century Literature*, ed. J. C. Hilson, M.M.B. Jones, and J. R. Watson (Leicester: Leicester Univ. Press, 1978), pp. 189-203, esp. pp. 194-95.

[155] See *The Providence of Wit*, p. 214.

great deal that cannot be neatly encapsulated in a theory. Typology is part—an integral part—of the system of signs that novelists found useful as a method of informing contemporary readers of special relationships and attitudes, of the qualities of certain characters, and of hints of certain expectations of plot. The novel places characters and their stories in a structure relating art and nature. Fictional structures, like molecules, contain smaller structures within them, and typology, in its various applications, is such a unit, whether it involves fictional characters, a preferred form of behavior, or the human condition. Arguments in favor of typological interpretation, as I said in Chapter 2, will not convince every reader. Scholars often strongly resist—correctly, in my view—the tendency to oversystematize, overchristianize, and overstructure literature; some of the most profound and elaborate systems of figural reading of the past are now regarded as mistaken (second-century allegorism is such an instance). Hence I view typology as being present in some eighteenth-century fiction, but also as something which interpreters should use sparingly and tentatively—figuralism should not come to dominate fable. I would not wish to make any larger claims for typology in the novel other than to say that its presence continues to be remarked long after the eighteenth century is over and that our awareness of that presence will help us to understand better the internal and external dynamics of prose fiction.

CHAPTER 8

Typology and Satire

IN THE FIFTH volume of *Tristram Shandy* (1762) there takes place an event of tremendous unimportance in Sterne's scheme of the novel, the death of Tristram's older brother Bobby. It is an event for which Sterne had prepared his more attentive readers —there is at least one foreshadowing of it earlier—and its momentousness lies in the fact that Tristram now becomes the heir to the Shandy name. Consequently, his sexual potency, already symbolically thwarted in the accidental flattening of the bridge of his nose during his birth, will assume ever more significance in the story. We have already seen Sterne's (or Tristram's) fascination with the subject in Slawkenbergius' tale (IV. init.) and in the fragment upon whiskers (V.i) and, shortly after Tristram enters his ministry, as bearer of the Shandy seed, as it were, we will hear more of his presumed ability to procreate in the account of the boy's accidental circumcision by a falling window sash. So when Obadiah delivers the letter containing the fatal news and cries out, "My young master in *London* is dead!" the cast of characters in the Shandy kitchen reacts with highly individualized associations. Corporal Trim, fresh from his triumphant reading of Yorick's sermon found in the pages of Stevinus, is present, and it is he who delivers the ultimate statement of the servants' hall upon the matter. " 'Are we not here now,' " he cries, "(striking the end of his stick perpendicularly upon the floor, so as to give an idea of health and stability)—'and are we not'—(dropping his hat upon the ground) 'gone! in a moment!'—'Twas infinitely striking! *Susannah* burst into a flood of tears. . . .—The whole kitchen crouded about the corporal." Sterne is obviously pleased with the corporal's eloquence, notes that there is nothing in Trim's actual words to arouse emotions, and concludes that the accompanying gestures or signs are entirely responsible for the emotional quality of his words. He goes over the passage again:

> —————"Are we not here now;"—continued the corporal, "and are we not"—(dropping his hat plumb upon the ground —and pausing, before he pronounced the word)—"gone! in a moment?" The descent of the hat was as if a heavy lump of clay had been kneaded into the crown of it.—————Nothing could have expressed the sentiment of mortality, of which it was the type and forerunner, like it,—his hand seemed to vanish from under it,—it fell dead,—the corporal's eye fix'd upon it, as upon a corps,—and *Susannah* burst into a flood of tears.[1]

Sterne knows that there are an infinite number of ways by which a hat may be dropped upon the ground without any effect, and he proposes that all meditate—all, even those who drive and those "who are driven, like turkeys to market, with a stick and a red clout"—on Trim's hat. Sterne is serious, of course, although he drops the subject at once and never returns to it, but he is also mocking, parodic, jesting, mercurial, and satiric. Thus the typology of Trim's hat assumes a special place in the narrative, if only for a moment, for the falling hat has become the "type and forerunner" of mortality. It is a standard phrase from the world of sermons and biblical exegesis, but Sterne and his audience knew that no serious exegete would apply a typological reading to a hat.[2]

What Sterne is doing with his figuralism here is representative of the secularization of typology in the late seventeenth and eighteenth centuries. Many writers—some of whom, like Swift, were trained as theologians, but others of whom, like Butler and Dryden, were laymen—discovered that typology could be turned to satirical purposes. It would be possible, they found, to satirize those theologians who introduced typology in over-frequent or excessive applications by imitating their figuralism in debased, ridiculous, or preposterous contexts. The parody of typology begins during the 1640s, when Anglican writers started to ridicule their Puritan antagonists by parodying the dissenting style and method of proceed-

[1] *The Life and Opinions of Tristram Shandy*, 9 vols. (London, 1760-67), V, 47-48 (V.vii).

[2] Benjamin Keach, in his monumental *Tropologia, or, A Key to Open Scripture Metaphors* (London, 1681), discusses the symbolism of the "crown" (p. 180), but even his thoroughness goes no further; nonscriptural terms were not deemed worthy of exegetical attention.

ing. Butler, Rochester, Oldham, Dryden, and Swift, to mention
only the major satirists of the later seventeenth and early eighteenth
centuries, attacked typological excesses by parodying the figural
mode in a variety of inventive and humorous ways. The same writers also used typology for satirical purposes by actually employing
a prefigurative style, and writing as if they were skilled exegetes
engaged in typological analysis. Prefiguration has its serious purposes for the eighteenth century, but it is clear that many authors
decided that there was no reason why it could not be used to ridicule and debase one's intellectual, political, or theological opponents.

Swift's techniques in the digressive and narrative portions of
A Tale of a Tub, as we will see, are a particularly effective form of
typological satire. Typology could be used for satiric purposes in
both theological and secular contexts. The typology of *A Tale of a
Tub* functions and is best understood in a theological milieu, but
that of *Mac Flecknoe* and *The Dunciad*, while it draws on theology
for its wit, has secular intentions. The typological character, which
so many novelists treated with the utmost sobriety, could equally
well be applied to satire; Butler, Pope, Fielding, and others do so
on a number of occasions. If novelists could draw typological portraits in their books, they could also create typological caricatures.
In an analogous fashion, we will find that typological satire appears
in the visual arts as well. Prefigurative devices are important in
eighteenth-century art, and political cartoonists often turn to typological subjects to enhance the satirical point of an engraving or
drawing. For example, a number of the political prints that appeared during the public clamor surrounding the repeal of the
Jewish Naturalization Act of 1753 deploy typological themes and
visual imagery for satiric purposes, the satire in this case being directed against Jewish customs and beliefs as well as against both
houses of Parliament which had, after all, passed the Act with re-
markably little controversy.[3] We may find typological themes and
techniques of prefiguration in the moral satire of Hogarth's *A Harlot's Progress*, where a subtle blending of biblical types, prefigurative characters (such as the Jew in Plate 2), and caricatures of well-
known principals in London prostitution of the 1730s combine to

---

[3] See Herbert M. Atherton, *Political Prints in the Age of Hogarth: A Study
of the Ideographic Representation of Politics* (Oxford: Clarendon Press, 1974),
pp. 162-67, and Plates 71 and 73; Atherton also cites other satirical prints
which he does not reproduce.

propose a typological moral commentary addressed to young women. These prints, Hogarth appears to be saying, figure forth and prefigure the doom of those who allow themselves to be ensnared by prostitution, a topic which receives its share of attention in the Bible and in eighteenth-century exegesis.[4]

First and foremost for our period, typology was always a system of exegesis. The many abstracted uses of it made by the writers of the age emphatically confirm its popularity and suggest the widespread recognition which it must have enjoyed among the contemporary audience. We can always be reasonably sure that the satirical object of a work of literature would have been readily comprehensible to the audience which its author intended that work to reach. The intricate typological satire of *A Tale of a Tub* would have been clear to many readers, but clearest of all to the very exegetes and biblical and classical scholars who are among its many satirical objects. Typology has its place in biblical exegesis but, in the hands of imaginative readers of Scripture, it could reveal layers of meaning that were far from obvious. We may recall that fourfold figural exegesis, as practiced in patristic times and in the Middle Ages, was often guilty of overinterpretation. To its eighteenth-century critics, typology was a form of excessive, mystical interpretation which, like cabalism, was capable of extracting prefigurative meanings from texts which never were intended to have them. The debate over Scripture prophecy in the 1720s, while it is conducted very much on the scholarly level, reveals the basis for popular ridicule of typology in the 1730s. Contemporary millenarianism and millenarian typology, in the view of Collins, Warburton, and others, went too far in their predictions of the Second Coming. It is therefore not surprising that typology would become important in some satiric literature during the political wars of the Walpole years. The original conclusion to the third book of *The Dunciad*, written late in the decade of the most severe reaction against typology, accurately recreates and ridicules the chiliasts and other features of contemporary popular culture:

> Signs following signs lead on the Mighty Year;
> See! the dull stars roll round and re-appear.

[4] See Ronald Paulson's discussion of *A Harlot's Progress* in *Hogarth: His Life, Art, and Times*, 2 vols. (New Haven: Yale Univ. Press, 1971), I, 235-59; without stressing the prefigurative quality of the series, Paulson nevertheless enumerates many typological qualities and themes in the six prints.

> She comes! the Cloud-compelling Pow'r, behold!
> With Night Primaeval, and with Chaos old . . .[5]

Pope describes, in a vision, the coming of the Millennium, one of the great desiderata of typological prophecy, but his "Mighty Year" heralds the advent of an eternity of Dulness, a New Jerusalem composed entirely of Grub Streets. In this context, Pope employs typology as if he were a sincere millenarian, for the essence of typological satire is to suggest the most ridiculous exaggerations of its figural basis as if they were completely appropriate and sensible.

In typological satire, the speaker or principal character is often a mock prophet, a flawed or counterfeit exemplar of genuine vision. The enthusiasts in Swift's *The Mechanical Operation of the Spirit* (1710), where a debased typology is part of the satiric method, are lunatics and, indeed, we will find that much satire involving typology, whether it is satire of typological excess or parody of typology itself, involves some hint of madness. The satirists clearly sought to imply that enthusiastic mystics like Boehme or Thomas Vaughan had gone mad and that typological excess—a deranged exegesis, as it were—was a symptom of their disease. The Scriblerian mock scholia to *The Dunciad Variorum*, which include typology, exemplify satire against the scholar-typologist. To understand satire of this kind, we must consult and become familiar with contemporary scholarly editions and the vast syntagmata which often evolved, over a period of a century, out of modest scholarly treatises. The scholia to scholarly works such as Poole's *Synopsis Criticorum*, Frantz's *Historia Animalium Sacra*, and a dozen others like them, and to major classical authors like Homer, Virgil, and Ovid often typologized the obvious, uncovered a plethora of secret meanings and Christian types, and in many other ways exceeded the bounds of rational inquiry. I have glanced at some of these developments in Chapters 5 and 6 and cannot go further into them here, but I should emphasize once more that all figuralism is open to criticism for its excesses. Satire against typology naturally exaggerates, and one of the traits of the typologist which satirists most liked to ridicule was his pedantry. Typology is closely linked with prophecy; often, in biblical exegesis, types are the very signs which confirm the accuracy of a prophet. But not all those who claim to be prophetical are genuinely inspired with the word of God or the Holy Spirit; some—indeed, many—are charlatans. Hence we will find

[5] *The Dunciad Variorum*, III.335-38.

that satire against typology also attacks it as a tool of the falsely inspired, used for deceitful ends with a show of great learning.

Let me revert to the typology of Trim's hat once more. In making the falling hat the "type and forerunner" of mortality, Sterne certainly ridicules some of the excesses of a figuralism which could discover such unseen—and unlikely—relations between apparently unrelated things. Yet there is also a pedantic seriousness to his identification. A hat dropped to the floor in any of ten thousand situations would be nothing, but in the context of young Bobby's death, Trim's action is exceptionally expressive. Perhaps, then, Sterne may suggest, there is something after all to the arguments of the inspirationalists that there is a pervasive predictiveness to everyday events, if only we were adept enough to spy it out. We have already seen that Walter Shandy is a pedant in the mold of Cornelius Scriblerus himself and that he plans to make (barring accidents) another Martinus Scriblerus of Tristram. Walter, then, is a harmless type of the pedantic worshiper of antiquity, a character whom a contemporary reader would have known from the character books and the stage, if not from *The Memoirs of Martinus Scriblerus*; his attitudes and behavior are reminiscent of those of Samuel Butler's most famous character, "An Hermetic Philosopher," which was first published early in the same year as the first two volumes of *Tristram Shandy*.[6] Trim's hat is more than a figure: it is a visual object as well. Typology almost always involves some hint of external signs or of things themselves, and Sterne, in finding prefigurative qualities in the falling hat, also ridicules typology by adopting its manner, by parodying it. I will return to *Tristram Shandy* later in this chapter. Let me make two points about it now, one particular, the other general. First, with regard to *Tristram Shandy*, Sterne's typological satire adequately reflects and even enlarges upon this interesting strain in English satire over the previous century. Second, more generally, satire of typology, from its beginning, makes much of the inspired prophetical nature of the texts and writers it attacks and magnifies beyond measure the riddling obscurity of this branch of figuralism.

6 Butler's characters were first published as part of his *Genuine Remains in Verse and Prose* (London, 1759). See the *Characters*, ed. Charles W. Daves, pp. 139-59. Walter Shandy's original name for his son was "Trismegistus," after Hermes Trismegistus, the leading philosopher of hermeticism, and some of *Tristram Shandy*'s scholastic nonsense is a satire on hermeticism.

2

The war-torn decade of the 1640s falls just before the acknowledged scope of this book, yet the contribution to English satire of John Cleveland, the major satirist of those years, is so important that a brief excursion to consider his interest in typology will be necessary. The first collected edition of Cleveland's poems appeared in 1651 and, by the end of the century, some thirty different collections of his verse had been published. His highly topical satires seem difficult and obscure to us today, but their popularity in the second half of the seventeenth century cannot be questioned; even after Dryden's well-known criticism of Cleveland in *An Essay of Dramatic Poesy* (1668) there were eight more editions of his poems.[7] Cleveland's satires deal with the religious and political issues of the Civil Wars from a Royalist point of view, so they would have had an attraction in the 1650s to a largely opposition group and, in the 1660s, to those who disliked Nonconformity in the Church. His famous obscurity is sometimes described as the last, worst excrescence of metaphysical poetry. Actually, it is something quite different. It is a glittering display of brief epitomes attacking the multifarious complexity of contemporary theological and political thought. Whenever possible, Cleveland uses an exaggerated obscurity borrowed from the very sects and schools which he attacks. Typological allusions have a definite place in such literature, for the typology of king and nation was a subject of much debate.

So, for example, in "The King's Disguise," which Cleveland wrote on the subject of Charles I's vain effort to escape in disguise from his adversaries in April 1646, he affects a riddling typology that deliberately sets out to prophesy the forthcoming tragedy of the Regicide. Other poets and writers, including Henry Vaughan, adopted the same theme of typological prophecy, but Cleveland was the only one to incorporate his typology into a satirical statement.[8] "The King's Disguise" plays on light and darkness, on the

---

[7] See *The Poems of John Cleveland*, ed. Brian Morris and Eleanor Withington (Oxford: Clarendon Press, 1967), pp. ix-xi. Most collections of Cleveland also contained a number of poems falsely attributed to him as well as satires by other authors.

[8] For Vaughan's poem, "The King Disguised," see *The Works of Henry Vaughan*, ed. L. C. Martin, 2nd ed. (Oxford: Clarendon Press, 1957), pp. 625-26. Morris and Withington, *The Poems of Cleveland*, p. 87, discuss other contemporary collections of "prophecies."

light of the sun (i.e., the King) being eclipsed by clouds of disguise, on this phenomenon as a foreshadow of apocalypse, and on the signs of kingship (texts of a sort) being obscured ("clear" types being made more complicated). Charles becomes a "shadow royall," a type whose deciphering is an exercise in mysticism:

> But pardon Sir, since I presume to be
> Clarke of this Closet to Your Majestie;
> Me thinks in this your dark mysterious dresse
> I see the Gospell couch't in Parables.
> The second view my pur-blind fancy wipes,
> And shewes Religion in its dusky types.
> Such a Text Royall, so obscure a shade
> Was *Solomon* in Proverbs all array'd.[9]

Charles's very sufferings and tribulations are transformed into texts, pieces of a narrative; it is significant that the narrative is like the parables or the Book of Proverbs, typological in some unexplained way. Cleveland's style here is not a parody of typology, but rather quite a serious application of prefigurative relationships to an historical event whose causes and consequences he laments bitterly. Cleveland, like a scorpion, always has a sting in his tail; he turns immediately from the typology of the King to snarl against "ye brats of this expounding age" to tell them why the typology of kingship is a lock that they cannot pick:

> Keyes for this Cypher you can never get,
> None but S. *Peter*'s op's this Cabinet.
> This Cabinet, whose aspect would benight
> Critick spectators with redundant light.
> A Prince most seen, is least: What Scriptures call
> The Revelation, is most mysticall.[10]

"The King's Disguise" is, in part, a satire on interpretation and the vain efforts of the Puritan exegetes to understand or explain the myths of monarchy, but, in ridiculing typological exegesis, Cleveland uses prefigurative techniques of his own which are a mixture of the serious and the jesting. His typologies in other poems are no less complex. "The Rebell *Scot*" (1644), perhaps his most popular single poem, draws fully on the tradition of the negative type, the character of Satan, in a way that is especially interesting. He sees the Scottish supporters of Parliament iconographically,

[9] *Poems*, pp. 8-9 (lines 91-98).   [10] *Ibid.*, p. 9 (lines 109-14).

> As in a picture, where the squinting paint
> Shewes Fiend on this side, and on that side Saint.

Scotland is a figure for Hell: the Scots are a cursed race, like that first type of Satan, Cain; and satirizing Scotland is to "wrong the Devill," so great is their evil.[11] In Cleveland's poems we find little to amuse, but much bitter use of typology, both for parodic purposes and as an integral part of satiric technique that will come to maturity in the next generation.

"*Synods* are mystical *Bear-gardens*," says Ralpho, and undertakes to prove it with an argumentative and interpretative skill worthy of Cleveland, but (helpfully, for those puzzled by Cleveland's conciseness) spun out to fantastic length. When Cleveland used typology, it was for brief illustrations; when Butler uses it, it is for verbose ridicule of what he considered one of the more obscurantist branches of mysticism. Typology, especially the typology of kingship, flourishes in the first years of the Restoration but, despite its popularity with monarchists, not every use of prefigurative imagery was acceptable. Writers like Butler disliked millenarianism, and Anglican apologists like Samuel Parker and John Eachard seized upon what they considered the mystical and figural excesses of some Puritan writers as evidence of an enthusiastic zeal which merited both parody and attack.[12] Ralpho's argument is clever—and, true to the style of *Hudibras*, he never gets to finish it—but ridiculous. Butler's squire is a mystic of profound depth who sees in the present-day synod and bear garden the completion (i.e., the antitypes) of a process that had its origins in the primitive Church. The bear, it seems, is like a persecuted saint (the term, of course, is derisive of the millenarian saints themselves) brought to the stake; the martyrs were accepted types of those persecuted for their beliefs in modern times; synods persecute the foes of the Presbyters just as the Romans persecuted the first Christians and as bear-baiters prick the bear; *ergo* synods are "mystical," that is, typological, bear gardens. Both synods and bear garden are antitypes of persecutions shadowed forth long ago. All this is proven from Holy Writ itself:

---

11 *Ibid.*, pp. 29-32 (lines 55-56, 57-60, 63-66, 81-82, 95-100, 121-24).

12 On the typology of kingship in the early Restoration, see Steven M. Zwicker, *Dryden's Political Poetry: The Typology of King and Nation*, pp. 17-23, 28-60. For comment on Anglican criticism of excesses in exegesis, see my "Swift and Typological Narrative in *A Tale of a Tub*," *Harvard English Studies*, 1 (1970), 70-73.

> This to the *Prophet* did appear,
> Who in a Vision saw a *Bear*,
> Prefiguring the beastly rage
> Of *Church-rule* in this later Age.[13]

The allusion to Daniel's beast vision is appropriate for several reasons. Anglicans and millenarians alike interpreted Daniel's vision as typological, but the types were usually taken to refer to the end of gentile domination and the beginning of Christianity.[14] There is certainly no reason to expect that the bear in the vision prefigures church rule or, for that matter, anything at all, but in the absurdist world of Ralpho's mind, typology is where you find it—or imagine you find it. As Hudibras says to his squire at the end of Part I, "thou art fallen on a new / Dispute, as senseless as untrue" (I.iii.1369-70).

Ralpho is a mystery-monger, a Neoplatonist, a hermeticist, a close reader of Thomas Vaughan's works on magic and of Alexander Ross's on myth. He is not so much learned as he is divinely inspired for the marvelous connections which he finds between disparate things. Hence it is not unreasonable to find that the basis for his associations is sometimes typological. The discussion about synods and bear gardens, for example, which is a motif running through the first three cantos of the poem, contains a number of references to mystical analogies from curious learning. Ralpho's method of proof is inspired: for every point about the modern bear-baiting, which he considers a "lewd, Antichristian Game" (I.i.794), he can find some pagan custom or belief which serves as its prototype and which prefigures the modern bear garden. Hudibras thinks differently from his squire, for he is an Aristotelian, a metaphysician, a logician. The memorable description of his intellectual skills (such as they are) in Part I, Canto i is so well known that I need not quote from it here. Moreover, Hudibras has typological qualities in his own right. Consider his beard,

---

[13] See *Hudibras*, ed. John Wilders (Oxford: Clarendon Press, 1967), p. 92 (I.iii.1117-20). The vision is that of Daniel 7.5; the second beast of his vision, "like to a bear," was usually seen as a reference to the empires of Media, Persia, and Babylonia.

[14] This is the view of Henry More, *A Plain and Continued Exposition of the several Prophecies or Divine Visions of the Prophet Daniel* (London, 1681) and Samuel Chandler, *A Vindication of the Antiquity of Daniel* (London, 1727). Daniel continued to be very popular as a source for millennial predictions throughout the nineteenth century; see, for example, Joseph F. Berg, *Prophecy and the Times; or England and Armageddon. An Application of some of the Predictions of Daniel and St. John to current events* (Philadelphia, 1856), *passim*.

> This hairy Meteor did denounce
> The fall of Scepters and of Crowns;
> With grizly type did represent
> Declining Age of Government;
> And tell with Hieroglyphick Spade,
> Its own grave and the State's were made.
> (I.i.245-50)

The description of Hudibras's beard consumes some forty lines, enough for us to glimpse the preposterous, mad symbolism behind it, for the knight wears his beard in defiance of his religious and political enemies, and will not relinquish it unless "the State should hap to reel" when it will be "consecrate / A Sacrifice to fall of State." But this hairy hieroglyphic is not merely symbolic of the present condition of the state; Butler would not have applied a word like "type" to it if he meant no more than that (for other satiric hieroglyphics, see Figure 11). A time-scheme of *Hudibras* shows that Part I, as the opening line of the poem tells us, refers to the 1640s, "When *civil* Fury first grew high."[15] So Hudibras's beard, in a curious way, actually *does* prefigure "Declining Age of Government," for Butler wrote with a fine sense of historical perspective. The Presbyterians, of whom Hudibras is a specimen, were at first supporters of Charles I, so Hudibras could well allow his beard to suffer "Persecution / And Martyrdome" with the state (and the King), at least until the late '40s, when the Independents disagreed with the Presbyterians on how to dispose of the King.

When Hudibras typologizes, he is less inspired, more doctrinaire than Ralpho. We have an instance of his style in Part II, when knight and squire encounter a skimmington (a village procession designed to humiliate an authoritarian wife and a henpecked husband by forcing them to ride back-to-back on a nag). Hudibras is offended by the pagan origins of this event and, after silencing the crowd,

> What means (quoth he) this dev'ls *procession*
> With men of *Orthodox* Profession?
> 'Tis *Ethnique* and *Idolatrous*,
> From *heathenism* deriv'd to us.
> Does not the Whore of *Babylon* ride
> Upon her *Horned-Beast* astride,
> Like this proud Dame, who either is

15 Earl Miner, *The Restoration Made from Milton to Dryden*, pp. 168-70, gives a helpful plot of the chronology of the poem with reference to English history.

A Type of her, or she of this?
Are things of Superstitious *function*,
Fit to be us'd in *Gospel Sunshine*?
(II.ii.759-68)

Like Ralpho, Hudibras despises vestiges of paganism in contemporary religion and society, but even as he debases typology he uses it more or less correctly. The squire is inspired to resolve the mysteries of the present by seeking prefigurations of them in the text of Scripture; Hudibras works from a New Testament source in Revelation, and follows the popular exegetical habit of the millenarians in applying the types of the Apocalypse to events in modern England. He even goes so far as correctly to differentiate between prefiguration and postfiguration, something almost no seventeenth-century writer except Swift bothered to do. The village termagant is either a "Type" of the whore of Babylon on her horned beast (a postfiguration) or the "Whore of *Babylon*" is a type of this "*Amazon* triumphant" (a prefiguration). Neither application has any justification, of course, and Butler's satire of typology gains from Hudibras's inventiveness. Just as Ralpho's use of typology which I discussed above abuses a scriptural source that was usually seen as prophetical of the Millennium, so Hudibras takes an allusion to another apocalyptic book and twists it into a mock-explanation of a piece of local folklore.

Perhaps Butler's skill, as some of his contemporaries thought, wanes in the "Third Part" of *Hudibras*, but his typological satire continues to flourish. In Canto ii, for example, in which Butler replaces the knight and Ralpho with an Independent and a Presbyterian politician, the discussion relates to events between the death of Cromwell and the arrival of General Monck at the head of his army. Butler analyzes the numerous schemes of government that different groups proposed, pausing to ridicule those who saw Oliver's death as a type of the New Jerusalem, the saints who were all for setting up King Jesus, those who saw the Rump Parliament as the type of all governments, and many more. "And now the Saints began their *Reign*," Butler tells us, pausing long enough to show us that all the crank schemes of 1658-59 have their origins in John of Leiden, who "Was made a Type by Providence, / Of all their [i.e., the Saints'] Revelations since" (III.ii.237, 249-50). The notion of prophetic fulfillment was widespread at the time and it was only a question of waiting so that people could see whose types would

turn out to have antitypes after all. As General Monck's troops—
and the accompanying rabble—march into London to put an end
to the Rump, Butler's statesmen are still debating how appropriate
it is that "Rumps [are] / . . . Symbols of State-mysteries" (1577-78).
It appears that the symbolism began with Egypt:

> For as the *Ægyptians us'd by Bees,*
> *T'Express their Antick Ptolomies,*
> *And by their Stings, the Swords they wore*
> *Held-forth Authority and Pow'r:*
> Because these subtile Animals
> Bear all their Intrests in their *Tails,*
> And when th' are once impair'd in that,
> Are banish'd their well order'd State:
> They thought, all Governments were best
> By *Hieroglyphick Rumps,* exprest.
> (III.ii.1587-96)

Students of hieroglyphics, from the sixteenth century to George
Stanley Faber, agreed that the glyphs were typological of later
events—just what, no one could say for sure—and Butler considers
a number of ridiculous governmental antitypes to his Egyptian
hieroglyphic, which is the type of the Rump, before the assembly
breaks up in tumult. It is fitting that the last part of Butler's satire
on the Interregnum should deal with hieroglyphic prefigurations
that, as usual, turn out to be wrong.

Mock-exegesis, distorted interpretation, and absurd misapplication of biblical texts to imaginary antitypes are the hallmarks of
Butler's satire in *Hudibras.* Hudibras and his squire are representative of different religious sects, but in Butler's satiric scheme, each
is also a character of the enthusiastic biblical critic, the exegete
gone mad. We may see in both heroes something of Butler's character of "A Hypocritical Nonconformist," who is not "so mean an
Interpreter of Scripture, that he cannot relieve himself, when he is
prest Home with a Text."[16] Butler's satire on biblical interpretation
is, next to Swift's, the best ever written, eminently worthy of more
attention than I can give it in these pages. When we look at *Hudibras* in the context of other seventeenth-century poems, we may,
like Earl Miner, find it "an altogether exasperating and terrible
poem."[17] But if we regard it as one step in a literary continuum

---

[16] *Characters,* p. 46.   [17] *The Restoration Mode,* p. 179.

running smoothly from Cleveland through Swift to Sterne, as a satire on mistaken ideas, false inspiration, and the babble of special languages and schools that characterize seventeenth-century England, it is a milestone. Typology was an integral part of the hieroglyphic systems and prophetical forebodings that make up these bodies of thought, and Butler's satire upon it, while sporadic rather than well-focused, comes just at the time when Royalist poets and divines took it most seriously.

The typology of *Hudibras* is distorted and abused; it is always recognizable for its absurdity. The situation with Dryden is somewhat different. The next major contribution to typogical satire is Dryden's *Mac Flecknoe*, where the author is one of the best typologists of the late seventeenth century. Unlike Butler, who regarded all methods of biblical exegesis with suspicion, Dryden took typology seriously. He had employed it for flattering the monarchy in his panegyrics of the 1660s, he would use it for sound theological reasons in *The Hind and the Panther* and, in various abstracted forms, it would have an important role in some of the major poems of his Jacobite years, the 1690s. The satire on typology in *Mac Flecknoe* does not come about because of the misapplication or distortion of the figure. Rather, the entire poem is an inverted prophecy, an annunciation of the Savior in reverse, in which the person of the Messiah is represented by Thomas Shadwell.[18] Marvell had already established the typology of Dryden's prophetical speaker, Richard Flecknoe, who is the subject of the satire, *"Fleckno,* an English Priest at *Rome"* (c. 1647). At the beginning of this poem, Marvell identifies Flecknoe as "some branch of *Melchizedeck"* and notes that his lodging is "at the Sign / Of the sad *Pelican."*[19] Melchizedik was a widely accepted type of Christ, and the pelican an emblem associated with Christ in the *moralia* of contemporary emblem books, so Dryden is able to proceed immediately into the stuff of satirical prophecy, without biblical allusions.

[18] The commentary to the California Dryden identifies the prophetical but not the typological qualities of the poem; see *The Works of John Dryden*, II, 310.

[19] *The Poems and Letters of Andrew Marvell*, ed. H. M. Margoliouth, 3rd ed. 2 vols. (Oxford: Clarendon Press, 1971), I, 87. Miner, *The Restoration Mode*, p. 399, says "Dryden had obviously read [Marvell's poem] when he wrote *Mac Flecknoe"*; either he saw a version in manuscript before he completed *Mac Flecknoe* in 1678 or he revised his text to show some verbal echoes of Marvell's satire after it was first published in Marvell's *Miscellaneous Poems* (London, 1681) the year before *Mac Flecknoe* appeared.

Mac Flecknoe consists of two long speeches by Flecknoe (lines 13-59 and 139-210) linked together by eighty lines of satirical description. The first speech is an ironic annunciation in the prophetic style of what twentieth-century theologians are wont to call the kerygma, that is, an heraldic pronouncement of news that affects the future of the state (in this case, Grub Street).[20] Much poetic typology of the late seventeenth century, including Dryden's own, can be quite complex, but that of *Mac Flecknoe* is similar to Butler's in *Hudibras*, as blunt as possible:

> *Heywood* and *Shirley* were but Types of thee,
> Thou last great Prophet of Tautology:
> Even I, a dunce of more renown than they,
> Was sent before but to prepare thy way;
> And coursly clad in *Norwich* Drugget came
> To teach the Nations in thy greater name.
>
> (29-34)

Earlier types, even Flecknoe himself, a kind of John the Baptist figure, were nothing but dim shadows of Shadwell's fullness; he is the "last great Prophet" of dullness, the antitype toward whom all prefigurations lead and, to double his significance, the perfection against whom all postfigurations of dullness, like all imitations of Christ, will be measured.[21] The prophet, we must remember, does not speak with his own voice but with the voice of a god or with the inspiration of the Holy Spirit. Dryden knows this fact well, but in his debasement of Scripture he complicates his prophet's message. John the Baptist addresses a simple text: repent now, for one greater than I shall follow me whose very shoes I am unfit to loosen (Luke 3.16). Flecknoe prophesies, but his foreshadowings are trivial and highly circumstantial. Dryden's prophet, then, is hardly filled with the divine logos; indeed, if his last words have any significance ("torture one poor word Ten thousand ways"), logomachia rather than logos may be his true meaning.

Dryden gives us, in *Mac Flecknoe*, a messianic character whose

---

[20] Sanford Budick, *The Poetry of Civilization: Mythopoeic Displacement in the Poetry of Milton, Dryden, Pope, and Johnson*, pp. 3-4, effectively brings *Mac Flecknoe* into the tradition of heraldic prophecy deriving from the Old Testament herald or *keryx*. See also my review of Budick's book in *ELN*, 17 (1979-80), 139-43.

[21] For comment on this interpretation, see Miner, *The Restoration Mode*, pp. 319-20, and my *From Concord to Dissent*, pp. 132-33.

incarnation will redeem an entire genre of literature, bad plays. His typological satire is based upon ironical distortion through proper application of the figure, but we should note that, whereas Butler satirized the exegetical qualities of typology, Dryden ridicules the prophetic, millenarian side of the prefigurative style. The satirical typology of *Absalom and Achitophel* is similar to that of *Mac Flecknoe* in this way, for it does not deal with exegesis either. Typology functions in two ways in Dryden's political masterpiece. The typology of David-Charles seems, at the start of the poem, likely to involve Dryden in difficulties, but this prefiguration is ultimately highly flattering. David's closing speech has typological associations, but they are affirmative, not satirical. Heaven thunders consent, a "Series of new time" begins, and "Godlike" David is restored again (1026-31). The "Series of new time" has orthodox typological qualities, for it suggests a new millennium, with David-Charles II-Jesus presiding over a New Jerusalem. Dryden's later words on the same topic, in "To the Dutchess of Ormond" (1700), show the richness of his own prophetic vein:

> When at Your second Coming You appear,
> (For I foretell that Millenary Year)
> The sharpen'd Share shall vex the Soil no more . . .
>
> (80-82)

Typology enters the poem as a satirical technique in the characterization of Achitophel, who is clearly Dryden's idea of the Antichrist, "Hells dire Agent" (373), a negative type representative of all evil. Shaftesbury's first speech to Monmouth, the poem's Absalom, persuades the youth that he is the people's "second *Moses*,"

> Whose dawning Day, in every distant age,
> Has exercis'd the Sacred Prophets rage:
> The Peoples Prayer, the glad Deviners Theam,
> The Young-mens Vision, and the Old mens Dream!
> Thee, *Saviour*, Thee, the Nations Vows confess;
> And never satisfi'd with seeing, bless.
>
> (236-41)

Achitophel's messianic language finds a ready ear, and shortly afterward Absalom makes his first progress around the country where "The Croud . . . / With lifted hands their young *Messiah* bless" (727-28). Legitimate temporal power was widely, if not universally, acknowledged as divine, so such flattering praise in the

mouths or on the pages of extreme Royalists would hardly be unusual, if applied to an anointed monarch. The great popularity of
a work like *Eikon Basilike* (1649) throughout the later seventeenth
century, coupled with many other circumstances in which Charles II
was presented as a second Moses and a postfiguration of the Savior,
are persuasive evidence that the typology of kingship had a wide
contemporary appeal.[22] Mosaic prefigurations were sufficiently popular in the early years of the Restoration that it seems consistent
with the time for Milton, in *Paradise Lost*, to have used the type
himself. He represents himself in the prologue to Book I as a postfiguration of Moses ("That Shepherd who first taught the chosen
Seed, / In the beginning how the Heav'ns and Earth / Rose out of
Chaos" [I.8-10]), as a second Moses leading a second chosen people.
However, at the same time that he used Mosaic typology to describe
himself, Milton was a foe of the typology of kingship, as he shows in
Eikonoklastes and *Paradise Lost*, Book II. In fact, there was widespread criticism of "vulgar prophecies," spurious enthusiasm, and
popular millenarianism from the Restoration until early in the
eighteenth century.[23] Achitophel's partially successful attempt to
mold Absalom into a popular messiah for the Jews may even relate
to the real efforts of European Jewry during the mid-seventeenth
century to establish the credibility of a genuine messiah, a quest
which, as I noted earlier, led to some question whether Cromwell
himself might have been the man.

Whatever the background to these lines and to the poem's messianic typology, it is clear that Dryden's audience would have been
intensely familiar with stories of local Absaloms. Dryden's typology
is again orthodox in every way but one—Absalom is not an
anointed king. Yet the poet chooses to use the exactitude of the
typological relationship for satirical purposes, confident that the
Jewish people of the poem, when apprised of their mistake, will
willingly accept "their Lawfull Lord." It was a risk, even for a

[22] The edition of *Eikon Basilike* that appeared in Dublin in 1706 is described
as "The fiftieth edition"; there were 25 editions in 1649 alone. See also Christopher Hill, *The World Turned Upside Down: Radical Ideas during the English
Revolution* (London: Temple Smith, 1972), pp. 285-86.

[23] John Spencer, *A Discourse concerning Prodigies* (London, 1665), pp. 394-408,
opposes the use of prodigies for promoting atheism and superstition; in his
A Discourse concerning Vulgar Prophecies (London, 1665), Spencer stresses the
distinctions between true and false prophecy, and notes that many recent so-
called prophecies are the result of melancholy (or, in twentieth-century terms,
mental disturbances).

writer so sure of his abilities as Dryden and, as it happens, someone attacked him for his ambiguity:

> First to begin with Top-Comparison [writes his detractor]
> Of Holy *David* to our *Soveraign.*
> The Type of Christ he makes our *Charles's Type,*
> Yet draws foul Figures of the *Antitype.* . . .

This unknown author of this crudely written verse critique, felicitously entitled *A Key (With the Whip) To open the Mystery and Iniquity of the Poem call'd Absalom and Achitophel,* scurrilously attacks Dryden for confusing type and antitype, for daring to make Absalom a presumed type of Christ, and for applying typology to matters outside of the literal text of Scripture.[24]

Dryden, we know, was sensitive to his critics, so perhaps the effect of the *Key* and other attacks upon *Absalom and Achitophel* was to persuade him to take fewer figural risks in *The Medall* (1682). Here he avoids the typology of kingship altogether and concentrates on "the Picture drawn at length" of his Satan-figure, the Earl of Shaftesbury. The portrait is not confined to Shaftesbury, however, but includes a denunciation of the dissenting sects of London which were responsible for Shaftesbury's support. Commemorative medals were engraved, and a contemporary synonym for engraving was "character," so we can regard the full-length portrait of Shaftesbury as an extended character, analogous to well-known characters of atheism and hypocrisy in the character books. The characters of evil in these compilations, as I have noted, are often negative types, that is, prefigurations of Satan and his mission. Dryden evidently alludes to this kind of figuralism which, like the obverse of a coin or medal, inverts traditional Christological typology:

> Five daies he sate, for every cast and look;
> Four more than God to finish *Adam* took.
> But who can tell what Essence Angels are,
> Or how long Heav'n was making *Lucifer?*
>   (18-21)

---

[24] See *A Key (With the Whip)* . . . ([London?], [c. 1682]), pp. 18, 19, 21, 40. This poem, which fills pp. 17-40 in the British Library's copy, from which pp. 1-16 are missing, is concerned solely with Dryden's figural inconsistencies, and makes no observations about his satirical methodology. The California *Dryden,* II, 293, speculatively assigns the *Key* to the Nonconformist minister Christopher Ness.

Other references ("A Vermin, wriggling in th' Usurper's Ear" [31]; "Hypocritique Zeal" [38]) and hints of papal domination corroborate Dryden's satanic picture, which he finally reveals himself: "And shews the Fiend confess'd, without a vaile" (81). There are glances at Milton's characterization of Satan here, but Dryden's typology is less an emphasis on individual character than it is an exposure of the evils of the crowd of sects, saints, seers, and factions.

The prefatory "Epistle to the Whigs," exposing the libelous writings of the antimonarchical factions, asks, "who made you the Judges in *Israel?*"[25] The "Shrieval voice" which announces "The Word" (14) is the heraldic declaration or annunciation of a messianic advent: "*Lætamur*, which, in *Polish*, is *rejoyce.*" The messianic prophecies of the Old Testament signal the coming of a time when the entire nation of Israel can rejoice, and Dryden carefully continues this prophetic style by nurturing the theme of typological prophecy *travestie*. Momentarily, he even echoes Butler when he shows what the excesses of typology can produce: "Since our Sects in prophecy grow higher, / The Text inspires not them; but they the Text inspire" (165-66). The famous address to London, the Israel of the poem (167-204), stresses the biblical notion of an Egyptian captivity from which the nation has been delivered by its Moses (Charles II) but which, through their sectarian idolatry, the sects continue to embrace. The sectarian controversy which envelops England is, for Dryden, a form of heresy, a subject which the pre-Nicene fathers had often attacked in typological terms. Origen, St. Irenaeus, and Arnobius of Sicca had allied the early heretics with anti-Christian impulses, the influence of Satan, and the Antichrist. Minutius Felix's ridicule of heresy actually approaches the satiric.[26] It is consistent with this tradition for Dryden to suggest that the New Jerusalem which Shaftesbury's sectarian priesthood paints is an inverted paradise,

> A Conventicle of gloomy sullen Saints;
> A Heav'n, like *Bedlam*, slovenly and sad;
> Fore-doom'd for Souls, with false Religion, mad.
> (284-86)

[25] *Works*, II, 39 (line 16). "*Israel*" here, as in *The Medall*, 167-204, refers not to England but specifically to London.

[26] See *Marcus Minutius Felix his Octavius; or, A Vindication of Christianity against Paganism*, trans. P. Lorrain (London, 1682), pp. 71-72.

The Medall, then, succeeds at last in debasing the coinage of the medal itself which is ostensibly the subject of the poem. A glance at the iconography of the Shaftesbury medal shows how the engraver included a well-known typological *topos* on the reverse, which depicts a scene of London from the Tower to St. Paul's, with London Bridge in the right foreground, and the sun emerging from a bank of clouds above the Tower.[27] The appearance of the sun, with its corona or rays, like an imperial crown or diadem, emerging from shadow, joined with the Latin motto and the date of the Whig grand jury's refusal to indict Shaftesbury for treason (24 November 1681), would undoubtedly have reminded a contemporary audience of the Sun or the Son triumphantly leaving a period of obscurity to commence his messianic ministry. The entire body of Dryden's text serves to debase this prophetic concept, and, to conclude matters, he closes the poem with a prophecy of his own, one which we may regard as his version of the truth. Dryden's attack on sedition is thus a critique of religious as well as political heresy: all opponents of the *status quo*, whether sectarian madmen or party zealots, abuse the normal typological qualities of prophecy.

Dryden takes heresy seriously and so he exposes it relentlessly although, one must also concede, without the picturesque wit of Butler. But there is another writer of the 1670s and '80s who satirizes heresy with such violence that, in comparison, Dryden appears clearly as the moderate he really is. This author is Oldham, perhaps the most severe and least appreciated of English satirists. Oldham's satiric range is considerable: his production includes satires on social evils and on the contemporary literary scene, the first genuine imitations of Boileau, Juvenal, and Horace and, in pindaric form, the famous "Satyr against Vertue." But he is best known for his *Satyrs upon the Jesuits* (1679-81), written at about the same time as Dryden's major satires, and the only one of his poems which has been adequately edited in the twentieth century.[28] Oldham is a son of Cleveland in scurrility but not in obscurity, for he was a skilled ecclesiastical controversialist who was well acquainted with the history of heresies, ancient and modern. Each of the four *Satyrs* presents a different view of the Jesuits through a *persona* who candidly damns the entire Society for its various alleged anti-Christian practices. It is all standard polemic against the "king-killing" poli-

27 The medal is reproduced in *Works*, II, facing 43.
28 An edition of the *Satyrs* appears in *Poems on Affairs of State*, II, 17-81.

cies of the Jesuits, but Oldham's satiric curses rise above (or sink below) the common run of attacks in their literary artistry and in their use of typology to intensify his satiric force.[29] Most of the typological satire of the *Satyrs* is confined to abusive representations of types of evil, like the following excerpt from *Satyr II*:

> When the first Traitor *Cain* (too good to be
> Thought Patron of this black *Fraternity*)
> His bloody Tragedy of old design'd,
> One death alone quench'd his revengeful mind,
> Content with but a quarter of Mankind:
> Had he been *Jesuit*, had he but put on
> Their savage cruelty; the rest had gone:
> His hand had sent old *Adam* after too,
> And forc'd the Godhead to create anew.[30]

Oldham's favorite technique is satiric inversion. Judas becomes a saintly martyr, paganism becomes Christianity, and Scripture itself becomes mere fable in the perversions of the Jesuits. In satire like Oldham's, which has a strong resemblance to the extended curses of Cleveland, it is important to exaggerate the evils of the satiric object. Indeed, if Oldham has any faults, one of them is surely that he magnifies the presumed evils of his foes too greatly. Typological satire, in the hands of Butler, is parodic and jesting; with Swift, as we will see, it may be part of a whimsical but bitter denunciation of heresy, and it is nevertheless very amusing. Oldham, like Dryden, makes use of the mock prophecy, most notably in the first *Satyr upon the Jesuits*, published separately as *Garnett's Ghost* (1679) but, once again, he is vengefully serious rather than jocular. Henry Garnett had been implicated and executed in the Gunpowder Plot in 1606; his ghost's extended monologue comprises the whole of *Satyr I*. Most apocalyptic prophecy foreshadows both eternal destruction and eternal salvation; Oldham's here foreshadows only destruction, hellish damnation, eternal torment, and the like. According to the plan of his inverted prophecy, the Jesuits are to

---

[29] The identification of the Jesuits with tyrannicide derives, so far as I know, from the Jesuit Juan de Mariana's *De Rege et Regis Institutione Libri III* (Toledo, 1599) which includes a controversial chapter (I.vi), "An tyrannum opprimere fas sit," approving of tyrannicide. De Mariana's work was instantly controversial; in later editions, the offending chapter is suppressed.

[30] *The Works of Mr. John Oldham, Together with his Remains* (London, 1686) [each of four parts, separately paged], I, 29 (II.105-13).

propagate a heresy even more noxious than those of ancient times and the Middle Ages. The novelty of Oldham's prophetical scheme is that it includes a full landscape of negative types—false martyrs, distorted saints, warped bodies of faith—as he twists all the groups and individuals traditionally associated with the *imitatio Christi* theme into figures of evil. Since he wrote most of his satires at a time of great national hysteria, perhaps we can explain his violently distorted typology by comparing it with the denunciatory style of much contemporary pamphleteering, but his particular brand of satire remains an aberration in the later seventeenth century. As Swift would demonstrate, there were more inventive ways of using typology for ridicule and satire.

The link between the typological satire of Butler in *Hudibras*, Oldham in the *Satyrs upon the Jesuits*, Dryden in *The Medall* and Swift in *A Tale of a Tub* may at first seem tenuous but, in fact, the four works have at least one common theme. They are united in opposing different strains of extremism in contemporary life and theology, and .they all use typology in differing ways to emphasize their opposition. Swift differs from his satirical predecessors in several important ways. He was, first, the only typological satirist of the late seventeenth century (here I shall regard *A Tale of a Tub* as a seventeenth-century work, despite its publication date of 1704) who was a professional theologian, in the sense that he had studied theology preparatory to taking holy orders. Swift is different from his colleagues in another important way: his typological satire is far more inventive and challenging to the modern student than that of any other writer of his age. It would be interesting to know precisely where Swift obtained his knowledge of typology, but we cannot be certain about his reading. It must be assumed that he learned of this branch of figuralism from a variety of sources—the basic works of patristic theology, Renaissance and post-Reformation exegesis and controversy, and contemporary Anglican and sectarian apologetics.[31] He was closely acquainted with sixteenth- and seven-

[31] For an example of Swift's reading for one year (1697) about the time that he composed the *Tale*, see *A Tale of a Tub*, ed. A. C. Guthkelch and D. Nichol Smith, 2nd ed. (Oxford: Clarendon Press, 1958), pp. lvi-lvii and, more generally, pp.. liii-lx.

teenth-century mysticism and the scholarly christianizing of pagan literature, as the complex allusions of the *Tale* clearly show. We may see from the sophisticated application of the abuses of typology that he scatters throughout the *Tale* that he was well versed in the Puritans' method of relating scriptural types to assumed antitypes in everyday life.

These blatant misapplications of typology tell us something about the expectations of an early eighteenth-century audience for, if Swift could produce such obvious distortions of traditional typology and yet embellish them with much subtlety, it is likely that the original audience for *A Tale of a Tub* was highly sensitive to the proper as well as improper uses of figuralism. The narrator of the *Tale* sometimes sounds like a Grub Street hack (in some modern studies, he is mistakenly identified as "the Hack" throughout), but at other times he is much more likely a fanatic Puritan with false pretensions to the role of scriptural exegete. It is the voice of the mock exegete that explains the device of the "Oratorial Machines" in "The Introduction" (Section I) in the mystical terms of figural exegesis:

> NOW this Physico-logical Scheme of Oratorial Receptacles or Machines, contains a great Mystery, being a Type, a Sign, an Emblem, a Shadow, a Symbol, bearing Analogy to the spacious Commonwealth of Writers, and to those Methods by which they must exalt themselves to a certain Eminency above the inferiour World. By the *Pulpit* are adumbrated the Writings of our *Modern Saints* in *Great Britain*, as they have spiritualized and refined them from the Dross and Grossness of *Sense* and *Human Reason*. The Matter, as we have said, is of rotten Wood, and that upon two Considerations; Because it is the Quality of rotten Wood to give *Light* in the Dark: And secondly, Because its Cavities are full of Worms: which is a Type with a Pair of Handles, having a Respect to the two principal Qualifications of the Orator, and the two different Fates attending upon his works.[32]

Students of Swift will immediately notice the parody of puritanical style and inspiration and the attack upon mechanist reductionism and the doctrine of the inner light. Furthermore, his manner and satirical style are obviously typological. True, he describes the "great Mystery" of the machines not only as a type, but as five other

---

[32] *Tale*, pp. 61-62.

terms as well, all taken from the terminology of contemporary biblical exegesis. But it is clear that the notion of adumbration applies particularly well to the mainly typological conception of early history as in some way prefiguring later or, in this case, modern history as a kind of consummation of an earlier promise. The typological narrative as Swift introduces it here is ridiculous, but it has certain basic satirical ingredients. These include the almost prophetic obscurity, the inventive foreshadowing of the future, the mystical and incomprehensible relationship between the type, sign, emblem, shadow, etc. and the antitype, that which is shadowed forth (in this case, modern learning, particularly the writings of the Puritans), and finally, the manifest absurdity of the interpretation of the type. Swift's typology in *A Tale of a Tub* is always parodic, and hence satirical of the extremes of figural abuse by Puritan exegetes and apologists.

Typology, moreover, is so familiar an exegetical device to Swift's narrator that he enters into its intricacies with an ease and naturalness born of long acquaintance, as in the first of the digressions in the *Tale*, "A Digression Concerning *Criticks*" (Section III). Here, as he traces the genealogy of the "True Critick," he makes the agreeable discovery that the history of modern criticism has been foreshadowed by the most ancient writers through a convenient application of typology to history.

> Yet whatever they touch'd of that kind, was with abundance of Caution, adventuring no farther than *Mythology* and *Hieroglyphick*. This, I suppose, gave ground to superficial Readers, for urging the Silence of Authors, against the Antiquity of the *True Critick*; tho' the *Types* are so apposite, and the Applications so necessary and natural, that it is not easy to conceive, how any Reader of a *Modern Eye* and *Taste* could overlook them.[33]

Swift's typological inventiveness here is quite obscure: his narrator uncovers prefigurations of modern criticism in texts of Pausanias, Herodotus, Ctesias, Diodorus, and Lucretius. The classical allusions themselves—asses with horns, an army put to flight by the braying of an ass, a plant with poisonous flowers—are less important than their method of introduction. To the enthusiastic narrator, these allusions are cunningly concealed allegories ("nothing can be

[33] *Ibid.*, p. 97.

plainer"), "cautious and mystical" signs introduced by the ancients
for the particular comprehension and guidance of the chosen *illuminati,* wise in the ways of obscurity. To the Modern they are clear
evidence of the prefiguration of the present by early history.

The abuse of scriptural typology consists in the narrator's imaginative interpretation of an extant, early text, charging it with symbolic, figural signification far beyond what seventeenth-century
hermeneutics, especially as practiced by the Church of England, considered permissible. Contemporary theory expressly rules out the
attribution of typical meaning to just *any* text, as Swift's narrator
does with such impunity in "A Digression Concerning *Criticks.*" According to the opinion of one exegete, "True types have God for
the Author of them. God bade the prophet here take one stick and
another stick, and write upon them; and thereby to type out the
houses of Judah and Israel. Had he [i.e., Ezekiel] taken these of his
own head, they had been nothing, bastardly types, not true types."[34]
The modern narrator is not simply guilty of devising false types,
but also of transgressing the boundaries of legitimate allegorizing
of a "dark" text. A plain scriptural text, according to an author like
Benjamin Keach or Samuel Mather, might legitimately be treated
as a type, and interpreted accordingly to educe the historical and
prophetical meaning of an Old Testament sign.[35] The narrator,
who here is the deranged exegete again, violates propriety in his
choice of texts, for not only is their meaning plain, but they have
nothing to do with Scripture. His abuse of typology appears in the
perversion of a standard hermeneutical device to prefigure not
Christ and his glory but rather modern learning and *its* glories.[36]
He justifies the need for typological interpretation of the plainest
passages in the Ancients: "The Reason why those Antient Writers
treated this Subject only by Types and Figures, was, because they

---

[34] See William Greenhill, *An Exposition of the Prophet Ezekiel, with useful
Observations thereon* (1645-62), ed. James Sherman, 2nd ed. (London, 1839), p.
746 (ap. Ezek. 37.20-22).

[35] See, in particular, Keach, *Tropologia* (London, 1682), pp. 26-29, 41-45.

[36] The narrator's allusions are to texts that are plain or literal in that they
are comprehensible without figural exegesis: "But *Herodotus* holding the very
same *Hieroglyph,* speaks much plainer, and almost *in terminis.* He hath been
so bold as to tax the *True Criticks,* of Ignorance and Malice; telling us openly,
for I think nothing can be plainer, that *in the Western Part of* Libya, *there
were ASSES with HORNS"* (*Tale,* p. 98). Such is the narrator's conception of
a "clear" prefiguration of modern criticism.

durst not make open Attacks against a Party so Potent and so Terrible, as the *Criticks* of those Ages were."[37] In this way Swift again creates, sustains, and justifies typological narrative for satiric purposes. His technique here is unique because, although typology is generally confined in the seventeenth century to scriptural and other theological concerns, Swift applies this branch of hermeneutics to modern learning, partly because his narrator personifies all the excesses of modern scholarship, both religious and secular, and partly no doubt because Swift is eager to correlate the abuses of modern learning with the enthusiastic zeal and self-righteousness of the Puritans.

The inspirational application of typology to all subjects, including the supposed perfections of contemporary learning, associates the obscurantism of the typologists, like Swift's exegete-narrator, with the similarly fantastic religious delusions of the occultists against whom portions of *A Tale of a Tub* are directed.[38] We find in the brief analogy between a tailor and a "True Critick" that typology may be used with good effect in any obscure allusion: "The *Taylor's Hell* is the Type of a Critick's *Common-Place-Book* and his Wit and Learning held forth by the *Goose.*"[39] In the satire on the sartorialists in Section II of the *Tale*, Swift presents their icons, a tailor-figure and his goose, as the objects of idolatrous devotion. So here the *"Taylor's Hell,"* the eschatological result of idolatry, prefigures the intellectual errors of modern critical documents, of which the commonplace book is the ideal representation. Typology becomes the essence of his analogical relationship between false religious inspiration and false learning. As a prominent device in biblical hermeneutics, its application to secular matters tends to disfigure them to the same degree that typological excesses blemish true religion. Hence when Swift refers to the Aeolists (Section VIII) as *"All Pretenders to Inspiration whatsoever"* he also alludes to those equal idolaters, the worshipers of modern learning. We see his satirical treatment of them best in Section VII of the *Tale*, "A Digression in Praise of Digressions," his longest and most

[37] *Tale*, pp. 98-99. The traditional seventeenth-century view of hieroglyphics, of course, held that they were a code devised by the priesthood to keep sacred secrets from being known and corrupted by the common people.

[38] For Swift's satire on occultism, see Phillip Harth, *Swift and Anglican Rationalism*, pp. 59-67; see also Guthkelch and Nichol Smith's appendix, "Notes on Dark Authors," in *Tale*, pp. 353-60, for a collection of some of Swift's more obvious allusions to occult writers.

[39] *Tale*, pp. 101-102.

effective attempt at typological satire, which is constructed in such a way that we may plausibly infer deliberate typological meaning throughout.

The principal typological *locus* in Section VII is the narrator's discussion of how modern scholars specialize in figural interpretation from the human genitalia:

> What I mean, is that highly celebrated Talent among the *Modern* Wits, of deducing Similitudes, Allusions, and Applications, very Surprizing, Agreeable, and Apposite, from the *Pudenda* of either Sex, together with *their proper Uses.* And truly, having observed how little Invention bears any Vogue, besides what is derived from these *Channels,* I have sometimes had a Thought, That the happy Genius of our Age and Country, was prophetically held forth by that ancient typical Description of the *Indian* Pygmies; *whose Stature did not exceed above two Foot; Sed quorum pudenda crassa, & ad talos usque pertingentia.* Now, I have been very curious to inspect the late Productions, wherein the Beauties of this kind have most prominently appeared.[40]

A marginal gloss to the words "antient typical Description" refers the reader to "*Ctesiae fragm. apud Photium,*" a parody of the scholarly gloss as it so often appeared in contemporary scholarship—the gloss is as arcane as the passage to which it refers. It happens that Swift's reference to Ctesias, Alexander the Great's physician who accompanied him on his Asian campaign and whose fragmentary histories of India and Persia are preserved only in the *Myriobiblon* or *Bibliotheca* of Photius, the ninth-century bishop of Constantinople, is genuine. True, Swift has doctored the doctor's Latin (actually a Renaissance Latin translation of the Greek of Photius) so that the line about the penises of the male pygmies would be clearer and easier for his audience to follow than the text of Photius. The abuse of typology in this allusion is similar to that in other mistaken, satirical applications of types in the *Tale.* To interpret an obscure, nonbiblical text in a typological sense is tenuous

[40] *Ibid.,* p. 147. Eds. 1-4 read "the *Genitals*" for "the *Pudenda* of either Sex" (5th and all later eds.).

and uncertain, to say nothing of being a flagrant violation of the rules of exegesis. To assert, as Swift's narrator does so categorically, that the grotesque pygmies, with their tiny bodies and exaggeratedly large genitalia, prophetically foreshadow the greatness of modern learning, or anything else, is absurd, if not obscene.

The only Latin text of Photius available to Swift, that of André Schott, does not present Ctesias' account of the pygmies in precisely the same words as Swift uses, although its meaning is substantially the same; evidently Swift wished to clarify the implication of Ctesias by deliberate economy of style.[41] More important, however, than the small alterations to Photius is his introduction of the gross physical image of the deformity of the pygmies as representative of the achievements of modern learning. The narrator is guilty of the modern failing "of deducing Similitudes, Allusions, and Applications, very Surprizing, Agreeable, and Apposite, from the *Pudenda* of either Sex, together with *their proper Uses*," while simultaneously he establishes the small body–large genitalia image of the pygmies as a suitable type of his own intellectual pursuits. We may also note that Swift does not refer to "the *Pudenda* of either Sex," but rather confines himself only to the typology of the male genitals.

Once we identify this image as Swift's debasement or parody of a true type, it becomes possible to discern a complex yet unmistakable strain of typological satire in Section VII constructed around analogies to this figural center. Analogous to the pygmy image are other images which utilize, in the same prefiguring or typological manner, a small body with exaggeratedly disproportionate genitals, posteriors, privities, or hinder parts. The swollen or erect genitals (*pudenda crassa*) of the Indian pygmies are latent with more than one typological meaning. These distended members hold forth not just the happy genius of the modern age of cant and hypocrisy, but a particularly inflated, enthusiastic kind of modern learning. The potential ejaculation of sperm which the pygmy-genitalia image

[41] See *Photius Bibliotheca. Sive Lectorum a Photio librorum recensio . . . e Graeco Latine reddita . . . Andreae Schotti Antuerpiani* (Augsbourg, 1606), p. 57: "Narrat praeter ista, in mediae India homines reperiri nigros, qui Pygmaei appellentur. Eadem hos, qui Indi reliqui, lingua uti, sed valde esse parvos, ut maximi duntaxat cubiti sum dimidio altitudinem non excedant. . . . Veretrum illis esse crassum ac longum, quod ad ipsos quoque pedum malleolos pertingat. Pygmaeos hosce simis esse naribus, & deformes." Swift's edition of Photius, ed. David Hoeschelius and André Schott (Rothomagi, 1653), pp. 145-46, gives the same text; see Harold Williams, *Dean Swift's Library* (Cambridge: University Press, 1932), where this work is Lot 104 in the sale catalogue.

implies closely parallels, in the imagistic scheme of Section VII, the discharge of the seeds of spiritual inspiration portended by the swollen bodies of Swift's Aeolists and by the inflated rhetoric of enthusiastic Puritanism and mysticism.[42] Sexual erection becomes clearly analogous to spiritual inspiration here, as it does in *The Mechanical Operation of the Spirit*, where Swift describes an enthusiastic fit in such terms: "The *Saint* felt his *Vessel* full *extended* in every Part (a very natural Effect of strong *Inspiration*)."[43] The association of carnality (physical excess) with fanaticism (false enthusiasm or inspiration) is common in seventeenth-century anti-Puritan writings, but it also is likely that Swift seeks to exploit an additional pejorative relationship, which draws as well on a rich figural tradition, between sexuality and idolatry. Prominent Anglican apologists like Parker and Stillingfleet allude to the idolatrous cults of phallic or priapic worship and their symbolism; the well-known studies of idolatry by Vossius and Kircher discuss the phallic myths of the ancient Egyptians and Greeks in detail; and Swift himself alludes to the "Types and Symbols" of the Osiridic and Bacchanalian rites.[44]

Analogous to the pygmy-type of modern genius is the equally obscure image of the Scythian mares which, with their artificially inflated privities, are also typical of the contemporary scholarship of which the narrator boasts so proudly. Yet everything unnaturally enlarged will eventually collapse: thus the small body of modern learning with its swollen appendages is essentially temporary, constantly in danger of running dry of newly invented matter. We have more than a figural joke here on the sexual and intellectual potency of Swift's contemporaries. The narrator's solution continues the typological relationship started by the pygmy image between the small body–large appendages concept and contemporary

[42] Sherman H. Hawkins, "Swift's Physical Imagery," unpub. doct. diss. (Princeton Univ., 1960), pp. 412-13, 423, makes the connection between inspiration and the discharge of semen, with interesting source materials.

[43] See *Tale*, p. 283; cf. pp. 280-82.

[44] See Samuel Parker, *A Free and Impartial Censure of the Platonick Philosophie*, pp. 99-103; Stillingfleet, *Origines Sacrae*, p. 591; G. J. Vossius, *De Theologia Gentili, et Physiologia Christiana; sive de origine ac progressu Idololatriae Libri IX* (1641) in *Opera*, ed. Isaac Vossius, 6 vols. (Amsterdam, 1695-1701), V, 12-14; Kircher, *Oedipus Ægyptiacus*, I, 223-30. For Swift's comments on the cults of Osiris and Bacchus, see *The Mechanical Operation of the Spirit* in *Tale*, p. 284. For general discussion of the Osiris and Dionysius cults and their phallic worship, see Sir James G. Frazer, *The Golden Bough*, 3rd ed. (London, 1935-36), VI, 3-23, 112-13; VII, 1-34.

genius. He proposes, therefore, "that our last Recourse must be had to large *Indexes*, and little *Compendiums*; . . . To this End, tho' Authors need be little consulted, yet *Criticks*, and *Commentators*, and *Lexicons* carefully must."[45] Once again, we continue with the prophetical foreshadowing of the present age by the "antient typical Description of the *Indian* Pygmies," since the greatest achievement of modern learning is a small compendium with a large, one is tempted to say a swollen, index.

The triumph of all this scholasticism is an author trained by the best methods of the modern school: "BY these Methods, in a few Weeks, there starts up many a Writer, capable of managing the profoundest, and most universal Subjects. For, what tho' his *Head* be empty, provided his *Common-place-Book* be full." The typological methodology prolongs the relationship adumbrated earlier. The accomplishment of the mysterious prophecy of the pygmy-type is achieved by a writer whose intellectual body (or head) is unnaturally small, but whose literary appendage, the universal compilation or commonplace book, is swollen with seminal thoughts derived from other writers. This is what Swift calls "the *Sieves* and *Boulters* of Learning," the intellectual detritus of scholarship. The traditional movement from type to antitype is one from prefiguration to fruition, from shadows to reality, from darkness and obscurity to light and truth. The narrator treats his text, the prophetic *dictum* of Ctesias, in the same way that the Puritans and the enthusiastic exegetes of the seventeenth century treat the Old Testament, as an obscure prophecy charged with mysteries. Are not all true types to be treated in this manner? The ultimate perfection of this type, the true modern work of genius, is a neat treatise which, "when the Fulness of time is come, shall haply undergo the Tryal of Purgatory, in order *to ascend the sky*." This mock glorification or resurrection of a desperate piece of hack writing, complete with somewhat sour scriptural echoes, recalls the enthusiastic prognostications of salvation which appear so commonly in the writings of the early Gnostics and more recent mystics like Boehme and Thomas Vaughan. It is also the final accomplishment of the type, from darkness to light, or from death to resurrection.

Typological satire, as Swift develops it in Section VII, is based on the creation of an absurd, mock-mysterious correspondence between the works of the ancients and the productions of his contemporaries. The pygmy-image, however, is the only one in the entire digression which the narrator clearly describes as "typical." A single

---

[45] *Tale*, pp. 147-48.

clear reference to a recognized type in a long argument is not unusual, for a seventeenth-century author employing typological exegesis could assume enough knowledge of the device among an educated audience to make corroboratory reference to types later in his text unnecessary. The exegete can thus mention the chief typical figures and events of the Old Testament without specifically informing us that these are types and that they prefigure certain later persons and situations. Such correspondences would doubtless have been obvious to many members of his audience. Through the guise of his narrator, Swift introduces allusions to the body of modern learning which, although we are never told of their "typical" nature (within the context of typological abuse that the narrator habitually favors), clearly relate to the prophecy-fulfillment conception of the digression and to the parodic, distorted typology of the pygmy image. Much of the satire on learning in the *Tale* consists of an ironical demonstration of the superiority of Modern over Ancient learning. Just as Ancient learning was partial and imperfect, so that of the Modern is the *pleroma*, the accomplishment of the prophecies which the works of earlier authors suggest.

Swift's description of contemporary intellectual methodology is, in figural terms, the achieving of an antitype:

> The most accomplisht Way of using Books at present, is twofold: Either first, to serve them as some Men do *Lords*, learn their *Titles* exactly, and then brag of their Acquaintance. Or Secondly, which is indeed the choicer, the profounder, and politer Method, to get a thorough Insight into the *Index*, by which the whole Book is governed and turned, like *Fishes* by the *Tail*. For, to enter into the Palace of Learning at the *great Gate*, requires an Expense of Time and Forms; therefore Men of much Haste and little Ceremony, are content to get in by the *Back-Door*. For, the Arts are all in a *flying* March, and therefore more easily subdued by attacking them in the *Rear*. Thus Physicians discover the State of the whole Body, by consulting only what comes from *Behind*. Thus Men catch Knowledge by throwing their *Wit* on the *Posteriors* of a Book, as Boys do Sparrows with flinging *Salt* upon their *Tails*. Thus Human Life is best understood by the wise man's Rule of *Regarding the End*. Thus are the Sciences found like Hercules's Oxen, by *tracing them Backwards*. Thus are *old Sciences* unravelled like *old Stockings*, by beginning at the *Foot*.[46]

46 *Ibid.*, p. 145.

We may disregard the first way of using books, for the narrator obviously finds the second method infinitely preferable. What is most striking about the second method and its ramifications is that all of them deal with the rear of learning, the hinder or lower parts of the body of contemporary intellect. Just as a knowledge of the index is the key to the book, so the posteriors of learning, wit, the arts and sciences, the human body itself, are the true entrance into the inverted world of modern genius. There is a parallel in this passage to the typology of the pygmy image, since the narrator sees learning and its acquisition, in figural terms, as virtually identical with what the pygmies shadow forth. The promise which the pygmies foreshadow is the stunted body of present-day originality with its large addition of commentary, appendix, and index. Analogously, through a group of deliberately imperfect types, the speaker describes the refinements of modern genius as a series of actions which stress the relative importance of the back door to learning and the relative insignificance of the proper acquisition of knowledge. These actions parallel and typify that modern vein of obscene allusion which is in danger of running dry unless modern wits emphasize still more the superficies of learning or have further recourse to indexes, systems, and abstracts.

Like the rest of Swift's typological satire, this section is filled principally with nonsensical figural interpolations whose meaning and application to the modern narrator's subject are purposely obscure. No doubt Swift intends to parody the obscure imagistic revelations of mystics like Vaughan and Boehme or writers of the alchemical school like Paracelsus, Agrippa, and Robert Fludd. But more to his purpose in this account of modern intellectual methodology is the knowledge of the nonsensical promise of contemporary greatness. He even creates a patrology of modern knowledge which is responsible for much of the felicity of the present age: "For this great Blessing we are wholly indebted to *Systems* and *Abstracts*, in which the *Modern* Fathers of Learning, like prudent Usurers, spent their Sweat for the Ease of Us their Children. For Labor is the Seed of *Idleness*, and it is the peculiar Happiness of our Noble Age to gather the *Fruit*." The early patristic writers, for whom typology was a central exegetical device, were important for seventeenth-century Anglicans as the first heresiologists, notable for their success in confuting the pre-Nicene heretics.[47] But in the twisted patrology

[47] On the early heresiologists, see Daniélou, *From Shadows to Reality*, pp. 1-7, and Berthold Altaner, *Patrology*, trans. Hilda C. Graef (Edinburgh and London, 1958), pp. 138-60.

of the *Tale*, the labor of the "*Modern* Fathers of Learning" is the seed or type which yields the fruition of "our Noble Age." The motion of typology, as I have shown, is a rising one, from promise to consummation. There is a clear parallel in the typological narrative of "A Digression in Praise of Digressions," for Swift moves from the partial and imperfect signs of modern genius, all of which point to the hinder parts of knowledge, to the ultimate accomplishment of modernity, "*Systems* and *Abstracts*." These are, after all, simply books in which the compilation of an index or other posterior pedantry has become the whole instead of the part.

The typological satire of *A Tale of a Tub* is not confined to the digressions. The allegory of the three brothers, which provides the narrative thread of Swift's story, is an elaborate typological parody of church history from its beginnings to the present day. First the three brothers, then the eldest, who becomes synonymous with Roman Catholicism, systematically distort interpretations of Scripture so that they may bring their unorthodox behavior into accordance with what their father's will had decreed and, in some cases, prophesied. The over-vivid imagination of the third brother, Jack, who is identified with numerous Puritan sects, tends "to reduce all Things into *Types*"; like other Puritans, he refines "what is literal into Figure and Mystery." When he can, Swift fiddles with the typology of the penis, as in a passage in Section XI where he manages to associate the size of a man's ears with the size of his genitals and his virility. His narrator assures us "that while this *Island* of ours, was under the *Dominion of Grace* [i.e., during the years of the Commonwealth], many Endeavours were made to improve the Growth of *Ears* once more among us. The Proportion of Largeness, was not only lookt upon as an Ornament of the *Outward* Man, but as a Type of Grace in the *Inward*."[48] Large ears—the Puritans, by cutting their hair short, exposed their ears—therefore become signs of grace as well as an indication that the possessor of them was well hung. Indeed, the custom in Puritan pulpit oratory of the preacher's turning to one side or the other, sometimes "to *hold forth* the one [ear], and sometimes to *hold forth* the other" is the reason why, among the sectarians, the operation of preaching "is to this very Day . . . styled by the Phrase of *Holding forth*." The joke might almost pass unobserved if we were unaware that "to hold forth" also refers, not only in the seventeenth century but elsewhere in *A Tale of a Tub*, to the functioning of typology; a type holds forth, or shadows forth, its antitype.

[48] *Tale*, pp. 202-203.

In the *Mechanical Operation of the Spirit,* too, Swift finds typology appropriate for sexual satire. In a detailed description of the "*Bacchanalian* Ceremonies" of the ancient pagans, we learn that these rites foreshadow modern fanaticism and contemporary Puritan worship. These mysteries are, plainly enough, typological:

> They [i.e., the Bacchantes] bore for their Ensigns, certain curious Figures, perch'd upon long Poles, made into the Shape and Size of the *Virga genitalis,* with its *Appurtenances,* which were so many Shadows and Emblems of the whole Mystery, as well as Trophies set up by the Female Conquerors. Lastly, in a certain Town of *Attica,* the whole Solemnity stript of all its Types, was performed in *puris naturalibus,* the Votaries, not flying in Coveys, but sorted into Couples.[49]

Swift had learned much from Butler's typological satire, but he carries the ridicule of *Hudibras* into far greater detail than Butler's poetic form could permit. Most verse satirists use typology, when they do introduce it, to emphasize the excesses of typological exegesis or to stress aspects of the typology of character (negative types, which shadow forth or postfigure Satan, are a special favorite). Swift follows the poëts, but the form of *A Tale of a Tub* allows him to parody the actual practice of enthusiastic and fanatic hermeneutics. As an Anglican priest, he was aware of the appropriate use of typology in genuine theological contexts. In this context, it is pertinent that none of his satirical adaptations of typology has anything to do with biblical interpretation. Every example, without exception, represents a misapplication or distortion of typological methodology to other, nontheological, forms of learning.

Seventeenth-century scholarship, as I have noted, included a sizable school of learned men who insisted on finding glimmerings of Christianity in the pagan mysteries and in such pagan authors as Homer, Virgil, and Ovid. To a large extent, Swift's attack upon Puritan inspiration is an attack upon this kind of scholarship, which could uncover secret resemblances, often by crude adaptation and debasement of typology, between texts, ideas, events, and entire bodies of thought that did not resemble each other at all. Typology, as students of figuralism know, builds a structure of relationship, the perception of a resemblance between *A* and *B.* The resemblance may really exist or it may not exist. The credulity of the interpreter

---

[49] *The Mechanical Operation of the Spirit* in *Tale,* pp. 284-85.

and the degree to which he or she imagines an act of foreshadowing will determine whether typology is used as a rational exegetical tool or as an agency of exaggeration and parody. Swift prefers to exaggerate the typologies which his narrators imagine, and so his technique is one of the most advanced parody. The most original quality of Swift's typological satire is that he includes as part of his satiric spectrum the very scholia of the learned works he ridicules. Just as most of the medieval typological interpretations of Scripture are to be found in the *postilla* and *glossa* of Nicholas of Lyra and other exegetes, so much contemporary typologizing is to be found in the scholarly additions to learned works—the moralia to L'Estrange's *Aesop*, the copious footnotes to Bochart and Kircher, the *problemata* to much-edited authors like Frantzius, and the numerous appendices and summaries to collections of biblical criticism, from Poole's *Synopsis Criticorum* to Letsome and Nichols's edition of the Boyle Lectures. If there is any eighteenth-century writer more proficient than Swift in dealing with the commentators, Alexander Pope is the man.

 5

Pope's knowledge of typology was considerable. He had a firsthand acquaintance with both Catholic and Protestant theology and with the exegetical traditions associated with both bodies of thought. We do not possess such precise notes on his reading or library as we do for Swift, but Maynard Mack's recent study of Pope's books reveals that he owned copies of Bochart's *Opera Omnia,* Huet's *Demonstratio Evangelica,* Thomas à Kempis's *Sermons,* and Vida's *Opera.*[50] His study of typological authors doubtless included many other relevant works.[51] It may be useful to consider for a moment Pope's practice in making serious typological allusions so that we may better understand his satirical methods. His first, and perhaps most famous, typological poem is *The Messiah. A Sacred Eclogue,*

---

[50] See "Pope's Books: A Biographical Survey with a Finding List" and Mack's "Appendix" to it, in *English Literature in the Age of Disguise,* ed. Maximillian E. Novak (Berkeley and Los Angeles: Univ. of California Press, 1977), pp. 209-32, 239, 266, 297, 303.

[51] Earl Wasserman, in a review of *The Twickenham Edition of the Poems of Alexander Pope,* Vol. I (London: Methuen, 1961), in *PQ,* 41 (1962), 615-22, argues persuasively that Pope was thoroughly schooled in pre- and post-Reformation traditions of biblical scholarship.

In Imitation of Virgil's Pollio. The first edition, in *Spectator* No. 378 (1712), includes modest marginal references to biblical texts, but when Pope reprinted the poem in his *Works* (1717) and thereafter, he added quite an elaborate *apparatus criticus*, consisting mainly of references to Isaiah and Virgil, interspersed with occasional comments on passages which he admired greatly. Other poets had written their own scholia for certain works, usually translations; Pope's *Messiah*, like Spenser's *Shepheardes Calendar*, with its typological "glosse," is a typological poem with a commentary that stresses its prefigurative qualities. Indeed, the *Messiah* is more than an "imitation" of Virgil's fourth *Eclogue*; it is a major transformation of a pagan text to a Christian exemplar of prophetic history. It is a reworking of Isaiah, a prefiguration of the story of Christ, and a prophecy which announces its antitypes as existing in the present rather than as forthcoming in the future.

Most millenarian interpretations of biblical prophecy dealt with Daniel or Revelation, and held forth the promise of the Second Coming sometime in the future. Not so Pope, who ends the *Messiah* with a concrete assurance that the antitype is with us now:

> But fix'd *his* Word, *His* saving Pow'r remains:
> Thy *Realm* for ever lasts! thy own *Messiah* reigns![52]

The poem derives from several traditions, of which that of the literary imitation is the most minor. Pope was clearly conversant with the vast literature dealing with the accuracy of scriptural prophecy, which was especially important during the first three decades of the century, and to which the works of the freethinkers and their orthodox Anglican confutors, including most notably the annual Boyle Lecturers, make major contributions. As I will discuss in greater detail in Chapter 9, the eighteenth-century controversy over prophecy affirmed and strengthened the position of typology in the figural language of literature. Pope's *Messiah* demonstrates his interest in and acceptance of the role of typology in contemporary Christian apologetics, and his presentation of the poem, with his own scholia, tells us how knowledgeable he was in curious theological learning. Nor is *Messiah* his only early poem to appear, in a later edition, with its own gloss. In *The Rape of the Lock*, Pope would add (in later editions) a scholarly note to the Midrash, and *The Temple of Fame* includes several learned footnote references

---

[52] *Messiah*, 107-108, in *TE*, I, 122.

to Egyptian paganism.[53] The Rosicrucian background to the *Rape* shows Pope's serious interest in the whimsical side of one of the mystery cults of Protestantism, one of those which Swift had ridiculed in *A Tale of a Tub*.[54] His experience as an annotator of his own poems, then, acquainted him at an early age with one of the central sources of typological figuralism, learned religious and literary commentary.

Pope's translation of the works of Homer, *The Iliad* (1715-20) and *The Odyssey* (1725-26), would train him even more thoroughly in traditions of typological commentary. The translation is to some extent a corporate venture, but Pope seems to have had a hand in all the notes that accompany the work, and there can be no question that he was familiar with most of the extensive scholarly commentary on Homer from Eustathius to the end of the seventeenth century.[55] Eustathius and other Christian commentators surrounded the *Iliad* and *Odyssey* with volumes of information, both pertinent and otherwise, and their massive scholia began the search for Christian undermeanings in the Homeric texts.[56] Most of the Christian allegorizing of Homer, as Allen shows, was the work of Renaissance, mainly sixteenth- and early seventeenth-century, editors and exegetes. These students of Homer's religion discovered surprising resemblances between the actions of the poems and key events in the Old and New Testaments. Some scholars thought that Homer had known Hebrew, and that his mythological personages postfigured the Old Testament, with which he must have been acquainted. Others decided that Homer was a more gifted seer, and that certain stories in both of his poems prophesied or typed out biblical stories. The scholia to Pope's *Homer* have little patience with these airy theorizings, but Pope, like other translators and classical exegetes of the eighteenth century, did not quite believe that this kind of mystery-hunting could be dismissed entirely. His prefatory comments on Homer's theology, to be sure, conclude simply that Homer was a

[53] See *Rape of the Lock*, I.145 (*TE*, I, 157) and *The Temple of Fame*, 109-18 (*TE*, I, 261-62).

[54] On Rosicrucianism in Swift's writings, see Philip Pinkus, "*A Tale of a Tub* and the Rosy Cross," *JEGP*, 59 (1960), 669-79.

[55] See Norman Callan, "Pope's Homer and the Greek Learning of His Time," *TE*, VII, lxxi-cvii, for a detailed analysis of Pope's knowledge of the Homeric scholia.

[56] Allen, *Mysteriously Meant*, pp. 83-105, tells the story at length. Eustathius and his followers were often euhemerists, but the exegetes gradually came to find typological figuralism in the Homeric poems.

pagan whose religious system has nothing whatever to do with Christianity.[57] But the commentary to his translation often cites, without qualification, the Christian allegorizings of his predecessors, especially Madame Dacier. Dacier tried to present Homer as a Christian moralist, and often suggests parallels between his dramatic events and apparently similar passages in the Old Testament.[58] In hundreds of places in his notes, Pope refers to Dacier's cross-cultural parallels between Grecian and Hebrew customs, learning, and traditions; many of these receive clear attribution, while he and his co-translators silently absorb others into the body of their commentary. The majority of these references are simply parallels between Grecian customs and Old Testament mores, between Homer's poetic language and the poetic style of the Hebrew poets, principally the Psalms and various historical books. Madame Dacier, like other seventeenth-century commentators, noted similarities between Grecian and ancient Egyptian learning, and saw a possible analogy between Homer and Moses, both of whom, she was sure, had been schooled in this mystic lore. Pope's friend and editor Warburton would later note this curious coincidence in the education of these two great authors and would make a great deal of Homer's learning, if not his actual Hebraism.

Pope is content merely to note the analogies between Homer and the Old Testament, yet the very fact that he chooses these observations from the thick forests of commentary available to him suggests that he found such parallels important.[59] For example, in Book V of the *Iliad*, Diomedes receives a severe wound, and prays to Minerva for assistance; the goddess restores his strength and, as an earnest of her affection for him, gives him vision as well: "Yet more, from mortal Mists I purge thy Eyes, / And set to View the warring Deities" (V. 164-65). Pope here adopts Dacier's parallel to the prophetic sight that God often gives to Old Testament prophets, but he adds a reference to the prophetic vision which Venus vouchsafes to Aeneas in *Aeneid II* and compares both passages to the Pisgah-

[57] "An Essay on the Life, Writings, and Learning of Homer," *TE*, VII, 67-70.
[58] See Callan, *TE*, VII, lxxvii-lxxx.
[59] For example, see *TE*, VII, 201, 235, 247, 274, 287-88, 291-92, 334, 337, 342, 351, 360-61 (these parallels are drawn from the commentary to *Iliad* V and VI only). Pope discusses Homer's Egyptian learning in a note to *Iliad* VIII (*TE*, VII, 394-95), agreeing with early scholiasts that Homer's fictions must embody allusions to Egyptian mysteries, but suggesting that he "might often use these Hieroglyphic Fables and Traditions as Embellishments of his Poetry only, without taking the Pains to open their mystical Meaning to his Readers."

sight which Milton gives to Adam in Paradise Lost, Books XI and XII.[60] Again, in an important note to *Iliad* VIII, on the "Tartarean Gulf," Pope observes that Homer might have had some notion of the underworld, "the Fall of the Angels, the Punishment of the Damned, and other sacred Truths which were afterwards more fully explain'd and taught by the Prophets and Apostles."[61] These instances, and a number of others like them, which allude either to Old Testament passages, pre-Christian traditions, or ancient theological mysteries which the prophets and Apostles would decipher later, tend to subscribe to the typological views of some seventeenth-century Homeric exegetes. Pope does not make a strong case for Homeric typology, and it is not my purpose to push him in that direction. Rather, I want to suggest that he was more than actively aware of the typological possibilities of ancient literature, especially in the parallels between visionary passages in the Homeric poems and typological sections of Scripture. He is careful not to force the analogy between Homer's visionary style and that of Milton's Pisgah-sight, but this contribution to Homeric scholia, which originated with him, lends prefigurative force to his commentary. Pope is not by any means a dedicated christianizer of Homer; he passes over some of the more obvious favorites of the exegetes, such as *Odyssey* XI (the voyage to the underworld) and Ulysses at the mast (*Odyssey* XII), with little or no comment. However, his protracted labors on the translation brought him into regular contact with the world of commentary, a world whose denizens were accustomed to make major interpretative observations in footnotes, glosses, and scholia. It is in this *apparatus criticus* to Homer that we find Pope's typological comments just as, in his mock-heroic, antiheroic poem of the later 1720s, *The Dunciad*, we will find much of his typological satire in the commentary to the text.

The Dunciad gave Pope the chance to write about the moneyed interests of the City, with the City-dominated theme of the man "who brings / The Smithfield Muses to the Ear of Kings." It was a subject that would attract much of his energy in the 1730s. For Pope, the tastes of the world of commerce represented deeply held antipathies; he had tangled during his years as entrepreneurial editor with the commercial values of rapacious booksellers, and he had not liked the encounter. Typology plays a role—indeed, a major role—in his satire upon these values and, in the context of *The*

60 *TE*, VII, 274-75.   61 *TE*, VII, 395.

Dunciad, perhaps no figural system would be better qualified for such a part. The exegetes had traditionally employed typology to bring out the links between the two Testaments and to reveal the pagan antecedents of Christianity; the mysteries of ancient Egypt and Greece somehow shadow forth for them the accomplishments of the Christian religion. In *The Dunciad*, Pope would invert traditional typology, so that the world of arts and letters, in short the classics, would become the types, and the antitypes would become the aspects of the modern-day paganism whose arrival the poem portends. Readers of *The Dunciad* in its unannotated state, the three editions of 1728, would have had little difficulty grasping the typological fable behind Pope's satire. Theobald's dream in Book III includes, encapsulated within it, the prophetic speech of Settle, the divinely inspired *vates* of the poem; the audience of the 1720s was perfectly familiar with the typological interpretation of such visions, whether they were the serious readings of contemporary sermons and students of biblical prophecy or the jocose Merlins of the popular press.

The Dunciad, we must remember, was not the only work to reflect the current learned quarrel over the genuineness and accuracy of Scripture prophecy. Iconography, scholars and men of letters discovered, was everywhere, from the prints of Hogarth and the frontispiece of *The Dunciad Variorum* (1729) to the most modest literary allusions and, finally, the fanciful representations of the past that adorned gardens and buildings. A contemporary viewer of William Kent's "Merlin's Cave" in Queen Caroline's gardens at Richmond, for example, wondered at the riddle of the thing, and noted ironically that it must therefore be profound: "We doubt not but that, like the works of the ancient *Ægyptians* frequently placed in their Royal Gardens and Palaces, it is wholly Hierogliphical [*sic*], Emblematical, Typical and Symbolical, conveying artful Lessons of Policy to Princes and Ministers of State."[62] Settle's speech in *Dunciad* III includes a full evocation of this mysterious East, mentioning both "Ægypt's wise abodes, / . . . where monkeys were the Gods" (III.203-204) and Moses, whom the exegetes saw as the fount of Egyptian learning to Jews and Grecians alike (III.102). In Pope's context, Settle's Pisgah-sight is an inversion of the usual typological vision that we would expect from such an account—

[62] *Fog's Weekly Journal*, 6 December 1735 (No. 270); see Judith Colton, "Merlin's Cave and Queen Caroline: Garden Art as Political Propaganda," *ECS*, 10 (1976-77), 1-20.

Egypt is a source of pagan error, Moses is bracketed with the pagan Christ, Pan, and the entire vision mocks standard typological prophecy.

The one clear reference to typology in Settle's speech is somewhat less than successful. Surrounding Wormius, Pope's name for the antiquarian Thomas Hearne, he beholds the fruits of modern learning:

> Round him, each *Science* by its modern type
> Stands known; *Divinity* with box and pipe,
> And proud *Philosophy* with breeches tore,
> And *English Musick* with a dismal score:
> While happier *Hist'ry* with her comrade *Ale*,
> Sooths the sad series of her tedious tale.[63]

Pope abridged this small aspect of the vision in the *Variorum*; even in the later version, these lines puzzle the Twickenham editors, who note that "the lines remain obscure, and have never, perhaps been generally understood, even by Pope's editors, who have no comment to make."[64] In the traditional Pisgah-sight, the visionary beholds types and their accomplishments, the later antitypes. Since Pope's figure of Settle offers an inverted Pisgah-sight, then we can explain this curious passage in the same way, remembering that each Science will hold forth a ridiculous modern fulfillment. The postfiguration or fulfillment of divinity is thus a snuffbox and tobacco pipe, suggesting modest addiction to stimulants but little to learning. The torn breeches of philosophy and the dismal score of English music postfigure the decay of those arts, and the vision of history is that of a feckless drinker. As typological satire, this passage is neither effective nor particularly clear, but in it we may glimpse the germ of the larger use of typology which Pope would introduce in the *Variorum*.

The 1728 editions of *The Dunciad* are almost entirely without scholia. Not so the 1729, and all subsequent versions, which are adorned with enough commentary to gratify the shades of Nicholas of Lyra, Stephanus, and Lipsius together. Now, the *apparatus criticus* to *The Dunciad Variorum* does many things; Pope certainly did not write it solely to clarify the typological satire of his poem. It satirizes many aspects of contemporary learning; the typology is incidental. Indeed, in this respect his scholia are unlike those of the

[63] *TE*, V, 172. In the 1728 editions, these lines follow III.200; in later editions, condensed to four lines, they appear as III.191-94.
[64] *TE*, V, 173.

Renaissance scholars who *claimed* to find Christian mysteries in Homer and Virgil, for his Scriblerian discussions of *The Dunciad* actually *do* describe, among other things, the typological relationships that are already present in the poem. Thus when Scriblerus himself tells us that "the Action of the Dunciad is the removal of the Imperial seat of Dulness from the City to the polite world; as that of the Æneid is the Removal of the empire of *Troy* to *Latium,*" the observation is not fanciful.[65] It is rather a fair statement of the poem's theme, without the embroidery endemic in the christianizing commentators. The analogy to Troy sets the scene for the debasement of traditional typology that follows immediately afterward in the "Dunciados Periocha," the arguments of the books. Of "BOOK the THIRD" the scholiast tells how Settle takes Theobald "to a *Mount of Vision,* from whence he shews him the past triumphs of the empire of Dulness, then the present, and lastly the future." The scenes of the future bring forth the most inexplicable "miracles and prodigies":

> On this subject *Settle* breaks into a congratulation, yet not unmix'd with concern, that his own times were but the types of these; He prophecies how first the nation shall be overrun with farces, opera's, shows; and the throne of Dulness advanced over both the Theatres: Then how her sons shall preside in the seats of arts and sciences, till in conclusion all shall return to their original Chaos: A Scene, of which the present Action of the Dunciad is but a Type or Foretaste, giving a Glimpse or *Pisgah-sight* of the promis'd Fulness of her Glory; the Accomplishment whereof will, in all probability, hereafter be the Theme of many other and greater Dunciads.[66]

This is the language of traditional typology which, it is now clear, Pope will use in *The Dunciad* in an orthodox manner for distorted, inverted purposes.

At the point in Book III when Settle summons his charge to the *"Mount of Vision,"* Pope adds a note to remind his readers of the passage in *Paradise Lost,* Book XI, when Michael summons Adam to the visionary hill from which he is to have his Pisgah-vision in the style of Moses (see III.53 and note). In a manner similar to that of Dryden in *Mac Flecknoe,* Pope is scrupulously correct in the way he applies typological relationships. As the argument to Book III

[65] *TE,* V, 51.   [66] *TE,* V, 56.

tells us, "the present Action" of *The Dunciad* is a shadowy pre-figuration of a glorious antitype which, stripped of mysteries, will arrive at some future time. The final lines of Settle's speech acquire the tone of millenarian rant:

> "Signs following signs lead on the Mighty Year;
> See! the dull stars roll round and re-appear.
> She comes! the Cloud-compelling Pow'r, behold!
> With Night Primaeval, and with Chaos old.
> Lo! the great Anarch's ancient reign restor'd,
> Light dies before her uncreating word. . . ."
>
> (III.335-40)

Aubrey Williams has accurately noted that this concluding passage, which Pope would remove from the mouth of Settle and assign to the general speaker of the poem in the expanded, four-book version of *The Dunciad*, presents an exact reversal of "the Christian positives—nature, Christ, Wisdom."[67] There are other reversals or distortions of traditional Christian themes in *The Dunciad*, many of them in both texts, some only in the enlarged, Cibberian version of the poem. They include the opening of Book III, where Theobald (later Cibber) sleeps with his "Anointed head" in Dulness's lap, curtained round with "vapors blue."[68] The scene recalls Madonna–Christ-child iconography, and reminds us that Theobald and Cibber are parodic types of Moses and the last prophet, Jesus. Just as Moses shadows forth Christ, so the leading Dunce of the poem, in both versions, holds forth "the Antichrist of Wit" (A-II.12; B-II.16). The parody of the Eucharist in Book IV (IV.549-64) is itself an antitype, for all of the fourth book, in the longer version of the poem, is an accomplishment of the apocalyptic prophecy of Book III.

Dunciad III, then, is not merely a series of reversals of traditional Christian symbols, but a type of "many other and greater Dunciads," which arrive in considerable detail in the final book. Pope leaves no doubt of his intention in the argument to "BOOK the

---

[67] See Aubrey L. Williams, *Pope's Dunciad: A Study of its Meaning* (London: Methuen & Co., 1955), p. 143 and, in general, 141-56. Most other studies of the poem virtually ignore Pope's mock apocalypse; see, for example, John E. Sitter's unadventurous reading, *The Poetry of Pope's "Dunciad"* (Minneapolis: Univ. of Minnesota Press, 1971), pp. 87-88. Dustin H. Griffin, *Alexander Pope: The Poet in the Poems* (Princeton: Princeton Univ. Press, 1978), pp. 269-74, comments briefly on some of the prophetic elements in *The Dunciad*.

[68] Williams, *Pope's Dunciad*, p. 149, makes this association.

FOURTH": "The Poet being, in this Book, to declare the *Completion* of the Prophecies mention'd at the end of the former, makes a new Invocation. . . ."[69] In the context of *The Dunciad*'s mock millenarianism, we should note that the poem falls squarely into the tradition of contemporary exegesis of the Book of Revelation, which deduced elaborate systems to show that the types foreshadowed in Revelation have had and *will continue to have* their antitypes in postbiblical secular history. Beginning in the seventeenth century, the exegetes were united in agreement on this point and Pope certainly would have known this persistent theme. "All the world believes it, and no one doubts it," wrote Pierre Jurieu firmly of the fact that all events of the New Testament had their types in the Old. Turning from general typology to the prefigurations of the Apocalypse, Jurieu went on:

> And therefore *Jesus Christ* hath had his *types*, without doubt *Antichrist* had his too, and that in great number. *Cain, Goliah, Pharaoh, Nebuchadnezzar,* and the other oppressors of the truth and the faithful, have been *types* of *Antichrist*. Among these *types* there was not any one more noted than *Antiochus*, who made the continual *sacrifice* cease for three *years* and a *half*, who made the *Church* desolate, who made almost the whole Nation fall into *Apostacy*, who prophaned the *Temple*, and cruelly persecuted those that persevered in the true *Religion*. So that as in the *types* of *Jesus Christ* we seek for and find his *Characters*, in like manner in *Antiochus* and that which the *Prophecies* say of him, we may find the *Characters* of *Antichrist*.[70]

The typology of the Book of Revelation, then, is a double one, prefiguring not only the Second Coming of Christ and his works but also the reign of the Antichrist and of all related evils (Antiochus is just one of many possible examples). Jurieu's view would receive regular confirmation and elaboration from later interpreters, including various Boyle Lecturers, especially Richard Kidder, William Whiston and his famous *Essay on the Revelation of Saint John* (1706), Charles Daubuz (1720), and Moses Lowman (1737).[71] Mil-

[69] *TE*, V, 337.

[70] See Pierre Jurieu, *The Accomplishment of the Scripture Prophecies or the Approaching Deliverance of the Church. Faithfully Englished*, 2 parts in 1 vol. (London, 1687), i, 234.

[71] For further discussion of the exegesis of Revelation, see Chapter 9, Section 3.

lenarian prophecy in New England was similarly based on the notion of relating the prophecies of Revelation to both good and evil
events in contemporary society. If millenarianism, in all its forms,
acknowledged that Revelation foreshadowed Antichrist as well as
the Second Coming, then Pope's including part of this tradition in
the parodic typologizing of *The Dunciad* must have intensified his
audience's pleasure in recognizing the figural depth of his own
vision.

The accomplishment of the types of Book III in the final book of
The Dunciad is clearly a triumph of literary, intellectual, and cultural evil; sins so pervasive as the cultural enormities of Book IV
may be ranked as a manifestation of Antichrist. Millenarian exegetes of Scripture were always quick to observe that the Apocalypse
would not come unless times were especially bad and evil doings
were especially predominant. The very fact that the dunces willfully
produce bad art, as Williams points out, is evil, a misuse of the
good, which is art itself.[72] The vast throngs that surround Dulness's
throne supply evidence that the bad times of consummate evil,
necessary as a prelude to apocalypse, have already arrived. First and
most important are the idolatrous:

> Nor absent they, no members of her state,
> Who pay her homage in her sons, the Great;
> Who false to Phoebus, bow the knee to Baal;
> Or impious, preach his Word without a call.
>
> (IV.91-94)

Following the false poets, whom Pope represents as pagan votaries
or dishonest priests, march many groups of worshipers. A note describes them as "The idolizers of Dulness in the Great," as well as
ill judges, ill writers, and ill patrons.[73] In them, we may find what
Jurieu called "the *Characters* of *Antichrist*," for in the realm of the
arts they do indeed profane the temple and persecute the followers
of the true religion. No single figure better personifies the idolaters
of art and learning than Aristarchus (Richard Bentley), with his
vaunting comment on the poet-priests of his own age: "Turn what
they will to Verse, their toil is vain, / Critics like me shall make it
Prose again" (IV.213-14). When Pope's Apocalypse finally comes,
after four hundred more lines of satire upon the freaks of Dulness,

[72] See Williams, *Pope's Dunciad*, pp. 155-56.
[73] *TE*, V, 351.

it is, as several readers have noticed, a reversal of the final chapters of Revelation. St. John's vision calls for the creation of a new heaven and a new earth, and a New Jerusalem of eternal light for "the nations of them which are saved" (Rev. 21.23). Generations of millenarians saw the conclusion of Revelation as a series of passages of great hope—for relief from persecution, for the coming of a utopia, for an eternal reign of justice. Pope's Apocalypse gives us none of these things. Instead, we see the extinction of the arts, the triumph of casuistry over truth, the annihilation of philosophy, medicine, and logic, and the death of religion and morality:

> Nor *public* Flame, nor *private*, dares to shine;
> Nor *human* Spark is left, nor Glimpse *divine*!
>
> (IV.651-52)

This Apocalypse is not an end to the world. To the contrary, Pope's point is that the world of profane things, tainted by paganism and idolatry, flourishes as never before. His universal darkness buries only the classical culture and humane studies of the world as he knew it—like most millenarian prefigurations of his day, *The Dunciad*'s last two books are a threatening sermon and a warning prophecy to an unconverted audience. Perhaps most significant for the student of typology is the fact that Pope, in the manner of Milton in *Paradise Lost*, Books XI and XII, and later Blake in *Jerusalem*, produces both the types and what he fancies to be their accomplishment, the antitypes of Book IV.

In the fourteen years between the publication of the unannotated *Dunciad* of 1728 and *The Dunciad in Four Books* (1742), Pope attacked entrenched privilege, corrupt behavior in public officials, and depraved private attitudes and tastes in a number of satires. There is no exact parallel in his other works to the typological inventiveness of *The Dunciad*, but we may see glimpses of typological satire of great power in various poems. In the third *Moral Essay*, the *Epistle to Bathurst* (1733), he creates one of the neatest typological pairings of the entire century in his portraits of the Man of Ross and Sir Balaam. The real-life model for the Man of Ross, John Kyrle, apparently followed the dictates of the *imitatio Christi* regimen in his daily life even more dramatically than does the character in *To Bathurst*.[74] He is a Christ type in the tradition of Dryden's

---

[74] See Howard Erskine-Hill, *The Social Milieu of Alexander Pope: Lives, Example and the Poetic Purpose* (New Haven and London: Yale Univ. Press, 1975), pp. 33-35, on how Kyrle's behavior on one recorded occasion almost amounts to the acting out of a New Testament parable.

figure of James II in *The Hind and the Panther* ("A Plain good Man, whose Name is understood"—III.906-43) or his memorable "Character of a Good Parson" in the *Fables*. Sir Balaam, on the other hand, is a satiric reversal of Job, one of the century's most canonical types of Christ. The Balaam of Scripture is a false prophet, a hireling, a lying teacher, and a man bereft of revelation. This character, which Pope created between his two versions of Antichrist in *The Dunciad*, shows some interesting similarities to both texts. The theme of Sir Balaam's temptation and fall is not quite analogous to the triumph of Dulness, but it is worth noting that Sir Balaam, "Rouz'd by the Prince of Air" (353), rapidly expands his wealth and influence, moves from the City to the Court (directly paralleling the central theme of *The Dunciad*), overreaches himself, and comes to a bad end. The final line of *To Bathurst*, "And sad Sir Balaam curses God and dies," is an exact reversal of the Job story (see Job 2.9, Job's wife to her husband: "Curse God and die."). Like Judas, one of the figures of the Antichrist most popular with the exegetes, Sir Balaam dies on the gallows, although not *felo de se*. The typological satire of *To Bathurst*, like that of other poems of the 1730s, is malign and foreboding; it lacks the sense of ridicule of the typological games of Butler and Swift. Perhaps, to Pope, the times were grimmer, closer in moral quality to the depravity of Juvenal's Rome and to the apocalyptic wickedness of St. John's Revelation, so that he could see no reason to play word games with sectarian doctrines. But history is a checkerboard: for every square of grim shadow in which all seems corruption, there are squares of light in which the gentle life goes on undisturbed. To see the 1730s solely through the lenses of Pope's poems is to miss much that made the decade peaceful and productive in many ways to many of his countrymen. Pope's use of typology for satiric purposes, I think, however gifted, is the high point of this kind of ridicule. We will continue to find prefigurative techniques satirized or used for satiric reasons later in the eighteenth century, but they are just a shadow of what we have seen in Pope.

 6

I began this chapter with a reference to the use of satiric typology in one novel of the eighteenth century, *Tristram Shandy*. We have seen that novelists tend to regard typology as a serious figural de-

vice; within the aura of Sterne's jocularity, there is undoubtedly a
sober awareness of what types are all about. Sterne had a firsthand
acquaintance with religious figuralism, so it is not at all surprising
that typology should come up somewhere in the vast hodgepodge
of his novel.[75] Does the typological style of Pope influence any of
the novelists of his generation? I think there is evidence that it does
affect Fielding. The typology of *Joseph Andrews* must owe something to the Man of Ross, and that of Squire Allworthy in *Tom
Jones* recalls Pope's praise of Ralph Allen in *Epilogue to the Satires,
Dialogue I* (1738): "Let humble ALLEN, with an aukward Shame,
/ Do good by stealth, and blush to find it Fame" (135-36).[76] Pope,
like other ethical thinkers of his time, thought that unostenta-
tiously performing charitable acts was one of the highest forms of
doing good and, in fact, private charity had a long series of typological parallels to support it and to associate it with the *imitatio
Christi* theme. The first dialogue of *Epilogue to the Satires* also includes a well-documented presentation of a negative type, a clear
prefiguration of the Antichrist, in the portrait of Vice. Once
adopted by "Greatness," Vice governs all of humanity:

> In golden Chains the willing World she draws,
> And hers the Gospel is, and hers the Laws:
> Mounts the Tribunal, lifts her scarlet head,
> And sees pale Virtue carted in her stead![77]

Like *The Vision of Camilick* (1727), an anonymous prose satire
ascribed to Bolingbroke, these lines evoke types of corruption drawn
from Revelation. Bolingbroke's satire stresses the viciousness of political venality; Pope's emphasizes the figure of the Whore of Babylon, "drunken with the blood of the saints, and with the blood of
the martyrs of Jesus."[78] The typological overtones of *The Vision of*

[75] See, for example, Sterne's Sermon XXIII, on the parable of the rich man
and Lazarus, *The Sermons of Mr. Yorick* (1760-61), in *The Works of Laurence
Sterne*, 8 vols. (London, 1790), VIII, 21-36; see also VIII, 199-201.
[76] See Erskine-Hill, *The Social Milieu of Alexander Pope*, pp. 204-40, esp.
224-32, and Benjamin Boyce, *The Benevolent Man: A Life of Ralph Allen of
Bath* (Cambridge, Mass.: Harvard Univ. Press, 1967), pp. 78-81.
[77] *Dialogue I*, 147-50; see *TE*, IV, 308-309.
[78] *The Vision of Camilick* appeared in *The Craftsman*, 27 January 1727 (No.
16); see *The Works of the late Right Honourable Henry St. John, Lord Bolingbroke*, 7 vols. (London, 1754-98), I, 185-88, where it is entitled "The First Vision
of Camilick." See also Isaac Kramnick, *Bolingbroke and His Circle: The Politics
of Nostalgia in the Age of Walpole* (Cambridge, Mass.: Harvard Univ. Press,
1968), pp. 22-23. Pope's text owes much to Revelation 17, esp. 17.6, quoted here.

Camilick help to enhance its satire of Sir Robert Walpole. Pope's treatment of Vice, with its hints of religious idolatry (cf. "See thronging Millions to the Pagod run," 157), also attacks Walpole, but in a broader and more general sense.

Fielding's *Jonathan Wild*, published the year after *Dunciad* IV appeared, owes parts of its satirical approach to both the particular and the general schools of anti-Walpole satire. Walpole is the man "with a purse of gold in his hand" in *Camilick*, whose power to corrupt enslaves mankind; the evil being that stalks through the pages of *Camilick* postfigures the beast out of the earth, the Antichrist himself (Rev. 13.11-17). The final line of Pope's description of Vice, " 'Nothing is Sacred now but Villainy' " (170), also figures forth the evils of Walpole's regime, but in these lines we see not the figure of Walpole so much as the abominations for which he is responsible. The story of Jonathan Wild, in Fielding's hands, acquires typological properties in the constant relating of Wild to well-known epitomes of evil. Fielding compares Wild to the devil, to a wolf in a sheepfold, to all great men, to a prime minister. There are hints of typology in these comparisons, but the best evidence that Pope's prefigurative satire in *The Dunciad* influenced Fielding appears in his extraordinary figural *tour de force*, Book II, Chapter vi, "Of hats." Wild, sensing dissension among his gang of thugs, correctly recognizes that "the difference [among them] lay only in the fashion of their hats":

"Gentlemen [he addresses them], I am ashamed to see men embarked in so great and glorious an undertaking as that of robbing the public, so foolishly and weakly dissenting among themselves. Do you think the first inventors of hats, or at least of the distinctions between them, really conceived that one form of hats should inspire a man with divinity, another with law, another with learning, or another with bravery? No, they meant no more by these outward signs than to impose on the vulgar, and, instead of putting GREAT men to the trouble of acquiring or maintaining the substance, to make it sufficient that they condescend to wear the type or shadow of it. You do wisely, therefore, when in a crowd, to amuse the mob by quarrels on such accounts, that while they are listening to your jargon you may with the greater ease and safety pick their pockets."[79]

[79] *The Life of Mr. Jonathan Wild the Great* (London, 1754), pp. 90-92.

Hats, simply enough, are outward signs, prefigurations of certain positive qualities; clothing, as Swift had proposed in his satire on the sartorialists in *A Tale of a Tub,* encodes a message about the person clothed. As words are the signs of ideas, so (presumably) hats are the signs of occupations, moral qualities, and so on. However, following the eighteenth-century tradition that the pagan mysteries and their hieroglyphic or emblematic signs were an invention of priestcraft to conceal religious truth from the common people, Wild introduces a similar mysterious interpretation of the gang's headwear. For Wild, types are not genuine, they are simply a figural imposition to allow criminals in high places to carry on their sublime task "of robbing the public." We might pass this speech by without further notice were it not for Fielding's deliberately calling attention to it with a lengthy Scriblerian footnote, the longest authorial scholium in any of his novels. The note, like many of Pope's interpolations in *The Dunciad Variorum,* merely ridicules scholastic pedantry, deliberately compounding the "mysterious" attributes of Wild's speech. We may glimpse for a moment Fielding's sympathy, in drawing his own character of the Antichrist-Walpole, with Pope's figural creations of Antichrist-Theobald and Antichrist-Cibber (one of Fielding's favorite satiric targets) in *The Dunciad.*

Walpole resigned as First Lord of the Treasurer (and hence as prime minister) in February 1742 so, by the time *Jonathan Wild* was published, Fielding's satire on the political differences of his ministry was old hat.[80] Political opposition for the rest of the 1740s would be less virulent than it had been from 1725 to 1742. Perhaps for this reason we do not again see typological satire of the complexity and harshness of Pope's later poems. The typology of *Jonathan Wild* consists, for the most part, of implied connections between Wild's criminal career and recognized characters of evil. The chapter "Of hats" is more jesting than it is serious typological satire. It may shed more light on the typology of Trim's hat in *Tristram Shandy* than it does on anti-Walpole satire. Jonathan Wild himself assumed an aura of implacable evil so intense that he becomes a type of wickedness to rank alongside Cain, Judas, and Satan. To-

---

[80] Bertrand A. Goldgar, *Walpole and the Wits: The Relation of Politics to Literature, 1722-1742* (Lincoln, Neb.: Univ. of Nebraska Press, 1976), p. 201, notes that Fielding abandoned work on *Jonathan Wild* in the second half of 1741, thus postponing its publication by at least one year, or until after Walpole's departure from office.

ward the end of the 1740s, Smollett even introduces Wild in such a context in *Roderick Random*. The scene is not a major one: Roderick, whom his employer has falsely accused of theft, applies to his former patron Mr. Concordance for help, but his accusers have informed against him and the patron dismisses him. "I must beg to have no manner of connection with you—my reputation is at stake —O my God! I shall be looked upon as your accomplice and abettor—people will say Jonathan Wild was but a type of me— boys will hoot at me as I pass along; and the cinder-wenches belch forth reproaches wafted in a gale impregnated with gin—I shall be notorious—the very butt of slander and cloaca of infamy."[81] Smollett, as we have seen, would later use typology in serious fictional contexts, but it seems obvious from this selfish hyperbole that, by mid-century, English writers had less patience with its intricate figuralism as a satiric device. From the virtuoso treatment of typology in the satires of Dryden, Swift, and Pope to what we see by the late 1740s, where satiric types are little more than humorous references, is a decline of sorts. The decline, however, has a great deal to do with changes in the forms and methods of English satire and does not imply a weakening of the English figural imagination. Antiquarian, mythological, exegetical, and millenarian interest in other applications of typology will be abundant well into the mid-nineteenth century.

The obscure figural jokes of *Tristram Shandy* may at first appear to relate to the satiric methods of Swift and the period around the turn of the eighteenth century. And, to be sure, there had been a certain disintegration in satiric typology after *The Dunciad Variorum*. But as a viable figural form changes, it gains as well as loses, and the enduring qualities of literary typology suggest that it was always in flux. *Tristram Shandy* does not have the earmarks of a piece of typological satire—not at first glance. We must remember that Sterne was intensely fond of mysterious figuration, whether for its own sake or for the purpose of ridiculing some form of intellectual endeavor he despised. One of the major themes of biblical typology is the foreshadowing of the birth of a certain child—an extraordinary, messianic child—whose birth will be announced to his parents and to the world by various strange signs and visitations. Other signs will prefigure the naming of the child, the initiation into his religion by circumcision, and the assumption of his min-

[81] *The Adventures of Roderick Random*, 2 vols. (London, 1748), I, 181.

istry. By virtue of Sterne's own principles of transformation, all of these events are present in *Tristram Shandy*, although not in the same sequence as in the Old and New Testaments. Tristram himself foreshadows his misfortunes early in Volume I: "I have been the continual sport of what the world calls Fortune . . . in every stage of my life, and at every turn and corner where she could get fairly at me, the ungracious Duchess has pelted me with a set of as pitiful misadventures and cross accidents as ever small HERO sustained."[82]

We hear of Tristram's birth a chapter or two later. Thereafter, Tristram's history is a crazy quilt of pre- and postfigurations. We will hear for three volumes of the circumstances of his conception, through a distorted form of annunciation, Mrs. Shandy's lying-in, and the mischance of his delivery. Present in the Shandy house to attend the child's birth are three pedantic magi—Tristram's father, Uncle Toby, and Dr. Slop—each of whom rides his own special hobbyhorse. The naming of the child is important. The young Messiah was to be called Immanuel, "which being interpreted is, God with us" (Matt. 1.24), a figure of light for the Gentiles (Is. 42.6), for the world (John 8.12). The young Shandy, as his father crisply puts it, parodying Isaiah 7.14, "shall be christened *Trismegistus*" (IV. viii). Which being interpreted is (since Hermes Trismegistus was the founder of hermeticism and a favorite dark author of Walter Shandy's), mysticism is with us, for the name would suggest mystery and darkness to all familiar with it. In fact, the local curate makes a mess of the naming ("—There is no *gistus* to it, noodle!"), and forthwith gives the child a name drawn from the pages of medieval Christian romance. Tristram, glossing the events surrounding his naming and baptism, cannot stay on the subject for more than a few words at a time:

> My mother, you must know,——but I have fifty things more necessary to let you know first,—I have a hundred difficulties which I have promised to clear up, and a thousand distresses and domestic misadventures crouding in upon me thick and three-fold, one upon the neck of another,——a cow broke in (to-morrow morning) to my uncle *Toby's* fortifications, and eat up two ratios and a half of dried grass, tearing up the sods with it, which faced his horn-work and covered way.—*Trim* insists upon being tried by a court-martial,—the cow to be shot,— *Slop* to be *crucifix'd*,—myself to be *tristram'd*, and at my very

[82] *Tristram Shandy*, I, 16-17 (I.v).

baptism made a martyr of;——poor unhappy devils that we all are![83]

Tristram will be circumcised later by an operation of which a pagan mystic like Hermes might have approved. The boy enters into his ministry by becoming the oldest male heir to the Shandy name in the typological passage I quoted at the beginning of this chapter, unless we are willing to concede that Tristram has been in his pulpit, giving the history of his opinions, from page one of the first volume. Baptism is a type of the Resurrection, and we have known all along that Tristram is going to suffer misadventures, but who would have expected him to become a martyr so young? If the misnamed young Shandy heir, a figure of parodic mystical darkness, can be "martyred" at his own baptism, typological satire is not dead after all—from type to antitype in three words!

Typological satire usually involves current topics in the church and religious affairs. The attacks of Cleveland, Butler, and Oldham focus on the figural excesses of seventeenth-century Puritanism; Dryden's typological satire ridicules millenarianism, messianism, and false prophecy; that of Swift criticizes Puritan exegesis directly. Pope's favorite medium for typological satire is the Apocalypse. Only the instances I have noted in the novelists do not fit an ecclesiastical pattern. Modern critical opinion tends to hold the view that the latter half of the eighteenth century, since it lacks a major satirist of the stature of Pope or Swift, is not a great period for English satire, as if the genre lay dormant until Byron's major poems. In fact, the reverse is true, as the satires of Churchill, Smart, Chatterton, Cowper, Burns, John Wolcot ("Peter Pindar"), and many lesser writers demonstrate.[84] The typological strain that I have elucidated in earlier satire continues to appear from Churchill to Byron, with one unifying subject predominant throughout the period. That subject is millenarianism, the theological subject of the widest popular appeal in the later eighteenth and early nineteenth

---

[83] *Ibid.*, III, 184-85 (III.xxxviii).

[84] Critical studies of the satire of the period are scarce. A relevant book is Thomas Lockwood, *Post-Augustan Satire: Charles Churchill and Satirical Poetry, 1750-1800* (Seattle: Univ. of Washington Press, 1979); see pp. 3-9.

centuries. Historical studies of advocates of the Millennium are quite numerous, so much so that the topic has assumed something of the status of an historical genre. And quite properly so: the millenarians flourished in the later eighteenth century as a part and later a tenuous branch of Wesleyanism; schemes of moral and social betterment around the time of the French Revolution hearkened to the notion of the coming doom; popular prophets of all stripes offered millenarian interpretations of the events in France and of the Napoleonic Wars; and the early struggles between labor and capital and the formation of the first labor lodges or unions were carried on in an atmosphere of millennial fervor.[85] Millenarian behavior often—although not always—leads to displays of enthusiasm, effusive prophetic utterances, and exhibitions of mental instability. Such elements of behavior need not be seen with a critical eye but, to the degree that they display human folly, satirists have often tended to attack them. Just as Dryden and Pope used millenarian themes as the basis for powerful and memorable satires, so satirists of the later eighteenth and early nineteenth centuries did likewise. The subject, indeed, is quite large, and I shall only sample this satiric tradition here, but there is much fruit for future study in the satiric and typological response to the Millennium.

Among the best—and most neglected—satirists of the later eighteenth century is Thomas Chatterton, who devoted the last year (1769-70) of his brief life to writing personal satires of considerable scope and ability. One of the most important of these poems is called "The Whore of Babylon," a long attack upon the new Babylonianism of government and the false interpretations of the Book of Revelation which the established Church countenanced. Chatterton did not publish "The Whore of Babylon" separately, but rather incorporated it almost entirely later in 1770 in an even longer satire, "Kew Gardens."[86] The chief clerical opponent of "The Whore of Babylon" is Thomas Newton, whom Chatterton disliked because, as Bishop of Bristol, he represented the Church establishment but who, appropriately for the poem, was also the author of several

---

[85] An illuminating study of this millenarian background is W. H. Oliver, *Prophets and Millennialists: The Uses of Biblical Prophecy in England from the 1790s to the 1840s* (Auckland: Auckland Univ. Press, 1978), pp. 25-41, 212-15.

[86] See *The Complete Works of Thomas Chatterton: A Bicentenary Edition*, ed. Donald S. Taylor with Benjamin B. Hoover, 2 vols. (Oxford: Clarendon Press, 1971), II, 1040, 1069-70.

volumes interpreting the Book of Revelation.[87] Chatterton's view is that Newton's prophecies of doom are blatant misreadings of Revelation and that, in fact, the Church actually serves and promotes the "Babylonish" harlotry of government. Bishop Newton, he writes, "with a good Intent / Discover'd hidden Meanings never meant"; a reader foolish enough to take the prophecies literally should

> read Newton and his Bill of Fare
> What Prophesies unprophesy'd are there.
> In Explanation he's so justly skill'd
> The Pseudo Prophets Myst'ries are fulfilld
> No superficial Reasons have disgrac'd
> The worthy Prelates Sacerdotal Taste . . .[88]

Chatterton, providing verbal echoes of Dryden and Pope, maps out a program of satiric attacks upon idolatries of church and state. It would appear that he saw himself as a prophetic scourge, a Jeremiah, assuring the people who took comfort from official blandishments like Newton's comforting exegeses of the prophets that the Millennium is not yet. Times are evil, but they must get a great deal worse before the people can hope to have the oppressors' yoke lifted.[89] Although Chatterton does not actually use typological figuralism in "The Whore of Babylon" the way earlier typological satirists do, he does criticize contemporary millenarianism for its excesses at the same time that he affirms the accuracy of some of the types of apocalypse present in his own time.

One of Chatterton's satiric missions was to label false prophets as charlatans, but it was not his only purpose. Antimillenarian satire plays a small part in what are essentially political poems. Such is not the case with William Blake's one major satire, *The Marriage of Heaven and Hell* (1790-93).[90] The *Marriage* is not only a satire

[87] Newton's main work is *Dissertation on the Prophecies*, 3 vols. (London, 1759-60), of which the third volume is entitled *Analysis of the Revelation*.

[88] *Complete Works*, I, 458-59.

[89] See Donald S. Taylor, *Thomas Chatterton's Art: Experiments in Imagined History* (Princeton: Princeton Univ. Press, 1978), pp. 209-14; see his excellent chapter, "Satiric Worlds and Modes," pp. 170-261, for an appreciation of Chatterton's satiric skills.

[90] There are many satirical passages in Blake's poems, as well as some shorter satires in *Poetical Sketches* (1783) and the largely satirical *An Island in the Moon*.

of religious ideas, somewhat in the tradition of *A Tale of a Tub,* it is also an attack upon the false (for Blake) millennialism of Swedenborg's *Divine Providence* and a presentation of Blake's own apocalyptic vision. Blake evokes a millenarian mood at once, in Plate 3: "Now is the dominion of Edom, & the return of Adam into Paradise," according to the prophecies of Isaiah 34-35. In order to effect the Millennium, Blake finds it necessary for mankind to reject existing religious codes and orthodoxies, a move which he accomplishes by inverting key texts of the Bible, reinterpreting *Paradise Lost,* and producing his own ironical scriptural book of proverbs, the "Proverbs of Hell." The Old Testament Book of Proverbs incorporates the wisdom of Solomon, who is the traditional type of wisdom and piety; while they are not explicitly typological, many individual texts of Proverbs make figural references to the Law, and some longer exempla present behavioral types of virtuous or evil actions.[91] The Proverbs of the Bible show that the wisdom and theology of Israel derive from experience and from generations of faith in the Lord; Blake's proverbs also derive from experience, but from an unorthodox approach to life whose central vision spurns traditional wisdom as tainted and therefore suspect. Whatever is part of an established religious code may be dangerous. Blake formally introduces his typology at Plate 14:

> The ancient tradition that the world will be consumed in fire at the end of six thousand years is true, as I have heard from Hell.
>
> For the cherub with his flaming sword is hereby commanded to leave his guard at the tree of life; and when he does, the whole creation will be consumed and appear infinite and holy, whereas it now appears finite & corrupt. ·
>
> This will come to pass by an improvement of sensual enjoyment.[92]

The types of Apocalypse, then, are true, "but first," Blake notes, mankind must prepare itself for the Day of Judgment by abandon-

---

[91] See Von Rad, *Old Testament Theology,* I, 345; for behavioral types, see Prov. 7.6-27 (on the evils of adultery) and 31.10-31 (a character of the virtuous woman). Harold Bloom, *Blake's Apocalypse* (Garden City, N.Y.: Doubleday & Co., 1963), pp. 83-88, attempts a reading of Blake's "Proverbs of Hell."

[92] *The Complete Writings of William Blake,* ed. Geoffrey Keynes (London: Oxford Univ. Press, 1966), p. 154.

ing orthodox notions of body and soul, religion and knowledge. Contemporary prophets—we must remember that Blake wrote on the rising flood tide of a great movement of popular prophecy— often set forth conditions of readiness for the Millennium; Blake's are unusual in that he does not call for a traditional repentance, according to the rules of established codes. As the devil points out to him in the fourth Memorable Fancy, "I tell you, no virtue can exist without breaking these ten commandments. Jesus was all virtue, and acted from impulse, not from rules."[93] It appears that Blake employs typology in *The Marriage of Heaven and Hell* with a double purpose, to satirize mistaken prophets and erroneous expectations of the Millennium and to present his own personal prophecies, which he describes as a reading of the Bible in its infernal or diabolic sense.[94]

No reading of *The Marriage of Heaven and Hell* should minimize the poem's many-faceted complexity or the various levels on which it can successfully be read. To a considerable extent, for example, Blake synthesizes his own prophetic voice by conflating together texts from Isaiah, Revelation, and *Paradise Lost*, making himself a prophet in the tradition of Old and New Testament writers and a major post-Reformation Christian visionary. In the longer perspective of Blake studies, the *Marriage* is obviously more important as a major prophecy than as a mixed-mode satire employing typological methods, but typology, in satire as in other major genres, often is present as a figural strain or pattern and seldom dominates a text completely. As works with satiric antimillenarian intentions go, Blake's prophecy is one of the most serious critiques of his century, for he allies himself with the forces of social protest, which would be the main wave of millenarian movements in the nineteenth century.[95]

Byron's *The Vision of Judgment* (1820), in comparison to Blake's visionary prophecy, is considerably less serious and more light-hearted. Byron's chase, like Dryden's, has his Flecknoe in view and

---

[93] *Ibid.*, p. 158.

[94] For a reading of the *Marriage* as a prophecy, see Wittreich, *Angel of Apocalypse*, pp. 189-99.

[95] Michael Adas, *Prophets of Rebellion: Millenarian Protest Movements against the European Colonial Order* (Chapel Hill: Univ. of North Carolina Press, 1979), pp. xvii-xxvii, esp. xix-xxi, offers a helpful perspective on the element of social protest; see also Harrison, *The Second Coming*, pp. 207-30.

like Pope's, his Cibber—both united in the person of Robert Southey. *The Vision* parodies not Judgment Day and the Millennium but the judgment rendered by Heaven on the late King George III and the accidental ascension of Southey to the celestial gate. However, Byron does recall millenarian visionary tracts, from Richard Brothers and Joanna Southcott to Edward Irving and Henry Drummond, which often visualize the scenes of final judgment in far greater detail than Revelation provides (Rev. 20). The judgment scene nicely suggests the millenarian satire of Byron's vision:

> And from the gate [of heaven] thrown open issued beaming
> A beautiful and mighty Thing of Light,
> Radiant with glory, like a banner streaming
> Victorious from some world-o'erthrowing fight:
> My poor comparisons must needs be teeming
> With earthly likenesses, for here the night
> Of clay obscures our best conceptions, saving
> Johanna Southcote, or Bob Southey raving.[96]

By 1820, Joanna Southcott had been dead for six years, but her popularity and the availability of her colossal outpouring of pamphlets continued unabated.[97] If she was the millennial prophetess of the age *par excellence*, then to link "visionary" Southey with her, as Byron does here, helps to tar the poet with the brush of fanaticism. Satan appears, summons a cloud of witnesses against George III, calls John Wilkes and Junius to the stand, when—like a pie thrown in a farce—Byron hurls his true satiric object, Southey, *in medias res*. The scene, until Southey's arrival, is reminiscent of the seventeenth-century "Session-of-the-Poets" verses; afterwards, it resembles the heroic and other games in *The Dunciad*. It comes as no surprise, in another Byronic parody of millenarian judgments, that during Southey's attempt to read his verse—he can manage only three lines before the immortals, one and all, flee for their lives—confusion breaks out and "King George slipp'd into heaven." No matter. Byron notes, "when the tumult dwindled to a calm, / I left

96 *The Vision of Judgment*, St. XXVIII.
97 For a recent appraisal of Southcott's life and works, see Harrison, *The Second Coming*, pp. 86-109. For her writings, see Eugene Patrick Wright, *A Catalogue of the Joanna Southcott Collection at the University of Texas* (Austin: Univ. of Texas Press, 1968).

him practising the hundredth psalm."[98] *The Vision of Judgment* is not good typology, but it is good satire on a well-known typological subject, with all the traditional characters, including the beast from the sea—Southey—firmly in place. It is especially noteworthy that some of the religious subjects against which Cleveland had turned his typological satire are also present in Byron's time, nearly two centuries later. A better proof of the endurance of typology is hard to imagine.

[98] *The Vision of Judgment,* St. CVI. Psalm 100, incidentally, is one of the four shortest psalms.

CHAPTER 9

Typology and Prophecy

WHAT IS A *Poetick Description fulfill'd*, but a Typical Prophesy *fulfill'd?"* asked Anthony Collins in the middle of his passionate defense of the typological interpretation of the Old Testament prophecies.[1] Writing as he does, in 1724, at the height of the debate over whether his contemporaries should interpret scriptural prophecies literally or allegorically, the Deist Collins shows us how eighteenth-century theological controversy could create curious and unlikely sparring partners. In a forty-page chapter in defense of "Typical or Allegorical reasoning," he writes particularly to confute the "literal Scheme" of William Whiston who, when he was not causing Anthony Collins grievous offense, had been a strong supporter of the typological reading of the prophecies in the Book of Revelation. It may seem paradoxical or ironical for a prominent deist to defend nonliteral exegesis of Scripture, especially against a former Boyle Lecturer known for his own advocacy of both literal and extended allegorical interpretation, but the cloak of deism in early eighteenth-century England is a wide one, and adversaries on one point could turn out to be allies on another. What is more important, I think, than the paradox is that Collins is simply articulating a view so widely held that few of his contemporaries would have wished to deny it—that all Old Testament prophecy and many other prophetical texts as well were typological. To doubt the prefigurative qualities of Old Testament prophecy was possible only if one wished to be charged, as Thomas Paine would be later in the century, with atheism, and even Paine, whatever he thought of the accusation, urged that his faith was not

[1] *A Discourse of the Grounds and Reasons of the Christian Religion*, pp. 238-39.

atheistical, but a brand of natural religion for which "there is a word of God [and] there is a revelation."[2]

As the century aged, members of the literal school of prophetical interpretation would be content to hold that it was correct to read biblical prophecy typologically, but that it was wrong to apply prefigurative interpretation to *all* prophetical utterances, whether canonical texts, the utterances of the Fathers, or events and texts in secular history and literature. However, for most men and women of letters, there was never any serious question that the New Testament showed the completion of prophecies shadowed forth in the Old and that, if the argument from design had any validity (which for most people it did), one could reasonably expect to find similar fulfillments of prophecies in the world around us. "The new and old Testament are one book," said Anthony Blackwall in a well-reasoned defense of the Bible. "In the first we have the type and shadow, in the second the antitype and substance: What in the first volume is prophecy, in the *last* is history and matter of fact: which at once clears all the obscurities and difficulties of the prophecies; and lets us know the reason why they were expres'd in obscure terms."[3] Typology and prophecy, then, are synonymous for Blackwall as they were for most students of sacred literature in the eighteenth century. Blackwall is a generalist whose sweeping equation of the two terms takes in more, perhaps, than some exegetes would have allowed. However, as I have suggested in earlier chapters, the confusion of terminology in the study of seventeenth- and eighteenth-century figuralism is a fact of life. In the strictest sense, many Old Testament types are not prophetical unless and until some writer argues that they are. Typology, as a system of exegesis, has two planes of existence: it exists, first, to the degree that the authors of Scripture acknowledge that they are using it and, second, to the degree that exegetes claim to have found it in the texts they analyze. Thus my study of typology and prophecy in this chapter will, like that of the relationship between typology and myth, discuss figural associations that people thought they saw, applications that they

[2] See *The Age of Reason; being an investigation of true and fabulous theology* (Paris and London, 1794), p. 22.

[3] *The Sacred Classics Defended and Illustrated: or, An Essay humbly offer'd towards proving the Purity, Propriety, and true Eloquence of the Writers of the New Testament* . . . (London, 1725), p. 349. Like Steele in *The Christian Hero*, Blackwall sought to praise the (hitherto neglected) virtues of Scripture and to criticize the use of pagan literature as a source of models for virtuous behavior.

claimed to find, and predictive structures some of which our eyes may miss entirely.

Early Christian allegorists like Philo and Origen had commented upon the presence of types and their fulfillment in Scripture, and even pre-Christian rabbinical interpretation recognized the types, with their promise of good things to come. Erich Auerbach proposes that, in the narrow figural sense, Tertullian is the first person, early in the third century, to treat Old Testament types as prophetic events foreshadowing accomplishments which would take place later.[4] And, indeed, in his *Adversus Marcionem*, Tertullian goes beyond treating the Old Testament as mere allegory; rather, to quote Auerbach, he believed that the text had "real, literal meaning throughout, and even when there was figural prophecy, the figure had just as much historical reality as what it prophesied."[5] We can readily understand why the early Christians saw prophecy in historical terms, for they eagerly sought tangible confirmations of beliefs for which they could—and did—suffer severe persecution. In the broadest historical terms, we will often find that sects of believers who happen to be in the minority at a given place and time attach historical validity to certain signs as a self-confirming value-judgment for their position. Tertullian's contribution is important for my consideration of typological prophecy in our later period because it emphasizes, for the first time, the historical dimension of Scripture prophecy. From his astute observation that the Old Testament types were *figures* whose *historical proof* occurs later, in the New Testament, grows the tradition of drawing parallels between figural events in texts of all kinds and supposed fulfillments or accomplishments in later texts, secular history, or contemporary life.

It was possible for the Fathers and for most exegetes until post-Reformation theology to confine their use of historical typology to the text of Scripture itself. Old Testament types and prophecies foreshadowed accomplishments in the New Testament, in the life and mission of Christ and his disciples. But there is always one conspicuous exception to the biblical types. These are the prophecies of Apocalypse or the Millennium in the Old Testament prophets, especially the Book of Daniel, and in the Book of Revelation. Millenarian visionaries, throughout the Middle Ages, carried the types from these books into historical contexts and, using a process of

[4] See "Figura," in *Scenes from the Drama of European Literature: Six Essays* (New York: Meridian Books, 1959), p. 29.
[5] *Ibid.*, p. 30.

thought which we may still see in use in the late twentieth century, they would argue, at different occasions in history, that the antitypes shadowed forth in Revelation and elsewhere were about to come. The process, as I will show later in this chapter, flourished in the seventeenth, eighteenth, and early nineteenth centuries, although I would not wish to suggest that millenarian prophecy necessarily reached its apogee during these years. Indeed, it would be fair to observe that millenarianism is a phenomenon of social protest and economic deprivation and that, because of this, historians, especially historians with an interest in class structures, have been able to find a typological side to many movements of social upheaval.[6] These movements are often specifically theological: not only are they sometimes based on the notion of regeneration and return to the simplicity of primitive Christianity, but they also draw their sustenance from a highly literal, fundamental, interpretation of apocalyptic passages in Scripture. The extensive literature on millenarianism stresses that these movements are not necessarily only Christian. The Jewish Sabbatean millenarian movement of seventeenth- and eighteenth-century Europe and Asia Minor, for instance, which derives from the acceptance of the Levantine Jew Sabbatai Ṣevi as the Messiah, flourished independently of Christian millenarianism at the same time.[7]

Apocalyptic movements, which advertise the coming of doomsday, have a figural basis as well as historical causes. The figural source is unquestionably a mystical exegetical act, whereby a popular prophet, zealous divine, or inspired layman saw fit to interpret a certain sign in the text of Scripture in terms of prophetical typology, as a type whose antitype was now imminent. The mental equipment which permitted inspired exegetes to draw such unwarranted conclusions will not be my subject in this study, for I shall be

[6] See Clarke Garrett, *Respectable Folly: Millenarians and the French Revolution in France and England*, pp. 2-6. Also important are three recent works on millenarianism: J.F.C. Harrison, *The Second Coming*, pp. 1-54; W. T. Oliver, *Prophets and Millennialists*, pp. 11-41; and Michael Adas, *Prophets of Rebellion*, pp. 99-121 (an interesting appraisal of millenarian protest movements in colonial —i.e., non-Judeo-Christian—societies).

[7] As Gershom S. Scholem points out in "The Messianic Idea in Judaism," in *The Messianic Idea in Judaism and Other Essays in Jewish Spirituality*, pp. 1-36, Jewish millenarianism goes back to the apocalyptic literature of the period of the Second Temple. See his *Sabbatai Ṣevi: The Mystical Messiah*, trans. R. J. Zwi Werblowsky (Princeton: Princeton Univ. Press, 1973), pp. 8-22 and, in general, pp. 1-102.

concerned in these pages with the figural rather than the psychological aspects of prophecy. The late George Rosen, in this context, noted that the behavior of prophets is related "to the needs of a particular situation within a given environment"; when social and other circumstances make prophetical skills desirable, people possessing these talents quite commonly appear.[8] Hence the critical political problems of Palestine in the seventh and sixth centuries B.C. heightened the frequency of prophetic utterances there in much the same way that the political uncertainties of England and France in the 1790s brought forth popular millenarian seers in greater than average numbers. These visionaries, to the established church and to most political and social thinkers, were curiosities; twentieth-century students of such phenomena might even regard some of them as deranged. Thus when Richard Brothers arrived at the door of the House of Commons in May 1792 with news of the impending apocalypse, which God had communicated to him in a private vision, the Sergeant-at-Arms refused to allow him to enter, and only one M.P., the millenarian and justly celebrated Orientalist Nathaniel Brassey Halhed, gave any credence to his appeals.[9]

But, while the establishment of church and state could ridicule millenarian thought, this very establishment combined to validate and vivify a strongly typological interpretation of the apocalyptic portions of Scripture. Richard Kidder, the second Boyle Lecturer (for 1693-94), clearly enunciated such an historical view. He noted that Jesus' own prophecies relating to later Christian history, dealing with the death of Peter and the destruction of Jerusalem, were fulfilled. Therefore, Kidder proceeded, "the *Apocalypse* contains many Predictions, a great number of which are already fulfilled, and the rest are approaching; and we doubt not, but they will, in the due Time, that is there prefixed and set down, be fulfilled also."[10] Sir Isaac Newton and Bishop Thomas Newton later take the same view. Far from being the anti-Semite that some historians have called him, Kidder actually sees the entire Jewish nation as typological of Christianity, argues that the conversion of the Jews will

[8] See *Madness in Society: Chapters in the Historical Sociology of Mental Illness* (New York: Harper & Row, 1969), p. 44 and pp. 21-70, *passim*.

[9] For thorough, recent accounts of Brothers' life and career, see Garrett, *Respectable Folly*, pp. 177-220, and Harrison, *The Second Coming*, pp. 57-85.

[10] *A Demonstration of the Messias*, in *A Defense of Natural and Revealed Religion: being a Collection of the Sermons preached at the Lecture founded by the Honourable Robert Boyle, Esq. (from the year 1691 to the year 1732)*. I, 95.

be a sure sign of the Second Coming and, to hasten this end, urges
Christians to undertake a greater study of biblical, rabbinical, and
talmudical Hebrew.[11] Other Boyle Lecturers joined Kidder in supporting the link between typological prophecy and history. George
Stanhope, whose translation of the *Imitatio Christi* was the most
widely read version of à Kempis in the century, was Lecturer for
two years (1701-02), and devoted two lengthy discourses to "The
Christian Interpretation of the Prophecies Vindicated." Stanhope
used a modified argument from design when he found it convenient: the fact that the New Testament fulfilled Old Testament
prophecies was persuasive evidence that the Millennium, when it
happened, would fulfill the prophecies of Jesus and the Book of
Revelation. The New Testament prophecies indicate that there will
be "some more glorious Demonstrations of the Power of Christ at
his second Advent, to be exhibited in the present World, but as yet
still to come."[12] Sir Isaac Newton, equally much a figure of establishment respectability, in his reading of Daniel and Revelation,
also argued for an historical meaning for the prophetical types:

> For as the few and obscure Prophecies concerning *Christ's*
> first coming were for setting up the *Christian* religion, which
> all nations have since corrupted; so the many and clear Proph-
> ecies concerning the things to be done at *Christ's* second com-
> ing, are not only for predicting but also for effecting a recovery
> and re-establishment of the long-lost truth, and setting up a
> kingdom wherein dwells righteousness. The event will prove
> the *Apocalypse*; and this Prophecy, thus proved and under-
> stood, will open the old Prophets, and all together will make
> known the true religion, and establish it. For he that will un-
> derstand the old Prophets, must begin with this; but the time
> is not yet come for understanding them perfectly, because the
> main revolution predicted in them is not yet come to pass.[13]

Elsewhere Newton argued that the mystical language of the prophecies was founded on an analogy between the natural world, as
described in Revelation, and the everyday world of human politics

[11] On Kidder's alleged anti-Semitism, see Margaret C. Jacob, *The English
Newtonians and the English Revolution, 1689-1720*, p. 166; cf. *Collection of the
Sermons preached at the Lecture founded by . . . Boyle*, I, 114-15, 148-49.

[12] *Ibid.*, I, 707; cf. I, 707-36.

[13] *Observations upon the Prophecies of Daniel, and the Apocalypse of St. John*
(London, 1733), p. 252.

and institutions. Thus the typological events shadowed forth by the prophecies must refer to antitypes that were yet to come. The Millennium, when it arrived, would be utopian, "a kingdom wherein dwells righteousness," a view which both Blake and Shelley would share. The Boyle Lecturers and Newton were deeply religious men, and their typological view of biblical prophecy found a large and sympathetic audience, although it must be acknowledged that this audience was a well-educated one, receptive to high rather than low culture. Prophecy, as George Stanhope put it, was "a light shining in a dark place," a glimmering of historical validation amidst the obscurity of Old Testament and apocalyptic style and imagery.[14] More important still, the chief impetus for the typological interpretation of scriptural prophecy comes not from millenarian sectaries and crackpot self-styled prophets, but from many orthodox Anglican writers and exegetes. The debate on scriptural prophecies in the 1720s, as I have already shown, regarded typology and prophecy as practically synonymous. The association of typology and prophecy, then, will have wide-ranging implications for various kinds of literature from the mid and later eighteenth century through the early nineteenth century. Indeed, if the scope of this book were wider than it is, I would be able to follow the broad path of typology and millenarian thought on into our own century.

The prefigurative style of prophecy will have many uses outside the theological sphere. Aided in part by the popularity of *Paradise Lost*, literary works, mainly on religious themes, will resound with typological presentations for the rest of the eighteenth century. Poems like Samuel Catherall's *An Essay on the Conflagration in blank verse* (1720), Edward Young's *The Last Day* (1713), the Seatonian prize poems of the 1750s at Cambridge (which are especially notable for the contributions of Christopher Smart), Smart's *A Song to David* (1763), Richard Cumberland's *Calvary* (1792), and translations of works like Vida's *Christiad* and the biblical epics of Bodmer and Klopstock represent only a small number of the texts which combine typology with some of the prophetic qualities of the Bible. More secular literature, from Thomson's *Seasons* and *Liberty* to Gray's *Odes*, Cowper's *Task*, some of Coleridge's few contributions to *Lyrical Ballads*, and *The Prelude*, is often colored by a prophetic, prefigurative style that owes much to the eighteenth-

[14] See *Collection of the Sermons preached at the Lecture founded by* . . . *Boyle*, I, 710.

century popularity of and fascination with typology. Prospects of
the future, like Thomson's Pisgah-sight of the future of liberty at
the conclusion to his *Liberty*, Book V (1735-36), are often secular
visions inspired by the prefigurative impulse to foreshadow the future from what we know of the present. And prospects of the past,
like Byron's evocation of the dead glories of Venice in *Childe Harold's Pilgrimage*, Canto IV (1818), frequently derive from the postfigurative vision of typology, that which makes the sorrows and sufferings of the past a grim foreshadow of present troubles. I will
discuss other examples of secular typology later in this chapter,
whose principal focus is the nexus of prophecy and prefiguration.

 2

The shape of the prefigurative style in later eighteenth- and early
nineteenth-century England is determined by several important currents in intellectual history. The first of these I have already mentioned, the debate over scriptural prophecy in the 1720s. As a result
of this lengthy controversy, biblical prophecy was established as an
accepted mode of rhetorical discourse. Solid antiquarian-historical
studies of Old Testament texts and languages, like Robert Lowth's
De Sacri Poesi Hebraeorum (1753; Eng. trans. 1787) and Sir William Jones's *A Course of Lectures on the Figurative Language of
the Holy Scripture* (1787), gave further historical justification for
the prefigurative style of Hebrew poetry. Jones also noticed the
prophetic style of Indian and Sanskrit poetry. Most influential of
all, however, in giving prophetic typology a popular basis for
everyday usage was the controversial William Warburton. *The Divine Legation of Moses Demonstrated* (1738-41) was Warburton's
most widely read theological work. Like many of his other writings,
it is primed for controversy—assertive, authoritative, argumentative. Warburton wrote to confute a generation of freethinkers and
deists who had suggested, among other heretical propositions, that
certain figural passages in the Old Testament could not be understood to refer typologically to Jesus or, in fact, to any aspects of
Christianity except in a secondary sense. In order "to shew the
Logical Truth and Propriety of *Types* in *Action*," Warburton enters upon an unusual justification of the intellectual and figural
bases of biblical typology.[15] As other students of antiquity since

---

[15] *The Divine Legation of Moses Demonstrated*, II, 626-27.

Richard Bentley and William Wotton had done, he attempts to supply an historical basis for symbolic language. His presentation is actually an early form of structural anthropology:

> In the gradual Cultivation of Speech, the Expression by *Action* was improved and refined into an ALLEGORY or *Parable*; in which the words carry a double Meaning; having, besides their obvious Sense that serves only for the Envelope, a more material and secret one. With this Figure of Speech all the moral Writings of Antiquity abound. But when it is transferred, from *civil* use into *religious*, and employed in the Writings of inspired Men, to convey Information of particular Circumstances, in two distinct Dispensations, to a People who had an equal Concern in both, it is then what we call a DOUBLE SENSE; and undergoes the very same Change of Nature with an *expressive Action* converted into a *Type*; that is, *both* the Meanings, in the *double Sense* are of *moral Import*; whereas in the *Allegory one* only is so: And this, which arises out of the very Nature of their Conversion, from *Civil* to *religious* Matters, is the only Difference between *expressive Actions* and *Types*, and between *Allegories* and *double Senses*.[16]

If we follow Warburton's definition (he does not go out of his way to make it clear), allegory is a figural equation in which the first term is clear but in which the second requires exegesis. Typology is a form of figural expression in which both terms of the equation have a double sense. Both type and antitype are obscure and require interpretation. Typology is an advanced form of figural expression, but it has arisen "in the gradual Cultivation of Speech." Thus the language of the types, for Warburton, evolved *naturally*, as a result of the nature of discourse in primitive societies. Although Warburton, like other ecclesiastical historians, thought that typology was primarily employed in religious contexts, his justification is so sweeping that it provides a reliable basis for typological expression in *any* context.

If we accept Warburton's contention that there was a *"logical Propriety"* for the existence of typology—that predictive structures are somehow inherent in patterns of human thought and expression—then it is but a short step to arguing that typology is part of

16 *Ibid.*, II, 629-30. Warburton's entire chapter on figuralism, II, 627-78, anticipates later eighteenth-century discussions of the rise and progress of language and the purposes of symbolism in primitive cultures.

the design of primitive religions, Christianity, and, indeed, secular societies. Two years before the publication of the first volume of Warburton's *Divine Legation,* Joseph Butler had already argued that the structural basis for typological imagery in pre-Christian Judaism and early Christianity was substantial. Furthermore, the "Mythological" and the "Satyrical" kinds of writing, according to Butler, were similar to scriptural prophecy in the way they shadowed forth future events; civil history was clearly analogical to the historical continuum of the Bible.[17] Butler's *Analogy* was one of the most popular theological treatises of the eighteenth century.[18] It was doubtless influential in the development of predictive and prophetic structures in theories of secular history, a process which would continue for the rest of the century. The use of the argument from design as a justification for the existence of typology received even stronger impetus from David Hartley, whose *Observations on Man,* first published in 1749, was republished in 1791, and whose writings were especially influential for English Romantic writers.

Like other Christian apologists, Hartley begins with the certainty of the Old Testament types, but he insists that there is a hidden logic in such complex structures: the design of typology is so intricate that no serious, considerate person could fail to believe them. Hartley goes even further than his predecessors in his argument from design: if God's scriptures are orderly in a predictive, typological way, then one would naturally expect an analogous order in the external world.[19] Scriptural typology, then, becomes the basis for the existence of abstracted typology or for other, analogical, predictive structures, not only in various kinds of literature and learning but in the works of Nature herself. Hartley's sweep is so broad that he prepares the way for the predictive structures of Blake, Wordsworth, Shelley, and Byron by extending typology far beyond the narrow theological sphere:

> As in the body, so in the mind, great and lasting changes are seldom wrought in a short time; and this the history of association shows to be the necessary consequence of the connection between body and mind. And yet he who made the blind to see,

[17] *The Analogy of Religion, Natural and Revealed, to the Constitution and Course of Nature,* pp. 250-56.

[18] There were more than a dozen full editions of the *Analogy* by the early nineteenth century.

[19] *Observations on Man, His Frame, His Duty, and His Expectations,* II, 160-61; cf. II, 162-66.

the lame to walk, the deaf to hear, the lepers clean, and the maimed whole, by a word, can as easily perform the analogous things, the antitypes, in the mind.[20]

Hartley continues his quest for analogies, and finds that animals and the brute creation in general function as types (a circumstance which the sacred zoologist Wolfgang Frantze had proposed on different grounds a century earlier). Secular history, for Hartley, is most typological of all, for what he saw as the wickedness of contemporary England was surely to be regarded as a prophetic type of Christ's Second Coming. We can see why Hartley, whose political sensibilities were acute, was reprinted at the time of the French Revolution. Hartley, it is also worth mentioning, theorized at great length on the typology of the Jews, whose restoration to their kingdom and conversion were widely regarded as sure signs of the Second Coming.[21] Later in the century, when the French Revolution was interpreted as a preparation for the Apocalypse, there would be further discussion of the regeneration of the Jews, a relaxation of traditional persecutions, and, in France, Napoleon would even reconvene the Sanhedrin.[22] The influence of prophetic typology on contemporary life could reach absurd lengths: in 1806 Napoleon issued a medal which, on one face, showed himself, dressed in Roman robes, receiving the tablets with the Ten Commandments from a figure who resembles Moses (see Figure 34).[23]

The situation of the Jews provides Hartley with matter for some of his most inventive use of prophetic typology, for he is convinced that the restoration of the Jews to their own land seemed to be predicted in the New Testament. He frames such questions as the following: "May not the two captivities of the *Jews*, and their two restorations, be types of the first and second death, and of the first and second resurrections?" The emphasis upon events mentioned in the Book of Revelation is highly significant, for the Book of Revelation was perhaps the most important single source of typological

[20] *Ibid.*, II, 413.

[21] *Ibid.*, II, 366-94, esp. 371, 374-75.

[22] See, for example, Henri Grégoire, *Essai sur la régénération . . . des juifs* (1789), trans. Eng. as *An Essay on the Physical, Moral, and Political Regeneration of the Jews* (London, 1791), p. 240. See also Richard H. Popkin, "La Peyrère, the Abbé Grégoire, and the Jewish Question in the Eighteenth Century," *Studies in Eighteenth-Century Culture*, 4 (1975), 209-22.

[23] For a facsimile of this coin, see Ismar Elbogen, *History of the Jews after the Fall of the State of Jerusalem* (Cincinnati, 1926), facing p. 167.

imagery and, particularly, of prophetic typology in the eighteenth century. Hartley continues his interrogatories: "Does it not appear agreeable to the whole analogy both of the word and works of God, that the *Jews* are types both of each individual in particular, on one hand, and of the whole world in general, on the other?"[24] This is sweeping prediction at its apogee. Here we must remember that the interpreters of Revelation had, for almost a century, habitually read their scriptural texts as predictive structures to signal the imminence of the storm that would soon break over the heads of the world's sinful nations, "Let no one deceive himself or others," says Hartley with assurance. "The present circumstances of the world are extraordinary and critical, beyond what has ever yet happened."[25] Hartley is simply a secular manifestation of a rich exegetical tradition: virtually every commentator on the Book of Revelation from Joseph Mede to Moses Lowman had done the same, only in more detail and with a greater wealth of documentation.

The idea of the apocalypse is the second major current in intellectual history that affected the course of prefigurative structures in late eighteenth- and early nineteenth-century literature. The types of the Old Testament apply, with few exceptions, to antitypes in the New. But the predictions of the Book of Revelation are different, for they transfer and transform traditional biblical typology from the religious to the secular sphere. The types of the Apocalypse can only refer to antitypes in history *since the writing of that book*. By the time of William Whiston's important *Essay on the Revelation of Saint John* (1706), the exegetes have universally agreed that Revelation is mainly a symbolical, predictive narration, a typological narrative, or a series of types whose antitypes can be located in the events of secular history since St. John or which are yet to be fulfilled.[26] The numerology of Revelation is also serviceable to the exegetes, for it permits them to fix, with an appearance of certainty, the date of the Second Coming and, in some cases, the country or

24 *Observations on Man*, II, 374-75.

25 *Ibid.*, II, 455.

26 See Whiston, *An Essay upon the Revelation of Saint John, so far as concerns the Past and Present Times* (Cambridge, 1706), pp. 30, 213, 228-33, 256-57.

countries most severely to be chastised. Whiston, in his 1706 *Essay*, proclaimed 1716 as the date of the Millennium; in his Boyle Lectures the next year, *The Accomplishment of Scripture Prophecies* (1708), his millenarianism is just as definite. In his post-1716 millenarian writings, he abandoned his earlier dating.[27] The German Pietist, Johann Albrecht Bengel, at mid-century, worked out exact chronological tables for all the predictions in Revelation, showing that the destruction of the beast was set for Sunday, 18 June 1836.[28] Moses Lowman, the most detailed historical exegete, intersperses his commentary with references to secular historians, both ancient and contemporary, for he is eager to establish what he calls "a Plan of Prophecy, and Order of History."[29] Chronology is vital for the exegetes: some find that the Second Coming will occur around 1800, others favor the more symbolical year 2000.

Anglican exegetes are more reserved in their typological readings of Revelation than are members of the various Nonconformist sects, who are often committed millenarians and who are always enthusiastic in their predictions.[30] But for Anglicans and Puritans alike, the interpretation of large portions of Revelation is historical. The ominous figural signs point directly to the Antichrist and, indeed, whenever the beast from the sea or the many-headed monster comes up, we are in for a thorough pasting of paganism and popery.[31] "This Beast was a *Pagano-Christian Beast*, and a *persecuting one*; because he spake and acted like a *Dragon*, the *Type of Paganism*

[27] See Jacob, *The English Newtonians and the English Revolution*, pp. 131-33.

[28] See J. A. Bengelius, *Bengelius's Introduction to his Exposition of the Apocalypse*, trans. John Robertson (London, 1757), pp. 236-51.

[29] Moses Lowman, *A Paraphrase and Notes on the Revelation of St. John* (London, 1737), pp. xii, xxiii, xxix-xxxiv.

[30] C. John Sommerville, *Popular Religion in Restoration England* (Gainesville, Fla.: Univ. Presses of Florida, 1977), attempts a statistical survey of the frequency with which various themes are mentioned in religious works from 1660 to 1711; references to the Second Coming and the Millennium in Dissenting works are more than twice as frequent as such references in Anglican works (see pp. 148-49). The author calls his categories "typologies" throughout the work with no figural intentions (see pp. 15-19); see also his "Religious Typologies and Popular Religion in Restoration England," *Church History*, 45 (1976), 32-41.

[31] On seventeenth-century views of the Antichrist, see Christopher Hill, *Antichrist in Seventeenth-Century England* (London: Oxford Univ. Press, 1971), *passim*; *The World Turned Upside Down: Radical Ideas during the English Revolution*, pp. 114-18; and *Change and Continuity in Seventeenth-Century England* (Cambridge, Mass.: Harvard Univ. Press, 1975), pp. 60, 70-71.

and Persecution," writes one anonymous commentator (obviously a Nonconformist of some stripe) in 1693.[32] Benjamin Keach, following a view that derives from Reformation commentary, has no doubts whatsoever that Rome and the Roman Catholic Church are the true antitypes of the persecutions carried out by *"literal Babylon"*; he is unquestionably among the most inventive of typologists, as he had abundantly demonstrated in his *Tropologia* (1681).[33] Perhaps the most frequently cited of the seventeenth-century apocalyptical typologists, however, is not English at all. He is the French ecclesiastic Pierre Jurieu, whose strongly typological reading of the Book of Revelation appeared, "Faithfully Englished," in 1687. Not only does Jurieu see much traditional typology in Revelation ("persons and actions *typical* of the good"), but he makes the helpful distinction of types of evil. *"Cain* was a *type* of the enemies of *Jesus Christ* coming of the seed of woman, he was a *type* of the seed of the Serpent; and his action against his brother was a *typical* sin, that representeth the persecution, which the Devil was to bring upon Jesus Christ and his Church."[34] Jurieu is more successful than any of his contemporaries in demonstrating that the types of Revelation foreshadowed contemporary European history and, since he focuses mainly on France as a particularly odious antitype, English writers in the 1790s would cite him frequently as one who had predicted the apocalyptic events of the French Revolution. With Jurieu as evidence, it is a relatively modest matter for contemporary theologians to conclude that the French Revolution itself is one of the antitypes forecast by the Book of Revelation.

The biblical prophecies, then, were widely regarded in a double sense: not only did exegetes and men of letters consider them true in the theological sphere, but many prominent theologians and literary men thought that the prophecies, especially those in the Book of Revelation, applied equally well to secular history, both past and present. Throughout the later eighteenth century, commentators

[32] *The Book of Revelation Paraphrased* (London, 1693), p. 290.

[33] See Keach, *Antichrist Stormed: or, Mystery Babylon the great Whore and great City, proved to be the present Church of Rome*, pp. 103-16. The alliance of popery and treason was hardly new, as John Miller demonstrates in his *Popery and Politics in England, 1660-1688* (Cambridge:University Press, 1973), pp. 67-90.

[34] Pierre Jurieu, *The Accomplishment of the Scripture Prophecies or the Approaching Deliverance of the Church* (London, 1687), Part I, pp. 233-34. See also Part II, pp. 245, 251-70. Jurieu deals with the typological relationship between ideas and language, between the sensible and the intelligible world (Part II, p. 331).

on Revelation echoed the conclusions of Mede, Keach, Jurieu, Whiston, Lowman, and almost a score of other divines. The old seventeenth-century pastime of drawing parallels between scriptural history and contemporary times, which flourished whenever times were bad, is succeeded, in the eighteenth century, by a new typological game. During times of instability—which means whenever street violence, governmental corruption, war and famine, immorality and dissolution, rose above their normal levels—eighteenth-century clerical and secular writers were fond of pointing out that the present days shadowed forth the Millennium. This imagistic tendency was by no means confined to the decade immediately following the French Revolution: important occasions like the American Revolution, or important books like Gibbon's *Decline and Fall of the Roman Empire*, provided an opportunity for an occasional person to make the expected association.[35]

Typology flourishes in another area of eighteenth-century thought which is of significance to the events of the period from 1790 to 1820: antiquarian mythology. In the last half of the eighteenth century, as we have seen, mythologists who focus on the mysteries of Eastern religions frequently suggest that ancient rites are in some way predictive of Christianity. Following Hartley, the syncretist Jacob Bryant, in a number of learned works, proposes that ancient Egyptian or Near Eastern religions and myths relate to the Hebrew and Christian Scriptures. Bryant is often extravagant, but, at his best, his notions of abstracted typology are splendidly broad, in a Blakean or Shelleyan sense. For example, in his study of the plagues of the Egyptians, Bryant presents an interpretation of the healing of Moses' leprous hand (Exod. 4.6-7): "From hence I should judge, that these miraculous representations had a covert meaning: and that they did not relate to the Israelites only and their deliverance from bondage: but to the redemption of the whole world; and to the means by which it is to be effected."[36] It is a small step from

[35] On the American Revolution, see Richard Price, *Observations on the Importance of the American Revolution* (London, 1784), pp. 5, 7, 27; on Gibbon's *Decline and Fall*, which provoked an outburst of theological refutations, see East Apthorp, *Letters on the Prevalence of Christianity before its Civil Establishment, with Observations on a late History of the Decline of the Roman Empire* (London, 1778), pp. 36-37. Apthorp rejects any suggestion that biblical prophecy might not be accurate.

[36] See *Observations upon the Plagues Inflicted upon the Egyptians* (London, 1794), p. 245. In general, pp. 193-306, on the divine appointment of Moses, are a broad defense of abstracted and prophetic typology.

Bryant and George Stanley Faber, another student of pre-Christian religions, to the universal historiography of Condorcet, who stresses, again as Hartley had done, the typological basis of human language, actions, and history. Once man has learned, Condorcet argues, the philosophical bases of the past, it is a simple matter to predict the future:

> If man can predict, almost with certainty, those appearances of which he understands the laws; if, even when the laws are unknown to him, experience of the past enables him to foresee, with considerable probability, future appearances; why should we suppose it a chimerical undertaking to delineate, with some degree of truth, the picture of the future destiny of mankind from the results of history?[37]

The past, for writers like Condorcet, becomes a pattern of types whose antitypes are either to be seen in history since the types, or which are yet to happen.

The message that came down to commentators on the French Revolution, then, was clear. In theological terms, the events in France had been predicted by Old and New Testament prophecies; in secular terms, history was to be seen as a series of predictive structures; and in figural terms, the prophetic types of Scripture were now having or about to have their long-awaited antitypes. In each of these conceptualizations abstracted typology is at work. The interpreters of the French Revolution, whether secular or clerical, found in the cataclysmic events across the Channel a series of unmistakable signs. The prophecies of Revelation were being realized: a new age was about to commence.[38] Among the clergymen were such as Mark Wilks, who declared that "Jesus Christ was a Revolutionist," a shadowy type of those who were bringing about present-day reformations; Richard Price, who thought that the events in France would lead to "the dominion of reason and conscience" in Great Britain; and Elhanan Winchester, author of a commentary on Revelation, who wrote a poem called *The Process and Empire of Christ* (1793) in pseudo-Miltonic blank verse stress-

[37] *Outlines of a Historical View of the Progress of the Human Mind* (London, 1795), p. 316.
[38] Meyer H. Abrams, "English Romanticism: The Spirit of the Age," in *Romanticism Reconsidered: Selected Papers from the English Institute*, ed. Northrop Frye (New York: Columbia Univ. Press, 1963), pp. 26-72, esp. pp. 30-37, discusses the spirit of the 1790s in interesting detail.

ing apocalyptic typologies and suggesting that Jesus prefigured modern innovators.[39] James Bicheno was more conventional, confining his predictions to the overthrow of the Pope, the end of despotism, the restoration of the Jews, and "the restoration of all things."[40] Bicheno was sometimes given to enthusiastic millenarianism. One of his later books, *The Probable Progress and Issue of the Commotions which have agitated Europe since the French Revolution* (1797), was a typological treatment of the 1790s, with the Book of Revelation serving as the typological text and the present as the antitype.[41] And Bicheno's millenarianism was moderate compared to that of Joseph Priestley, who quoted liberally from the typological fancies of David Hartley's *Observations on Man*, and urged politicians to heed the signs of calamity.

Finally, to complete this catalogue of figural adventurers, I must mention Richard Brothers, the demented chiliastic visionary. His whole work is an extended Pisgah-sight, his speech a prefigurative-postfigurative garbling of the Book of Revelation. Brothers does not deserve to be neglected, but he demonstrates that the ultimate stage of prophetic typology, as Swift had hinted a century before in *A Tale of a Tub*, is madness. Brothers writes with the confidence of infallible inspiration. "On the second day of the first month, being deeply engaged in pondering on the state of the sublunary world, and the nations thereof, as walking in the fields, I insensibly bent my course towards a high hill . . . [where, at its summit] lo, and behold! I had a Vision of the Most High God, who appeared to me face to face, as a man to his friend—(as to Moses)."[42] In the ensuing

39 See Mark Wilks, *The Origin & Stability of the French Revolution* ([London], 1791), p. 5; Richard Price, *A Discourse on the Love of Our Country* (London, 1789), pp. 49-50; and Elhanan Winchester, *The Process and Empire of Christ* (London, 1793), pp. 136-37. See also Winchester's *The Three Woe Trumpets*, 2nd ed. (London, 1793), pp. 33, 35, 43, for the argument that the French Revolution fulfilled the prophecies of Revelation.

40 *The Signs of the Times: or the Overthrow of the Papal Tyranny in France, the Prelude of Destruction to Popery and Despotism; but of Peace to Mankind* (London, 1793), Sig [π] 4ʳ. The restoration of the Jews was a popular notion; cf. note 22, above.

41 *The Present State of Europe compared with Ancient Prophecies* (London, 1794), pp. 18, 20-21, 27, 31-33, 35-44.

42 See Brothers's *Prophecy of all the remarkable and Wonderful Events which will come to pass in the present year* (London, [n.d., but c. 1794]), pp. 3, 4-8, and *passim*, and *A Revealed Knowledge of the Prophecies and Times* (London, 1794), pp. 45, 47, 67, etc. On Brothers, see also Morton D. Paley, "William

dialogue, God predicts all sorts of apocalyptic events to Brothers—famine, pestilence, earthquakes, and the like—and helpfully pinpoints forthcoming political crises in France, Italy, Spain, Portugal, Turkey, and Russia. When it suits his purposes, Brothers brings his prophecies closer to home. In one of his works, he has a vision of "Satan walking leisurely into London . . . he was dressed in White and Scarlet Robes" (rather like a fashionable rake off for an evening at a West End gambling club). In this work, he sees the spiritual Babylon of Revelation 17 as London rather than as the more traditional Rome. The vehemence of Brothers's popular prophecies accords well with the turmoil of the 1790s, but I should emphasize that the substance of his typology had appeared in less enthusiastic contexts over the previous century in writings on the Apocalypse.

A rare verse example is Samuel Catherall's Miltonic *An Essay on the Conflagration* (1720). Catherall writes of the Last Judgment as an accomplishment of all the types of the Bible, and offers many examples of how the entire creation, in its final hours, becomes a type of Hell. Catherall's purpose is similar to that of the popular prophets: his poem is meant to warn the audience that the time for conversion is now. In the second of his two books, a disembodied voice in a dream warns the author that his "Vision lofty, and Prophetick" is a high call to obedience to God's commandments. Catherall replies,

> O Vision bless'd,
> To me vouchsafe'd by Heav'n! a Type so true
> Exhibiting of *Future Judgment*! Sent,
> No doubt, to warn *Me* of my *Grand Concern*
> By strongest Motives: representing Hell
> To me, if disobedient found, but Heav'n,
> And all it's Glory, if faithfull to the End.[43]

Blake, the Prince of the Hebrews, and the Woman Clothed with the Sun," in *William Blake: Essays in Honour of Sir Geoffrey Keynes*, ed. Morton D. Paley and Michael Phillips (Oxford: Clarendon Press, 1973), pp. 260-93. This predictive style has become a staple of Christian fundamentalism, of which many inspirational examples might be cited. An especially interesting specimen is a curious octavo entitled *The Doom of Britain. A Divine Warning. The German Conquest of England Foretold in the Scriptures* (London, 1911), an anonymous effort whose author treats events in Revelation as types of conquest by the Kaiser.

[43] See *An Essay on the Conflagration in blank verse* (Oxford, 1720), p. 61; cf. pp. 52-53, 58-60.

Many other writers associate millennial prophecies with urgent calls for conversion; what is unique, of course, about the texts of the 1790s is the political atmosphere in which they exist. Catherall calls for personal repentance; Brothers reaches out to embrace whole kingdoms, and he confidently predicts that the monarchies of Europe will fall by 1798.

The politicizing of prophetic typology was not carried on without dissent, although the dissenters were few and scattered. The most eminent of them was Edmund Burke, who mocked the prefigurative style of Richard Price and generally ridiculed typological millenarianism (see Figure 22). He recognized with great clarity how easy it was for an inspired preacher to parallel a contemporary event with the Book of Revelation and then to assure a credulous audience that the same event was a precursor of the Millennium or the Fifth Monarchy. Burke describes the capture of Louis XVI and Marie Antoinette in gory detail, and criticizes the dissenting ministers whose sermons have praised the event:

> —These Theban and Thracian Orgies, acted in France, and applauded only in the Old Jewry [where Richard Price preached], I assure you, kindle prophetic enthusiasm in the minds but of very few people in this kingdom, although a saint and apostle, who may have revelations of his own, and who has so completely vanquished all the mean superstitions of his heart, may incline to think it pious and decorous to compare it with the entrance into the world of the Prince of Peace, proclaimed in a holy temple by a venerable sage, and not long before not worse announced by the voice of angels to the quiet innocence of shepherds.[44]

Prophetic typology, then, could lead to dangerous excesses in civil order, and it was precisely this misdirected millenarian zeal which members of England's political establishment most feared.

Thomas Paine also ridiculed typological excess. Like a few others, he revived an earlier deism in arguing that the style of Hebrew

[44] See *Reflections on the Revolution in France* (London, 1790), p. 107; cf. pp. 96, 97-98, 108.

prophetical poetry had been misunderstood (a view for which Lowth had provided a basis in fact) and twisted by modern expounders, by the "whimsical conceits of sectaries." To these distorters, "Every thing unintelligible was prophetical, and every thing insignificant was typical. A blunder would have served for a prophecy; and a dish clout for a type."[45] Burke's contemptuous view of Price's typologizing was part of his strongly conservative reaction to Price's sermon, *A Discourse on the Love of Our Country* (1789), the work which was the immediate catalyst of *Reflections on the Revolution in France*. But Paine was himself a revolutionary whose criticism of prefigurative fancies sprang from an effort to vindicate himself of the charge of atheism. Thus he presented himself as a theist who finds typology acceptable enough in poetical fictions but inappropriate when it becomes a basis for political thought or action. Paine's rejection of typological figuralism was similar to the criticism of biblical prophecy by the English deists in the 1720s in one interesting way. Once again, opposition to typology did nothing whatever to diminish its prevalence in religious discourses or, for that matter, in other imaginative literature. Paradoxically, criticism of this sort tended to *solidify* the position of prefigurative imagery. If it was permissible for the ancient Hebrew poets to employ typology because it was a traditional form of discourse for them, then could not contemporary writers do the same?

The typological design of the years 1789-1805, then, comprised several genres of literature and several styles within those genres. We see the strict, almost teleological millenarianism of self-anointed prophets like Brothers and Joanna Southcott, the prophetic apocalypticism of divines like Price, Wilks, and Winchester, with the antitypes always near at hand, and, thanks to the skepticism of writers on both flanks of contemporary politics like Burke and Paine, we see too the further evolution of what I have called *natural typology*. The theological opponents of the eighteenth-century Deists, Warburton, Hartley, and a decent-sized phalanx of other worthies, had urged that typology was basically logical, inherent within the structure of the religious systems that preceded Christianity, and therefore all but canonical. In the 1790s, this developmental argument is resurrected by such poets and scholars interested in the origins of religions as Charles Dupuis, C.F.D. de Volney, and Blake. The Comte de Volney's *Ruines* (1791), translated into English during the 1790s, may be taken as representative:

[45] *The Age of Reason*, p. 53.

Now, if you take a retrospect of the whole history of the spirit of religion, you will find, that in its origin it had no other author [than] the sensations and wants of man: that the idea of God had no other type, no other model, than that of physical powers, material existences, operating good or evil, by impressions of pleasure or pain on sensible beings. You will find that in the formation of every system this spirit of religion pursued the same track, and was uniform in its proceedings; that in all, that dogma never failed to represent, under the name of God, the operations of nature, and the passions and prejudices of men.[46]

The basis of typology is natural and, indeed, universal: de Volney indicates that there is a basis for prefigurative structures in *all* religions and in *all* cultures. The discovery that typology is a structural component of the way men build systems of religious belief may explain the casualness with which Romantic poets employ it.

Blake, as we know, was well acquainted with biblical and prophetic typology, both literary and iconographical. Swedenborg and Mosheim, whom he read closely, use typological expositions in a standard theological way; Jacob Bryant and Jakob Boehme, by whom Blake was profoundly influenced, are among the most proficient typological innovators since Nicholas of Lyra.[47] He knew Spenser and Milton well and was acquainted with traditions of visual typology in eighteenth-century illustration and illumination, and, to a limited extent, introduced typological scenes (highly telescoped, as they must always be in any visual art less ambitious than a large altarpiece) into his own engravings.[48] Yet his presentations of typology in his poems are seldom accompanied by the external ritual of signs that had been popular earlier in the eighteenth century, and even as recently as the 1770s in Christopher Smart's

[46] See C.F.C. de Volney, *The Ruins, or a Survey of the Revolutions of Empires* (London, [1795]), p. 296. De Volney regularly employs typology to demonstrate how primitive tribes applied euhemerism.

[47] See, for example, Ruthven Todd, *Tracks in the Snow: Studies in English Science and Art* (London, 1946), pp. 29-55 ("William Blake and the Eighteenth-Century Mythologists"); and Desirée Hirst, *Hidden Riches: Traditional Symbolism from the Renaissance to Blake*, esp. Chaps. IV, VII, VIII, and IX, for the mystical background with which typology has often been associated.

[48] Wittreich, *Angel of Apocalypse*, pp. 109-13, indicates some of Blake's acquaintance with typological iconography. For the visual perspective of several religions merged into one typological scene, see Figure 16.

poetry. Blake mentions *types* infrequently, but so pervasive is his effort to explain the hidden meanings of the biblical myths that he introduces the traditional typological characters of the Old Testament—Adam, Moses, David—on many occasions with clear prefigurative import. In his *Description of a Vision of the Last Judgement* (1808), for example, the kneeling figures of Adam and Eve, Abraham and Moses are types of the Throne of Christ, as is everything else in this design.[49] The typological structures of *The Everlasting Gospel* (1818) appear throughout, in every question and every answer, indicating that Jesus was the fulfillment of earlier prophecies.

One of the rare occasions when Blake actually mentions typology, in the "To the Public" before *Jerusalem*, is complicated, practically Miltonic in its promise of didactic accomplishments:

> Therefore I print, nor vain my types shall be:
> Heaven, Earth & Hell henceforth shall live in harmony.[50]

Blake's "types" are, of course, his works, which he images forth as prefigurations of the eternal, universal harmony which is the ultimate goal of *Jerusalem*. Everything in this world is, or should be, "some Mental pursuit for the Building up of Jerusalem," the heavenly Jerusalem toward which everything in the poem seems to lead. Blake's message "To the Christians" (Pl. 77), a more specialized subgroup within the "Public" he first addressed, is an excellent instance of natural typology: "I know of no other Christianity and of no other Gospel than the liberty both of body & mind to exercise the Divine Arts of Imagination, Imagination, the real & eternal World *of which this Vegetable Universe is but a faint shadow*, & in which we shall live in our Eternal or Imaginative Bodies when these Vegetable Mortal bodies are no more."[51] This notion emanates originally from Boehme, but the belief that quotidian things in some unexplained way foreshadow an eternity is traditionally part of meditative Christianity. More inventive is the cry of Los, later in *Jerusalem*:

> "But General Forms have their vitality in Particulars, & every
> "Particular is a Man, a Divine Member of the Divine Jesus."[52]

---

[49] *Complete Writings*, p. 443.   [50] *Ibid.*, p. 621.
[51] *Ibid.*, pp. 716-17 (italics added).
[52] *Ibid.*, p. 738 (Plate 91.30-31).

The sweeping generality of Blake's typological equation testifies to the central position that prefigurative structures occupy in his poetry. In *Jerusalem*, Blake becomes St. John of Lambeth: his vision of the Apocalypse stresses not so much the Last Judgment as it does the New Jerusalem. His typological prophecies therefore emphasize antitypes rather than types, the accomplishment of prophecies rather than their foreshadowings. When the figure of the Saviour speaks of Jesus, he refers to the risen lord, not the typological martyr on the cross: "We call Jesus the Christ; and he in us, and we in him / Live in perfect harmony in Eden, the land of life."[53]

The importance of prophetic typology for Blake is therefore enormous, but his figural system is less self-consciously literary than the typologies of other eighteenth- and early nineteenth-century writers. His types, when they occur (and they are pervasive in his major prophecies), resemble the silent iconographical systems of painters and other graphic artists. Blake's address "To the Jews," for example, which forms Plates 26 and 27 of *Jerusalem*, is a heraldic annunciation to God's chosen people, informing them that the lamb of God has returned to Albion and urging them to fulfill their historical destiny:

> If Humility is Christianity, you, O Jews, are the true Christians. If your tradition that Man contained in his Limbs all Animals is True, & they were separated from him by cruel Sacrifices, and when compulsory cruel Sacrifices had brought Humanity into a Feminine Tabernacle in the loins of Abraham & David, the Lamb of God, the Saviour became apparent on Earth as the Prophets had foretold, The Return of Israel is a Return to Mental Sacrifice & War. Take up the Cross, O Israel, & follow Jesus.[54]

Both the prophesied Jesus and the risen Christ appear throughout *Jerusalem*, from the epigraph on the first page (John 8.9) to the Christ-Jehovah figure in the final plate. In his message to the Jews, Blake's pictorial presentation suggests that the Old Testament types (here Abraham and David) and the sacrifices associated with them prefigure the millennial events which now have come to pass. Like Hartley, Blake sees the Jewish people as typological of Christianity, but he treats them as an antitype as well—the Jews "are the true

[53] *Ibid.*, p. 665 (Plate 38.20-21).

[54] *Ibid.*, p. 652; cf. *The Poetry and Prose of William Blake*, ed. David V. Erdman and Harold Bloom (New York: Doubleday & Co., 1965), p. 850.

Christians," the prophecies have been accomplished, and they can now "Take up the Cross" with safety.

"To the Jews" concludes the first chapter of *Jerusalem*. A companion section, "To the Deists" (Pl. 52), finishes the second chapter. Just as "To the Jews" mentions Abraham and David and "the compulsory cruel Sacrifices" of the Jews, by which Blake probably means the sacrifice of Isaac as typological of the Crucifixion, so "To the Deists" acts out the antitype, the martyrdom of Jesus itself. The Deists of history—Locke, Newton, Voltaire, Rousseau, Gibbon, and their ilk—are the Pharisees and hypocrites responsible for human suffering: "Those who Martyr others or who cause War are Deists, but never can be Forgivers of Sin." Even more emphatic is Blake's quatrain on the symbolism of martyrdom:

> For a Tear is an Intellectual thing,
> And a Sigh is the Sword of an Angel King
> And the bitter groan of a Martyr's woe
> Is an Arrow from the Almightie's Bow.[55]

The martyr's sighs and the Almighty's arrow are part of Blake's own typology, which goes beyond tradition at times. He is fond of uniting type and antitype in the same text: Jews as Christians, Isaac as Jesus, Abraham's sacrifice of his son as the Crucifixion. Other poets allude to these figures as types alone; Blake is considerably more inventive. Thomas Zouch, for instance, in *The Crucifixion* (1765), gives a more traditional presentation:

> On Revelation's sacred page intent
> The eye of faith surveys the mighty deed
> Shadow'd in mystic type, when Abram urg'd
> By heaven's all-wise behest, with eager zeal
> Snatched from a mother's weeping care the child
> Of laughter, on Moriah's secret top
> Binding the spotless hands of innocence.[56]

Blake's friend, Richard Cumberland, in *Calvary* (1792), makes the same typological point.[57] Plate 76 of *Jerusalem*, however, is a dra-

---

[55] *Complete Writings*, p. 683 (Plate 52.25-28).

[56] See *Musae Seatonianae. A Complete Collection of the Cambridge Prize Poems, from their first institution . . . in 1750, to the Present Time* (London, 1773), p. 229.

[57] See *Calvary; or The Death of Christ. A Poem, in Eight Books* (London, 1792), p. 203: "Now God by the' off'ring of his only Son / The type of Abraham's sacrifice fulfill'd." On Blake and the Crucifixion, see Jean H. Hagstrum,

matic representation of the Crucifixion; Blake follows it with his final address, "To the Christians" (Plate 77), an explicit statement of the typological properties of the true Christian life. All the types are but "the end of a golden string" which, rolled up, will lead the Christian pilgrim "in at Heaven's gate / Built in Jerusalem's wall."[58] In Blake's uniquely harmonious vision, prefigurations and accomplishments are all but synonymous. We have seen prophetic types until now as traditional foreshadowings. But *Jerusalem* as a poem is typological and descriptive of the Millennium simultaneously. The innovations of Blake, which result from a careful study and reworking of the old millenarian traditions of prophetic typology, show why this ancient figural system has endured so long— it can constantly be reworked into new forms.

As I noted in the previous chapter, Blake's prophecies coincide with a great flood of popular prophetic energy in England, a tide which was to continue almost undiminished for the first half of the nineteenth century. Two of the leading voices of Blake's era are those of Richard Brothers and Joanna Southcott, the "Nephew of the Almighty" and "The Woman Clothed with the Sun." The contemporary audience for the small editions of Blake's prophetic works was obviously miniscule, whereas the cheap pamphlets of the popular prophets poured forth from London's presses by the dozens and in thousands of copies. Blake, who excites many readers today, agitated few in the 1790s; Brothers, whose printed works have all but disappeared today, gained much public attention and even attracted the notice of the government. In early 1795, the government had Brothers arrested; a committee of the Privy Council examined him; he was found to be insane; and he passed the next eleven years in a private insane asylum.[59] Blake escaped such notoriety and such bitter treatment from the establishment, but his links with the popular prophets are nevertheless very close. He was not actually a follower of Brothers or Southcott, but he certainly did read some of their tracts; like them, he interprets the Bible as a series of types and shadows vouchsafed to the original authors in visions. Blake's own system of scriptural exegesis is likewise visionary. The popular prophets borrowed an important portion of their doctrine from

---

William Blake, Poet and Painter: An Introduction to the Illuminated Verse (Chicago: Univ. of Chicago Press, 1964), pp. 116-17.

[58] Blake's design for this page, as if to emphasize the pilgrimage of life, shows a child following the golden string and rolling it into a ball.

[59] See Harrison, *The Second Coming*, p. 60.

seventeenth-century Puritanism and millenarian prophecy, the view
that many of the most important types of the Old Testament and
the Book of Revelation referred to antitypes in present-day England. But they carried this point further than their millenarian
predecessors had done. For the prophets of the 1790s, it was not
enough to say that Israel *foreshadowed* England; Israel *was* England,
and the English were the Jews of Old Testament times mysteriously
transplanted. Brothers's schemes amount to an "Israelization" of
England in which the New Jerusalem was to be a reconstructed
version of London, for which he produced lengthy and detailed
architectural specifications. The notion of London as Jerusalem
seems curious today, yet as recently as 1970 the National Theatre
presented a musical pageant derived from the writings of Blake
entitled *Tyger, Tyger* in the second act of which the entire cast, as
I remember, constructed a very London-like Golgonooza on stage,
while softly chanting, "For every thing that lives is holy."

Blake subscribed to views like those of Brothers and Southcott
with regard to the Israel-England identification; he describes them
in his chief piece of prose theory on his system of scriptural exegesis.
This work is his remarkable *A Descriptive Catalogue of Pictures,
Poetical and Historical Inventions, Painted by William Blake in
Water Colours* . . . (1809), the exhibition catalogue for a showing
of his graphic works in London from May to September 1809. The
exhibition consisted of sixteen works for which the catalogue provides descriptions, a few very brief, a handful very long. Here, in the
prose gloss for his watercolor of "The Ancient Britons," Blake
announces his ideas of British antiquities:

> The antiquities of every Nation under Heaven, is no less
> sacred than that of the Jews. *They are the same thing*, as Jacob
> Bryant and all antiquaries have proved. How other antiquities
> came to be neglected and disbelieved, while those of the Jews
> are collected and arranged, is an enquiry worthy both of the
> Antiquarian and the Divine. All had originally one language,
> and one religion: this was the religion of Jesus, the everlasting
> Gospel. Antiquity preaches the Gospel of Jesus. . . .[60]

The efforts of Bryant in *A New System* had to do with tracing
Christian origins and seeking shadows of Christianity in pagan religious belief. Nowhere does Bryant arrive at the inspired conclusions

[60] *Complete Writings*, pp. 578-79 (italics added).

which Blake attributes to him, although he devoted most of his long career to the quest for correspondences which might lead to such a conclusion. Bryant's types, then, are true. Blake follows another idea of the popular prophets, namely that during the ancient, post-Babel dispersion of tribes and confusion of tongues certain pagan nations migrated to England, and that later they were followed by some of the twelve tribes of Israel.

Hence he writes with assurance, "Adam was a Druid, and Noah; also Abraham was called to succeed the Druidical age, which began to turn allegoric and mental signification into corporeal command."[61] If the patriarchs were ancient British figures, whose names the confusion of tongues had altered, then it follows, logically enough, that we can find still closer Israel-England correspondences. Blake accordingly presents them in *Jerusalem*, which he wrote and engraved during the years when he was preparing his exhibition. The counties of England, Wales, and Scotland, according to Blake's account, are assigned "Gates" named after the twelve tribes of Israel, thus carrying Old Testament typology specifically into Great Britain.[62] The types of the Bible enter into London itself: "I behold Babylon in the opening Streets of London. I behold / Jerusalem in ruins wandering about from house to house."[63] Blake would say elsewhere that Jerusalem was an emanation of the Giant Albion, England, almost as if, for him, types and antitypes were the same thing simultaneously. The "Preface" to *Milton* (1804) had already asked, rhetorically,

> And did those feet in ancient time
> Walk upon England's mountains green?
> And was the holy Lamb of God
> On England's pleasant pastures seen?

> And did the Countenance Divine
> Shine forth upon our clouded hills?
> And was Jerusalem builded here
> Among these dark Satanic Mills?[64]

Blake answers in the affirmative: England was the location of Eden, of Israel, of Jerusalem, the place where the Old Testament types took place, foreshadowed, and were accomplished in the person of

[61] *Ibid.*, p. 578.
[62] *Jerusalem*, Plate 16 (*Complete Writings*, pp. 637-38).
[63] *Ibid.*, p. 714 (74.16-17).   [64] *Ibid.*, pp. 480-81.

Jesus. In Blake's scriptural exegesis, then, the Bible is a text about Albion just as the pre-Christian mysteries led to and actually took place in England (for another visual representation of the New Jerusalem, see Figure 15).

The longest discussion in the *Descriptive Catalogue* is devoted to the watercolor of "Sir Jeffrey Chaucer and the nine and twenty Pilgrims on their journey to Canterbury," which includes a striking analysis of character:

> The characters of Chaucer's Pilgrims are the characters which compose all ages and nations: as one age falls, another rises, different to moral sight, but to immortals only the same; for we see the same characters repeated again and again, in animals, vegetables, minerals, and in men; nothing new occurs in identical existence; Accident ever varies, Substance can never suffer change or delay.[65]

Chaucer's characters, however, are not merely universals, they are predictive figures with typological qualities for, shortly afterwards, Blake anatomizes the pilgrims one by one and finds that Chaucer has derived many of his people from figures in ancient mythology such as Bacchus, Silenus, Aescupalius, and Hercules. Alexander Ross had long ago revealed the typological aspects of virtually all of the members of the Greek Pantheon, and now Blake, recalling that tradition, concludes that "Chaucer's characters live age after age. Every age is a Canterbury Pilgrimage." Just as he sees all religions deriving from one original, Blake sees all human characters emanating from one universal or one group of universals whose types and antitypes appear again and again. The Chaucerian characters which derive from ancient mythology are, in fact, visions of eternal attributes or divine names, but all characters may be unified into one universal, "for when separated from man or humanity, who is Jesus the Saviour, the vine of eternity, they are thieves and rebels, they are destroyers."[66] I know of no other student of character between 1650 and 1820 who so successfully states the typology of character as Blake does here—all characters are united in the human breast, all characters are one. Hence different *characters* are both postfigurations of emanations from that One as well as prefigurations of that One into which all will blend again at last. The millennial pronouncement in the last plate of *The Marriage of*

[65] *Ibid.*, p. 567. [66] *Ibid.*, p. 571.

Heaven and Hell, "EMPIRE IS NO MORE! AND NOW THE LION & WOLF SHALL CEASE," states effectively for the animal creation what Blake has presented for humanity in his reading of Chaucer. At the Millennium, all human differences will disappear; there will be both a universal raising and a universal leveling, not merely of social disparities but equally of variations in personality. Every age is a Canterbury Pilgrimage written in a different kind of cipher; the language of the types, for Blake, is the key for decoding people as well as for interpreting texts and religions.

Blake's methods of exegesis blend together in *Milton* (1804-08), his great prophecy on the intellectual's role in public life, the influence of Milton on his own writings, and the coming of the end of days. When Blake started *Milton*, he was living away from London at Felpham, a Sussex coastal village, and here an event which links him with Richard Brothers took place. In 1803, a soldier named John Schofield had an argument with Blake and, in the course of the dispute, had him charged with sedition, a most serious charge at the height of the Napoleonic Wars. Blake was actually tried for the charge and, with the aid of his friend and patron William Hayley, was acquitted in January 1804.[67] So Blake, unlike Brothers, escaped imprisonment, but he must have noted the analogy between his own fortunes and those of the popular prophet. Furthermore, Milton, after the Restoration, was thought to have escaped the persecutions of the Royalists only through the intervention of Marvell. The historical Milton was one of the eternal character types with whom Blake identified himself, but he was aware that Milton, after supporting liberty against tyranny in his republican prose writings, had upheld religious orthodoxy in his epic poetry. Blake describes *Milton* in a letter to Thomas Butts as "a Sublime Allegory . . . I consider it as the Grandest Poem that this World Contains,"[68] but, in order to show Milton's expiation for his mistakes in supporting orthodoxy, he conceives of an elaborate scheme for the poem in which Milton acknowledges his errors and his emanation returns to earth a century after his death. As a shooting star, Milton descends, enters Blake through his left foot, and inspires him with a true vision of the Resurrection, the Last Judgment, and the Millennium.

[67] See Michael Davis, *William Blake: A New Kind of Man* (Berkeley and Los Angeles: Univ. of California Press, 1977), pp. 106-11.

[68] *Complete Writings*, p. 825 (letter of 6 July 1803).

The typology of *Milton* is ubiquitous. The "Preface" states Blake's belief that the ruins of a fallen Jerusalem exist in England and that the "Mental Fight" of the poem will be to build—actually, to rebuild—Jerusalem "In England's green & pleasant Land." But the types of the poem are greater than the Israel-England figuration. Poetic creativity and the divine Creation, which are different versions of the same action, lead to a typology of creativity: "And every Space smaller than a Globule of Man's blood opens / Into Eternity of which this vegetable Earth is but a shadow."[69] Milton prefigures Blake and both prefigure Jesus, the last and greatest prophet. Blake, merged with Milton and inspired by Los, foreshadows the Millennium, the Last Vintage of the poem:

"I am that Shadowy Prophet who Six Thousand Years ago
"Fell from my station in the Eternal bosom. Six Thousand Years
"Are finish'd. I return! both Time & Space obey my will.
"I in Six Thousand Years walk up and down; for not one Moment
"Of Time is lost, nor one Event of Space unpermanent,
"But all remain: every fabric of Six Thousand Years
"Remains permanent, tho' on the Earth where Satan
"Fell and was cut off, all things vanish & are seen no more,
"They vanish not from me and mine, we guard them first & last.
"The generations of men run on in the tide of Time,
"But leave their destin'd lineaments permanent for ever & ever."[70]

Six thousand years, in Blake's computation and that of millennialists since the seventeenth century, was the full term of the created world, after which the Millennium would commence. Blake sees himself as a combination of other prophets—or their emanations—who were his types: the original fallen angel, Satan, Milton, and Jesus. One of Blake's speakers in the poem, the Divine Family, his term for the Communion of the Elect, assures Milton's emanation, Ololon, that the Millennium is nigh (21.51-60), and Blake then hints at the forthcoming union of Ololon with Jesus. The returned Milton, combined with Blake, and inspired by the types of other prophets, is, in the words of Los, "this Elected Form who is return'd again, / He is the Signal that the Last Vintage now approaches."[71] At the end of the second book, Milton's emanation Ololon descends to Blake's environs, the vale of Felpham, envelops Jesus the Saviour

---

[69] *Ibid.*, pp. 516-17 (29.21-22).
[70] *Ibid.*, p. 505 (22.15-25).   [71] *Ibid.*, p. 509 (24.41-42).

in the form of clouds on which are written "the Divine Revelation in the Litteral expression, / . . . the Woof of Six Thousand Years." Immediately after this last accomplishment of the types, the Four Zoas "Applied their Four Trumpets & them sounded to the Four winds."

At this critical point in the poem, we see that all of *Milton* has been a typological allegory of the poem's own creation, for we return at once to Blake himself in his garden at Felpham:

> Terror struck in the Vale I stood at that immortal sound.
> My bones trembled, I fell outstretch'd upon the path
> A moment, & my Soul return'd into its mortal state
> To Resurrection and Judgment in the Vegetable Body,
> And my sweet Shadow of Delight stood trembling by my side.[72]

Catherine Blake, the poet's "sweet shadow of Delight," helps her husband back into his chair, and the great harvest and vintage of the nations goes ahead without further delay. The clap of the apocalypse, the final antitype, has brought Blake back into consciousness for a moment from his fourfold vision and, struck by the imminence of the Millennium to his physical self, he swoons. In an intensely real sense, the shadows of the end of days encompass him much as the shadowy types and figures from his prophetical reading embrace and inform all that he writes. Like the other prophets of the time, Blake lives a life of *figura*, an existence permeated by typology, that closely parallels the worlds of his visions.

 5

The aspect of this figural system which appealed most to English Romantic poets is natural typology, or typology abstracted from theological concerns to natural phenomena and normal aspects of human behavior. Natural typology often associates the secular and the theological spheres in an obscure manner; such a style is popular with mystical writers like Boehme. Blake was adept at using such typology as, for example, he does in the "Lark" and "Wild Thyme" passages at the beginning of *Milton*, Book II. In these brief sections, he presents the lark as the first and chief worshiper of Nature among the birds—"He leads the Choir of Day" (31.32). The wild thyme is analogous to the lark among the vegetable creation

---

[72] *Ibid.*, p. 534 (42.24-28).

(31.51-53). Blake's animal and plant typology is well developed, part of the carefully articulated prefigurative structure of a lengthy prophecy. To find some of the poetical forerunners of this figural system, we must look back to the poets of the 1760s and '70s. An early example of this tendency would be the following stanza from Christopher Smart's *Song to David* (1763):

> O DAVID, scholar of the Lord!
> Such is thy science, whence reward
>   And infinite degree;
> O strength, O sweetness, lasting ripe!
> God's harp thy symbol, and thy type
>   The lion and the bee![73]

The typological qualities of many animals—including, as it happens, the lion and the bee—have been noted in commentaries to editions of Frantze's *Historia Animalium Sacra*, but these animals have no direct prefigurative association with David. The sacred zoologists' figural systems invariably show that the lion and the bee possess, among their many qualities, certain traits which foreshadow Christ and his mission. Smart's typology here, however, leads us to Samson's riddle to the Philistines in Judges 14. David's leonine qualities (strength) and his apian characteristics (sweetness of song) are indeed prefigurative of Jesus. Hence Smart himself, like any other poet who captures the Davidic style of rhapsody, is acting out virtuous Christian behavior which, in turn, is a structure both predictive and postfigurative of the life of Christ.[74] Smart's typology is very involved, and may not be theologically correct, but the fact that he chooses to embody it in a poem about one of the chief prophetic figures of the Old Testament, David, reveals yet another facet of prophetic typology in the last half of the eighteenth century. The explanation of the relationship between Smart's David and his types is less important, I think, than the existence of such predictive structures in eighteenth- and nineteenth-century literature. Thanks to the labors of Warburton, Butler, Hartley, and others, who had suggested that there was a prefigurative basis to human thought and speech, it was now possible to place such structures in works of literature without a second thought about their theological accuracy.

[73] *A Song to David* (London, 1763), p. 10 (St. xxxviii).
[74] On the typology of *A Song to David*, see Christopher M. Dennis, "A Structural Conceit in Smart's *Song to David*," *RES*, n.s., 29 (1978), 257-66.

Smart's animal typology finds an apt echo in *The Task*, William Cowper's secular epic. Cowper's skillful and enlightened typological imagery pervades his *Olney Hymns* (1779), and his longer poems of 1781-82, especially "Truth," "Expostulation," "Hope," "Charity," and "Retirement," often mention typological themes from both Testaments. *The Task* is less ostensibly religious than these early works. Cowper's miscellaneous, conversational style embraces furniture, architecture, "God made the country, and man made the town" (I.749), retirement, luxury, freedom, and dozens of other traditional *topoi* of eighteenth-century discursive poetry. He praises seclusion and, from within his retirement, he turns abruptly to talk of himself:

> I was a stricken deer, that left the herd
> Long since; with many an arrow deep infixt
> My panting side was charg'd, when I withdrew
> To seek a tranquil death in distant shades.
> There was I found by one who had himself
> Been hurt by th' archers. In his side he bore
> And in his hands and feet, the cruel scars. . . .[75]

The deer or hart is a traditional type of Christ; authors of bestiaries and commentators on texts which mention the hart, especially Psalms 42.1 ("As the hart panteth after the waterbrooks, so panteth my soul after thee, O God"), had first made the association in patristic times.[76] The stricken deer is a type of the Christian seeking the sacramental cleansing of baptism. That Cowper, in his quest for solitude, should then meet a savior-figure marked with the stigmata and that he should compare himself with this Christ-figure ("one who had *himself* / Been hurt by th'archers") intensifies the personal typology of these lines. Just as Smart had identified himself with his typological hero, David, Cowper merges himself with his healing savior. Cowper's self-identification with the hero of *The Task* is a significant step in the development of the Romantic idea of the poet as theme of his or her own poetry, but it is also important in the evolution of typology.[77] In *The Task*, Cowper fulfills the

[75] *The Task*, III.108-14.
[76] On the typology of the hart, see Beryl Rowland, *Animals with Human Faces*, pp. 94-101.
[77] On the notion of the poet-hero, see Robert Folkenflik's forthcoming essay, "The Artist as Hero in the Eighteenth Century," *Yearbook of English Studies*, 12 (1982).

imitatio Christi theme, and both meets and becomes the poem's Christ-figure simultaneously, so that type and antitype for the moment are coevals. Cowper's self-image, then, as a personal type of Christ, is identical with the voice of the prophet, for Jesus is the last prophet. The secular world of *The Task* is not so secular after all—Cowper, like Gray before him and Blake after him, thought himself divinely inspired. Rather than announce himself, as they do, as a prophetic speaker, he codes his message with the help of typological signals. Cowper does not breach a tradition; the convention of the poet-prophet is ancient. However, without the benefit of visionary fireworks, he calmly reveals a typological dimension to everyday life. It is an aspect of natural typology which will be popular with English Romantic writers.

 6

The notion of typological places, a form of natural typology, continues to develop during the later eighteenth century, and becomes relatively common in Romantic landscape poetry. This concept derives from seventeenth-century Puritan treatments of Egypt, Babylon, wanderings in the desert, various biblical captivities, and other scenes related specifically to *places* as types of the Puritans' contemporary persecutions and from the personal typology which permits clergymen, self-styled prophets, and poets like Smart and Cowper to identify events or places in their own lives as prefigurations of millenarian happenings or of Christ and his works. Later in the nineteenth century, Ruskin would make similarly sympathetic readings of history and would interpret the destinies of Venice and Tyre as types for the England of his own generation, while Victorian painters would make equally widespread use of the typology of place.[78] Wordsworth, who frequently refers to types in the theological sense, is especially sensitive to the possibilities of prophetic typology in landscape poetry, as in his famous description of the Simplon Pass in *The Prelude*:

> Brook and Road
> Were fellow-travellers in this gloomy Pass,

[78] The typology of nineteenth-century painting has recently started to attract scholarly attention; see George Landow, *William Holman Hunt and Typological Symbolism* (New Haven: Yale Univ. Press, 1979), and "William Holman Hunt's 'The Shadow of Death,'" *BJRL*, 55 (1972), 197-239.

And with them did we journey several hours
At a slow step. The immeasurable height
Of Woods decaying, never to be decayed,
The stationery blasts of waterfalls,
And in the narrow rent, at every turn,
Winds thwarting winds, bewildered and forlorn,
The torrents shooting from the clear blue sky,
The rocks that muttered close upon our ears,
Black drizzling crags that spake by the wayside
As if a voice were in them, the sick sight
And giddy prospect of the raving stream,
The unfettered clouds and region of the heavens,
Tumult and peace, the darkness and the light—
Were all the workings of one mind, the features
Of the same face, blossoms upon one tree,
Characters of the great Apocalypse,
The types and symbols of Eternity,
Of first, and last, and midst, and without end.[79]

Symbolic landscape is a venerable poetic technique: Wordsworth can scarcely be said to operate within a new tradition. Landscape, however, although frequently endowed with symbolic values, is seldom so explicitly prefigurative as it is here. The motion of the passage is manifestly typological, from a torrent of circumstantial details to unity and the unanimity of great eternal facts (*"one* mind ... the *same* face ... *one* tree"), from tumult to peace, darkness to light, type to antitype. Wordsworth's "types," even more significantly, are also "Characters," predictive structures drawn from natural phenomena. Finally, since these types look forward to the Apocalypse and the Millennium, we may see them as yet another manifestation of the prophetic figuralism that occurs so frequently in English life around the turn of the century. His types, then, are ready-made, and lie open to the reader of the great book of nature. Their purpose, as if part of a great physico-theological scheme, is to foreshadow the glories of the author of that book, God the Father.

Since prophetic typology often involves the blending of themes, theological and secular, Christian and pagan, it may be well for us to consider one further example in the earlier nineteenth century —Shelley. Like Wordsworth, Shelley often writes with a heightened awareness of mysterious prefigurative meanings in natural existence.

[79] *The* Prelude, VI.621-40.

In *Mont Blanc* (1816), for instance, he meditates, "The wilderness has a mysterious tongue / Which teaches awful doubt, or faith so mild . . ." and suggests that, while this voice is not understood by all, "the wise, and great, and good" may interpret it.[80] From his reading of Milton and seventeenth-century mystics, Shelley extracted the notion of types as shadows; thus he often alludes to shadowy forms or intellectual concepts as suggesting larger, more fully developed entities in the future. *Mont Blanc* may hint at an apocalyptic revelation, but Shelley's prophecy lacks the assurance of Wordsworth's.

Typological figuration, as Hans Frei has recently suggested, declines in popularity around the turn of the nineteenth century because "it strained credulity beyond the breaking point by the suggestion that sayings and events of one day referred predictively to specific persons and events hundreds of years later."[81] Frei, however, speaks primarily of typological exegesis as a tool in the interpretation of Scripture. Paradoxically, during the same period that biblical exegetes laid an ever-growing emphasis on literal and historical reading, enthusiastic millenarians make progressively greater use of the figural system which draws on Old Testament types, the *imitatio Christi* tradition, and both pre- and postfigurations of Jesus. One symptom of Frei's decline in theological typology is a change from pure to abstracted typology in literary situations. Another is the gradual amalgamation, in the early nineteenth century, of pagan myth into typological situations or narratives, as with Coleridge and Shelley. Typology and pagan myth have profound seventeenth-century associations (I need mention only Alexander Ross), and in this context I must note again the popularity of seventeenth-century mysticism with English Romantic writers. Where Shelley fails to uncover typological qualities in natural landscape, he evokes them successfully through his combining of pagan and Christian myths in *Prometheus Unbound* (1818). The signs that surround Shelley's presentation of the pinioned Titan are typological signals. At first, Prometheus appears as a type, almost paradoxically, without an antitype. As the Chorus observes in Act I, "And the future is dark, and the present is spread / Like a pillow of thorns for thy slumberless head."[82] The typological sign, the pillow of thorns, is

---

[80] *Mont Blanc*, lines 76-83.
[81] *The Eclipse of Biblical Narrative*, p. 6; see, more generally, pp. 1-16.
[82] *Prometheus Unbound*, I.562-63.

present and there *is* a future, although at the moment it promises nothing.

The signs multiply. Panthea reports shortly afterwards that she has seen "A woeful sight: a youth / With patient looks nailed to a crucifix."[83] Prometheus becomes an "emblem" (I. 594) of those who suffer for the wrongs of men, and the Titan himself recognizes his role in a pagan drama of expiation and salvation:

> Thou subtle tyrant [i.e., Jupiter]! Peace is in the grave.
> The grave hides all things beautiful and good:
> I am a God and cannot find it there,
> Nor would I seek it: for, though dread revenge,
> This is defeat, fierce king, not victory.
> The sights with which thou torturest gird my soul
> With new endurance, till the hour arrives
> When they shall be no types of things which are.
>
> (I.638-45)

The more Christ-like Prometheus becomes, the more numerous are the signs of typological affirmation that surround him. Toward the end of Act I, the Chorus of Spirits enunciates the refrain of prefigurative promise: ". . . the prophecy / Which begins and ends in thee!" (I.690-91, 706-707, 799-800). The types of *Prometheus Unbound* are crowded together on the canvas of Act I, a situation which is fitting indeed for a predictive drama fusing pagan and Christian elements. The reason for this concentration is that the first act serves as an iconographical prefiguration of the achievements of Acts III and IV—the dethronement of Jupiter and the jubilant cosmic dance of the finale. The dialogue between The Earth and The Moon suggests the accomplishments of the prophecies. The key speech of Earth concludes:

> And the abyss shouts from her depth laid bare,
> Heaven, hast thou secrets? Man unveils me; I have none.
>
> (IV.422-23)

The removal of the veil is complete, just as an antitype explains and removes the mystery of its type.

The intricate backgrounds to Shelley's mythmaking, both Christian and pagan, Western and Oriental, reveal the rich typological vein available to the creative artists of the later eighteenth and

---

[83] I.584-85. Prometheus as the crucified Christ was an enduring Renaissance emblem. See Stuart Curran, *Shelley's Annus Mirabilis: The Maturing of an Epic Vision* (San Marino, Calif.: The Huntington Library, 1975), pp. 53-58.

early nineteenth centuries. Shelley relies not only on the syncretic mythologists, but on a host of later scholars and commentators the fruits of whose researches had been unavailable to Swift, Pope, and Johnson.[84] Indeed, the seventeenth-century students of euhemerism and the pagan origins of Christianity like Gerhard Vossius, Samuel Bochart, Athanasius Kircher, and John Owen, whose writings were never translated out of the Latin, and Stillingfleet and Theophilus Gale, who wrote in English, are to a large extent subsumed and continued by this later generation of scholars in a language open to all readers. Thus the typology of Shelley's *Prometheus* is extraordinarily complex, embodying the mysterious lore of the professional mythologists and much of the familiar prefiguration of Old Testament exegesis. Robert Lowth, speaking half a century earlier of Old Testament typologizing, exemplifies the vein that runs to the more biblical sort of abstracted typology: "Hence that truly Divine Spirit, which has not disdained to employ poetry as the interpreter of its sacred will, has also in a manner appropriated to its own use this kind of allegory, as peculiarly adapted to the publication of future events, and to the typifying of the most sacred mysteries."[85]

If Shelley's Prometheus resembles the typologically resonant heroes of late eighteenth-century biblical epic, we should not be surprised at the similarity. The central characters of the biblical epics by Friedrich Klopstock, Johann Jakob Bodmer, Richard Cumberland, and in fresh eighteenth-century translations, the sixteenth-century Bishop Vida, help to promote the popularity of prophetic typology in the Romantic era.[86] Klopstock's *Messiah* and Bodmer's *Noah* may owe their form and subject to Milton, but their visionary style recalls the ever-popular Ossianic fragments. Lowth's observations about the style of the biblical narratives are especially

[84] Curran, *Shelley's Annus Mirabilis*, pp. 33-94, 212-30, thoroughly documents Shelley's reading of Bryant's *A New System*, Faber's *The Origin of Pagan Idolatry*, and dozens of other available sources.

[85] See *Lectures on the Sacred Poetry of the Hebrews*, trans. G. Gregory, 2 vols. (London, 1787), I, 238, and 234-49, *passim*, Lowth's important chapter "Of the Mystical Allegory."

[86] Klopstock's *The Messiah*, trans. Joseph Collyer, 2nd ed., 2 vols. (London, 1766) is laden with typological import, much of it original with its author. See II, 101, 174, 213, 263. Collyer also translated Bodmer's *Noah* as *Noah, Attempted from the German of Mr. Bodmer*, 2 vols. (London, 1767), in which see esp. II, 191-255. Both translations are in prose. Cumberland's *Calvary; or The Death of Christ* presents a complex Jesus who, like Shelley's Prometheus, is surrounded by iconographical detail from various mythologies. An especially fine passage is the one in which the resurrected Jesus addresses the souls of the

relevant in the evaluation of late eighteenth- and early nineteenth-century reworkings of Old and New Testament stories. It will not be at all novel for me to note the vast difference between the style of early and late eighteenth-century biblical poems. Sir Richard Blackmore, Edward Young, Samuel Catherall, and Elizabeth Rowe introduce typology into their verse—indeed, they could scarcely make do without it—but they are always narrative reporters observing the scene from afar.[87] The German biblical poets, Smart, Blake, and even—in his dramas—Byron become profoundly self-involved as personal visionaries. Typology is no longer merely an exegetical system; it has changed into a personal style, one which, to paraphrase Lowth, the Holy Spirit did not disdain to use, a symbolic expression of the figuration of life itself.

In the study of literature it is a relatively easy matter to find similar forms, motifs, themes, and structures in diverse texts, cultures, and traditions. Typology, as I have said on many occasions, has much in common with motifs and structures; typological themes certainly repeat themselves, and predictive structures without doubt foreshadow later antitypes that may be very similar to their types. A structuralist student of the Bible would be likely to interpret sacrifice stories—I take a convenient example here—as all basically similar. Abraham's sacrifice of Isaac, which actually becomes a nonsacrifice, would, in the language of structuralism, be similar to Jephthah's sacrifice of his daughter (Judges 11.30-40) and to God's

---

patriarchs and welcomes them (incongruously) to eternal life: the antitype holds a conversation with the types (see pp. 266-67, ap. VIII.170-201)! Moses responds with a stirring recollection of all his typological actions (pp. 282-85; VIII.568-650). It would appear that typology so caught the fancy of many writers that they embroidered upon it freely. Vida's *Christiad*, translated several times in the later eighteenth century, is also prefigurative in an inventive manner; see *The Christiad: An Heroic Poem; in Six Books*, trans. Edward Granam (London, 1771), pp. 35-36, 131-72.

[87] I refer here to Blackmore's *Creation* (1712), Young's *The Last Day* (1713), Catherall's *Essay on the Conflagration* (1720), and Rowe's *History of Joseph* (1736). Rowe's poem is a good standard: the invocation states, "The sacred lays a mystick sense infold, / And things divine in human types were told"; Joseph, imprisoned by Potiphar, has a prophetic trance in which the Angel Gabriel visits him and vouchsafes him a Pisgah-vision of some length. See *The History of Joseph. A Poem in Eight Books* (London, 1737), pp. 3, 20, 59, 60-66. Rowe is always the reporter, distanced from her subject, personally uninvolved.

permitting his own son to be sacrificed.[88] Typology is capable of being similar to structuralism—it, too, can be a closed system, a code for which there is one standard key that will open all occurrences, wherever they may be. But in the period which this book covers typology does not operate this way. It is a code, one which many audiences were surely capable of deciphering, but there was no universal key. What makes prophetic typology such an interesting subject for scrutiny, I think, is its number of variations. Prophetic typology, as I have shown, embraces nearly every form of literature from 1650 to 1820: it includes exegeses, sermons, and Christian apologetics, every kind of poetry, and, toward the end of the eighteenth century, children's books, popular narratives, and millenarian tracts intended for the less cultured reader.

At the beginning of the century, writers who seek the prophetic voice are most likely to model themselves upon Milton and the high heraldic style of *Paradise Lost*. By the end of the century, the shape of prefigurative style still recalls Milton, but it now embodies low culture, too, and includes among its voices those of Bunyan, modest emblem books, and the hymns and ballads of the age. Prophetic typology is no longer a specially coded message for the well educated; it is Joseph Priestley preaching on the Millennium to thousands at the Gravel Pit meeting at Hackney, it is Richard Brothers reaching an audience of tens of thousands through his cheaply printed pamphlets with their crude, childish woodcuts, and it is even the Romantic poets speaking to their somewhat more select audience in plain stanzas and on utopian themes. The prophetic typologist comes out of the study and the library and into the street, where popular prophets, whether in ancient Judea, medieval Europe, or mid-seventeenth-century England, have always spoken most effectively. I do not wish to minimize the popular appeal of *Paradise Lost* at the turn of the nineteenth century, or to suggest that its complex prophetic typology did not affect many readers, but there can be little doubt that the simple, moving types of Augustus Montague Toplady's beautiful hymn, "Rock of Ages" (1776), affected still more.

Warburton, Butler, and Hartley, to mention three theologians whose theorizing about typology in the first half of the eighteenth century contributed to our understanding of prophecy throughout the period of this book, were widely read, but they did not reach

[88] Howard Gardner, *The Quest for Mind: Piaget, Lévi-Strauss, and the Structuralist Movement* (New York: Knopf, 1973), pp. 151-57, discusses various structuralist theories as they are applied to biblical narratives.

an audience so large as did the writers of hymns like Watts and Toplady, the authors of gothic and other popular fiction, and the major Romantic poets. Nevertheless, these writers do more than theorize about types; they also help us to understand the natural bases for typology. Warburton discusses how typology is a natural figural development in the growth of languages and societies; Butler treats, among many other subjects, the analogies between the book of Scripture and the book of nature; and Hartley notes that typological reasoning corresponds to reasoning by analogy. "A type," he writes, "is indeed nothing but an analogy, and the scripture types are not only a key to the scriptures, but seem also to have contributed to put into our hands the key of nature, analogy."[89] These men, in different ways, help to broaden the base of prophetic typology so that, by the end of the eighteenth century, we do not find prophetic types only in exegeses of Revelation but also in a wide spectrum of popular literature.

Northrop Frye has observed that popular literature usually "indicates where the next literary developments are most likely to come from."[90] The broadening of prophetic typology over a period of more than a century may therefore be an instructive guide as to the direction which this branch of figuralism will take. As with all such changes, the evolution is gradual, but we can detect the signs of change long before it is finally complete. The signs that I have in mind relate to the emergence of what I have called elsewhere natural typology. The natural typologist finds prefigurative forces and relationships at work in the world at large, often without either a theological or a popular prophetic context. Prophetic typology always recalls and draws on biblical, mainly apocalyptic, foreshadowings. The prophetic typologist looks forward to an antitype, preferably one in the near future. Hence there is an urgent utopianism to the millenarianism of Price and Priestley, a thread which is closely woven into the texture of contemporary life. Natural typology is usually more aloof, and is relatively distant from politics. Writers who employ this kind of figuralism—like Marvell, Coleridge, and Shelley—are sometimes intimately engaged with political life or with the art of swaying public opinion, but they seldom choose to employ natural typology in their more public writings. While natural typology may use biblical type-scenes, its narrative source is not the Scriptures, it is everyday life itself.

[89] *Observations on Man*, II, 165.
[90] See *The Secular Scripture: A Study of the Structure of Romance* (Cambridge, Mass.: Harvard Univ. Press, 1976), p. 28.

CHAPTER 10

The Typology of
Everyday Life

1

ONE OF THE many qualities of typology which this study has
sought to illuminate is its ability to seek order, pattern,
arrangement, and correspondence between things which
may not seem to be related. As an ordering device, however, typology is not so simple as other methods of classification. The standard
methods for creating a taxonomy call for assigning a comprehensible name to a phenomenon, for generating what is essentially a
metaphor. But typology is a more complicated kind of tropology
than other forms of figuration. As Warburton pointed out in his
important speculations on language in *The Divine Legation of
Moses Vindicated,* in typology both terms of the figural equation
may require explanation. Both the type and the antitype may be—
and often are—obscure. As seventeenth- and eighteenth-century
writers, scientists, divines, and philosophers sought to classify an
ever-increasing multiplicity of literary characters, themes, and motifs, flora, fauna, and natural phenomena, and religious and philosophical categories, we know that they faced problems with terminology. Among the results of those problems are the elaborate
schemes of classification which the authors of learned works drew
up so that they could deal with their topics in an orderly way. The
Linnaean system is one such scheme; the detailed table of the arts
and sciences which appears as the foldout frontispiece to Diderot's
Encyclopédie (1751) is another.[1] The compilations of fables and
books of characters that I mentioned earlier are not the syntagmatic

[1] See *L'Encyclopédie, ou Dictionnaire Raisonné des sciences, des arts et mé-
tiers,* 17 vols. (Paris, 1751-65), I, frontispiece. For another ordered tree. this one
with typological qualities, see Figure 18.

collections that they might have been in Renaissance Europe, but arrangements of texts with a certain order. And narrative itself, during the period of my focus, gradually develops a greater concern for plot and structure. Even *Tristram Shandy* contains authorial protestations about form—nothing is more highly structured than a work which mocks the very concept of order. In this general current of intellectual history, typology plays a unique role, for types too represent an effort to classify. The first typologists knew that they were bringing a sense of order and relationship to two diverse bodies of narrative, the two Testaments of the Bible. As early as the sixteenth century some exegetes started to use typological methods to interpret texts other than theological. Their reasoning for this expansion of the uses of typology was perfectly sound, so far as they were concerned. After all, the exegetes believed, there were religious meanings in many texts besides the Holy Scriptures. The argument from design encouraged still more adventurous typologizing. If the Bible, which was of divine authorship or inspiration, contained hidden prefigurative relationships, then it followed that one might find similar relationships not only in other texts that might have an inspired core to them, but in natural phenomena, historical events, and ultimately, all aspects of human experience.

It is easy for us to ridicule seekers after hidden relationships that we now know do not exist. Students of Egyptology have learned to laugh at Kircher's puzzling over the hieroglyphics on the obelisks brought from Egypt to mid-seventeenth-century Rome, for we know today that all his typological and mystical readings of the glyphs are nonsense. Early Renaissance readings of hermetic texts have no standing in the twentieth century. Aldrovandus's efforts to classify the entire creation in eleven folio volumes are without basis in modern paleontology. The figuralists who found types of heavenly glories in all created things, as did Jakob Boehme and Thomas Vaughan, may also seem like strange artifacts from the past. For the student of typology and literary figuralism, however, these writers and their confusing distinctions over literary terminology are very important. From their confusion over terms like type, symbol, emblem, hieroglyphic, allegory, and so on, we may derive the growth of natural typology, the typology of everyday life. Type-scenes (which may be emblems, symbols, or glyphs) naturally repeat themselves in many texts: scenes that recall the beginning of Christian's pilgrimage, for example, in *The Pilgrim's Progress*, occur hundreds if not thousands of times in the structures of narrative beginnings from the seventeenth to the nineteenth centuries (see Figure 14).[2] Type-myths, type-characters, and type-behavior also recur constantly, as authors continue to find them useful or attractive. These things recur not only because we—the readers, the universal exegetes of reality—want them to, but because in fact the fabric of human experience *does* consist of repetitions. Again and again, I have quoted texts whose authors were aware that figural qualities of texts represented reality as, indeed, the nature of mimesis tells us they must. David Hartley, for one, was certain that there was a natural typological relationship among all created things:

> All the works of God, the parts of a human body, systems of minerals, plants, and animals, elementary bodies, planets, fixed stars, &c. have various uses and subserviences, in respect to each other; and, if the scriptures be the word of God, analogy would lead one to expect something corresponding hereto in them.[3]

This passage does not simply make grandiose claims for the argument from design; it also states rationally what mystics like Boehme, Vaughan, and William Law had said enthusiastically, that the order of the world and our lives in that world are arranged according to a rational code. The person who can decipher this rational code is capable of understanding the language of things—"signatura rerum," in Boehme's happy phrase—and of *predicting* future behavior, events, characters, conclusions, and history.

The analogy of things to the prefigurative order of the divine plan is a concept which derives first from the neoplatonic syncretists and afterwards from the physico-theologians and natural theologians. Seventeenth-century religious and linguistic thinkers, believing that the events surrounding Babel were responsible for the confusion of tongues and likewise for the confusion of mythic types, sought to recover the *Ur-Sprache*, the key whereby they would be able to decode all the mysteries of the gentile cults as well as the secrets of the creation.[4] We may find a good expression of the search

2 On the opening scene of *The Pilgrim's Progress* and its structural qualities, see Wolfgang Iser, *The Implied Reader: Patterns of Communication in Prose Fiction from Bunyan to Beckett* (Baltimore: Johns Hopkins Univ. Press, 1974), pp. 1-14.

3 *Observations on Man*, II, 160-61.

4 On the confusion and multiplicity of languages, see George Steiner, *After Babel: Aspects of Language and Translation* (New York: Oxford Univ. Press,

for a lost unity in Sir Thomas Browne's *The Garden of Cyrus* (1658), an important treatment of horticultural, linguistic, and religious origins. After discussing the significance of "shadowing" and "shades" in horticulture, Browne becomes expansive:

> The greatest mystery of religion is expressed by adumbration, and in the noblest part of the Jewish Types, we finde the Cherubims shadowing the Mercy-seat: Life it self is but the shadow of death, and souls departed but the shadows of the living: All things fall under this name. The Sunne it self is but the dark *simulachrum*, and light but the shadow of God.[5]

Browne's typology is unconventional so far as his terminology is concerned, and he appears to use the notion of shadowing forth in both directions, as life shadows forth death and as dead souls are "shadows of the living." However, it is certain that he believes that he has found extensive relationships between types and antitypes in the created world just as such relationships already exist in religion.

We may find further hints of prefigurative analogies in Cudworth's major work and then much more commonly in the eighteenth century. William Derham's approach to natural phenomena, for instance, is to treat all of nature's wonders as signs of the greatness of God, as marks and badges which acknowledge the existence of God to the believer.[6] Writers like Derham, Butler, and Hartley were principally concerned with proving that the creation revealed God and, typologically, prefigured his attributes. Other students of the pagan past like Warburton, Bryant, Jones, and Faber were more interested in the predictive bases of language and, through language, of a wide variety of texts, sacred and secular. Faber's system is especially interesting. He is certain that all pagan mysteries and symbolism derive ultimately from a body of natural prefigurative structures, whether symbols, glyphs, or ancient fables. The great confusion of the types, for Faber, springs from Babel, the source of

---

1975), pp. 58-63, part of an excellent chapter entitled "Language and Gnosis." Mystics like Paracelsus and Boehme, who worked deeply in the alchemy of speech, expected that divine providence would one day restore the unity of tongues; commentators on Revelation pick up and elaborate upon this notion.

[5] See *The Prose of Sir Thomas Browne*, ed. Norman J. Endicott (Garden City, N.Y.: Doubleday & Co., 1967), p. 335.

[6] See his *Physico-Theology: or, A Demonstration of the Being and Attributes of God from his Works of Creation*, 3rd ed. (London, 1714), pp. 428-47.

all corruptions and abominations. "In the Christian world," he writes,

> the figurative Babel has been the mother of an idolatrous apostasy, which, reviving under a new name the ancient pagan demonolatry or worship of deified men, long disfigured in almost every part of the Church universal the pure simplicity of the Gospel. Therefore the literal Babel must have been the mother, in the patriarchal world, of that mixed system of demonolatry, which seduced men from the truth, and which was then diffused over every part of the habitable globe.[7]

The linguistic confusion of Babel becomes the basis of all pagan mythologies. Faber has read Bochart, but he is not an etymologer. Rather, he believes that the ancient tongues and their descendants possess retained typological obscurities, types that had been passed on unseen and unknown from earlier periods of history. Like Warburton, Faber thinks that the very nature of language, as it developed from its early stages when it was less copious, has led to much figural expression and hence—inevitably—to typology. Typological codes, according to this theory, may be found in any figural speech, far beyond the theological sphere and, as if to demonstrate the accuracy of his speculations, Faber even analyzes various type-myths for their prefigurative elements.[8] These writers of the eighteenth and nineteenth centuries were responding to the ages-old idea of the book of nature. It is a theological notion that originates in the Middle Ages, which Paracelsus and Boehme popularized in the sixteenth century, which Marvell knew when he referred, in "Upon Appleton House," to *"Natures mystick Book,"* and which Sir Thomas Browne recognized when he spoke of the "common Hieroglyphicks" of nature.[9] Wordsworth, when he visualizes the sublime landscape of the Simplon Pass in typological terms, is actuated by the same tradition. However, he feels no need to tell his readers that he makes this association because, to use Quarles's phrase, the world's a book in folio printed on God's press. There is a reason for his silence on the source of his tradition; I think it is simply that natural typology had become so common by 1800 that there was no longer any *reason* to mention it.

[7] *The Origin of Pagan Idolatry*, I, 77.

[8] *Ibid.*, I, 145-51, 488-98; III, 314-55.

[9] See Ernst Robert Curtius, *European Literature and the Latin Middle Ages*, trans. Willard R. Trask (New York: Pantheon Books, 1953), pp. 319-26.

Faber's system of languages and types is fairly well-developed, although he admits that his discussion of typological motifs in the texts of romances is nothing more than a few scattered notes. Let me therefore turn briefly to a parallel development, the study of figural language in that most popular of prophetical books, Revelation. Almost all of the numerous commentaries from the mid-seventeenth century devote some space to the language of prophecy; I have already had occasion to allude to some of these discussions. Among the most important considerations of prophetic language are the commentaries of Henry More and Sir Isaac Newton. More's *Apocalypsis Apocalypseos* (1680) stresses that Scripture is an uncultivated field rather than an orderly garden from which meaning must be wrought with difficulty rather than gathered with ease, provided that the reader is in possession of the key to its code:

> A *Revelation* may be a *Mystery*, that is, *mystically* or hiddenly conveyed, but yet plainly be known by them that have the *Key*. As it is in *Steganography* by which Secrets are certainly conveyed or revealed, but in such a mysterious way that none but they know the *clavis* or *Key* shall be ever the wiser. Wherefore it is not all repugnant that the *Apocalypse* may be a *Revelation* and yet a *Mystery*, that is, a Revelation *Mystically* conveyed. . . .[10]

One of the most significant treatments of the subject of prophetic language appears in Charles Daubuz's *Perpetual Commentary* (1720), a well-known work which Warburton, Hartley, and Bryant must have read with attention. Daubuz's preliminary discourse on "The Origin of the Symbolical or Prophetical Language" makes good reading even today:

> Now if we find, that in the Prophecies and Visions of the Old Testament and of the New, and particularly in those of the *Revelation*, the Holy Ghost has made use of such Symbolical Terms, Images, or Types, as were in use amongst the *Egyptians* and *Chaldeans*, or other Nations, which followed those Studies and Learning, and practis'd all those Sorts of Divination that are Consequences of that Learning; we have all the Reason

10 From the "Epilogue" to *Apocalypsis Apocalypseos; or the Revelation of St. John the Divine unveiled* (London, 1680), p. 302.

in the World to think, that the Holy Ghost has therein adopted this Symbolical Language; whether they be Visions and Prophecies given to the *Israelites*, or afterwards to the Christian Church. So that it must needs happen, that the Symbolical Language of the Holy Ghost; and consequently, that the *Revelation* of St. *John*, being written in that Symbolical Language, and giving an Account of Visions suitable to the Symbolical Character, may be illustrated thereby, and ought indeed to be explain'd accordingly. . . .[11]

Perhaps it does not matter that Daubuz reasons circularly; he is certainly not alone among his contemporaries in doing so on such topics. What does matter about this passage is that the Holy Ghost, in dictating the Revelation to St. John, apparently chose to employ the figural style of ancient Egypt and Chaldea, the pagan idolatry from which Faber would later derive all linguistic, mythological, and figural confusions. If the Holy Ghost could use such symbolic speech, borrowed from such an obviously mystical source, then contemporary writers might reasonably argue that they could not be censured for doing likewise. Hence we will find that many writers who claimed to be inspired simply adopt a symbolic style, charged with natural typology, as a matter of literary tradition and undoubted right.

Collins, Gray, Akenside, Smart, and Macpherson all use a prophetic style that, on various occasions, deliberately echoes the primitive typologies of the sacred books. Collins, in his *Odes on Several Descriptive and Allegoric Subjects* (1747), frequently evokes the mystic figure of the poet or bard possessing visionary powers. The accounts of these figures habitually employ a "Symbolical Language and Character" which at first glance we might not consider typological, but Collins's mood is both prophetic and predictive. In his "Ode to Fear," for instance, he calls on Fear as follows: "Dark power, with shuddering meek submitted thought / Be mine to read the visions old, / Which thy awakening bards have told." He begs that Fear might be his muse, his inspiration; he asks to be touched like Fear's earlier prophet Shakespeare, of whom he would become a postfiguration.[12] The normal signs that customarily accompany

[11] Charles Daubuz, *A Perpetual Commentary on the Revelation of St. John* (London, 1720), p. 13.

[12] *The Poems of Gray, Collins, and Goldsmith*, ed. Roger Lonsdale (London: Longmans, 1969), pp. 422-23.

typological scenes appear to be absent here but, in Collins's view, divinely inspired poets are all "prophets," types and antitypes of each other and of the sources of their inspiration. In the more elaborate "Ode on the Poetical Character," in a passage which recollects typological interpretations of human creativity in Akenside's *The Pleasures of the Imagination* (1744) and anticipates similar passages in *The Prelude,* Collins seeks the bard capable of recreating divine rhapsody:

> Where is the bard, whose soul can now
> Its [i.e., Heaven's] high presuming hopes avow?
> Where he who thinks, with rapture blind,
> This hallowed work for him designed?
>
> High on some cliff to Heaven up-piled,
> Of rude access, of prospect wild,
> Where, tangled round the jealous steep,
> Strange shades o'erbrow the valleys deep,
> And holy genii guard the rock,
> Its glooms embrown, its springs unlock,
> While on its rich ambitious head,
> An Eden, like his own, lies spread;
> I view that oak, the fancied glades among,
> By which as Milton lay . . .[13]

The Bard of the poet's search is evidently himself—a traditional identification—and the earlier literary figure, the type of whom he would like to be the antitype, is now Milton. The subject of sacred inspiration is Paradise itself, which Collins represents as a mount of inspired vision (the Eden of *Paradise Lost,* as is traditional in exegesis of Genesis, sits atop such an eminence). Thus the inspiration of the poet is analogous to a prophetic vision from a height, a Mount Pisgah. Collins follows Moses, Jesus, Milton, and all those who have had visionary sight from the heights and, it is important to note, the *place* of inspiration has now become part of a natural typology.[14] We can trace visions from mountaintops back to the

13 *Ibid.,* pp. 433-34.

14 Marjorie Hope Nicolson, *Mountain Gloom and Mountain Glory: The Development of the Aesthetics of the Infinite* (Ithaca, N.Y.: Cornell Univ. Press, 1959), ignores the mount of vision as a literary subject; her account of mountains, instead, is devoted principally to the natural sciences and geology, but see pp. 274-76 (on *Paradise Regained*), and pp. 354-58 (on Gray, Collins, and other mid-eighteenth century poets).

Bible and the pagan classics, but Collins is not merely a landscape poet; he is a pilgrim seeking the sacred and the inspirational, for whom the typological style is an appropriate way to display his quest. What is significant about his expressions of vision is that, while they relate to a lengthy tradition, they are also part of one of the confusions of Babel by which the prefigurative style gradually ceases to be a special dialect and becomes more like the language of everyday speech.

I have already discussed this kind of typologizing in Smart's inspirational poetry, and there are similar examples in Gray's *Odes*, Akenside's discussions of human creativity in *The Pleasures of the Imagination*, and Macpherson's epic fictions. Along with other writers, they represent the gradual refinement of type-language, or the symbolical side of ordinary speech. Type-language exists in every age, but it varies from one period to another, depending upon the things to which a given culture assigns predictive values. In the period I have been studying in this book, the poets who discuss matters of vision and personal involvement in their poetry introduce certain subjects—the mount of vision is just one of them—with coded, prefigurative significance.[15] In one sense, we may say that these poets were using a special dialect; for writers in different literary periods or milieux these terms might not have the same predictive qualities. I do not have the space in this volume to examine the specialized languages of the many nonliterary genres that flourish in the eighteenth and early nineteenth centuries but, as scholars classify some of these genres in more detail, we will notice that such codes are common. Already, thanks to the new taxonomies which the monumental *Eighteenth-Century Short-Title Catalogue* has been applying to the more than one-half million printed works published in English between 1701 and 1800, we can see emerging persuasive evidence that each genre had its own predictive language. The authors of manuals on gardening, pamphlets on the Hanoverian Succession, handbooks on trade and commerce, annual court

---

15 Visionary poets have a small armory of coded terms which comprise their type-language. Gray favors Apocalypse ("The Bard"); Smart refers to different animals, musical harmonies, pearls, and various flora; and Cowper mentions thorns, the worm, tempests, the fig tree, fetters, scenes of battle, and streams or fountains. In this context, see Patricia Meyer Spacks, *The Poetry of Vision: Five Eighteenth-Century Poets* (Cambridge, Mass.: Harvard Univ. Press, 1967), pp. 165-66, where she notes that many of Cowper's coded words "are commonplaces of Evangelical discourse."

calendars and almanacs, and treatises on food and cuisine—five non-theological genres each consisting of more than one thousand exemplars in the eighteenth century alone—all have their own predictive codes appropriate to their specialized audiences which these reading publics understood. In the study of the High Enlightenment—the works of literature on which, for the most part, I have focused in the foregoing chapters—type-language is relatively easy to detect and understand. It will be in the study of the Low Enlightenment, which embraces the vast majority of printed materials, that the recognition of these codes will provide the greatest challenge to scholars and students of the past.

In tracing the typology of everyday life, we must seek more than type-language, for literary texts consist not only of words, but of themes, plots, and characters as well. I have already had occasion to speak of biblical type-scenes and stories relating to such well-known *topoi* as betrayal, persecution, exile, pilgrimage, sin and repentance, sacrifice, and death and resurrection. Themes and motifs deriving from and relating to obviously biblical type-scenes clearly had prefigurative impact on eighteenth- and early nineteenth-century readers of literature, from the simplest periodical essays to the most elaborate novels. Indeed, recent study of biblical type-scenes suggests that even the original audience of the Bible read (or listened) typologically. Much of the art of the Bible, and the art of all narrative works, "lies in the shifting aperture between the shadowy foreimage in the anticipating mind of the observer and the realized revelatory image in the work itself."[16] Type-scenes, which alert the reader of a work to little prefigurative dramas within its essential fabric that allow an audience to predict certain vital conclusions, are, as Theodore Ziolkowski has shown us, universal in modern literature (as they are in all literatures).[17] A twentieth-century audience awake to these possibilities would recognize such types in cinematic narratives as well. An excellent—perhaps an obvious—example is the Western film *High Noon* (1952), in which Kane (Gary Cooper); the good but beleaguered marshal of a frontier town in Texas, faces the threat of death at the hands of four evil men, one of them a convicted murderer whom he had helped to imprison. Kane seeks the support of the townspeople but, like

16 See Robert Alter, "Biblical Type-Scenes and the Uses of Convention," *Critical Inquiry*, 5 (1978-79), 355-68, esp. 368. I quote Alter slightly out of context here but, I think, without doing harm to his argument.

17 See *Fictional Transfigurations of Jesus*, pp. 3-29.

Jesus, he is spurned three times. First, the churchgoing members of the community refuse to help him form a *posse comitatus* (the Pharisees, as the Sanhedrin, reject Jesus—Matt. 26.59-66); next the men in the town's saloon refuse him (the Roman populace requests freedom for Barrabas and crucifixion for Jesus—Matt. 27.21-22); and finally one of his own posse refuses to serve him (Peter denies Jesus —Matt. 26.69-75). Films are the popular narratives of twentieth-century Western culture, and in the popular stories of every age we will find similar type-scenes and plots with prefigurative qualities. The viewers of *High Noon* may realize, dimly or acutely, that the author of the film has made prefigurative hints which will help to predict the conclusion, although, of course, the tradition of the Western film requires that the Jesus-figure will dramatically reverse the sacrifice of which he is the intended victim.[18]

Popular writers of the eighteenth century were strongly aware of the need to communicate with their readers in terms of prefigurative codes, so that even works which might seem to lack a moral foundation could possess a didactic purpose. Sir Roger L'Estrange, in the century's most popular collection of fables (whose typological qualities I have already noticed), argues that mythologists, fabulists, and writers of fiction are bound to write prefiguratively in order to teach proper behavior:

> Now as there are Good and Bad of all sorts, their good Behaviour and their Misdemeanours are to be set forth, circumstanc'd, and distinguish'd in such sort, as by Rewards or Punishments, to Encourage the One, and to Discountenance the Other, in Proportion to the Dignity of the Action, or the Degree of the Offence; by conferring Marks or Characters of Honour, Offices of Trust, or Beneficial Commissions on one hand; and by inflicting Sentences of Shame, Infamy, Pains, Corporal or Pecuniary, on the other. Without this Distribution, one main end of the Emblem is lost; *neither is it the true figure of Life.* For, Wicked Men, False Brethren, Unnatural Parents, Disobedient Children, Barbarous Husbands, Unduti-

---

[18] It is a commonplace of criticism of *High Noon* that screen writer Carl Foreman and director Fred Zinnemann deliberately analogize the action of the film—the stalking of Marshal Kane by the gang—to the McCarthyite persecutions of Hollywood artists in the early 1950s. Critics have noted that the murderer who leads the gang actually resembles Senator McCarthy. See Mark Crispin Miller, "What Happened in the Sixties?" *New York Review of Books,* 22 (4 Aug. 1977), 17-22.

ful Wives, Tyrannical, Weak, or Fantastical Governors, Rebellious Subjects, Cruel Masters, Faithless Servants, Perfidious Kindred and Acquaintants: All these Lewd Characters are as absolutely necessary to the Design, as the most Laudable Excellencies in Nature.[19]

Vice, as Johnson would say in *Rambler* 4, "is necessary to be shewn" but "wherever it appears, it should raise hatred by the malignity of its practices, and contempt by the meanness of its stratagems." In scores of *moralia* to his *Fables*, L'Estrange emphasizes that these stories and the characters they present are type-themes and type-characters. A work that ignores the proper arrangement and distribution of these types is emphatically not "the true Figure of Life." L'Estrange, other fabulists, the collectors of characters, and most eighteenth-century novelists seem to have shared similar views. Narratives imitate life and, in order to be "true" or probable, they must, according to L'Estrange, be figural and predictive. From this conclusion, which merely echoes the argument from design in the literary sphere, it will be obvious that life itself, the subject rather than the result of mimesis, must be a fabric of prefigurative emblems, events, characters, and themes. Eighteenth-century students of narrative and reality realized that experience—the basis of all narrative, of all literature—is predictive. We anticipate the conclusion of the circumstances that we encounter or in which we take part, basing our expectations on an elaborate typology of previous experience, whether consciously remembered or subconsciously sensed, which allows us to make predictive judgments about the likely outcome of events, characters of individuals, and meanings of words or signs. One might describe the mixture of psychology and semiology whereby the human mind predicts—whether rightly or wrongly—such conclusions as the psycho-typology of everyday life.

 3

The literary contexts for this kind of typology are many—so numerous, in fact, that I will give only a brief perspective on them here,

[19] *Fables of Æsop and Other Eminent Mythologists with Morals and Reflections*, I, 445-46, from L'Estrange's *moralium* to Fable 413, "The Kingdom of Apes" (italics added).

for this chapter is a conclusion, not a beginning. It would be fair to say that all seekers after the sublime in the works of nature, especially those who attach a sacramental meaning to emotionally charged scenery, whether landscape or cityscape, may be classified as natural typologists. Denham, viewing London beneath its cloak of smog from the modest eminence of Cooper's Hill, has religious musings and, in some of them, the circumstances assume prefigurative force. Nearly every topographical and prospect poem after *Coopers Hill* (1642) includes some awareness of the infinite, the Supreme Being and his attributes, and their predictive import to man. The Creation, after all, was a book, and English writers, particularly Protestants, were very much people of the book. Therefore it is a commonplace for writers of our period, from 1650 to 1820, as it has been throughout the centuries, to analogize the typology of The Book, the Bible, to the book of nature. When Thomas Gray visited the Grande Chartreuse in the late 1730s, he was thoroughly seduced by the mountain scenery, just as John Dennis had been and as the several generations of English visitors who followed him would be. He wrote to Richard West in a tone that would later become the familiar coin of such descriptions: "Not a precipice, not a torrent, not a cliff, but is pregnant with religion and poetry."[20] Wordsworth, as we have already seen, also was moved by the typological possibilities of these landscapes. But the key poet for our understanding of the typological qualities of secular life and landscape is not the religiously inspired Smart, or Gray and Collins in their rhapsodic moments.

It is far more likely Cowper, highly respected for his *Olney Hymns* (which are often typological) and an important secular voice of the 1780s. He could say, with assurance, at the end of his "The Progress of Error" (1782), "I am no preacher." Nevertheless, he sees the sacramental aspects of life as no other secular poet before Wordsworth did:

> The cross, once seen, is death to ev'ry vice:
> Else he that hung there suffer'd all his pain,
> Bled, groan'd, and agoniz'd, and died, in vain.[21]

Cowper has an uncanny ability to bring divine figuration into his secular verse. In this poem he undertakes to lecture the English

[20] *The Correspondence of Thomas Gray*, ed. Paget Toynbee and Leonard Whibley, 3 vols. (Oxford: Clarendon Press, 1935), I, 138.
[21] "The Progress of Error," lines 621-24.

establishment on philosophy, ethics, and politics, just as Coleridge would begin to do, a decade later, in prose. There is, or should be, a prefigurative lining to contemporary events which, Cowper believes, may be found in analogies to Christian typology. In another poem of the same period, "Expostulation" (1782), his focus is slightly different but his method is the same. "Expostulation" is a discussion of the decline of English liberty in the problem-filled years of the American Revolutionary War, a period during which Paine, Price, Priestley, and many other political and religious thinkers spoke strongly and often of political and social crisis and the fulfillment of ancient types. "Wherefore weep for England?" Cowper asks (31), and answers with a long parallel which begins with the coded phrase, "The prophet wept for Israel." Israel—a chosen people, delivered by a Savior, its glory now faded and dispersed—becomes a type of contemporary England, except that England, an exporter of slavery and tyranny, is worse than its type, for antitypes are usually greater than their shadowings in one way or another.

Cowper, without the strong prophetic utterance and fanfare of Blake, Brothers, or Southcott, associates himself with Jeremiah, who prefigures Jesus, and issues forth his word,

> Mark'd with the signature and stamp of heav'n,
> The word of prophesy, those truths divine
> Which make that heav'n if thou desire it thine . . .
>
> (685-87)

Since Cowper does not cultivate the religious sublime in his poems of 1782, students of religious verse have found far better examples for scrutiny; but in his plain, conversational, sometimes confessional manner he manages to make both himself and his subject manifestly typological.[22] His typological method extends through more than ten thousand lines of ostensibly secular verse, so it is difficult, if not unjust, to epitomize his prefigurative attitudes. Perhaps the epitome may be found in the final lines of "Conversation" (1782), a droll essay on language, forms of narrative, and social intercourse. Good conversation, Cowper tells us, is heavenly, and is meant to pursue the course "that truth and nature teach." At its

---

[22] Even so excellent a study as David B. Morris's *The Religious Sublime: Christian Poetry and Critical Tradition in 18th-Century England* (Lexington, Ky.: Univ. Press of Kentucky, 1972) overlooks Cowper's contributions, perhaps because his theological message is so secularized and so coded in terms of natural typology.

best, everything else "is made subservient to the grand design, /
For which heav'n form'd the faculty divine" and, carried on by a
gifted artist, "It sounds Jehovah's name, and pours his praise
along."[23] Conversation thus becomes sacramental, a coded activity,
best meant for the praise of divine things and, in its purest form,
a foreshadow of them.

At this point another example of natural typology from *The
Prelude* may be helpful. I have in mind another passage from Book
VI where, still recalling his days at Cambridge, Wordsworth remem-
bers the pleasures "Of geometric science":

> More frequently from the same source I drew
> A pleasure quiet and profound, a sense
> Of permanent and universal sway,
> And paramount belief; there, recognised
> A type, for finite natures, of the one
> Supreme Existence, the surpassing life
> Which—to the boundaries of space and time,
> Of melancholy space and doleful time,
> Superior, and incapable of change,
> Nor touched by welterings of passion—is,
> And hath the name of, God.[24]

Wordsworth does not quite argue for the typological basis of everyday life in these lines; geometry, after all, is a highly symbolic system of notations and proofs. Nevertheless, we catch a glimpse here
of God as Supreme Geometer. Natural typologists from Collins to
Coleridge reserve the right to epitomize their themes with specifically focused examples. Collins stresses the prophetic power of his
verse with comparisons to mounts of vision; Cowper shows that conversation is typological by presenting Luke's account of the two
travelers on the road to Emmaus who converse with the resurrected
Jesus; and Wordsworth speaks here of how one of the favorite subjects of the physico-theologians prefigures God. The English Newtonians had not mentioned geometry as part of Newton's natural

---

23 See "Conversation," lines 881-908. Earlier examples in the poem hint at
more obvious typology: Cowper recounts the conversation of Cleopas and his
friend with the unknown stranger (the risen Christ) on the road to Emmaus
(lines 505-36), an elegant version of Luke 24.13-35, and makes this occasion a
type of all good converse on heavenly things. The Cleopas of Luke 24 is presumably the same person as the Cleophas of John 19.25.

24 *The Prelude*, VI.129-39.

philosophy, but Whiston had seen Newton's mathematical and scientific discoveries as proof of natural phenomena that confirmed the prophecies of Daniel and Revelation.[25] Wordsworth does not speak of the Apocalypse here—he does mention it in his typological description of the Simplon Pass, also in Book VI—but that is because his discovery of geometry is just one of the happenings of everyday life, what might well happen to any collegian reading a textbook.

The typological learning of Coleridge was probably greater than that of any other Romantic poet, including Shelley. Not only did Coleridge closely read a welter of English, German, classical, and patristic authors who favor and use typology, but he also annotated (and we have preserved, mainly at The British Library) the works of Boehme, Warburton, Hartley, and Bryant, to mention only some of the authors whom I have dealt with most prominently in this study. He early recognized the multivalent nature of typology, but his rare discussions of it in his philosophical prose, most of them from the second decade of the nineteenth century, show that he was not entirely certain how to apply the language of the types. For example, in his Bristol lectures of 1813-14, Coleridge delivered a talk of more than usual miscellaneity, entitled "Asiatic and Greek Mythologies—Robinson Crusoe—Use of Works of Imagination in Education." Here he speaks of hellenistic mythology as "a mythology in itself fundamentally allegorical, and typical of the powers and functions of nature, but subsequently mixed up with a deification of great men and hero-worship,—so that finally the original idea became inextricably combined with the form and attributes of some legendary individual."[26] Warburton, Herder, Bryant, and Jones all discuss the decline of Greek, and other, mythology as a result of euhemerism, but Coleridge's perception that these ancient narratives prefigure "the powers and functions of nature" is an important step beyond the mythographers. As we know from *Biographia Literaria*, Coleridge tried to develop a theory of creativity according to which one force or agent had the power to receive perceptions and to figure forth an artistic representation of them. It may be that his comments on Greek myth were meant to be an early stage of this theory—the evidence is insufficient—but in their surviving form they show that he was aware of the typological

---

[25] See *The Accomplishment of Scripture Prophecies*, p. 95.
[26] Lecture XI in "A Course of Lectures," *The Literary Remains of Samuel Taylor Coleridge*, ed. Henry Nelson Coleridge, 4 vols. (London, 1836-39), I, 185.

possibilities of narrative and of natural phenomena. Coleridge makes a stronger statement on prefiguration in *Biographia Litera-ria*, at the end of his famous chapter "Of the Imagination, or esemplastic power":

> The IMAGINATION then I consider either as primary, or secondary. The primary IMAGINATION I hold to be the liv-ing Power and prime Agent of all human Perception, and as a repetition in the finite mind of the eternal act of creation in the infinite I AM. The secondary I consider as an echo of the former, co-existing with the conscious will, yet still as identical with the primary in the *kind* of its agency, and differing only in *degree*, and in the mode of its operation. It dissolves, diffuses, dissipates, in order to re-create; or where this process is ren-dered impossible, yet still at all events it struggles to idealize and to unify. It is essentially *vital*, even as all objects (*as* ob-jects) are essentially fixed and dead.[27]

The primary imagination is clearly Coleridge's shaping force, a re-flection in the human mind of divine creativity ("the infinite I AM"), but finite and a diminution of something infinitely greater. In the sense that the primary imagination is typological, it prefig-ures the secondary imagination, which is the antitype of the pri-mary. The secondary is identical with the primary imagination, except that it is the created, idealizing, unifying, embodying force, a representation in plastic terms of what the primary imagination has perceived. Coleridge slightly distorts his typology here: the usual relationship between type and antitype is one between lesser and greater, but he proposes that the secondary imagination is "an echo of the [primary]." Thus Coleridge's prefigurative relationship, at least in this instance, involves a declining rather than a rising structure, for we must assume that an echo is a slight diminution of its original.

Difficult as are Coleridge's speculations in the *Biographia*, they become even more clouded in his *Hints towards the formation of a more comprehensive Theory of Life* (1818) where, once again at the very close of a complicated argument, he brings up the subject of figuration. In Chapter XIII of the *Biographia*, there are several hints at a typological subject before the final paragraph on primary

[27] *Biographia Literaria; or Biographical Sketches of My Literary Life and Opinions*, 2 vols. (London, 1817), I, 295.

and secondary imagination: the epigraph from *Paradise Lost* deals with gradations of creation, from lower to higher, and the letter from "a friend" (actually from Coleridge himself) mentions shadows several times and suggests that Chapter XIII is but an idea of a much larger work. The *Hints* does not have quite the same kind of structure—to do it justice, I should say that it rambles more than Coleridge's shorter works—but his suggestions are audacious and deserve our attention:

> Life, *as* Life, supposes a positive or universal principle in Nature, with a negative principle in every particular animal, the latter, or limitative power, constantly acting to individualize, and, as it were, *figure* the former. *Thus,* then, Life itself is not a *thing*—a self-subsistent *hypostasis*—but an *act* and a *process*; which, pitiable as the prejudice will appear to the *forts esprits,* is a great deal more than either my reason would authorise or my conscience allow me to assert—concerning the Soul, as the principle of both reason and conscience.[28]

To interpret, I would say that the negative, or limitative, power in all animals is the figuring power, the type which prefigures the positive, or universal principle in Nature, the antitype. The limitative power constantly individualizes, figuring forth specialized forms from the increate formlessness; Coleridge says earlier in the *Hints* that "the individuation itself must be a tendency to the ultimate production of the highest and most comprehensive individuality."[29] Thus this typological or figuring power leads from less formed to "the most comprehensive" particularized forms—from shadowy or imperfect type to completed antitype. This universal typology of forms seems very distant from the usual theater of prefiguration but, as I hope to show in a moment, it has its own peculiar relevance to the typology of everyday life. Coleridge's process of figuring is itself predictive and typological, for lower forms presuppose higher, more complex forms, of which Man is the highest. No wonder, then, that Coleridge should call Man "a revelation of Nature!"[30]

At this point, I should note that the main trends in biblical criticism and exegesis in the early nineteenth century were toward extreme literalism and the capturing of the spirit of the author of a text. David Strauss's *Life of Jesus* (1835) completely rejects all fig-

[28] *Hints towards the formation of a more comprehensive Theory of Life,* ed. Seth B. Watson (London, 1848), pp. 93-94.
[29] *Ibid.,* p. 50.   [30] *Ibid.,* p. 86.

ural interpretations of Jesus's life and mission, which means, more bluntly, that Strauss scuttled typological interpretation. Friedrich Schleiermacher, in biblical hermeneutics, thought even less of typology than Strauss and his historical school of exegesis, and believed that continuity in the biblical narratives about Jesus could be found by trying to grasp the spirit of the author and their inner form or organic connections.[31] Coleridge was acquainted with the major trends of biblical hermeneutics in Germany and England, and would have been aware, too, that even English exegetes, who were less advanced than the Germans in the early nineteenth century, had turned from traditional exegesis to studying the generation of myths, language, and literary forms. So when he writes in the *Hints towards the formation of a more comprehensive Theory of Life* of the figurative process in the development of different forms of life, it is significant that he continues to retain an interest in prefigurative systems and not at all surprising that his typology, such as it is, is so closely involved with the evolution of higher forms of life.

The typology of Coleridge's poetry is of at least two kinds. What we see in *The Ancient Mariner* and *Cristabel* is similar to much of what I have discussed in earlier chapters—Coleridge uses the prefigurative traditions of myth, the sacraments, and biblical type-characters and scenes in both poems. In neither case do we find a system of prefiguration that can be described as natural typology. However, some of the shorter poems that appeared for the first time in *Sibylline Leaves* (1817)—a title with obvious prophetic implications—although written earlier than his prose speculations on figuration, are worthy of attention here. The "Hymn before Sunrise in the Vale of Chamouni" shows Coleridge's natural typology at work, profoundly emotional yet much less formal than that which either Wordsworth or Shelley displayed when writing about the same Alps. The poem is not prophetic and gives no hint of prefiguration, but its motion, as Coleridge worships the vastness of Mont Blanc and as he exhorts the mountain and all its attendant glories to praise God, is continually rising. Coleridge clearly sees Mont Blanc as a type and figure of eternity, of heaven, and of the mighty hand that made them both, but we can only surmise such a conclusion from the sacramental meaning with which he enwraps every object. If the "Hymn before Sunrise" is to be seen as a psalm of praise, and there is no question that Coleridge intended it to be such, then we

---

[31] See Frei, *The Eclipse of Biblical Narrative*, pp. 310-16.

can regard Coleridge himself as Davidic lyricist, a typological figure of the last and most inspired of prophets.

Even more expressive of the typology of everyday life is "Frost at Midnight," in which Coleridge broods over his child's cradle as the frost on a winter's evening "performs its secret ministry." The poem's prefigurative devices are explicit: the fluttering fire on the grate takes Coleridge back to his own childhood, when he would watch the same fluttering of the flames in the schoolhouse fire as if they were "Presageful" of a visit by a stranger, when he would hear the ringing of church bells "like articulate sounds of things to come!" The promise of "things to come" is a close recollection of the language of typology in the New Testament, particularly Paul's assurance to the Hebrews that "the law [has] a shadow of good things to come, and not the very image of those things" (Heb. 10.1). Coleridge proceeds to prophesy the good things which his child will enjoy:

> So shalt thou see and hear
> The lovely shapes and sounds intelligible
> Of that eternal language, which thy God
> Utters, who from eternity doth teach
> Himself in all, and all things in himself.
> Great universal Teacher! He shall mould
> Thy Spirit, and by giving make it ask.[32]

This prefiguration is consistent with Coleridge's later theories of types—his child will be a higher form than he, and will see and hear more than he has known. In his own childhood, he dreamed of antitypes, things to come, but he is certain that his child will achieve a union with the godhead that he has never enjoyed. Coleridge's visionary style, then, is prophetic in a manner far different from that of his contemporary prophet-poets, for he is less the heraldic figure with a trumpet and more the quiet prefigurant with an aeolian harp.

If Coleridge is uncomfortable with the style of prophetic typology, he doubtless had good reason for his attitude. His own millenarianism, which he expresses elegantly in "Religious Musings" (1794), must have led to disappointment by the turn of the century, when he realized that the Millennium had not come.[33] "Religious

---

[32] "Frost at Midnight," (1798), lines 58-64.

[33] See Garrett, *Respectable Folly*, pp. 142-43; his chapter, "The Millenarian Tradition in English Dissent" (pp. 121-43) is highly relevant to Coleridge's early millenarianism.

Musings" is an intensely typological meditation, written on Christ-
mas Eve 1794; it is a study of the redeeming virtues of Christ's crucifixion, and a certain promise of eternity. Coleridge's climactic account of the Apocalypse may be his best typological passage:

> Believe thou, O my soul,
> Life is a vision shadowy of Truth;
> And vice, and anguish, and the wormy grave,
> Shapes of a dream! The veiling clouds retire,
> And lo! the Throne of the redeeming God
> Forth flashing unimaginable day
> Wraps in one blaze earth, heaven, and deepest hell.[34]

Life and its concomitant sufferings and joys are but a prefiguration
of an eternal Truth, the apocalyptic unification of all, heaven and
hell, at the moment of Eternity. The typology of everyday life could
scarcely be expressed more dramatically. But Coleridge, after 1800,
became disenchanted with millenarian politics and its prophetic
style. Despite his admiration for Price and Priestley, he found himself doubting the efficacy of the prophetic role. In his lines "To
William Wordsworth" (1807), he specifically rejects the voice of
public prophecy which Blake was cultivating so successfully and
which Shelley would later adopt. "That way no more! and ill be-
seems it me," he cries, "Who came a welcomer in herald's guise, /
Singing of Glory, and Futurity."[35] "Glory, and Futurity" are the
stock in trade of the millenarian seer, and the kerygmatic style is
the prophet's traditional voice—heraldic and annunciatory. Prophetic typology continues long after Coleridge—it is with us yet—
but I know of few writers who so categorically reject its messianic
stance as he does. Nevertheless, despite his rejection, Coleridge
never ceased to think prefiguratively, as his efforts to demonstrate
the existence of a prefigurative basis to life and the creative force
reveal.

The chronological focus of this book, barely 175 years of literary
and intellectual history, is small in terms of the lifespan of typology
but it is long enough, I think, to illustrate the progress and changes

---

[34] "Religious Musings," lines 395-401.
[35] "To William Wordsworth," lines 76-78.

of the language and uses of the types. I have alluded earlier to the restrictive definitions of the Fathers, and it may be well, at the conclusion, to mention them again. Augustine, who kept typology known in the West at a time when the mode was most common in the Eastern Church, used typological exegesis very extensively. He was fully aware that types hint and foreshadow the future. A type "cannot fully be known at the time of the occurrence," writes a recent commentator on Augustine, "although there may be no realization of that fact at the time of the occurrence. Clearly, only God may be the author [of types] since he alone certainly knows the future."[36] The view that God was the author of the types, as he was the author of the book of nature, may be found in eighteenth-century theology as clearly as in that of Augustine. But there is another conception of typology that originates in the Middle Ages. It is that typology is not simply a method of biblical exegesis, but that it is a world view, a way of reading sacred history and, by extension, secular history as well. The application of the types to sacred history leads to prophetic and millenarian typology; their application to secular history opens a much larger area of inquiry, for this approach leads to the study of prefigurative elements in every branch of secular literature. I have emphasized throughout that types are codes which not every member of a given audience may be able to decipher. Since writers who introduce typology into their texts usually accompany it with various signs, symbols, images, or other hints of its presence, our awareness of the use of typology may depend upon our knowledge of these signs. And, when we understand them, we may perceive types elsewhere, in nonliterary contexts.

It is now appropriate to ask the most speculative of questions: what kinds of writers can we expect to use typology, and why? Why do some writers in the later seventeenth century, like Dryden, use typology frequently in secular contexts, while others in the same period, like Pepys and Evelyn, use it very seldom? Why, in the early eighteenth century, does Pope use typology so often, while his contemporary Gay uses it practically not at all? Smart introduces types on almost every possible occasion; his contemporary Samuel Johnson almost never uses them. Cowper's secular poetry is rich in typology, that of his contemporary Crabbe is nearly bereft of it. Coleridge, Shelley, and Byron use different kinds of typology often, but

[36] See Raymond Carter Sutherland, "Theological Notes on the Origin of Types, 'Shadows of Things to Be,'" *Studies in the Literary Imagination*, 8 (1975), 1-13. esp. p. 12.

Keats almost never introduces it into his poetry. We could make similar observations about many other writers specializing in a number of genres. Typological source materials, as I have shown, are always available, and certain subjects—kingship, prophecy, the Millennium—seem to summon forth the typological imagination more than other topics for, indeed, the typological propensity is very common to the human condition. The typologist need not have a great deal of learning: some of the best and most inventive secular types are the work of writers whose formal education was almost non-existent, like Bunyan, Blake, and Brothers.

Let me venture a few answers, equally speculative. Since typology, in the English Enlightenment, is always most closely associated with the religious faith of the dissenting sects, secular writers with a dissenting background or interest will be more likely to employ typology than others. Typology, in addition to being a system of exegesis, a hermeneutic device, a method of linking together the two Testaments of the Bible, is also one more thing that I have not previously mentioned. Typology is a method of presenting evidence, an evidentiary technique. A writer who employs typology in secular literature is using it for purposes of proof, demonstration, and convincing. But typology, with its analogical basis, specializes in demonstrating or suggesting relationships between things that do not readily have resemblances. The typologist, as Warburton noted, does not say "A suggests B" or even "A (which is obscure) suggests B." Rather, the user of prefigurative imagery says "A (which is obscure) suggests—or shadows forth—B (which may also be obscure)." Hence the writer who introduces typological figuralism into a work of literature is proving something, but he or she is not going about it in a direct way. The writer who will use typology, then, is someone whose evidentiary methodology is—at least for the moment—indirect. The typological relationship is one of the world's oldest literary codes and, potentially, one of the most difficult to decipher. Thus the typologist asks an audience to work harder at interpretation, to read more closely. The writer who uses types, finally, seems to me to be asking for commitment from his or her audience—from those who are able to decipher the code, that is—for some readers will have the mental equipment to interpret the typological relationship while others will not. Not all types are equally difficult, of course, but, then, not all readers are equally intelligent. The typologist, like any other figuralist, takes the risk of painting pictures to the imagination, and some writers, who do not fear being misunderstood by a portion of their readers, will take such a risk. Typological codes, after all, are a challenge to both author and reader and, as such, they can be an intricate part of writing and interpreting.

Outside the literary milieu, a type does not have the same prefigurative functions that it has in a text; it has little or nothing to do with a narrative story and it will have small value in interpreting language or character. Yet typology exists in nonliterary contexts; in theological situations, it has flourished in iconography since late Latin antiquity, indeed, for as long as there has been a Christian iconography. Can it be found outside the religious sphere? There is no doubt that it can, as the iconology of Ripa and George Richardson shows. The wide acceptance of the syntax of visual symbols in literature, through the influence of Ripa, the popularity of emblem books (a Renaissance vogue that continued during the eighteenth century), and the gradual diffusion through English culture of certain standardized notions of ornament, helps to create an anatomy of prefiguration whose magnitude scholars have just started to grasp. Addison, who did so much to popularize for the eighteenth century one of the greatest of English typological authors—Milton —may serve as an example of the importance of another kind of typology, that of nonliterary forms. Let me look for a moment at his *Dialogues upon the Usefulness of Ancient Medals* (1702), a branch of study more popular in the eighteenth century than in our own. Addison discusses particular medals and general principles of iconography. Of one image he writes, "The next figure I present you with is *Eternity*. She holds in her hand a globe with a Phænix on it. How proper a type of Eternity is each of these you may see in the following quotations [which illustrate phoenix-imagery]." Or again, "The woman underneath represents the earth. . . . The *Cornucopiae* in her hand is a type of her fruitfulness."[37] Later, Addison takes a broader historical view of ancient and modern coins and medals, as he speaks of medallic symbolism in France:

> It is certain . . . there is the same mixture of Christian and Pagan in their Coins; nor is there a less confusion in their customs. For example, what relation is there between the figure of a Bull, and the planting of a French colony in America? The Romans made use of this type in allusion to one of their own customs at the sending out of a colony. But for the *French*, a

[37] See *The Works of Joseph Addison*, 4 vols. (London, 1721), I, 462, 491.

Ram, a hog, or an Elephant, would have been every whit as significant an emblem.[38]

Besides the mildly disparaging tone, I would note that Addison's medallic *types*, thanks to the confusion of terminology that often surrounds the term, are perhaps more appropriately *emblems* than prefigurative elements. Yet the types on old coins do have an aura of predictiveness—Addison notes that the Romans used the figure of a bull with a particular purpose—though sometimes we may not understand the code behind them completely. Addison detects a "confusion" in French medallic figuralism, and confusion there may indeed be. However, as we struggle with the meaning of such types, there is always the possibility that the relevant code, some orderly sense or arrangement, just may exist, but that we have not entirely discovered how to decipher it.

Visual codes are always puzzling, as Addison and other amateur antiquarians of the seventeenth and eighteenth centuries found when they began to study a mysterious past without professional skills or vast technical knowledge. In the same manner, predictive codes that were understood by specialists in the eighteenth century may still be lost to us in the twentieth. Printing types, for example, once may have been used by typographers with prefigurative and predictive force, as part of a printers' code or a semiotics of print. Such a tradition appears to have been relatively strong in the sixteenth century, when the type font in which a book was printed was often a key to its subject, a predictive element to guide the reader in his or her assumptions about the book's seriousness. Some printers used a single font for Bibles, another (usually brevier) for prayer books and missals, one for secular romances, one for sermons and exegeses, and still another for classical texts. Further keys to a book's purpose would be found in subtleties relating to layout, format, and title-page design. Hence when a new genre evolved, printers would often demand a new type font for it, so that the uniqueness of the new class of books would be clear to readers. The civilité font was introduced in this way, in early sixteenth-century France, for the purpose of printing children's textbooks and guidebooks.[39] By

[38] *Ibid.*, I, 537.

[39] See Elizabeth L. Eisenstein, *The Printing Press as an Agent of Change*, 2 vols. (Cambridge: Cambridge Univ. Press, 1979), I, 201-207, 430. The confusion of printers' types and biblical types exists in the eighteenth century, but it is difficult for me to say how common it was. For example, Philip Freneau makes

the late seventeenth century, this figural tradition was all but lost except for the finest printing (which was rare in England before Baskerville), but I am sure that some of my readers may remember, as I do, feeling a sense of mystery at the discovery that the types in which Bibles, dictionaries, and encyclopediae were printed differed from that used for *Robinson Crusoe*. Familiarity lessens the surprise, and the mystery, for most of us, is "lost in kindly heat of lengthned day."

Visual codes are especially common in architecture and here, too, types have their importance. Architectural types change over the centuries, so that a library of the Middle Ages does not at all resemble one of the twentieth; but if we examine, as a group, eighteenth-century market buildings, law courts, royal palaces, libraries, theaters, and so on, we will indeed find visual codes that contemporary architects used so that an audience would understand, without need of an explanation, the purpose and ceremonial function of a given building.[40] As the world of print becomes ever more complex, that of visual symbols slowly recedes. This gradual process was at work during the years 1650-1820. Iconic symbols, that is, visual symbols of invisible entities, thus become more shadowy throughout the eighteenth and early nineteenth centuries. We may still see these old signs on monuments and public buildings, but they are now nearly as meaningless as the abstractions they were meant to represent.[41]

In the Middle Ages, as Jacob Burckhardt saw, "Man was conscious of himself only as a member of a race, people, party, family,

---

a series of complex puns on scriptural types and printers' types in his "Epigram occasioned by the title of Rivington's Royal Gazette being scarcely legible"; see *The Freeman's Journal*, 13 February 1782. Printers' flowers and ornaments, since they often qualify as pieces of iconology or iconography, sometimes convey typological meaning. See Keith Maslen, *The Bowyer Ornament Stock*, Oxford Bibliographical Society Occasional Publications, No. 8 (Oxford: Bodleian Library, 1973), pp. 13, 18, 25, 28 (Nos. 5, 20, 70, 114-20 [a series of tailpieces incorporating the phoenix]).

[40] Nicolaus Pevsner, *A History of Building Types* (Princeton: Princeton Univ. Press, 1976), shows in remarkable detail the evolution of models and architectural styles in buildings designed for different purposes. Pevsner himself is aware of the hidden codes I have been discussing, which he describes as elements of design. See esp. his chapter on national monuments and monuments to genius, pp. 11-26.

[41] See E. H. Gombrich, "*Icones Symbolicae*: The Visual Image in Neo-Platonic Thought," *JWCI*, 11 (1948), 163-92.

or corporation—only through some general category."[42] Typology answered to this need for, by its very nature, it allows readers to make general connections between one category of events, people, or things, and another. In the Middle Ages and Renaissance, typology linked pagan authors to the Christian temperament. Even when the Enlightenment put an end at last to such general categorizing, and allowed the growth of individuality, typology continued to flourish and to grow in new and unforeseen directions. The novelists, creators of the genre that more than any other heightens the individual, adapted and used it, and so did learned men and poets from Dryden to Coleridge. Its popularity continued after the end of the Enlightenment. We may read the novels of the 1850s, books like Charles Kingsley's *Hypatia* (1853), Cardinal Wiseman's *Fabiola* (1854), or George Eliot's *Adam Bede* (1859), and find these authors using typological figuration in a somewhat altered form. And the decade of the 1850s is by no means unique—similar evidence for systems of prefiguration appears in almost every decade of English and American literary history. As we study the history of typology, I hope that I have shown that the types are ever-present, a silent language waiting to be unlocked.

[42] *The civilization of the Renaissance in Italy*, trans. S.G.C. Middlemore, 2 vols. (New York, 1958), I, 143.

CHAPTER 11

Typology: A Bibliographical
Essay

T<small>HE INDEX TO</small> this book includes all authors and works to which I refer in both text and notes. If the reader wishes to know whether I mention a given work, or to find my first reference—with bibliographical information—to a work, he or she should look there. The following bibliographical discussion, therefore, does not merely present, in a different arrangement, the books and articles that I note elsewhere. I do mention a few items that I have already cited but, for the most part, I discuss materials for which there was no room in my notes or no convenient reason to cite, even though I made good use of all of them. I have classified a small number of the basic sources, both primary and secondary, for my work on typology, with an emphasis on subjects that others have treated in greater detail than I have done here and on topics for which definitive treatment is still lacking. The thoroughness of my own research will have to speak for itself; in the following pages, I intend my commentary to provide both the casual reader and the serious student with some useful guides for the further study of typology, typologies, and their applications in theological and nontheological contexts.

1. *Bibliography*. No scholar has yet compiled a thorough bibliography of typology and its manifold applications. Sacvan Bercovitch's "Annotated Bibliography: Typology and Early American Literature" in *Typology and Early American Literature*, ed. Sacvan Bercovitch (Amherst: Univ. of Massachusetts Press, 1972), pp. 245-337, provides a most helpful beginning for the modern student, but the compiler notes in several places that his work is selective, focuses principally on early American literature, and is restricted mainly to

396

the typology of the two Testaments. Hence Bercovitch quite properly omits most millenarian works and virtually all figural applications of pagan myths (this work also contains an unusually large number of errors for a bibliography). Pre-1800 scholarly works seldom are bibliographically rich, but I have found compilations assembled for the use of divinity students and clergymen to be a good source of typological exegeses. Of these, one of the best in English is that by John Wilkins, Bishop of Chester, *Ecclesiastes: or, A Discourse of the Gift of Preaching* (London, 1646; many subsequent editions), a work that gives good contemporary references for most aspects of theological study as it was then constituted. Another important early resource that scholars often ignore is the wealth of eighteenth- and nineteenth-century catalogues of large private libraries. Unlike the contemporary auction catalogue, which auctioneers usually prepared hastily for their sales, the library catalogue often has considerable pretensions to scholarship and a scheme of classification that makes it easy to use. One of the largest and best arranged of these is the *Bibliothecae Harleianae Catalogus*, 5 vols. (London, 1743-45), which William Oldys and Samuel Johnson compiled for the bookseller Osborne; its scheme of classification is one of the best ever conceived before the age of modern librarianship. The student should consult the sections on the Bible and its interpretations in Volumes 1-4; Volume 5, however, is nearly worthless. Three others that I have used extensively are [Carolus a Firmian,] *Bibliotheca Firmiana*, 6 vols. (Milan, 1783), [Maffei Pinelli,] *Bibliotheca Maphei Pinelli Veneti*, 6 vols. (Venice, 1787; the Pinelli sale, which took place in London over sixty days in 1789, has a one-volume sale catalogue, *Bibliotheca Pinelliana* [London, 1789]), and [Samuel Parr,] *Bibliotheca Parriana* (London, 1827). In the realm of library catalogues, I have started most of my work with the *General Catalogue of Printed Books* of the British Library (known to specialists, in its present state, as GK3): its three massive volumes on "Bible," with hundreds of appendixes and subsections, and its entry on "Jesus Christ" should be standard sources for all typologists. The De Backers' great bibliography of the Jesuits, Augustin and Alois De Backer, *Bibliographie de la Compagnie de Jésus*, 11 vols., 3rd ed. (Brussels and Paris: O. Schepens, 1890-1909), with Volume XII, "Supplement," ed. Ernest M. Rivière (Louvain: Editions de la bibliothèque S.J., 1911-30), provides more than 10,000 pages of listings, but it is useful only when one's author happens to be a Jesuit. The bibliographies in *The Cambridge History of the Bible*, 3 vols.

(Cambridge: Cambridge Univ. Press, 1963-70), while brief, are relatively current, but are stronger on textual than on exegetical matters. Henkel and Schöne's supplementary volume to their monumental *Emblemata* (Stuttgart: J. B. Metzler, 1967), is a splendid iconographical bibliography: Arthur Henkel and Albrecht Schöne, *Emblemata: Supplement der Erstausgabe* (Stuttgart: J. B. Metzler, 1976). The notes and bibliographies of secondary sources also deserve attention; of the hundreds of such works that I cite in my own notes, I have found the books—and bibliographies—of Berthold Altaner, Jean Cardinal Daniélou, Barbara K. Lewalski, and C. A. Patrides especially detailed guides to typological study.

2. *Source Materials for the Study of Typology.* In addition to mainly bibliographical guides, there are a number of authors whose works are typological sources in that they refer to or analyze large bodies of prefigurative materials. The annotated Bibles and scholarly syntagmata of the European Renaissance are often vast thesauruses of primary materials. I have used the *Biblia Sacra, cum glossis, interlinearia et ordinaria, Nicolai Lyrani postilla,* 7 vols. (Venice, 1588), but any Renaissance edition of the Bible that includes Nicholas of Lyra's enormous fourteenth-century commentary will do as well. Among the syntagmata, there are three that I would mention here: Salomon Glassius, *Philologia Sacra,* 5 vols. (Jena, 1623-36), Matthew Poole, *Synopsis Criticorum,* 4 vols. (London, 1669-76), and Johannes Cocceius, *Summa Doctrinae de Foedere et Testamento Dei* (Leyden, 1648). Among post-Renaissance studies, the classic work of Patrick Fairbairn, *The Typology of Scripture,* 2 vols. (Edinburgh, 1845-47), Daniélou's many books, especially his *Sacramentum Futuri: Etudes sur les Origines de la Typologie Biblique* (Paris: Beauchesne, 1950), trans. Wulstan Hibberd as *From Shadows to Reality: Studies in the Typology of the Fathers* (London: Burns & Oats, 1960), Richard Longenecker, *Biblical Exegesis in the Apostolic Period* (Grand Rapids, Mich.: Eerdmans, 1975), Beryl Smalley, *The Study of the Bible in the Middle Ages* (Oxford: Clarendon Press, 1941), Henri de Lubac, *Exégèse Médiévale: Les Quatre Sens de l'Ecriture,* 4 vols. (Paris: Aubier, 1959-64), and the references to biblical and patristic typology that Bercovitch gives ("Annotated Bibliography," pp. 250-52, 257-59), all merit close attention. Among them, they tabulate and analyze thousands of typological texts and examples and discussions of them. The student who seeks more general approaches should start with Hastings's

Encyclopedia of Religion and Ethics and the *Catholic Encyclopedia*, both of which include exemplary studies of typology.

3. *Theories of Typology.* Modern theoretical discussions of typology begin with Fairbairn's *The Typology of Scripture* (see Section 2, above); to it must be added another nineteenth-century work, Frederic A. Farrar's *History of Interpretation* (New York: E. P. Dutton, 1886). Theoretical treatments in this century begin in the late 1940s with Henri de Lubac's " 'Typologie' et 'Allégorie,' " *Recherches de Science Religieuse*, 34 (1947), 188-226, and continue in the '50s with Daniélou's books, Robert C. Dentan's "Typology— Its Use and Abuse," *Anglican Theological Review*, 34 (1952), 210-17, Woollcombe and Lampe's two long essays in their *Essays on Typology* (1957), and the first appearance in English of Erich Auerbach's seminal essay, "Figura" (1959). Other important treatments of the theoretical backgrounds of exegetical typology are the books on Origen by Daniélou and Hanson. Three more recent studies are James S. Preus, *From Shadow to Promise: Old Testament Interpretation from Augustine to the Young Luther* (Cambridge, Mass.: Harvard Univ. Press, 1969), Hans Frei, *The Eclipse of Biblical Narrative* (1974), and E. S. Shaffer, *"Kubla Khan" and the Fall of Jerusalem: The Mythological School in Biblical Criticism, 1770-1800* (Cambridge: Cambridge Univ. Press, 1975).

4. *Typological Backgrounds: Jewish, Christian, and Pagan.* For more than a century, scholars have identified pre-Christian Jewish millennialism and messianism as early manifestations of typology. In addition to the writings of Harry Austryn Wolfson and Gershom Scholem, I have profited from reading and studying the backgrounds cited in Maurice Vernes, *Histoire des Idées Messianiques depuis Alexandre jusqu'à l'Empereur Hadrian* (Paris, 1874), R. H. Charles, *A Critical History of the Doctrine of a Future Life in Israel, in Judaism, and in Christianity* (London: Adam and Charles Black, 1913), and Joseph Bonsirven, S.J., *Exégèse Rabbinique et Exégèse Paulinienne* (Paris: Beauchesne, 1939). Important eighteenth-century treatments of the Jews and Judaism with typological implications are Jacques Basnage's *The History of the Jews from Jesus Christ to the Present Time*, trans. Thomas Taylor (London, 1708), Hartley's *Observations on Man*, the Abbé Henri Grégoire's *Essai sur la regénération physique, morale, et politique des Juifs* (Paris, 1788), and some of the pamphlets spawned by the contro-

versy over the Jewish Naturalization Act of 1753, especially *A Collection of the Best Pieces in Prose and Verse against the Naturalization of the Jews* (London, 1753). Three modern studies will also be helpful: Thomas Perry, *Public Opinion, Propaganda, and Politics in Eighteenth-Century England* (Cambridge, Mass.: Harvard Univ. Press, 1962), Ursula Henriques, *Religious Toleration in England, 1787-1833* (London: Routledge & Kegan Paul, 1961), and Mel Scult, *Millennial Expectations and Jewish Liberties*.

The blending of pagan and Christian typologies can best be viewed as a single topic, starting with Hugo Rahner, *Greek Myths and Christian Mystery*. Daniélou's three volumes of his *History of Christian Doctrine before the Council of Nicea*, especially Volume 2, *Gospel Message and Hellenistic Culture*, trans. John A. Baker (London: Darton, Longman, & Todd, 1973), are invaluable. Other important studies include Allen's *Mysteriously Meant*, Douglas Bush, *Pagan Myth and Christian Tradition in English Poetry* (Philadelphia: American Philosophical Society, 1968), Henry Chadwick, *Early Christian Thought and the Classical Tradition* (Oxford: Clarendon Press, 1966), and Arnaldo Momigliano, *Paganism and Christianity in the Fourth Century* (Oxford: Clarendon Press, 1963). Most secondary works draw, at least in part, on the large compilations of Gronovius, Graevius, and Montfaucon, all of which the modern student may continue to consult with great profit: Jacob Gronovius, *Thesaurus Antiquitatum Graecarum*, 13 vols. (Amsterdam, 1697-1702), G. J. Graevius, *Thesaurus Antiquitatum et Historiarum Italiae*, 45 vols. (Leyden, 1704-25), and Bernard de Montfaucon, *L'Antiquité expliquée et representée en figures*, 10 vols. (Paris, 1719-24). Finally, late Renaissance editions of classical authors are often—usually—generous compilations comprising numerous scholia; later editions of Homer, Virgil, and Ovid are particularly fruitful in their efforts to link Christian and pagan.

5. *Typology and Renaissance Backgrounds*. Despite the existence of many studies of typology in individual authors, especially in Milton and the English metaphysical poets, it is surprising that no single study of typology in the European Renaissance exists. Helpful for the later Renaissance, and with a good bibliography, is Joseph A. Galdon, S.J., *Typology and Seventeenth-Century Literature* (The Hague: Mouton, 1975). Important for Renaissance backgrounds are Auerbach's classic essays, "Figura," "Typological Symbolism in Medieval Literature," *Yale French Studies*, 9 (1952),

3-10, and "Figurative Texts Illustrating Certain Passages of Dante's Commedia," *Speculum*, 21 (1946), 474-89. Most of Auerbach's published writings shed significant light on European figural traditions; a complete list appears in his *Literary Language & Its Public in Late Latin Antiquity and in the Middle Ages*, trans. Ralph Manheim (Princeton: Princeton Univ. Press, 1965), pp. 393-405. Several essays in *Seventeenth-Century Imagery: Essays on Uses of Figurative Language from Donne to Farquhar*, ed. Earl Miner (Berkeley and Los Angeles: Univ. of California Press, 1971), are relevant: Maren-Sofie Røstvig's "Images of Perfection," pp. 1-24, and Pierre Legouis's "Some Remarks on Seventeenth-Century Imagery: Definitions and Caveats," pp. 187-97. Victor Harris's essay, "Allegory to Analogy in the Interpretation of Scriptures," *PQ*, 45 (1966), 1-23, remains one of the best statements ever written on late Renaissance typology. The essays in *Literary Uses of Typology* provide a generous perspective on typology in this period, while the scholia to Wittreich's *Visionary Poetics* cite nearly all typological studies of English Renaissance literature. For another thorough survey of the Renaissance background, see also Barbara K. Lewalski, *Protestant Poetics and the Seventeenth-Century Religious Lyric*, pp. 449-56. Somewhat peripheral to my subject, but nevertheless, like all his books, most useful is D. P. Walker's *The Decline of Hell: Seventeenth-Century Discussions of Eternal Torment* (London: Routledge & Kegan Paul, 1964). Among the books on aspects of Renaissance learning that I have found helpful are J. R. Jacob, *Robert Boyle and the English Revolution: A Study in Social and Intellectual Change* (New York: Burt Franklin & Co., 1977), F. Secret, *Les Kabbalistes Chrétiens de la Renaissance* (Paris: Dunod, 1964), and R.J.W. Evans, *The Making of the Habsburg Monarchy* (Oxford: Clarendon Press, 1979), especially his four magnificent chapters on "The Intellectual Foundations" of the Empire (pp. 311-446).

6. *Typology and Puritanism.* Bercovitch, "Annotated Bibliography," is detailed in his coverage of typological aspects of American Puritanism; also excellent are the essays in the same volume (*Typology and Early American Literature*) and in several special issues of the journal *Early American Literature*. On British Puritanism, there are several fine studies: U. Milo Kaufmann, *"The Pilgrim's Progress" and Traditions in Puritan Meditation*, Mason Lowance's introduction to Samuel Mather, *The Figures or Types of the Old Testament* (1705) (New York: Johnson Reprint Corp., 1969), and

William G. Madsen, *From Shadowy Types to Truth*. As I noted with regard to typology in the Renaissance in Section 5, above, there is no single study devoted to Puritan figural traditions and exegetical methods in England. The many books of Christopher Hill (most of them cited in the notes) deal with these as well as with many other aspects of Puritanism. Three of Hill's works that are particularly relevant to typology are *Antichrist in Seventeenth-Century England* (London: Oxford Univ. Press, 1971), *The World Turned Upside Down: Radical Ideas During the English Revolution* (London: Temple Smith, 1972), and *Milton and the English Revolution* (New York: Viking Press, 1978), especially the section on "Milton's Christian Doctrine" (pp. 233-337). I have also learned much from Michael Walzer's *The Revolution of the Saints: A Study in the Origins of Radical Politics* (Cambridge, Mass.: Harvard Univ. Press, 1965), the essays in *Puritans, the Millennium, and the Future of Israel: Puritan Eschatology, 1600-1660*, ed. Peter Toon, and Bryan W. Ball, *A Great Expectation*. William Haller's *The Rise of Puritanism, Or, The Way to the New Jerusalem . . .* (New York: Columbia Univ. Press, 1938) and Horton Davies's *Worship and Theology in England: From Andrewes to Baxter and Fox, 1603-1690* (Princeton: Princeton Univ. Press, 1975) are two indispensable classics for the study of Puritan backgrounds. Among primary sources, I recommend the typological handbooks of Keach, Mather, Guild, Worden, and others and the British Library's GK3 under the headings that I cited in Section 1 above, as well as under "Charles I, King of England" and "Oliver Cromwell."

7. *Typology and Myth*. Both Allen in *Mysteriously Meant* and Richardson and Feldman in *The Rise of Modern Mythology* give bibliographies (Allen's is sometimes unreliable). The bibliographical references in Frazer's *The Golden Bough* and his *Folklore in the Old Testament* are dated but nevertheless excellent for the study of backgrounds relevant to prefigurative uses of myth. Theodore H. Gaster, *Myth, Legend, and Custom in the Old Testament* (New York: Harper & Row, 1969) is a fine compendium, worth consulting, but unfortunately thin on bibliography. Mircea Eliade's *A History of Religious Ideas. Volume 1: From the Stone Age to the Eleusinian Mysteries* (1976), trans. Willard R. Trask (Chicago: Univ. of Chicago Press, 1978), pp. 376-479, gives a first-rate summary of recent scholarship on myth, with some relevance to typological matters. Three background studies that I have found invaluable are Frank

E. Manuel, *The Eighteenth Century Confronts the Gods* (Cambridge, Mass.: Harvard Univ. Press, 1959), Frances Yates, *Giordano Bruno and the Hermetic Tradition* (London: Routledge & Kegan Paul, 1964), and D. P. Walker's stimulating *The Ancient Theology: Studies in Christian Platonism from the Fifteenth to the Eighteenth Centuries* (Ithaca, N.Y.: Cornell Univ. Press, 1972). Walker's study of Neoplatonism, freemasonry, hermeticism, and many other subjects often associated with the occult sheds light on the association of myth with narrative forms, especially prose fiction and satire; from his researches we can clearly see the contemporary bases for the satire on polymathia in *The Memoirs of Martinus Scriblerus* and in the relentless antiquarianism of Walter Shandy. Among more recent studies of myth that I have found helpful for their continuation of structural motifs are Claude Lévi-Strauss, *The Savage Mind* (Chicago: Univ. of Chicago Press, 1966) and his essay, "The Structural Study of Myth" in *Myth: A Symposium*, ed. Thomas Sebeok (Bloomington: Indiana Univ. Press, 1974), Edmund Leach, "Genesis as Myth" in his *Genesis as Myth and Other Essays* (London: Jonathan Cape, 1969), and Herbert Schneidau, *Sacred Discontent: The Bible and Western Tradition* (Berkeley and Los Angeles: Univ. of California Press, 1976).

In this book, I have used as primary sources the vast compendia on myth, Christian origins, and the religion of the gentiles by seventeenth- and eighteenth-century writers, including those of Stillingfleet, Vossius, Bochart, Kircher, Gale, Warburton, Bryant, and (later) Faber; also relevant for the student of typology and myth are the appropriate entries in Bayle's *Dictionnaire philosophique* and in *L'Encyclopédie*. The polymaths moved steadily eastward in the quest for Christian origins—Kircher, for instance, wrote extensively on Chinese religion—and, in this context, another compendium may be useful: Theophilus Spitzel's *De Re Literaria Sinensium Commentarius* (Leyden, 1661). The orientalist Sir William Jones often compares Indian and Persian myths to Christian history; see his contributions to *Asiatick Researches* (1788-94) and his study of the Bible, *A Course of Lectures on the Figurative Language of the Holy Scriptures* (London, 1787).

Typology is associated with the early transmission of myth through the study of hieroglyphics, a subject that seventeenth- and eighteenth-century mythographers pursued with vigor. The two most important modern studies of the glyphs are those of Madeleine David and Liselotte Dieckmann (cited in the notes). The attraction of early methods of writing to modern grammatologists is the route whereby Jacques Derrida has revived interest in Warburton's *The Divine Legation of Moses Vindicated*: see Derrida's *Of Grammatology*, trans. Gayatri C. Spivak (Baltimore: Johns Hopkins Univ. Press, 1976). The link to China is provided by A. H. Rowbotham, *Missionary and Mandarin: The Jesuits at the Court of China* (Berkeley and Los Angeles: Univ. of California Press, 1942), and "The Jesuit Figurists and Eighteenth-Century Religious Thought," *JHI*, 17 (1956), 471-85. Hieroglyphics, hieratic codes, mystical writing, steganography, and codes in general are topics often connected with typology that helped to spread prefigurative notions through many aspects of eighteenth-century life and literature; further study of all of them would be most welcome.

8. *Typology and the Visual Arts.* Visual representations of types and typological symbols have appeared in the arts since early Christian antiquity, starting with illuminated manuscripts of the Bible and other sacred writings and, no doubt, with early frescoes. In the Middle Ages, visual typology appears as well in stained glass, painting, coins, and book illustration. The late medieval and Renaissance altarpiece, with its tableau of scenes from a single biblical—usually New Testament—story, provided a rich source of visual typology and, like stained glass, the altarpiece has had fascinating revivals in the nineteenth and twentieth centuries (see Figures 25 and 26). The Renaissance adds emblem literature, ceramics, iconology, and various kinds of prints to the arts in which typology turns up, if not flourishes (see Figures 1-3, 28, and 29). Scholarly documentation of these manifestations has thus far been uneven. Broadly synthetic studies include the books of Seznec and Grabar, but these, like many works in art history, touch rather lightly on prefigurative images. A scattering of essays by art historians—including Gombrich, Wallis, and Boase, all cited in my notes—deal with specialized topics. See also Bercovitch's section on "Art and Architecture" in his "Annotated Bibliography," pp. 322-27. D. J. Gordon's essay, "Ripa's Fate," in his *The Renaissance Imagination*, is also stimulating. The student should consult seventeenth- and eighteenth-century editions of Ripa's *Iconologia*, George Richardson's *Iconology: or, A Collection of Emblematical Figures*, 2 vols. (London, 1779), Lionardo Agostini's *Gemmae et Sculptae Antiquae* (Amsterdam, 1685), and Obadiah Walker's *The Greek and Roman History Illustrated by Coins and Medals* (London, 1692). Allen, *Mysteriously*

Meant, pp. 256-62, also deals with numismatics. On stained glass, the various volumes (arranged by country and in some cases by city) in *Corpus Vitrearum Medii Aevi*, which have been appearing since the 1930s, are an essential resource. Rosemary Freeman, *English Emblem Books* (London: Chatto & Windus, 1948), is a fine source for the study of emblems, but she does not stress their prefigurative elements. An excellent, but unfortunately nearly unknown, account of emblems and their application is Brendan O Hehir's *Expans'd Hieroglyphicks: A Study of Sir John Denham's Coopers Hill, with a Critical Edition of the Poem* (Berkeley and Los Angeles: Univ. of California Press, 1969), pp. 16-24. Two more general studies of the visual arts in literary contexts are Ronald Paulson, *Emblem and Expression in Eighteenth-Century Art* (Cambridge, Mass.: Harvard Univ. Press, 1975) and George Landow, *William Holman Hunt and Typological Symbolism* (New Haven: Yale Univ. Press, 1979); Landow is one of the few modern scholars with a broad interest in typology and the visual arts. See also his chapter, "Ruskin and Allegory" in his *The Aesthetic and Critical Theories of John Ruskin*. There are many visual contexts for typology in the eighteenth and early nineteenth centuries, but the only subject that has received considerable and detailed attention in this respect is William Blake. Among the many scholars whose books have discussed Blake's visual typology, Jean Hagstrum and Kathleen Raine in the 1960s and Joseph A. Wittreich, Jr. in the 1970s—all are cited in the notes—deserve particular mention. Much study of Blake consists of articles and essays, including the following that I have found especially helpful: Mary Lynn Johnson, "Emblem and Symbol in Blake," *HLQ*, 37 (1974), 151-70; Frank M. Parisi, "Emblems of Melancholy: *For Children; The Gates of Paradise*," in *Interpreting Blake*, ed. Michael Phillips (Cambridge: Cambridge Univ. Press, 1978), pp. 70-110; John Beer, "Influence and Independence in Blake," *ibid.*, pp. 196-261; Leslie Tannenbaum, "Blake and the Iconography of Cain," in *Blake in His Time*, ed. Robert N. Essick and Donald Pearce (Bloomington: Indiana Univ. Press, 1978), pp. 23-34; and Joseph A. Wittreich, Jr., "Painted Prophecies: The Tradition of Blake's Illuminated Books," *ibid.*, pp. 101-15. A great many other contributions to Blake studies deal with prefigurative materials, but often without much emphasis on them; a book devoted to Blake's typologies is a desideratum. We can expect that, as scholarly sensitivity to typology grows, there will be more and better analysis of the visual art of the period covered by this book.

9. *Typology and Millennialism.* Many writers have regarded typology and the Millennium as practically synonymous (and not without reason). The primary literature, which deals mainly with interpretations and applications of the prophetic and apocalyptic books of the Bible, is extensive; since others have fully catalogued it, I shall not list again here works that I already cite in text and notes. There are some seminal studies, including Norman Cohn, *The Pursuit of the Millennium: Revolutionary Messianism in Medieval and Reformation Europe and Its Bearing upon Modern Totalitarian Movements* (London: Secker and Warburg, 1957; rev. ed. 1970), Marjorie Reeves, *The Influence of Prophecy in the Later Middle Ages: A Study in Joachimism* (Oxford: Clarendon Press, 1969), and Ernest L. Tuveson's two studies, *Millennium and Utopia: A Study in the Background of the Idea of Progress*, and *Redeemer Nation: The Idea of America's Millennial Role* (Chicago: Univ. of Chicago Press, 1968). I have already referred to the books of Clarke Garrett, W. H. Oliver, J.F.C. Harrison, and Michael Adas. Others that I should mention here are James W. Davidson, *The Logic of Millennial Thought: Eighteenth-Century New England* (New Haven: Yale Univ. Press, 1977), Ernest R. Sandeen, *The Roots of Fundamentalism: British and American Millenarianism, 1800-1930* (Chicago: Univ. of Chicago Press, 1970), especially Chapter 1, and Margaret C. Jacob, *The Newtonians and the English Revolution, 1689-1720*, Chapter 3. Studies of individual millenarians are often semipopular in character and fundamentalist in perspective, so I shall not cite any of them here; Garrett's chapters on Richard Brothers and Joanna Southcott are, by contrast, excellent scholarly treatments. On some of the leading figures, see also Alan Smith, *The Established Church and Popular Religion, 1750-1850* (London: Longmans, 1971). A forthcoming book, *The Apocalypse and English Renaissance Thought and Literature*, ed. C. A. Patrides and Joseph A. Wittreich, Jr. (Manchester: Univ. of Manchester Press, 1982), should also be noted here, especially for Wittreich's comprehensive bibliographical appendix on the exegesis of Revelation and its myriad applications. The relationship of millennial and utopian thought makes it appropriate for me to mention the Manuels' *Utopian Thought in the Western World*, while there is a bibliography of "Utopias and Dystopias, 1500-1750" (a number of them millenarian) in *St. Thomas More: A Preliminary Bibliography of His Works and of Moreana to the Year 1750*, comp. R. W. Gibson (New Haven: Yale Univ. Press, 1961). The relationship of typology to

prophecy, which I discuss in Chapter 9, is documented in many works, of which one of the most important is LeRoy E. Froom, *The Prophetic Faith of Our Fathers: The Historical Development of Prophetic Interpretation,* 4 vols. (Washington, D.C.: Review & Herald, 1946-54). Of many secondary interpretations, I will mention Wittreich's *Visionary Poetics,* Murray Roston, *Prophet and Poet: The Bible and the Growth of Romanticism* (Evanston: Northwestern Univ. Press, 1965), Hillel Schwartz, *The French Prophets: The History of a Millenarian Group in Eighteenth-Century England* (Berkeley and Los Angeles: Univ. of California Press, 1980), and Rupert Taylor, *The Political Prophecy in England* (New York: Columbia Univ. Press, 1911). There are many contemporary sources, some of which I have cited in my analysis; two other relevant works are the anonymous epic, *The Prophets: An Heroic Poem* (London, 1780), and a little-known—and scarce—collection, *Prophetical Extracts,* 6 parts (London, [1804]) (the British Library shelf mark is 3187.d.42).

10. *Typology and Literature since 1820.* Although I end this book at about 1820, at the height of the Romantic movement in England, I chose that *terminus ad quem* for reasons of scholarly convenience rather than because typology dries up and blows away after 1820. It is true that there are major changes in the literary adaptations of the mode in Victorian England, but the growth of religious fundamentalism alone in England and America would have been enough to keep it alive. The reader of Wordsworth's "Ecclesiastical Sonnets"—if there are any readers of these poems—will find numerous instances of typology in them. Dickens, Thoreau, and Eliot often refer specifically to types or, paraphrastically, to typological situations. The religious and ethical novelists of the mid and later part of the century, whom Robert Lee Wolff collects in the Garland reprint series, *Victorian Fiction: Novels of Faith and Doubt,* frequently use typological themes and characters; see also Wolff's somewhat pedestrian study, *Gains and Losses: Novels of Faith and Doubt in Victorian England* (New York: Garland Publishing Co., 1977). The vast field of Victorian religious poetry deserves attention; G. B. Tennyson, in *Victorian Devotional Poetry: The Tractarian Mode* (Cambridge, Mass.: Harvard Univ. Press, 1981), deals with the typology of some of it, especially Keble and Newman. George P. Landow's *Victorian Types, Victorian Shadows: Biblical Typology in Victorian Literature, Art and Thought* (London: Rout-

ledge & Kegan Paul, 1980), is of major importance to anyone who seeks to understand the nineteenth-century passion for prefiguration. The essays in *Literary Uses of Typology* by Karl Keller, Landow, and Theodore Ziolkowski illustrate further applications of types after 1800, as do the later chapters of Bercovitch's *American Jeremiad*. Ziolkowski's *Fictional Transfigurations of Jesus* does more for recent applications of typological themes than any other study; the student of post-1820 typology should read his *Disenchanted Images: A Literary Iconology* (Princeton: Princeton Univ. Press, 1977) as well. And the creating of typological themes and their exegesis does not stop there: to take a recent example, when Graham Greene's *The Human Factor* appeared in 1978, a number of reviewers, remembering the typological qualities of *The Power and the Glory*, successfully identified the types in Greene's story of Maurice Castle, his counterintelligence work, and his flight to Moscow. Nor, if my guess is shrewd, will it end soon.

INDEX

THIS Index includes references to works that I cite in text and notes; I often use abbreviated titles. A page number in parentheses indicates the location of the most complete bibliographical information about a book or article.

Abraham, 350, 366

Abrams, Meyer H., "English Romanticism: The Spirit of the Age" (1963), (343)

An Account of Some Passages in the Life of a Private Gentleman (1708), 207, 208, (209)

Achilles, 5, 135, 140

Adam, 30, 96, 107, 181, 219, 349; typology of, 71, 80, 82, 237

Adams, Thomas, *The Works of* (1629), (124); character sermons of, 124

Adas, Michael, *Prophets of Rebellion: Millenarian Protest Movements* (1979), (325), 331, 406

Addison, Joseph, 23, 125, 126; *Dialogues upon the Usefulness of Ancient Medals* (1702), 392, 393; *The Spectator* (1965), (126), 150; *The Works of* (1721), (392)

Adonis, 135, 136

Aeneas, 5, 135, 140, 148, 149, 151, 307

Aesculapius, 135, 355

Aesop, xv, 126-29, 141, 162, 208, 262, 303

Agamemnon, 78

Agostini, Lionardo, *Gemmae et Sculptae Antiquae* (1685), (404)

Agrippa, Henry Cornelius, 300

Aikin, John, 264

Ainsworth, Henry, *Annotations upon the Five Bookes of Moses* (1629), (230)

à Kempis, Thomas, 197-208, 209, 228, 239, 250; *De Imitatione Christi*, 197-202, 333; editions of *De Imitatione Christi*, 215; *The Christians Pattern* (1657), (197); *Sermons*, 303

Akenside, Mark, 375; *The Pleasures of the Imagination* (1744), 376, 377

Alcibiades, 120

Aldrovandus, Ulisse, 370

Alemán, Matteo, 210

Alfred, 108

Alkon, Paul K., 216-17; *Defoe and Fictional Time* (1979), (9), 217

Allen, Don Cameron, xiv, 78, 127, 150; *Image and Meaning* (1969), (40); *The Legend of Noah* (1949), xiv; *Mysteriously Meant* (1970), (xvii), 8, 42, 54, 55, 84, 108, 122, 127, 135, 136, 138, 148, 150, 305, 400, 402, 404-405

Allen, Ralph, 231, 316

Altaner, Berthold, 398; *Patrology*, trans. Hilda Graef (1958), (300)

Alter, Robert, "Biblical Type-Scenes and the Uses of Convention" (1978-79), (378)

American Art: 1750-1800 . . . (1976), (21)

American Revolution, 32, 342 and n. 35, 382

Amphion, 107

Anglicanism: exegesis in, 111; rationalism; 43; typology and, 48

Anne, 108, 118, 149-50; marriage of, 118; death of, 119; *Hymenaeus Cantabrigiensis* (1693), (118)

Antichrist, 190, 311-15, 318

Antiochus, 312

apocalypse, idea of, 68, 221-24, 235, 311-14, 321, 324, 330, 338, 339-46, 350, 362, 377, 384, 389

The Apocalypse and English Renaissance Thought and Literature, ed. C. A. Patrides and Joseph A. Wittreich, Jr. (1982), (406)

Apollo, 135

Apthorp, East, *Letters on the Prevalance of Christianity before its Civil Establishment* (1778), (342)

architecture, 20-21, 394; church, 20;

Index

Hanson, R.P.C., *Allegory and Event* (1959), (93), 399

Harrington, James, *Oceana and Other Works* (1700), (50); *The Political Works of James Harrington* (1977), (50)

Harris, Jocelyn, 194 n. 15; "Learning and Genius in *Sir Charles Grandison*" (1979), (238); "*Sir Charles Grandison* into *Mansfield Park*" (1980), (238)

Harris, Victor, "Allegory to Analogy" (1966), (401)

Harrison, J.F.C., *The Second Coming* (1979), (35), 65, 325, 326, 331, 332, 352, 406

Harth, Phillip, *Contexts of Dryden's Thought* (1968), (41); *Swift and Anglican Rationalism* (1961), (43), 293

Hartley, David, 11, 29, 37, 174, 176-77, 178, 180, 203, 267, 342, 343, 347, 359; *Observations on Man* (1791), (177), 337, 344, 367-68, 370, 372, 374, 399

Hawkins, Sir John, 72

Hawkins, Sherman H., "Swift's Physical Imagery" (1960), (297)

Haydon, Benjamin Robert, *Christ's Triumphant Entry into Jerusalem*, 22

Hayley, William, 356

Hector, 140

Henkel, Arthur, and Albrecht Schöne, *Emblemata* (1967), (86), 141; *Supplement* (1976), (398)

Henriques, Ursula, *Religious Toleration in England, 1787-1833* (1961), (400)

Henry V, 108

Henry, Matthew, *An Exposition of the Old and New Testament* (1829), (249)

heraldry, 102

Herbert of Cherbury, Lord, 77

Herbert, George, 53, 63, 80; "Jordan (I)," 53; *The Temple*, 57; *The Priest to the Temple*, 57

Hercules, 5, 81, 82, 105, 107, 118, 131, 135, 141, 147, 172, 173, 190, 355

Herder, Johann Gottfried von, 384

hermeneutics, 43, 75, 100; hermeneutic gap, 106; Puritan, 43; typology as a branch of, 100

Hermes Trismegistus, 274, 321

hermeticism, 29, 48, 161, 182, 274, 320, 370, 403

Herodotus, 292

hieroglyphics, 5, 29, 54, 55, 83, 86, 102, 107, 152, 159 n. 57, 160, 165-72, 178, 181, 281, 294, 307, 370, 372, 373, 403-404; Fig. 18; book of nature, typology of, and, 87; character and, 124, 167; code and, 5; Egyptian and Chinese, 152, 189, 281, 370; fable and, 127; Kircher and, 83, 138, 370; learning and, 48 n. 18; mythology and, 169-70; natural, 87, 372, 373; natural typology and, 87; and romance, 189; satiric view of, 279; Fig. 11; terminological confusion and, 85, 165; typology and, 86; writing and, 170-72, 178

High Noon (1952), 378

Hill, Christopher, 143, 402; *Antichrist in Seventeenth-Century England* (1971), (69), 142, 340, 402; *Change and Continuity in Seventeenth-Century England* (1975), (340); *Milton and the English Revolution* (1978), (65); *The World Turned Upside Down* (1972), (65), 285, 340, 402

Hirst, Desirée, *Hidden Riches* (1964), (18), 348

history, English, as discipline, 108; narrative of, 108; change, historical, 40; prophetical properties of, 92; as prefiguration of later events, 92

The History of Charlotte Summers (1749), (210)

Hobbes, Thomas, *Leviathan*, 45

Hogarth, William, 308; *A Harlot's Progress*, 271

Homer, 28, 60, 90, 151, 155, 159, 187, 273, 302, 305-307, 310, 400; *Iliad*, 78,

Index

history, 109, 330; of Jewish
history, 203, 332, 338, 350, 352-55
secularizing of, 5, 23, 24, 26, 34-35,
266, 270, 335, 390
and semantic enclaves, 106, 112, 130,
166
and structuralism, 12, 21, 22, 38, 152,
153, 162, 165, 236, 258, 267, 336,
337, 366-67
survival of, 8, 39-74 *passim*
traditions of, 8, 35, 39-74 *passim*
typological patterns or situations,
34, 112, 186, 199, 216, 221, 222-23,
226, 227, 240, 325, 368, 370; in
Bible, 61
typological reasoning, 116, 390-91
typological stories, 216, 245-60
passim, 261-65; and recognition
scenes in, 230
typological thinking, 34, 390-91;
Gerhard von Rad on, 34

VI. *In historical periods or in
the manner of individual
writers or groups*
and Anglicanism, 48
in colonial America, 7, 24
of French Revolution, xv
Jewish use of, 4, 27, 28, 30, 32, 75,
143, 337; *see also* Judaism and
Jews
medieval and Renaissance modes of,
63
in Milton, importance for, 70-72
of patristic period, 186-87
Pauline, 28, 136
pre-Christian, 29
Puritan use of, 103
after Restoration, old style of, 67
Romantic, 169
twentieth-century examples of, 11,
15, 24, 407-408

VII. *Of particular characters,
people, and places*
Abraham, 229; Adam, 71, 80, 82,
96, 107, 231, 237; Charles I, 32,
59, 119-21, 151, 193; Charles II,
71, 81, 105, 284; Cromwell, 31, 59,
68; Cyrus, 161; Daniel, 120; David,

117, 231, 359; Eden, 117, 220, 354;
Hercules, 105, 173; Fig. 30; hydra,
118 n. 42; Figs. 30, 33; Isaac, 200,
229; Fig. 28; James II, 147;
Jerusalem, 52, 352-55; Fig. 15;
Job, 231, 249-50, 255-60; Jonah,
120, 180, 188, 217, 220; Fig. 19;
Joseph, 228; Judas, 246-47;
London, 63, 64 n. 45, 96; Mary, 95;
Melchizedik, 261, 282; Noah, 83,
117, 214; Orpheus, 81, 136;
phoenix, 115, 142; prodigal son,
229; Prometheus, 117, 231, 359;
Satan, 246, 276-77; Saturn, 149;
Socrates, 153 n. 46; Venice, 98;
William the Conqueror, 108

VIII. *Books associated
with typology*
bibliography of, 13, 30-31, 396-408
passim (*see also* Wittreich,
Joseph A., Jr.); collections of
types, 36, 80 n. 8; scholarly
editions, 273; typological handbooks, 36, 156

*Typology and Early American
Literature*, ed. Sacvan Bercovitch
(1972), (31), 75

Van Ginnekin, J., *La reconstruction
typologique des langues archaïques
de l'humanité* (1939), (104)
Vaughan, Henry, 40, 57, 63, 80, 146,
275; "The King Disguised," 275;
Poems, ed. L. C. Martin (1957),
(275)
Vaughan, Thomas, 46, 77, 167, 273,
278, 298, 300, 370, 371; *Magia
Adamica* (1650), 167
Venus, 307
Vernes, Maurice, *Histoire des Idées
Messianiques* (1874), (33), 399
Vespasian, 119
Vico, Giambattista, 170, 172-74, 177,
178, 189; and hieroglyphics, 171;
The New Science, 172-74; *The New
Science*, ed. Thomas G. Bergin and
Max H. Fisch (1968), (170)
Vida, Marco Girolamo, 303, 365;

This book was composed and printed by
Princeton University Press

Title-page border and chapter headpieces adapted
from Frederic Warde, *Printer's
Ornaments* (London: Lanston
Monotype Corp., 1928), p. 60
Floral design in chapter subsections adapted
from The Monotype Corporation's
18-point series, no. 203

Typography: Linotype Baskerville
Paper: S. D. Warren's 1854 Text

Designed by Jan Lilly